Harvard Historical Studies · 130

Published under the auspices of the
Department of History
from the income of the
Paul Revere Frothingham Bequest
Robert Louis Stroock Fund
Henry Warren Torrey Fund

FRANCE

in the

ENLIGHTENMENT

❧

Daniel Roche

Translated by Arthur Goldhammer

HARVARD UNIVERSITY PRESS

Cambridge, Massachusetts
London, England

First Harvard University Press paperback edition, 2000

First published in France as *La France des Lumières*
©Librairie Arthème Fayard, 1993

Published with the assistance of the French Ministry of Culture.

LIBRARY OF CONGRESS CATALOGING-IN-PUBLICATION DATA
Roche, Daniel.
[France des Lumières. English]
France in the Enlightenment / Daniel Roche ; translated by Arthur Goldhammer.
p.   cm. — (Harvard historical studies ; 130)
Includes bibliographical references and index.
ISBN 0-674-31747-5 (cloth)
ISBN 0-674-00199-0 (pbk.)
1. Enlightenment—France.   2. France—Intellectual life—18th century.
3. France—Politics and government—18th century.   4. France—Civilization—17th century.
5. France—History—Louis XIV, 1643–1715.   I. Title.   II. Series.
DC33.4.R61515   1998
944'.034—dc21   97-42550

To Fanette

CONTENTS

FRANCE IN THE ENLIGHTENMENT

Introduction

"THE CORPSES of the kings of France serve as excellent chronological markers," Pierre Goubert used to joke. The remark is applicable to more than just the research of historians keen to find some coherence in the periods they study. The death of a monarch forces any society to interrogate itself. In politics it marks a time when the pluses and minuses of the reign thus ended are summed up and the possibilities of a new beginning are assessed. Reading about the death of Louis XIV teaches us about the nature of politics in his time and the way in which political life was being transformed in Enlightenment France: beyond the event itself we glimpse the first stirrings of a social crisis.

Let us turn first to Saint-Simon. His account of Louis XIV's death comes at the end of a long period of anxiety. The year 1715 was an exceptional one, providing material for more pages of the *Mémoires* than any other.[1] The event was awaited patiently and impatiently; its brilliance obscured the skies of court and kingdom alike:

> On Saturday, August 31, both night and day were detestable; moments of consciousness were rare and brief. Gangrene had reached the knee and now spread through the entire thigh. The medicine of the clever abbé de Saint-Aignan was administered, a medicine sent by the duchesse du Maine that was excellent for smallpox. The doctors agreed to everything because there was no hope. At about eleven in the evening, the king's condition was so bad that last rites were pro-

I

nounced. The ceremony revived him. He recited the prayers in a voice so loud that it could be heard over the voices of the many ecclesiastics and others in the room. When the prayers were over, he recognized Cardinal de Rohan and said: "Those are the last rites of the Church." This was the last time he spoke to any person. He repeated the words *"Nunc et in hora mortis"* several times and then said, "Oh, my God, come to my aid. Hasten to my rescue!" Those were his last words. All night unconscious, then a long agony, which ended on Sunday, September 1, 1715, at eight fifteen in the morning, three days before he would have completed his seventy-seventh year, in the sixty-second year of his reign.

This account is followed by a brief biographical sketch stressing the length of the reign. Then four hundred pages go by before we come to the very short note on the transfer of the king's remains to Saint-Denis and the funeral, reduced "to the utmost simplicity in order to avoid the expense, the trouble, and the length of the ceremonies."

This text calls for several remarks. A nugget extracted from a rich lode, the passage by itself is not enough to tell us much about the philosophy of history and time that guided Saint-Simon's narration of the year 1715. Yet it does reveal the essence of such a philosophy: everyone looked upon the sovereign's death as a public event; various still customary practices accompanied it; and Louis's death was exemplary, accepted and experienced as a Christian death subject to the laws of the Church. The king still established for his kingdom the meaning of a history docile to the decrees of Providence. His death was the final act of an ascent toward ultimate ends. The writing, punctuated by expressions such as "never" and "the last time" repeated over and over, creates a morbid atmosphere. It thus focuses attention on the crucial objective for the community, the kingdom, and all nations, whose future and fortunes were directly dependent on the king's death. The memoirist was reporting for all his readers on the mystical and material force of the king's passing away into eternal life. The passage takes for granted, yet at the same time questions, an ancient, Christian, absolutist concept of power. Time was the judge of all things.

While power was passing into the hands of young Louis XV, who caught a cold as he stood on the balcony at Versailles, Saint-Simon was creating a tradition: the judgment of the previous reign. His reference to the public state of mind was the first appeal to the court of a yet-to-be-born public opinion. Another passage of the same text is well known: "Louis XIV was missed by few people apart from his lesser servants and those mixed up in the Affair of the Constitution," that is, the most orthodox, anti-Jansenist elements of the Catholic Church. The court went through the motions required by custom. Paris lived in hope "of some liberties," and in this the capital was not alone: "The provinces, in despair over their ruin and annihilation, jumped for joy, the *parlements* congratulated themselves on their liberation, and with scandalous enthusiasm the ruined, oppressed, desperate people gave thanks to God for the deliverance that, in their ardent hopefulness, no longer seemed in doubt." Here is the true crux of an exceptional story that revealed what in ordinary times was hidden by hagiography and the effects of memory. It brings together Saint-Simon's experience of the world, his cyclical vision of time, compatible with his religious philosophy, his tragic conception of human history, and an image of timelessness in which "everything is circle and period." Death, which always proclaims eternity, is nevertheless in this case the prelude to a new era.

The testimony of Saint-Simon, a man of the seventeenth century (he was forty in 1715) who would die at the height of the new age and whose ambitions for public life had been disappointed, offers us a picture of the old world, to be sure, but one that, as Montesquieu would say, "unraveled the sumptuous enigma of Louis XIV." In so doing, Saint-Simon gives historians the means to understand a point of departure: he shows us the illustrious symbol of power at the very moment when that power was beginning to disintegrate under the impact of a variety of forces.

The death of Louis XV, barely sixty years later, was a less sumptuous occasion. The abbé de Véri, who knew the court as well as the *petit duc* (Saint-Simon), and who possessed an audience as well as a capacity for keen observation, was a liberal and enlightened economist, but he lacked the vitriolic talent and style of the great memoirist.[2] He nevertheless cuts straight to the heart of the matter, as he too sets the king's text in the context of a broader narrative. His intention, however, is not to situate the end of Louis XV's reign in relation to the beginning of eternity, to measure it against an absolute "mirror of truth," but to relate kings as individuals to the march of progress, quite apart from the episodes of any particular reign or the great deeds of any particular monarch: "Buffon, Voltaire, and Jean-Jacques Rousseau will outlive Louis XV," he wrote. As

3

before, the announcement of the king's death points up the uncertainty of the future and more than ever justifies a summing up:

> The contrast between his death and the danger he courted when he fell ill in Metz in 1744 is a very striking lesson for sovereigns. One of the men assigned to deliver his funeral oration said that a people has no right to disobey but does have a right to keep silent when ill governed. Never has such silence been more deafening in the Churches. Everywhere, the Forty Hours was called for during his illness, and everywhere the temples were empty. Meanwhile, the provinces and the capital were united in a common sentiment.

Subsequent pages of the text offer a version of Louis XV's death that can be compared with those of his confessor Abbé Mandoux and the young duc de Liancourt. Central to all these accounts is the issue of the sacraments received by the dying king. They affirm, some more forcefully than others, the king's comparative virtue and the triumph of the Christian religion. Véri, who relates the confidences of Bordeu and the duc d'Aiguillon, sees the king's tranquillity of soul after receiving the sacraments as nothing more than the insensibility of a man about to succumb to smallpox. In recounting the king's final agony, which lasted from Saturday, April 30, to Tuesday, May 10, 1774, Véri emphasizes two things: the story of the extreme unction and the expulsion of Mme du Barry. Death as physical event outweighs all political considerations, and the writer stresses the climate of ambiguity and uncertainty as to the king's religion: no one denied that he believed, but what was astonishingly new was that the quality of that belief could be a subject of discussion. The abbé de Véri does not narrate the monarch's final moments. Instead, he prefers to enter into a broader discussion of the reactions provoked by the king's death:

> The body of the king, who died on Tuesday, May 10, was so corrupted by the nature of the disease that it had to be buried as quickly as possible. It was unceremoniously transported to Saint-Denis the following Thursday and placed in its vault. No one missed him as sovereign; a few people close to him did miss him, however, as a good master. His personal service was in fact quite mild: to do him justice, it must be said that he had acquired the virtue of containing the wrath to which he was inclined by nature. The churches that remained empty

during the prayers prescribed while he lay ill were the prelude to the indifference that greeted his death. The word *indifference* is not correct. The vast majority of his courtiers and people felt joy. Nevertheless, the prospect of a boy king in his twentieth year who had as yet shown no sign of capacity for government must have been worrisome.

This text is noteworthy not for its factual content (it contains hearsay and echoes inaccurate rumors concerning, for example, the corruption of the king's body) but for the ways in which it differs significantly from the *Mémoires* of Saint-Simon. Is Louis still identical with the state? And the writer indicates that the new king will require capacities that he may not possess! The relation between the monarchy and its subjects had come to be conceived in a new way. The representation of the monarchy had also changed: a complex, symbolic figuration had given way to a simpler image; rituals had become less frequent; and even reports of the king's death had become relatively impoverished compared to earlier ones, reduced to criticism and stereotypes. These changes represent different aspects of a broader process of desacralization.

When did the French cease to believe that the mysteries of government were impenetrable? It is more important to understand the whole range of processes that allowed the development of a political culture that permeated the entire society. The king is dead, long live the king! But when the unpopular Louis XV died, people could sense the ambiguity inherent in different expressions of an event that marked a major turning point for the government as well as the people. Absolutism, said Marc Bloch, is a kind of religion, which can be defined as the consubstantial union of king and kingdom for the common good. When monarchs died, the unraveling of certain ways of conceptualizing that union became apparent. What was most evident was the erosion of the sacred value of monarchy by philosophical criticism.

These two snapshots of crucial historical moments reflect the basic choices that shaped this book as an intellectual project. For me, and of course for the discipline within which I work, the goal is to understand the various levels of historical reality as it was experienced by men and women in the eighteenth century. I want to interpret eighteenth-century

France by comparing points of view that historians have usually kept separate.

With that in mind, I want to make several points. First, despite the accumulation of a large number of monographs, it is still possible to doubt generally accepted beliefs. In our search for coherence, for the creative power of the age, the Age of Enlightenment, we must constantly bear in mind the dizzying expansion of curiosity that accompanied it. The only real certitude is that we will never know what the people of the past experienced as they did.[3] What makes the historian's craft interesting is the limitation imposed by its central problem: How can we understand change without being influenced by what has already happened and what we now know about the future of a world that was necessarily ignorant of it? We must not sacrifice to the idol of teleology; we must not write the history of an age in the light of what came after it.[4] Thus, to analyze the possibilities of transformation in eighteenth-century France is not the same thing as to investigate the causes and origins of the French Revolution, thereby establishing a causal connection between totally different orders of facts and events simply because one is chronologically prior to the other.[5]

If our amalgamating eye scrutinizes change, it is also to try to see how change became possible in a world that saw itself as stable, changeless, and coherent by virtue of ancestral principles and age-old values: the worship of a God, the power of a king, and the reign of Christian mores. In other words, is it possible to compare the forces and tensions that existed in an inegalitarian, holistic society (to borrow an expression from Louis Dumont), a society governed by the moral principle of "everyone in his place," with those of the new world that emerged gradually in its midst, the world of the Enlightenment, of the individual economy, of new freedoms, and of mobility of men and things?[6] Can we compare the world of the past even partially with our own? It is important to bear in mind the lesson of one of Karl Marx's greatest works, the *Contribution to the Critique of Political Economy* (1859):

> In the social production of their existence, men inevitably enter into definite relations, which are independent of their will, namely relations of production appropriate to a given stage in the development of their material forces of production. The totality of these relations of production constitutes the economic structure of society, the real founda-

tion, on which arises a legal and political superstructure and to which correspond definite forms of social consciousness. The mode of production of material life conditions the general process of social, political, and intellectual life. It is not the consciousness of men that determines their existence, but their social existence that determines their consciousness. [Trans. S. W. Ryazanskaya (New York: International Publishers, 1959), pp. 20–21.]

Although materialist metaphysics is not our subject here, it is worth noting the exhortation to understand simultaneously that which unifies and that which differentiates. How were human and social relations intertwined in eighteenth-century France? We must explore the inevitably historical relation between freedom and dependence, between individual independence and mechanisms of social determinism.

A second methodological option will be to consider the relation between society and culture in terms not of infrastructure and superstructure but of complex interactions. We will move from social history to history on a broader scale, a history in which culture weaves the fabric of society just as surely as social bonds and clashes, a history in which realities and representations interact.[7] The history of Enlightenment France becomes the history of the way in which men and milieus variously appropriated mental structures and cultural values in a permanent confrontation of economic and social horizons that was the very root of their existence. The aim is not to study ideas and behaviors as "reflections" or rationalizations of social interests, but to perceive the intrinsic values and interrelations that placed them at the point where discourses, texts, and practices came together. Thus, the analysis of cultural facts, broadly understood, may allow us to bring together matters having to do with the constitution of opinions and their manifestation in a new cultural space and matters having to do with new opportunities for diffusion and reception. Any appropriation is of course a free act, and in the realm of cultural exchange, texts carry multiple meanings and are open to contradictory interpretations. Instead of blurring contradictions, we will try to consider them as a source of richer understanding. Finally, we must try to understand the possible connections between facts of intellectual culture and facts of material culture. A single process affected all aspects of life and reality: understanding and knowledge organized reality, and pragmatic activities were shaped by empirical and theoretical knowledge.

Despite many uncertainties and questions, a book ultimately reflects a choice. This book is organized around three major themes. The first is space and time, which is examined in relation to social roles and governmental action. The aim is to show how perceptions and conceptions, customs and practices, expressed what the people of the eighteenth century saw as a homogeneous construction, one that we can interpret as a key to their thinking. The second major theme is the relation of the monarchical state to subjects and corporations *(corps)*. More than institutional history, the goal here is to study political and administrative action, conflicts, crises, and protests in order to understand how enlightened absolutism worked and thus to grasp the nature of the continuity that Tocqueville emphasized between the Ancien Régime and the Revolution. The third major theme concerns changes in fundamental values. Here we shall try to reinterpret the relations among the essential and the biological, production, and material civilization in an age that believed in prosperity as the basis of universal enlightenment.

This book would not have been what it is without the support of many friends. Foremost among them I would place Jean-Claude Perrot, and I offer him this remembrance of our conversations. I offer my heartfelt thanks to Philippe Minard and Dominique Margairaz, who were always quick to arouse my curiosity and renew our debates; and to Alain Guéry and Dominique Julia for their unstinting assistance. Finally, I want to mention Aline Fernandez and the IHMC, Agnès Fontaine, Olivier Grussi, my first and always attentive reader, everyone who was involved with the book at Editions Fayard, and of course Julie Groleau.

PART ONE

Times, Spaces, Powers

1

Knowing France

FRENCH HISTORIANS, we are told, have lately been rediscovering politics and its history. The case may be overstated, because there has always been a tradition of political history. Despite changes in paradigm, it has been perennial and active, and its pages are rich with both anecdote and passion. The eighteenth century lends itself particularly well to this sort of exercise: a series of great ministers—Dubois, Choiseul, Fleury, Sartine, Necker, and Calonne—has attracted the attention of biographers. The versatile Edgar Faure's books on Law and Turgot deserve more than a tip of the hat: they are carefully researched and pondered works, original in their way of studying political actors in relation to the situations they faced. What emerges from work of this kind is the history of a political culture, a history that shows how institutions and individuals, ideas and ideologies, representations and practices interact. In the background we glimpse a history of governmental institutions in a "pre-constitutional" age, that is, a time when customary constitutions and fundamental laws existed implicitly but were not yet gathered together in homogeneous form, a time when it was common to deduce constitutions from institutions rather than the other way around.[1]

England was a favorite reference of the philosophes because its Magna Carta and Bill of Rights gave it an explicit constitution: these texts defined the relations between nation and state, people and sovereign. Voltaire, Montesquieu, and the many translators of England's fertile crop of seventeenth- and eighteenth-century political writing taught this tradition to France. To be sure, the lesson depended on a certain ambiguity. Neither Montesquieu's aristocratic liberalism nor Voltaire's proposal for an alliance between the liberal Enlightenment and enlightened absolutism (not despotism) had much in common with either British liberal theory or the practical realities of Hanoverian England. From England nevertheless the philosophes drew examples, testimonials, and whatever else they needed to illustrate such new ideals as freedom of opinion, religion, and conscience to a receptive public. "*Liberty and property*—that is the English cry . . . the cry of nature," exclaimed the philosophe of Ferney, who was more interested in civil liberties than in political ones, more interested in concrete but limited administrative reforms than in challenging unwritten constitutional traditions.[2] He constructed civilization through action.

This interaction of institutions and principles, action and theory, held implications for the relations between subjects and princes, people and their rulers. Over the long run, from monarchy to republic, the sources of sovereignty and legitimacy shifted while at the same time a new sensibility and identity emerged, at first (though not exclusively) among the elites who managed, controlled, and thought about the activities of the state. Tocqueville had a knack for explaining this slow, centuries-long change, "which is the remote source of events."[3] Here I want to examine the connection between these political relations and a moment in the history of knowledge: how, given the fabric of economic and social equilibria that structured the kingdom and the lives of ordinary French men and women, the political structure of the time encouraged or impeded thinking about the nature of society and the state.

Of course, the knowledge that rulers and officials needed in order to act filled archives with masses of documents whose number vastly increased over the course of the eighteenth century: published and unpublished texts circulated throughout the society and influenced contemporary perception and even fiction. This profusion of mirror images reinforces our confidence in our understanding but at the same time forces us to question the limits of our perception. Eighteenth-century France is indeed contained in the documents, but we need to think about what kind of knowledge of the past is available to us through study of contemporary theory and practice; we need to investigate the forms and categories in terms of which the men and women of that time apprehended the world: space, time, history. These are concrete historical objects, or, rather, aspects of a more general object: the conviction that a particular portion of the earth's surface has been singled out for a distinctive destiny.[4]

This investigation will help us to understand the origins of a descriptive and classificatory technique that still shapes French consciousness even today. Science helped the monarchical administration to understand people, their living conditions, and their needs, and in turn the administration helped science. Certain resistances and fears were uncovered. If the Enlightenment represented modernity, Enlightenment social science revealed inequalities in regard to cultural heritage and the understanding and justification of social roles, needs, and routines. The desire to learn and understand that is so apparent in contemporary reports and discussions was not limited to the elites; it also motivated many ordinary people of a practical and realistic bent. And women as well as men were involved: this awakening, of which we find evidence in the autobiographies of common people, definitely had an impact on home and family life.

Montesquieu, in his *Pensées*, noted that "states are governed by five different things: religion, general maxims of government, particular laws, customs, and manners. These things are mutually related. Change one and the others follow, but slowly, thus creating a ubiquitous dissonance." One has to hear the history of these dissonances in order to understand "how a general spirit is formed and what results follow from it,"[5] as the point was reformulated most clearly in *L'Esprit des lois* before 1743, with the addition of "climate and the example of things of the past" to the list of items to be investigated.[6]

Knowing the Kingdom

Despite the will to unity, one cannot speak of a unique knowledge of the kingdom. In the first place, France was too complex for any such knowledge. It involved too many issues and subjects ranging from the material to the spiritual, the empirical to the theoretical, everyday practice to matters of management. In describing these relationships, we will follow changes in perceptions and customs and their representation at a time when three things were still confused: *France,* as a collective entity and historical heritage; the *space of the kingdom,* as framework and object of analysis; and the *territory,* a structure built up over the centuries and maintained by the will of the prince, defined and enclosed by borders.[7] We will then compare this series of structures with another, for knowledge of the kingdom was stratified by social and cultural status, which determined the need for and access to information. Those at the top of French society did not require the same information about France as those at the bottom. One's view varied with one's position, which affected one's relations to the rest of the world and to other people. The historian of eighteenth-century France is fortunate in that "France" was by then a stable entity: it did add Lorraine in 1766, completing a diplomatic exchange first imagined nearly thirty years earlier (1738) and capping a royal policy initiated in the previous century, and then Corsica in 1768, in connection with a policy of maintaining a presence in the Mediterranean and maintaining a constant watch over an island that had long been a dangerous powder keg.

The chevalier de Jaucourt contributed an article on "France" to the *Encyclopédie*, and from it we can learn a great deal about how people thought about the nature and use of space:

> France: *(Geography)*, great kingdom of Europe, bounded to the north by the Netherlands; to the east by Germany, Switzerland, and Savoy; to the south by the Mediterranean Sea and the Pyrenees; and to the west by the Atlantic Ocean.

Writing as if he were merely noting an obvious fact, the versatile scribe begins by describing France as a political unit situated at the center of a world characterized as much by natural geographic features (sea, ocean, mountains) as by historical entities possessing a certain physical unity. This opening is followed, however, by four paragraphs with a rather different focus. The first raises a key question: What is the size or extent or surface area of the kingdom? Jaucourt answers by quoting Cassini: "France, from east to west and north to south, covers 400 square leagues." This is obviously a misprint: the figure should be 48,400 square leagues, the value obtained by squaring 220 leagues, the average distance between the northern and southern and eastern and western borders (equivalent to 957,874 square kilometers). Following this erroneous figure is a discussion of the whys and hows of calculating the kingdom's area. This can be interpreted as a politics of spatial knowledge, an example of the confluence of science and administration, of territorial management using a particular set of analytical instruments, agents, and modes of diffusion.[8]

Jaucourt's article continues with a brief geographical description from the standpoints of both naive and administrative observers: "Over the extent of this territory, the air is pure and healthful, and the weather is temperate almost everywhere . . . It has high mountains and beautiful rivers. Its fertile and delightful land abounds in salt, grains, vegetables, fruits, grapevines, mines, etc." Here the accent is on the country's "charm," and the description is full of stereotypes, reinforced by a rapid survey of religious and judicial institutions: Jaucourt has been leafing through his almanac. Finally, he turns to history, where France's destiny is revealed:

> The history of this kingdom shows the power of the kings of France growing, dying twice, reviving each time, then languishing for several centuries; but then, imperceptibly gaining strength, it increased everywhere and attained its highest point, like a river that loses its current as it flows or disappears beneath the earth only to reappear swollen by other streams to the point where its swift current sweeps away anything that stands in its way.

Jaucourt thus draws together in a geological and hydraulic image the vagaries of centuries of history, identifying the formation of the kingdom and territory of France with a natural phenomenon which, flowing on from the Capetians to the Bourbons, grew so powerful that it simply swept up various groups of people who thereby came to share a common history. Moreover, that history was a history of liberation, of people delivered from the tyranny of their lords by the efforts of the monarchs, and of a kingdom freed from material dependency by the efforts of absolutism. The France thus praised and held up as a model to other nations was the wealthy France of Colbert, with its "immense riches" but also its inequalities, "the peasant crushed by poverty, the propagation of the species threatened." In other words, the apparently rigorous, if flawed, definition of the beginning of the article has given way to a myth of progress linked to the fate and fortunes of the monarchy, leading to a program for remedying the ills of "the French nation, a flexible nation, which grumbles more readily, obeys more fully, and forgets its misfortunes more quickly than any other nation." This was a fundamental tendency of contemporary thought expressed in the commonplace rhetoric of reform.

For the royal administration as well as the Encyclopedists, there was only one way to modernize the state and develop its resources: action required knowledge, knowledge of the kingdom and its people. Men and resources had to be evaluated before they could be exploited. But the gathering of such knowledge was subject to influences of many kinds: from the state (what were eighteenth-century geography and statistics like?), from various agents, and from the desires of the very people who were the subjects of investigation.

Knowing Space: Mapping the Territory

Knowledge of the kingdom was abstract. It had little to do with the kind of serendipitous discovery a tourist might make, even though travel within France was on the rise and more organized than ever before. Travelers' accounts proliferated: Boucher de La Richarderie counted more than 20 for the seventeenth century (and his list was not exhaustive) and more than 150 for the eighteenth century, most of them published after 1750. Increasingly complex individual reports gained readers but were still overshadowed by the sciences of geography and cartography, which remained the chief instruments for understanding space. Moreover, those instruments were wielded by the state and thus afforded the state tight control over this type of knowledge.

The Royal Journey

State control was no longer exerted personally in the course of royal visits. From Louis XIV on, the royal residence changed frequently, and the organs of state power moved with the king, but these moves were orchestrated in a distinctive new way. There was a regular seasonal rhythm to them, a rhythm linked to the exigencies of the hunt and the economy of the royal estates. But not everyone associated with the government followed the king. Increasingly, the central organs of the administration continued to operate in Versailles and Paris. Major departments were installed in the capital in the second half of the eighteenth century as the government took over old seigneurial *hôtels*. The king's travels were essentially limited to the region around Paris. Most important of all, the old custom of using royal journeys as symbols of a political project and demonstrations of the union between the monarch and his kingdom had vanished. French kings no longer traveled with the whole panoply of court, royal family, intimates, troops, valets, and clerks. The purpose of this pomp had been to compensate for the tenuousness of the administrative network, the weakening of the chain of command induced by distance from the center of power and its agents, the inadequacy of communication, and the isolation of elements of the population. When the king traveled, he discovered the kingdom with his own eyes, experienced it with his own senses, and at the same time monitored the workings of royal institutions and symbolized his power with royal entry ceremonies. But royal mobility had diminished in the seventeenth century, and by the eighteenth century it was limited to specific, well-defined objectives. The locus of power became fixed; the government no longer traveled the highways because it could now avail itself of well-developed channels of communication, because everything important now took place at Versailles to the detriment of other places, and because all things now revolved around the absolutist Sun.[9]

To be sure, Louis XV and Louis XVI did travel, but their journeys no longer had the same meaning as in the past. The regular departures for Marly, Fontainebleau, and Compiègne were a routine feature of court life, which rewarded a select elite with private celebrations away from the vast caravansary that was Versailles. The characteristic features of the old mobility did appear on rare occasions, however, when the king, showing himself to his people, asserted his authority while at the same time entering into an implicit contract.[10] While making himself known to his subjects, the king also recognized local corporations and governing bodies and allowed them to participate in ceremonies in a manner that reflected their rights and privileges. The knowledge gleaned from such occasions depended on direct contact with people and places. Two occasions were particularly well suited to a replay of the old scenario: the coronation journey and the military expedition.

The journey from Versailles to Reims was brief but still long enough to establish the kind of festive atmosphere in which the king and his subjects could come together. On October 16, 1722, Louis XV left his palace and went to Paris, where he was acclaimed by the crowd. The spectacle created a portrait of the monarch: the handsome young king was greeted by joyous Parisians, still jealous of Versailles, and the solemn procession heralded the glorious future of his reign. A peculiar physical, almost palpable relationship developed both in Paris and along the highways between Louis XV, already "well loved," and the people of France. That relationship would later come undone as a new political culture emerged and sacred authority eroded.

En route to his coronation, Louis XV passed through Dammartin-en-Goële, Villers-Cotterêts, and Soissons. There, on October 20, the young king climbed up to the top of the cathedral and found the sight so beautiful that he ordered a bird's-eye sketch.[11] The cartographer king, pupil of the abbé de Longuerue and Guillaume Delisle, can be seen in this anecdote. It demonstrates that the head of state himself was interested in knowing his country scientifically: maps were an instrument of power, and one began the study of the arts of warfare and fortification by learning how to calculate and survey. The education of Louis XV shows us a social need. The king and nobility studied drawing, geometry, and astronomy as introductions to strategy and tactics, but at the same time they gained competence as engineers and architects. Indeed, the king and his nobles embodied talents that the century would disperse as it gained ever greater mastery over space.[12] Eventually the architect, whose goal was to create something distinctive and aesthetically pleasing, came to be opposed to the engineer, whose mission was utilitarian, goal oriented, and dedicated to improvement. The sumptuous coronation ceremonies in Reims (October 22–29) completed the first phase of a journey whose joyous return leg culminated on November 8 in Saint-Denis, where the king paid his respects to the entire dynasty. The next day he returned to Paris, and the day after that he reached Versailles.

For another example of a royal journey reuniting king and people we must wait until 1744. War was the reason this time—war and Louis XV's desire to don the boots of his warrior ancestors. It was a strange journey, for which the groundwork was carefully laid: the queen and dauphin and most of the court were excluded, matters pending before the various councils were dispatched, and commands were distributed. The king joined the army in Flanders in three days: on May 7 he was in Condé, on May 8 in Le Quesnoy, and on May 12 in Lille. He inspected and evaluated his forces, and his conduct vis-à-vis the local populations and the army made him quite popular. In July he went to Lorraine and set up headquarters in Metz. Illness put an end to the journey, however, and provoked a crisis within the court over the king's morals and public respect for religion. Sacrificed to the critics, Mme de Châteauroux hastily left Metz. The king's popularity reached new heights, but there is food for thought in the enigmatic conjunction of criticism (the king's morals subjected to scrutiny) with praise (Louis le Bien-Aimé was never better loved).

After 1744, Louis XV did little traveling. In this, Louis XVI emulated him. He did travel to Reims for his coronation and anointment, a matter of importance both to him and to the young Marie Antoinette. Turgot had suggested celebrating the rite in Paris, but tradition won out. There were no innovations in the itinerary or in the organization of the celebrations and ceremonies of entry and welcome in Châlons and Reims. The holy city of the monarchy was decorated with symbols exalting the virtues of the sovereign and reflecting the hopes of his people. The royal carriage passed through the gate of the "kingdom's happy economy." Sumptuousness and spectacle were mobilized to make the journey and its attendant festivals unforgettable for both participants and spectators and to give concreteness to the dreams and hopes of both sovereign and people. Here, the manner in which the king made the acquaintance of his kingdom was at the root of a fundamental ambiguity, because it masked more than it revealed the real problems of the hour and the growing discrepancy between the vision of leadership circles and the critical demands of public opinion. A brief trip to Normandy to inaugurate a major military construction project in Cherbourg filled the same purpose in Louis XVI's reign as military expeditions had done in earlier reigns. The monarch, no doubt deceived by his hope of winning the affection of his subjects and spurred on by the American challenge, proved no more lucid on this occasion than on others. In any case, he was not really rediscovering France, since before the Revolution the government's mastery of space depended on facilities, networks, and institutions to link Versailles and Paris to the provinces and establish the sovereign's presence everywhere: "Travel should be relied on only sparingly."[13]

Geographers and Cartographers: The Evolution of a Practical Science

The young king's training and instruction included lessons in the abstract understanding of space. From these early lessons Louis XV retained a taste for geography and a determination to protect the cartographic initiatives of the Académie des Sciences. Louis XVI studied with Philippe Buache, who provided his illustrious apprentice with "eight manuscript maps and explanations of each" extending to twenty or thirty quarto pages. The titles of these explanatory documents give an idea of the range of subjects treated and the way in which the young sovereign and other high-ranking individuals learned about the world: subjects included a view of the globe, first *mappemonde* with indication of geographical terms, second *mappemonde* for the history of the early patriarchs, third *mappemonde* of astronomical geography and mathematics, first hemisphere inhabited by different animals, map of early tribes, map of countries and cities for sacred history, and a general map for the history of the patriarchs. By the time Louis XVI was seven, he could write fluently and had acquired a basic general knowledge of space that was at once physical, natural, historical, and religious. History thus served all sorts of purposes, as did geography. Philippe Buache, one of the great scholars in this field at the time, was the son-in-law of Delisle, the teacher of Louis XV. He provided the tutors of the dauphin and the comte de Provence with all that was needed to teach a geography based on ancient principles as well as more recent developments.

After studying descriptive general geography and various notions about the formation of the world, the royal children moved on to regional study of Europe and its kingdoms, Germany, Italy, and France, with lessons on climate, political organization, economics, products, history, and monuments. For this purpose Buache created veritable geographical jigsaw puzzles to fix the political and administrative subdivisions of Europe in his pupils' minds. The king learned his trade well: Buache inspired in him a true passion for hydrography, sailing, and exploration (less well known, however, than his passion for mechanics). Louis XVI was skilled with the cartographer's tools: pen and brush, sextant and surveyor's chain, graphometer and alidade. He also took an interest in important contemporary works in the field, which he was able to read and understand. In this princely curriculum we see a reflection of the century's interest in educational reform. Along with history, the key discipline for learning the art of government, concrete geography, from the theoretical treatise to the practical exercise, taught mastery of space in a manner that combined serious study with amusement, and it was in space, after all, that political forces operated and military forces deployed. Geography also instilled curiosity about the world. Although there was a sharp division within the discipline between the studious scholar and the explorer, between the authors of maps and textbooks and the discoverers of new worlds, these distinctions were somewhat blurred in practice. All explorers knew how to make maps, and while not all cartographers traveled, many did and few were uninterested in new discoveries.

The linchpin of research in this field, where description of the world was brought into contact with scientific progress in general, was the Académie Royale des Sciences. It trained the indispensable experts in geography as well as in other fields of learning essential to the monarchy. With encouragement from Louis XIV, Colbert, and their successors, much had been accomplished since the academy's foundation. Work continued throughout the eighteenth century. Three characteristics stand out: astronomical observation was corroborated by exploration, as exemplified by the work of J.-D. Cassini; emphasis was placed on empirical observation, not only to correct astronomical tables but also to describe natural and human conditions (scholarly geography was absolutely dependent on the information gathered by royal missions and collected through a network of correspondents spanning the entire globe); and there was no sharp distinction between historical and geographic research. The Académie des Inscriptions and the Académie des Sciences complemented each other; ancient geography coexisted with modern geography, and the two societies exchanged honorary members, ordinary members, and correspondents. Until 1743, Abbé Bignon offered encouragement to all the learned institutions for which he enjoyed responsibility, delegated by his uncle Louis de Pontchartrain. Travelers and sedentary geographers came together in the academies, as well as in the reading of a cultivated public enamored of travel literature and in the administrative offices that dealt with the navy and the colonies, where their services were essential. Although this encounter did not always result in new concepts, it contributed greatly to mobilizing the intellectual elite, which was slowly converted to a positivistic and philosophical geography.

At first, until 1760 or so, the emphasis was on transforming the legacy of the humanist geographers. Knowledge of the globe was now based on numerous solid observations. Expeditions had determined the shape of the earth, and cartographers had rid themselves of fantasies still prevalent in maps of the world only a short while before.[14] What is more, a systematic effort was made to bring observations together in a unified way, an effort facilitated by the needs of colonial expansion. In areas where France was dominant—the rim of the Mediterranean, the East and West Indies, and to a lesser degree Canada—numerous expeditions were launched. Literature followed close behind, impelled by an expectant public, for reading about travel "pleased everyone, and although it usually served as an amusement, shrewd people relied on it to learn about geography, history, and commerce," Abbé Lenglet-Dufresnoy recalled in his *Méthode pour étudier la géographie,* of which four editions appeared between 1715 and 1768. No part of the world escaped the public's curiosity, and the new literature of course stimulated dreams of exotic places and fascination, real or utopian, with faraway places as well as reflections on the origins of society and the physical world.

Buffon, in his *Théorie de la Terre* (1749), sought to explain the original chaos, taking a position between the Plutonians (who believed that orogeny, or the process of mountain formation, originated in the earth's "central fire") and Neptunians (who emphasized the role of water and the primitive ocean). Buffon was thus critical of Scripture, questioned the Flood, and proposed a totally new chronology. He was a reformed Neptunian, which is to say a Neptunian without a systematic philosophy. The erosive effects of water were, he believed, the only way to explain the distribution of the continents and the relief of the earth's surface (the subject of stratigraphy, a science developed by Stenon in the seventeenth century). Buffon's success already owed much to a sensibility evident in *Les Epoques de la nature* (1778): for him, the earth was a living organism, whose component parts interpenetrated one another and whose evolution was not yet totally distinguished from a revolution still envisioned in cyclical terms. This way of seeing things became an aspect of the culture of the period. Buffon added to that vision through the questions he posed, just as Buache, in his essay on "physical geography" (1752), proposed a geometry of relief formation in which orography was deduced from hydrography and relief was understood systematically in terms of the action of river basins—not without a certain exaggeration that led him to place mountain ranges where none existed (across the Beauce between the Loire and the Seine, for example) in order to demonstrate the correctness of hydrography. But even his errors aroused curiosity about matters that went beyond generally accepted principles. In contrast to the old, erudite geography, whose only limits were political and historical, Buache proposed a "natural geography" based on deduction and a geometrical topography derived from simple principles. He thus initiated a debate that drew in the mineralogists, who, following Guettard, would abandon deductive explanation in favor of geological observation as an inductive method for understanding topographical relief. Meanwhile, travelers in France and throughout the world provided descriptions that contradicted Buache's conjectures. By the middle of the century, interest in geography had not subsided, as Numa Broc has argued, but rather shifted its focus. There was more continuity than discontinuity: positivist, abstract geography lost some ground, but that ground was occupied largely by various kinds of speculation concerning both distant discoveries and the vogue for scrutinizing local nature. The cultivated elite participated in a geographic enyclopedism that preceded the *Encyclopédie* and inspired the many varieties of research that followed its publication.

One sign of change was the transformation of textbooks and popular scientific literature. The humanist geography exemplified by works devoted to the "delights" of France or Italy, which favored erudite historical and cultural essays over the scientific study of space, were supplanted by works marked by their insistence on method, or, in other words, by a determination to pose problems and to seek understanding through classification. Among the latter were Le François's *Méthode abrégée* (1722), the *Nouvelle Méthode pour enseigner la géographie* (dedicated to the dauphin in 1732), and above all the publications of Father Buffier, who taught at the Collège Louis-le-Grand and whose work remained popular long after his death. All these works attest first of all to the enthusiasm for popular science among both authors and public. Writers tailored their approaches to the expanding interests of their audience and included maps as aids to visual memory and questionnaires and lists for rote memorization. Many of these devices were quite old, but as in historical chronology, efforts were made to bring them up to date, thereby bringing space into the sphere of classification and taxonomy. Geography, it was felt, had to be relieved of its "repellent aridity" and "scientific thorns" if it was to become appealing and accessible. In working toward that end, schoolmasters and tutors contributed to the taxonomic effort of the age.

Another sign of change was the success of the great classics of descriptive geography. Take, for example, Lenglet-Dufresnoy's *Méthode pour étudier la géographie*, first published in four volumes between 1715 and 1718 and reprinted in 1736, 1742, and 1768. Lenglet was a scholar, an indefatigable writer, and something of a spy, a jack-of-all-trades who absorbed a wide range of materials and reshaped them to suit his needs.[15] His method was encyclopedic, with reflections on the nature and utility of geography, bibliographies, maps, a guide to the globe, an ancient geography, a "geography for children," and a methodical description of the continents.[16] His aim was to localize, delimit, subdivide, and enumerate; his geographical nomenclature included everything from climate to relief, from populations to products. Through classification the scholar-investigator brought order to confusion.

A similar success was enjoyed by Piganiol de La Force, whose *Description de la France* was first published in 1715 and reprinted several times through the 1750s and accompanied by an abridged companion volume for travelers, the *Nouveau Voyage de la France*. The work incorporated a wealth of knowledge organized in the form of provincial travel itineraries. Despite various difficulties, the project met with success:

> A precise description of France that can be read with pleasure is not an easy undertaking. It must contain full details about a large kingdom yet be reliable enough to have nothing to fear from an infinite number of readers, each one perfectly informed about the canton he happens to live in, and who, taken together, form a corps of critics apt to daunt even the most careful of writers.

Three characteristics of Piganiol's work probably account for its success. First, the book was a gold mine of information: drawing on administrative sources, it made economic and statistical data a part of the respectable gentleman's cultural capital. Second, Piganiol knew how to use the resources of descriptive nomenclature in a lively, forceful manner. Each province was described in picturesque terms, and its products were detailed at length. Finally, the image of France that emerged from the work was a balanced one, in which productive forces, commerce, and forges were not neglected. Piganiol contributed to change by extending the range of knowledge.

The work of the provincial academies can be seen in a similar light. Already before 1750, thirty or more stable learned societies had begun to put science to work toward understanding and improving the environment. Private communications and, even more important, dissertations submitted in prize competitions added observations and experience to the fund of geographical knowledge. Here, the important thing to notice is the fertile link that developed between local research and general problems posed by provincial amateurs. Montesquieu owed a great deal to discussions at the Académie of Bordeaux, as Rousseau did to the prize competitions of the Dijon academy. Here, too, there was a desire to compile vast documentary resources that combined observation of nature (climate, geology, physics of the earth) with agronomic, economic, and, increasingly, social statistics.

Besides the geography found in textbooks, best-selling descriptive texts, and academic papers, there was also the geography of the dictionaries and *répertoires*. The *Encyclopédie*, in its first edition as well as successive revisions, has its place here. It shared in the desire to explore difference rather than identity and delighted in the discovery of foreign, not to say exotic, places as a way of achieving self-knowledge and overcoming prejudice. This interest found an echo in the government's *dessein de savoir*, or science policy, which encouraged officials to subsidize countless surveys. In the last third of the eighteenth century, a new way of looking at the world emerged from these convergent desires. The curiosity of the cultivated elite expanded to embrace the entire world and inspired detailed exploration of France and Europe. For naturalists, economists, agronomists, travelers, and other observers, part of this new interest was undeniably utilitarian. In the quest to understand how the earth's natural features related to human geography, few provinces went unexplored: Faujas de Saint-Fond roamed the Alps, Alléon Dulac explored the Beaujolais, and Legrand d'Aussy plunged into the heart of Auvergne.

As contemporaries confronted issues of population and resources, they began to ponder questions of cause and effect: Rousseau did so in the *Social Contract*, for example, as well as Buffon in the *Epoques de la nature*, also Ramond, who explored the Pyrenees, and Volney, who analyzed the Middle East, traveled in America, and wrote *Ruines*. The new thinking drew on knowledge of familiar territory as well as far-off lands, natural as well as human causes, and on the transformation of natural philosophy into a doctrine of political progress. Man discovered that civilizations are mortal (Montesquieu proved this in the case of Rome, Volney in that of the Middle East). At the same time, however, people wanted to believe that man's action on nature (from which sprang the need for knowledge) paved the way for future progress. As increasingly efficient technologies were developed and techniques for acquiring useful knowledge were perfected, officials and scholars, professionals and amateurs alike asserted a positive belief in the evolution of man's spatial sense.

Our problem is to understand geography, the science of that spatial sense, in relation to Enlightenment categories rather than the epistemology of the nineteenth or twentieth century. The emerging science was of course shaped by new concepts and methods developed in other disciplines and subsequently imported into geography. The Revolution did not interrupt this process, moreover: the qualitative statisticians of the Napoleonic period, many of whom had been geographers before the political upheaval, carried it on. Prefects sent surveyors into the field to compile figures and charts, in part to assess any damage that the Revolution might have caused. They also sought information useful to both the government and the general public, and in the process rediscovered both the methods and the limitations of prerevolutionary surveys: there were plenty of descriptions, lots of picturesque detail about local variety and chaotic customs, and a great deal about the certainties of nature and the uncertainty of tradition. The interaction of social, political, and cognitive practices from the Enlightenment to the Revolution and beyond tells us a great deal about how modern administration and social analysis developed in parallel.[17]

Knowing the Population

Today we can see this geographical curiosity about space and its heterogeneous characteristics as an aspect of the "spirit of the time." In due course we will need a more precise definition of what this might mean. For the time being, we may view man's relation to space as one manifestation of a more general development of eighteenth-century speculation in relation to the history of the monarchy.

Two strands of tradition have to be unraveled. On the one hand, knowledge and action were associated in the representation of space: to know the kingdom was to draw a map of it. It was to apply methods similar to those of botanical or mineralogical classification, and, before long, of chemistry as transformed by Lavoisier. These methods offered an instrument that was more than just a mirror in which to contemplate the extent and diversity of France; it was also a means of action. Geography, people used to say, was useful for making war, and cartography, which made it possible to map old battles and prepare for new ones, even more so. Clearly, the tools—the map and the discourses associated with it—cannot be separated from the purpose for which they were developed.

Yet the purpose of knowledge was not just to develop tools and explore their variety and limitations but also to act. Classificatory schemes assigned each object to a place in a logical, rational framework, but the map added a spatial dimension whose function was to afford the king a homogeneous grasp of his realm. Maps and surveys were used in the same way: the extent of the king's territory and the ratio of population to resources were important ingredients of the king's power. The ideas of *density* and *average* emerged in response to the need for indexes of royal power and justifications for political reform. "As the notion of wealth as a source of princely power was joined by the notion of wealth as a source of prosperity for his subjects,"[18] that is, as people became aware of the dialectical relationship between the strength of the sovereign and the capacity of his subjects, the responsibility of the former and the obligations of the latter, works appeared to provide the necessary scientific capital. From Vauban, who was read continuously, to Lavoisier, whose *Richesse territoriale* may be taken as the end point of the period (published in 1791, the book was of course the product of considerable prior work),[19] a tradition was forged, with its associated sites, agents, and practices. Its history remains to be written, but the high points can already be indicated.

Maps of France

As we have seen, geography, once the science of places, gradually developed into an interpretation of the local. The old geography of position was strikingly different from the new concrete, active "reading" of space by many types of scholars. This reading was inevitably influenced by the cartographic tradition, as was only to be expected since the project of representing France was inextricably intertwined with the affirmation of monarchical power. Daniel Nordman, following the work of Father de Dainville, demonstrated this, but unfortunately for the eighteenth century there is no equivalent of the work of Pastoureau, the historian of the Sanson dynasty (1630–1730) and the successive editions of atlases. Three major features of the period emerge from the work of these historians: the development of cartography as a profession; the hierarchy of tasks involved in mapmaking; and the importance of Cassini's map of France in revealing the hopes, tensions, and resistances characteristic of the whole enterprise.

A glance at the professionals of geography, the old cosmographers and new cartographers, is enough to suggest how professional qualifications in the field became stricter as the division of labor increased. At the top of the profession were the royal geographers: the Sansons, Duval, Delisle, Buache. The position of royal geographer first emerged in the seventeenth century as part of the king's immediate service. With the Sansons, whose energetic dynasty symbolized the growing importance of the charge and definition of its responsibilities, the office became sedentary and essentially civil in character. The royal geographer became heavily involved in the publication of maps and atlases. The Sansons and their successors—Pierre Duval, the nephew of the dynasty's founder Nicolas Sanson, his brother-in-law, Father Placide, Alexis Jaillot, and the Sanson grandnephews Robert, Gilles, and Didier de Vaugondy—exploited this legacy from the reign of Louis XIV to the Revolution; they reproduced the traditional works. Louis XV appointed his teacher Guillaume Delisle as first royal geographer, and Delisle helped to modernize the post by taking account of work done by the Académie des Sciences. Buache, Delisle's nephew, continued in this direction and offered his services to the government as an expert consultant on matters as diverse as the Paris floods and the future of the colonies. D'Anville and Buache de Neuville continued this tradition.

At the grassroots level were the less well known but equally essential surveyors, *leveurs de terriers* (title clerks), and feudists, who could subdivide great estates into parcels and establish titles to land. Once again the *domaine royal* and royal administration set the example with their *arpenteurs-géographes du roi* (royal surveyor-geographers), an office held throughout the eighteenth century by the Matis family, as well as the *maîtres des eaux et forêts*. The need for the latter developed in the wake of Colbert's forest reforms, where everything depended on the accuracy of the surveyor. The royal administration subsequently devoted considerable effort to the enforcement of ordinances governing the marking and recording of plots and land titles. Two types of surveyors oversaw the exploitation of royal forests: those who reported to the *grand maître des eaux et forêts* and those who reported to a local *maître*. Their functions were similar: to designate certain parts of forests for logging and to ensure that there was no cutting outside designated areas. The routine work of marking cuts and noting violations was not unrelated to the more exalted task of devising an overall plan for forest use, but the latter mission, to which we owe some splendid maps of France's forests, was more often than not assigned to specialists reporting directly to the *grand maître* rather than to local forest surveyors.

The administrative infrastructure developed gradually. In Avallon, the first surveyor, a lumber dealer, was appointed in 1715 (he purchased his office). In 1723 a second *officier* was named, and a third in 1766. The number of surveyors and other forest officers varied from district to district, however, and it was not until after 1750 that the overall situation improved. The number of agents increased, as did their competence. In Nevers, twenty-five commissions were registered between 1730 and 1790. Important economic and social issues lay behind the growing power of the surveyors and increasing frequency of forest surveys: urban growth had raised fears of shortages of wood, and relations between landlords and peasant communities grew increasingly tense. Surveyors were expected to meet higher intellectual standards, and their work improved correspondingly. Crude sketches gave way to careful color-coded plots and eventually to the large-scale maps that were essential for planning the exploitation of vast mountain forests; mapping techniques slowly improved as topographical geometry was universally adopted, not without aesthetic embellishment. These improvements no doubt owed a great deal to growing general interest in the subject (an interest shared by Louis XV and Louis XVI personally), as reflected in the publication of textbooks such as Doyon's *Géométrie de l'arpenteur* (1767), Ginet's *Manuel* (1770–1783), and Dupain de Montesson's *Science de l'arpenteur* (1766–1802) and *Art de lever les plans.* Plots of every variety proliferated (Babeuf estimated that two-thirds of the kingdom's *seigneuries* were "mapped" in the eighteenth century), and the level of technical perfection was unprecedented.[20]

Between these two extremes, which communicated through networks of administrative information and theoretical training, were the intermediate echelons, about which we know more. Practical on-the-job training supplemented by the study of mathematics and drawing was the norm at all levels. In the army, young topographers trained in the field, perhaps drawing on bits of theory learned at school. The schools responded to the requirements of builders, the economy, the military, and the provincial administration. In the late 1740s, Trudaine created the Bureau Topographique of the Ecole des Ponts et Chaussées, founded during the Regency. This geographical institute began as a school of cartography. In 1748 the Ecole de Génie (military engineering school) at Mézières was instructed to train future officers in the use of the plane table, compass, and watercolors. The technique of mapping heights in the plane with respect to the highest point was not unrelated to Monge's work in projective geometry, embodied in that masterpiece, the *Atlas des places fortes.* Finally, field-trained engineer-geographers were sent to Versailles itself for advanced training. Topography was in demand everywhere, at all levels of society, for building roads, canals, cities, and manufacturing facilities. Cassini was obliged to train his own engineers. Provincial assemblies and governors in Guyenne and Rouergue sent mapmakers into the field. A fruitful dialogue with the more sedentary geographers could thus begin.

The proliferation of projects gave rise to a hierarchy of uses and functions of manuscript and printed maps. For forest owners, maps were a defensive weapon, a form of protection: they offered a precise accounting of an economic asset. The evolution of estate and plot plans, which Marc Bloch studied, linked lists of assets and taxpayers to land registers and maps.[21] Economic equilibrium and social relations depended on information of this kind, and what has been called the "feudal reaction" in the period from the end of the seventeenth century to the Revolution was nothing more than a tightening of estate management in light of the newly available kinds of information: changes in the land had to be recorded. The spread of scientific methods spelled an end to less precise management techniques. Mapping sometimes led to more disciplined land use, reflected in ever more detailed, extensive, and complex plot plans. In case of litigation, these could be introduced as evidence in court. In any event, they gave concrete expression to the boundaries that existed between private plots, parishes, *seigneuries,* farms, and types of crops or terrain. It was as if the century wished to prove that it was not afraid of Rousseau's anathema on boundary markers, said to be the source of inequality: "The first man who took it in mind to fence in a field and say this is mine and who found people simple enough to believe was the true founder of civil society . . . Beware of such impostors." The mapping of private property countered such thinking and played its role in the rise of "possessive individualism." It was also related to the constant dispute between proponents and adversaries of mobility, as well as to the debate about economic development and even luxury. From plot plans to the *plans d'intendance* envisioned by Turgot and partially completed in Auvergne, Limousin, and Ile-de-France, maps established the relationship between individuals and space as a matter of ownership and law. The basis of the present-day cadastre (Savoy, a foreign territory, first adopted its cadastre in 1728), these maps also figured in thinking about egalitarian tax reform. But in France the time was not yet ripe for that.[22]

Other customs also contributed to the creative vitality of the eighteenth-century cartographic movement. In the army, royal engineers, trained in "descriptive" techniques at the Ecole at Mézières, helped to plan maneuvers and attacks and played an important role in the development of topography as well as military and civilian cartography.[23] Mézières was a research institution that took its data from staff officers at royal fortifications. Military maps had to satisfy certain requirements: they needed to indicate topographical relief, pinpoint the location of natural obstacles, identify passages, and provide information about resources. Mathematics, geography, statistics, and even economics helped to supply these needs in ways that call for further elucidation.

In the cities the work of cartographers was crucial. Whether trained by the army or the Ponts et Chaussées, they responded to the needs of modern urban construction.[24] Engineers, draftsmen, and construction foremen belonged to the party of change, which waged a successful battle against the forces of tradition led by city aldermen, the Church, and, to a lesser degree, the army. Urban modernization called for new streets, broader vistas, and the building of new monuments, and such projects required maps, plans, sketches, plot analyses, and vast material resources, and, to keep track of all this, countless documents and files that fill hundreds of archives. In Caen, from the seventeenth century to the Revolution, the city's visual odyssey was recounted in nearly seven hundred maps, plans, and sketches: of these, barely fifty date from before 1715, while four-fifths are from the second half of the eighteenth century. The archives record the phases of urban development, along with the aims of the developers and the changing tastes and comprehension of the public.

Pastoureau and Nordman have shown how a wide range of scientific and utilitarian literature found a large audience. Maps, portrayed in paintings since Vermeer, became fashionable with the publication of atlases. Publishers aimed these works at extensive audiences with a variety of purposes. Atlases collected diverse documents in a global or, increasingly, national framework. The Sansons, Jaillots, Defers, and Duvals made atlases their specialty. For wealthy amateurs they produced sumptuous volumes that presented official documents in a unified, rational manner, emphasizing two themes appreciated by the public: maps of administrative boundaries and historical geography. Leading eighteenth-century publishers such as Jaillot and Desnos (who bought out Jaillot's operation) popularized "postal maps" and a traveler's guide known as the *Indicateur fidèle*. Geography counted on increased mobility even as it helped people to know exactly where they were. Its audience grew, starting with kings and princes on down to military men, magistrates, and professional geographers who needed to collect reference materials. Schools acquired atlases and travel guides and developed new ways of teaching about space. Space itself was rationalized: think of the numbering of houses and the posting of street names in cities.[25] Students learned the practical benefits of scientific discoveries and administrative rationalizations.

Meanwhile, central government officials from Colbert to Orry promoted a unified, centralized, systematic national cartography. This was not only a scientific project but also a political one: the state was in charge, even if the Académie des Sciences shouldered much of the responsibility, since modern mapmaking required rigorous measurements and expert skills. The preparatory work—measurement of altitudes and meridians and triangulation of the territory—took three-quarters of a century; it took fourteen years just to establish the network of triangles necessary for mapping. By 1744 this work was complete, and Cassini III was able to publish part of a first map at a scale of 1/886,000. Further progress depended on a curious partnership between public initiative and private organization. Cassini had the support of the king and a subsidy from the royal treasury, but "he founded a joint stock company that benefited from the enthusiasm of the court as well as the more durable backing of the scientific community. He would therefore have to endure the consequent vagaries of fortune."[26] This national map, intended as a royal monument, was still incomplete at the time of the Revolution, despite the efforts of a team of some twenty engineers recruited, trained, and set to work throughout France. Apart from financial difficulties, the project soon ran into two obstacles: lack of real support from the provincial authorities, many of which were involved in rival ventures, as in Languedoc, and conflict between the map and established local customs.

Cassini (as of 1756) hoped to distribute 2,500 copies of the map to three audiences: the king, his subjects, and a local clientele. For the king it was "advantageous and necessary to know the country under his rule." For his subjects, it was "useful to have accurate knowledge of the location of places to which their interests might take them." As for local clients,

Cassini hoped to sell each sheet of the map to 500 customers (and with a projected 182 sheets, this meant distribution to some 100,000 buyers, a considerable and no doubt exaggerated number). Cassini believed that they would be "curious to have maps of their territory and the surrounding area." Sales did not meet expectations and declined steadily from 1760 to 1765. Profits were not as great as predicted. The army, stripped of exclusive control of one of its key instruments, persuaded the revolutionary government to confiscate the map, thus reinstating the military monopoly on topographic information, which became a state secret.[27] France had its unified map, but it was a map that reflected the criteria of geometers and only partially met the needs of the majority of its users: it was behind the times in regard to "indications of terrain," details of roads, and reliefs. The opposition of the military was reinforced by the provincial authorities' open distrust of an instrument that failed to accommodate all of their interests. All in all, Cassini's undertaking reflected many changes and needs typical of eighteenth-century society; it was a public project that crystallized tensions between the public and private, Paris and the provinces, the army and civilians, and geometers and topographers.

From Map to Survey and Survey to Classification

Maps are useful for location and measurement. They give us indications of how space was conceived of, organized, and related to surrounding space. Eighteenth-century mapmaking suffered from two limitations. First, there was no available technique for representing spatial networks and thus for representing relational systems on a unified national scale. The effects of this can be seen in the postal routes of the period, which reflect a fragmentary idea of space with no conception of hierarchy or functional complementarity. Second, Enlightenment cartography found it difficult to bridge the gap between representation of content and representation of the container. Few maps indicate regional productive output or divide space along thematic lines. In this respect, maps lagged behind qualitative and quantitative statistics, for the data relevant to such thematic mapping had been available for some time. Indeed, since Colbert, the government had gathered such data in order to keep track of the workings of the administration and control the flow of resources. The *intendants'* survey *(enquête des intendants)* of the late seventeenth century was a model of the genre, one that left an indelible mark on French intellectual and administrative tradition.

The *intendants'* survey was typical of monarchical practice. Its purpose was to educate the heir to the throne, and the stakes were nothing less than the general prosperity and grandeur of France. The man who would be king was obliged to learn about his kingdom, for, as Fénelon said, "any king ignorant of such things would be only half a king: his ignorance would leave him incapable of correcting what was wrong and do him more harm than would corruption in those who governed under him."[28] In order to know the present "state of the kingdom," the future king needed a general picture of how things stood: quality of the land, number of inhabitants, aptitude for work, customs, professions, stability of *corps.* The survey mirrored the kingdom in any number of ways: the manner in which it was conducted, from center to periphery, prince to *intendants;* its basic categories; and its guiding fiscal and mercantilist concerns. The *intendants'* survey revealed the state of France at a specific and difficult moment in time: the decade of crisis from 1690 to 1700, when statesmen and reformers worried about the poverty of the people, the future of the economy and of commerce, and the consequences of war and religious turmoil. It was accompanied by such forward-looking initiatives as the establishment of *capitation* in 1695.[29]

The *intendants'* survey continued to influence eighteenth-century administrators and has been used by historians ever since. Although much depended on the personality of the *intendants* who responded to the king's questionnaire, the survey tells us a great deal about the culture of those who confronted the difficult tasks of government at the time. Its very structure offers a good example of this. Despite the diversity of questions and answers, the survey as a whole was shaped by a consistent descriptive conception: after a brief historical review and rapid topographical evaluation, each author was expected to explore first institutions (ecclesiastical, military, judicial, and financial) and then fiscal resources, described in terms of the province's aptitude for commerce and manufacturing. The survey reveals the inherent limitations on royal action and the possibility of unification in a still heterogeneous state. To know the present state of the kingdom was to apprehend the body politic, and to a lesser extent the body social, in terms of administrative and economic function. The task also called for painting a portrait of the king's subjects: How civilized were they in comparison with court society, and what state of development had they achieved when measured in utilitarian terms? Parts of France were still crude and wild (drunken Bretons, lazy, crude southerners), while other parts were civilized (Angevins, for example, were mild-mannered and literate); the hard-working, industrious, and even prosperous portions of the realm stood out from the regions that were listless, indolent, and underdeveloped. The value of this sort of portrait depended on the conviction that such stereotypes reflected the "natural" character of the inhabitants of each region, a character that was important to identify even if impossible to change.[30] "Numerous, hard-working, docile subjects in a prosperous, efficiently administered kingdom: this, for the time being, was what interested the king and his officials far more than the variety of customs, beliefs, and dialects."[31]

This tradition of gearing surveys to administrative districts would endure to the end of the Ancien Régime and beyond with the collection of statistics by *département*. In the epistemological debate that pitted description against counting, the influence of the *intendants'* survey under Louis XIV was decisive. Instead of mathematical abstraction, the survey or local monograph purported to be a portrait drawn from nature. It could accommodate everything from natural conditions to social conditions to provide a composite portrait by which the king's representatives could gauge their actions. Each place was defined by the changing interrelationship among these constituent elements. This approach was well suited to the capacities of an administration that lacked survey personnel of its own and was obliged to rely on information provided by subdelegates, curés, tax collectors, manufacturing inspectors, and engineers of Ponts et Chaussées. Increasingly, the information they provided was supplemented by information from private sources: large landowners and wholesalers contacted through royal societies of agronomy and consulates; after 1750, moreover, local doctors played a major role. The resulting "descriptive statistics"—typified by the surveys of 1730, 1745, and 1764 initiated by *contrôleurs généraux* from Orry to L'Averdy, as well as by the *intendants'* survey—were shaped not so much by scientific logic as by competition among ministerial departments and local agents.

The interests of the state were served by the spread of Enlightenment culture by way of local academies, agricultural societies, reading rooms, lodges, and philosophical salons. The elites who were drawn together by recognition of their cultural power shared not only the same educational baggage but also the message of the *Encyclopédie*, which provided them with both a vocabulary and a classificatory scheme, that of d'Alembert's Table of Knowledge, as well as a firm belief in the idea that the government was willing to listen to reason and inform itself in order to reform itself. They were its legitimate counselors, who believed that the sciences of man were to be used for the benefit of man. Hygienists, geographers, physicians, administrators, and economists all contributed. For them, it made sense to understand social relations in the terms made popular by the very works of "natural history" that these academicians often discussed in their meetings. Listen to the geographer Darluc: "The natural history of a province whose only purpose was to study that province's fossils, climate, and products could at best do little more than satisfy our curiosity. By contrast, a natural history that could tie all these aspects together and attempt to draw conclusions pertinent to the human species and if possible relevant to public utility would be far more valuable."[32]

A compendium of knowledge in which the facts would speak for themselves and yield all their implications: this faith, which owed a great deal to Montesquieu's *De l'esprit des lois,* lay at the heart of the system of descriptive statistics. It belonged to the same conceptual universe as the dictionary, the agronomic topography (one model for which was the book of Arthur Young), and the scenic journey. Another type of survey came out of a different universe: its purpose was to collect data necessary for the administration of the kingdom. The hope was to compute averages, constants, and arithmetic regularities—in short, to work toward homogenization and abstraction, to go from the particular to the general rather than the reverse. This second type of survey, which drew its inspiration from English "political arithmetic" rather than German "cameral science" *(Kammerwissenschaft),* developed primarily after 1750. It inherited some of its methods from the seventeenth century, from Vauban's initiatives and from the sources of the *contrôleurs généraux* and other major administrative departments such as Bignon's *librairie,* and developed standard techniques for counting the population, evaluating available foodstuffs, gauging the health of industrial sectors, and monitoring prices and trade volumes. From Louis XIV to Louis XVI, the royal administration thus gathered records and statistics based on varying periods of measurement (a year, a semester, a month) in response to the need for specific data about a specific problem such as the state of the printing industry or paper manufacturing, mines or forges, tanneries or agricultural output.

These standard accounting practices fostered two characteristic attitudes. First, they encouraged continuous communication on specific issues between local administrations and the central government. Study of these sources thus always reveals the discrepancy between the political interests and economic and social concerns of the local and central authorities. Second, the surveys encouraged belief in the idea that statistical information could provide a basis for enlightened government action. Whether the goal was to monitor the food supply, count the population, or keep track of criminal behavior (as the Montyon survey did from 1775 to 1786), the goal clearly was no longer just to record for the sake of knowledge and classification but to collect social data in order to develop the means to respond to short-term emergencies as well as pursue long-range objectives.

In various ways, moreover, survey results moved from the realm of state secrecy (where information was kept in manuscript form and circulated by copy, slowly and at great cost) into the public domain. The results of the *intendants'* survey, for example, were contained in an imposing volume of documents, copied and recopied sometimes with slight revisions and kept both in central government repositories (for comparative purposes) and in local archives or even collected by senior state servants such as M. d'Argenson and the duc de Croÿ. By 1727, excerpts began to be published and used. Boulainvilliers's *Etat de France* is typical of this process of diffusion: a dozen copies are known to have been dispersed across France. The first published edition appeared posthumously in English. It gave rise to a tradition of political criticism. Dictionaries and other works revisited various incomplete aspects of the original survey. Thus, administrative secrecy ultimately gave way to the demand for knowledge, with the result that information fifty or sixty years out of date was made available to a public that often interpreted it without the necessary detachment. This was the case with Savary's *Grand Dictionnaire du commerce*, first published in 1723 and subsequently reprinted and often plagiarized; it gave wide currency to information collected between 1695 and 1715. At the end of the Ancien Régime, the archives were gradually opened to investigators. Necker set the example with his *Compte rendu de l'état du royaume*, which captured the attention of the public and thus expanded the terms of political debate.

The stakes were considerable, even if the results did not become apparent until later. The goal was to end the isolation that had left arithmeticians starved for data and forced them to resort to abstract computation and logical deduction. We see this in the history of the census, where demographic issues were slow to disentangle themselves from questions of marriage and taxes. Administrators needed the proper conceptual tools to collect good data. A brief "golden age" resulted from "the cooperation of power with intelligence, which made it possible to go beyond economic and human science."[33] France became less elusive.

Administer and Classify

Central to the relationships established by the new science and its associated technologies were two things that bear emphasizing. First, the need for classification was felt in many areas: François Dagognet wrote a book about the period entitled *The Catalogue of Life*.[34] Second, there was a vast gray area between everyday action and perception and scientific knowledge and theory, a frontier where ordinary spatial habits and perceptions crystallized.

With its surveys, measurements, and bookkeeping, the administration propagated a way of seeing and technique of management whose logic was based on counting, inseparable from classification. Determining the magnitude of the tax base, the size of the population, and the number of crimes or cases of disease required schemes of classification. Inventories and incomes, ages and sexes, crimes and punishments, nosologies and remedies are all categories that reveal not only a set of facts but also a way of organizing them. This is important for understanding phenomena as various as a poll-tax register, a library catalogue, or a parish inspection report. For the historian, no classification is neutral: each one reveals something about how the people who used it thought about what they were doing, how they justified their choices, and what effects those choices may have had. In medicine, one cannot treat what one does not recognize, which leads to the classification and naming of diseases; but every taxonomy of disease is also a recipe for change. So the Société Royale de Médecine was really promoting change in 1776, when it produced its "medical topographies" of France. The aim was to improve the health of the public in both body and mind. Knowledge was a prelude to change.[35]

Hence there was a connection between administrative science and natural science. In both it was important to discover the essence of things, to find operative criteria of selection, to grasp the connections between the visible and the invisible, the outside and the inside: in other words, to make a diagnosis. To that end, cameral science, like botany and medicine, chemistry and mineralogy, developed a vocabulary that allowed its practitioners to interpret and deduce properties and predict future developments. All of nature was read as a code, and taxonomy became an instrument of progress. Everything was systematically summarized in tables so detailed that nothing escaped. "It shaped the destiny of society." Collections, whether of plants, books, or objects, not only delighted people fascinated by the mysteries of profusion, the aesthetics of spectacle, and the joy of ownership, but also promised in the long run to grant mastery over nature and things; it linked material culture to intellectual culture. "Natural order is like the philosopher's stone of the chemist," wrote Antoine Laurent de Jussieu.[36] The realm of the living was captured in catalogues, transforming the world: the new catalogues had repercussions on the production and economics of plants and animals, reshaping markets and confronting government officials with new problems. In the late eighteenth century, a strong affinity emerged between botanical and zoological classification and nosology.

Gardens, hothouses, and herbariums brought civilization to vegetal nature. Techniques first tried out in the forests were later extended through the use of substances derived from organic chemistry and the study of fossils. Animals were important because they provided the energy on which the whole system of production and distribution depended. These are the characteristic features of what might be called the "ecotechnical" phase of technological development: change came about through the extension of existing science and technology. Later, the industrial revolution accelerated these changes and led to an environmental crisis. Before that, however, logging and forestry dominated the trades; wheat preoccupied the agronomists; and the history of the harvest was the main preoccupation of managerial theory. The large "manufactories" were dependent on farming: on sheep for wool and on dyestuffs made from plants. The state encouraged travelers and experimenters. As François Dagognet has shown, the period was crucial in several respects:

> Botany became as different from what it had been as it was from horticulture and herb gardening: it went from the empirical stage to a more rigorously deductive one. In fact, it was the advent of the term

"plant" that set things in motion and justified the change. The word stood for more than the "vegetal" that it replaced. Anyone who knew the correct name could use it as a sort of talisman to discover the thing itself and everything related to it. This is what a successful intersection looks like.[37]

The work of the Adansons, Jussieu, Linnaeus, and Tournefort, as well as, on a smaller scale, Rousseau, whose letters made botany popular among the elite, made deduction as well as naming possible. It promised more rapid progress in a variety of areas.

Work in zoological classification by Vicq d'Azir, Cuvier, Bourgelat, and later Geoffroy Saint-Hilaire similarly made a place for animals in the world of civilization, and just as in botany this work was conceived as having a utilitarian purpose. Medicine developed along similar lines from nosology to the clinic. The catalogues and methods of the neo-Hippocratics exposed the wounds of the body social (as in Tenon's 1788 survey of Paris hospitals) and raised the hope that scientific methods of classification and separation might provide a remedy. All these various ways of knowing and acting were related. Knowledge was organized around sense data, primarily derived from the sense of sight, and used to develop a system of rational classification as well as a rational cartography of the living. Administrative intelligence thus fueled both scientific projects and social aspirations and shaped the questions that men of learning asked and the diagnoses they offered.

2

❧❧❧❧❧❧

Mastery of Space

THE PRESENT AGE has mastered space: near space, in which nothing more stands in the way of our movement, and outer space, in which time has no limit. The world is at our doorstep. By contrast, the people of eighteenth-century France experienced distance as an everyday problem and a cost in human and monetary terms. It took a long time for orders, news, and information to reach their destination. Space caused "congestion" in the human relations of the past, and we must learn to recognize this. The whole era would join forces to achieve the fluidity necessary for the kind of social development that people dreamed of and strove to achieve.

From household to village, village to province, and province to kingdom, space figured centrally in economic thinking. Mercantilists vied with physiocratic and liberal innovators. Economic descriptions were spatialized: the concept of an economic "circuit," central to contemporary analysis, had been discussed since the seventeenth century.[1] As trade and manufacturing evolved, markets were defined by the ability to move goods. Roads, canals, rivers, ships, and port facilities were the instruments of a trade policy that was essential to the creation of a national market.

Here as elsewhere, England set the tone. Nature had blessed the British Isles: valleys once verdant with farm and pasture might now be gloomy with industrial plants and coal mines, but these facilities enjoyed easy access to the sea. Local shipping linked London to countless other ports, and improved rivers (more than a thousand miles of navigable waterway in 1750) made it possible to ship heavy commodities at relatively low cost. Speculators made money on canals, and road construction, though a matter of local or even private interest, drew capital from landowners, farmers, industrialists, and merchants across the nation. In short, England witnessed a veritable revolution in transportation.

In France the transportation revolution took a different form. The kingdom countered regional isolation through improvements to its transportation infrastructure. It did so because isolation was an obstacle to growth. Since growth is more than simply an economic matter, we cannot measure circulation simply in terms of the flow of raw materials and manufactured products. "Commerce" had two meanings: whether domestic or foreign, it was the driving force in the development of markets and the consequent development of manufacturing (it was not until the nineteenth century that the cause and effect relation was reversed); and, in a more general sense, it was a force that promoted reciprocal social relations, a key factor in sociability. Véron de Forbonnais made this very point in the *Encyclopédie:*

> Infinite Providence, whose work nature is, sought, through the variety it established in nature, to make men dependent on one another. The Supreme Being bound nation to nation in such a way as to preserve the peace and promote love for one another, and also, by filling the universe with marvels, to garner their praise by demonstrating his greatness and his love for all. And so it came to pass that human ideas and passions found their place in the unalterable order of eternal decrees. Because men can supply one another with a variety of goods, they become mutually dependent; this is true not only of real needs but also of the need for a variety of opinions.[2]

In a style not very far from that of Abbé Pluche and the *Spectacle de la nature,* and with a teleology capable of reconciling the mercantile order with the divine, the author of *Eléments du commerce* (1754) and *Observations sur l'esprit des lois* (1753) clearly indicated the importance of social and cultural factors in the thinking of those who defended the free market system and the role of "natural circulation." From Montesquieu to Condillac, "gentle commerce," civilizing commerce, had not only an economic meaning but also a connotation of "civility," discipline, and useful participation in social life. This richly evocative term, which Marx would hold up to ridicule in his account of primitive capital accumulation,[3] thus expressed the culmination of the process of circulation and overcoming of isolation, defragmentation and expansion, which linked the local economy to the world economy.

Hence the study of the material aspects of communication should also disclose broader transformations that affected the realm of thinking and ideas. How did mobility affect progress and the construction of new social relations? At a time when "philosophies," propounded by men of action as well as philosophes, sought to give men roots—stable homes, vital statistics, official papers—we must try to understand how factors of stability and movement interacted. After exploring these factors, which were crucial because of their social impact, we will turn to the men who created the new social space and networks of communication, the builders and artisans of circulation: architects and engineers. And among them we will find a conflict that reflected the clash between two principles of improvement, two ideas of space: on the one hand, an aesthetic ideal, an idea of culture as the primary collective expression of a collective consciousness, of the "spirit" that Montesquieu ascribed to each nation—in short, the classical ideal according to which "utility is not the same thing as propriety"—and, on the other hand, an idea of space associated with a demiurgic will embodied in a new territorial reality and a far-reaching project. In the end, economic conceptions of space were overturned.

Roads and Water: A Policy of Communication

By the time of Louis XV's accession to the throne, the country's rulers were already concerned with the rational organization of French space. Since the time of Colbert, *contrôleurs généraux* and *intendants* and to a lesser degree *trésoriers*, who shouldered local responsibility for France's roadways and who were somewhat slower to respond than those above them, had given thought to increasing France's domestic and foreign trade by improving "circulation" throughout the nation. Roads were classified according to their economic value, and specialists calculated their profitability.[4]

Within a world still governed by custom emerged the idea that space has different qualities as it pertains to the circulation of men, ideas, and commodities, a circulation that could be aided by conveniently located facilities. The early triangulation surveys led to uniform maps and thus helped pave the way for the elimination of local particularisms. The anarchic juxtaposition of such particularisms inevitably gave way to the modern conception of the nation's territory, which could be measured and conceptualized in technical as well as economic terms.[5]

Such was the ideal as it existed at the dawn of the Enlightenment, but the means available for its realization were mediocre.

Early eighteenth-century roads were more like the rudimentary trails that one finds today in the Third World than they were like modern superhighways. Most roads were natural rather than constructed, except in the vicinity of Paris, which needed better roads to handle its huge volume of supplies. The road network around the capital was well developed in all directions, even toward the northeastern border. Users of roads were obliged to cope with natural obstacles. Roadbeds were narrow and capricious and tended to snake their way through valleys wherever possible or follow ridge lines when necessary. Dense in the plains, roadways were sparse in mountainous areas and in isolated parts of western France. Improvements depended on fortuitous coincidences between needs and resources, as well as on local capabilities, generally mediocre, and of course encouragement from on high. Strictly speaking, the idea of a road network did not yet exist, for it depended on the concept of a hierarchy of interconnections, and this was slow to develop.[6] The road also competed with the waterway, although travel by water faced similar difficulties and obstacles. In the absence of improvements, natural impediments raised the cost of travel. If roads and waterways were sometimes competitors, they could also work together. Highways and rivers became increasingly interdependent, and with that interdependence came a new obsession: how to link arteries of communication to life in the regions they passed through. This was the problem that Arthur Young posed, not very objectively, on the eve of the Revolution, on his first journey, even though the data gathered by the engineers contradicts his hypothesis:

October 9–10–11, 1788. Returning by way of Beauvais and Pontoise and entering Paris for the fourth time, I confirmed that the roads leading to this capital were deserted compared with those leading to London. What sort of relation do they have with the countryside? Either the French are the most sedentary people on earth, who, once they are in a place, remain there without any thought of going anywhere else, or else the English are the most mobile, and take greater pleasure in running from one place to another than in remaining at rest to enjoy life.[7]

It is clear that the economics of travel is also a matter of national psychology, hence of culture.

The Road: From Means to Ends and Concept to Technology

Roads had long been the business of the state. The organizational work begun by Colbert continued after him. In 1713 the status of the various technicians recruited in the provinces was standardized. Each *généralité* had one engineer and ten inspectors general. A hierarchy took shape. The Regency reorganized this hierarchy and in 1716 instituted a *corps* that subsists to this day.

From that date on, the *généralités* were placed under the authority of an inspector general, a first engineer, and twenty-one additional engineers; three inspectors maintained liaison among the various departments of the agency. Before the Revolution, however, the provinces with their own Estates General (*pays d'Etats* as opposed to *pays d'élections*) were not included in this hierarchy, so that in Burgundy, Languedoc, Brittany, and Provence a competition developed that was hard to manage. Roads were a means of asserting autonomy in the face of expanding royal power and, after 1716, in defiance of the *contrôleur général*, who was in charge of finances and highway planning.

A second milestone came in 1728, with the creation of the Bureau des Dessinateurs and the appointment of Trudaine as *intendant* in 1743. The training of engineers is a good example of the economic, technical, and pedagogical accomplishments of the enlightened French administration. Trudaine (1703–1769) was a magistrate, *intendant,* and civil servant committed to scientific progress. In 1747 he added another man to his staff whose role would prove to be even more important than his own. Perronet (1708–1794) was the son of a Swiss Guard cadet who lacked the fortune necessary for a career in the corps of fortifications. He worked for the city of Paris in the department of quay architecture and joined the road administration in 1735. After 1747 he played a greater role in the reform of the highway system than did Trudaine. A mathematician, architect, *Encyclopédie* collaborator, and member of the Académie des

Sciences and the Académie d'Architecture, he was a very important official, an empirical and prudent man aware of the latest scientific discoveries but more pragmatist than scientist.

Perronet's efforts were concentrated in two main areas. First, he improved the training of engineers by requiring instruction in mechanics, hydraulics, calculus, and draftsmanship. His vision was reflected in project competitions, where geometry and draftsmanship reigned supreme.[8] It was the first time that anyone concerned himself with the specific needs and requirements of a regularly appointed corps of engineers. The military engineering school at Mézières, the rival of the school of Ponts et Chaussées, was not established until 1848. Perronet's work was also crucial in the creation of the Assemblée des Ponts et Chaussées. In 1747, for example, this group discussed highway policy and technical matters. A steadily increasing budget made it possible to move from the planning stage to realization: in the early 1700s, the average annual expense on roads was under a million livres; by 1740 it was close to 5 million, and by 1786 it was up to 9 million.[9]

Road policy during the Enlightenment would attempt to respond to the difficulties that had plagued the highway infrastructure in the age of Louis XIV. Irregularity gave way to regularity; discontinuous itineraries were replaced by continuous ones that ended the need for unnecessary loading and unloading. The program that was discussed in meetings, developed in plans, and little by little implemented on the ground reflected a desire to dominate nature and end regional isolation by improving the flow of goods and people.

These goals were furthered by a series of regulations, whose main points deserve to be summarized. In 1720 the hierarchy of roads was defined and widths specified for each type of road: royal roads *(routes royales)* were 60 feet wide (19.4 meters), highways *(grands chemins)* 48 feet, royal ways *(chemins royaux)* 36, and crossroads 30. Establishing these standards made it possible to develop priorities and organize work schedules. Meanwhile, engineers worked on ways to stabilize the roadway so that traffic would no longer be subject to the vagaries of the seasons, mud, and rutting. Stone fill and paving were the favored techniques, and then basic maintenance was required to keep the roads dry and hard in all seasons. Among many important works from this crucial period in the history of roadbuilding, one that stands out is that of Pierre Marie Jérôme Trésaguet, a collaborator of Turgot in the Limoges years around

1670, whose 1775 *Mémoire sur la construction et l'entretien des chemins* became the engineers' bible. Trésaguet solved two key problems: he showed how roads could be economically covered with a thin, carefully smoothed layer of pebbles in such a way that passing carriages did not pull up paving stones and dig deep ruts; and he provided for regular maintenance by establishing a corps of road workers whose job was to repair minor damage before it got worse.

Although the Trésaguet system took time to catch on (it was only after 1787 that its true impact was felt), it nevertheless marked an important step forward. The road system was now seen as a systematic, organized project, one element in an ongoing technological process that would eventually reduce costs, save effort, and permit travel at greater speeds. Carriage makers and mechanics began to think about improvements they could make: wider rims, lighter suspensions, and improved steering, along with the kinds of amenities on display in works such as the *Parfait Cocher*. A whole civilization took to the road.

Roads, Economics, and the Enlightenment

These developments highlighted a variety of arts and crafts. Royal roads, with their straight lines, bridges (another major area of theoretical activity), and other structures were like monuments.[10] They etched the power of the monarchy into the landscape itself. They also served a military and strategic purpose, extending military power from its central headquarters in Paris toward the frontiers over a network of roadways. Military convoys traveled over paved roads and various shortcuts across the axial network. The movement of troops was thus disciplined.

Meanwhile, the government extended its control over the territory. In the *Encyclopédie méthodique* the chevalier de Pommereul wrote: "Roads are to the state what arteries are to the human body." The organic metaphor suggests that the viewpoint of the physician and anatomist influenced that of the economist and engineer and vice versa. Major roads served as conduits for laws, civilization, and commerce. The royal authorities maintained way stations *(relais de poste)*, which punctuated the journeys of couriers, riders, carriages and their passengers. Their location and density reflected regional needs: they were more numerous, for example, around Paris and along the approaches to mountainous regions. At these stops, travelers could refresh themselves and change horses. From fewer than 800 in 1700, the number of such way stations grew to 1,426 in 1788, an average of one per one and a half to two posts (13–17 kilometers), depending on the route. The *Indicateur fidèle*, published regularly by Desnos, enabled travelers to calculate their routes. Postmasters and innkeepers, those stock literary characters, were also real personages who did their part in opening up the kingdom to foreign and domestic travel.

Finally, roads had a crucial "multiplier effect" on a wide range of activities. They facilitated the transmission of economic and political information and accelerated the circulation of monetary and financial instruments. Safe roads, free from bandits, attracted gold and paper and lowered interest rates. For merchants and manufacturers, improved roads opened up urban markets and allowed the scale of business to increase. Political and economic theorists called for the abolition of private toll-gates as an obstacle to trade. A royal commission set to work on this issue in 1725 and eliminated many such tolls. As roads increased trade and made new speculation possible, their presence or absence introduced inequalities that spurred discussion among the enlightened public. With a network of some 6,000 leagues (or 26,000 kilometers) of roads, France seemed a model for other countries in the mastery of space. Debate centered on two issues, inequality of service and the cost of road maintenance, which revealed latent social conflicts.

The work of the engineers had focused on the major axes, leaving many secondary roads in substandard condition. The economists Cantillon and Galiani foresaw perverse effects if roads were improved without systematic network planning. Instead of an interconnected network of solid trunk roads, complementary and distinct routes were built on an ad hoc basis. The nationwide network planned by the administration was never built. Reasoning in terms of flow, circulation, and arteries, technicians inspired by medical, anatomical, and hydraulic analogies laid the groundwork for a longer-term policy. What was achieved before the Revolution reflected shorter-term thinking, but its effects were still visible. Regional differences were accentuated (single-crop grain production increased to meet the needs of Paris). The price mechanism adjusted relations between different markets and led to increased local trade that allowed a greater social and geographical division of labor. Livestock could be moved into cities, with consequent effects on urban diets. Finally, the major roadways played a key role in the deeper evolution of material civilization by enhancing the value of the land and its products in this proto-industrial society. New and improved roads led to a homogenization of much of the market and merged the various elements of the social and economic system into a totality. Roads and maps unified the territory. "Thanks to these improvements, the mosaic of regions characteristic of the Ancien Régime would eventually give way to a more homogeneous space marked by improved facilities and increased commodity flows."[11]

Because roads, once built, entailed a series of further transformations, they were at the center of political and administrative debate. The road system was crucial in debates in provincial assemblies that put decentralization to the test between 1787 and 1789, as well as in the *pays d'Etats*, which were sometimes quicker to take the initiative than were the *pays d'élections*. In Languedoc, for example, Mme de La Tour du Pin discovered the beauty of southern roads while driving about in the *berline* of her uncle, Archbishop Dillon. Roads also figured in new forms of social conflict. Landowners clashed with the administration, whose proposed routes in some ways offended physiocratic beliefs and, at a deeper level, challenged faith in the land as the source of all wealth, to be preserved at all cost. And later there were noisier, more energetic clashes between peasants and engineers, rural communities and royal authorities such as *intendants* and treasurers, over the issue of *corvées*, or compulsory labor details instituted in the *intendances* to supply labor for building and maintaining roadways.

The *corvée* was a response to the need to finance the government's road-building policy. Whereas the English had adopted a system of payment by users (through tolls and turnpikes), the French royal administration preferred to finance roads through taxes. The issue was at once financial, economic, and political. Orry, the *contrôleur général*, who took his inspiration from the abbé de Saint-Pierre, believed that the *corvée* was an easy way to mobilize those subject to the *taille* (tallage), even if its application varied from one *généralité* to the next. Requiring a few days' work each year made it possible to avoid a tax increase while hastening construction projects that would benefit local populations. This expedient thus allowed the government to economize on scarce cash while sparing peasants the need to dig deeper into their meager hoards. According to Necker, the *corvée* in 1789 produced the equivalent in labor to 20 million livres in cash, and everyone in the administration agreed that this was a reasonable price to pay for an end to regional isolation.

Among the populace, however, the *corvée* was very unpopular because the burden was unevenly distributed and because it hindered productive work by consuming up to ten days of labor per year. The debate now shifted ground: economists and philosophes made the *corvée* the symbol of arbitrary rule and a sign of the persistence of feudal practices. In an article entitled "Corvée" in the *Méthodique*, Guillaume Grivel emphasized the strange analogy between archaic medieval servitude and major road-building projects. The *corvée* met with passive resistance as early as the 1760s, a decade that witnessed a growing number of people taking positions for or against it. Among the adversaries were the *parlementaires* of Normandy, Toulouse, and Bordeaux, the Physiocrats, the *Ami des hommes*, the marquis de Mirabeau, and Dupont de Nemours, all of whom attacked the hidden taxation and the penalty imposed on production. Among the proponents were the engineers, led by Perronet, Viallet, Diderot's friend Duclos in 1762, and Bourgelat, one of Bertin's close collaborators.

Broadly speaking, we may say that two distinct conceptions of the political clashed over issues of economic development and the mastery of space. The administration of Ponts et Chaussées paid the price for all the discontent. The protests were slow to disappear despite reform policies initiated locally by *intendants* and extended by Turgot in 1776 and later by Necker and his successors. As a result, taxation eventually replaced the *corvée*, but with concessions for the privileged, including the Church and noble landowners. France did not heed the lesson of Adam Smith (1776), according to whom commerce does not pay for roads. France's course of action was justified by the chevalier de Pommereul in the *Méthodique* (1781, 1787): it was consistent with the idea of egalitarian centralization and with a distribution of burdens fair to both rich and poor regions. Mutual cooperation and taxation (in cash after the 1787 abolition of the *corvée*) would provide the means for road improvements in France.[12]

These conflicts had a further dimension in addition to those already mentioned. The *corvée* made it necessary to find new ways to compute mass labor employed in tasks that had nothing to do with the corporate tasks of an earlier era. Although there were geographic variables, the nature of the work was the same everywhere, and engineers could accurately predict how much labor would be required and how long a given project would take. Hence road building contributed to the standardization of the labor market. What is paradoxical is that this took place under the aegis of the administration, not the entrepreneur. Engineers and their culture thus shaped the future of French society.

Rivers and Ports

In the political and economic debate over modernization, rivers, streams, and canals were not neglected, but their development did not stir as much controversy. For one thing, river craft and coastal fleets had long been used to supply major cities: "Without the Seine, the Oise, the Marne, and the Yonne, Paris would not eat, drink, or for that matter keep comfortably warm."[13] For another, the assistance of the administration was not called upon as frequently in this area, despite projects dating all the way back to the time of Colbert. Waterways, or "moving roads," were advantageous for heavy transport and, to a lesser degree, for the movement of lighter goods and passengers. One mule could carry about two hundred pounds. A wagon drawn by a team of two or three fragile and costly horses could carry four to six hundred pounds. But since the time of Vauban, people knew that a boat of reasonable size with a crew of six could be hauled along a canal by just four horses and move as much freight as four hundred cart horses.

The economic consequences of the success of water transport were evident on the Loire. The price of a boat rose sharply throughout the century, and the sailors who hired on for the duration of a voyage or by the year were among the best-paid workers.[14] In 1780, when an ox driver earned about forty livres per year, a sailor could pocket fifty-four livres for a voyage of average duration, say, from Moulins to Paris. The river stimulated hiring, created jobs, and provided work for many trades: boatbuilders, barrel makers, stevedores. Freight costs favored shipping, even if navigation was still slow and not very reliable: during the summer, low water closed canals and halted traffic; during the winter, ice and floods slowed travel and made rivers dangerous. The length of a voyage was unpredictable: it took five days to go from Tours to Orléans if all went well, but if the winds were unfavorable, it could take five to six times that long. Thus, the advantage of shipping by water was calculated on a shipment by shipment basis. Cartage was not so much a competitor as a supplier of cargoes to the boats. France, with its 8,000 kilometers of navigable rivers and nearly 1,000 kilometers of improved canals, was blessed with an important natural and artificial waterway, but it was not developed as intensively as the road network, which often ran parallel to rivers. Coastal shipping also remained attractive, despite the imponderables of weather and warfare. Quesnay praised it in the *Encyclopédie*.[15] In his view, France's 2,700 kilometers of coastline, the English example, low prices, and the existence of a large number of small ports and major trading centers all contributed to economic growth.

The dynamic changes stimulated by the spate of road building were not duplicated in the realm of shipbuilding, navigational technique, or waterway improvement. Most of the major construction projects in this area were complete before 1725, and it was not until the late 1760s and 1780s that other projects came to fruition: the canal du Nord and the canal de Franche-Comté. There was no shortage of initiatives on paper, however, and many of these plans survive in the archives of provincial administrations. La Lande, a member of the Académie, remarked on some of these in his 1778 *Traité des canaux de navigation*. Perronet's pupils drew up plans and blueprints for locks and dikes, especially after 1781. Their work belongs to a great French tradition going back to the "age of scarce water" and "hydraulic architecture."[16] Mingling the military tradition with that of the mechanic, the art of the engineer here relied less on mathematical computations than on the geometry of proportions. Technicians were still steeped in the traditions of the arts. Bélidor's construction can be seen as the ultimate expression of this attitude. As d'Aviler wrote in his *Dictionnaire* (1755): "The principal purpose of hydraulic architecture is to build in water and to make the use of water more convenient . . . the construction of bridges, reefs, quays, dikes, locks, and mills . . . We deal with natural as well as artificial streams, both to make them navigable and to bring them to the places where they are needed."

Mastering water also led to improvements in machinery. It was still directly linked to all the objectives of architecture (monuments, gardens landscaping), but increasingly it had to do with harnessing energy for the purposes of both transportation and manufacturing. Machine building had been associated with thinking about modernization ever since the Renaissance. Belidor proposed to perfect the hydraulics of Vitruvius, and his future lay not in the domination of space but in the transformation of water consumption.[17]

For the engineer of Ponts et Chaussées, the introduction of mathematical analysis undermined the traditional maxims. The work of Antoine Gaspard de Prony and Pierre Simon Girard contributed to this change. Water flow, canal profiles, and piping layouts had to be calculated in accordance with formulas dictated by the principles of applied hydrodynamics. By the end of the eighteenth century, the crisis in the Vitruvian art was over, and the new consensus was evident in the design of bridges and canals. The mastery of space and the struggle to build over water[18] were in many ways related to urbanization and the consequent need to supply adequate food and water and to contend with the challenges of building ports, docks, and locks.[19] Like road building, hydraulic construction was conceived as a process; it required the measurement of volumes of water and distribution of forces, and the velocity of the fluid had to be tamed. Technological progress had to be quantified and construction work rationalized.

What place did water occupy in the Enlightenment? Rivers were calm and controlled: floods were fortunately rare, but when they occurred allowed geographers and hydraulic engineers to make otherwise impossible observations. Canals and ports were improved. All this created a double image of man's relation to nature. One image highlighted tradition and the experience of the past century. The other heralded the triumph of trade and the progress of industry. The first image reflected the social history of the riverside populations of the Seine, Rhone, Loire, Garonne, and Dordogne: these microsocieties lived in harmony with the seasons and depended on the river's flow and moods. A river is not just a waterway; it is also a region that provides people with work and subsistence. It drives mills, soaks hemp, brings fishermen their aquatic harvest, floats rafts of logs and barges of stone downstream, and carries feed, merchandise, wheat, and coal. It draws traffic from an entire region and links the ocean and the exotic lands beyond to the hinterland upstream, but slowly, without exacting an unbearable price on those who live beside it. The inhabitants of the regions flanking all of France's major rivers were enticed by the rapidly growing volume of trade. A hierarchy developed, separating the sedentary from the wanderers and, among the latter, the merchants who controlled the flow of traffic from the transporters and shippers who always had one foot in the water and the other on land.

The river was a crossroads where needs and goods came together, a place where the interests of farmers, artisans, and merchants could meet, a territory still marked by such feudal vestiges as tolls and other duties but now open as well to the new dynamic of trade. Riverside populations were subjected to a variety of pressures operating on different time scales: from major traders, from old settlements, from the administration with its penchant for control and modernization. Outdated practices were swept away, but the riverside populations paid the price of progress: after 1780 they were subject to the *régime des classes*, which they found hard to tolerate.[20]

River and ocean ports symbolized the spirit of expansion and mastery of the water. In the minds of the engineers, port cities deserved special attention because they could galvanize the development of whole regions. In Nantes, Bordeaux, and Marseilles, and to a lesser extent in Lorient, Le Havre, La Rochelle, and Dunkerque, urban development programs gave concrete expression to an ideal of modernization that reflected both the civilizing power of commerce and new social needs. In a fever of private building and real estate speculation, docks and stock exchanges, theaters and public monuments symbolized the ambitions and dreams of these new cities. Meanwhile, in activities ranging "from shipbuilding to the construction of harbors, jetties, and dry docks, ports drew the most advanced technological activities of the day."[21] The engineers therefore turned their minds to the possibility of rationalizing port operations such as shipbuilding and cargo storage and proposed grandiose plans for reorganizing ports from top to bottom. In the realm of planning, they combined an aesthetic ideal with a dynamic economy and a philosophical vision in which technology and progress were compatible.

Vernet's *Ports de France* offers the same message. Born in Avignon, Claude Joseph Vernet quickly won international recognition after a long stay in Italy (1738–1753). He was the son of an architect and decorator, whose seascapes, luminous and open urban landscapes, country scenes, and paintings of picturesque landmarks (although the word "picturesque" did not yet exist) made him one of the chief proponents of the new concept of civilized nature. Nature, as Abbé Goujenos put it in his commentary on the Salon of 1748, was the place most susceptible to the representation of action and variety, most apt for capturing the quick play of light. A "physicist" with a shrewd eye for nature, whose most distinctive moments he was able to catch in paint,[22] Vernet could credit his success, together with the admiration of the entourage of the marquis de Marigny, the new *contrôleur des Bâtiments du roi* (consisting of Cochin the engraver, Abbé Leblanc the aesthetic theorist, and Soufflot the architect), with earning him a commission to paint a series of large paintings of

France's ports. This commission marked a decisive step in art patronage, heralding a new determination to honor commerce, urbanity, and urbanism through serious painting. All the major and picturesque ports were included: Toulon, Marseilles, Bandol, Sète, Antibes, Bordeaux, Bayonne, La Rochelle, Rochefort, and Dieppe. In each case Vernet hit upon a virtuoso solution to the problem of composition posed by the need to portray the business of each port while also providing "snapshots" of major sites and monuments. His "views" were successful because they captured ships, people, and port activities in horizontal perspectives ideally suited to the depiction of architecture and contrasts of light and shadow. The use of the sky as a dominant element, together with the topographical precision and realism of the painting, resulted in an extraordinary reconciliation of art and nature. In addition to the fifteen port paintings, Vernet spent ten years making preliminary studies in city after city, works that express the combination of the naturalist aesthetic championed by Diderot ("Everything is true, one feels it," he wrote in 1767) with the civilizing design of "gentle commerce" promoted by the monarchy of technicians and their admirers. In these works the navy and commerce stand for the glory of France and its dreams of prosperity.

Stability, Mobility, Action

Mastering space had many purposes, and it would be wrong to focus only on the economic aspect of things. To be sure, economic progress was both a stimulus and a result, as is evident from the increased speed of travel and the reduction in its cost. News and merchandise flowed more rapidly and more cheaply than ever before, as did travelers of every stripe. In 1789 stagecoaches rolling day and night covered ninety kilometers at a stretch and brought Lyons within five days of Paris and Marseilles within nine days. There was not a city in France that could not be reached in under fifteen days. Everywhere the limits of space seemed to recede, regardless of whether one started from Paris or from provincial capitals such as Toulouse, Lyons, Rouen, Bordeaux, and Rennes. Cargoes followed: in 1715 it took twenty days to send a package from Lyons to Paris; by 1787 it took no more than fifteen. On other routes, however, gains were less dramatic, and according to Paul Léon the cost of shipping changed little, although there were important variations from region to region. In this respect France lagged behind England, and this delay put the two powers at loggerheads. The transportation bottleneck sustained the regional fragmentation of France, and one wonders whether the reality, in terms not only of transportation but of life in general, was not more static than the dynamic, idealized, at times utopian vision of the modernizers would lead us to believe. To investigate this question further, however, we have to change the scale of our analysis to look more closely at the movements of individuals and to determine what role mobility and openness played in the culture of the time.

Obstacles to Circulation

Obstacles to circulation were not all of a material order. They did not depend solely on the state of the transportation infrastructure. The whole organization of human relations also played a part, as did the perception of space. The very idea of mobility remained crucial, even as changes were under way. We can, for example, measure the resistance to defragmentation even as some barriers were coming down.

Broadly speaking, three factors influenced mobility: frontiers, which both united people and separated them; the allure of home; and the desire to travel, whether out of necessity or in search of freedom. Let us turn first to frontiers. In the eighteenth century there were "hot frontiers" and "cold frontiers," but by the end of the expansive age of Louis XIV, France's frontiers had stabilized and been transformed into "boundaries."[23] One can follow this process by looking at how the border with the Austrian Netherlands was adjusted by peaceful negotiations. After the Treaty of the Pyrenees, some 350 sites remained in dispute. By 1789 the status of only a few enclaves remained unsettled. Wherever possible the idea of natural boundary—a river or ridge line—was discussed. Frontiers defined in this way naturally kept people apart, especially when kept under military surveillance. The "iron frontier" was a defensive strategy aimed at controlling communications. It required a series of defensive outposts, with customs stations backed by military patrols. Young *fermiers généraux* such as Helvétius in 1738 and later Lavoisier were expected to inspect these border outposts personally by means of long and instructive frontier tours. Along the border with the Netherlands and the principality of Liège, the frontier included both areas where outposts were relatively spread out, as from Vouziers to Rethel, and critical areas where their density was higher, for instance along the Meuse near Sedan and Rocroy. The customs border still functioned like a boundary.

Frontiers probably brought people together more than they kept them apart, however, because traditionally borders could be crossed without formalities. Cross-border circulation was free, and *frontaliers* (a word in common use in 1785 for border-crossing workers) were statutorily entitled to free passage. The state of international tensions determined when borders were open and when they were closed.

Frontiers are therefore an ideal place to study foreign relations. From Peter Sahlins's work on the French frontier in the Pyrenees, two things clearly emerge.[24] First, the shift from a vague frontier zone to the more modern concept of a "borderline" did not occur everywhere in the eighteenth century. Between France and Spain a borderline had existed long before nation-states began to make use of it, symbolically and practically, to define their territory. Furthermore, the existence of a line did not altogether do away with the concomitant existence of a border zone or cross-border relations and local trade in defiance of precise boundary lines. Communal identities were built on both sides of the border. Such identities were not imposed by the central government; they developed in response to local processes and customary relations.

Until 1789 a jurisdictional and territorial conception prevailed; afterward, however, sovereignty was defined exclusively in terms of territory. In eighteenth-century Cerdagne (Cerdanya in Catalan), new social relationships developed within what had been a unified geographical and linguistic area. On the Spanish side people situated themselves in relation to Madrid or Barcelona, while on the French side they situated themselves in relation to Paris or Perpignan. Old local contrasts and oppositions between villages and communities defined a second axis of cross-border relations. Little by little the frontier transformed the identities of the people who lived near it, because social and cultural evolution differed according to which side of the border one happened to be on. For the Catalan and Spanish residents of Cerdanya, the French enjoyed a prosperity that eluded them but that they hoped to match, and nationality gradually came to be defined in terms of interests and conflicts over water, inheritances, communal lands, and customary rights. Thanks to linguistic plurality, moreover, everyone could claim local or national identity at any point in time. The frontier both brought people together and kept them apart, but above all it prevented homogenization of the space of identity-defining traditions that could lead to conflict. It was those conflicts that shaped the frontier and made it an obstacle, since to resolve them there was no choice but to appeal to national authorities. There was localization of the national and nationalization of the local. This interpretation, which gives due weight to the role of border dwellers determined to civilize cross-border relations and eliminate sources of dispute, emphasizes "customs." The Pyrenees themselves were not a barrier; mountain passes were subject to treaty regulations. Yet collective decisions inscribed differences in the landscape. This history teaches us something about the relation between local communities and remote central authorities and between geography and identity.

The "allure of home" had a negative effect on mobility. It was probably just as common in cities as in villages, for it grew out of the ties that individuals formed over the course of their lifetime with family members and neighbors. When Jacques-Louis Ménétra left Paris on his tour of France, he confessed that after "passing through the *barrière d'Enfer,* I frequently turned and looked back, and it occurred to me that anyone who saw me must have thought I was afraid to let my village bell tower out of my sight." Such sentiments of attachment are quite common in traditional societies, which think of themselves as stable and fixed systems in which each person has his or her place and must remain in it. France was thus a country of 36,000 parishes, to take Vauban's figure, each established on a piece of the territory with its own local customs and allegiances—so many "static villages" to which change could come only from outside.

Now we can understand the importance of the debate about the extension of the infrastructure from highways down to rural roads. We can also see the degree to which the ideal of self-sufficiency, of France as a series of villages with "closed horizons,"[25] threatened economic development. How could innovation and all that it required be reconciled with the old tradition of "household economy" taught by countless books on the subject? How could rural villages be brought into contact with the outside world? When it came to opening themselves up to change, peasant communities depended in large part on social and cultural ambassadors, that is, people whose line of work brought them into contact with more animated spheres: the lord and his family, the curé, or perhaps a schoolmaster or village worthy who happened to know the *grand vicaire* of the diocese or the *subdélégué*. This was the terrain on which the relationship between the local community and the authorities was played out, and it affected attitudes toward outsiders, as can be seen from incidents that made it into the courts, as well as in settlements drawn up by notaries and reports prepared by administrators.[26]

This was also the traditional setting in which the problem of cultural isolation arose as the principal obstacle to communication. Neither the parish school nor religious training prevented old local traditions from being passed on from generation to generation.[27] In the village, it was daily contact between individuals that shaped the "social personality." Such contact instilled values and attitudes whose legitimacy derived from the force of example, the authority of words and actions, and the content of myths and folk tales. Mobility opened up new horizons and introduced new values from other places, values potentially different from those in force at home. In this transformation, what rural people saw was already filtered by earlier changes in the cities.

Mobility increased the urban population; the social division of labor and commodity trading encouraged a different organization of urban space. Listen to young Restif de la Bretonne's stupefaction at discovering Paris for the first time:

> We saw a huge expanse of houses beneath a cloud of steam. I asked my father what it was. It was Paris, a big city, so big that not all of it could be seen from where we stood. Oh! How big Paris was! My father said it was as big as from Vermanton to Sacy and Sacy to Joux. At least that big. Oh! What a lot of people! There are so many people that nobody knows anybody else, not even in the same neighborhood, not even in his own house.

Paris and other cities had none of the familiar landmarks of village life. The scale of urban mobility was different from that of the village. In peasant society, mobility existed against a background of overall stability. Rural people traveled on familiar occasions, in connection with events that were an integral part of rural life; they also traveled in less usual circumstances, sometimes connected with political or religious incidents. War and persecution had always uprooted people and forced them to take to the roads. Fortunately such occasions were rare in the eighteenth century. In studying such processes, historical demographers prefer to speak of "migrations." They draw on a wide range of sources. Parish registers enable scholars to study moves due to marriage; hospital admission records, notarized documents of all sorts, judicial archives, passport registers, and constabular lists all have their uses. With the help of such sources, one can estimate the number of people on the move, the routes they took, and the ebb and flow of the population with the seasons or over longer time intervals. This is not the place to study the history of migration, but it is worth pausing to point out that understanding population movements is essential to achieving a proper vision of space.

Short Moves and Long-Term Mobility

For convenience, people often distinguish between seasonal, multiannual, and lifetime moves, but these categories obviously pertain to distance as well as time. Moreover, they fail to take account of "habitual forms" of mobility, which can serve as an apprenticeship in the skills required for more extended moves. The nature of the peasant's work required mobility on a daily basis. Various factors influenced the extent of that mobility: the size of the farming region, the relation between ownership and exploitation of farmland, the ratio of cultivated to uncultivated land, and livestock-rearing practices. The countryside was thus a place of constant movement—movement that depended on the seasons and on the mosaic of fields and paths. Day after day the peasant followed the same trail to his field, and this routine made the local farming region seem less like a composite of diverse elements (physical environment, array of crops, collection of fields, juxtaposition of vineyards and grain fields, and so on) than a series of interrelated subspaces linked by a network of trails.

> In the way they divided up space, ancient peasant communities forced to rely on themselves for all their needs also broke up their daily chores, punctuating periods of effort with intervals of rest at the edge of the field or vineyard, where one paused not only to relax but also to contemplate the finished work, whose extent was just large enough for the eye to take in. "The end is in sight" was a country saying with lots of emotional overtones: it was enough to encourage a tired farmer to make one final effort to get the job done. "The horse smells the barn" was another expression reflecting the same idea, that big jobs are accomplished one step at a time.[28]

Fields and trails, the material correlates of effort and movement, structured the syntax of the land. Trails were of fundamental importance because they determined how much land could be used and how long it took the peasant to reach his field with his team, wagon, and/or livestock without encountering obstacles or damaging property along the way. Rights of access, a burden that had to be borne, sometimes gave rise to social tension or conflict, but more often than not they reflected a basic agreement about land use. Regulations governing rights of access differed from region to region. In open-field regions such as the plains of northern France, access rights were communally regulated. Grape-growing regions tended to be more individualistic. Studies of trail networks in Beaujolais show how the daily movements of peasants and grape growers were organized: pastures were linked directly to the main trail network; forests rarely were; while the density of connections to fields and vineyards varied, with the most accessible always being those worked most routinely.

Urban workers were also subject to limitations of mobility. The glazier Jacques-Louis Ménétra's autobiography shows how his mobility evolved as he grew up. As a boy he was largely confined to his neighborhood, the small area of Paris between Saint-Germain-l'Auxerrois and the Seine, as he traveled from home to school and school to play. As an adolescent apprentice and adult journeyman he roamed Paris from shop to shop, uncle to uncle, master to master, in search of work. His recreational activities further extended his range: chasing employers and chasing girls were the principal activities of a stage of life that lasted until marriage settled him down. Thereafter, space shrank once again, and the journeyman's movements were confined more to the center of the city. Court records tell a similar story: three-quarters of those who stole food and clothing traveled long distances each day in search of plunder. The lives of the poor were characterized by instability, mobility, and discontinuity. Necessity kept people on the move until they found both secure work and a permanent home.[29] The search for food and housing was a basic element of the poor man's life.

The time spent on this search was looked upon not as "wasted" but as an integral part of life itself. Different classes moved at different speeds, as Louis Sébastien Mercier was quick to note: the rich traveled rapidly in carriages, workers walked at a deliberate pace, and both shared a taste for leisurely strolls. For Mercier, space was organized in concentric circles. The innermost circle was the home itself, whether the peasant's humble cottage or the rich man's apartment. Here, around the hearth, everything was familiar and reassuring. Outer circles were progressively less familiar. A peasant, for example, would have relations with other people in his village and the surrounding region. Some of these relations would be with people he knew fairly well, others with people whom he hardly knew at all. As social space expanded, the nature of social relations changed with it. New rules, customs, and surveillance (by the Church and charitable organizations, the sheriff, and the lord) held the old spontaneity in check. In other words, power took the place previously occupied by influence. Even economic relationships changed, as formal accounting replaced trust. The family, nuclear or extended, was the key social (and fiscal) unit in rural areas, where it coincided with the farm, or unit of production. The family circle was also important in the urban environment, where the "warmth of the hearth" was a central feature of popular life in eighteenth-century Paris.[30] Of course, this fundamental social unit was subject to breakdown in the face of life's uncertainties, especially given the high death rate characteristic of Ancien Régime demography. In the cities, where life was even more "fragile" than in the countryside, the high death rate had important social and economic consequences. In particular, it meant that people had to look about more broadly to fulfill their matrimonial and economic needs. This, too, contributed to the expansion of space.

The choice of a spouse was governed in part by rules, in part by what was available. In mapping the rural heart, the demographer is primarily aware of constraints such as the size of the population and the insistence of families on consolidating property. Accordingly, in a parish of 400 to 500 residents with 80 to 100 baptisms annually, there were in any given year roughly 20 to 25 eligible bachelors and a slightly higher number of marriageable females. Since social requirements further limited the possibilities, the number of possible proposals over a three- to four-year period was fewer than 75. Although the vast majority of rural people took spouses with whom they had grown up, the numbers were a source of anxiety. Only about a third of young people could marry, and marriage possibilities were further limited in families where considerations of wealth and social rank were even more stringent. Bands of young men traveled about this "prenuptial space," availing themselves of holidays and dances to call on nearby villages in search of marriage prospects; sometimes these visits erupted in brawls.

The autobiography of a weaver named Louis Simon tells how all this worked in the Maine. The story of his engagement takes up three-quarters of his text, which shows clearly how parental influence vied with youthful freedom. Simon and his future wife, Anne Champeau, reacted to the situation in very different ways. She fell in love, to hear him tell it, at first sight. For him, things progressed more gradually. There was a regular ritual of courtship, and violence played its part. The whole idyll unfolded in a space defined by the homes of the two families, the inn, the cemetery where the two lovers met, holiday celebrations attended by bands of youths, and taverns and farmhouses over a radius of four to six miles. The love affair almost ended when Simon was set upon by a gang of rivals: this drama took place on "the highway."

Broadening our scale of observation from the individual to the regional level, we can begin to understand how matrimonial mobility was regulated. In the Vendômois, between Perche and Beauce, Jean Vassort examined some 3,000 marriage certificates: of these, 35 percent of the grooms and only 8 percent of the brides did not live in the parish at the time of their marriage. Nearly all of these came from neighboring parishes, moreover. Examination of census data, however, sheds further light on these figures. Men traveled anywhere from tens to hundreds of miles in search of wives: 10 percent of the men were born outside the Vendômois, and 4 to 5 percent outside the area that would be included in contiguous *départements* after the Revolution, a distance of 20 to 50 leagues. For women, these proportions decrease to less than 4 percent and 1 percent, respectively. The geography of this mobility was dictated by line of work and social position: 27 percent of notables came from outside the region, as did 69 percent of soldiers, 20 to 26 percent of artisans and wage earners, but fewer than 10 percent of the group as a whole. Workers migrated from the *bocages* (hedge-enclosed fields) of western France to fill in as hired hands. But there were also more specialized immigrants: soldiers, masons, medical men, lawyers, teachers—an "enlightened mobility" whose definition was primarily social and cultural. From the west came forest workers, from the Massif Central masons, and from the northeast and southwest notables and graduates of the Ecole Militaire. Marriage settled all these restless people.

Interparish exchange took place on a smaller scale, between cantons, and was more uniformly distributed through the population: it involved 34 percent of the men and 30 percent of the women, and in all social categories except soldiers, vintners, and textile workers the rate of exchange exceeded 40 percent; in this category, nonagricultural populations were not much more mobile than agricultural ones. The territory covered was the same for both sexes: most of the mobility was from west to east along the valley of the Loire and from northwest to southeast, from Perche to Beauce. The multitude of short-range moves owing to marriage followed the same axes as the longer-range moves dictated by the economy and the need for work. If we were to consider marriages within the parish and between adjacent parishes, the rate of mobility would be even higher. The rate of endogamy was very high: 65 percent for men, 90 percent for women; but census figures show that more than 50 percent of the people counted were not born in the same parish in which they lived, and this intercommunal mobility was approximately the same for both sexes. Women were more likely to make short moves, and the propensity to move varied with age, women being likely to move up to age twenty-five and men up to age thirty, after which marriage settled both sexes down.

The Vendômois is not France, but study of the region has highlighted a more mobile society than previously described. Movement was a major element of social life for both those who moved and those who did not. Before turning to longer-range movements, such as those involved in feeding urban populations, let us look at another aspect of the phenomenon: movement owing to economic inequalities and trade.[31]

People can acquire experience of other places in a variety of ways. Here we see one of the privileges of the privileged, people of rank, culture, and wealth and city dwellers generally. But various forms of inequality can also be an impetus to mobility. Peasants often left their villages to buy and sell goods at fairs and markets. Some also came and went with the seasons or in cycles extending over several years. Eighteenth-century economists from Cantillon to Turgot were of course greatly interested in trade and places of exchange. This interest shaped their thinking about the differentiation of space and the role of the city.

In the *Encyclopédie* Turgot proposed a definition of fairs and markets that involved mechanisms of mobility. The market was defined in terms of a natural region: consumers and producers lived close together, knew one another, and were aware of one another's needs. The advantages of traveling some distance to a large marketplace largely outweighed the costs. Monitoring stocks and prices, essential to the operation of a free market, was a function performed by consumers, part of their social and political culture. They insisted that dealings be open and aboveboard, and this necessitated repeated trips to marketplaces to compare price and quality; this frequency of travel multiplied opportunities for making new contacts.

Economists looked on fairs as more artificial than markets, for they depended on privileges granted by the authorities and required special exceptions or franchises. Hence they were instruments of a controlled economy, of regulated trade. Turgot believed that free competition would cause them to disappear, yet they remained attractive despite transformations of the economy. At places such as La Guibray near Caen, Beaurecaire, and even Paris and Saint-Denis, they continued to serve as regional redistribution centers for incoming goods. In fact, their role in the economic circuit was different from that of the market. Nevertheless, the importance of fairs did decline as markets increasingly became attached to permanent urban locations, from which wholesalers found it easier to trade with manufacturers. Large cities had markets of many kinds, while intermediate centers tended to specialize. One attraction substituted for another.

Until the Revolution, whose statistics are invaluable for measuring how things stood beforehand, travel to markets and fairs was an important source of mobility.[32] In some 9,000 towns, the statisticians computed some 16,000 fair days and nearly 160,000 market days (based on their weekly frequency). Market locations reflect the economic geography of France: they were dense in northern and western France and along the major rivers; elsewhere they were less frequent. Fairs were most common in the west and southwest, central France and Burgundy, and the southeast. Cities of more than 2,000 inhabitants boasted only 20 percent of the fairs but 30 percent of the markets. The location of fairs and markets also reflected the network of roads and waterways, although the frequency of market days in some cases compensated for deficiencies in transportation. The map also reveals the range of influence of various markets: the ability to meet a variety of consumer needs drew clients from long distances.

The great multipurpose fairs stood at the top of the trade hierarchy. They offered enough of a show to attract customers for all sorts of merchants, including increasing numbers of wholesalers. Fairs offered a window on the burgeoning economy that helped to encourage consumption. Rural fairs often played a more specialized role. Many were devoted to the sale of livestock: cows, horses, mules. They were also a first stage in the collection of local goods for shipment to other provinces or even abroad. Many fairs also attracted customers with "notions," "haberdashery," china, and manufactured goods. Servants could be hired, and hawkers could replenish their supplies. Some fairs were associated with pilgrimages, others with theater troupes and magicians. Fair dates often coincided with holidays. Market days were more frequent: markets were for buying and selling fresh produce and necessities (grain, vegetables, meat), activities that encouraged different patterns of mobility. Peasants shipped food to the cities and engaged in trade with regions whose products were complementary: thus there was a trade between plains regions and mountainous regions, as there was between the city and the countryside.

Men and women also came to fairs and markets to socialize (in their different ways) as well as to speculate and lay in needed supplies. Fantasy and desire played their part. Material needs were influenced by taste as well as calculation. Each person's sense of belonging to a particular place was challenged by awareness of difference and distance. Tensions sometimes erupted in riots, as local people rose up against the authorities or foreign speculators. Sometimes the market itself was a subject of controversy (over grain prices, behavior of sellers, or access), but the market was also a place where people exchanged information and discussed politics in a basic, down-to-earth way.[33]

Beyond this regular but local, limited market travel, people began to experience space and distance in a new way. In the cities, journeymen workers *(compagnons)* certainly experienced the greatest mobility. It was customary for apprentices to learn their craft by embarking on a "tour of France," whose pace and duration varied widely. A considerable proportion of young urban men under the age of thirty thus found themselves on the road. There were sound technological as well as economic reasons for the tour. Apprentices could learn techniques in use in different parts of the country and improve their methods, while the system effectively guaranteed work for younger craftsmen. The tour had its own distinctive social rituals and symbolic practices, and of course there were also tensions associated with restlessness and youth. Jacques-Louis Ménétra left a remarkable memoir of his years on the road, and the papers of the Société Typographique de Neuchâtel tell us about young printers motivated not only by a desire for work but also by the hope of seeing new things, the idea of "profitable freedom."

In the countryside there were "people movements" of much greater size that involved far vaster territories. These movements were a deeply ingrained feature of rural life.[34] The rhythms of agricultural life itself contributed, as did the lack of work after the harvest and the need for additional manpower during the harvest. Mobility was influenced by the ratio of resources to population; where resources fell short of needs, people had to look elsewhere to make up the difference. The combined effects of natural poverty, heavy taxes, and demographic growth caused many people from the mountains to head for the plains, while everywhere the unemployed took to the roads in search of work. One sees this, for example, in the regular migration of masons from the Marche to Paris and the fringes of the Massif Central: they numbered 6,000 per year in 1700 and 15,000 in 1789, most of them reliable adult workers.[35] These migratory movements rarely extended beyond France's borders, although they did frequently reach as far as Spain and Italy. The longer the migration, the less likely the worker was to return home, but the majority of migratory workers did return home regularly.

The use of space cannot be gauged accurately without taking account of the degree to which different localities organized and facilitated migration. In Paris, Auvergnats and Limousins formed coherent communities which controlled certain levels of various trades such as water carriers and masons. Members of these communities were willing to do disagreeable jobs because they returned home regularly and hoped one day to go back with enough set aside to remain in better circumstances than they began. Those who participated in this "temporary mobility" did not reject their origins. The same was true of the countless itinerant peddlers who roamed the Alps, the Pyrenees, and the Massif Central yet never gave up their ties to their native villages.[36] Yet it was possible for people who left home for any number of reasons to sever their roots and stay away for good: migrants became settlers. Life changed.

Migration swelled the population of growing eighteenth-century cities. Bordeaux, for example, became a great regional capital, as its population increased from 45,000 under Louis XIV to more than 100,000 under Louis XVI. The availability of work attracted a growing volume of immigrants, some 35,000 of whom died in the city between 1737 and 1791.[37]

Most of them were unmarried men who came for brief periods of work: the city did not hold on to everyone it attracted. Nearly all came from southwestern France, and a third traveled less than 25 miles. This was both a mobility of necessity and a mobility of freedom: not all migrant workers were driven to the city by poverty and ignorance. The influx of migrants to Caen suggests how attractive that city was. Census figures show that its population increased from 38 percent immigrant in the seventeenth century to 51 percent by the end of the eighteenth century. As in the Vendômois, migration affected all segments of the population. Similar rates of migration can be found almost everywhere: in Lyons, Paris, Nancy, Strasbourg, and Rouen, for example. Surely there were individual as well as economic motives: the urban dream was promoted by such major writers as Marivaux in the 1740s, Rousseau in the 1760s, and Restif de la Bretonne in the 1780s. Cities drew the boldest individuals, in part because they offered a different relation to mobility and space than did the old rural society from which they drew their populations and the labor essential for their growth.[38]

We are now in a position to draw some provisional conclusions about mobility as a key social phenomenon of the time. Certain large trends are discernible. The Vendômois case study attests to both the movement from mountainous regions to lower elevations and the more significant flow of population from west to east, from the *bocages* to the great plains of the Paris basin, and of course to the appeal of Paris itself. This attraction is also evident in criminal records. Witnesses to a bloody crime that occurred in 1788 told the sheriff that "the murderers were thirty in number and came from Brittany." Whether real or imagined, such a migration was plausible; that is the important point to note. It was related to the border turmoil that separated the west from the rest of France, a turmoil that encouraged smuggling, violation of the salt laws, and nocturnal hauling in the Beauce. Migration in the opposite direction, from east to west, was less common. We note a difference between regions where dwellings tended to be isolated and regions where they tended to be grouped: dispersion alienates, grouping attracts. There are also differences depending on the density and type of farming: wheat fields and vineyards, hedged fields and sparse pasture gave rise to specific types of mobility. Regions in which mobility is limited are regions open to trade. Residents of cities stabilized by the advent of proto-industrial labor and commercial networks tended to be less mobile. Mobility must always be seen in context, in the light of complex social situations, before we can say to what degree it was voluntary or involuntary. Even in societies where the majority of the population is firmly rooted, the potential for hope and adventure exists.[39]

Yet as we learn more about mobility, we begin to understand that different people perceived space in different ways. Only a minority traveled long distances, and the sedentary majority were at once wary of and curious about those who traveled. Thus the small minority of travelers could make the larger number who stayed home aware of new horizons, just as "a minority of readers can bring some forms of culture to an illiterate majority." At the same time, short-distance local travel took people well beyond their own parishes and thus contributed to the circulation of information from a variety of sources.

An example will help to illustrate these remarks. A Lancé farmer, Pierre Bordier, kept a diary for many years, and by comparing this text with his regular activities, we can identify three main horizons in his perception of space. First came the horizon of family life. This encompassed more than just his own parish; he had relatives who lived three or four leagues away in places such as Crucherny and Saint-Amand (in the direction of Beauce in the case of the men) and between Longpré and Saint-Cyr-du-Gault (toward the Gâtine in the case of the women). Second came a horizon defined by the purchase and lease of land (recorded in notarized documents): of twenty instances, two-thirds were in Lancé and Vendôme, while the rest were as scattered as Bordier's relatives. And third came the horizon defined by markets, about which we know from Bordier's diary: Vendôme was his favorite, but he also went on occasion to Montoire, Herbault, and Château-Renault, all of which were the same distance from his farm. He was seldom able to travel as far as Blois, seven leagues away. In the course of his travels he picked up rumors and news from afar. His vision of space thus took in both proximate regions, which he could visit physically, and faraway places, which he knew only by hearsay. Of the most distant places he had only the vaguest knowledge.

Circulation and Control

Two phenomena typify the eighteenth century: circulation accelerated everywhere for growing numbers of people, and procedures and methods for controlling mobility were established. Maps and local descriptions familiarized people with space, but in an abstract way. The new approach was slow to filter down through the population, however: it remained the exclusive province of the educated elite, beyond the reach of the masses. We must be careful not to contrast a popular view of space rooted in the concrete with an elite view available only to the more cultivated. There was indeed a split, but it is not clear that everyone in the cultural elite was quick to adopt the new methods. What mattered was whether people understood space intimately or externally, and the external approach was frequently adopted by the elite. The educated learned to deal with space in new ways, and their experience reveals a certain ambivalence about stability and mobility.

The Enlightenment marked the culmination of a long-term process whereby societies learned to restrict the movements of troublesome individuals. The war on vagrancy began at the municipal level in the sixteenth century. The "great confinement" of the late seventeenth century hastened the change, though not without difficulty. This history has many points in common with the history of poor relief, whose central institution, the general hospitals, also served to confine potential troublemakers and to provide work and religious instruction to able-bodied beggars, the homeless, vagabonds, and criminals destined for the galleys. The royal administration, urban police, and Catholic and Protestant churches saw social exclusion in a new light: potential troublemakers were declared to be a social, medical, and moral danger to be excluded from society. This contrasted with the traditional religious view of the poor as unfortunate human beings created in the image of Christ and therefore deserving of hospitality. At all levels of society, the old traditions of hospitality withered: the effects on the collective consciousness deserve further study.

Similar changes occurred in the countryside. Before 1724, however, repressive regulations against the poor were left to the discretion of local aldermen. In that year a royal declaration extended limited earlier regulations to the entire kingdom and established a Bureau Général de Correspondance in Paris for the purpose of collecting information from provincial poorhouses. The royal government subsequently declared war on begging and vagabondage. It launched investigations in 1724, 1753, 1764, and (under Turgot) in 1774 to study the cost of various means of stamping out begging. And it issued various new ordinances intended to improve the implementation of the royal decree of 1724. In particular, beginning in 1764, it established *dépôts de mendicité*, which Turgot was forced to maintain after the upheavals of 1776. The police now had a weapon to use against beggars.

Policing of the highways was the job of the *maréchaussée,* which was reorganized in each *généralité* beginning in 1720. Brigades of marshals made regular rounds to ensure the safety of travelers on the king's highways, which they did despite a shortage of manpower (just a few thousand marshals for all of France). The records of their activity tell us a great deal about the world of the vagabond. Two things stand out. The distinction between illegal vagabondage and acceptable travel dictated by economic needs and customs was a tenuous one. The gendarmes did not always arrest the people they should have arrested. What is more, the central files in Paris did not yield the expected results, and recidivists proved difficult to spot. Nevertheless, the work of the brigades tells us where the key junctions in the transportation system were located, what regions were most attractive, and how frequently vagabonds were picked up on the royal highways around Paris or Lyons or near major fair sites and festivals or at suburban inns and taverns, where many arrests were made. Given the increase in the flow of traffic and the relatively small number of checkpoints, it is easy to see that the repression of vagabondage was spotty at best, since the police already had their hands full with real criminals.

The attitude of the *maréchaussée* was not all that different from that of the rural population.[40] There is little evidence of peasant revolts against the gendarmes, even in the early eighteenth century, when we do find evidence of urban resistance to the *archers* of the police. To peasants, still susceptible to being forced to take to the roads in times of hardship and used to sending their children off in search of temporary work, vagabondage and begging were normal activities. Beggars were not rejected so long as they were known and identified. But peasants took a different attitude toward unknown tramps, who were often denounced as "insolent" for no reason, and all the more so if they acted up or seemed threatening. Vagrants were accused of theft, poaching, and setting fire to barns and crops, which further exacerbated fears and tended to curb mobility. All in all, the eighteenth century straddled the line between ending isolation and reinforcing it. What people wanted was not always clear.

Society's efforts, the role of the state with its surveys and policies, and the aspirations of a portion of the social elite, primarily in the cities, tended in the direction of greater openness. But they also mobilized forces that localized and controlled the flows that were supposed to fuel development. Between stability and mobility a war raged, a war that determined what it meant to enjoy concrete freedom through acceptance of constraints. There can be no doubt that much Enlightenment legislation favored stability: improved vital statistics, increased surveillance of residences, issuance of various certificates and passports to monitor people's movements. Everywhere disorder diminished. In Paris the police dreamed of keeping records that would ensure more effective control of a larger, more mobile population, as Inspector Guillauté, a contributor to the *Encyclopédie,* indicated in his *Mémoire sur la réformation de la police en France.* In the end, the goal of vigilance was to achieve happiness and prosperity through virtue. Theorizing about police work was directed toward the same end as philosophizing about space or about the difference between nature and urban civilization. It is interesting that we find the same men who were protagonists in other battles pitted against each other here: Voltaire against Rousseau, economists against the Christian philosophers. The war against property and luxury and the denunciation of city dwellers as useless parasites went hand in hand with praise for vagabondage and the historical myth of denatured man.[41] Another version was linked to urban development and the local struggles it engendered.

Among the adversaries of change were the military men who defended citadels and ramparts and who mobilized in Caen, for example, to save that city's fortifications; the Church, which, not without internal opposition, defended its symbolic heritage against urban modernization and reacted to threats leveled at monastic property by some *intendants* and other advocates of change; ordinary people who opposed exhuming the dead to make room for new construction on former cemetery sites and who enlisted the support of the parish clergy; and finally aldermen, who favored order over change, opposed administrative innovations, saw the *intendants* as agents of oppression, and insisted on traditional liberties.

Opposing this heterogeneous coalition, which proved ineffective in the long run yet capable in the short run of using financial weapons to wage effective guerrilla warfare in defense of its privileges, were the modernizers. Socially they were no more homogeneous than their adversaries, but the supercharged economy drew them together. United by a broader cultural vision as well as their own self-interest, officials connected with the *intendances*, economists who met in local academies (which brought together citizens of the Republic of Letters throughout France), physicians, lawyers, administrators, a few entrepreneurs, the odd enlightened cleric, builders, and above all wholesale traders and shippers and of course engineers, whose esprit de corps was heightened by struggle.

Two cultures thus clashed over the question of openness: one looked to the wider world and to a France without internal barriers and drew its examples from Paris, while the other remained devoted to the traditions, not to say privileges, of a society of *rentiers* and *corps* and displayed an attitude akin to that of the *parlementaires* at war with the reformist monarchy, favorable to local interests, and wary of mobility and circulation.[42] Hence the stakes were larger than the urban changes that were directly at issue. The clash revealed the triumph of special interests and the antagonism between cultural and professional groups over the transformation of the kingdom. It highlighted the frenetic activity of the engineers, the new masters of space, whose triumphant rhetoric exalted the possibility of progress in the face of recurrent opposition, prejudice, natural obstacles, and economic bottlenecks. "The optimism of the engineers seemed to indicate that the significance of their work lay in its perpetual incompleteness, in their pursuit of an end that always lay just out of reach. It makes sense to ask whether this situation did not already anticipate some of the uncertainties of the next century."[43]

By replacing the monolithic concept of modernization, which was taken from classical architectural theory and remained dominant up to the middle of the eighteenth century, with the implementation of technical efficiency and specialization, the triumph of the modernizers turned out to involve a change of society. A stable, orderly vision based on a hierarchy of status and embodied in absolute sovereignty—a society of orders and compromises based on separation, compartmentalization, and negotiation—was supplanted by a mobile, unstable, comparatively chaotic world in which conflicts of interest and utility were settled by experts. These experts claimed to represent the hopes of the citizenry as reconciled in the "general will." Joining theory together with practice, the experts designed projects to control flows, movements, and production processes. Thus the mastery of space, jointly achieved through technology and administration, left a lasting mark on the development of France and indeed on French civilization generally. The dream of an "economic monarchy" that one finds in *L'Esprit des lois*, among other great texts, was

73

sustained not only by the enthusiasm of entrepreneurs, merchants, and bankers but also by the energy of engineers and administrators. Men whose instruments were classification, specialization, and calculation, they brought all their powers to bear on the problem of bringing regularity and order to the circulation of men and resources—in short, the problem of mastering space.[44]

3

❦❦❦

Time and History

THAT A CONNECTION exists between the mastery of space and the mastery of time is implicit in the history of attempts to study and improve circulation and control mobility. Literate people in the eighteenth century knew that time had been measured in terms of movement since Aristotle: chronometry, by relating time to space through an appropriate "movement," made time measurement possible. Enlightenment scientists and technologists speculated at length on this concept. They did so because, in the mathematization of the world that began with the formulation of Kepler's, Galileo's, and Newton's laws in the sixteenth and seventeenth centuries, time figured as a measurable quantity in universal laws involving other measurable quantities such as length, force, and mass.

The scientific revolution affected different people in different ways. Classical chronometry began with Huyghens's publication of *Horologium oscillatorium* in 1673 and with speculation on the relation between terrestrial time and celestial time. This was grist for the academies. But how many cultural mediators stood between the leading scientists of the day and the man in the street? Theories may have been less important than the effects of their gradual popularization. People's attitudes toward time changed, and research was undertaken in areas dictated by the needs of the government, the economy, the army, and the navy. Historians are understandably interested in these matters and in contemporary cultural changes, as well as in the great "chronosophies," or philosophies of time (and therefore of mankind's future). We cannot understand the eighteenth century without understanding how different conceptions of time were interrelated.

Temporality defines the quotidian, just as the philosophy of time—the relationship between past, present, and future—defines history. Between these two dimensions of time, invisible currents circulate, currents that stimulated awareness and fueled debate at major turning points. In this respect, the century of Enlightenment was a time of transition: everyday practice had been evolving for several centuries, yet people still related their daily lives to older cosmic, religious, and mercantile frames of reference. Meanwhile, the concept of history changed, in part because its foundations were questioned and in part because its practice was transformed.

Consider the dictionaries of the time. For the Jesuits of Trévoux, history was the art of narrating the most memorable facts and most celebrated deeds of the past. The word could be applied to the description of natural as well as human phenomena, and the best example was still Pliny's *Natural History*. History was defined by its subject matter—natural, sacred, or civil—as well as by its form, which could range from the simple chronological list to the historian's rhetorically complex narrative. A key distinction separated narrative history, whose subject matter was true, from fabulous or fictionalized history. François Furet has shown that this ambiguity runs through a whole range of books with the word "history" in their title as recorded in applications for the privilege to publish.[1] In the thought of the period there was a shift from natural history to the history of human events observed both chronologically and geographically. The old hierarchy of types of historical discourse and historical subject matter was still in place at the beginning of the eighteenth century: sacred history was still the basic, primary reference; civil history covered the evolution of institutions, customs, and knowledge; personal history dealt with individuals; and singular history dealt with events. Broadly speaking, history taught men about the influence of the past on the present. Tomorrow was the "future of the past," essentially determined by the sacred foundations of civilization.[2]

Now let us turn to the *Encyclopédie*. Voltaire transformed the intellectual landscape of the age.[3] For him, history was a narrative based on facts assumed to be true, in contrast to myth, which was a narrative based on facts assumed to be false. The history of opinion was a compendium of human error; by contrast, the history of art recorded what was most useful in the development of civilization, most conducive to progress. As a historian, Voltaire treated sacred history as one of those "respectable subjects" that had best be left untouched. He thereby secularized the field of history and cleared the way for a history of prejudice based on an epistemological distinction between truth and mere opinion. Natural history was transferred to the realm of natural science on the basis of another epistemological distinction, this time between nature and culture. In the realm of history proper remained the arts, the whole range of technology and science, and events "stripped of any transcendental presupposition." Henceforth the human world was to be categorized in terms of human history. Voltaire ensured that history would become a modern discipline by defining historical knowledge as that which could be proved and basing it on the same fundamental distinctions that still shape our understanding. History was redefined in terms of secular chronology—history is what men make of it—and certain criteria of truth.

In view of the conceptual gap between these two definitions, the fact that they coexisted suggests that a transformation occurred in man's relation to time, which, like space, was seen in more secular, rationally pragmatic terms. Yet a series of conceptions of history subsisted for everyone, and the incompatibilities among these were not always apparent. The Encyclopedist Jaucourt defined the adjective "historical" as follows: "That which belongs to History. Opposed to mythical [*fabuleux*]. One says "historical times," "mythical times." One also says "a historical work." A "historical painting" is a painting that represents an actual fact, an action drawn from History, or even, more generally, an action that takes place among men. It does not matter whether that action is real or imaginary."

The transition from the realm of historical discourse to that of painting is interesting, and this approach to ways of interpreting the passage of time is worth looking at a little more closely. The passage demonstrates the difficulty of defining history solely in terms of its pursuit of the truth: the term had other uses, which broadened its meaning. Cyclical, linear, and evolutionary conceptions of individual and collective time all were brought to bear on a changing reality. In practice as well as theory, different aspects of time were joined together in the eighteenth-century mind.

Human Time

Anthropology has taught us how to interpret the "everyday quality" of human time. Temporality is defined by three contrasts found in all civilizations. The first of these is repetition versus event. Ordinary time is cyclical, a regular distribution of works and days succeeding one another in tranquil monotony. This gives rise to the idea that a time such as the Ancien Régime or period such as the eighteenth century or civilization such as that of the Enlightenment can be characterized in terms of the way in which time is managed. Note, however, that it is no easy matter to find out how individuals and families budgeted their time. In pursuing the quotidian and the way in which people protected themselves from the unexpected and unusual, we would do well to be suspicious of evidence purporting to demonstrate progress or rationalization; evolution is better understood in terms of a more amorphous logic.

The second contrast that defines time is that between repetition and rupture. When we trace the boundary between order and disorder, between what was regulated and what was not regulated, we see that time consisted of periods of monotony punctuated by moments of rupture: in modern societies this is the function of holidays and vacations. In Enlightenment society this opposition touched on a fundamental issue, because what was at stake in the contrast between the liberation of leisure and holiday time and the time of work was again the effectiveness of social control and the possibility of change, particularly economic change. In other words, the different rhythms of working time and idle time are central for understanding the patterns of cultural evolution.

Finally—and this is the third of the contrasts I mentioned—we need to look at the opposition between the quotidian and time itself. Eighteenth-century society had ways of managing human time, including both control of change through discipline and concealment of the consequences of action through routine. Two concepts are key for understanding eighteenth-century notions of human experience: Newton's idea of absolute, universal time which flows uniformly in accordance with a mathematical, mythophysical model (God remains as master of time), and Kant's idea of time as the "medium of all change," a subjective, metaphysical theory. The very attempt to make sense of the notion of time made philosophers aware of how different aspects of knowledge were intertwined. Pascal agreed with Augustine that it was pointless if not impossible to define time: "Time is of this kind. Who can define it? And why undertake to do so, when everyone understands what one means in speaking of time without designating it further."[4]

The historian of culture is left with the possibility—or impossibility—of finding out about how individuals and groups dealt with time. What we find is that different time schemes were superimposed, just as different conceptions of space coexisted.[5] The perception of time varied with place and cultural sophistication. Each notion of time was associated with characteristic forms of behavior and a distinctive relationship to nature and culture. There were two principal dimensions: that of natural, cosmic time and that of measured or clock time.

Cosmic Time, Natural Time

The temporal architecture of the eighteenth-century French mind was complex. One problem in investigating the history of sensibility is that, according to Piaget and other psychologists of knowledge, the perception of time begins in early childhood, before the child is even conscious of a self; it takes shape along with language and memory and is reinforced by experience of the world and knowledge of both inanimate objects and living things. The historian has little chance of clarifying the way in which this intimate, individual, internal experience is constituted. He is better equipped to describe the collective experience that structures individual experience, although the pace of life and personal or family context may vary from individual to individual. The organization of the calendar, for example, reflects both autonomous factors, astronomical observations made for utilitarian or scientific purposes, and religious and even political influences. In rural villages different people perceive the calendar in different ways; in cities these differences are even more striking. In eighteenth-century France the measurement of time was influenced by two traditions, one stemming from the peasant's immemorial relationship with nature and the other from the doctrine of the Church.

In any society dominated by rural life, time is above all the time of seasons and days. The calendar of work and apprenticeship reflects the regular cycle of the seasons and the kinds of work characteristic of each. Memories, good or bad, tend to become associated with the milestones that one passes as the years unfold. The years of scarcity in the heart of

79

the reign of Louis XIV left their mark well after the king's death: what people remembered, according to Vauban, was the horror that reduced one-tenth of the population to begging and a series of hecatombs that claimed millions (1.5 million in 1693–94, 800,000 more in 1709–1711). As late as 1750, 1760, and beyond, elderly people still remembered those dark times. When misery reigned and the land failed to provide people with enough to eat, Nature herself was called into question, and God along with her.[6] We shall see that as the pressure of these bad memories abated over the course of the eighteenth century, the measurement of time became more fluid. Bordier le Vendômois measures time in his diary not in terms of abstract units but in relation to his own experience and concrete activities.[7] Seasons relate not only to the calendar but also to the sequence of agricultural chores: Pierre Bordier speaks of the "August of wheat" and the "August of oats." More generally, the rhythm of the seasons influenced the rhythm of liturgy and tradition.

Man's sense of time and primitive measurement of it are linked to the force of nature as mediated through the daily work process and routine of domestic chores. Bordier's diary and other sources teach us about the cycle of hours as experienced by farmers and shepherds. Throughout the year, the day's work unfolded between "sunup" and "sundown," not only in the country but also in the city. Consequently, winter wages paid by the day or job were higher in hourly terms than summer wages, when days were longer. The year was divided into two parts: a brief but active four months from Saint John's to All Saints', followed by eight long months of waiting. These two periods of unequal duration were nevertheless perceived as having equal importance. In addition, the contrast between the slow season (or dead season) and the active season was attenuated by the fact that the former encompassed all the major dates of the religious calendar.

Pierre Bordier recorded nearly everything that happened in both seasons, from the commonplace to the memorable. From 1748 to 1767 he wrote down his observations on agricultural activities ranging from the *couvrailles* of October (when fields were manured, plowed, and sown) to the harvests of August to the threshing and storage of the grain. The coming of spring was a moment of intense renewal of chores and rotations: plowing for quick-growing grains and oats was done in March. In June came haymaking. October was also for grape picking and nut gathering. The passing of the seasons determined the pace of life in the

Vendômois, just as tides and winter storms set the pace for the life of sailors elsewhere. When days were short, the hours seemed to pass more quickly: the opposition of night and day defined a boundary of multiple significance. Bordier's records of transactions show the importance of fairs and the seasonal use of hired labor: domestics were hired at Saint John's for the year, while *scyeux* (wheat cutters) signed on in July for the harvest. Rents and leases ran from All Saints', as did tenant-farming contracts.

The Church calendar was the other main influence on the perception of time. Religion imposed a weekly rhythm on the passage of the hours: Sunday was the day of rest, Monday was for weddings, and Tuesday was for Mardi Gras on the eve of Lent, during which sexual intercourse was forbidden for many long weeks. Communities everywhere came together for Sunday mass and high holidays. Strong-willed drinking men deserted church services for the local tavern, which the authorities could never keep closed. There, matters of common interest were discussed and news was exchanged. Along with the markets and fairs, Sunday services provided the occasion for individuals and groups to get together for social purposes as well as to buy and sell goods and exchange information. The major religious holidays—Easter, Pentecost, All Saints', Christmas—marked the passage of time. The frequency of notations in Bordier's diary is similar to that in the diary of François Latron, a vine grower from Naveil, but we also find differences between the farmer and the vintner because one was fond of a particular religious ceremony or felt a professional obligation not shared by the other. Certain entries present in one case but not in the other can be explained by differences of sensibility or proximity to the city. Nevertheless, in both diaries the festive entries are concentrated mainly in the first half of the year (67 and 54 percent, respectively). The harvest months have the most entries. Both grain farmers and vine growers lived in anticipation: for them the present was always hostage to an uncertain future, because the fruits of their labor were at the mercy of the elements.

The fact that time was organized in terms of natural rhythms and religious celebrations had two consequences. First, the seasonal distribution of weddings, baptisms, and funerals followed well-defined patterns: the number of births peaked in springtime and reached a low ebb in autumn, and the death rate followed a symmetrical trajectory, so that the season of life and the season of death were juxtaposed. Weddings were less rigidly determined, yet they had to reckon with the triple constraint of agricultural necessity, popular beliefs and traditions, and prescriptions of the Church. Two-thirds of all marriages took place in just four months of the year: January and February and June and July. Second, peasants (and to a lesser degree city dwellers) also marked the seasons with folk celebrations that the Church, after unsuccessfully doing battle against them, finally incorporated to one degree or another. For example, the winter solstice was celebrated with rites involving torches, mistletoe, and logs, while other folk celebrations marked the season from Lent to Saint John's, after which they became less frequent.

The "time frame" that most strongly affected society as a whole was thus the annual cycle. This cycle influenced the way in which events were remembered: think of the role played by anniversaries. It also accounted for the uneven density of events. The only rival to the great cycle of the seasons was the measurement of time in terms of work. In plowing his *journal* (the amount of land that could be plowed in a day), the peasant demonstrated his direct, concrete grasp of time: ancestral tradition determined how much land the *journal* comprised. The relation of time to labor was an observed necessity.

In this kind of work there was less of a gap between work life and social life. The pace of work defined a kind of freedom to which people were attached; it was something they valued. Was it legitimate to waste time? Clergymen, administrators, landowners, and economists answered this question in different ways, but all were scandalized by "popular unemployment" and the misuse of holidays to squander time. To add new holidays to the calendar and extend leisure time was to profane time from which all that was not sacred was to be banished. Listen to the curé de Faye in the diocese of La Rochelle: "On Sunday, within the octave of the parish patron, Saint Vivian, a group of people assembled in the doorway and in front of a tavern of the town, and various insolent words, indecencies, and drunken oaths were uttered, along with fighting and swearing, and so little care was taken to celebrate the holy day that no person from the parish went to vespers."[8]

The festival was at the heart of cultural and religious conflicts over time. Repression of celebration was a concern of the ruling elite, which dreamed not only of disciplining behavior in order to improve morals and productivity but also of creating holidays and other occasions for celebrating the new values. When time became money, the loss of labor power (of youth, primarily) was recognized as a loss of wealth. Countless works of the Enlightenment made this point: Montesquieu, Voltaire, the marquis de Turbilly, Faiguet de Villeneuve, Chomel, and Rouillé d'Orfeuil all concurred. More subtle, *L'Ami des hommes* defended festivals as a "spur to work" and "divine institution." The *Encyclopédie*, the academies (like the one in La Rochelle), and the agricultural societies were opposed to idleness. It is not at all certain, however, that those opposed to celebration triumphed over habit. "The bachelors of the Center-West never danced as much as in the final years of the Ancien Régime," according to their historian.[9]

It is not accurate, moreover, to assume that rulers and ruled divided along class lines over conceptions of time, work, and leisure. On both sides, everyday material culture, though expressed in different forms, had similar roots. The elite temporal order was not immune to natural accidents; because time was one component of ruling-class power, landlords, priests, and policemen joined together in opposing excessive celebration. The fact that time is finite was a political as well as an economic problem, a religious as well as a secular issue: everything was intertwined. Many factors went into the definition of social time: the sun, the liturgy, and the political calendar all played a part. Although the ruling minority dreamed of controlling the common man's leisure time and staged elaborate shows to promote the virtue of work, rulers did not live in a different world from the people they ruled.

The *fête des rosières* was a festival in which wreaths of roses were awarded to virtuous maidens, a sort of rustic cult of virtue; wreaths were also awarded to deserving youths and elderly people; and Rousseau and Marmontel are often credited with having inspired a great communion with nature: all these things suggest a persistent arcadian nostalgia for the world of eclogues and pastorals. Nature poetry was fixated on the eternal order; so were almanacs. Such phenomena deserve attention because they describe a conception of time different from the one that eventually prevailed.

The Seasons of the Poets

The "nature poem" survived the coming of modernity. Did its popularity after 1769 signal the birth of a new interest in nature or simply the rebirth of an old interest? To raise this question is merely to underscore the importance of nature poetry as a major cultural interest of the period from the baroque era to the Enlightenment, despite certain changes in form and tone.[10] Didactic, descriptive poems by both minor and major poets remained popular, *pace* Boileau (La Fontaine and Father Rapin were still read in eighteenth-century *collèges*), as did the great ancient tradition of Virgil, Lucretius, and Hesiod. A vast array of Greek and Latin models, translations, and imitations fueled the ardor of modern imitators of Virgil's *Georgics,* and philosophers borrowed questions and examples from Lucretius' *De natura rerum.* For schoolboys and provincial academicians, Virgil remained the inimitable model of perfection; the cardinal de Polignac and the atheist Sylvain Maréchal both drew on Lucretius; and Ovid inspired generation after generation of imitators in French and less frequently in Latin. Foreign writers such as Haller and Gessner from Germany and Young and Thomson from England introduced new accents from abroad, where the intense effects of the scientific revolution were experienced differently, and where the picturesque was quicker to win adherents than in France (the word *pittoresque* came to French from the English *picturesque,* an adjective applied to landscape painting). From theological epics such as the poem of seven thousand lines that the merchant Dulart submitted to the academy of Marseilles, entitled *De la grandeur de Dieu dans les merveilles de la nature* (published in five known editions, the first of which appeared in 1751), to secular verse with apologetic subtexts such as *Religion vengée* by Cardinal de Bernis (whom Voltaire called "Babet la Bouquetière"), readers were inundated with verse about nature, the cycle of the seasons, and the regular progression of works and days—poetry filled with metaphors of forests and rivers and lakes. "Naturalism took its place at the heart of didactic poetry and filled it with light." Poetry thus kept alive a persistent feeling for the land.

The French muse stimulated a diverse array of talents, including painters as well as poets, to take up the subject of time. There was Watelet's *Art de peindre,* for example, and Joseph Vernet's *Quatre Saisons.* A major shift from warmed-over imitation to genuine lyrical invention occurred in the 1750s: the *Discours sur l'inégalité* was written in 1753; Saint-Lambert's article "Génie" appeared in the *Encyclopédie* in 1757; Helvétius pondered his great poem *Sur le bonheur* from 1740 to 1771; and Saint-Lambert worked the new harmonies into his *Saisons.*

The cycle of the seasons was a constant theme of poetry in this period, a theme that one also finds in painting and music (Vivaldi, 1725; Haydn, 1801). Bernis explored this territory in 1748 with his *Quatre Parties du jour* and *Quatre Saisons,* but in terms of intellectual ambition he was surely outstripped by the marquis de Saint-Lambert, Voltaire's fortunate rival in the competition for the affections of that tender Emile, Mme du Châtelet. Poetically, Saint-Lambert was an innovator who replaced traditional genres with mannered verse and was less interested in descriptive didacticism than in developing a naturalistic art in which love of nature was coupled with love of man. Saint-Lambert's *Saisons* was a poem by a philosopher with the ardor of a moralist and the talent of a poet whose subject was the common understanding of time. Saint-Lambert the moralist called for "relief for the countryside" and for a return to nature and the château. In *Automne,* for example, he celebrated the grape harvest and the deer hunt, but his music being no longer ours, it takes effort to appreciate the charm of his verse:

> Il vient [l'automne] environné de paisibles nuages,
> il voit du haut du ciel le pourpre des raisins,
> et l'ambre et l'incarnat des fruits de nos jardins.
> De coteaux en coteaux la vendange annoncée
> rappelle le tumulte et la joie insensée.
> J'entends de loin les cris du peuple fortuné
> qui court, le thyrse en main de pampres couronné.
> Favoris de Bacchus, ministres de Pomone
> Célébrez avec moi les charmes de l'automne
> l'année à son déclin recouvre sa beauté . . .

> [Autumn] comes wreathed in tranquil clouds.
> From his lofty perch in the sky he sees the purple of the grapes
> and the amber and red of our garden fruits.
> From hill to hill news of the grape harvest spreads,
> awakening memories of tumult and wild joy.
> I hear from afar the shouts of happy people,
> who come running, thyrsis in hand and crowned with vines.
> Favorites of Bacchus, ministers of Pomona,
> come celebrate with me the autumn's charms.
> The waning year regains its beauty.

Beyond the indispensable cultural references, we have here a good example of the themes of nature and time that made such "painting poems" successful. Poetry of this sort accounted for the intellectual and academic reputation of Abbé Delille, the very type of the poet produced by the *collège* and promoted by the provincial academies (he was crowned in Marseilles). His translation of the *Georgics* met with astonishing success in France and throughout Europe. After 1769, Lemierre's *Fastes* and Roucher's *Mois* (both published in 1779 and both good examples of the new genre of epic descriptions of the seasons and of time) and, later, Delille's *Plaisirs de la vie champêtre* and *Homme des champs* as well as the 1782 *Jardins* were read and reread because they showed how poets could draw on old literary sources and still argue in favor of moral regeneration; these poems touched on matters that concerned agronomists yet maintained contact with the concerns of ordinary people. "The images that human beings discover evolve slowly," Gaston Bachelard once said. The history of nature poetry shows us how the discontinuity in the calendar gave rise to a vision of man in nature and in the temporal order—a vision that could be interpreted differently by different people.

Exchange Time and Clock Time

It may seem paradoxical to exalt lyricism in the age of reason, but only if we forget the basic assumption of this book, which is that ideas and things influence one another in a variety of ways. It is a matter of taste whether one prefers Rousseau's grape harvest (at Clarens in *La Nouvelle Héloïse*) to the harvests of Saint-Lambert or the Abbé Delille, but history obliges us to understand past successes as well as those prepared or ratified by the evolution of taste. There is no need to condemn descriptive rapture in the name of intellectual progress. Indeed, calling attention to the rapture has the useful benefit of reminding us that at any given moment, thinking and behavior may be influenced by very different sets of ideas and values. What we find when we look at time in the eighteenth century, at the height of early modernity, is that many people were still attached to old chronosophies, to Aristotelian and Augustinian conceptions of time, which combined change and stability, permanence and variation. These older conceptions contended with the Church's idea of time, as well as with conceptions of time associated with the rise of cities and merchants. Precise, measured, calculated time—the time of clocks and watches—eventually triumphed, but slowly, so that ultimately a linear, quantified concept of time was superimposed on the cycle of the seasons.[11]

Along with countless other published and unpublished diaries, Pierre Bordier's compendium demonstrates the psychological importance of the Church's conception of time, marked by recurrent festivals and stretching inexorably from the advent of Christ to the Last Judgment. Over the years, clerical and other writers, breaking with Augustine's tendency to view time as cyclical, had shown that the Christian concept of time was compatible with history and chronology. The teaching of the catechism, the practice of the faithful, and the spread of rites intended to sanctify life and death allowed individuals to internalize these new ideas of time to varying degrees. Ever since the fourteenth century, under the impact of reform, both theology and profane understanding had come to recognize the value of life and hence worldly time as necessary to salvation. Christian teaching sought to link sacred history to individual lives, and the liturgy was designed to give individuals a part in sacred history. Time was one, whether dealing with individual souls or mankind as a whole: this was the deeper meaning of hourly devotions and other repeated rituals of sanctification. Although such rituals were more easily observed in quiet cloisters and monasteries than in the world with all its bustle, they nevertheless left their mark on the world. Think, for example, of the role played by church bells in the noisy cities as well as the quiet countryside: ringing bells marked the hours of the day and life's important moments. Bells pealed for everyone's everyday joys and pains as well as for the great disasters and high points of communal and national life. They spoke a language to which we no longer possess the key, a language that imparted a particular value to time.

The old symbols were under pressure, a pressure that did not so much challenge their continued presence as modify their meaning. We know that social time in the cities, and to a lesser extent in the countryside as well, was transformed by the impact of trade, monetary circulation, transmission of news and information, the rise of credit, and speculation on the value of money over time.[12] The world of immediacy receded before the necessities of regularity, hence of quantification of time. The man who knew how to use time without wasting it gained an advantage. The new conditions triumphed in the analysis of labor: both the mobility and duration of labor had to be regulated. These regulations were a

permanent source of conflict between masters and journeymen, employers and employees, administrators and their clients. Labor regulation was
one aspect of a society in the process of conquering irregularity in all its
forms. The effort in this area also had its intellectual counterpart in
economic thinking about numbers of men, production volumes, and flows
of material—ideas borrowed from physics and applied to economics.[13]
Use generally preceded theory: witness the development of techniques
such as Arabic numerals, quantification, averages, statistical tables, and so
on. Society used time as well as arithmetic as a metaphor. Innovation was
slow: the calendar was sacred (even the Revolution was frustrated in its
efforts at reform), while the organization of the working day was not.
Gradually, other reforms became possible.[14]

The triumph of exactitude grew out of the proliferation of technology. New instruments for measuring time were perfected, but older ones
did not become outmoded all at once. The men of the eighteenth century
continued to look at sundials and to turn hourglasses upside down, and
they still greased the wheels of ancient clepsydras. They still measured
time by watching smoking candles slowly burn down or by noting the
leisurely movement of the stars. The great triumph of the modern age
was the mechanical clock and its companion, the watch, which made it
possible to measure time even when skies were cloudy or people were
inattentive or asleep. The new clocks reflected the idea that the world,
indeed the universe, as well as the human body, could be understood in
mechanical terms. The visualization of time by way of a mechanical
clockwork was merely one aspect of the visualization of astronomical
movements, and the very common trope identifying God as the "Great
Clockmaker" expressed this rational, mechanical view of the universe.
The metaphor of the cosmic clock found application in all fields of
thought: it was applied to human freedom and the mechanics of society. It
may well be that growing familiarity with watches—a material fact—had
"a concrete impact on the subtleties of theory."[15] The clock, *machina
machinarum*, was the most autonomous of machines, a machine that
regulated itself. Hence it could be invoked to justify the notion that the
universe, once set in motion by the Great Clockmaker, regulated itself in
accordance with independent laws. This idea had great appeal for a world
fascinated by craftsmanship and automata. Real or cosmic, pocket watch
or theoretical entity, the clock encouraged regularity and harmony. For
readers of Newton, it was a successful prototype of a generalized expla-

nation of how things worked. For the man in the street, it was a useful tool for dealing with movement, space, and even appearances.

This is not the place to retrace the technical evolution of clocks and watches.[16] Timekeeping instruments became increasingly powerful as new techniques were discovered and publicized. Key developments included the escapement (fifteenth to seventeenth century), which made it possible to divide the hour into fractional parts, and improvements in pendulum and spring mechanisms, which by the end of the seventeenth century, thanks to the work of Huyghens and Coster, reduced timekeeping errors to a few seconds. The royal academies in Paris and London as well as the naval ministries encouraged work on improved timekeeping in the hope of solving the problem of longitude measurement. By the end of the eighteenth century, all the innovations had been assimilated: time was quantifiable. Hence it was now the property of man rather than God, even though the Church was more keenly aware than ever of the importance of controlling time. Study of popular devotional literature may someday help us to understand how religion helped to perpetuate various discontinuities in the perception of time. Prayerbooks, guides for retreats, and pastoral literature for the terminally ill embraced a philosophy of time that also influenced secular pursuits.

In the transfer of control over time from sacristans and city governors to individuals, the effects of the market and economic activity proved to be crucial. Clockmakers, whether French, English, Dutch, or Swiss, were sons of capitalism. Also crucial was the impact of communication, as well as the growing regularity of transportation and improvements in the quality of vehicles. Coach schedules were now posted, published, and read, and what is more the schedules were kept. Bear in mind, however, that each region, and in some cases each city, kept its own time. The working day began at different times in different places. National standardization did not come until the nineteenth century. Before that, people set their watches to a variety of time zones. Another important factor was the role of armies and navies in the use of time to synchronize troop and ship movements. Watches enabled commanders to avoid the confusion caused by the uncertain hour of the dawn and made coordinated attacks possible. They were indispensable in synchronizing troop movements with artillery barrages. Clocks were also an instrument of discipline, as British labor regulations make clear. Watches and clocks were found wherever discipline and management were required. The need to keep time gave rise to a flourishing industry and brought business to shrewd merchants in Switzerland (think of Rousseau's father), England (home of Harrison's masterpiece, the chronometer), and France (Bréguet).

Not all the buyers were rationalizers, though. Clocks and watches were also a matter of fashion, articles of distinction. In Paris ordinary workers owned them, as did wealthy bourgeois: practical needs were not incompatible with aesthetic desires. Clocks were ornamental as well as practical and useful. Watches were jewels as well as instruments. Appearance was therefore as important as accuracy, if not more important. A watch showed that a man was cultivated and disciplined. In the countryside it marked its wearer as a prominent personage. Interestingly, peddlers everywhere hawked watches along with eyeglasses, books, icons, and ribbons: all of these things were tools for transforming individuals and the world. In Paris, the prostitutes in the bordellos frequented by Jacques-Louis Ménétra were crazy about the watches worn by Swiss commercial travelers, and some coachmen wore English watches. In 1786, Berthoud deplored the fact that the French watchmaking industry had succumbed to competition from Swiss and English manufacturers who supplied the "best shops in Paris," but everyone still wanted French-style timepieces. Bréguet watches were coveted by the cream of European society, but cheaper, sturdier models were available from London and Geneva. From their places of manufacture, European timepieces traveled to the far corners of the earth.

What ultimately proved crucial was that the ubiquitous watches did not simply measure time, they manufactured it. Listen to Ernst Jünger, who had important things to say about the subject:

> This claim seems to run counter to idealism, which has conclusively demonstrated that time is a form of human representation. But the representation of time depends on nationality and period, and it determines not only the technique of measuring time but, more generally, the value ascribed to it. For we can still perceive time in ways very different from measuring it. If man as a practical subject (to borrow a formulation of Kant's) conceives of a new kind of time, it has an effect on his theoretical conception of time. The place where that effect makes itself felt is the clock, understood in the broadest possible sense.

In this respect the eighteenth century witnessed the birth of a new form of sovereignty.

The Historian's Time

The history of the perception of time has demonstrated the complexity of a temporal architecture in which individual, religious, social, and collective times were intertwined, while the need for and ability to provide regularity and control increased steadily. This history cannot be divorced from questions about time itself—the historian's raw material. As customs changed, there were major changes as well in the way history was written, in part to accommodate changes in the conception of politics. The eighteenth century consumed large numbers of history books. Whether ecclesiastical or profane, history drew on a wide range of associated disciplines. Contemporary catalogs and libraries included geography and travel writing under the head of history, which occupied a respectable place among applications for authorizations to print: roughly 10 percent of 1,700 titles listed for the period 1723–1725, 10 percent again for the period 1750–1754, and nearly 18 percent in 1788 (among public permissions). The proportion of tacit authorizations was more stable, varying between 10 and 15 percent over the period from 1750 to 1784.

These figures show that history was not one of the dominant categories of the period: it ranked far below belles lettres and arts and sciences. But journal reviews confirm that it was a central category of knowledge: history accounted for 30 percent of the books reviewed in the *Mémoires de Trévoux* and 23 percent of those reviewed in the *Journal des savants* at the beginning of the century (1715–1719); hence it ranked as a major discipline for the literate public. The majority of these titles fell under the head of profane history, although the categories themselves were not well defined. If one goes by Chancellery records, for example, the number of works of secular history published annually remained steady or rose as the century progressed, but the Jesuits of Trévoux held that this number declined; the discrepancy probably indicates that many writers fell back on "safe" subjects such as ancient history. In any case, the figures attest to the existence of a readership for historical works, a demand that conceals a variety of interests ranging from the needs of students to the desires of citizens. Certain groups found history books more appealing than did others: the nobility, for instance, in both Paris and the provinces liked to fill their libraries with historical works.[17] Of the 5,000 books in Turgot's libraries, more than 1,200 were works of history. Those Parisian nobles who read were mainly interested in the past, especially the French past

(40 percent of all titles). In Brittany, Languedoc, Franche-Comté, and Provence, among both *parlementaires* and the *noblesse d'épee,* the proportion of history books in estate inventories varied from one-quarter to one-third and tended to increase over time.

There were differences, however, between the history of the historians and the history of readers, and these tell us both how people in the eighteenth century perceived time and how they represented it. Two examples will suffice to illustrate this point: they concern, first, the historical vision of two provincials and, second, the place of history in almanacs, which were widely distributed and drew on (as well as promoted) vast cyclical mythologies of time. These examples show how little space was reserved for history in the *Encyclopédie*'s "system of human knowledge." They also tell us something about the sources of intellectual crisis in a century during which historians learned to reason and to view old certitudes with a skeptical eye.

Vision of Time, Vision of History

Like other men who kept diaries, Pierre Bordier recorded the trivial details of rural life in a compendium and diary he kept from 1741 to 1781. Compared to other texts of the same type, Bordier's has one advantage: time was at the center of his reflection, and cyclical time is interrogated by events.[18] In the diary especially, Bordier displayed a unique ability to write about the passage of time and its preservation in memory. A peasant who every year recapitulated the main features of his agrarian existence, he encountered in the course of his intellectual development a text that he copied out at length and referred to frequently: the *Prophéties perpétuelles* (of which Prault's 1743 edition shows that the text was in circulation at the time), a work attributed to Pythagoras, Joseph the Just, and Daniel the Prophet and typical of the kind of book that met with popular success. The text offered a theory of cyclical recurrence: history repeated itself, the book claimed, every twenty-eight years. For Bordier, this suggestion was the key to interpreting both the generational cycle (twenty-eight was the average age of marriage) and the accidents of agrarian life. In the eyes of the peasant, the return of wheat rust and unusually heavy rains proved that the prophets were right, and even if the interval was not always the predicted twenty-eight years, Bordier returned to the text repeatedly in the hope of understanding the cycles of history.

In pursuit of this cyclical structure, Bordier patiently recorded the recurring sequence of the seasons while carefully noting each isolated event, as if the history that interested him were unfolding simultaneously on two levels: slowly and cyclically on one level and in the form of brief noteworthy events on the other. In interpreting events, Bordier looked for both local and global explanations of exceptional occurrences. In his diary he emulated clerics who, between official notations in their parish registers, made similar annotations: the cold winter of 1709, wars, royal coronations. The events recorded by the rural chronicler constituted the history he considered to be memorable: it included deviations from the norm (with respect to prices and harvests, say) as well as the aftermath of memorable celebrations and exploits. Time was conceived in terms of norms and deviations from the norm, and Bordier's concept of history was formed by the type of information to which he had access: prognostications, royal proclamations, and gazettes that he came upon when visiting inns. The facts he recorded meshed neatly with his cyclical vision because they pertained to the biological events of the dynasty and to major religious events (jubilees, holy years). In Bordier's vision of historical time, inertia was far more important than the unexpected.[19]

If we compare his attitude with that of Abbé Michel Simon, the learned author of the *Histoire de Vendôme et de ses environs*, who was born in Vendôme in 1712 and died there in 1782, we note both differences and similarities. Simon's vision was that of a city dweller, cleric, and scholar. First curé and later canon of the collegiate church of Saint-Georges, a man with a comfortable benefice, Abbé Simon had interests typical of a prominent member of the middle class, the kind of man who elsewhere would have belonged to an academy. He was a man of taste who owned paintings, as well as a man of science and observation. His library, composed mainly of works of theology and law, included a large proportion of history books (27 percent). An Augustinian, he loved the classics more than the works of the Enlightenment.

His attempt to write local history was similar to many others, although Simon himself did not belong to any group of scholarly researchers. He died, moreover, without publishing his text, so that it remains for us a model of historical compilation. Simon was clearly concerned with historical method, verification, and criticism, but he worked with an outdated historical vision. His study, devoted mainly to analyzing the role of illustrious counts, dukes, and abbots from his region, focuses primarily on two medieval institutions: the county and the abbey. Counts and dukes asserted their power against outside powers and were judged for their initiatives. By contrast, abbeys were places that departed from the will of their founders only to return to their original conception, cyclically for a time and then definitively after the sixteenth century. The tone of the narrative changes with the advent of the modern era, as the local vision is integrated into the history of France; Louis III, the last duc de Vendôme, is praised, but allusions to the achievements of the Bourbons become obligatory.

Compared with Bordier's diary, Simon's history is more localized and more closely geared to institutional chronology. It is history seen from above, and primarily an account of the destiny of counts and dukes whose actions are judged in terms of moral and religious values. Explanations of major events are rare, because those events are related to a particular conception of time. For Simon, time was stable and repetitive. Its beginning was repeated in various types of foundational events: the foundation of the abbey, the county, and the duchy, followed by the annexation of the duchy to the kingdom of France in 1712. Time is also governed by cycles based on generations, on the biographies of prominent local personages. The generational cycle is the normal mode of the passage of time, a mode that allows Simon to reconcile continuity with change, with progress as defined by the scholar or moralist. For Abbé Simon, history was largely a story of scarcely questioned immobility over more than a millennium. His understanding of time is not all that different from that of his neighbor the farmer: both men emphasize continuity over evolution, cyclicity over change. This finding raises two questions: How did the Enlightenment develop a new vision of change, and how did it spread that new vision? In this respect, the conventional social and cultural hierarchies are not very rigorous; almanacs, to which we turn next, reveal yet another aspect of the situation.

Almanacs and History

Almanacs have attracted the attention of historians of popular culture since Charles Nisard in the nineteenth century and Robert Mandrou thirty years ago. We are less certain today than in the past about how the large urban and rural readership of this category of literature was divided up, since the boundaries between groups shifted from the seventeenth to the eighteenth century. Almanacs and similar publications are quite revealing in this respect. They may also help us to answer our question about the relationship between instruments of learning and their social distribution.

The primary purpose of the almanac was to publicize the dates of church holidays, agricultural events, and phenomena related to health, along with information about festivals, seasons, and the phases of the moon (which were believed to affect the body). The almanac also contained a view of life, described in terms of different ages, and of history, in the form of more or less extensive chronologies. Almanacs sought to give a detailed breakdown of time, and calendars occupied a central place in all versions of the genre. The *Almanach ou pronostication des laboureurs,* the *Almanach des bergers,* the *Messager boiteux,* and the *Almanach liégeois* (or *Mathieu Laensberg*) clearly offered a cyclical, cosmic conception of time. Astrology was used to interpret and predict character and temperament, and the present could not be understood in isolation from probable future revolutions.

In the eighteenth century, however, almanacs evolved in two ways. First, their widespread use by all social classes gave rise to increased precision and specialization. And second, having been prophetic, almanacs became historical, partaking of the same deep-seated cultural changes that we have already encountered in Bordier and Simon. Almanacs were successful both locally and nationally. Following the example set by the *Almanach royal,* specialized almanacs, calendars, and yearbooks addressed audiences in specific provinces, cities, and even groups (hunters, poetry lovers, admirers of fashion, women). This change began in the first half of the eighteenth century but accelerated after 1750. The bibliography of almanacs and administrative and military yearbooks lists a hundred or so titles before 1700 and more than three hundred by 1750.[20] During the reign of Louis XVI approximately three hundred additional titles were added. These included the *Calendrier historique de la cour, Etrenne de la province, Etat royal pur, Etrennes militaires, Etrennes ecclésiastiques,* and *Etrennes curieuses.* Everyone now had access to sources of information that could help them cut through the complexity of the administration (urban and economic growth had made such information more necessary than ever). Time still played a central role in these new almanacs, but calendars were reduced to essentials as texts were called upon to provide all sorts of new information.

The transition from the *Compost des bergers* to the yearbook of scientific knowledge was a slow one. At the beginning of the century the *Almanach de Milan* was still published in Toulouse: this was a "true universal almanac . . . by the great preacher de Chiarvalle, containing observations on the year with indications of predictions that came true exactly as foretold." We are still in the realm of popular cosmogony: the predictions of the future attest to a cyclical conception of history. The *Almanach très curieux pour la ville de Toulouse* perpetuated this tradition as late as 1750, but it already faced competition from the *Calendrier de la cour du parlement*. Two imitations probably had a decisive impact on this change, namely, the *Almanach royal*, which was a best-seller in Paris, and the *Ordo ecclesiasticus;* the staff of both was the same, as was the organization of the court calendar, based on the model of the diocesan calendar of services and holidays. Nonreligious and social concerns combined to yield a similar division of time and space, a classified listing of urban life. After 1750, the yearbook formula came into its own with the *Almanach historique et chronologique de Languedoc.* The almanacs with the most useful contents sold the most copies. There was something for everyone, from dates of fairs to addresses of bailiffs, merchants, and trade guilds. Some almanacs were pocket-sized, others rugged enough for daily use. Custom dictated a variety of formats and packages: for fifteen sols one could by the *Calendrier* alone, and for six sols one could buy the *Messager boiteux* at a bookstore. For one livre ten sols one could purchase the complete version. The almanac-yearbook and yearbook-almanac attest to the mingling of old traditions with the new utilitarian model.

Along with their new relationship to space and consumption, almanacs also discreetly reflected the rise of history. We can trace this development by looking at the almanac most representative of the cyclical, cosmological conception of time, the *Messager boiteux,* known in the seventeenth century for its Basel and Alsace editions and then in the eighteenth century for countless publications in Switzerland and France. Like its chief competitor, the *Mathieu Laensberg* from Liège, from which the *Messager* tried to distinguish itself both physically and editorially, it was sold everywhere. As was traditional, a good deal of attention was devoted to the calendar, along with features from the old *Compost* (twenty-four pages, or about a third of the 1770 edition) and a few pages on the human body and astrological topics that still appealed to readers. In general, however, the *Messager boiteux* became increasingly "historical" by design. Might there have existed at the time a "popular" version of history, where the word "popular" is to be taken as broadly and imprecisely as possible?

What is striking is that events are simply juxtaposed rather than woven into a narrative. Bordier did the same thing: he noted accidents and deviations from the norm, although the information at his disposal hardly allowed him to achieve the exhaustive presentation that an almanac editor could aspire to. The *Messager boiteux* offered four kinds of chronicle: the life of people of rank, with their banquets, festivals, and ceremonies (10 to 15 percent of the text from 1764 to 1789); political events, including wars and treaties, history of nations and great men (18 percent); current events, including techniques, recipes, remedies, and inventions (5 percent); and the legal chronicle, listing laws and edicts (barely 2 percent of the text); but above all oddities, natural disasters, monsters, announcements of pregnancies, prolonged pregnancies, crimes, and acts of virtue (more than 60 percent). What we see, then, is the development of a vision centered on the immediacy of the nonquotidian and geographically focused on Europe, primarily France, though without excluding the occasional report from one or another exotic locale. The important point is that the news in almanacs was already placed in a context of distance, yielding something like a "spontaneous history of the present." Editors drew on the usual sources: not only gazettes and newspapers but also broadsides and satirical publications. It was generally impossible to identify a clear source for any particular fact. Almanacs simply filtered the news that the gazettes reported as it happened. The coherence of their vision lies not in any rhetoric of historical narrative (which is not present) but in the persistence of certain themes.[21]

War was one ever-present source of information. Although France was increasingly spared its direct consequences, it remained a fundamental source of anxiety. It was the backdrop to history itself, full of lessons for princes and their subjects. War was the theater of high politics, a stage for noble as well as ignoble deeds. It was also a theater of passions and a cyclical punishment visited upon mankind. And already there was criticism of war, whose horrors revolted not only people of sensibility but also the popular heart. Princes with the power to start and end wars occupied an important place: they made history. "Let us thank heaven that peace has been restored to a Europe governed by gentle, enlightened, equitable princes," declared the *Messager boiteux* in 1760. Princely deeds and edicts mobilized the "imposing apparatus" of royal representation with its attendant ceremonies and festivals. Some almanacs availed themselves of the opportunity to describe the good or bad prince and thus to give voice to the expectations of their subjects. Happy were the peaceful and beneficent, but bellicose braggarts like Frederick II were condemned. In this way a note of political criticism, still highly moralistic in character, slipped into the almanacs.

Moralism also colored reports of the news, crime, and sentimental events: people liked to read about highway robbers and great loves thwarted, about edifying deaths with lessons for all, about exemplary tortures and revered old men. The almanacs in general painted a very conservative portrait of society, yet they incorporated many of the lessons of the day. While they still embodied "prejudices" and "superstitions" denounced by men of enlightened views, they also published news of change and of the breakdown of walls between cultures. They praised the invention of new machines, promising remedies, scientific discoveries, good hygiene, and the benefits of inoculation. The *Messager boiteux* condemned torture and slavery in 1787 and 1789, respectively. Almanacs not only gave wide currency to new ideas but also made palpable their acceptance by large numbers of people.

The *Messager boiteux* placed history on the boundary between passing time and past time. It arranged facts in more or less precise chronologies and alongside a yearly list of key historical dates. This history remained approximate when compared to the traditional precision of the calendar and essential chronological facts: "Since the birth of My Lord Jesus Christ, we count 1,787 years, or 5,736 since the creation of the world and 4,080 since the Flood . . . 847 years since the invention of the art of printing in Strasbourg by Jean Gutenberg . . . 973 years since Charlemagne . . . 12 years since the alliance with the United States of America." With the exception of the last date, the rest (including both sacred and profane events, mainly dynastic and political) remained unchanged throughout the century. There was nothing especially "popular" about this chronology. It was merely a simplified form of scholarly history, some aspects of which, and especially of sacred history, were challenged. While the chronology might evoke history, it was not directly related to the listing of the year's events, which continued to be defined by strictly annual limits.

Almanacs did not evolve much, but they did gradually incorporate a more complex and critical historical discourse by creating a "memory of the present," an anticipated vision of the future in which the present became a memorable past worthy of celebration.[22] The *Messager boiteux* was now expected to cover temporal ground, where tradition could be contested, thereby giving rise to a new vision of political, social, and national history. While preserving both a cyclical vision of time and a morally edifying linear representation, the almanac made its expanded readership aware of public life. The history it adapted combined immediate information with lessons for the future, experience of the present, and utility. Like Bordier's compendium and Simon's *Histoire du Vendôme*, the almanacs raised the vague possibility of gradual change. These three types of practice survived both the calm stretches and the more tortured phases of the century. They survived because they embodied different forms of social instruction from which individuals could draw on memory and custom in accordance with their resources and needs.

History, Memory, and Custom

There is constant exchange between temporal traditions and practices and historical discourses: the linear time of the Church, a time of slow, irreversible evolution, was compatible with a repetitive, cyclical reading of natural and human history. The cumulative linear time of the philosophers, men of letters, and scientists was compatible with regression owing to corruption of taste, degradation of morals, perversion of religion, political decadence, and alienation from nature.[23] The Moderns and the Ancients clashed over such matters in a dispute that outlived Louis XIV. Attitudes changed in the eighteenth century, but the change was fueled by a variety of arguments that could justify quite contradictory behavior. The important point is to understand how the linear vision of time gained ground at the expense of the ancient traditions, and how this in turn fed into a broader philosophical vision based on the idea of progress. We must restore the complexity of contemporary historical practice by looking at institutions as well as actors and at how the choices of historians revealed the connection between history as written for the Church and history as written for the king in the period before it was taken up by the philosophes. Traditional historiography, focused on works but neglecting social institutions, as usual emphasizes certainties while leaving debates and compromises in the shadows.

From the Age of Louis XIV to the Age of Enlightenment, two protagonists shared not only Clio's favors but also a common conception of
history: the Church and the monarchy. Both took a utilitarian view of
history: from Bossuet to Mably, from the *Discours sur l'histoire universelle*
to the *Projet d'étude de l'histoire dédié au prince de Parme*, history offered
sage advice to princes, and beyond political wisdom it also revealed the
nature of man. The purpose of studying the past was to corroborate the
views of moralists and religious apologists. A whole segment of the
public remained under the sway of the historical catechism that Bossuet
composed in the service of theology. For Bossuet, history was meant to
protect the world as God willed it against change. The rationality of
history was solely a consequence of God's plan, even if events in this
world were connected by natural and human causalities. What this history lacked was perhaps the essential thing, namely, a sense of time and
evolution.[24]

What Bossuet and his imitators used to justify their religious ideas,
others, sometimes acting at the express request of the monarchy, sometimes not, used to ratify royal policy or, even more broadly, the idea that
God had entrusted France's destiny to its Bourbon kings. History as
handmaiden to politics was called upon to justify specific royal attitudes
or decisions. For example, the issue of the Constitution pitted two distinct
systems against each other: the Romanist thesis of Abbé Dubost and the
Germanist thesis of Boulainvilliers. Both were rife with consequences for
the future. Debates about the history of France were among the liveliest
parts of eighteenth-century culture, because they arose out of civil society's drive toward power and became involved quite early in the search
for a source of legitimacy.[25] The crux of the matter was the usurpation of
power by the absolute monarchy. This was an authentic debate, even if it
projected issues of the present into the past, and even if the chief participants twisted the evidence to suit their positions. Not even Montesquieu
avoided the controversy: he devoted three books of *De l'esprit des lois* to
it. When seen in the context of the work as a whole, these three books
reveal a general design ultimately intended to rescue history from utilitarianism in order to study it for signs of the "laws" regulating governmental practices as well as customs.

Hence it would be wrong to set up an artificial boundary between
history as conceived by the philosophers and history as conceived by
adepts of religion and monarchy. It is just as misleading to lump the

history produced by erudite scholars together with that written by men of letters: positivist historians tend to do this without considering differences of audience and sources of recognition. Within the cultural community there were different uses for different kinds of history.[26] As the supremely intelligent Montesquieu said, and as countless hardworking scholars and an even greater number of amateur history buffs discovered in their studies, it was through critical study of the sources that historians came to understand change in nontheodical terms. The Enlightenment believed in history because its intellectuals were able to separate historical facts from supposedly natural theories of history. This enabled them to think against contingency and dominate both the general and particular causes of events. To say that history suffered from the importation of foreign ends is to fail to recognize that, among the many areas on which historians do research, there is a connection as powerful as rationalism and equally much a driving force, namely, erudition and philological criticism. This fact cannot be avoided by anyone who wants to understand the fate of Enlightenment history in terms other than those of nineteenth-century epistemology.

The primary goal of the eighteenth-century historian was to instruct, and according to rhetorical tradition he needed to please in order to convince. The strength of literary prejudice was responsible for the success of practices that to us seem surprising but that had pedagogical value and linked the historian to the orator and history to eloquence. So said the scholar Nicolas Lenglet-Dufresnoy in his *Méthode pour étudier l'histoire*, first published in 1713 and frequently reprinted: "In what way should history be written, if not with the sort of male eloquence and elevation of style that has its place not in private memoirs but only where it is necessary to describe the actions of a people that distinguished itself by its grandeur and dignity?"[27]

Was this view of the matter ever entirely abandoned? There is reason to doubt it. Neither the persistence of rhetorical prejudice nor the argument of utility should be allowed to mask the heterogeneity of practice. There was little in common between the practice of a secondary school teacher such as Rollin in his best-seller, *Histoire ancienne*, and that of facile historians such as the abbé de Vertot, who saw archives as so much "useless paper." Everyone knows Vertot's response to the person who asked him for new details about the siege of Rhodes: "My siege is finished." Think, too, of Voltaire and Montesquieu, who in their different ways helped to bring history and philosophy together and thus furthered the cause of analysis and explanation. Like other writers, they were historians, but not all historians reasoned in the same way or pursued the same ends. But isn't what makes them similar just as important as what makes them different, namely, the period's fascination with accumulating systematic knowledge? When we study the "press," or writing about the present in all its forms—gazettes, broadsheets, literary newsletters, and so on—what we find if we choose a sample year, say, 1734, is the prominence of history as a reference, its recognition as an important instrument of knowledge, and its capacity for improvement as attested by criticism of its own methods, objectives, and classifications. "The triumph of history is the triumph of the modern spirit in the form of acute consciousness of time and evolution."[28]

The Institutions of Critical History

The change in historical method came about somewhat before the turn of the eighteenth century. It was undoubtedly connected with the religious schism that tore Europe apart and with the "crisis of consciousness." Catholic erudition was condemned to history, just as Protestant science was condemned to biblical hermeneutics. The aggressive criticism of Pierre Bayle, the symbol of early eighteenth-century intellectual debate, is to be understood in this context and in relation to the proliferation of knowledge and philosophical systems in previous years.[29] Our desire to understand the rationalization of history should not be allowed to mask the enormous work that was accomplished in its institutions; study of those institutions is perhaps the only way to rediscover a major component of the culture. In this area we can distinguish four circles, even though they never functioned in total isolation from one another: first, the religious congregations, especially the Benedictine order; second, the Académie des Inscriptions et Belles-Lettres; third, the king's servants, employed either as historiographers or by the Cabinet des Chartes; and finally, provincial learned societies and academies. A more detailed study would point out the correspondences that developed among these various networks and indicate points of contact as well as divergence. Here, however, the best we can do is to show how the intellectual community operated. We will not attempt to restore a unified theory of history, implausible on its face.

The Benedictine monks of Saint-Maur constituted an archive by following the principles laid down by Dom Mabillon in *Diplomatique* (1681).
Between the first generation of "Maurists" (Mabillon died in 1710) and
the Revolution, the work of the Benedictines was carried on in the major
abbeys of the order, especially Saint-Germain-des-Prés. The Maurists
poured their energy into three projects: first, the history of their order
and of the ecclesiastical sciences from patristics to liturgy; second, led by
Dom Montfaucon and Dom Tarrisse, the introduction of historical study
in France through the *Histoire littéraire*, ecclesiastical history (the *Gallia
Christiana*), and provincial history (of Languedoc, Brittany, and Burgundy); and third, an anthology of the historians of the Gauls. The
publication of numerous Maurist texts gave the Benedictines a role in
contemporary debates such as the one about the concept of origins and
the one about the place to be assigned to the study of the ancient world.

The wide-ranging work of the Benedictines points up three important
principles for understanding cultural practices. First, the work required
lengthy professional training, including apprenticeship in complex techniques and methods. This training enabled scholars to collect, sort,
authenticate, and copy manuscript sources. These activities were consistent with royal policy, and the energy with which they were pursued
cannot be separated from the sense of importance they derived from their
association with the monarchy and the Church. Second, the Benedictine
enterprise created a social network; the monks' work depended on their
ability to correspond, travel, and meet others doing similar work. That
ability attests to the unflagging vitality of the regular orders.[30] Finally, the
epistemological basis of the Benedictine project linked it to other innovations in the natural sciences, for example, as well as in efforts to understand and control space. Classification and criticism of source documents
depended on careful observation, comparison, and identification of common characteristics. This work confirmed the superiority of writing over
speech and public over private. A preexisting order was reconstituted for
the purpose of documentary work. Antiquarians and archivists achieved
an intellectual revolution in their own right: the work of Mabillon gave
them an instrument for discovering the truth based on a kind of reasoning
different from that involved in mathematics.[31]

Social contacts and correspondence created numerous ties between the
Benedictine network and the Académie des Inscriptions. In a sense, the
Académie, founded by Colbert, took over from the Maurists when their

activity slowed or was impeded by the Jansenist crisis, which was partially resolved by a shift of responsibility to the Cabinet des Chartes. Created to contribute to the "glory of the king" by means of inscriptions and medals, the "Petite Académie" became under the leadership of Abbé Bignon a dynamic center in which all disciplines were represented: archaeology, epigraphy, paleography, ancient and modern history, and the history of orientalism. Forty members, ranked according to function and celebrity as in all academic cenacles, worked under his control. In exchange, the monarchy guaranteed them compensation and places in its various administrations. Everyone who was anyone in the world of historical erudition eventually wound up here: Nicolas Fréret, Antoine Galland, Abbé Jean-Jacques Barthélemy (who on the eve of the Revolution published the *Voyage du jeune Anacharsis en Grèce dans le milieu du IVe siècle*), Bourguignon, Bougainville (the abbé, not the sailor), Foncemagne, and La Curne de Sainte-Palaye. The group consisted of professionals drawn from various quarters of society, including members of the clergy and Third Estate; it owed its influence to the fact that it served the monarchy.

The Académie promoted the development of scholarly criticism and laid the groundwork for archaeology and other sciences auxiliary to history. At the same time it reoriented ancient history and oriental studies through its publications and competitions. As a *compagnie* of the Ancien Régime, it investigated history on behalf of the state, but unlike the Académie des Sciences in the realm of science or the Académie Française in the realm of language, it never became the supreme arbiter in its domain. The unsuccessful political agenda of the Académie des Inscriptions was to make the study of classical antiquity the basis of all scholarship on behalf of the state and essential preparation for work on the history of France. The Académie was neither a closed group of marginalized scholars hostile to the Enlightenment nor a conservative cenacle suspicious of heterodox views. A few (very few, to be sure) of its members personified the Enlightenment: Caylus, de Brosses, Duclos, Pastoret. As an institution it was quite active in defending the aristocratic interpretation of the Enlightenment until it took a more liberal turn. The Boulainvilliers and *parlementaire* circles agreed about certain basic intellectual values: they were against the rhetorical view of history and for criticism, rational inquiry, classification of research subjects, emancipation from prejudice, and promotion of talent and merit.

All in all, the Académie carved out a zone of liberty for itself, a space where intellectual audacity was possible if tempered by practical and tactical prudence. As Lionel Gossman has shown, it was not far from the *parlementaire* opposition in its critique of absolutism but could not follow the philosophes in their more radical commitments. In other words, one reason for the marginalization of the Académie was that it failed to make a clear-cut ideological choice and sought instead to achieve some degree of reconciliation with traditional views of nature and history. Nonconformist scholars somehow always got off on the wrong foot, as the example of La Curne de Sainte-Palaye shows: his critical erudition laid the groundwork for medieval history, yet all he saw in society was the old order and traditional hierarchy. For these scholars history was an end in itself, whereas for both the philosophes and the monarchy it was a way of justifying action aimed at achieving progress. The Académie stood for noninterventionist liberalism.

These two marginalizations (of the Benedictines and other clerical scholars mired in theological disputes and of academic scholars left in the dust by philosophes bent on progress) had an impact on the formation of the third circle mentioned earlier, the Cabinet des Chartes. Its history illustrates the development of historical research for well-defined administrative purposes. One of the most reputable adversaries of the philosophes, J.-N. Moreau, was entrusted with the task of investigating the legal and historical foundations of the monarchy. Moreau, a lawyer steeped in classical culture, an associate of the d'Aguesseau circle, and the author of the famous satire *Les Cacouacs*, inherited several missions: to manage the archives that had been set up under the auspices of the Contrôle Général des Finances in 1759; to locate and collect in a central repository all documents needed by the administration; and, as the program of 1762 states, to establish a "repository of public law and history": "The discoveries of historians shall provide legal scholars with grounds for argument, and specialists in both domains must lend one another a helping hand." In this way the government would be able to justify its actions and settle disputed matters.

The so-called *dépôt des chartes* became an active administrative archive. The collection of documents mobilized many Benedictine scholars as well as Parisian and provincial academicians. Drawing on institutions of all kinds, from libraries to parish charter rooms, the new repository collected thousands of copies from all the provinces of France. Some forty thousand of these can still be consulted today in the Cabinet des Manuscrits of the Bibliothèque Nationale, but many came from abroad. The Cabinet des Chartes had a budget, salaried employees, and an executive committee, the so-called Conférence des Chartes, which brought administrators (such as Bertin, Paulmy, and d'Aguesseau) together with scholars; there was also a program of publications. Professionalization was thus the watchword of this particular conjunction of history and politics. When Bertin submitted a proposal for legal reform to Louis XVI in 1774, scientific and scholarly history was expected to support the monarchy in its increasingly urgent search for legitimacy, roots, and principles. In 1778 the Comité d'Histoire et de Droit Public was charged with codifying French law for the purpose of developing a constitutional framework. It was no doubt too late for the state to reform itself, but the work of the Cabinet des Chartes and its director is a good example of why any judgment on the history of the Enlightenment must be ambivalent: this institution, which helped to develop new historical methods and lines of inquiry and which promoted documentary expertise, could not sever its ties to the government and its policies of legal reform, even after the idea of basing a more equitable law not on history but on reason had gained public support.[32]

We find a similar contradiction in our fourth and final circle of historians, the provincial academicians. Provincial academies always reserved a large place for history, which for them always numbered among the human sciences in Furetière's sense. To be sure, this taste for the past was not immediately distinguishable from historical rhetoric and pedagogy. Several factors encouraged the development of historical work on a broad front. First, the provinces invoked the past in order to define themselves in opposition to Paris. Second, the academies spontaneously embraced the ideal of progress and reform that animated both men of the Enlightenment and administrators. History, the guardian of the past, now became mistress of the future, justifying attempts to measure the degree to which the human spirit had been transformed. It was therefore obliged to teach a mode of thought and way of life that looked forward to greater independence and promoted a new "clergy." Based on reconciliation of social antagonisms and internalization of the values of aristocratic sociability, it guaranteed liberty, while as a "bourgeois" mode of thought it made change thinkable. History thus found its way into the schedule of activities of academies everywhere; some of the most active in this area were the academies of Toulouse, Besançon, Dijon, Marseilles, Nîmes, and Lyons, which distinguished themselves by sponsoring well-known prize competitions. Not surprisingly, *parlementaires* and other erudite magistrates played a certain role here. If I had to choose one among hundreds of possible examples, I would mention François Droz, a *conseiller* in the *parlement* of Besançon and correspondent of the Benedictines and the Cabinet des Chartes. He was responsible for a great deal of activity that could not have developed to the extent that it did without widespread interest in the subject.

In the end, what mattered was the role ascribed to history and the status accorded to it. It retained, first of all, the function of granting the "capacity to govern to those entitled by birth to do so." It also justified the privileges of the ruling elite but at the same time expanded the liberty of all vis-à-vis the state and thus became "the school of the true citizen." That is why the majority of historians were provincial and secular in their outlook, and that is why history served the Enlightenment. Being provincialist, history expanded the study of the past to the study of customs and mores, and the history of the provincial neo-Immortals reconciled Mabillon and Voltaire. History shared Mabillon's concerns with critical inventories and verified chronologies, but it also shared Voltaire's ambition to serve humanity and promote progress in keeping with a linear conception of time:

> Common woes or public prosperity, the growth or decadence of empires—these things assume slightly different appearances in the various provinces that compose great states, because climates, mores, customs, and a thousand other natural and moral causes yield detectable variations. These traits often escape disinterested eyes. One would look in vain for them in general histories. But he who has made it his duty to conduct a serious study of the national territory and genius inevitably discovers them in the original memoirs he ponders and in the monuments that survive for him alone.

In tracing the advent of various forms of modernity in history, we have seen that erudition and reason, *érudits* and philosophes, cannot be contrasted in any simple way. If their positions do not always agree, their practice reflects similar cultural changes. Ira Owen Wade was right to emphasize the importance of the meeting that took place at Senones when Voltaire, in the course of writing his *Essai sur les moeurs* (1756), went to consult references in the library of Dom Calmet.[33] This meeting points up the deep kinship between rival approaches and the unresolved debate. Voltaire challenged "reasoning reason" in the name of empirical historical reality, but he conceived of history as the history of the human spirit. All of his historical work is in this vein, from the *Histoire de Charles XII* (1732) to the *Siècle de Louis XIV* (1739–1751) and from the *Précis du règne de Louis XV* (1751) to the *Histoire de Pierre le Grand* (1763).[34]

Conceived as the history of civilization, Voltaire's history laid the groundwork for later attempts to demonstrate how the logic of development of man's faculties was hidden behind history's vicissitudes and crimes. Voltaire's work cleared a path for Turgot to write the *Tableau philosophique des progrès de l'esprit humain* (1750) and for Condorcet to write the *Esquisse d'un tableau historique des progrès de l'esprit humain* (1794). When all is said and done, it may be that history teaches us only one law: that with the passage of time, man develops his faculty of reason and expands his freedom and therefore his ability to transcend the past.[35]

4

Peasant France and
Merchant France

THE EFFORTS of eighteenth-century Frenchmen to understand geography and population, to master space by developing roads and waterways, and to conceptualize time in new ways suggest that the French culture of this period was full of variety and contrast. A majority of the population lived narrowly circumscribed lives. For most people, the only contact with broader social networks came through a circulation of commodities and men, orders and information—a circulation that depended on an organized system of transportation, an extensive administrative infrastructure, and a willingness and ability to travel. Within a populated world whose contours had been largely defined since the fourteenth century, the boundaries of rural society were essentially fixed: call this the spatial dimension of rural life.[1] Geographers tell us that relations between villages were defined primarily by the distance between them: call this the linear dimension.[2] Natural resources and the trade that flowed from them define a third dimension of rural life, a dimension linked to supply and demand and productive capacity relative to current needs: call this the qualitative dimension. These three dimensions shaped both the peasant's relation to the land and social relations to others.

Rural society, which still bore traces of its feudal origins in social relations between peasants and landlords and between lords feudally subordinate to surviving suzerains jealous of their rights, had since the sixteenth century been largely taken over and restructured by the administrative monarchy. Because the power of the Bourbon territorial state depended on its population, royal administrators were obsessed with studying and controlling the territory in order to collect taxes more easily and recruit soldiers when necessary. In this respect the kingdom's growing cities and towns formed part of an administrative and military, fiscal and bureaucratic network capable of marshaling men, money, and services for the benefit of the state. The monarchy thus became the primary consumer of productive surpluses as well as a source of cash revenues. The associated process of territorial integration brought a broad range of peasant economies into contact with one another: the "peasant kingdom," the *royaume profond*, is not only the primary object of agrarian history but also the key to unraveling the important relationship between stability and change.

Meanwhile, another society within France created new social structures and tugged French life and culture in new directions. This was the society born of the growth of trade and commerce, the society of the great port, manufacturing, and trading cities. Coastal cities and inland trading centers formed part of a very different network of communication and information. Access to Mediterranean and Atlantic shipping routes, inland trade, commodity transport, and the circulation of news was an important factor in economic development, especially in the commercial sector, but it also defined a distinct sphere of cultural development. While enlightened *intendants* tried to make *la France profonde* more efficient through more rigorous—and vigorous—implementation of improvements and reforms, there arose "another France," more open, more mobile, and equipped, if not with its own culture, then at least with its own form of communications and social relations characteristic of a commercial society.

Simply to state this contrast, however, is to give too crude and static a picture of eighteenth-century French society and culture. Many other differences have to be taken into account (differences of religion and sociability, for example). Sometimes the analysis seems to support the classic antithesis between the Protestant ethic and the Catholic model of a Christian economy. In any case, this line of questioning is useful for bringing a number of problems to light.

First, there is the problem of how different modes of social organization within the old rural society as well as in the relatively new commercial cities interacted. One aspect of this interaction was the emergence of political economy. By studying political economy we can find out how the two systems perceived each other. Without such study we know less about how different social actors may have thought about one another and have to rely on isolated cases to measure the tensions between them. This leads us to look at "two dreams of commerce," where we discover the world of business divided between the old society of privileges (the social expression of rural France and state arbitration) and the new logic of free enterprise, the world sometimes facilely characterized as "laissez-faire" and described in Book 1 of *Capital* as the realm of "naked exchange," the sphere of commodity circulation, the "veritable Eden of the natural rights of man and the citizen, where what reigns unchallenged is liberty, equality, property, and Bentham."[3] What remains to be uncovered is the relation between the world of interests and the old society.[4] This line of inquiry also brings up the old question of "bourgeois betrayal," raised many years ago in a different context by Fernand Braudel. This is useful for discussing the important phenomenon of rising social mobility, which is difficult to measure using historical methods alone. Did the flow of individuals from merchant families into the nobility, carefully promoted by the monarchy through the sale of offices, ever stop?

This brings us to a second problem: the emergence of the industrialist, who soon moved into the front ranks of society. Expanding his business depended largely on the accumulation and reinvestment of commercial capital. It also depended to an equal extent (and at least until the second half of the nineteenth century) on the merchant's ability to control the production of essential items: think of the textile trade. But industry's responses to commerce were largely determined by the actions of *le royaume profond*, of the France of administrators and privileges, of entrepreneurs (including "industrial nobles") and primary investors (whose funds often came from capital in land), and of peasants willing to become workers in the proto-industrial economy. There were many points of contact between the two societies, the two economies, and the two cultures in both the countryside and the city. By studying these we can learn how use value lost out to exchange value and how the modernity of the Enlightenment can be interpreted as a transition from a stationary state to a dynamic society.[5]

Peasant France: Structures of Stability

Great revolutions also occur in silence, unnoticed perhaps by anyone. France, today part of the European Common Market, is in the final phase of a major chapter of its history which the Age of Enlightenment helped to launch: the rural France of old has become an urban country with no hope of turning back the clock. The forces that formerly maintained the rural and urban populations in equilibrium were gradually reversed: whereas the population was once, roughly speaking, 80 percent rural and 20 percent urban, the proportions are now the opposite (and the contrast is even more dramatic if we look at the working population). An ancient system of civilization has all but vanished. To understand the beginnings of this process is one of our goals. The *Homo rusticus* of the eighteenth century did not experience the "agricultural revolution," which existed only as a theoretical model for explaining various aspects of change that began before 1750, accelerated thereafter, and continued for many generations until the twentieth century and its "second French Revolution" did away with the peasantry almost entirely.[6] What we have to explain is how slow transformations could have occurred in a stable society and how those transformations induced a shift from a static equilibrium to a series of unstable states.[7] In other words, we need to understand how peasant society worked.

Peasant society was hamstrung by a series of constraints and traditions. We will be looking at only the early stages of change, for the economic Ancien Régime did not simply disappear at the end of the eighteenth century. Still, we can hardly avoid considering various aspects of rural life in which modernity began to challenge the past. Finally, the village was the basic cell of French life, so we have to ask about changes at the village level. Various factors influenced local changes, factors ranging from the desire for change to the resources available for implementing it. Cultural differences were important here, because the determination to change reality, which drove the cultivated ruling elite and led it to picture rural happiness as it was painted by artists and poets, had to contend with the exigencies of the real. Some enlightened individuals delegated shepherds to live out their dreams of happiness, but sometimes literary forms obscure the truth, no matter how good the documentation or how subtle our reading. We sense this difficulty in the "Essai sur la pastorale" that introduces the novel *Estelle* (1788) by the fabulist Florian: "A shepherd who chokes with rage at the gate of his sheepfold is not a pastoral image, because shepherds are not supposed to be familiar with the degrees of passion that lead to such rage . . . They have their own language. It is seldom heard outside their high valleys."[8]

Ancient, persistent, slow to change: these are the adjectives that characterize the separate language of rural society generally. Yet these same characteristics apply to the unchanging character of the landscape and to methods of tilling the soil. The ancient social order had as much influence on peasant culture as the disciplines required by the still inexpert science of nature. Interesting in this respect is the journey of a traveler like Arthur Young from England, whose attention was focused not only on agricultural matters in the hope that these might bolster his faith in English progress in agronomy but also on customs and mores that revealed France's actual backwardness. Peasants were also subject to historical and geographic factors. Young left a series of maps which still speak to our senses and reveal some of the major aspects of spatial organization. Let us briefly recall the chief contrasts in Young's account.

Large villages with houses grouped around a central church dominated the landscape of northern and northeastern France, where fields were open and laid out as long ribbons. Traditionally, peasants in the north grew cereal grains, which entailed a pattern of stable fields, regular crop rotations, communal restrictions on land use, and small herds of livestock. In richer soil, the horse was master: where ownership of horses once designated the lord of the manor, it now signaled the well-to-do yeoman farmer. The only remaining extensive forests belonged to the king, princes, and other lords. Smaller patches of woodland provided villagers with fuel, wood for tools, an area for animals to graze, and sometimes refuge. In this highly individualized region, only soil of poor quality—crystalline, granitic, or otherwise mediocre—escaped the tyranny of the plow. Such poor land defined the "boundary" of the arable zone, because it could be cultivated only with powerful teams of many horses and therefore required a considerable investment. These poorer soils were found in the damp regions of Le Bray and the sandy parts of Sologne. There, villages were organized differently, and cultivated patches were more irregular. Traveling southward, Young did not pass without transition from this first type of landscape to the better-shaded, less densely populated regions of the south and west. Wherever he went he found "little Beauces" and "mini-Champagnes," along with variations in the intensity of cultivation. Nevertheless, what he found more and more as he traveled southward across the Limousin and then northward again toward Brittany were fields enclosed by earthen berms or vegetation and hamlets scattered across the largest parishes in France. Grouped houses were of relatively recent construction, and except in mountainous regions where communal constraints were strong, customary easements played a smaller role than in the north. Historians of Brittany and the Midi have taught us to see these regions—dominated not by the *ager* and the "necessary evil" of cereals[9] but by *saltus* and marshland, woods, pasture, and livestock—not as zones of grinding poverty but as places where there was room for peasants to exercise their practical intelligence and organizational skills. These enabled the populations of the south and west to avoid the most serious of the ills that afflicted northern villages after every phase of increased mortality, resulting in a temporary recession: such was the reward of mediocrity and the beneficial equilibrium it fostered.

Most peasants accepted the basic conditions of life as essentially immutable, all but impervious to change. But change in those basic conditions was necessary if new crops and methods were to be introduced, if families were to move beyond providing for their own subsistence and escape their dependency on others, and if people were to become less fearful of crises. It was at this level that calls for economic development had to be heard, at this level that backwardness would be overcome. But the inertia of the agricultural system impeded progress. In the cereal zones, demographic pressures and fear of famine encouraged farmers to stick with traditional crops, on which the yield was low (2 or 2.5 to 1) for want of fertilizer. Revolution was impossible owing to legal and fiscal obstacles, shortage of capital (since ground rents were seldom reinvested), technological backwardness, and lack of equipment. How could communities do without fallow fields and common pastures? In poorer but more balanced cantons in western and southern France, the rudimentary nature of many farms scarcely encouraged changes likely to disrupt an equilibrium achieved only by dint of great effort.

France was thus a difficult place for innovators to make headway. The Orry survey of 1745 was a superficial study of the standard of living in different parts of France. The results, recorded on a map of the "faculties of peoples," contrasted a relatively prosperous, open, and economically advanced northern and eastern France with a poorer, less progressive southern and western France. These same findings were repeated on any number of other maps compiled well into the nineteenth century, including maps of illiteracy and morphological contrasts. Another contrast was thus superimposed on that between peasant and commercial France: the contrast between developed France and underdeveloped France. The dividing line between the two would shift somewhat over the course of the eighteenth century, but there was no revolution. Inertia and constraint on the one hand, the adventure of change, movement, circulation, and communication on the other: these were the forces that determined individual fates.

Recall the three dimensions of rural life enumerated earlier. The village, as basic agricultural unit, and the peasant villagers themselves depended on the availability of land, which depended on distance from the village. Beyond a certain distance the efficiency of exploitation diminished; hence development was limited by density of population. Since this limit could not be circumvented, the only way to increase production was through division of labor and specialization. In this system the network of market towns providing facilities for trade and services was essential. Cities were less accessible to peasants, and distribution depended crucially on the system of transportation. Similarly, geographic mobility, which was not greatly hindered by distance as such or by natural obstacles of the sort that impeded transportation, was hobbled by social and economic constraints. A village's propensity to mobility affected its aptitude for development and its respect for social hierarchy. It determined the limits of autarky and of marginal development through specialization and the occasional speculative venture such as a quality vineyard or the emergency food supply afforded by a chestnut grove. Also involved were such fundamental phenomena of the eighteenth century as the total domestication of forests, which were exploited in rational ways to meet the needs of the navy and the cities, and the spread of new crops such as corn, which conquered Languedoc and the southwest; legumes; and, after 1770, potatoes. A process of transformation was launched, and the driving force behind it was the new use of fallow land, where new crops were *secretly* introduced: peas, broad beans, green beans, string beans, turnips, beets, as well as fodder crops that could be fed to livestock. "Changeless villages" everywhere seemed to be grazed by the winds of change, but inertia remained a formidable force which, together with the conservatism of social hierarchies, inhibited expansion.

Land and Respect

What were the consequences of the relative autarky of peasant society in the eighteenth century, when peasants lived "like potatoes in a sack," to borrow Marx's celebrated image?[10] Change could come about only indirectly, and innovation had to be introduced from outside, because everything tended to reinforce the stability of the system: everyone in the village knew everyone else, social relations were more personal than functional, and the socioeconomic hierarchy was such that the most prestigious places were occupied by non-peasants. "In this kind of social system, individuals do not have to adapt to new situations or make decisions. They also do not need to express or reveal themselves in front of others who know them intimately. Hence people tend to maintain their identities and conform to the images that other people have of them. The expression of personal feelings or opinions is not encouraged by the prevailing value system."[11] In a society of this kind, material change and intellectual change must go hand in hand.

The moral center of the peasant economy was domestic. If new values were to be embraced, the economy had to be opened up. The clash between urban values and peasant values was particularly visible on three fronts: attitudes toward land, attitudes toward work, and attitudes toward prestige and the society of notables. "To hold on to the land" was the immemorial dream of the peasantry, for the peasant's life was shaped by the land he inherited, with its physical peculiarities, quality of soil, exposure, and difficulty of access. It was peasant labor that turned mere land into valuable fields. Land symbolized the supreme value for the entire society, but in the village that value was reinforced by the experience of season after season of hard labor. The land was often compared to a woman, and fertility was interpreted in sexual terms: this emphasis on the female qualities of farmland is yet further evidence of the force of the fundamental allegiance to the soil: words like "land," "estate," "inheritance," and "farm" were similar in meaning but not interchangeable. Land was the essential form of capital, the only sure investment, the only reliable form of wealth.[12]

The evolution of peasant land ownership in the eighteenth century is therefore absolutely fundamental. It is commonplace to say that France was already a nation of small landowners, but it is more important to keep in mind that very little property was owned outright (allodial property accounted for only 10 percent of the total arable land) and that the peasants who bequeathed, sold, rented, or gave away their rights to the soil were never absolute masters of it. Seigneurial rights persisted everywhere, and the battle to win independence from copyholders was frequently hindered by the eminence of the landlord. Through fiscal records, *compoix*, and estate maps it has been possible to estimate the total amount of land owned by the peasantry: peasants owned perhaps as much as half the land they cultivated, but there was considerable diversity from region to region. The rate was much lower in the west (13 percent in Les Mauges), somewhat lower in the Paris basin and the north and east (20 to 30 percent), and higher in the Midi and mountains. Within this total, however, there was a whole range of types of ownership and therefore a hierarchy of types of exploitation. And the type of exploitation determined the nature of the peasant's labor, the independence of his family, and the degree of landlord control.

Even on land they owned, peasants owed various dues to the landlord: the *cens*, or quitrent, was not very onerous but stood as a reminder of the peasant's personal subjugation to the lord, a subjugation that was renewed whenever a new landlord took possession, at the time of the so-called *aveux et dénombrements;* other dues included the *lods et ventes,* a fraction of the sales price owed to the lord, and the *champarts,* a sort of tax on the harvest rather than the property itself. These dues varied widely from place to place. The range of landlord exactions diversified the national mosaic at least as much as the variety of customs. Bitterly resented, these exactions hindered development everywhere, although the problem is not without its complexities. Regions in which the institution of seigneury was weak or degraded often fared no better than regions where it was oppressive, including the whole south of France and much of the west and center-west, exhibiting equally passive behavior and achieving barely enough increase in output to compensate for demographic growth.[13] Regions such as Burgundy, where landlords were aggressive, rose in protest against speculation by economic competitors. The seigneurial reaction, which began throughout the country in the seventeenth century, became a decisive factor when new landlords increased their prosperity by exploiting their estates and "reserves" more rationally; increased scrutiny of dues on land also helped. When seigneury was "modernized," as it was in the plains of the Paris basin, seigneurial rights gave rise to economic monopolies or persisted as symbolic obligations; though less onerous than traditional dues, such rights were frequently contested. In short, French society was roiled by a variety of currents: the peasant reaction to the seigneurial reaction was but the latest episode in a centuries-long battle for ownership of the land and preservation of the family farm and therefore the family, which was not always protected by the standard farming and sharecropping contracts. Only the most prosperous peasants were immune from this worry.

Clocks and watches were introduced into rural areas by notables and gradually transformed the traditional representation of time in which the calendar, as Marcel Mauss once said, was the "code of quality," and old almanacs divided the year into propitious and functional periods and indicated good and bad days. Time was related to a person's line of work or product: day laborers were paid by the day, domestics by the year, but the yearly wage was no greater than that of the farmhand who hired on from Saint John's to All Saints'. Labor on the land defined not just surface measurements but lifetimes. Peasant society was as uncertain about the difference between work time and leisure time as it was about the difference between production and consumption, productive activity and productive family leisure. For rural people, work was more a matter of morality than of rationality. Rationality figured only in the account books of physiocratic enterprises, which were kept to prove the theory that large-scale cultivation was more profitable and yielded a higher net product than small-scale cultivation.[14]

From Works to Days

The land and the work done on it defined both the quotidian and the future and thus influenced all sorts of representations. Good management ensured the prosperity of future generations and was a guarantee of survival: "The peasant is worth as much as his land; it is his life."[15] The eternal order of the countryside was a product of eternal recurrence,[16] and change was inevitably seen as a break with the past and a potential threat to the stability of the family. There has been much speculation about the influence of different family models. Areas such as the south and west of France and Alsace in which extended families predominated were less developed than regions in which nuclear families predominated and to which modernity came early.[17] In the eighteenth century as well as today, the past influenced the present. While comparisons of this sort rest on shaky ground, it is clear that certain customs did affect social mobility and the willingness of families to accept change. Peasant marriages were matters of interest, inclination, social arrangement, parental coercion, and individual choice. The factors that weighed most heavily were different from what they are today. The main consideration was perhaps the chance to take over a family farm or create a new business. After the wedding came the assignment of responsibilities to each spouse in their joint effort to earn their daily bread. Work assignments inevitably gave more weight to continuity than to change, which was difficult to imagine.

Sons learned their roles by working under their fathers: living and learning were part of the same experience. What differentiated the farmer from the hired hand was the farmer's knowledge of things and people. The ability to rise above the daily grind and speculate about times and quantities enabled the peasant to buy and sell shrewdly at fairs and markets. The ability to take in new information was crucial: without it, the peasant had little choice but to continue as his forebears had done, and most peasants did just that. Strict autarky was impossible: there were always items that one could not produce, and the market, which created needs, dictated the domestic economy. Fidelity and stability were supreme values because true wealth was to be found not in trade but in meadows, fields, and shrewd additions to existing properties. As Jean-Claude Perrot has pointed out, this kind of "alienation" was no less influential than the kind defined by Marx, because it immobilized the village.[18] In a stable economy, two factors played a more or less decisive role from the bottom to the top of the social hierarchy: first, the family as economic ideal, and second, respect for hierarchies associated with the land (which extended the sphere of stability well beyond the economy).

In this type of economy, the household was held out as a model in both private account books and early works on agronomy such as those of Oliver de Serres and Liébault, which continued to be reprinted in the eighteenth century. The household model was basically an aristocratic one, with the family unit under the authority of the father. Two authorities thus ruled rural life: the landlord controlled work, while the paterfamilias saw to the needs of the family. This authority relationship covered both people and things, since the family was dependent on its material possessions. Out of it grew social relations that were neither entirely relations of production nor seigneurial or feudal relations. The head of the household occupied a special place: he was in charge of the family's work as well as its support, and his ultimate goal was clear, namely, to maintain and if possible increase the family patrimony, consisting of people as well as property. "Any decent man is obliged to preserve as much of his patrimony as he can for his children, and it is necessary to leave them this example," according to Henri de Forbin, Baron d'Oppède. This goes to the heart of the old economy, a subsistence economy in which personal and social relations overlapped. Fathers saved for the future: they liked to hoard cash and hated to borrow. Alongside them stood their wives, whose role was educational, especially in the eighteenth century after Fénelon, but at the same time dependent. The only way that innovation could occur in such a society was for some of its members to become converts: peasant France had to be brought into contact with merchant France. This was Turgot's dream.

A further impediment to any change in social representations or behavior was the fact that the existing social order was venerated because it was based on the prestige of land: "The land gave families their names, their titles, and their coats of arms; it symbolized their substance and longevity. It sustained and breathed life into a complex system of fiefs and seigneuries which defined the social hierarchy all the way up to the king, France's ultimate landowner. The Physiocrats made land the basis of their new political constitution."[19] It was the village social structure, based on material reality, that defined the still fluid frontiers between social groups: noble lords; bourgeois and clerics, who were more present on the scene than many people think, or at any rate well represented by their officers and agents; notables more fully integrated into village life; priors and bailiffs; notaries and tax collectors; wholesalers; yeomen and merchants, who invariably managed real estate and other holdings; farmers and sharecroppers who owned some land and whose fate depended on their ability to rotate crops and livestock; artisans with one foot still on the soil and the other in the changing economy and who were essential for maintaining equilibrium; and finally the mass of day laborers and domestic servants who lived on the fringes of the village and at the bottom of the hierarchy and who were not only mobile but also vulnerable to every economic vicissitude. This was a rigidly stratified society: wealth stood out, lifestyles varied, and social and geographic mobility were limited. Social inequalities were a source of energy, conflict, and protest, but "the hierarchy and its privileges were widely internalized, because submission had become traditional." This conservatism, which was understood and experienced in different ways by Frenchmen with no common root identity, was the leading characteristic of rural culture.

Rurality and Culture

Given this state of affairs, how could an agricultural revolution take place? Against the peasants, in part, from outside, through the pressure of economic forces (the market economy), social forces (exchange and mobility), and cultural forces (countless efforts to teach). These progressive factors must be understood in relation to two other developments: first, the growing tendency to see the rural world as the principal theater of change, and second, the emergence of a division between the stable culture of village communities and the reformed, modernized culture of the cities and their rural satellites, the notables.

Criticism of prejudice was associated, in agronomy as in religion, with criticism of superstition. The state was no more interested in depriving people of their culture than was the Church. Its goal was rather to "invent modern man."[20] The difference between the two approaches is more than just a matter of vocabulary. It is the difference between an abrupt change of comprehension and the analysis of a complex process. The capacity or incapacity of rural society for change must be measured not only by examining what the cultivated, privileged, and powerful said but also by probing patiently for signs of material and intellectual change. There is no other way to understand how conservatism and conformism could coexist with the first indications of change in the peasant mentality. Yves Castan's analysis of hundreds of trials in Toulouse shows this clearly.[21] These cases show the difficulty of change, for it was no easier to produce or acquire new property in the eighteenth century than before. Social and personal relations were shaped in part by this sense of stagnation. Urban society itself was not totally free of it, different as its customs and outlook were. It was nevertheless still hampered by a state of mind shaped in large part by rural society, and its exploitation of the countryside only reinforced that state of mind.

In order to break with the past, other forces had to intervene. Economists set themselves the task of enumerating them, while others, in the hope of unleashing those same forces, attacked popular prejudices. Intellectual progress reveals both tensions within society and shifts in people's behavior along with the energies that drove the process forward.

The Possibility of Change

Two examples will help to clarify these remarks. First, I want to compare the physiocratic analysis of society with the concrete reality it attempted to describe. And second, I want to look at a clash between two cultures and the related problem of reconciling education with nature.

The Physiocratic Hope

Anyone interested in the eighteenth century has to read the Physiocrats, because their work develops a parallel between the natural and the human order. Physiocratic thought reflected the thinking of landowners and in fact confused the figure of the landowner with that of the noble. Its ambition was to halt time. It ascribed little weight to history (whose absurdity the Physiocrats often compared to the orderliness of things) even as it sought to change history's course. In his *Introduction à la philosophie économique,* Abbé Baudeau, one of the most eminent members of the sect, discussed a pedagogical mission that involved the king, his agents, and the owners of land and that was directed at the other two classes of society: the "sterile class" of industrialists and merchants and the "productive class" of peasants and growers. Baudeau's "social art" filled three functions: instruction (which was entrusted to "ministers" of the "cult"), administration, and security. Sovereignty, nobility, and property were thus inextricably linked. What the Physiocrats hoped to teach was in essence a new "economic morality." Therein lay "the fundamental understanding that ought to guide universal instruction." Behind the words we clearly make out the natural law of property and the immutable order of universal reason, a utilitarian vision that served the practical interests of landed property, an effort—not without risks—to adapt the society of privilege to an economy of circulation and social change.[22] This viewpoint was consistent with the role of an active minority within the state apparatus, a minority that attempted to convert the ruling classes and create a climate of opinion favorable to its views and perhaps ultimately to seize the levers of command before and after Turgot's ministry.

The primary value of physiocratic analysis, however, is that it shows how the rural order was opposed to the urban and commercial order point by point. Two distinct economies were superimposed, and we may surmise that no transformation was possible without some reconciliation of the two cultures. Hans Lüthy's *Banque protestante*[23] shows how Quesnay's *Tableau économique* explained this issue:

> The economy [read: agriculture] is the wheat field or olive grove in which nature's fruits ripen in the sun, and where God is present as the bestower of all goods, distributing a portion to the farmer, to the lord, and to the clergyman in accordance with His justice, which is not the justice of *do ut des* [tit for tat]. For not even the farmer makes the fruit; he simply serves as a humble agent in accomplishing the miracle of the harvest and is not its sole owner. Chrematistics [read: commerce, trade] is the market, where anonymous buyers and sellers meet and communicate solely through abstract signs, where goods are merely commodities passing from hand to hand, commodities that represent nothing more than the sums of money that they cost or will fetch, and where the only driving force is the profit to be made by the intermediaries, and God is no longer present or at most present only through the tablets of the law: a code of morality and commercial honesty, the rule of impersonal equity.[24]

True morality and tranquil happiness had always rested with the land and nature, while passion and instability were associated with the city, commerce, and culture. This conflict was central to eighteenth-century ideological and political dispute and to the crisis of the Ancien Régime. It shed a powerful light on the way society actually worked.

Quesnay's *Tableau* revealed what the Physiocrats took the real hierarchy to be, the hierarchy that determined society's evolution.[25] At the top was the "class of landowners," the Ancien Régime itself, in its constituted orders: king, nobility, clergy, rentier bourgeoisie, officeholders, and others with a claim on the "net product" or income from agriculture. Their expenditures governed all economic change. Below them Quesnay listed yeomen, farmers, and other members of the "productive class," as well as merchants, wholesalers, industrialists, artisans, and other members of the "sterile class," who earned their living with products and services rather than with what they grew on the land, which in the eyes of members of the physiocratic "sect" was the only source of genuine wealth. All other wealth derived from the land, and it was mobilization of the "net product" that fostered circulation and commerce. Large-scale popular consumption of imported and manufactured goods did not yet exist; it developed first in England and only later spread to France. In the countryside and lower strata of society, artisans and small merchants limited themselves to meeting needs of physical subsistence. The technological and intellectual equipment on which they relied was rudimentary. There was no major market here for either nascent industry or colonial commerce, although the winds of change had begun to blow, first in the cities and then in the countryside. Countless intermediaries carried the news into the most isolated *bocage* country and the most out-of-the-way valleys. With the army, court, and city, expenditure of the "net product" set everything in motion. Ultimately, the whole economy depended on the labor of Louis XV's millions of peasant subjects, a portion of which was siphoned off by the landowning class and redistributed.

Quesnay's *Tableau* put things in their place and explained how, beyond needs of subsistence and reproduction, the social product of peasant labor provided a surplus to cover society's noneconomic expenditures: on luxury, prestige, administration and the army, religion, and art. This revenue of sovereignty upheld the political order, and the political order was in turn obliged to encourage the growth that sustained it. Therein lay the key to a whole refined and brilliant civilization. It linked cultural and economic as well as social and intellectual history by demonstrating that everyone was both producer and consumer. Trade developed only because the upper strata of society consumed, and the goal of ending the cultural isolation of rural society turned out to be fundamental to both the future of the state and the increase of the tax revenues on which it depended. Quesnay was perhaps the last theorist before Karl Marx, who "stood him back on his feet," to try to develop a philosophy that treated state and society, economy and nature, as parts of a whole, at the center of which, in Quesnay's case, was rural society.

Peasant Wisdom, Stability, and Growth

Before attempting to measure the possibility and limits of change, we need to examine the key features of a peasant culture that was only semipermeable to innovation and therefore resistant to history and change. The household economy's need to reproduce and aggrandize itself dictated respect for custom and tradition. The same crops had been grown in the same fields for centuries, perpetuating landscapes that could only be nibbled away at the edges where new techniques were tried. The litany was always the same: "In order to do away with fallow lands, you need fertilizer. To get fertilizer, you need animals. And to feed the animals, you need either natural or artificial pasture." The rural economy was caught in this vicious circle.[26] The yardstick of agricultural progress was the amount of land allowed to lie fallow, and its corollary was the shortage of livestock.

We also know, however, that tradition was challenged by the insistence on modernization. Young's astonishment at discovering a rural landscape dominated by wheat fields and fallow land points up the conflict, for behind the fallow land and cleared land, things were happening. Late eighteenth-century agronomy was at odds with peasant practice: for agronomists, there was only one road to progress, namely, the open field model with continuous crop rotation. But peasants nearly everywhere had experimented with other forms of equilibrium: nonrotational systems had been tried in Flanders, for example, while elsewhere fields had been planted with corn rather than allowed to lie fallow. Agronomists, however, favored cereal grains and disapproved of corn. Finally, as Jacques Mulliez has shown, a great deal of arable land had been given over to livestock: the "prejudice in favor of fallow land" that the agronomists denounced did not exist in all regions. In the face of development, rural tradition, "barbarian agriculture," stuck with proven techniques for adapting to natural conditions. Farmers rotated crops slowly, carefully collected fertilizer and manure, risked letting fields go to pasture in order to raise livestock when the markets for dairy and meat products seemed promising, and, in the west and the northern edge of the Massif Central, raised horses. These practices were characteristic of mountainous areas and high plains, where husbandry was more important than farming, and still more important in Brittany, Poitou, Maine, Perche, and the Gâtine, where fallow land supported livestock.

The critique of the agronomists demonstrates two things. First, that prejudice, taken to be indicative of backwardness, was defined in relation to a norm, namely, the assumption that growing grain was the correct way to farm. Second, that the peasant tradition was in fact the result of earlier adaptations: grass versus plowing, long fallow periods versus wheat. Furthermore, the tradition suggested possibilities other than the one enforced by the terror of famine and the coercive designs of the enlightened administration. Thus, the very constraints responsible for the stability of peasant society can be interpreted as signs of the possibility of change. Prudence is always an issue in social transformation.

Other indications of prudence can be found in the almanacs and in the continuity of behavior required by agricultural life and the rural economy. Almanacs were not used exclusively by peasants, although their rural circulation did increase over the course of the eighteenth century, probably because the images and astronomical and astrological signs they contained made them accessible even to people who could not read. They were nevertheless read by people of all stations, including urban landowners and investors in land as well as rural folk. Geneviève Bollème has put her finger on the crucial point: that although the almanacs reveal an obsession with cyclical time, a gradual transformation had begun (we have already considered its historical dimension).[27]

Almanac titles began to emphasize their utilitarian and encyclopedic qualities and their value as sources of news. The relation between the text and everyday life changed: what the almanacs now purported to offer was not so much prognostication as specific, practical advice. The advertised contents were an invitation to readers to ask questions about themselves and about the world. Take, for example, the titles of two successful agronomic almanacs. From the late seventeenth century we have *The Perpetual Calendar for Good Farmers and Almanac for the year of grace One Thousand Six Hundred Seventy-Eight, composed by Master Antoine Magin, also known as the solitary hermit, containing general and perpetual prognostications for all years. Convenient and useful for farmers, gardeners, and all other persons, for all the true remarks and observations herein contained, including information on sterility and prices, with the abundance of grains, wines, and moneys and all other necessary utilities.* Neither townsfolk nor countryfolk were excluded, but prospective readers were enticed with promises of prognostications along with useful information: magic for everyone. Compare this title with another from the late eighteenth century: *Almanac of Agriculture, essential for farmers and growers of all sorts, with chapters devoted to every element of agricultural science and every aspect of raising livestock, cultivating land, using fertilizer, plowing the soil, plant-*

ing seeds, reaping harvests, preserving grains, and, in general, information pertaining to all aspects of rural labor, at Paris (Le Prieur, 1773). The target audience is more clearly identified, the allure of prophecy has been abandoned, and the utilitarian aim is patent: this almanac offers readers physiocratic precepts and practical advice.

Between the covers, however, the content of the two almanacs is less different than their titles would suggest: the later volume still offers the same venerable philosophy as the earlier one. There are two noteworthy differences, however: the amount of space devoted to astrology has diminished, and moral teaching focuses increasingly on life in society. At one time, astrology offered everyone a way of coping with the future. It met the need for understanding in an age when the world was governed by analogical thinking rather than science: the movements of the stars revealed the foreordained destinies of individuals and societies. In the eighteenth century, prophetic discourse dwindled, and time, fertility, accident, and disease became subject to the will of God. The poor prayed to God to preserve the nation from calamity and reward those who through their labor demonstrated their worthiness. A process of desacralization began, as age-old anxieties gave way to belief in a merciful God who bestowed his blessings on men of action as well as men of prayer. In short, a new idea of God took hold, an idea compatible with that of linear time and progress. Those who embraced the new faith could freely devote themselves to the work needed to improve life in this world and to make men more prosperous.[28] To be worthy of God's goodness was now to think, observe, and learn.

At the same time, the moral advice in the almanacs was increasingly directed toward social behavior. Instead of long didactic texts one found proverbs, adages, and maxims. These generally counseled prudence and obedience. Admonitions to honor the great without scorning the poor were commonplace, but almanacs gradually shifted the focus of their advice to living in society, not to say fashionable society. For example, the *Messager boiteux* offered this advice in 1776:

Love without self-interest, pardon without weakness. Be obedient to the great without abasing oneself. Cultivate thy neighbor's friendship, and never argue with any person . . . Lend with good grace and discernment. If compensation is necessary, be generous, and no matter how you wish to appear, do so without excess and without forgetting your place . . . Boast of nothing; keep your own counsel. That is the quickest way to perfection.

Here we read the traits of a respectable country squire, conscious of appearances, wise in his choices and actions, and not uncalculating ("Make no decision without weighing it carefully") or devoid of practical judgment ("Render unto God what one owes" and "think before embarking on any enterprise"). Almanacs thus shared one fundamental characteristic with other widely read "popular" literature: by imitating the court, they spread civilized, urbane manners to a wide audience. Morality meant breeding above all, and the almanacs therefore taught good manners, time-honored adages, the secrets of living well. The adages generally counseled prudence, thrift, and restraint, hence stability through virtue. Listen to the calendar advice in the 1787 *Messager boiteux:*

> August: thunder in this month signifies great prosperity, so praise God for his bounteous goodness.
>
> September: purge, bleed more than ever, to keep your blood fresh; conduct your life wisely and you will walk free of disease.
>
> October: drink wine in moderation for your best hope of good health.
>
> December: praise God from whom all things come and who never forsakes us.[29]

Even more interesting is the fact that in addition to this innocuous advice, never verifiable and always true, we increasingly find observations that pointed readers toward a more active concern with social and even political morality, hence with change. A discreet critique of society found its way into this anodyne advice. Consider the following, from the May–June 1788 issue of the *Messager boiteux:*

> It is good to bathe and bleed
> and dress well, within reason.
> Be happy, take courage,
> but watch out for your household
> In an orderly state one tries to prevent
> disorder; the soldier should be guided
> by honor and reasonable ambition.
> . . . .

Eat herbs and drink good wines;
moderate exercise is useful and necessary.
Banish laziness in order to prevent
the vices to which it gives rise.
A generous man takes an active interest in the fate of the unfortunate.

This excerpt is a confused mixture of the virtues of the "static society," the maxims of the "culture of appearances" (according to which people should dress soberly in a manner appropriate to their station), praise for patience (the primary attitude of citizens of the "stationary state") as well as for useful labor and profitable good works (as opposed to charity), and, finally, a quick call for change. Country people, even if educated, could both be served a philosophy thought to be compatible with their nature and exhorted to pay heed to a world that it was up to them to improve.[30] Publishers, authors, and readers began to play it both ways: the best way to ensure the continued success of the old formula was to bring it up to date. Almanacs offered people a "philosophy," that is, a course in manners and good behavior. They taught people that even humble folk could be happy, so why should anyone remain resigned to his fate? Here is the new ideal as proclaimed by the *Messager boiteux* in 1766:

May the new year and those that follow bring happiness and peace to the hearts of all men. We can be certain of this happiness if philosophy continues to enlighten the world and if men of all nations, joined together by talent, cultivate the arts and humanity more and more. These are the miracles that talent and art have wrought: let us cultivate them in peace, and the social bond will encompass more and more of us as mankind enjoys unprecedented prosperity.

In other words, culture, sociability, and enlightenment were beginning to take hold in the countryside. No longer was the almanac an instrument for perpetuating an indestructible tradition, which could still be found readily in the realm of proverbs and adages pertaining to daily life and various occupations. To the extent that we can judge (given the difficulty of dating proverbs collected by scholars and folklorists), these essentially counseled resignation, patience, and distrust of mobility and its companion, irony toward those in power as well as toward God, his saints, and his priests: "Le bailli vendange, le prévôt grappe, le procureur prend, le sergent happe, le seigneur n'a rien, s'il ne leur échappe" (roughly: "The sheriff picks, the judge grinds, the prosecutor takes, the constable snatches, and unless the lord escapes them, he is left with nothing"). It may have been pleasant to think of the fat cats devouring one another, but the burden always fell on the peasant's back.[31]

Members of the eighteenth-century elite took one of three attitudes toward almanacs: scorn, curiosity, or a desire to use the medium for pedagogical purposes. Almanacs were scorned along with other purveyors of prejudice, and accordingly they help us to locate the dividing line between the popular and the non-popular in literature, religion, and agronomy. The eighteenth-century almanac was not a pure cultural object. It was read by different groups of readers for different purposes, and since it communicated heterogeneous norms, its intellectual impact helped to transform the daily and spiritual life of many of its readers. Bibliophiles bought almanacs out of curiosity and read them in order to find out what "the people" who owned land and whose income depended on it were thinking. This practice was not incompatible with a need to be entertained or to understand rural life or to turn to it as a possible source of happiness. As almanacs began to attract wider audiences, they became more specialized. As pedagogical instruments, they inculcated both new and old values. Almanacs reached people who otherwise read very little. The model of all almanacs, the *Grand Calendrier compost des bergers*, was more than a symbol in this respect: it claimed to be the work of a man who did not know how to write, "the great shepherd of the high mountain." The author and his readers were equals: the former provided the latter with the means to live in accordance with the dictates of natural wisdom. What changed in the eighteenth century was the ends and means of that wisdom.

In order to break down the cultural barriers that made France into a nation of "changeless villages," people had to overcome the attitude of hostility and pity that the cultivated elite of clergymen, city folk, and people of privilege felt toward rural life. At Sennely in Sologne in the diocese of Orléans, an episcopal order issued in 1728 enjoined curés to "redouble their efforts to confiscate from the faithful in their charge pernicious writings with which the diocese is inundated."[32] This order indicates both the influence of popular pamphlets and the suspicion with which they were viewed. If we are to understand the rapid spread of that influence, we must look at the conditions that made it possible. What follows will be a chapter in the history of rural reading, a topography of places in which ideas were exchanged. After that we will look at the sudden vogue for "agronomy." In both approaches we will be interested in the interplay between individual freedom and social constraints and at how people behaved on the borderline between two worlds.

Rural Reading

Changes in attitude depended largely on opportunity and circumstance. The market for printed matter—including newspapers, topical publications, almanacs, and images—played a part, as did the availability of news in written or oral form. But emulation of others was also important, and emulation was encouraged by the increase in circulation encouraged by the government's transportation policy. It was not entirely accidental that the great ministers of agronomy, Orry and Bertin, were also interested in roads, or that the Physiocrats and those they influenced, such as Turgot, were zealous champions of improved roads as a means of reducing transportation costs and bringing new inventions such as the two-wheeled plow into the most out-of-the-way provinces. Roads, as we have seen, exert a "multiplier effect" on cultural development.

An example will help to bring this subject to life. Let us look, along with Anne Fillon, at the autobiography of Louis Simon, a cloth maker. The setting of Simon's life story is the very type of the stable community.[33] The majority of the inhabitants of La Fontaine (a town not far from Le Mans) spent their entire lives there, and the parish registers contain the names of families going back over three generations: the Piverons, the Le Bouls, the Cosnards, the Morins, the Lefrancs, and the Fougerys. Some families could trace their roots back to the fifteenth century. Mobility did exist within the village, however. Families moved if they grew in size and had the money to do so. This society was not static, and Louis Simon chronicled its changes in a chapter entitled "Novelties That Came to France during My Lifetime." Note, first of all, that his view encompasses not just his local region but all of France. What is particularly interesting is that Simon links the expansion of his view to the opening of the royal highway: this was the event that changed his life. "I witnessed the construction of the great highway from Le Mans to La

Flèche, across fields, meadows, and marshes: this road was built by the people, whose labor was requisitioned." "Peasant labor and toil"—which, Simon insisted, "ruined the people"—were lavished on the great road from 1750 to 1762, mainly in building embankments (paving was left to specialists). Once the heavy cost was paid, however, the village reaped the benefits: previously, when September's heavy rains fell, carriages and wagons could not pass; but now carters hauled produce out and brought in essential wood and beverages along with other, less essential items such as cotton goods and calico, which we begin to find in estate inventories at around this time. The whole pattern of consumption changed. Despite the difficulties of the prerevolutionary crisis, the quality of life improved: this contrast—or contradiction—became the major focal point of a society torn between its rapidly expanding needs and its slowly increasing capacities.

Louis Simon also witnessed a rapid acceleration in the speed of news delivery: it became easier than ever for letters and newspapers to reach his village. The Angers stagecoach left Paris on Tuesday mornings at six. Passengers dined at Le Mans and slept at Foulletourte on the following Saturday and reached Angers on Monday at ten. The schedule published by Desnos in *L'Indicateur fidèle* for 1785 was respected. This particular route set no national records, but travel was considerably faster than it had been in the seventeenth century. The regular coach service sustained a series of inns. At Foulletourte, the Ecu de France emerged from the ashes of the Croix verte, and the marquis de Broc "built a coach house in his courtyard with all the conveniences of a hotel." Fontaine, somewhat off the main route, had to make do with an inn and tavern, which was kept by none other than Louis Simon, who simultaneously held down a dozen other jobs in the hope of improving his lot. In addition to running the Plat d'étain in 1786, he also made cloth and served as sacristan, tax collector, and fence mender. A key figure in the village, he became its *syndic* in order to defend a community that had undergone profound changes since the beginning of the century: it had opened itself up to the outside world and had seen its habits turned upside down, and it had also been plunged into poverty after some landowners left and many sharecroppers found themselves in difficult straits. Simon was not exaggerating when he said that "people here had no choice but to come to me, because I was the only one who could write and who had a head for business." The innkeeper served the village in many ways. The opening of a second inn, the Cheval blanc, shows that the level of need was rising in this area as in others.

There was of course no clear-cut boundary between the influence of more rapid circulation of news and the influence of books. Printed materials attracted readers. Books reached villages through the efforts of booksellers in distant as well as nearby cities; some were purchased directly at fairs or markets, while others were ordered by mail. The Dôle bookseller Tonnet supplied the rural elite of the entire region with pamphlets and religious materials. Books could be bought at the village grocery store as well as from the stalls of itinerant merchants who displayed them along with other wares such as fabrics, nails, mirrors, powder, and rosaries. Peddlers played a particularly important and well-known role.[34] They traveled everywhere and had three essential qualities: first, they knew their territories well and carried rumors, news, and confidential information wherever they went; second, their willingness to extend credit allowed them to tap a larger market; and third, they sold not only printed matter but also trinkets and cosmetic items. Peddlers carried all sorts of merchandise and came in many varieties, from the simple *mercelot*, or seller of notions, to the full-fledged *libraire forain*, or itinerant bookseller. Some sold shoes, others frocks and boots, and, like Noël Gilles, who was arrested for selling "naughty books," frequented fairs and markets in towns and cities. There was something for everyone in this trade, as M. de Malesherbes noted in 1752: "The taste for literature is so widespread that it would be hard, indeed quite difficult, to prevent this sort of commerce entirely. To do so would be to deny a great convenience to aristocrats living on their estates, country priests, and many individuals living in towns and villages where there are no booksellers."

Here we have identified the chief markets and principal cultural intermediaries: the presbytery, the chateau, and the home of the notable. The mention of country priests reminds us of the educational role of the Catholic Church and the operation of its networks. The largest rural book collections and best news sources were clearly to be found in the shady cloisters of monasteries and abbeys rather than in the homes of modest priests, but all clergymen had access to reading matter. The itinerant glazier Jacques-Louis Ménétra acquired the rudiments of culture in monastic and priestly libraries and met other similarly cultivated journeymen in the inns where he stayed. He could hold his own in argument, as when he found himself at the home of the curé of Montigny in the

Cévennes in 1758. He and the priest engaged in learned theological conversations: "I often went [to his house] on the pretext of looking for books. One day when I thought he was at the chateau, I went to the presbytery. After sweet-talking the housekeeper, I was holding her tight in my arms when I heard him coming. I dashed straight for the nook beside the fireplace and with one hand buttoned myself up while with the other I held a book."

This enlightened journeyman knew how to read and write. The episode he describes does not lack for spice: it shows that he knew where to borrow books and how to make the most of every opportunity, and there is no reason to think that his colleagues were any less clever.[35] Thanks to improvements in the education of priests and to their role in teaching and in spreading both official and unofficial news, the lower-ranking clergy played a crucial part in transforming rural culture. There can be no doubt that eighteenth-century curés owned more books than their counterparts a century earlier.

Although libraries in castles and in the homes of notables were not open to the public, they were nevertheless a potential resource. Reading incontestably became a feature of rural life: the number of aristocratic libraries increased, and their contents grew more diverse. People read not only for themselves but also for others, as in Mme de Genlis's "evenings at the chateau." To be sure, for every erudite chateau there was another without books; some libraries served the needs of bibliophiles, while others were kept for utilitarian purposes. The important point, however, is that the very existence of a library created possibilities for borrowing or stealing books, hence for the transfer and circulation of knowledge; thus the nobility, like the clergy, participated in a development whose essence was to foster change. What mattered was the availability of books and pamphlets, which bore the seeds of innovation and made people interested in things other than what they already had. This dynamic process was aided by any number of intermediaries: stewards, agents, butlers, valets, servants, and even coachmen. Through such channels reading matter reached rural villages and farms.

The overall interpretation I have just proposed has two limitations. The first of these is the limit to cultural transmission established by the rudimentary level of education. This was overcome, I think, by the establishment of a public space in which the transfer of information from books to readers, from the printed page to the individual mind, was part of a larger transfer of culture from the cities to the countryside. The second limitation has to do with the question of what sorts of things rural people read. What we know about small farm libraries does not suggest that farmers read much technical or agronomic literature, except in the highest strata of rural society in the most highly developed regions (for example, among the yeomen of Ile-de-France studied by J.-M. Moriceau). Hence reading must have had an indirect effect on modernization: for one thing, access to reading matter changed people's habits; for another, the contents of such widely read publications as almanacs and newspapers changed over time; and finally, reading was a source of examples that could be emulated. Consider inns. Among subscribers to the *Mercure*, in addition to 250 nobles living in their castles, we find fifty postmasters, and we can only speculate how many potential readers those fifty represented. For the postmaster was at once a "functionary" and an entrepreneur, an inhabitant of the *royaume profond* (often a substantial farmer and breeder of horses) and a well-placed agent of circulation and exchange; he was both reader and informant, conversationalist and man of letters—an apt illustration of the many forces reshaping rural life.

There is a case to be made for a history of practical examples, of actions undertaken either on orders or on advice from others. Studying this history might be a way of understanding how rural structures evolved, how people learned by watching what other people did and adopting improved tools and equipment. Unlike agronomic science, practical agronomy was not confined to books and laboratories. Intellectual and practical advances and changes in social organization went hand in hand. The rural economy after 1750 was a melting pot in which economic doctrines, social hierarchies, political structures, and technological transformations were boiled down and reconstituted. These ingredients became so thoroughly mixed that progress in one area was impossible without progress in the others.[36] The spread of theoretical agronomy led to a revolution. It triggered changes in the structure of land ownership and of rural space. Landowners—not a new class exactly, but one imbued with aggressive new ideas about "English-style development" and eager to emulate the country squires of Norfolkshire—moved into the countryside. This led to an interaction between capitalism and the revitalized countryside: prices began to shift, calls were issued for free trade, and fiscal choices had to be made. These developments pitted Necker against Turgot, the past against the future.

Here, however, we are interested not in these battles but in the influence of agronomy on the culture. Two important factors (just how important we will see later on) were the role of notables and the explosion of agronomic reading matter. Notables (and here I am using the word to refer to anyone with an economic interest in the "net product" of the land) were seldom discoverers of new ideas. They depended on thinking done by others. I will have more to say later on about the role of the agronomic network in stimulating growth.[37] Peasants had good reason for defining themselves in relation to city folk. As a general rule they had little room to innovate, because the inertia of the social system and constraints of tradition prevented them from doing so (we know how slowly leases reflected progress). By contrast, the non-peasant landowner operating on the fringes of the system had more opportunities to innovate and thus to teach by example.[38] Aristocrats, bourgeois landowners who acquired seigneurial estates, and ecclesiastical landlords had a very different outlook from their farmers and sharecroppers: they were educated, they had traveled, and they could compare one thing with another. If a landlord was traditionalist, it was because he refused to change or was too conservative.

This brings us to a crucial problem of the eighteenth century, the residence of landlords. The degree of absenteeism, presumably made necessary by the requirement that many nobles live at court, has perhaps been exaggerated. A careful study of noble life is needed to clarify the situation. As with bishops in the realm of religion, the absentees may not always have been in the wrong: administrative structure, representation, initiative, and the possibility of dialogue have to be taken into account. It is possible that a majority of the landowning class consisted of full-time or part-time "peasants" (some of whom may have done their farming "indirectly"). The cyclical annual rhythm of aristocratic life was not incompatible with farming: nobles fled the city and the court in August and were present on their estates for wheat and grape harvests, as well as for hunting in the fall. Aristocratic careers were also compatible with rural life: country squires became soldiers, gentlemen farmers became sailors or administrators who took up temporary residence in town. What is more, the role of women needs to be explored in greater detail: when the master was away from the chateau, his wife took over his responsibilities. This was what Fénelon taught, and it was what the young ladies of

Saint-Cyr learned and passed on to others: the two priorities of a woman's life were Christian education and household management.

Notables who made their lives at least as much outside the village as in it had an active role to play. Many became "improvers." Two things drove them toward modernization: their way of life and their economic advantages. To keep up an estate, secure a future for one's children, and maintain one's rank took money, and living in the city during the winter hastened its redistribution. Notables could not live in autarky or on small surpluses. Pressing needs and excessive consumption forced some into speculation. To what extent did notables (including aristocrats and clergymen) participate in the market economy? They had both the opportunity and the means to do so: with agricultural profits on the rise, they could afford the risks of investment, purchase better tools, and experiment with new seeds and fertilizers. Success was the best persuader, and some converts set out to proselytize others. For example, Duhamel du Monceau's *Traité de la culture des terres* (six volumes, 1753–1761) drew on the experience that the author and his brother had acquired in running their estate at Denainvilliers in the Gâtinais:

> Let no one suspect me of treating the workers with disdain [he is speaking here about forest workers]. Born in the forests and put to work as children, their only concern is with their work. No, I have not allowed myself to be misled by the sweat and dust with which they are covered; or by their skin, burned by the sun or gnawed by the cold; or by the rags they wear. I have talked with these good people and found them gifted with natural good judgment and capable of accurate thinking about their work . . . but, since they are limited to a fixed set of ideas, their natural judgment does not allow them to draw all the consequences they might from what they do.[39]

Drawing those consequences and persuading people through success was precisely the work of the evangelists who spread the gospel of agronomy by way of their experimental farms. Think of Lavoisier, who applied the mathematical methods of the laboratory chemist to the work of agriculture, discovered a method for dispelling illusions, and hoped to revitalize the rural economy by means of education.

A second factor in the conversion process was the explosion of writing about agronomy. Texts of this sort were of course aimed at the enlightened class. They came in a variety of forms ranging from theoretical treatises to practical periodicals. For a more complete picture of the range of publication, we can turn to Musset-Pathay's bibliography,[40] from which I have compiled the following chronology of production:

Before 1500	26
1500–1599	111
1600–1649	55
1650–1699	91
1700–1749	96
1750–1799	1,105
After 1800	491
Subtotal	1,975
Undated	159
Total	2,134

In other words, the majority of the nearly two thousand titles in the bibliography were published in the second half of the eighteenth century. These publications revealed the attractiveness of innovation; they complemented and to some extent anticipated the influence of specialized newsletters and governmental propaganda aimed at notables. Agronomic publishing really took off after the transition from the reformist programs of the 1750s to a reality of slow and steady progress that would pay off a hundred years later. When crisis came, that progress halted briefly, then hastily resumed after 1800. Agronomy gained popularity within a certain social group, but its ultimate fruits would not be borne until the Empire.

One ought now to move from this first, macroeconomic scale to focusing on the improvers themselves. Unfortunately, in the current state of research, this is impossible. There is no doubt, however, that such an approach could help us understand the location of trials and errors and the source of resistance to the challenges raised to traditional ways of life. Change in the countryside was slow because it was invariably experienced as a threat to stability and tradition. Overcoming this fear was the goal of those who defined agriculture as the quintessential art. Listen to the "Ami des hommes," the marquis de Mirabeau:

Agriculture is not only the most admirable of all the arts, the most necessary to the state, and to society the most primordial; it is also, in the most complicated form that this society can accept, the most profitable and remunerative. It is the type of work that brings the greatest reward to human industry through the use to which it is put. What nobility, what generous hospitality we find in the manners of men who spend their lives leading their reapers and their flocks . . . Here I am talking morality only insofar as morality is pertinent to interest properly understood; indeed, what is most correct morally is always what is most real in terms of interest.[41]

Our next order of business will be to measure the impact and extent of the clash between tradition and innovative utility.

5

❦ ❦ ❦

The Kingdom of Exchange:
The Culture of Privilege and the
Culture of Commerce

VOLTAIRE DISCOVERED ENGLAND; Voltaire discovered commerce. He stayed in London from May 1726 until the fall of 1728. It was not his first trip abroad: he had been to Amsterdam four years earlier. He was therefore alert to the economic realities of Europe in his time, for he had visited the center of one of the great commercial powers. Recall the tenth of his *Lettres philosophiques:*

> On commerce: Commerce, which has made the citizens of England wealthy, has also helped to make them free, and that freedom has in turn expanded commerce. This has made the nation great. Little by little, commerce established the navy that has made England master of the waves. At present the English have nearly two hundred warships.[1]

The letter begins by positing a sort of Copernican revolution, reversing the traditional mercantilist view of the relation between economics and politics: in opposition to mercantilist ideas about the control of borders and import duties, Voltaire implied that free trade brought wealth to both states and their citizens. It was commerce that made a small island "with nothing of its own but a little lead, tin, fuller's earth, and raw wool" into a world power capable of holding its own against Louis XIV on both sea and land. It was the merchants of England whose credit network had enabled them to lend Prince Eugene the £50 million he needed for his Italian campaign: "Afterwards, he delivered Turin and defeated the French and wrote this little note to the men who had lent him the money: 'Gentlemen, I have received your money, and I am confident of having used it to your satisfaction.'"

From that day on, war became a matter of business, and a nation's independence rested on the contacts of its merchants:

> All this has made the English merchant justly proud, so that he dares to compare himself, not entirely without reason, to a citizen of Rome. Accordingly, a younger son of a peer of the realm would not disdain to engage in trade . . . In France anyone who wishes to be a marquis may become one, and anyone who comes to Paris from a provincial backwater with money to spend and a name ending in -*ac* or -*ille* can say: "A man such as myself, a man of my quality," and look down his nose at the merchant. The merchant hears his profession scorned so often that he is foolish enough to blush at the thought. Yet I cannot say which is more useful to the nation: a well-powdered lord who knows at precisely what hour the king rises and goes to bed and who gives himself airs while groveling like a slave in some minister's antechamber, or a merchant who enriches his country, issues orders to Surat and Cairo from his office, and contributes to the world's prosperity.

What we have before us is one of those rare texts in which we actually see things in the process of changing. Voltaire knew what he was talking about: he was a scion of the Parisian bourgeoisie and heir to the dynasty of the notary Arouet. He was a wealthy man, who made his money originally from bonds and speculation. And he was the protégé of the quartet that did in John Law, the brothers Pâris, of whom the youngest, Duverney, was a "sort of dictator and absolute master of people and property" in the 1720s. It was the brothers who made Mme Pompadour what she became and who advised the young Arouet about his investments. He repaid them with an *Ode à la Chambre de justice*, which whipped up public enthusiasm for a "Saint-Bartholomew's [massacre] of *traitants* [tax farmers]." Voltaire stood at the center of an economic system at the point where revenues poured in from rural France and were redistributed by way of state expenditure, the actions of the "sterile class," and speculation. His sincere praise for the commerce that had made him rich was dictated in part by his social background (recall that he had only recently been bludgeoned by the chevalier de Rohan's lackeys and briefly imprisoned for having made the mistake of thinking that talent could erase social distance and that genius could vie with birth), and in part by his powers of observation. His letter ends with a series of implicit demands linked to his call for freedom—of trade as well as individuals. It reveals both what united and what divided the two economic, social, and cultural groups that shaped French identity in the eighteenth century, two distinct families in both spirit and behavior: on the one hand, those who believed that "France alone can supply the needs of France," including Vauban and the *intendants,* and on the other hand, those with a subtler view of the relation between economics and politics, who believed that circulation and change were both necessary. The mercantile kingdom and the agricultural kingdom stood in opposition because each embodied a distinctive social structure and mentality.[2] Conflict between the two societies had emerged with the formation of the territorial state and the organization of a royal administration obsessed with its fiscal powers and with controlling the flow of wealth through ports and trading centers. At stake was not only control over the circulation of men and commodities but also the economic and cultural significance of that circulation.

Like Montesquieu, Voltaire saw England with new eyes, for both men were associated with maritime cities and merchants. And both drew the same lesson from what they saw: namely, that the economic system is what enables us to understand the deep nature of the monarchical state and its relation to the nobility and its privileges. Yet from this lesson they drew different conclusions: Voltaire's political and social liberalism went farther than Montesquieu's respect for the implicit constitution and intermediate bodies. Crucial to both social reality and intellectual debate was thus the influence of trade and the way in which the economy impinged on two distinct subcultures.

The Rise of Commerce: Structures of Change

The rise of commerce breathed life into French ports along the English Channel, Atlantic coast, and Mediterranean as well as into inland cities such as Lille, Metz, Nancy, Strasbourg, and Lyons, which were connected to the commercial capitalist economy that had developed across Europe from the shores of the North Sea to the Low Countries to the prosperous Rhineland and southward into northern Italy. In the center of all this, Paris, a capital of finance and banker to the monarchy, played an essential but little-known role. For Fernand Braudel, Paris was not a metropolis of the "world economy" on the same order as cities such as Venice and

Genoa in the past or Amsterdam and London in the eighteenth century—cities that had been centers of exploration, shipping, and crucial economic developments. Whether or not Paris deserves to be excluded from this company awaits the verdict of a true economic history of the French capital. It is worth remembering, however, that economic convulsions in Paris—from the collapse of "Law's system" to the impact of Calonne's decisions to the twilight of the Ancien Régime—regularly shook the rest of France, including its port cities and merchants. In Paris, at the Conseil de Commerce, in the offices of financiers and trading companies, in the *hôtels* of Protestant and Catholic bankers, in the cubicles of commercial clerks, in the warehouses of the great textile merchants of the rue Saint-Denis or the big trading houses on the place des Victoires, the nation's business was often decided: credit was negotiated, major loans became matters of high diplomacy, and the peasant economy interacted with the commercial economy.

Although Parisian intervention began to break down economic barriers, allowing certain regions to specialize in certain types of production (Provence could grow grapes, for example, while other regions could import grains and specialize in raising livestock), contemporaries continued to see a stark contrast between the remote interior of France and the periphery and major trading routes. Take, for example, Abbé Galiani's *Dialogues sur le commerce du blé* (Dialogues on the Grain Trade, 1770), a crucial text by an Italian so Parisianized that he probably understood France better than the French themselves: "All the wealth of France has moved toward its frontiers; all its great, opulent cities are on its borders; the interior is frightfully thin."

Commercial Circuits, Commercial Cultures

The expansion of commerce can already be seen in the effort to build new roads, the capillaries that extended the circulation of goods into the nation's interior. Improvements to waterways—canals and rivers—served the same purpose. Unfortunately we lack readily available statistics for evaluating the relative volume of internal trade as compared with imports and exports from abroad. The foreign and domestic markets formed a single, organic whole; the two cannot be separated, regardless of whether we are talking about goods or labor. Urban manufactured goods spurred trade in wheat; sugar and other comestibles from the

Antilles and spices from China and India began to reach cities in the heartland of France and even, through fairs and markets, made their way into the hands of the more sophisticated country folk. Trade began to have an impact on daily life. Traders who bought and sold abroad were mindful of their reliance on domestic commerce: merchants in Marseilles, Bordeaux, Nantes, Rouen, and Le Havre looked to the seas for goods that could be sold inland. In Lyons traders looked for outlets on the Continent as well as across the seas, but they also attended to the domestic market, not only in the immediate vicinity of the city but all across France.[3] Commercial circuits for various products intersected, and the flow of goods shifted to accommodate regional economic expansions and contractions. In this respect, mercantile culture was fundamentally different from rural culture: merchants and those who depended on them had to contend with a variety of geographic and cultural factors. What defined space and social relations for the merchant was the restless search for profit and the law of supply and demand.

Merchant *(marchand)* and trader *(négociant):* the terminology is important, because by the late seventeenth century distinct roles had begun to emerge within a single overall function. Both were practical men, but their spheres of action differed. Their businesses, unlike the work of peasants not yet involved in speculative activities, were not stable and immutable. The warehouse of a great Bordeaux trader might well contain "products from around the world." The smell of sugar and cinnamon was apt to fill the air, while the floor was likely to be piled high with fabrics, manufactured goods, and various kinds of produce. Foreigners were drawn to this world of strange smells and exotic individuals, a microcosm of the vast world in which the trader transacted business. The business world in which traders and merchants operated was complex, rational, formalized, and abstract. They relied on money in all its forms, and the free circulation of monetary instruments was an absolute necessity. This involved them in an international circuit driven by profit. The goal was not to reproduce wealth but to generate a surplus; to reinvest and develop, not maintain. Traders also relied on written orders and correspondence and therefore needed specific training and distinctive skills. They could not operate without direct or indirect relationships with "independent merchants," and maintaining these called for an ability to negotiate and compromise. Traders also needed to be acute observers capable of analyzing whatever information came their way.

In mercantile cities it is easy to imagine the kinds of competition that must have existed between leading traders and representatives of the monarchy, which had a hierarchy and value system of its own. When Quesnay protested that "the trader is a stranger in his own land," he was suggesting that the two value systems were incompatible. What he forgot, however, was that traders and government officials had for a long time shared many common interests. Consumption by the state had offered merchants a unique market that yielded steadily increasing profits. Through loans to the government and to state officeholders (who purchased their offices), merchants became creditors of the state and therefore increasingly concerned with its fiscal and financial soundness. Men of commerce lived in both the world of privilege and the world of freedom. They needed independence, but they also needed protection.

To explore this interpenetration of cultures, I want to look at two examples. One is the story of an individual, Benoît Lacombe, a merchant from Gaillac who came to do business in Bordeaux.[4] The other is the story of a community: the traders of Lille.[5]

Along with countless other individuals, Benoît Lacombe moved from the mountains in which he was born to the sea, driven by dreams of riches and the attractions of the growing city of Bordeaux. He was a native of Gaillac, one of the large market towns of southwestern France, where his family had slowly worked its way up the social ladder. His grandfather began as a cooper and later became a merchant. His father owned a coopering business and eventually became a substantial trader and consul and ultimately *secrétaire du roi*, on the threshold of nobility. This change in status reflected the family's rise and demonstrates the interpenetration of values: profit was the driving force; land, patiently acquired, was a guarantee of status; and official appointments were symbols of prestige. Benoît Lacombe would not have been what he was without his family background and connections. He had contacts with wealthy landowners and merchants who sold grapes from vineyards and wheat from small farms in the region. He could tap into the sources of credit amassed by coopers and peasants. And he was familiar with the maze of state loans and municipal and state offices. The merchant's son grew up to be a consul, trader, and *sous-fermier des greffes* (an office associated with the law courts). All sectors of the economy were in communication with one another: money, land, commerce, and government. Knowledge gained from study was also important, as was the state administration, "and above all that priceless commodity, honor."[6] Two generations of Lacombes had amassed fortune and position, and it was left to Benoît to take the final step, the leap to nobility. This he would never do, however, because the Revolution intervened.

One cannot describe his time in Bordeaux in detail, so let us focus on the essential. The most important change was one of outlook: his horizon expanded from that of a small city to that of a great port in communication with the four corners of the earth. The certitude of dealing with local markets held on fixed days gave way to the uncertainties of international trade and the difficulties of carving out a niche for oneself in a worldwide market. Benoît Lacombe's correspondence reveals the pressure he felt to squeeze profits out of dealings that ranged in scale from minuscule to immense. Deals, profits, the honor of the firm—all these were important. But what really held the whole thing together was human contacts: men and families mattered more than commodities. Success really depended on people. By the 1780s, what Benoît wanted from the state was less interference and less oversight. He dreamed of open, free trade with as little state intervention as possible. When needed, however, he expected effective protection from the state. When revolt smoldered in the islands or his exclusive rights to certain markets were threatened, the merchant grumbled, and the state stepped in as arbitrator. Free exchange and protectionism could easily coexist at the level of individual businesses: everything was a matter of scale and ability to control the market.[7] A weakened state could only harm the interests of the group. The crisis of 1788–89 left Benoît stranded on the shoals of the *royaume profond*—in Gaillac, the "burial ground for men of talent."

Let us shift our attention now from the story of an individual to that of a group, from Aquitaine to Flanders. Both "commercial dreams" faced the same realities. In Lille, the economic order was based, as in other cities, on *corporations* (guilds). But the traditional guild methods of privilege, monopoly, and oversight had been partially supplanted by the capitalist free market. The city's traders controlled trade and dominated the economy, but they did so in a way that delegated some powers to the traditional guilds. Artisans and shopkeepers went about their business as they had always done, employing journeymen to do the work, but a few emerged as major players. Among thread makers, for example, the small number of men who controlled the guild also controlled markets and sources of supply over a region that extended beyond the nation's borders. Most masters in this craft depended on these few for the sale of their wares, even though the work was done mainly by female spinners from the country. The "guild" continued to exist while an industry was developed not in opposition to it but within it, under the leadership of men who served the municipality as aldermen or members of the chamber of commerce. "The overall structure of commerce was one of cooperation and interaction among people of every status."[8]

Furthermore, the expectations of traders with respect to monopoly raise a series of questions that are fundamental for understanding the final crisis of the Ancien Régime. The first of these has to do with the decline of the guilds. Although it is true that guilds in Paris, Valenciennes, Toulouse, and Caen closed their ranks to all but sons of those who were already master craftsmen, and guild wardens found themselves in difficult straits owing to the monarchy's overly greedy tax policies, there was no general crisis of the guilds in the face of calls for freedom of enterprise. The social situation was in fact much more complex. Labor legislation was not the archaic "barricade to industrial society that is so often described." For one thing, the regulations were easily circumvented wherever mercantile capitalism was on the rise. For another, the guild system was not as rigid as many people think; in fact it was capable of absorbing all sorts of individuals, from wage earners to businessmen, from proletarians to capitalists. In Caen, whenever the real productive forces of the city exerted their muscle, the guilds retreated; their economic power was quite limited compared with that of capital. In Lille the world of profit simply made its peace with the guilds. The crisis lay in the future.

Guilds also provided a reasonable solution to the "problem of quality." Syndics, clerks, and in Paris even police constables checked to make sure that products met certain standards of quality. Such oversight was not merely a matter of routine: it gained the confidence of buyers by upholding high standards and honest measurements. Inspections could even be adapted to the changing needs of customers. Output did not suffer from this discipline to ensure the quality of the goods produced.

Interestingly enough, we find the same conflict within the agency of government assigned to regulate industry, the Inspection des Manufactures.[9] Within this Colbertian agency an antiregulatory attitude held sway, while champions of the good old days sought to maintain regulations, privileges, inspections, and marks of quality—the whole panoply of oversight of guild labor and proto-industrial production. At issue in this debate was obviously the entire relationship between the state and the economy, with implications for France's ability to overcome obstacles to development and make use of industrial innovations. Since the end of the seventeenth century, the corps of inspectors had been guided by an oversight policy on which some producers, including the Lille traders, depended as a guarantee of quality and security. The presence of inspectors in the workshops certified conformity with standards of quality. At the same time, the inspectors kept the royal authorities informed about economic developments. Acting as go-betweens, the inspectors were like economic advisers, agents of development. As well-placed observers at key points in the production process, these fifty men were divided in their views: some missed the stringent regulations of the past, while others believed that a freer economy meant greater growth. The latter group included Roland de La Platière, who served first at Villefranche near Lyons and later in Amiens. Until Turgot launched his reform effort, economic policy only became more and more uncertain. After 1775 regulation was all but suspended, but the minister's departure left the administration in shock.

An investigation ordered by Necker revealed the depths of the malaise: the guilds wanted to reinstate stringent regulation, but any such reinstatement was a practical impossibility. The liberal policy desired by some economic actors and advocated by some economists had reached the highest levels of government. The Inspection des Manufactures, which generally favored reinstatement of the rules, backed into the "intermediate system." The inspectors' worldview was based on two principles: first, in order to sell, one has to manufacture good products—quality creates markets; and second, in order to increase profits, merchants deceive consumers, thus putting future markets and especially exports at risk. The government's job was to protect the "general good," which no automatic law of self-adjusting markets could guarantee. As the regulator or arbiter between the kingdom of peasants and the kingdom of commerce, the monarchical state had to continue to play its role. It had no intention of giving in to those who called for absolute freedom of trade, such as Clicquot de Blervache, for whom the consumer's taste was the only rule, "the torrent that must be followed," while the only worthwhile inspection was to put a variety of products on the market and allow the consumer to choose.

The "intermediate system" tried to grasp both ends of a chain that was already stretched to the breaking point. The method was to classify textile products according to their conformity to quality standards and then to sell the goods thus classified via two different distribution channels. This was a compromise whose success depended in part on persuading the Inspection des Manufactures to change its attitude. Instructions issued throughout the 1780s emphasized advice rather than oversight, persuasion rather than micromanagement, and incentives rather than repression. This procedure reveals the realities of the commercial and manufacturing economy as it existed on the eve of the Revolution. Clearly it would be wrong to confuse guilds with regulations: regulations could be justified as necessary to protect markets, and guilds could be either tolerated or rejected depending on local conditions.

This was a crucial debate because tampering with any element of a system risks undermining the entire system, and because it reveals the real nature of economic relations. Guilds and regulations were good for more than just oversight: they created zones of solidarity, credit, and trust in which family and matrimonial strategies played an important role. They brought wealth together with know-how to form a prosperous community that afforded protection in hard times. Not only wealth but also networks of clients and interpersonal relations created unity among "traders" in Lille, Bordeaux, Marseilles, and other cities. Individuals relied on these networks for information, resources, support, recommendations, and contacts. As Jean-Pierre Hirsch observes, "Immersion in the market was not enough; success depended as much on the quality of a man's contacts as on his ability to calculate." In this respect state intervention played a distinctive role in France as compared with, say, Great Britain.[10]

In Britain, agrarian capitalism and mercantile captalism developed simultaneously, allowing trade to develop and a greater division of labor to emerge. England was the first large market in which money for capital, loans, and wages was able to circulate freely. In France, the structure of society (slow to change, rooted in the soil, and ruled by conflicting rights, forms of land tenure, customs, and types of exploitation) was such that the economy relied not so much on division of labor and circulation as on hierarchical distribution of the income from land. The exchange economy at the time was nothing more than a supplementary circuit for distributing the surplus harvest.

By the end of the eighteenth century, three-quarters of French commerce was devoted to domestic transactions involving homegrown products, primarily agricultural goods and textiles. Maritime and industrial development occurred on the margins, with help and oversight from the government since the time of Louis XIV. State needs—for the army, the navy, and *la grandeur*—continually imposed certain requirements on the economy. Colbert and later officials created and maintained monopolies, operating trading companies such as the Compagnie des Indes and state-protected firms that to one degree or another were immunized against competition. Did government intervention distort French economic growth? This question cannot be answered here.

Intellectual and Social Debates: Mercantilism, Physiocracy, Liberalism

Not all traders and manufacturers were men of theory, though a few were economists. Some 1,800 authors produced works on economics between 1700 and 1789: of these, 43 were manufacturers, 64 businessmen, and 51 landowners actively engaged in farming. The vast majority of these works were written by government officials, military men, scholars, physicians, and clerics—that is, by and large, people employed by either church or state. Biographical analysis, moreover, shows that what mattered more than occupation was affiliation with one or more informal networks in which the study of economics was valued. For example, Jean Gabriel Montaudouin de La Touche, one of the biggest shippers in Nantes, was also a correspondent of the Académie des Sciences and founder of the Rennes Société d'Agriculture, de Commerce, et des Arts, which was subsidized by the Estates. Because of the nature of his business, he had a hand in everything. Money men and speculators such as John Law, Richard Cantillon, Nicolas Barrème, and especially Joseph Pâris-Duverney were in the spotlight more for their actions than for their writings. They had reputations as dazzling adventurers in the world of writing no less than in the world of politics. But where should we categorize competent financiers and *fermiers généraux* such as Dupin, Helvétius, and Lavoisier, who had their hands in every pot of gold? Fortunes were made from tax revenues as well as from land and speculation, and the remarkable upward mobility that such wealth made possible was the source of many a reputation. Businessmen, merchants, and manufacturers such as Dassier, Hubert, and Morainville took part in reflections on the nature of the economy. What they wrote was a direct outgrowth of what they had learned from acquaintances, contacts, and other sources of information over the course of their long careers as much as from professional experience in the narrow sense.

Occupation had little to do with economic thinking for two reasons. What came first was action or enterprise; the doctrine to legitimate it was developed only afterward. Second, it was perfectly possible for the message of a social group to be delivered not by members of that group but by active intermediaries: lawyers, writers, and officials who frequented and received information from the various circles in which theories were distilled from experience. Historians clearly need to be cautious about assuming that economic ideas can be correlated in any simple sociological sense with practice. Politics influenced commerce and enterprise, but economics also played a commanding role.[11] No conciliatory worldview clearly articulated the differences between bourgeois consciousness and the inegalitarian aristocratic spirit or ascribed a simple, socially derived structure to the realm of economic ideas. What we need to understand is who had access to the "language of principles" and what methods and breakthroughs were involved in the evolution of economic thinking. "In this respect, texts only summarize outcomes understood in terms of perceived realities."[12]

Mercantilists, Physiocrats, and liberals clashed in both action and doctrine and were perceived as different by contemporaries. The polemic that divided salons and academies at midcentury developed slowly in reaction against long-dominant attitudes. Representatives of the different schools were involved: the wealthy Baron d'Holbach (a friend of Diderot's), Mme d'Epinay, and Mme Geoffrin, all of whom were associated with the Ferme Générale, criticized the Encylopedists Galiani and Condorcet, Morellet and Raynal, Turgot and the marquis de Chastellux. Three salons welcomed economic thinkers of various stripes. In Paris during the winter and at La Roche-Guyon during the summer, the duchesse de La Rochefoucault-Liancourt received elite members of the "sect" (that is, the Physiocrats), including Quesnay, Abbé Baudeau, the marquis de Mirabeau, Bertin, Dupont de Nemours, and, later, Turgot and Condorcet. More attuned to the world of finance was the salon of Mme Blondel, the daughter of a *receveur général des finances*. Her sister married a *fermier général*, her son was an *intendant de commerce*, and her husband was a diplomat. At her side was the comtesse d'Angivilliers, the daughter of another *fermier général*, whose salon served economists as a stepping-stone to the Académie Française.

The several schools vied for the support of well-known writers and for the ear of journalists who could spread the word. Each group had its provincial intermediaries and booksellers. These networks created an audience for works of economics that extended far beyond Paris. The 267 contributors and correspondents associated with the *Journal d'agriculture* reflect this diversity, even if Paris still predominates: 35 percent were provincials, two-thirds lived in the more developed northern and eastern parts of France or in a leading commercial city, and one-quarter belonged to one or more *sociétés de pensée*. Few were rentiers or entrepreneurs, although a third enjoyed privileges of one sort or another. Commoners in the group included magistrates, officers, physicians, scientists, and writers. Thus the membership reflected not the orders or classes that made up society nor any particular set of occupations but rather the kind of people who were attracted to the "Republic of Letters."[13] This brings up two questions. How much distance was there between the everyday activities and speculations of traders and the realm of cultural practice? And did traders and merchants have a distinctive cultural identity?

The boundary lines between physiocracy, mercantilism, and liberalism were not clear-cut, because the different schools were influential in different periods and to different degrees and were not organized in the same way. By the Age of Enlightenment, mercantilism already came in various forms and had behind it a considerable tradition and experience with economic realities stretching back to the great upheavals of the sixteenth century, when the modern economy emerged (and the first economists along with it). As in any intellectual mode, mercantilist thought varied, and there was as much difference as there was similarity between the bullionism of the early Renaissance economists (for whom gold and silver, precious metals and their associated economic and symbolic values, remained the sole form of wealth) and the calculations of the English political arithmeticians such as Petty and Tucker (who were read in France in the early eighteenth century): "The error [is to say] that money is wealth, when in reality industry is wealth and money is the easiest way to transfer the product of industry from one person to another." Mercantilist thought was never codified as the doctrine of a school, although it was crystallized in the writings of English-style commercialist economists who favored importation of precious metals coupled with prudent protectionism. The chief contrast between the British mercantilists and the liberals was the mercantilists' certainty that spatial concentration of men and production yielded wealth and power. Until the eighteenth century and the consolidation of absolutism in France, mercantilism was not so much a unified school of thought as a set of concurrent pragmatic measures; this was because of the geographic dispersion of mercantilist writers and the need for a strong interventionist state. The Navigation Act, together with Colbert's legislative and economic program, are often cited as examples of mercantilist policy, which depended on bureaucratic administration.[14] Mercantilism was defined chiefly by the doctrines that opposed it.

Physiocracy, by contrast, was soon seen as a school, not to say a sect. After an initial phase in which many authors from Vauban to Boisguilbert extolled liberty, growth, and agricultural wealth, physiocratic doctrine solidified around Dr. Quesnay, a contributor to the *Encyclopédie*, protégé of Mme de Pompadour, and author of the *Tableau économique* (1758). The school thereupon broadened its theoretical ambitions to include not only the circulation of wealth but also the theory of taxation (in response to the state's financial crisis) and eventually hit on its "rural philosophy." Meanwhile, its audience also expanded in the wake of scandal (Mirabeau was imprisoned because of his conflict with the Ferme Générale), and influential economic administrators such as Bertin, Trudaine de Montigny, and any number of *intendants* began to consult the physiocratic doctors.

It took a decade or so for the school to develop into a sect. It published its own journals: the *Gazette de commerce*, Dupont's *Journal d'agriculture, commerce et finance*, and Abbé Baudeau's *Ephémérides du citoyen*. These, together with books such as Quesnay's *Despotisme de la Chine*, Mercier de La Rivière's *Ordre naturel et essentiel des sociétés politiques*, and Dupont's *Réflexions sur la constitution essentielle du gouvernement*, spread the new gospel to political circles. Its influence became ubiquitous, for there were Physiocrats in all branches of the administration; Turgot (who to be sure had some reservations about physiocratic thinking) was foremost among them. The sect encouraged the new agronomic thinking, but meanwhile its attacks on the "sterile class," its alienation of a segment of the public in the luxury debate, certain ambiguities in the writings of the Encyclopedists, and the failure of the liberal experiment forced the Physiocrats onto the defensive. If the mercantilists were not so much a school as a spectrum of opinions, the Physiocrats were often tempted to express doctrine as science based on natural, absolute, universal, immutable laws. Only a social as well as intellectual analysis of economic debate can show how certain thinkers such as Bertin and Turgot managed to reconcile seemingly contradictory values.[15] One needs to move from the level of doxology to the "archaeology of knowledge."[16]

The liberals advanced with even less discipline in the ranks. Although the liberal cause received an immense boost in 1776 with the publication of Adam Smith's *Wealth of Nations* (which was immediately translated into French), liberal thinkers had already been speaking out for some time. Unlike the mercantilists, who were everywhere and nowhere, liberals turned up wherever mercantilist social, political, and economic principles stood in need of criticism. They drew their arguments from the writings of adversaries of French economic policy in the crisis years such as Vauban, Boisguilbert, and Fénelon, and maintained relations with powerful men engaged in the renovation of France's fiscal and monetary system in the wake of the collapse of Law's System: Silhouette, the *contrôleur général;* Jean Frédéric Phélypeaux de Maurepas, who was minister of the navy, a member of the important Conseil du Commerce, and one of Gournay's protectors; and René Louis, marquis d'Argenson, who was secretary of state for foreign affairs. Two figures were the very incarnation of liberal principles: Jacques Claude Vincent de Gournay and François Véron de Forbonnais.[17]

Gournay was a trader from a wealthy, ennobled family of Saint-Malo shippers. He was therefore deeply involved in a sector of the capitalist economy that had experienced the socioeconomic tensions born of economic growth. The triumphant expansion of the market that marked the seventeenth century was slowed in the eighteenth century by the implosion of the mercantile elite (the number of active traders in Saint-Malo declined from 150 in 1710 to 50 in 1740). Enterprising Malouins (as the inhabitants of the city were known) now left their native city for larger French cities or for the islands or for Cádiz, while others abandoned commerce, the wealthiest and most talented for places in the courts, the army, the world of finance, or idle leisure. This social mobility disrupted the link between economic development and social success. Born in 1712, Vincent de Gournay left Saint-Malo for Cádiz in 1730. Upon his return to France, he made his way into the public sector and became one of Maurepas's main informants while continuing to keep a hand in private business affairs. In 1751 he purchased an office as *intendant du commerce* and until his resignation in 1758 became one of the bureau's most energetic members. His specialty was monetary exchange, a crucial factor in international trade. As a high-level functionary, he influenced legislation and dealt with the regulation of privileges and monopolies. This experience led him to believe that growth of the domestic economy depended on population, employment, and trade and was best served by a doctrine of "laissez faire, laissez passer." His thinking was also shaped by his efforts to convert other officials and thinkers in the salons and academies, such as the academy of Amiens, whose members included the principal leaders of the liberal movement—Abbé Coyer; Duhamel de Monceau; Butel Dumont, Montesquieu's son; Montaudouin, another trader; Cliquot de Blervache, an important merchant; Abbé Carlier; Abbé Morellet—a fair sampling of the enlightened elite consolidated by the academies and its connections with the provincial administration (the *intendant* and governor of Picardy) and its Parisian counterpart. Véron de Forbonnais was of course also a member.

Gournay's writings, unpublished to this day but analyzed by Simone Meysonnier,[18] tell us about the principles of an economist who believed in both the free market and regulation. The writings of Véron de Forbonnais, published in the *Encyclopédie* from 1754 to 1767 (including articles on commerce, exchange, contraband, and so on), in the *Eléments du commerce* (1754), and various essays on trade with the Levant, painting, and the trade aristocracy in *Principes et observations économiques* (1767), represent the ultimate version of egalitarian liberalism; their publication helped to give currency to the ideas of the school.

Forbonnais (1722–1800) was also a trader from a family of Le Mans manufacturers whose ancestors were wealthy drapers. For twenty-five years he worked for an uncle in the shipping business in Nantes and later did stints at the firm's branch offices in Italy, Spain, and France. His outlook was thus similar to Gournay's and quite different from that of the great Physiocrats: Quesnay, a physician with ties to the court; Mirabeau, a landowner "feudal in background and temperament,"[19] who wanted to prevent commoners from purchasing fiefs; and even Dupont, the son of a watchmaker, whom Mirabeau and Quesnay made presentable enough to allow him to pursue a career that attracted many men of talent in those days, that of secretary to the great of this world. A translator of Latin and English economists, as well as a man familiar with the markets of the day, Forbonnais was an individual whose whole career sheds light on a primary issue of Renaissance history: How is it that human societies contribute to social order without thwarting the natural order of things? Forbonnais was already close to Gournay when he joined the *administra-tion des finances* in 1755. In 1756 he became inspector general of the Mint. He would remain in state service.

The liberal movement was never anything more than a series of iso-lated administrative actions to deal with market distortions coupled with increasingly radical pronouncements by intellectual proponents of lais-sez-faire. Gournay and Forbonnais became public intellectuals when they moved from the world of trade to the world of government. As intellec-tuals of trade, they worked out a program within the government and sold it to other government officials. In this way they became mediators between the world of government and the world of scholarship and between the world of thought and the world of work. A veritable turning point was reached in 1755, when the *vingtième*, a fiscal reform proposed by Machault, failed to produce the desired results—a defeat for the administration in the eyes of a public seduced by the *parlements* and clergy, that is, by men of privilege. Another reason for the turn was the publication of Rousseau's *Discours sur l'origine de l'inégalité*, which forced liberals to reflect on the reintroduction of morality into the economic and political order after Physiocrats and liberals had tried to replace it with the values of science and utility. Two controversies, one over the "com-mercial aristocracy" and the other over painting, reflected a hardening of positions that would endure with little change from 1760 into the 1780s: the conflict of intellectual and social interests would reemerge in various guises as reform programs and pragmatic experiments from Turgot to Calonne.

Meanwhile, the old confidence in state mercantilism remained. Social organization was justified if it enriched the state and private individuals. The ultimate goal remained an "economy of grandeur," that is, a family economy expanded to the dimensions of a kingdom. The object of eco-nomic as well as political policy being to make the king rich, merchant France was obliged to accept the values of rural France with its network of controls. Meanwhile, egalitarian liberals argued the case for the market and utility as compatible with both state interests and economic growth. But trade depended on connections and family alliances and personal ambitions driven by profit as well as honor. It was at home in a world of unlimited competition among people as well as commodities. Adam Smith's book demonstrated the greatness of the market order, and insofar as it encouraged comparison of the "theory of the wealth of nations" with the "theory of moral sentiments" based on sympathy and impartiality, it showed that the market was compatible with an individualistic morality. For adepts of the Scottish philosopher, it was the construction of the sphere of self-interest that made possible the existence of disinterested sentiments as the expression of free and equal individuals.[20] "Every man obeys his own sensation because he is free," said Mercier de La Rivière, in this case anticipating Smith.

How to reconcile liberty, individualism, and harmony of public and private interests? The Physiocrat establishes his principles in the space between public and private. His theory of value, unlike that of Gournay and Borbonnais, is based not on utility, labor, and movable capital but on land, or immovable capital; and unlike that of the mercantilists, his theory rests not on monetary wealth transposed from the books of the family to those of the nation (and not even on money as "stimulus"), but on landed property as the only source of new value. English commercialism and French industrialism (the legacy of Colbert) yield the same end by the same means: intervention and protection. Although these principles could be modified in practice (as we saw in the case of the Inspection des Manufactures), their overall tenor was protectionist, an attitude that we find more or less continuously at the highest levels of the state and quite frequently at the base, but which physiocracy rejected.

Jacques Necker's eulogy of Colbert before the Académie Française, for which he received that body's prize on August 25, 1773, can be understood in this light. The occasion marked the culmination of both Necker's philosophical career and the reaction against physiocracy, the last school of reformist thought encompassed entirely within the monarchy. Ten years earlier, the Académie had awarded its prize to a eulogy of Sully by the master of academic eulogies, Antoine Léonard Thomas, who actually offered a disguised apologia for Quesnay. In 1773 Necker defended monopolies, the Compagnie des Indes, and Colbertian statism. He vehemently attacked the primordial title of landed property, the cornerstone of monarchic and physiocratic society. He praised movable wealth and the work of a great minister of finance. His text was a declaration of his own candidacy for the post as well as a programmatic statement and self-affirmation: as Grimm put it in a letter, "M. Necker has found out the soul of this great minister by measuring it against his own," and the virtuous banker and adept of trade became the only man capable of gaining the confidence—that is, of attracting the money—of the world of commerce and industry.[21]

The liberal experiment had begun in 1760 with Bertin and Laverdy: wheat circulated freely until a series of crises from 1764 to 1776 caused prices to skyrocket and discredited the liberal ideal. By 1770 Terray had given up on the free market. The conflict between *delamarisme* and laissez-faire resurfaced in this period: it was a fundamental clash between two worlds. Gradually, however, a new symbiosis took shape. It became possible at one moment or another for interventionists and liberals, Physiocrats and mercantilists to join forces. What made this possible was the secularization of the economic realm: it was now up to intellectuals and legislators to propose social values in which society could invest for the good of all, without reference to divine authority. Free trade and protection were no longer just opposing positions in the debate on protectionism but a matter of the protection of liberties by the state acting as arbiter. Gournay's laissez-faire was not the laissez-faire of the traders. Like mercantilism before it, liberalism became eclectic, but in so doing the cardinal points of its social interpretation changed. If liberalism was less of a force than physiocracy in debates from 1750 to 1770, it was because Quesnay had proposed a sufficiently sweeping reformulation of economics to change the basis of economic interpretation completely: although he started from land, he paradoxically reasoned in terms of a capitalist system in which questions of distribution and demand were relegated to secondary importance, after questions of supply and production. From now on only profit could regulate growth. Rich and poor became locked in struggle. The issue thus became one of regulating the economic role of the state in an increasingly unstable society.

Trade Culture and the Culture of Traders

The profit seekers did not ignore the fundamental debate altogether, and some even played a leading role in it, as we have seen. On the whole, however, they seem reticent when compared with the cultivated class in general. I have given evidence for this elsewhere, and there is no need to revisit the subject here.[22] I do want to explore the education of traders, however, and to compare the culture of traders in two cities, Bordeaux and Marseilles.

Before doing that, however, we would do well to recall what economic historians have discovered. The eighteenth century was the golden age of commercial capitalism despite the fact that business in those days was individual and family-oriented, personalized, divided, and rarely corporate. In no city did joint-stock companies outweigh family-owned "houses," nearly all of which were self-financed. It took a long time before commodity trading availed itself of major sources of credit. The backwardness of French banking may have had something to do with this, but so did the attractiveness of the monarchy's need for credit to prospective financiers. The history of Protestant banking, studied by Hans Lüthy, clearly shows that different areas of finance were closely interrelated: commissions on *rentes*, insurance business, maritime business, the grain trade, bills of exchange and banker's acceptances. Recall what Abbé Morellet, who dined with Necker and sought newcomers to invite to his salon, said about the minister: "Necker owed his fortune to banking and to some profitable business with the Compagnie des Indes before he became one of its directors. Profits of this type, however low the interest rate, are always considerable when the sum of capital is large; and . . . only ignorance or maliciousness or most likely both can turn it into a crime."[23]

Commerce at the time was growing rapidly in all the major ports (Bordeaux, Nantes, Marseilles, and Rouen divided 90 percent of large-scale Atlantic trade among them) and many lesser ones: from 1716 to 1789 the volume of trade grew by perhaps 400 percent, or 2 to 3 percent annually. This fabulous growth made the leading diversified capitalist traders among the wealthiest men in France.

Remember, too, that there was variable but undeniable growth in industry, especially textiles (cotton goods, prints, and silks), where the growth rate was about 1 percent annually. To be sure, industrialists and traders were not part of the same circle, but the quest for profit united all entrepreneurs, as did the need to search out new markets. Age-old rural France was gradually penetrated by a variety of proto-industrial entrepreneurs with a distinctive way of accumulating capital and putting workers to work. Whether dispersed or concentrated in "proto-factories," rural workers felt the effects of distant markets on their wages. The trader's culture and worldview thus left its stamp on the rural France of hedgerows and scrub. In the iron industry, one of the most technologically advanced of its time, the culture clash was even more acute. Factories were located in the heart of rural and forest areas. Innovative techniques attracted the attention of technologists and scientists: the naturalist Buffon, for example, was responsible for the forges of Montbard. Last but not least, the landed nobility played a crucial role in this area: 56 percent of factories were owned by men of privilege. Even if they did not run the businesses themselves, they did come into contact with the requirements and vicissitudes of a different kind of society. This clash, similar in nature to that which took place in commercial centers between wealthy landowners, rentiers, and officeholders and people involved in trade—between rural France and merchant France—inevitably forced people to take a more complex view of the relation between society and economy.[24] When viewed broadly, the growth of the French economy, whatever its pace and weaknesses may have been, was a dynamic process involving entrepreneurs engaged in many activities at once. Although these entrepreneurs were not entirely left out of the cultural movement of the time, their role in it was secondary.

Was the trader a pioneer in the formation of a bourgeois ideology? Perhaps; but his social role guaranteed that his position in the various cultural societies would remain inferior. These societies implicitly confirmed the existing social order. Their honors went to acknowledged notables and later to capitalists: one-third of the cultural societies never elected an entrepreneur, and the other two-thirds accepted either the occasional dynamic personality, as in Toulouse, where trade was absorbed by the nobility, or else small groups that enjoyed the respect of the community, as in Amiens, Bordeaux, Caen, Cherbourg, Dijon, Lyons, Marseilles, Nîmes, Orléans, La Rochelle, and Rouen. In this way recognition came to merchant culture. The list does not include Lille, even though the Collège des Philalèthes (originally a Masonic lodge that turned itself into an academy) at first accepted traders, who were gradually supplanted by the usual enlightened notables.[25]

Two things are worth noticing here. First, trade and enterprise can be situated within broader circles of sociability, chiefly centered on Masonic lodges. Masonic sociability was above all transferential: for initiates, true nobility depended on virtue, feelings, and behavior. Traders initiated into Masonic lodges became people of significance, and for some this social integration had the impact of a spiritual revelation. Second, was the opposition between *negotium* (trade) and *otium* (leisure) completely clear? Certainly not: there were many ambiguous cases. Ideas and values did not necessarily correspond directly to social groups: debates and questions focused simultaneously on both ideology and practice, as we saw in Lille. We are comparing systems governed by distinct rules, systems that did not evolve at the same pace; hence we cannot translate the terms of one into the terms of the other in any straightforward way. In the second half of the eighteenth century, a growing segment of the merchant class enjoyed the benefits of accumulated cultural capital and was therefore able to define its own cultural objectives. This ability fostered new hopes of social integration, which took a variety of forms: it could as easily lead to the embrace of classical ideals as to their rejection, and it could alter the prevailing state of mind. The choices that individuals made were reflected in the way they educated their children.

The Businessman's Education: Between Pragmatism and Integration

What made a good businessman was a reputation for competence and skill.[26] The requisite abilities could be learned by observing a wide range of behavior and attitudes and acquiring certain intellectual accoutrements. Making a profit required a variety of skills. As the market expanded, so did the number of commodities for sale. Manufactured products became increasingly diversified, and standardization was impossible under existing conditions of production. The young trader therefore had to become a judge of quality. If in the textile business, for example, he had to learn the range of available wools and fabrics, the hierarchy of grades, and the acceptable trade-offs between quality and price. This kind of knowledge was acquired mainly on the job rather than from books, although more and more people did begin to read manuals and dictionaries of commerce. Systems of measurement varied widely within France and across Europe, and one had to learn to sort these out and to distinguish between the genuine and the counterfeit. Business knowledge was a matter of observation, expertise, and flair gained through contacts with other people. It was important to specialize in a particular section or geographical region. The young man who focused on one part of the world—the islands, the Orient, the north of France—and on a limited range of products—wine, say, or textiles—could be reasonably certain of a successful apprenticeship and a good future in business. The emergence of so-called *grands crus,* or great vintages of wine, can be understood in terms of the growing expertise of both buyer and seller, and this kind of expertise could be passed on from generation to generation: expert knowledge and keen observation could fill the coffers of a business with profits.

As the range of commodities available for trade grew, traders needed a wider range of skills. Honest dealing was a way of ensuring the loyalty of clients. The goal of apprenticeship was still to learn the art of making money, even if there were no specific rules for doing so. People were quick to see a link between the necessity of commerce and the need for education. Reading, writing, and arithmetic were essential skills at all levels of business; other sorts of knowledge were clearly essential for climbing to the top. Arithmetic and accounting were influenced by advances in mathematics. Businessmen mainly needed to perform computations, and the use of new tools such as tables of logarithms did not necessarily imply a high level of mathematical competence, as Condorcet observed. The trader's finesse can be measured in other areas, however. Knowledge of foreign languages was a necessity, and children were sent abroad to acquire the requisite fluency.

Practice, which is more difficult to pin down, reveals a broad range of oral and written linguistic competence from the barely literate to the refined. The bare minimum of necessary skill could be learned from textbooks of commercial correspondence in conjunction with on-the-job training. Pierre Jeannin considers it a distinctive feature of the eighteenth century that merchants wrote well and adopted the refined tone of men of quality. Knowledge of geography and the world and of the law could be useful socially as well as professionally. Learning acquired value only through action, where what counted was what was needed to win. This kind of knowledge could be gleaned from either textbook precepts or firm archives. The law had specifically commercial uses, just as there was a special math for business or accounting. The problem for the historian is to know what people of different social stations learned. The ability to engage in complicated financial transactions such as currency exchange and arbritrage set some firms apart from others, as did connections with banks and other sources of credit and the ability to analyze market developments, which remained rather rudimentary. Generally speaking, access to knowledge became broader in the eighteenth century without becoming deeper. The typical French trader was little better educated than the typical businessman of the sixteenth or seventeenth century. One problem was that business had its own specific set of needs, and these conflicted with calls from other quarters for broader public education.

From Counting Room to *Collège*

Merchant practices in port cities have been studied by many people: Bardet for Rouen–Le Havre, Butel for Bordeaux, Carrière for Marseilles, Lespagnol for Saint-Malo, Cabantous for Dunkerque, and even Garden for Lyons. These studies have demonstrated the educational importance of the family, the business, and the extended educational journey. In an age when residence and place of business were not necessarily separate, the home was center stage in the world's theater. The young man who, with his father, uncles, cousins, and employees, made the rounds of cellar, loft, warehouse, and storage areas learned his calling at home. Success depended on maintaining the family's good name. On-the-job training often led to an early start on a business career. In Saint-Malo it was common to say that "going to school is neither useful nor convenient." Education in and for business came in stages, generally between the ages of fifteen and thirty. The owners' sons might be sent to sea to serve as apprentice seamen or junior officers aboard one of their father's ships. Danican de L'Epine (1656–1734) worked his way up from supercargo to shipowner. From Bordeaux children were sent as far as the Antilles, although it was more common to send them for a stint with a sister house in London, Amsterdam, or Hamburg. When the trader's sons returned home, they continued to live in an open, cosmopolitan environment. Thus the family environment prepared them to meet future as well as immediate business challenges. The key to success was readily available at home. Socially, the reproduction of the group was assured. Sons had no choice but to continue in the family business, although the best might be chosen for the most difficult tasks. There was little chance for escape, because peer pressure was quite strong. The only danger was that a boy might be tempted by some opportunity in the outside world, for society itself was changing. He might then seek an education that could be had only outside the family, primarily in the *collège*, or secondary school.

Between the end of the seventeenth century and the Revolution, the contempt of merchants toward secondary education diminished. Although it was still common to say that literature turned young men away from business, this attitude was tempered by a hunger for social advancement that only the dominant culture could satisfy. The fact that *collèges* were not as common in port cities as they ought to have been reflects the strength of the antieducational bias, just as the makeup of secondary school classes in mercantile cities shows that the demand for additional education just barely held steady. The sons of traders sought education from various sources. Some enrolled in Jesuit or Oratorian institutions, where the curriculum was accelerated. In Bayonne, only 10 percent of the forty pupils who entered at the sixth-grade level graduated. Where it is possible to study *collège* students in some detail, as at Belley or Grenoble, we find that pupils stayed for relatively short periods, and that merchants' sons were more likely to attend boarding schools such as La Trinité in Lyons that offered enticing subjects such as history, geography, and decorative arts.[27]

Most merchants' and traders' sons supplemented early home instruction with more sophisticated formal lessons in reading, writing, and arithmetic. After 1740 many were sent to urban boarding schools, which can be studied (and counted) by way of advertisements and brochures: there were three in Dunkerque, around twenty in Lille, five or six in Bordeaux, and several dozen in Paris. All of these schools offered instruction that marked a partial departure from earlier methods of teaching the humanities: technical and professional proficiency was valued, as were foreign languages and geography. For the same reason the proportion of traders' sons increased from 15 to 25 percent in elite institutions such as Juilly as well as in the "military" schools that were created in Vendôme (50 percent), Pontlevoy (25 to 30 percent), and Sorrèze. The sons of the leading French traders were after the same thing as the sons of international traders in England, Ireland, Germany, Italy, and Spain. At a lower level of society, the Christian Brothers opened a dozen boarding schools, two of which, in Rouen and Marseilles, welcomed several hundred pupils each year. Commercial subjects at last made an appearance in the classroom, with courses in commerce, finance, mathematics, commercial geography, and even architecture and military art. In Marseilles accounting, applied physics, navigation, foreign languages, drawing, arms, and algebra were taught.

Education stood at the center of merchant culture. A major cultural divide originated here, with the denial of access to Latin and the humanities. Social and cultural differentiation was the result of choices made by families. The cultural baggage that was more easily acquired in the new institutions than in the old *collèges* bestowed on merchants' children an ease abroad that no brief stay could provide. Traders needed skills of two kinds: technical skills and cultural skills. Accordingly, different members of merchant society appropriated courtly ideals in different ways. Interestingly, in some schools we find both sons of the nobility being educated for military careers and sons of traders being educated for commercial careers. When humanities as taught in the *collèges* became associated with pedantry and fell out of favor, a new, elitist aristocratic model of schooling combined the advantages of both public and private instruction, somehow miraculously squaring the circle. Innovations in teaching made it possible for students to acquire both expertise and manners.

Merchant Sociability and Culture in Marseilles and Bordeaux

In order to understand trader culture in general, we would have to study the group's intellectual output and the books and paintings that influenced it. We know from the work of Jean Quéniart on the cities of western France that merchants and traders in Nantes, Rouen, Angers, Rennes, Le Mans, and Saint-Malo read little, generally late in life, and chose what they read selectively. In the late seventeenth century traders everywhere began to amass libraries, but these were quite modest and inferior to the libraries of the traditional elites. By the middle of the eighteenth century, however, they were among the leaders in terms of both numbers of books owned and scholarly interests. Their collections exhibited a distinctive character, moreover: professional books took up a large part, as did works on science, technology, geography, and exploration. Adepts of new, more public forms of reading such as lending libraries, the traders of western France led the way in reading works about politics and economics as well as newspapers. At the same time, they invested heavily in works of recreation and escape such as novels and plays. The Bordeaux libraries analyzed by Paul Butel yield similar results, and it would be good to have corroborating data from other sites. In Lyons, by contrast, only major traders amassed substantial libraries in the first half of the eighteenth century, and these libraries were barely distinguishable from those of the aristocratic elite. After 1750, libraries were more numerous and more responsive to the taste of the moment as well as to contemporary debates, scientific writing, and practical works.[28] Reading developed in two directions: utility and recreation. Religion never took up much space in these collections beyond a minimum imposed by convention. This was probably not because merchants substituted secular tastes for religious ones but because they tended by necessity to be men of pragmatic tolerance, not to say relativism. Their choices in part reflected those of other elites—the atmosphere of the time—and in part their own new social aspirations: the worldview of a social group.

These processes and differences stand out even more clearly when we look at sociability in Bordeaux and Marseilles. Both ports had experienced substantial commercial growth, but there were differences between the two. Marseilles was all business, even if it lacked the Manchester-like coldness that struck Grimod de La Reynière in Lyons. Bordeaux, with its *parlement* and judicial aristocracy and its *intendance,* was more typical of the mixture of landed France and commercial France. Despite their very different histories, both cities were cultural centers whose influence extended far beyond their walls and beyond the hinterland that supplied them with men and goods. Hence these are good places to look at two institutions that helped to change traditional patterns of sociability, namely, the Masonic lodges and the museums.

It is worth pausing to point out certain features of Bordeaux's growth in order to make clear what was distinctive about its traders. Recovering from the fluctuations of the reign of Louis XIV, commerce quickly picked up steam. The elite of Bordeaux could not choose between the temptations of the sea and its traditional attachment to the land. Wine and other local specialties gave the land its value and afforded a dominant place to the judicial and landed aristocracy. The city's economic growth, encouraged by tax advantages granted by the government in 1717, depended on this tension between the lure of the land and the call of the colonies. For certain types of goods, Bordeaux was France's leading port, but its prosperity depended on international relations stretching across Europe: it grew into a leading international port with a growth rate of 5 percent annually from 1715 to 1765 and 3 percent thereafter. Drawing in new citizens and stimulating various kinds of economic activity in the hinterland, Bordeaux took off; the city outstripped all others in the region, including La Rochelle and Bayonne.

Marseilles, the leading port of the Mediterranean, also experienced phenomenal growth. It, too, enjoyed privileges granted by Colbert, including an authorization to engage in commerce without derogation from nobility. Traffic in Marseilles did not grow quite as fast as in Bordeaux—only 1.6 to 2 percent annually. The city's trading zone expanded to the west in spite of opposition from other major powers. As in Bordeaux but to a lesser extent, the growth of the port encouraged other types of activity, drawing new workers into the city. To a greater extent than the Aquitainian capital, Marseilles had commerce in its soul: land was of only marginal importance here, and one had to move well inland—to Aix, with its *parlement, intendance,* and Estates—before the cultural climate changed. Traders in the two cities therefore played different social and cultural roles.

In Marseilles, the whole economy was organized around the port, and trading was more important than manufacturing. Among the city's inhabitants (who numbered 50,000 after the plague but 120,000 in 1789), major traders were few in number: less than 4 percent of the population, some 300 families, or 750 major traders who paid more than 700 livres in taxes. Two features characterized this group: its membership turned over rapidly, and many of its members came from outside—from Languedoc, Provence, the Dauphiné, and even abroad, mostly from northern Europe, Switzerland, and Italy. Cosmopolitanism and mixing were real, encouraged by religious affiliation, endogamy, and notoriety based on success and wealth. The new trading class was the force behind the Enlightenment, according to one of its scions, Guys, speaking to the academy in 1775:

> Let no one judge the superior and distinguished men of this profession by those who are its artisans and who, accustomed to filling orders that, like needs, continually recur, are condemned to live in narrow-minded ignorance. Incapable of broadening their views or perceiving causes other than prosperity or fate, they creep, labor, obey, and all their lives perform a necessary duty that does them little honor. The trader of whom I am speaking, whose status is not incompatible with the most ancient nobility or the most noble sentiments, is the one who, superior by virtue of his views, his genius, and his enterprise, adds his fortune to the wealth of the state . . . While his vessels, laden with our foodstuffs and the products of our factories, travel in search of goods from the most varied foreign climes, his ministers follow him everywhere, keeping him informed and carrying out his orders. His agents transmit his

orders to all the markets of Europe. His name on a circulating note causes funds to be disbursed and multiplied. He orders, he recommends, and he protects.

This collective portrait proclaimed the glory of capitalism in the very heart of the academy. It hailed the triumph of the distinguished businessman, setting apart those who merely followed orders from those noteworthy men whose "instinct" was responsible for both prosperity and Enlightenment, as Quesnay wrote in his article entitled "Grain."

In Bordeaux, out of a population that increased from 45,000 in 1715 to 110,000 in 1790, traders were not much more of a presence than in Marseilles: they figured in only 10 to 12 percent of marriage contracts. There were perhaps 900 substantial traders in 1730 and more than 1,300 by 1780, of whom only 400 to 500 were truly important. This was larger than the number of aristocrats, for the traders accepted outsiders from the surrounding region and abroad and admitted Protestants among their number. Traders stood on an equal footing with the judicial aristocracy, which had profited from the growth of the economy, and the wealthiest traders increasingly moved in the same circles as the nobles of the robe. As in Marseilles, but without enjoying social supremacy, traders in Bordeaux breathed life into high society and oversaw the renovation of the city, but they were obliged to share political power with *parlement*, the *cour des aides*, and the *intendance*. In Bordeaux, the guild wardens were obedient to the central government, whose views they expressed more than those of commerce. The king's men made their authority felt not only in the guilds but in fiscal and administrative institutions as well. Social competition was intense, but mobility was moderate. The trader, at odds with traditional society, was not as close to it as he was in Marseilles. In Provence, despite monarchical oversight, the city retained some of the spark of the republic it once had been. Merchants were in control of municipal institutions, and the chamber of commerce played a more active role than in Guyenne. Merchants ran the city, and the affairs of the city were the affairs of businessmen, a source of rancor among the old nobility.

At the turn of the eighteenth century, both great metropolises were therefore illustrious, but within them the internal divisions were different. In Marseilles the culture was that of the kingdom, but marginal and backward in three areas: religion, where a new order had yet to be imposed; language; and integration into the emerging networks of scholarship, science, and publishing. Traders were marginal, and their culture was the culture of the countinghouse. By contrast, Bordeaux had long been integrated into the national culture and the Parisian orbit in regard to intellectual and educational matters. The administrative and parlementary elite dominated cultural life, and everyone was quick to accept the leadership of Paris in this realm.

Academic Life and New Forms of Sociability

Academic life was institutionalized much more rapidly in Guyenne than in Provence. The circles of learned amateurs and salons of literary people underwent a transformation at the turn of the century. In 1712, under the protection of the governor, the duc de La Force, the academy received its patents. It brought the parlementary elite (which throughout the century would revere the name of Montesquieu) together with the wealthy: dues of three hundred livres were required until 1732. In Marseilles attempts were made to organize an academy before 1720, but a small group of scientists with close ties to the world of trade clashed with the bishop and hero of the plague, Monsignor de Belzunce, over the issue of Jansenism. Hence the founding of Marseilles's academy came later, in 1726, and it was dominated by literary men, owing to the need to integrate this southern city into the culture of France. In both cities the departure from spontaneous sociability excluded traders, who were men of the world, and so did the influence of traditional elites and the culture of the *collège,* so different from the traders' practical expertise. The chief difference between the two cities had to do with municipal support, which in Bordeaux was hesitant and at times a source of conflict, whereas in Marseilles it was unstinting. In this we see the effects of two different political traditions.

The two academies differed in the same way as to recruitment. Over the course of the century the Bordeaux academy elected 181 members of all categories, among whom the parlementary and officeholding nobility dominated until 1763; after that it accepted men of talent, but all the directors of the academy were still nobles, and only four traders were elected. In Bordeaux the Enlightenment was an aristocratic affair, sustained by the solidarity of a hundred or so families and justified by the predominant role of *parlementaires,* landowners, and a few merchants. It was at the academy that Montesquieu, a vine grower, met Melon, an *inspecteur général des Fermes* who became John Law's secretary and whose *Essai politique sur le commerce* was a milestone in liberal thought. Admission to the academy of Marseilles was far more inclusive: there were only 137 noble members, compared with 135 non-nobles. But the composition of the noble membership was different: there were as many military men as officeholders. More than that, there was a place for traders alongside other talented bourgeois such as lawyers, physicians, teachers, and prosecutors: 25 percent of the members came from the world of trade, including two noble merchants. We find some of the leading names of Marseilles commerce: Bertrand, Dulard, Guys, Seymandi, Borelli, Grosson, Louis Necker, the brother of the *contrôleur général,* and above all Dominique Audibert, who was a Protestant from the Gap region and a major shipping magnate with a hand in all the growth areas of the economy. Broadly speaking, the tone and independence of the world of trade came to dominate the Marseilles academy. "The spirit of commerce breaks down all inhibition," Audibert wrote to Abbé Bignon. The continual presence of traders transformed the assembly into an economic and political tribunal. In the academy of Bordeaux, where the traditional elite dominated, economic concerns were heard for three reasons: landowners had a responsibility to derive the best value from their harvests through commerce; administrators were responsible for managing the economy; and intellectuals were responsible for cultural change. In Marseilles commercial expertise offered its own judgments; in Bordeaux its judgments were filtered through others. The activities of both academies need to be seen in the light of broader alliances and common interests and in terms of wider social networks, as well as in relation to cultural ambitions stemming from a desire for recognition and integration as much as from the specific culture of a distinctive subgroup.

In Bordeaux the traditional elite clearly took charge of its common interests with the new elite of traders. The nature of Montesquieu's curiosity as well as his success assisted in this. He lectured the judicial nobility on behalf of scientific and technological culture, which had become essential for commerce and economic growth. The influence of traders made itself felt in two areas: applied research, which gave rise to an endless series of papers on maritime timekeeping, ship handling, cosmography, meteorology, the problems of the slave trade, and useful commercial products; and empirical utilitarianism, which stimulated theoretical discussion of the unification of the market, the commercial nobility, protectionist legislation, economic systems, and infrastructural improvement.

In Marseilles the trader class looked out for its own interests in the academy, especially after 1750. This can be seen, for example, in prize competitions, most notably in the rhetorical acclamation accorded to the success of "gentle commerce." In 1777 a competition on the influence of commerce on mores drew twenty entries, which revealed a division of opinion: some offered Rousseauian descriptions of urban depravity, while others praised civilization. In other respects, however, the entries demonstrated a unity of opinion: a conciliatory impulse elicited praise for Sully as well as Colbert and for local trade as opposed to international trade. Switzerland and Holland were praised at the expense of England. On the eve of the Revolution, the municipal government asked the academy to ponder the subject of "education for trade," and Abbé Raynal proposed a prize competition to "analyze the causes of the growth of its commerce and means for ensuring continued prosperity." In Bordeaux as well as Marseilles, economic interests and debates were successfully incorporated into academic programs, but the social background against which this took place was more divided in Guyenne than in Provence. New social patterns took shape differently in the two cities, but the trading class enjoyed success in both.

Freemasonry welcomed traders. Masons looked with approval on the openness, mobility, and cosmopolitanism of the trading class. In the lodges traders found a place where their vague longings as well as explicit demands for social recognition were accepted. In part this desire for social recognition was compensation for the social marginalization of economic affairs by the *royaume profond,* and in part it was also a response to the shattering of religious consciousness. This attraction has been corroborated by regional monographs such as Gérard Gayot's on Sedan and Charleville, social monographs such as Guy Chaussinand-Nogaret's brilliant analysis of the world of financiers and businessmen in Languedoc, and broader studies of Masonic recruitment in academic cities.

Freemasonry in Marseilles and Bordeaux was consistent with these hypotheses. There had long been a Masonic presence in both cities, since at least 1732 in Bordeaux and sometime between 1730 and 1740 in Marseilles. English and trader influence played a role in both cases, and some traders in both cities were affiliated with English and other foreign lodges. Finally, Masons in both cities came predominantly from the world of commerce: in Bordeaux there were some two thousand Masons, probably a third of whom were merchants or traders. In Marseilles there were more than a thousand, a good quarter of whom were in trade and another 20 percent in the navy. Finally, in both cases, the world of trade joined forces with its rival the nobility to oversee and if need be limit Masonic expansion, which threatened to devalue the distinction conferred on "the royal art." Thus, Freemasonry helped to integrate traders into society and taught them to accept the values of the new sociability.

In Marseilles traders triumphed in the academy as well as the lodges, achieving undeniable unity among the thirty or so who sat on the benches of the academy. In Bordeaux, however, traders created a cultural institution of their own, the museum, which, in opposition to the academy, quickly acquired influence over the culture and society of the city. An institution typical of the period 1775–1789, the museum of Bordeaux was founded in 1783 at the behest of an agent of the *intendance* and with the support of an active group of traders. It provided the city's elites with a new venue for cultural exploits. Here, however, the public would be able to measure the contribution of the "sterile class," the triumphant society of entrepreneurs and their clients: lawyers, engineers, architects, and enlightened clerics. In short, the museum served the open society that delighted in poetic celebration and practical pedagogy (mathematics and foreign languages), the reading of newspapers and reviews, and debates about luxury, civilization, science, and music. The difference between the academy and the museum was not just sociological; there was also a shift in sensibility that was central to trader culture, a shift that is clear in debates about Rousseauism, apologias for trade, and the commingling of a passion for nature with a Promethean enthusiasm for science and progress.

Our study of the marginality of traders in a culture dominated by the economic and social values of rural France has called attention to two convergences: one on the level of conduct and behavior, the other on the level of debate and theory. We have tried to understand how such a fundamental change in values should have come about, and how intellectual and practical exchange could have been arranged between "two dreams of commerce." We have also seen how closely two different societies were intertwined, a closeness that needs to be explored further on a different scale. To that end, we now turn our attention to the modern city, whose genesis was perhaps one of the fundamental forces for change.

6

❦〜❦〜❦

The City, Crucible
of Change

THE CLASH BETWEEN peasant France and the France of trade revealed the difference and superiority of the urban world. "The urban superstructure was a system perched upon, and explained by, the underlying peasant society, which was condemned to carry it on its shoulders," wrote Fernand Braudel.[1] In the eighteenth century this ancient relationship took on a new meaning, as once again the new was about to emerge from the old: within the fabric of urban France the features of an urban and industrial nation had begun to appear, even though persistent old hierarchies became entrenched and older cities maintained their preeminence.

The period has bequeathed to historians three main criteria for defining a city: architectural, legal, and demographic. (The relative importance of these criteria shifted over the course of the century.) Jaucourt alludes to all three in the *Encyclopédie,* in which we see that for a man of the Enlightenment, a city was first of all a matter of topography coupled with civil and military architecture, an "assemblage of a number of houses arranged by streets and enclosed by a common barrier ordinarily consisting of walls and moats. More precisely, a city is a space enclosed by walls, within which one finds various neighborhoods, streets, public squares, and buildings."[2]

What created the city, first and foremost, was its enclosure, which separated it from the rest of the world. This could be a physical barrier of walls and moats, once required as military defenses, or it could be defined by law. The Encyclopedist went on to enumerate various legal aspects of urban status, some defined by custom, others by the fiscal authorities. Within a city's limits the law was different: Jaucourt's focus accordingly shifts from topography to law.

The citizens of a city enjoyed certain privileges that rustics did not, and various institutions were required to see to it that these rules were enforced. Public law classified cities according to the extent of their privileges. For example, *villes abonnées* were cities in which the *taille* (tallage) was set at a certain annual sum: this was a fiscal privilege, which was an enormous benefit because it authorized cities to shift the tax burden onto the surrounding countryside. In topographical terms, this privilege was translated into boundary markers and tollhouses. A *ville d'arrêt* was a city whose inhabitants enjoyed the privilege of securing, without a formal court judgment, a warrant for the arrest and seizure of the property of any foreign debtor. This was an economic privilege (embodied in article 173 of the customary law of Paris, for example), which allowed urban businessmen to seize goods from their debtors, thus strengthening their hand in case of dispute and guaranteeing their economic autonomy. The list of privileges is a lengthy one: there were privileges for so-called *bonnes villes,* successors of the ancient communes recognized by the king as entitled to magistrates, juries, and *bourgeois; villes chartées,* recognized by charters of emancipation; *villes jurées,* with elected administrations and guilds run by wardens; and *villes de loi,* such as Lille in Flanders, which enjoyed special liberties and franchises. Two features stand out: first, city dwellers enjoyed a right of inspection that helped them manage their business affairs, and this right posed an obstacle to any extension of royal oversight; and second, citizens were as jealous of their city limits as they were of their fiscal, military, and economic privileges.

In the area of social representation, urban citizens enjoyed a variety of guarantees. Laws and practices were as varied as traditional cities themselves. In order to understand this variety, one has to be aware of the hierarchy that distinguished village from town *(bourg)* and town from city. Each type of city or town had a different function and fostered a different type of relationship between residents and inhabitants of the surrounding countryside. Cities were able to play a transformative role and to spread both cultural and economic aspects of the new civilization of trade only because they did not cut themselves off from the hinterland. City dwellers and peasants thought of themselves as different, and what they saw with their own eyes corroborated this belief. Some city folk envied the peasantry: "Happy is the peasant who knows how fortunate he is," Virgil had said. But everywhere the youthful energy of the enlightened city kindled enthusiasm for change.

City and country cannot be understood in isolation. Yet in the eighteenth century the relation between them was in the process of change: cities were bustling, fortunes were being made, and old prestige was on the wane. A primary reason for (and excellent index of) change was the growing size of the urban population. In Jaucourt's definition, population was the third fundamental criterion of urbanity (and what was novel about his definition was the way it moved from urban architecture to urban function). Urban growth worried both traditional administrators and new demographers; some, from Necker to the officials who conducted Napoleon's census, tried to specify the minimum population needed to constitute a city. At one time or another the figure ranged from 1,500 to 2,000. Such debates are interesting because they shed light on contemporary thinking. The debate on population paralleled the rethinking of the traditional idea of the city that took place in the second half of the eighteenth century, a rethinking that led to a more functional view of urban phenomena.[3]

Urbanization, Density, Population

How did the image of the city change over the course of the eighteenth century, and how did that change in image relate to the underlying reality? The map of urban France changed little: urban sites and contours had long been settled, and the last major wave of construction ended in the seventeenth century with the building of Versailles, the classical era's model of the new city; Richelieu, an abortive utopian dream of the cardinal's; Lorient, which flourished as the Compagnie des Indes prospered; Rochefort; and Sète, which lived on seafaring activities. Along the northeastern and eastern borders of France, the cities that Vauban had created along with some three hundred fortresses stagnated within their walls. The Enlightenment built few new cities, but it altered the status quo in many existing ones. The key problem of urban development was how to accommodate the growing population that came with economic change without sacrificing social stability. What encouraged people to move, what held them back, and what could be changed?

Counting People

Urban population figures are plentiful, but most are based on estimates rather than regular census data. City people were hard to count: this was one of their privileges, for the fiscal exemptions or *abonnements* that most cities enjoyed cast suspicion on any attempt to count the population. Urban France learned statistical rigor with difficulty, and administrative surveys invariably ran up against the suspiciousness of residents and the opposition of magistrates and notables. Census surveys supplanted estimates only at a relatively late date and in conjunction with projects of various kinds—military, administrative, political, economic—which were not always compatible. Still, the census figures from 1791 to 1806 do not prevent us from attempting to supplement earlier, inadequate data, whether based on estimates or calculated by demographers such as Montyon, Moheau, and the academic arithmeticians.

The history of urban demography is the history of a discipline that tried to evaluate law-like regularities in what it saw as a scientific manner despite a variety of social and political pressures.[4] The calculations, comparisons, and classifications in Moheau's *Recherches et considérations sur la population de la France* (1778), for example, yielded hard numbers that served as a basis for speculation on the laws of social progress. "The political machine cannot run smoothly, nor can administration be enlightened, in a country whose population is unknown." The future of both peasant France and urban France was at stake. To ponder either, one relied on actual counts (based on parish registers of baptisms, marriages, and deaths) as the basis for calculated extrapolations. The figures were published in economic journals and academic memoirs and used by the administration when, for example, it became necessary to convoke the Estates General.

"What is the number of inhabitants of the cities and countryside?" Moheau asked in the third question of his study. For our purposes we can safely ignore the debate about the paternity of the *Recherches:* Was the author Montyon, a philanthropic *intendant*, or his secretary Moheau, who accompanied him on his journeys? What interests us is the fact that the work was administrative in origin and yielded certain kinds of information:

> The inhabitants of cities and the inhabitants of the countryside constitute two different species of men. The former are more industrious and lead less unhappy lives. The latter are more robust and hardworking, more subject to custom, and have more children. Agriculture spreads and disperses men in the countryside; commerce and the arts concentrate them in the cities . . . Since agriculture requires more hands than any other kind of employment, all our provinces count a larger number of inhabitants in villages than in cities. But the superiority of their number is more or less marked according to the quantity and quality of manufactured goods, the facility and needs of commerce, the abundance of riches and variety of pleasures. Finally, it is of the essence of cities to recruit new citizens in the countryside and drain its population, although there is no corresponding desire to return that would drive the children of city dwellers to repopulate the countryside.[5]

Here, urbanity and rurality are contrasted both in terms of a complex, antagonistic definition (based on economic, social, and cultural considerations) and in a relation of exchange that is a factor in a larger social transformation. How was this long-term, steady, partially hidden population movement to be measured, given the threat it posed to stability in all its forms? Moheau followed his definition with examples: the *généralités* of Tours, Poitiers, and Alençon; Franche-Comté, Lorraine; the *généralités* of Rouen and La Rochelle; Flanders; the Artois. With the minimum population of a city taken to be 2,500, the proportion of the population living in cities varied from one-fifth to one-quarter depending on the region, but what these figures showed, even with their variability taken into account, was the growing conflict of interest between city and country. Hence, "after examining the population that is being absorbed by the cities, legislation should either encourage or halt further growth and promote either increase or decrease in the number of inhabitants."[6]

Other demographic studies corroborated these findings: in 1725, towns of more than 2,000 inhabitants accounted for some 4 million out of 24 million French subjects; in 1789 they accounted for more than 5 million out of nearly 29 million. Depending on the method of calculation, the urbanization rate ranged from 15 to 20 percent. On the eve of the Revolution, nearly one Frenchman in five lived in a city or small town.

From 1700 to 1750, urban growth remained slow as the countryside caught up with the cities and its population expanded. This was a period of "agricultural revenge" and the tail end of a depressed phase of the urban economy that began in the seventeenth century. But from 1740 until perhaps 1775, urban growth accelerated rapidly, after which it slowed again as cities felt the effects of the prerevolutionary crisis that marked the reign of Louis XVI.

These shifts can be related to two other sets of phenomena. The first of these was regional differentiation, which was accentuated by the urbanization of plains and valleys, of the developed regions of the north and east, and of the coastal regions, along with the overurbanization of southern France—phenomena that reflect geographic conditions and the influence of the past. Traditions of housing played a key role: southern cities stood out from cities elsewhere because of their strong traditions of sociability. Social and functional differences were also important because they established clear distinctions and separated cities into groups: the Paris basin extended its influence into Flanders, Alsace across the Rhine, and the cities of Normandy across the channel into England. Growth itself implied regionalization, because the larger the city, the larger the production and population basin on which it drew.

Second, urban growth was highly differentiated: stagnant cities co-existed with flourishing ones. In 1720 Marseilles, Toulon, Aix, Arles, and Avignon were ravaged by the plague, and afterward growth resumed at a different pace in each. Rouen grew slowly, as did Beauvais, Angers, and Chartres. Valenciennes, whose population was 19,000 under Louis XIV, had slipped to perhaps 18,000 under Louis XVI. Caen grew until 1775, after which expansion slowed. What did not change was the conception of urban power or the picture of the ideal city, which in this case was in harmony with the vision of traditional France. The source of urban power was not production but unearned income *(rentes)* and the administration; the city's power over its rural hinterland was mediated by commerce and taxes.[7] The beginnings of change were apparent in areas of dramatic growth, whether regular or irregular, including ports great and small such as Bordeaux, Le Havre, Marseilles, Nantes, Brest, Lorient, and Sète; industrial cities such as Saint-Etienne and Nîmes, which grew from a population of 20,000 in 1730 to 50,000 in 1789; great regional capitals such as Lyons, whose population exceeded 150,000; and of course Paris, which may have doubled in size from 400,000–500,000 inhabitants in 1700 to 700,000–800,000 under Louis XVI. A hierarchy developed among cities depending on whether the "urban motor" could accelerate sufficiently to attract people and goods.

The Urban Network and Standardization of Behavior

The urban network and hierarchy were highly stable. If one city was reclassified, the overall pattern did not change much, because it reflected long-standing equilibria and the relationship of cities to the all but static rural landscape. The geography of urban functions captures not only this relationship but also the relationship among zones of unequal development, trans-European trade patterns, and urban locations. The maps established by Bernard Lepetit show the changes that took place north of the Nantes-Lyons line as well as the relative backwardness of the south and southwest (except for port-related occupations). Nationally, three things stand out: the overwhelming importance of Paris, the more or less marked feebleness of the provincial capitals, and the flourishing of middle-sized cities (whose number increased from 65 in 1750 to 88 in 1780 and 95 in 1794). This may serve as a generalized demographic index of the increasing density of economic and cultural exchange. The primacy of Paris—with 7.6 percent of the urban population in 1750 but only 6.5 percent in 1790 (though unstable populations are drastically underestimated in these calculations)—diminished overall as well as in relation to the leading regional capitals: Bordeaux, Lille, Lyons, Marseilles, Nantes. This delay can be interpreted as marking the triumph of the kingdom of exchange over the *royaume profond,* the increase of revenue from urban commerce and industry as opposed to ground rents and tax income. The exchange economy surged into the lead over the monarchy's peasant-centered political economy, and a society open to the world replaced the enclosed territorial society of old.[8]

The advent of the open society established a system whose key variables were behavioral: increased migration into the cities intensified division of labor between cities and countryside. Cities grew, but in order to sustain themselves they needed a regular influx of men and women from all walks of life. In fact, as we can now see, things were not as simple as they once appeared: the relation between natural demographic factors (births and deaths) and social ones (migration rate) was complicated, influenced as it was by descriptions of the city as burial ground and sinkhole of poverty. The coin had two sides, but the dark side was not exactly the negation of the bright side: urban mortality was real, but what drew people to the cities was not reality but hope. The triumph of the urban can of course be read in the gap between the descriptive and the normative, a gap that is reflected in the "galloping statistics"[9] concerning urban population and economic development. In fact, it is much easier to estimate the influx of new residents than the outflow of both the native-born and former immigrants. Yet calculating these flows and relating them to birth and death rates is the only way to understand the new cultural relationship between villagers and city folk.

Urban Realities and Rural Hopes

In Caen, which has been studied by Jean-Claude Perrot, calculations of population changes due to natural causes and migration show that the city fell out of favor as rapidly as its fortunes had risen: between 1775 and 1790, when the population dropped from 40,858 to 37,795, departures accounted for six times as many lost residents as did the excess of the death rate over the birthrate. Over the course of the eighteenth century, moreover, the nature of migration changed. Initially it was young people who moved, while married couples and the elderly stayed where they were. Socially, moreover, most migrants were wage earners. This fact reflects both the influence of the labor market and the city's role in training apprentices for new tasks. By the end of the eighteenth century, when census figures showed that 51.8 percent of the population consisted of nonnative residents, migration clearly affected categories other than wage earners and small peasants from the *bocage* country: it affected all social and occupational groups and had its own motivations. Those who came to seek their fortunes in the city were bolder than those who stayed home as well as better educated and for the most part young, even though more than 20 percent of them were now over thirty (compared with just 6 percent a century earlier). Every year some of the newcomers left, mostly young women following their husbands or their abandoned children. But others left, too, mostly in the wake of failure but occasionally on account of success. Two conclusions can be drawn from this preliminary analysis. First, the cities that flourished were those that managed to hold on to their immigrants. This was true of Rouen,[10] Bordeaux,[11] Lyons,[12] and many other places. Second, those who left were not entirely equivalent to those who arrived: the urban dream did not always come true, but even when it did not, there is reason to believe that some part of it remained intact: those who departed left with new skills, judgments, and views of the world. By encouraging immigration, cities transformed the rest of the society.

The effects of immigration will become even clearer if we focus on a particular case: immigration from the Limousin to Paris, a small part of the overall influx into the capital. The Limousin immigrants formed an ill-defined, temporary group within the city's population. For our purposes such a group may be the most interesting of all, but it is not easy to study because Ancien Régime officials never analyzed it in detail. Newcomers to Enlightenment Paris rubbed shoulders with people from all parts of the social spectrum. Students mingled with the poor in the hospitals; military men sat next to functionaries; harried travelers sat down with idle tourists, wanderers, vagabonds, and rootless individuals. Repression of vagrancy intensified as the economy declined and demands for law and order began to be heard in the cities. At the same time, however, the undeniable growth of the population reminds us of the crisis years 1770–1790. Public opinion was aware of it, and so were the police, who surveyed the mounting peril with alarm.

Workers constituted a less agitated, more ordinary portion of this carefully scrutinized migrant population.[13] They were attracted to the capital by the wage differential: the same worker who could earn twenty-five sols per day in Limoges in 1750 could earn as much as two livres in Paris. At midcentury some ten thousand made the trip every year, and by 1790 the figure may have been as high as twenty thousand. Migration was spurred at the point of departure by scarcity of food and land and at the point of arrival by the need for skilled workers. They left home in groups, intending to stay for only a few months and finding lodging in furnished rooms kept by *marchands de sommeil,* or "sleep merchants." Hard times at home and a construction boom in Paris kept up the flow of migrant workers, who were not rootless individuals but people trying to help out their families. A mason from the Limousin who returned home from Paris could pay off his family's tax obligations and debts, marry, and augment his patrimony. People who owned small amounts of property were likely to leave home in search of temporary resources in order to hold on to the land needed to support and raise a family.

In migration there were risks, however: not everyone returned home.

There were also opportunities: many came home transformed, and some settled into new roles as craftsmen or small-time entrepreneurs. People came back from the city with more than just money in their pockets. They changed in other ways, which affected tastes and even customs. If as many as a quarter or even a third of urban immigrants picked up stakes again and returned home, it was not simply because they failed to make a go of it in the city. Such instability reflected the allure of freedom as well as the fear of poverty and crime. The problem for the historian is that the sources that tell us about this migration, sources produced by agencies concerned with the associated social problems, tell us more about crime than about expectations of cultural advantages ardently desired and painfully acquired. Immigrants lived in a social system that extended all the way from the point of departure to the point of arrival. On the way from his parish in the Limousin to Paris, the young mason's apprentice acquired new habits: he tasted new wines, saw new shows, and discovered a world in flux. All these novelties stayed with him even if he later returned to the provinces. The city taught him about freedom, initiating him into a new world of consumption and new kinds of social relations. Even if he was confined to a hospital or locked up in a jail, his experience changed him. The issue of punishment, of the appropriate sentence for various crimes, was of intense topical interest. In hard times, when cities were besieged by armies of the penniless, harried urban authorities had to contend with a chaotic situation. Their response was not always to exclude, to ward off a potential peril; philanthropy and charity sometimes welcomed those in need and offered them help in finding new homes. Cities were both a laboratory for public assistance and a breeding ground for poverty.

Those who came, whether to stay or to return home, had to learn how to behave in a new demographic setting and how to deal with a more complex set of social relations than they were used to. Recall the essential features of eighteenth-century urban demographics. First, the proportion of unmarried men and women was high, in part because cities attracted young people (particularly to work as domestic servants and unskilled laborers) and in part because of the disproportionate numbers of clergymen and other celibate groups. The age of marriage was relatively high everywhere, twenty-seven for women and twenty-nine for men, but immigrants in Lyons married even later than natives: they might not wait until their fortunes were made, but they did wait until they had "dowry in hand." In Nantes, Reims, and Rouen, prudence and calculation made headway as the century progressed; some notables set an example by marrying very young girls.

For everyone, the city multiplied the contraceptive effects of celibacy and delayed marriage. It also accelerated the spread of techniques such as coitus interruptus and other "dark secrets" of which confessors complained. Prostitutes, of whom there were more than forty thousand in Paris, risked using pessaries. Dominant groups took steps to plan their families and improve the upbringing of children, thereby setting an example if not establishing a norm. The urban birthrate was stabilized or even reduced: it was 32.5 per thousand in Bordeaux in 1788 but 39 in Lyons. In Rouen families had an average of four to five children in 1700 but only three to four by 1780. The decline in the birthrate matched the hierarchy of wealth and status. It also extended beyond the city walls, because geographic mobility, together with less common social mobility, facilitated cultural change. Infant mortality did not decline much, and the number of abandoned children increased (often resulting in unintended deaths). Together with other signs such as increased illegitimacy and frequency of broken families, especially among the urban poor, at least in Paris, these statistics show that the demographic situation was unstable and liable to change.

City ways were different from rural customs: infants were put out to nurse, for example. If women in Paris, Lyons, Reims, and Rouen gave up their infants, presumably temporarily, it was because they had a different conception of what it meant to live and work alongside their husbands. *Le Retour de nourrice,* painted by Greuze and engraved by Hubert, shows that bourgeois families had no compunctions about sending their children out to nurse, even though 40 percent of urban babies dispatched to live with their wet nurses never returned. Yet the painting was intended to be a picture of progress and optimism: innovations in parenting represented new opportunities for the urban bourgeoisie.[14] Although urban mortality rates remained high for people of all classes, things began to change in the eighteenth century. Changes of which few people dreamed when they left their native villages were becoming possible.[15]

The perception of new social relations therefore turned out to be of the utmost importance. The city seemed to be a good place from which to observe society and learn about the whole range of human relations. Louis-Sébastien Mercier made this point in his *Tableau de Paris:* "A man

. . . who knows how to think has no need to go beyond its [i.e., the city's] walls . . . He can learn about the entire human race by studying the individuals huddled together in this immense capital."[16] Although urban growth also meant difficulties and dangers, the city made social relations apparent to observers and residents alike. As in the village, newcomers learned the various value systems that people used to understand society. Urban society had its orders, of course: nobility, clergy, commoners. But the social fabric became increasingly complicated in the city, where daily life revealed the importance of alliances and reputation and the influence of talent and money. Fiscal classifications, which were rudimentary in the countryside, were more sophisticated in the society and familiarized people with the idea of wealth as an element of social status. In the city people of different conditions mixed, and everyone took note of the external marks of success, which no longer simply confirmed the ancient order of things. As a result, the prevailing value system changed. The complicated, confusing urban status hierarchy began to replace the simpler rural one. Meanwhile, the ancient "processional" representation of the French social hierarchy could still be seen on holidays.

The manner in which urban space was organized helped to change people's outlook. Two structures were emphasized. Occupational divisions were still reflected in street names as well as in work and recreational patterns. In addition, there was vertical stratification of living space, with the wealthy occupying the so-called noble floors of buildings and the poor relegated to garrets and basements. Rich and poor therefore met daily. It was not until the end of the century that horizontal segregation by neighborhood made its appearance, especially in Paris. This did not exclude concentrations of immigrants, which were also social groupings. Immigrants were not quick to blend into the population at large. Mixing jeopardized traditional allegiances, although other kinds of associations could be established. Nevertheless, the city offered access to a new culture, whose potential benefits depended on the migrant worker's energy and ambition.

From Functions to Culture

We still have to measure the psychological and social effects of these new urban social relations. For the first time in history, the old solidarity among those who lived off the land was challenged by new solidarities among those who lived on profits and wages. The speed with which people adapted to these new realities and the potential of urbanization to bring about change cannot be studied in isolation from the various sources on which urban life drew, along with its organization, history, and manner of inculcating social deference. Change depended on a city's ability to enter in one way or another the circuit of economic growth.

Two models will help us not so much to explain the extraordinary diversity of urban France as to orient our thinking. Consider, then, two ideal types: the "Ancien Régime city," defined by a wall and privileges and home to rentier notables, and the "commercial city," the city of the future, characterized by economic development and its associated instabilities. Obviously the two were not different in every respect: there was of course a certain continuity of urban function. In the eighteenth century, however, the growing intensity of economic activity gave rise to a new kind of urban life. Indeed, this history can be interpreted as the "genesis" of the modern city, as Jean-Claude Perrot showed in his remarkable study of Caen.

Historians have noted two important developments. First, there was a shift in the analysis and description of urban life from terms of superiority and privilege to terms of role and function. Space was henceforth organized not in terms of historically justified privileges but in relation to activities that integrated urban and rural life at various levels. Second, instability was frankly recognized. What counted was not the founding event, whether repeated or not, but success or failure. The new urban image emerged at the same time as the economic concept of urban functions. Between the two the relation was, as one might expect, dialectical.[17]

The Continental and Maritime Models and the *Bonnes Villes*

The ideology of the capital dominated representations of the relations between city and country and city and city. The urban tradition was essentially based on the idea of the city as a gathering place for landed elites, a place for the exercise of power, and a nexus of social interaction. Call this the "continental model" of the city, in which the role of the city was to transmit power outward from the central authorities; in this role cities played an important part in the development of the European nation-state. Despite the advent of a competing "maritime commercial model," the continental model continued to define the urban hierarchy and the idea of interurban relations. Cantillon has shown how cities can be classified in this respect on the basis of three variables: the presence of landowners, spending their income from the land in the urban setting; the presence of magistrates and other agents of the central government; and the presence of entrepreneurs and wage earners engaged in production and trade to meet the needs of consumers. The fate of any given city was determined by the distribution of these various sources of revenue, which were also sources of power. Using factor analysis, we can compare major cities on the basis of institutions reflecting various types of activity. In cities of the Ancien Régime type we expect to find *intendance, subdélégations,* courts of justice, administrative offices, ecclesiastical institutions, and military garrisons; in commercial cities we expect to find schools and cultural institutions (an index to the circulation of knowledge and information), post offices, shipping offices, facilities for river and ocean shipping, consulates, chambers of commerce, fairs, and businesses of various kinds.

Having examined these variables for a hundred French cities, Bernard Lepetit was able to show that the urban network was organized in terms of functional complementarity rather than stark opposition between continental and maritime cities. Often one finds aspects of both models: most of the twenty-eight territorial capitals were also local market towns. The analysis confirms the existence of two models of urbanization, sometimes in combination (as in Paris and Bordeaux), sometimes not (as in Marseilles, which had neither a *parlement* nor an *intendance*). Note, moreover, that manufacturing was not a key variable in determining the urban hierarchy: it was a factor in increasing economic specialization and in attracting additional population, but a dependent variable determined most notably by a dynamic commercial economy.

At the top of the urban hierarchy stood thirty or so governmental and commercial metropolises, all cities of twenty thousand or more inhabitants, with the exception of Poitiers, Perpignan, and La Rochelle. These thirty-odd cities, which covered the entire country, including central France, were quite diverse in character: they included Montpellier, Rouen, Toulouse, Besançon, Lille, Lyons, Strasbourg, Aix, Nancy, and Orléans. What earned them their status was the way in which France had grown, by progressive annexation of new territory to the original kernel of the kingdom. As a result, the old urban hierarchy had survived a series of historical, economic, and social changes.

The base of the urban pyramid consisted of a hundred or so cities in which the tertiary sector predominated: administrative and cultural institutions and trade (as opposed to production) were central. Territorial administration meant success in other areas as well. What distinguished these cities from the metropolises at the top of the hierarchy was that they administered smaller regions. On the urban map we find an unequal density of these smaller regional centers: one group clustered around Paris, from Châlons to Amiens and Chartres to Beauvais; another, oriented toward the south, penetrated the Massif Central via the Loire and Allier and included Nevers, Riom, Moulins, and Clermont; a third reached into the southwest. In the east and south, Ancien Régime–type cities were rare, because here the logic was one of *bonnes villes* attached to the royal domain. These were *pays d'élection* rather than *pays d'Etats,* in which the cities were centers of royal power and as such dominated by royal institutions. What was novel about the eighteenth century was that it imposed a logic of change on these areas of "solidified time." We caught a glimpse of this earlier when we looked at urbanization rates and regional distributions. During the eighteenth century, the relative importance of Paris decreased while the great multifunctional commercial metropolises triumphed. At the same time there was confirmation of the role of many smaller cities whose development and prosperity were linked to the state, "consumer cities" as opposed to "producer cities."[18]

Thus, the presence of administrative agencies exerted a strong influence on urban development. The administration did not compete with commerce, however, and in the early stages of commercial development even encouraged it. It is therefore difficult to define a completely satisfactory typology of the total or even the active population in terms of social differentiation. Over the past few decades historians have looked at tax records and notarial archives to evaluate the number of people in each social group and estimate their wealth and ability to pay taxes. Nevertheless, we do not yet possess sufficiently homogeneous data for the hundred-odd cities that constitute the urban network to allow us to understand the relation between socioprofessional structure and growth, which did not so much destroy the older network of interurban relations as superimpose a new one on it. Growth also made urban institutions themselves less stable, more permeable to mobility, and therefore more difficult to evaluate.

Within the urban network we find two types of social organization, cities in which the degree of segregation was low, and cities in which it was high. Cities of the former type tended to be smaller administrative towns. In places like Guérande and Châteaudun, Guingamp (in Brittany) and Tulle, social differences existed but within relatively narrow limits: there were neither too many rich nor too many poor. Nor were differences of wealth reflected in residential patterns. The hierarchy was defined by relationships with the nobility and clergy and by networks of patronage. In cities where the population was growing and where social and economic differentiation, reflected in the proliferation of socioprofessional categories, was high, social relations and residential patterns were more complex and status differences increased. In cities dominated by administrative institutions and where economic activity was weak, the privileged classes and the rentier bourgeoisie dominated. Examples included Châlons-sur-Marne and Valence, to take two academic towns notorious for "the indolence of [their] traders and manufacturers." In cities where the bourgeoisie was more energetic and aggressive, where, for example, the "*Verlag* system" flourished and merchants were bent on extending their city's influence, more resources were available. This made the city more attractive, but the hierarchy of notables was such that new and old business activities clashed. Dominated groups became caught up in shifting but confining circuits of dependence where the iron law of wages and profits was in effect. At the very top of the urban hierarchy, dominating all other cities, were the great metropolises, the nodal points of all the lower-level networks. Here all the social hierarchies coexisted: ecclesiastical, judicial, economic, and administrative. And then as now, Paris dominated everything. To illustrate how all this worked, I shall focus on four examples: Ussel, Angers, Caen, and Lyons. But one could just as easily cite any number of other examples from the rich literature about provincial cities.[19]

Ussel, Angers, Caen, and Lyons: From Stalemate to Progress

Ussel was the center of the world for people who lived in its corner of lower Limousin. "Lo païs d'Ussé," as this region of mountains cut by streams was known in the local patois, revolved around the city, which was linked to a host of surrounding towns and villages. With its tottering ramparts, beautiful churches, two convents (Ursulines and Recollects), one- and two-story houses, narrow streets, shops, stalls, cellar-entrepôts, inns and taverns, Ussel was Jerusalem to hardworking shepherds and pastors. It drew people from twenty miles around—a distance that meant a day's walk via rudimentary footpaths. An influx of men (33 percent of marriages involved men from outside the city) and women (18 percent) compensated for deaths and departures. The city employed its new citizens in stores and workshops: there were forty-six small businesses whose inventories seldom exceeded a thousand livres. Neither commerce nor craft work sustained an economy dynamic enough to stimulate a large volume of trade. Merchants served as distributors of agricultural produce. They sold grain, livestock, wine, wax, and wool and imported goods of all kinds for those who could afford them, especially wines and luxury items. But the volume of trade was not large, and what drew people into the city was the work for craftsmen created by the consumption of noble and bourgeois notables.

The social hierarchy was defined in part by land: the city controlled 30 percent of the farmland in the *sénéchaussée*. Tax rolls show that different social groups owned roughly equal amounts of land but that nobles and bourgeois enjoyed a marked advantage in income because their land included pastures. Income and status also influenced the social hierarchy. At the bottom of the ladder were tenants who rented their homes and usually owned no land, day laborers without hope of advancement, and domestic servants, some of whom were clever and enjoyed certain advantages. In the middle were merchants and artisans who had to pay the tax known as the *vingtième* on their gross income, which ranged from nine to three hundred livres, two-thirds above twenty livres. And at the top were the notables, the clergy with benefices, the noble magistrates associated with the courts of the *sénéchaussée*, a small group of professionals (doctors, surgeons, notaries), and eleven bourgeois families, of whom the upper crust aped the manners of the five families of the *noblesse de robe,* who did not mingle with the bourgeoisie. Such was the society of this stagnant backwater town, which slumbered on undisturbed throughout the century. With 491 households in 1715 and 409 in 1775, Ussel was the very type of the "Ancien Régime city," not totally closed to the outside world but not really open either, and barely touched by growth.[20]

With Angers we move to a larger scale but find a city no less somnolent or parasitic, a city in hibernation. In 1770 it was found to have 25,000 citizens (16,879 of whom lived inside the walls). The city maintained an active if predatory relationship with a prosperous agricultural region. Boats and barges plying the Loire and the Maine brought produce from the rich farming areas to the west and south. External mobility was limited (grooms in only 25 percent of marriages and brides in only 10 percent came from outside the city), as was upward mobility, while downward mobility was unknown (or at any rate unverifiable). The city was growing slowly at the end of the eighteenth century, with perhaps as many as 27,000 to 30,000 people at the time of the Revolution (but this was 5,000 less than in 1650). The capital of Anjou had little to do with industry. The muslin, stockings, and knit goods that had replaced the fabrics of the seventeenth century did not make it a great textile center. Sugar refineries survived thanks to provincial markets, and by 1789 there were as many as four, but Angers was caught in a squeeze between Nantes and Orléans. Slate quarries languished for want of entrepreneurs. Development efforts (spurred by Pierre Boreau and Danton Moreau) that affected all sorts of businesses bogged down. There was no shortage of cash, but wealthy people were anxious and preferred the security of real estate and fixed-income investments. The *receveur général des finances* of Tours apparently had every reason to offer this judgment: "The residents of Angers prefer the indolence in which they were raised to the diligence and hard work required for major undertakings and bold speculation. Short of energy [the word was new at the time], the current generation is vegetating as did the generation that preceded it and as will the generation to follow."

The society of the city reflected this assessment. Among the 21,567 inhabitants counted in the census of 1769, the active work force of 9,371 included a substantial number of domestics (25 percent). Most workers were employed by small shops making either textiles or clothing, yet spinners found themselves in a precarious situation. There was also a fair number of notables, including bourgeois rentiers and professionals, minor nobles, and clergymen. The tax burden on the lower and middle levels of taxpayers was heavy: 78 percent of the assessed paid less than twenty livres yet bore nearly half of the total tax burden. The city worked primarily for itself and secondarily for the region. The tone was set by well-to-do bourgeois and nobles who lived modest but regular lives with one foot in the country and the other in the city. Many spent a part of the year living on their estates, from which they derived an appreciable portion of their income in cash or in kind. Overshadowing all of this was the clergy, with its churches, bishopric, convents, monasteries, canons, schools, seminaries, and university. Angers was a clerical city, which over the centuries had evolved a tranquil, stable way of life based on ecclesiastical privilege and tradition.[21] Its calendar was primarily the church calendar, with holidays marked by the ringing of bells and the spectacle of religious processions. If Angers had a history in the eighteenth century, it was a history of missing the significant changes that marked the century as one of openness to the outside world.

In short, Angers was a model of the sleepy mid-sized city of which one could easily cite dozens of other examples. Its officeholders, landowners, nobles, bourgeois, and clergymen led comfortable lives, but the bulk of the population had at best a dreary existence, living precariously on the edge.[22] Yet the memoirs of François-Yves Besnard show how it was possible for at least one man living in this environment to broaden his cultural ken.[23] Born in 1752, he was in his thirties when he discovered how much the world was changing outside this closed provincial society. The son of a wealthy merchant and farmer, Besnard had trained for the clergy at a time when customs were stable and fashions changed slowly. Yet already Angers, though barely affected by economic growth elsewhere, was gradually transforming people who in one way or another came into contact with the winds of change.

Those winds also blew in Caen, though not steadily. Surrounded by fertile farmland, Caen was a city of many artisans and a bustling port, whose population grew from 26,500 in 1700 to 40,858 in 1775, only to decline somewhat thereafter. It stood somewhere between hibernation and openness. Its stability was abetted by its domination of the surrounding countryside, which supplied most of its needs for food. From produce to wheat and meat to drink, the Caen region proved to be a Norman cornucopia. Bread was never in short supply, and indeed almost always in excess of what the city needed. The *octroi* records show that supplies flowed in from a number of different areas, and merchants earned handsome profits. Drugs, groceries, dry goods, sugar, coffee, fabrics, and luxury items came from Le Havre and Rouen, while many less costly goods were purchased from suppliers along the banks of the Loire and as far off as the border with Brittany:

This was a region in which industrial products were traded more than foodstuffs, and it is not surprising that a modest urban commercial demand made itself felt, facilitated by the existing commercial network for textiles and already proven by the periodic fairs in Guibray and Caen. Indeed, it was predictable that these marginal, composite products, for which demand was quite elastic, would already give rise to a commercial structure similar to the industrial economy in which the city ceased to be what Loesch classically described as a purchasing center surrounded by a continuous supply belt and became instead part of a loose network of trade centers and axes of exchange.[24]

The city, situated at the center of its own food supply, was thus able to afford a welcome to industry, which came in four waves: luxury fabrics, caps and bonnets, linen, and finally lace. Each new wave brought its share of entrepreneurs, who were almost immediately replaced by others. The conditions necessary to attract labor were all present: there was a decent supply of capital, and except at the end of the period, the economic climate was generally favorable. Of course the very agricultural richness of the region was not without difficulties. It did not provide an adequate supply of raw materials for the textile industry, since there was more money to be made in supplying food. The success of agriculture in the region drew capital and a portion of the labor supply. Investment in land therefore yielded good profits, but it dampened economic development.[25] Despite calls for innovation by local economists, Caen was slow to awaken; initiative came in waves. And the local economists being Physiocrats, their predilection was of course to invest in land. But there were also administrators, a few traders, lawyers, and engineers who became involved in both improving the economy and thinking about the consequences of change such as usury and pauperism. The focus of their thought shifted from the rural economy not to the industrial economy but to questions of moral economy and economic philosophy. In Caen the guilds did not impede change. It was the culture of the city itself that posited land as the primary value and preached caution, inaction, and suspicion of risk.

The social hierarchy reinforced this tendency: it was dominated by the nobility and rentiers, a small but active group of traders, and a fair number of artisans and shopkeepers who had done well supplying local needs. Between 1750 and 1760, the number of people working was only 8,932, compared with 20,000 who were idle (including rentiers). Throughout France the working population averaged 37 percent of the total population. The figure for Caen was lower (32 percent of the population was active in 1792 and only 28 percent in 1760), primarily because of the concentration there of the idle rich. The gap between those with economic capital and those with intellectual capital grew wider owing to the development of a semi-proletariat of wage earners paid by the job. The city employed laborers drawn from the surrounding countryside under "the impression that the only possibility was to hold their own" rather than to invest in growth.[26]

Circulation and trade not only stimulated economic development but also encouraged architectural innovation. This had a profound impact on the city, which became an instrument of instruction, a source of information that changed the people who lived or came to do business in it. It also exacerbated conflicts of interest and antagonism between professional and cultural groups. Utilitarian values began to take hold even before the transformation of society by the industrial age. New demographic factors emerged, and attitudes toward space changed. People waited longer to get married. Hygiene and medicine began to have an impact on daily life in Caen as elsewhere. The city's historian notes the importance of the city as a cultural mediator in linking economic change to demographic evolution.

With Lyons we come to the summit of the urban pyramid: 97,000 inhabitants in 1700, 146,000 in 1785, with a notable acceleration after 1750. With support from outside, the growing city drew population primarily from the parishes of its *généralité* and to a lesser extent from beyond. This dramatic growth was countenanced and supervised by the authorities. Necessity imposed its laws. The silk factories and related industries of Lyons required two quite different types of worker: male apprentices who would someday replace the master craftsmen in their specialties, and female workers, girls and women, whose participation in the silk trade, where their contribution was essential, was not subject to regulation. The hiring of apprentices had a direct bearing on the future of the sons of the master craftsmen of Lyons. Lyons had become the European silk capital. Its prosperity depended on the market for luxury goods, and this depended in part on finding talented designers and in part on changing fashions. Unskilled peasants had to serve a long apprenticeship, and they also had to compete for jobs with the sons of well-to-do artisans and burghers eager for work in Lyons's better ateliers.

Newcomers to Lyons settled down and got married. The proportion of immigrants varied with type of work: only 40 percent of ordinary silk workers were born in the city, compared with 80 percent of master *fabricants* and 75 percent of traders. Unmarried young women came to work as servants, which was a dangerous profession, and were continually replaced, as the records of the Hôtel-Dieu indicate. Lyons was thus a city with a mobile population, and that mobility was a response to economic demand. It was primarily driven by a desire to settle down, a hope of trading rural misery for a somewhat better life in the city, or by the idea that more was possible in the city. Louis Tolozan, the last *prévôt des marchands,* was the son of a man from the Dauphiné and was himself ennobled after the birth of his own son. It was thus possible, if rare, to rise to nobility in just two generations. But what was important was the amplitude of the movement and the fact that by the end of the century there were more immigrants than native Lyonnais in nearly all strata of society. The total number of immigrants, four-fifths of whom came from the Lyonnais, Bugey, and the Dauphiné, may have exceeded 120,000, and even more people may have left the city than arrived. This turnover had an important cultural consequence: populations of diverse backgrounds lived together in the city and its streets and houses.

This melting pot effect can be seen in the data for one street, the rue de la Barre, from a late eighteenth-century census. A tavern at the head of the street was kept by two vintners from Millery. The next shop belonged to a used-clothing dealer from the Dauphiné. The landlord, who lived on the entresol, had come to Lyons from Bugey sixty years earlier. Proceeding up the staircase, one met a man from Franche-Comté married to a Swiss woman, a metal turner from Bugey, a carter from Saint-Etienne, day laborers from various villages in the Lyonnais, a hairdresser from Nevers, a cabinetmaker from Vesoul, a mason from Auvergne, and a peddler from Guéret. On the fifth floor lived a hatmaker from the Lyonnais, a craftsman from Forez, and another hatmaker from the Dauphiné.

Thirty-six households and only six natives of Lyons! This mixing of the population turned the city into a place where anything could happen. Despite the reshuffling, however, the cards were not always equitably distributed. Tax records reveal the growing gap between poor and rich neighborhoods. Notarial records disclose widening social disparities: day laborers, domestics, and women constituted the bottom 15 to 20 percent; silk workers made up the next 25 percent; artisans about a third. The remaining 20 to 25 percent consisted of wealthy and titled notables, traders, magistrates, professional men, and ecclesiastics. The average *capitation* was two to three livres for the first three groups, nine livres for the artisans, and fifty livres for the notables.

Factories, ateliers, shops, and trading rooms employed many citizens of Lyons. Because the city depended so heavily on trade, this diverse population was necessary. More than two-thirds of the total population (and a higher proportion of the working population) made its living directly from trade. Yet the social hierarchy also reaffirmed traditional privileges: the nobility led all other groups in both income and expenditure. In many respects it remained the group to emulate, despite the fact that many titles in Lyons were of recent origin and many nobles were connected either directly or through marriage to the world of commerce. In a city that lived on business, prosperity deepened the gap between the wealthy minority and the masses of poor workers. Within each specialty, master craftsmen and others who controlled the promotion of journeymen grew wealthy. In manufacturing, stable wages meant increased profits for merchants. Because of this bourgeois monopoly, Lyons society was largely closed despite the rapid turnover of population. The bourgeois economy and class society became established in Lyons through a process different from that which we saw at work in a growth-oriented Ancien Régime city such as Caen. Yet here as elsewhere, the crucial change was the transformation of peasants into city dwellers.[27]

To sum up, let us consider once more the relationship between city and countryside—a relationship of solidarity as well as conflict. The exploitation of rural society was at once the motor of development, without which nothing could be done, and the brake on that same development. The old bonds between city and country endured and continued to influence behavior, even as literature made fun of the rustic and bestowed nobility on the city dweller. The urban calendar continued to mark the wheat and grape harvests, despite the city's walls. Even with those walls, the city invaded the country every day and vice versa. The closing of the gates, which forced men such as the young Jean-Jacques Rousseau to spend the night outside, reflected continuing anxiety and a determination to control entries and exits. The stasis of the countryside gradually succumbed to the expansion of proto-industry and commerce, while the very existence of the city depended on the productive capacity of the countryside (agricultural at first, industrial later). The city drew its growing population from the rural population, and complaints about this were heard only in hard times, when vagabondage was prohibited. At the same time, however, urban charity and wealth attracted vagabonds. Thus the city simultaneously fabricated failure and success. It antagonized as well as attracted. Some new arrivals married and settled down, others failed to marry and left. Economists have translated such phenomena into their own jargon: "pull factor" and "push factor." Employment and adaptation were one possible outcome, unemployment and deviance were another.

Unlike rural France, urban France was both a buyer and a seller. Cities owned part of the countryside and helped themselves to part of the peasant's income. The rest returned in the form of wages and advances to the countryside, but not before the city deducted taxes from the amount available for redistribution. Those taxes financed facilities and roads, but the countryside paid a disproportionate share for these infrastructural developments. Rural labor paid for the progress of nonrural France. The city-country relationship was one of growing imbalance and unequal exploitation on the one hand and reduced inequalities and economic and cultural development on the other hand. One cannot neglect the stimulus effect of urban consumption, which made it possible to break out of the circle of stagnation. The demand for goods from Paris and the regional metropolises helped to transform the rural economy, diversify taste, and spur further demand for more sophisticated products. The urban network was where it all began, before towns and villages were affected. The cities also gave rise to processes of acculturation about which I shall have more to say later on.

Features of Urban Change

If the city was effective in transforming human beings, that was because it offered a new kind of space for living and culture and a new way of organizing life. The city had its own dimensions, its own rhythms, its own sense of the normal and abnormal. Its principal characteristic was that people lived in close proximity and became mutually involved with one another. Hence the cities fostered a range of new forms of sociability that allowed individuals to enter into discussion with their fellows. City dwellers became estranged from the countryside and from nature: as populations grew, buildings proliferated and city limits expanded, the pace of life changed, and people lost touch with nature, plants, and animals. As the countryside receded, people began to imagine it in a new way, and the relation of city to countryside was stood on its head. But this happened only after the urban way of life had come to be seen as superior to the rural way because less dependent on hard labor and less impervious to change. The city meant development. It was a nerve center where energies for transforming the material, spiritual, and intellectual worlds came together: "The air of the city makes you free!" In the eighteenth century three things lent credence to this ancient belief: the city's cultural advantages, attested to by its taste for reading; a shift in the literary image of the city from an ancient ideal of civilization to a more functional, and at the same time more controversial, representation; and the perpetuation of old municipal political practices that provided an arena in which new conflicts could emerge.[28]

The City and the Press

Earlier I discussed the growth of the rural readership. In provincial cities as well as Paris, reading made still more rapid progress. Schools were better in the cities, and it was also easier for people to learn how to read outside of school. Cities harbored a public of virtual readers, people who did not buy books or read assiduously but who became accustomed to reading printed matter of various kinds readily accessible in an urban setting. Scholars have for too long focused on book reading and neglected other forms of printed matter associated with a range of social and cultural practices. What organized the circulation and appropriation of printed matter (which in the eighteenth century proceeded at an accelerated pace) was the central tension between private activities and the definition of collective spaces and customs. Over the course of the century the equilibrium between the two shifted. Two different styles of reading emerged, one individualized, the other related to social intercourse in the family, at the workplace, or in literary societies. City dwellers not only had greater access to printed matter than did country people but also through reading learned about various possibilities for social change.

Private Ownership of Books

Numerous studies, for the most part based on estate inventories, allow us to measure the increase in book ownership, although what the indices tell us is not always clear. Take for example the percentage of estates including at least one book: in the cities of western France (Angers, Brest, Caen, Le Mans, Nantes, Quimper, Rennes, Rouen, Saint-Malo) it was 33.7 percent in the eighteenth century, compared with 22 percent in Paris in 1750. How can we explain that fewer than a quarter of Parisians owned at least one book at a time when a far higher percentage of provincials could make the same claim? It may be that the Parisian notaries who compiled estate inventories were more blasé about books, or it may be that Paris had already moved to a culture in which books were just one form of printed matter among others: broadsheets, lampoons, signs, and posters. Ownership of books increased but not steadily: in the west the rate was the same in 1788 as in 1728, namely, 35 percent. It varied, moreover, with the extent of transformation of the urban population and level of literacy. In the eighteenth century the culture of print jumped one major hurdle, but its subsequent history was not without setbacks.

In addition to inequalities between cities and periods, there were also inequalities of condition. In Paris in 1700, the proportion of book ownership was 13 percent for wage earners, 32 percent for magistrates, and 26 percent for nobles of the sword. By the second half of the century these figures had risen to 35, 58, and 53 percent, respectively. Two rules with few exceptions governed this growth. The first rule was that the higher the average wealth of a given social group, the greater the percentage of its members who owned books. And the second was that within each group, book ownership again varied with wealth. These rules were corroborated in Paris, Lyons, and the west of France. Books made deep inroads everywhere, reaching ordinary workers and artisans. At the same time, the average size of book collections increased. There were more readers, more homes with a single book, and larger libraries. The number of texts on sale also increased, a change that was not without effects on the ways in which people read.

Another aspect of urban practice in this period was a shift in the reading habits of different sociocultural groups. Take the urban clergy. There were important differences between Paris and the provinces as to size of collections and above all range of contents. The overall homogeneity of clerical reading was a result of religious teaching. That teaching was in turn dictated by a program of reform, which in Paris had had to compromise with other traditions. Parisian canons and priests were less conservative than their provincial counterparts. Noble privilege also existed in this area, but it tolerated numerous infractions for those who were less wealthy, younger sons, and widows. What is striking everywhere is the strong contrast between the *noblesse de robe* and the *noblesse d'épée* in regard to reading. Over the course of the century, the size of book collections increased for both groups but especially for the magistrates, although their rivals later sought to make up the ground they had lost. A gap remained, however, a gap that was reinforced by differences in content with respect to religious and historical matters. Female bourgeois readers also exhibited differences depending on whether they belonged to the world of professionals or to the world of trade. In the former case professional books dominated, but a growing number of collections included works of history, plays, and novels. In the latter group, books on commerce and economics were collected for business purposes, while novels, poems, and travel literature fed the need for escape. Among the lower classes works of religion were most prevalent, particularly where there was only one book in the house, although signs of broader tastes can be found in Paris, Lyons, and the urban west. What counted most of all was the accumulation and comparison of different styles and choices. Reading became a regular and familiar practice.

Public Access and Practical Changes

In the city even people who did not own books had greater access to reading matter than in the country. One could read a book without owning it, and institutions and practices that made this possible proliferated in the eighteenth century. Books could be borrowed from friends and relatives and often passed through many hands. We have evidence for this in correspondence of the period and indeed in libraries themselves, which often contained more than one copy of a book in order to facilitate loans. Public libraries served an even broader public. A list of these may be found in the *France littéraire* for 1784: Paris led the way with eighteen collections, primarily religious but some secular as well. Some twenty-odd cities had at least one public library: in Lyons the *collège* had one, in Rouen the academy, in other cities a convent or monastery. The opening of major religious collections such as that of Sainte-Geneviève in Paris further encouraged reading. So did the libraries of major collectors, for whom the king set an example, and the civic spirit of those who bequeathed their private libraries to municipal institutions. Lyons, for example, inherited the collections of Aubert, Brossette, and Adamoli.

Libraries served mainly men of letters. They were supplemented by a second network of *cabinets de lecture* and bookshops with "reading rooms" where browsers could read without purchasing in the hope that reading would eventually create new clients. Other reading rooms were created by private initiative, especially in mercantile towns. People who paid a small fee to join could use these rooms to read, discuss books, and exchange information in an informal setting. By the end of the Ancien Régime such reading rooms were quite common, usually found in conjunction with cultural societies of one kind or another. People avid for reading matter and learning got together and created them. These were the kind of readers who rented books by the day and virtually devoured best-sellers such as Rousseau's *Héloïse* and who also borrowed newspapers and magazines and read texts aloud to others. The breadth of this movement led some people to reflect on ways to reform public reading. Two reforms were frequently proposed. One was that some sort of oversight be imposed on reading, which was proliferating for better and for worse. We find this, for instance, in Louis-Sébastien Mercier's utopian writing. The other was a call for a sacred repository in which all books would be collected. We find echoes of this in the plans of architects such as Boullée. Such a library-temple was envisioned as occupying a central place in each city, where knowledge would be available to anyone who wanted it.

Urban reading practices changed as the availability of books increased. Reading was an intimate, private act, depicted in paintings by artists such as Fragonard, Baudouin, and Hubert Robert as a symbol of intense investment. Reading became a symbol in portraiture, where it was generally represented as an activity to be enjoyed in comfort and leisure. In contrast to the gratuitousness and frivolity of urban ways, reading was a serious matter in which readers participated actively; it changed their thinking. So said Rousseau to his readers and correspondents, male and female alike. In opposition to this view, writers and artists such as Nicolas Rétif de la Bretonne and Jean-Baptiste Greuze proposed scenes in which a mediator, usually the father in a rural household, relays the content of the printed work to illiterate or semiliterate listeners. This representation offered a transparent, communal counterimage to the representation of urban reading as a silent, individual, elitist practice.

In the cities countless intermediaries gave voice to the written word and caused it to circulate among the populace: songsters, poster hangers who read their texts out loud before posting them for all to see, and authors of the seditious texts that appeared in abundance in times of political and religious crisis. Even societies of the wealthy and learned made room for public readings. Texts were read aloud in homes as well as in academic meetings and friendly gatherings. City people read collectively in workshops, apartments, and public places. There was a growing volume of circumstantial writing, pious and utilitarian images, broadsheets, almanacs, and yearbooks to choose from. The reading public grew and accommodated new readers who read relatively little. Meanwhile, institutions proliferated. Over time, however, printed matter began to circulate from the cities into the countryside, so that the difference between the two diminished. The effects of this wider diffusion may have been contradictory: on the one hand, it made it possible to teach new disciplines in matters of religion, manners, and work, but on the other hand, it opened people's minds, bringing them new information or imaginative fiction that allowed them to escape from the dull daily round. In so doing, printed matter lost its symbolic value even as it gained in utilitarian efficacy. As printed material became more common, ways of appropriating it tended to become more and more differentiated as people sought new forms of distinction.

Images of the City, Metaphors of Change

The increase in urban reading also points up changes in representations of the city both in the culture at large and in economic thinking. Marx saw the fate of Western society as bound up with the division of labor between city and country: "The division of labor within a nation first entails the separation of industrial and commercial labor on the one hand from agricultural labor on the other, and this leads to the separation of the city from the countryside and to an opposition of their interests."[29] This process separated cultural practices as much as forms and spaces of labor. The eighteenth century witnessed a shift from a cultural discourse to a functional one. The transformation of rhetorical images and themes reflects the degree to which public opinion saw the city and its functions in terms of a new interpretive framework.[30]

The seventeenth-century city was above all a locus of civilization, warmed by the breath of spirit. According to literary sources (which expressed themselves in the same terms as administrators), the city was a mirror, a microcosm in which what mattered was beautiful architecture, pleasant society, and erudite learning. From the Renaissance on, rhetoric of all orders received exalted advancement—collective as well as individual—through urbanity. Enlightened minds lived in cities, to whose revival they gave voice. The words "pagan" and "peasant" frequently referred to the same backwardness. By the end of the seventeenth century, however, the old unified cultural vision was already giving way to a multiplicity of points of view: the city was a variety of histories, a plurality of destinies. It was an economic center as well as a place of awakening. Definitions proliferated.

Men of letters and scholars began to focus on themes relating to urban functions. In Caen, Father Charles Gabriel Porée, the brother of Voltaire's teacher, wrote for the *Nouvelles littéraires* a *Discours sur la naissance et le progrès des sciences* in 1744, in which he developed an analogy between the beauty and symmetry of the urban organism and the canons of the human body. A city was supposed to possess the "beauty of utility," and to make cities attractive without harmful, corrupting side effects would, it was argued, take thinking. At the same time Rousseau was already mulling over ideas that he would develop later in *La Nouvelle Héloïse:* he coupled an apology for the city of modest size, close to nature, with a critique of corrupting capitals such as Paris, which were undermining morals and destroying the human race. Echoes of these changes can be heard in the poetry submitted to a competition organized by the University of Caen, a contest that had counterparts in the academies. From 1666 to 1792 a thousand poems were submitted: 25,000 lines representing 278 authors, mostly (71 percent) from Caen, expressed the attitudes of the well-to-do classes, which had been restructured by the process of urban development. Until 1740 Caen identified with Athens and saw itself as the capital of the Muses. After that date a variety of new themes began to appear: the government of the city, its public works projects, its growing prosperity, the obligation to assist the poor; at the same time poems began to be submitted in praise of nature and in criticism of overpopulated cities. Two kinds of rhetoric were attached to the city: an organic, biological rhetoric that made systematic use of traditional bodily metaphors for describing the world (a development that reflects the rise of the medical community), and a rhetoric of the rediscovery of nature, cultivated by elites eager to flee the new problems created by urban growth, problems that were the focal point of a moral and economic debate that developed around the unavowable reality of persistent poverty. In Paris moralistic commentators such as Rétif and Mercier, disciples of Rousseau, attest to a similar diversification. Both were fascinated by the urban organism, suspicious of the separation of rich and poor, obsessed with the dehumanized dregs of society, and possessed of a new vision for the future: in a rural Arcadia lay the salvation of mankind.

Even pamphleteers joined in the debate. A hundred or so pamphlets, some dating back to the seventeenth century, were reprinted again and again. These featured a series of representations of the city that were duly transmitted to the countryside. The city appeared as a stage on which different social groups expressed their "troubles," "difficulties," "pain," and "misery." The pamphlets presented kaleidoscopic images of a city such as Paris or Rouen in the throes of progress, portrayed in a series of impressionistic scenes. Their purpose was didactic: the city's monuments recalled the glories of civilization; its trade and industry served useful ends. Such pamphlets inspired dreams even in the minds of those villagers who would never make the journey to the big city. They gave people reason to hope and believe, and for those who were ready to make the leap they gave encouragement. Popular pamphlets were read by everyone, but mainly by the poor, and they thus made urban values a part of the general culture, the fantasy life of mankind. Individuals interpreted their social experiences in terms of what they read in pamphlets.

Increasingly, however, there was also emphasis on the troubles of urban life: instability, social stalemate, conflict, poverty, and degradation of standards of morality and dress as described in the superb series of *Cris de Paris*.[31] The annoyances of urban life became not only the butt of humor but also food for thought. When pamphlets discussed cities, they wondered about their future. They noted that people not only learned new rules but also learned how to break them. The pamphlet literature was not static. Its themes changed over time and according to the audience it addressed. Readers also read the pamphlets in different ways. Whereas some saw the dream of a better world, others saw the specter of decay. By the end of the eighteenth century, there was no single popular vision of the city but many diverse visions.

A similar shift took place in the interpretation of the urban economy, which inspired the work of city planners and reformers, including government officials, medical doctors, engineers, and architects. The functionalism prevalent in these disciplines stemmed from a grasp of the city's unique role in redistributing wealth, concentrating population, and spurring consumption and development—in short, from a view of the city as economic "multiplier."[32]

This view originated with Cantillon, whose *Essai sur la nature du commerce en général* was written between 1720 and 1730 but not published until 1755. The argument was pursued by Condillac (*Le Commerce et le gouvernement considérés relativement l'un à l'autre*, 1776) and taken to its logical conclusion by Adam Smith, whose *Wealth of Nations* was immediately translated and soon given wide currency by the use made of it in the article entitled "Ville" in the political economy section of Panckoucke's *Encyclopédie méthodique* (1788): the city, it was argued, was a consequence of the division of labor and of man's natural propensity to engage in trade. This idea stemmed from a spatial theory of production, in which labor and capital sought the most advantageous employment, the emerging urban hierarchy reflected capital accumulation, not all cities were equally productive, and commercial cities were contrasted with rentier cities. Where rentier income predominated, idleness was the rule; where capital and productive investment dominated, industry and development followed.[33] Condillac stood Smith's analyses on their head: for the Frenchman the key was not production but consumption and circulation, which led to an organic functional theory in which infrastructure fostered increased trade. Boerhaave's disciple Quesnay used this "medicalized" view to describe the "urban obstruction" caused by accumulation of wealth without redistribution into agriculture and natural reproduction.[34]

The city was thus obliged to protect its role by promoting an optimistic economic view of its function. Modern thinking rejected isolation, and one segment of urban thinking shifted responsibility for communication from the cultural to the economic sphere. In this connection the culture of print took on an even more novel significance: its role was not simply to accumulate knowledge in books but to create new connections between ideas. The mission of the city was to bring one form of knowledge in contact with another in order to make things happen. Commerce sprang up where two kinds of thinking came together: just as conversation was an outgrowth of sociability and culture, exchange of labor and commodities was an outgrowth of political economy in which the city was to play the role of economic accelerator. Against the Physiocrats, Cantillon and Condillac argued that the city transferred wealth, created new value, and ensured redistribution of profits, thus giving rise to a "revolution in lifestyles." For Condillac, two factors were at work. First, the pleasures of consumption made cities more attractive and led to further diversification of consumption; and second, rural output gravitated toward the cities, and increased demand accelerated agricultural production, increasing farm incomes and ground rents, which in turn stimulated further growth.

Urban economic thinking accordingly rejected the idea of economic space as consisting of adjacent, isolated districts interacting only at their mutual boundary and replaced it with a new spatial vision. Within the economic circuit, price variations spurred production and stimulated successive waves of development. According to the new view, the economy was driven by demand and not, as in the mercantile tradition or the Christian, moral view of the economy, by supply. Relations between cities were built from the top down, by function.[35]

Urban Authorities, Cohesion, and Conflict

The administration of the city had to deal with conflict in a context of liberalism. The urban administration became the very symbol of the city. Its interventions fostered social cohesion and development. But the urban nobility and bourgeoisie fought for control of the government and therefore of development. Types of municipal government varied widely. Broadly speaking, responsibility for government was shared among three bodies: a general assembly of residents (which as time went by tended to exclude all but notables and representatives of parishes, guilds, and other corporate bodies); the councils; and the *corps de ville,* or city corporation. Although cities had been under royal tutelage since the seventeenth century, they did still enjoy some measure of liberty. When the government clamped down on the diversity of urban institutions in 1764–65, it merely recognized the existence of quasi-republican traditions controlled by urban elites. The urban authorities enjoyed prestige and power: they collected taxes while at the same time defending the fiscal privileges of their citizens; they maintained food supplies if necessary by taxing rural parishes; they managed ordinary courts of law, regulated commerce, administered the guilds, oversaw urban planning, accepted or rejected the poor and sick, monitored teaching, and supervised public health and morals. In short, municipal governments handled a wide range of matters which in the eighteenth century fell under the head of *la police* (public order), as discussed in a long tradition of *traités de police*. Delamare's *traité* provided a model for France and Europe. The work was essentially a treatise on moral economy, seen in terms of managing space and social groups.

Clashes over urban policy were therefore serious matters. Usually they pitted the privileged against the oppressed, but sometimes the nobility vied with the bourgeoisie. In Caen the nature of the confrontation was not always clear because the different social groups did not always act in accordance with what we take to be their own interests. The conflict over development there has already been discussed. The city corporation, dominated by a noble mayor and six aldermen, two of whom were nobles, two bourgeois living in noble style, and two traders, generally opposed the initiatives of the active bourgeoisie and the royal administrators who supported them. The municipal government, with support from its citizens, was able to slow the expansion of trade in defense of its landed interests. The municipality won backing by conceding portions of its estate to individuals who supported its conservative policies. It waged war against the *intendance* and the Ponts et Chaussées on major as well as minor issues. The conflict was one of independence versus dependence, status quo versus change, and vested interests versus zealous entrepreneurs. The issues were most clearly posed in debates over development projects and above all in discussions of taxes, especially after the nobility joined forces with those in favor of development and public works.

The blockages that one finds at the municipal level in Caen did not exist everywhere to the same degree. In Nantes, Bordeaux, and Rouen, municipal elites and traders shared a desire to "change the city" and, as long as special interests did not get in the way, often acted jointly in everyday matters of maintenance and management. In the great Norman port, for example, cooperation was more apparent than conflict. Thus, there was nothing to stop construction of new docks, improvements to warehouses and enrepôts, and clearing of passages for new streets that showcased the importance of the city as a driving force for change. And there was also agreement about erecting prestigious monuments, promenades, squares, fountains, theaters, and concert halls—places where older social networks could make contact with people involved in the newer modes of circulation.

Among the cities of Flanders studied by Philippe Guignet, we find numerous examples of an urban civilization at the crossroads of development.[36] We also see the role of urban oligarchies in the controversial management of development issues. Until the middle of the eighteenth century, the municipalities of Flanders subsisted in an urban civilization based on oligarchical rule by the *senior pars* (representatives of privilege) and on the economic and religious principles of the Counter-Reformation. Charitable organizations and guilds took care of social needs, and competition was limited. Increased central control and the transformation of the economy plunged this system into belated but lingering crisis. The traditional, conservative, interventionist spirit survived because municipal elites took in new members without losing their cohesiveness, which was reinforced by the domination of social groups that lived on income from land and bonds and owed nothing to trade or industry. Large-scale trade circumvented the authorities because in Lille, Valenciennes, Douai, and Cambrai, aldermen largely refused to accept changes in the nature of manufacturing. The urban environment was constricting and ill adapted to innovation, even if traders still found ways to make profits.

This conflict brings us back to the question raised at the outset. The interests of traders were not always compatible with the interests of fixed-income investors. The new economic logic frequently undermined the existing basis of urban solidarity. Repeated incidents occurred in the early 1760s. Static France, the France of "the three orders," was forced to confront change in the form of new networks of circulation and new modes of communication. In the resulting conflict not all cities were on the same side. We can explain the ensuing tensions. For the moderns, the city was a tool, and the goal was calculated profit. The ancients, by contrast, opted for a nostalgic, old-fashioned pastoral and rural philosophy. "All phases of urbanization were accompanied by one form or another of an apologia for nature."[37] This dictum certainly applied to the period in which cities became the motor of economic development.

7

꙳꙳꙳

The Regulated Kingdom:
Paris and the Provinces

IN THE ORGANIZATION of space, the opposition between trade and land, city and country, is not sufficient to characterize what was distinctive about the changes that occurred in eighteenth-century France. Another dimension existed, a dimension that played a central role in intellectual debate and literary representation and had a direct effect on the routine practices of government: namely, the contrast between Paris and the provinces. Montesquieu put it well in his *Pensées:* "In the provinces, Paris is a North Pole that attracts you, the *intendant* a South Pole that repels you."[1] In the tug of war between the provincials, whom Montesquieu can reasonably be taken to represent, and the Parisians (the *intendants* being the local representatives of royal power), it was the role of the capital that was at issue—or should I say *capitals,* for the problem was not uniquely French. It arose throughout Europe in conjunction with the genesis of the modern state and the development of its institutions. Montesquieu elaborated his thinking in a text entitled "The Grandeur of the Capital":

> In a republic, a city that is too large is extremely pernicious, because morals always become corrupt there. When you bring a million men together in one place, the best you can do by way of keeping order is to make sure that each citizen receives some bread and needn't worry about having his throat slit. Put men where there is work and not where there is lust. In despotic states the capital necessarily grows . . .

The prince is a singular star: come close and find warmth, keep your distance and be burned . . . In a monarchy the capital can grow in two ways: either because wealth from the provinces draws people there (as in a certain maritime kingdom), or because poverty in the provinces forces people into the capital . . . A monarchy ruled by law will not be destroyed by its capital. It may even derive splendor from it. The prince has a thousand ways of restoring equilibrium and enticing people back into the provinces. To mention only those that come first to mind, let him decrease the taxes on food in the provinces and increase them in the capital; let cases before the provincial courts be concluded in those courts and not appealed endlessly to his councils and special tribunals; let him send back to their posts those who are in any way employed in the provinces; and let him bear in mind that the more people leave a place, the more others will desire to do so, because the pleasure of those who remain is diminished.

Montesquieu, a keen observer of the realities of history and of the links between political organization, population movements, and wealth, put the question in its proper context. Some difference between the capital and the provinces is inevitable, regardless of the nature of the government and the principles (republican, despotic, or monarchic) on which it is founded. The harmful effects of the capital on production, population, and morals as well as on provincial culture (note the word "pleasure") vary little from one type of regime to another. The cure for these ills depends on administrative intervention. The king and the *intendant* must see to it that the institutions of government work effectively to maintain a proper balance between the capital and the provinces. There can be no doubt that for Montesquieu this was a major feature of any regime's social policy and one of the fundamental issues facing the French monarchy after a century of absolutist rule.

Commentators have pointed out how important it is to take note of the unique features of the French monarchy. Having no constitution to define hierarchical relationships, the monarchy was simply a juxtaposition of institutions bearing no clear relation to one another: ancient institutions inherited from the Middle Ages coexisted with more modern ones founded in the sixteenth and seventeenth centuries. Despite its lack of unity, this institutional structure was not without a functional principle: there was a sort of "institutional spirit" of modern France, a spirit that was challenged by the spirit of Enlightenment in the middle of the eighteenth century. So just as we need to work hard to comprehend the thought processes of people who must have had a difficult time finding their place in the amorphous aggregate of subcultures of which Mirabeau spoke in 1789, we must also make an effort to see institutional inconsistencies and conflicts as an integral part of the political culture of the time.[2] It is easier to think of the institutions of the monarchy in terms of organic metaphors (head, members, body) than in terms of mechanical analogies (motors, belts, gears) or electrical ones (transmitter, receiver, network). Georges Durand has given an exemplary if little-known analysis of those institutions that can help us understand the various functions of the state apparatus.

In reviewing the main institutions of the monarchy, it is useful to follow the itinerary proposed by Montesquieu, from the attractive North Pole (the center of deliberation and decision making) to the South Pole of routine administrative activities directed by various governmental agents and/or bodies, activities in which large and small issues were inextricably intertwined (and still are, as we all know from our daily lives). High-level governmental decisions, bureaucratic routine, and public reaction and pressure were all parts of a single system from which we can learn a great deal about social values, shared beliefs, and an administrative and political culture that unified the French but at the same time created antagonisms among them. Out of this mix came the legendary contrast between the unhappy provincial and the arrogant Parisian.

Paris and Versailles: The Centralized Monarchy

All of eighteenth-century Europe saw France as the perfect monarchical state, an ideal hierarchical organization that facilitated the transmission of orders in one direction only, from center to periphery. "A king, ministers who are nothing more than clerks, councils which are nothing more than bureaus, a *parlement* which is politically nothing more than a rubber stamp, and a hierarchy of tribunals and financial institutions that enforces edicts and collects exactions from the *brevet* to the *taille* to the extent that the economy can bear."[3]

This model, which allowed the monarchical state to quell the turbulent aristocracy, vanquish economic instability, and survive the military emergencies of the reign of Louis XIV, was based on two principles: unity through fidelity (but how was it established?) and negotiated solutions to recurring conflicts. The impulse to independence remained powerful because it was rooted in a higher common principle: the idea of an organic society of corporations and estates. The shared dream of all was for the king to act as arbiter in all disputes in such a way as to maintain an equilibrium respectful of tradition and custom: the nobility wanted to protect its social and political preeminence; the bourgeoisie wanted a favorable hearing for its diverse interests and guarantees of some measure of upward mobility; and the people wanted the protection and prosperity that it was only natural for children to expect of their father.

Louis XIV decisively altered this ancient conception of the monarchy by refusing to share power: no more Estates General, no more *assemblées de corps* (except for that principal ally of the monarchy's glory, the clergy), and no more *assemblées de notables*. The dominant classes were depoliticized, and from that point on nobles and clerics, magistrates and notables, were exhorted to accept the new model of government according to which the role of the central authority was to unify all special interests. The stakes, as one might expect, were fundamentally political, but they were not only political: there was also a cultural aspect, involving the unification of the language and the elaboration, by Parisian and provincial academics, of a veritable political ideology of *absolute* but *enlightened* monarchy.[4]

Once that model was in place, two problems arose. First, how effective were these principles in practice, given such obstacles as distance; variations of land quality, custom, and law; alienation of judicial and fiscal authority through the sale of offices, which limited the monarchy's capacity to act; and the limits of royal officials, of whom the *intendants* were only the most visible? In addition, the political history of the eighteenth century raised an even deeper question. Given the hesitancy of the government and its inability to steer a firm course between conservatism and reform, people began to question the legitimacy of the monarchy itself. New controversies, coupled with the "belated, disillusioned image that the elites formed of a system they were no longer willing to tolerate,"[5] revealed the existence of partial critiques and special interests that overshadowed the general interest. By 1715 the early criticisms of aristocrats such as Fénelon and Saint-Simon, the invocation of Christianity, the systematic recourse to history, and the insistence on the customary role of various orders and corporations added up to an influential critique of absolutism at its very core. This critique had a profound impact on the historians who continued the debate (Boulainvilliers versus Abbé Dubos, aristocratic liberalism versus elite liberalism) and on the parliamentary opposition through an endless series of disputes that were seized on as pretexts to confront the central government, religion, the tax system, and even the courts themselves. Enlightened despotism, or rather absolutism, was never able to choose between the forces of conservatism and the forces of progress, and this failure reflected a partial institutional dysfunction, a gap between spirit and practice.

The Councils as Expressions of Authority

What unified the kingdom and the crown, the territory divided up without rhyme or reason into a veritable jigsaw puzzle of administrative subdivisions (*bailliages, sénéchaussées, gouvernements, généralités,* and jurisdictions of various courts and agencies), was the delegation of sovereignty. The state was distinct from the royal person from whom authority emanated. This separation was authenticated by ancient rituals distinguishing the "king's two bodies." The state survived the death of the mortal individual who embodied it. "I am going," said Louis XIV shortly before his death, "but the state will always remain." Leaving aside abstract principles of authority and the apparently illogical structure of state institutions, what remained was the will to act. That will was embodied in institutions as well as individuals—individuals who tended to form a political class. These were the people who made the decisions and took the initiative, a group of wealthy men with strong ties to one another and fingers everywhere, whose only desire was to "find out the details of everything that was happening and settle everything in Paris," as Tocqueville remarked.[6] This group naturally became the focal point of all resentment, since the king was rarely challenged directly: "He does not know."[7]

Absolutism inherited one ancient principle of feudal government: no decision or intervention without consultation. Apart from the Maison du Roi (royal household), the principal political organism was the Conseil du Roi (King's Council), the offspring of the ancient Curia Regis of vassals, jurists, and scribes. In theory the Council was an intellectual appendage of the political person of the monarch: "My Council is neither a body nor a tribunal apart from me: I myself act through it," was the way it was phrased by Louis XV's legal experts.[8] It was in council that the will of the prince was made known. "He [the king] is one [a prince] because he is king." The Council functioned as an invisible entity, without an official role of its own, without existence apart from the monarch, who invited whomever he pleased to each meeting according to the nature of the matters to be discussed.

Monarchical power evolved in two ways. On the one hand, it relied increasingly on deliberations and decisions by a group of loyal servants from which princes and other high aristocratic personages were eliminated. The membership of this group was determined by the needs of the moment and the caprices of royal favor. On the other hand, it could not altogether forsake consultation with the "born representatives" of the people (de jure or de facto): certain high officials of the crown such as the chancellor and the *surintendant des finances*, and certain powerful individuals close to the monarch, the royal family, and the highest-ranking members of the nobility. During the Regency the "born representatives" regained some of the power they had lost under Louis XIV. Louis XV and Louis XVI generally backed the legal specialists and technicians, but they were not always able to refuse the princes and other aristocrats. Indeed, in practice as well as theory, the ancient function of the *consilium* in regard to both preparation and execution of decisions was far broader than just described: this was what distinguished monarchy from despotism.

In regard to the preparation of decisions, the broader conception of the Council involved irregular consultation with the Estates General, but the king had closed the book on these in 1615 and would not reopen it until 1788. There were also consultations with assemblies of corporations and notables. More generally, the sovereign courts *(parlements, chambres des comptes, chambres des aides)* also claimed the king's ear and insisted on their right to file remonstrances and to issue independent judgments. The recording of royal edicts, which was intended simply as a means of making laws public, became the basis of what the *parlements* claimed as a duty and a right: to negotiate with the king about laws that appeared to deviate from the traditions of public law or to be inopportune, and possibly to amend them. This "political diplomacy" failed because the right of remonstrance was interpreted differently by the king and his parlementary magistrates, who owned their own offices. For the monarch, this was nothing more than a customary right inherent in members of the expanded royal council, not a means of opposition. For the jurists it was a right to review laws and to take part in the legislative process. Eventually it came to signify a right to represent the people, a right that reflects all the ambiguity of the old political culture, for the general good and common interest were to be defended by the *sanior pars*, that is, by representatives of privilege, who wielded governmental and economic power at the local level and had special interests to defend.

After the failure of the Polysynody during the regency of Philippe d'Orléans, the real decision-making organism became the handful of counselors chosen by the prince to serve in the government. This body was compatible with the established traditional distinction among "conseils d'administration, de justice et de gouvernement." It was here that important affairs of state were decided in the presence of the monarch, flanked by trusted advisers to whom various political and military responsibilities had been assigned. In this respect the reign of Louis XIV had marked a crucial milestone, although it was still possible for one individual to hold positions on several advisory bodies or to be recruited from one to another.

Let us concentrate on what was essential. After 1660 the principal figure in the governmental hierarchy was no longer the chancellor, the incarnation of the judicial conception of royal power, whose role was somewhat limited. Part of the chancellor's former powers were shifted to the Garde des Sceaux (Keeper of the Seals), despite the fact that some very important personages would still serve as chancellor: d'Aguesseau, Lamoignon, Maupeou. The Garde des Sceaux was a royal officer who enjoyed exorbitant financial and symbolic privileges, including the lucrative emoluments of the seal. Thanks to his triple role as initiator, censor, and guardian of the law (although his role as initiator declined somewhat over the course of the century), he wielded important powers, especially in ideological matters, from within the Chancellery. As chief of the courts and secretary of the Privy Council, he was an essential cog in the machine.

The most important servant of the administrative monarchy was in fact the *contrôleur général des finances*. As the direct descendant of an office to which Colbert had attached a wide range of responsibilities, the *contrôleur général* was not an *officier* (who owned his office and therefore could not be removed) but a *commissaire* who served at the pleasure of the king. Indeed, no one survived in the position very long: sixteen men held the post under Louis XIV, fifteen under Louis XVI, with an average term of two years. The king chose his *contrôleur général* from among his *conseillers d'Etat, intendants de finance,* and representatives of a variety of other institutions: the Church, with Abbé Terray or Brienne, the archbishop of Toulouse; the *intendance,* with Calonne; business, with John Law; and banking, with the Protestant Necker (who did not officially bear the title). Although the *contrôleur général* did not order government expenditures or make final spending decisions (the king did that), he enjoyed de facto power to guide financial policy: he prepared all fiscal and economic edicts; he was authorized to make payments in the king's name; and in general he supervised economic policy.

His authority was exercised through *directions,* or departments, of the Contrôle Général that were headed by *intendants de finance:* Fermes et Aides, Domaines, Ponts et Chaussées, Hôpitaux, Tailles et Impôts, Trésor, Commerce. The power of the *intendants* in disputed matters spelled their doom: in 1777 Necker eliminated these posts as offices and preserved only their administrative functions. It is not certain, however, that the reform had the desired effect.[9] In this episode we see the conflict between docility and efficacy, centralized control and the reformist imagination, in conjunction with the primary function of the *contrôleur,* who gradually took over all economic matters.[10] One whole aspect of the eighteenth century's thinking about reform was conducted in conjunction with such solid dynasties as the Ormessons, the Boullongnes, and the Trudaines. By controlling the budget, the *contrôleur général* controlled the secretaries of state and ministers. Through his fiscal and regulatory powers he influenced economic policy, as can be seen in the case of Orry and even more in the case of Terray or Turgot. The prospects for change were determined in part by what went on in the bustling, well-informed offices of the *contrôle général.*

Gravitating around the *contrôleur général* was the world of ministers and secretaries of state. At times royal favor might single out one of these as a prime minister without the title, as was the case with Abbé Dubois, the duc de Bourbon, Cardinal Fleury, and later Choiseul. These men headed major departments of government: War, Navy, Foreign Affairs. The king could promote them by inviting them to join the Conseil d'en haut (High Council), and he could add to or subtract from their authority whenever he pleased. They were at the heart of the business of state and close to the source of all favor, but they still functioned in the context of the larger King's Council, in whose deliberations they might or might not participate, depending on the nature of the meeting and the matter under discussion. In "government," and with the king present, they sat as the Conseil d'en haut, membership in which conferred the title of minister of state, a considerable pension, and the confidence of the monarch.

By custom, secretaries of state were considered to be ministers. They could sit on the Conseil des dépêches, a veritable cabinet for domestic affairs, whose meetings the chancellor also attended. They went to the Conseil des finances to hear the reports of the *intendants* with the *contrôleur* in the chair. They were rarely present at meetings of the Conseil de conscience, whose membership was reduced after Louis XIV to the king, his confessor, and one or two designated prelates. Other councils came under the heads not of government but of justice and administration. The "Conseil d'État, privé, finance et direction" was the name given to the highest civil court, a sort of supreme court that heard special cases and cases removed from the jurisdiction of lower courts under a procedure known as *évocation;* it had final jurisdiction in all fiscal and administrative matters.

Here was the culmination of the effort of centralization in a typical compromise between the principles of the judicial state and the financial state. The Conseil issued some four to five thousand judgments a year, and by studying these we can follow in detail the work of a group of men who owed their positions to both birth and talent. Assemblies of various sizes gathered ministers of state, secretaries of state, and on occasion princes, dukes and peers, high-ranking officials, and state councilors authorized by special letters or warrants, along with provincial governors, laymen and ecclesiastics, *maîtres des requêtes, huissiers, greffiers,* and clerks—perhaps two thousand people all told. Some one hundred to two hundred of these tracked cases prepared by regular bureaus and commissions (such as the financial *directions*) or special commissions (on tolls or reform of the regular clergy, for example). The Conseil extended its reach to the provinces by dispatching *maîtres des requêtes* and established a centralized geopolitical kingdom that appeared to be part of Nature herself. In France the debate over centralization grew out of the action of an administration in which orders were transmitted from center to periphery, where local officials had to contend with ethnic diversity and geographic and historical heterogeneity.[11] This system, in which France was administered by a political class gravitating around the governmental center, reached its apogee in the eighteenth century.

From Political Class to Bureaucracy

The King's Council became the center of a large group of political figures on whom the future, and to an even greater extent the present, of the kingdom depended. At the heart of this group, which Michel Antoine has studied,[12] were the *maîtres des requêtes*, but they were only the most important figures in a much broader collection of individuals who assisted the various councils in their work, including a variety of office-holders, appointees, delegates, and clerks—in short, major and minor administrative personnel. There was constant interchange between people who owed their positions to the personal favor of the king and people who had worked their way up through the ranks of state service; many careers involved both personal favor and regular service.

The *robe du Conseil* included everyone who had been, was, or would be a *maître des requêtes: intendants*, members of the Conseil d'Etat, some ambassadors, the *premiers présidents* of the courts, secretaries of state, ministers, the *contrôleur général*, and the chancellor. Contemporaries were struck by the ubiquity of these *maîtres des requêtes*. In terms of institutional origins they were associated with the judicial function, heirs of the so-called *juges de la porte* of the Curia Regis, and their *tribunal des requêtes* judged many cases referred to it by the Council. Because of this, the Parlement of Paris, with whom they had many connections, was not overly fond of them as a group. Those who had been magistrates in Parlement and who had left without giving up their offices rarely sat on the bench. They sometimes sat on the Grand Conseil, which, along with the Conseil du Roi and Parlement, had jurisdiction over civil suits. They were also close to the Chancellery, to which they presented edicts for affixing of the royal seal, and which they sometimes represented in dealings with provincial chancelleries. In other words, what distinguished the *maîtres des requêtes* was their versatility in preparing and carrying out the orders of the king. About them Chancellor d'Aguesseau had this to say: "They resemble the desires of the human heart. They aspire to be no longer. Theirs is an estate that one embraces only to abandon, a body that one joins only to resign. Anyone who grows old in this employ dies a little each day and vanishes into oblivion." The irony of this characterization conceals the fact that many *maîtres des requêtes* continued in their positions and went nowhere: this was the case with 128 of 309 between 1715 and 1774. Nevertheless, it does point up the advent of the idea of a professional bureaucracy in which it was normal to expect to move up in grade: 90 percent of the *conseillers d'Etat* who belonged to the *robe* (that is, who were neither clergymen nor members of the *noblesse d'épée*) were *maîtres des requêtes*. Socially, they shared three primary characteristics: they were Parisians and nobles, and they came from a highly homogeneous milieu.

Parisians: of 348 cases identified by Michel Antoine, 240 were born in the capital, and most of these young magistrates had gained their first experience with the Parlement of Paris. The remainder came from other cities with *parlements* and courts, which contributed two to five each, except for Lyons with ten *maîtres* and Bordeaux with eight. Hence this was to a certain extent an open *corps*, but entry was screened by the provincial sovereign courts. Recruitment to the two financial councils, the *cour des aides* and *cour des comptes*, did not follow this rule, however. Two factors were at work here: the interests of the administration, which was eager to secure the services of men with knowledge of local customs and laws, and the ambitions of family dynasties such as the La Bourdonnayes of Rennes, the Gourgues of Bordeaux, and the Perrignys of Dijon, who were keen to see one of their own promoted to Paris and ultimately to the Council.

All *maîtres des requêtes* were nobles, but the nobility of the Council included both old families such as the Argouges and the Argensons, whose nobility dated back to the thirteenth or fourteenth century, and bourgeois dynasties recently ennobled through the purchase of royal offices. Thus the Council was a melting pot which in some ways paralleled Parlement, where the old families of the *grande robe parisienne*, the Ormessons, Lamoignons, Joly de Fleurys, and Amelots, coexisted with the recently cleansed heirs of fortunes made in trade and finance. Becoming a *maître des requêtes* was like a confirmation of a family's noble status. It was no handicap, moreover, to be a royal secretary (as were 52 of 374 *maîtres des requêtes*). The Council could serve as a springboard to a brilliant and lucrative career. The Chaumonts de La Galaizière rose to nobility in just two generations, for example. The majority of Council members joined with two degrees of nobility; access to the Council was easier than access to the sovereign courts, and the prestige of wealth was more likely to be recognized. All *maîtres des requêtes* were wealthy: it took between 100,000 and 200,000 livres to buy one's first office. And all added to their wealth while in office, availing themselves of privileges granted to those who were both noble and rich: property, valuable estates, well-stocked libraries, and polished manners.

Finally, nearly all councilors were related: everyone was somebody's cousin or married to somebody's cousin. A few individuals married outside this network, occasionally taking a mate from the impecunious high nobility, as was the case with the Phélypeaux. Two traditions stand out: some councilors married within the *robe*, shunning the frivolous court and the dubious world of finance (thus the Gilberts de Voisin were directly related to seventy-one families in the Parlement of Paris); while others chose brides from the worlds of finance and business from which they sprang. These marriage practices tended to unify the milieu and to bring noble families into closer relationship with trade and finance. Here the role of Paris as capital of finance and state disbursement was essential.

The threefold unity of the Council milieu, which was further reinforced by intellectual affinities, made the central government quite culturally homogeneous. All councilors had studied what they needed to know in order to wield power, and it was power more than background or career history that made them what they were. As Parisian or Parisianized *robins*, they were beholden to the state. The state was their *raison d'être*, just as *raison d'état* was their justification. As intermediaries between the people and the government and between Paris and the provinces, they were potent agents of centralization, emblems of a social transformation that involved economic and bureaucratic organization, recruitment of talent, and a combination of individual and dynastic ambition under the king's protection and with his blessing.[13]

Two changes need to be considered, however. First, the Council itself changed. It no longer dealt with important matters in plenary session, which, as d'Argenson said, was "only for trifles and current business," but rather in private committee. In important respects the Council of Louis XV was a fiction. Bureaucratic logic had won out over the notion of the "king as judge." Officers once attached to the king by an almost religious bond of loyalty became functionaries. The king granted his approval to work done by "ministry committees," whose status was un-official until 1737 but officially recognized thereafter. In other words, the old belief in the need for an open, plenary *consilium* faded within the

Council itself as political power was usurped by agencies of the executive. That is why the monarch's choice of individuals was so important, and why his entourage fought so bitterly over every appointment. Study would show how priorities and individuals from the worlds of finance and commerce, from the *ferme générale* to reform-minded modernizers, gained influence with the administrative structures of the judicial state. In 1775, when M. de Malesherbes submitted "remonstrances" denouncing "financiers set up as legislators," he put his finger on the essential: confronted with a shortage of resources and problems of development, the financial state modeled itself on the organization of the financial and economic administration. The rise of Necker, who was not required to abjure his faith or become naturalized like John Law before him, can be interpreted as the promotion to the very summit of a man radically alien to the society underlying the monarchy. To be sure, his success would not have been possible without a lobby of interested groups indispensable to the finances of the monarchy, but it also required internal evolution of the Council milieu and upper levels of the administration.

This second change played a part in throwing the entire system into crisis. It can be interpreted as the rise of a "bureaucracy" (the word was coined by Gournay, Turgot's teacher), which in a sense supplanted the administration unified and justified by the king and his ties to the underlying society. Eighteenth-century centralization produced bureaus and archives, investigations and formalities, and spurred ritual protests against swollen government and useless paperwork. It also had other consequences: power was redistributed, and conflicts were settled according to rules that at least in part reflected not an inegalitarian society but a society of classes hierarchized by function and utility. The administrative spirit cut the monarchy off from the active forces within it,[14] but it was the administration to which people turned for change and reform. A debate broke out over freedom and memory as embodied in archives, surveys, and documents. People became obsessed with arbitrary changes to laws and with blocked decisions. Bear in mind, however, that most administrative edicts played a useful role in unifying the society. Society could not live without laws, and good laws required good information. Society could not live without development, and proper development required surveys and rules, identifications and definitions. Means and ends are not the same: everything was a matter of intelligence and equilibrium. And the Age of Enlightenment had those qualities in abundance.

From Center to Periphery: Officials and Functions

Officiers, Commissaires, and *Fonctionnaires:* The Conflict

The evolution of the Council reveals the development of a major contradiction that hampered the action of the monarchy: those responsible for the executive function ceased to share a single conception of the state. Until the eighteenth century, three types of government agents played roles now filled by bureaucrats. The first was the *officier,* or officeholder, whose role was justified in two ways: by broad interpretation of the right of the king to seek counsel and by the organization into *corps* and *compagnies* of men who owned offices purchased from the state. The *officiers* of the sovereign courts, who insisted on their right of remonstrance (reinstated in 1715), were both judges and administrators. The fact that these men purchased a share in the authority of the monarchy reinforced both their collective interests and their local authority; it also tied them closely to the sovereign. Roland Mousnier gives an excellent definition: "An office was thus a lifelong distinction that carried with it a public function, which could either be conferred on a notable or make a notable of the man on whom it was conferred."[15] This definition has the merit of emphasizing the social influence that went along with the exercise of power. As a result, most officeholders upheld the interests of their *corps* by defending custom and tradition; in other words, they instinctively assumed a conservative function. As professional administrators and judges, they also tended to feel that a representative function had been vested in them: "They speak to the nation in the name of the king and to the king in the name of the nation," as the *parlementaires* of Rennes put it in 1757.[16] As early as the Regency, this partial alienation of the administration from the monarchy created a kind of dysfunction.

In order to remedy this defect, absolutist government (with its insatiable need for more revenue from taxes) had relied on a more direct form of administration using *commissaires* chosen by the king and invested with limited powers defined by letters of commission. Although the majority of royal *commissaires* were also officeholders, the two forms of agency came to be seen as antithetical even if inextricably intertwined: officeholders were part of the normal, ordinary mode of administration, whereas *commissaires* served in a more temporary, extraordinary capacity. It was only when the tenure of *commissaires* was extended—with the transition from the *intendant* on temporary mission to the permanent *intendance* covering the entire kingdom—that the monarchy entered into conflict with itself, that is, with the society of *corps*. The new type of *commissaire* combined all powers (justice, police, finance) in a single person. The *intendant* was not "the king in the provinces" but "the King's Council in the provinces." He transmitted information to the Council and carried out its instructions.

Two issues arose. First, officeholders felt that their power was being challenged. The conflict between *officiers* and *commissaires* became a routine theme of administrative and political life. But the activities of the *commissaires* did not always involve conflict; *intendants* had no choice but to strike some sort of compromise with provincial realities. The history of the *intendances* in the eighteenth century is a story of negotiation and compromise on the one hand and confrontation on the other. The "procès de trois cents ans" to which Chancellor Maupeou referred in 1771 while alluding to the systematic opposition of the sovereign courts and their officeholders and lesser officials was only the reverse side of a coin whose face was an enduring modus vivendi periodically disrupted by temporary disputes.

All administrators in the center or in the provinces, whether officeholders or *commissaires,* recruited and paid a small army of clerks, secretaries, and scribes. Government offices in Versailles were full of them. The *contrôleur général,* for example, relied on the services of thirty or so head clerks, men feared for their long experience of government. A hierarchy developed with department heads at the top, chief clerks next, and simple scribes last. In Paris a host of clerks, secretaries of state, and *intendants de finance* invaded former aristocratic *hôtels* made over into bureaucratic offices. In the provinces *intendants* similarly surrounded themselves with clerks and *subdélégués,* though on a lesser scale.

Three significant developments occurred in this area. First, the clerks were professionalized, their positions became permanent, and their authority was recognized: "The clerks," said the marquis d'Argenson, "are in charge of the store." They were not hampered by the constraints that applied to judicial procedures, and they acted with express written authorization (often signed in advance, according to Roland Mousnier, leaving details to be filled in later by the clerks themselves). This freedom allowed them to act decisively. The administration was transformed from a group of assemblies governed by custom to a group of individuals organized in a hierarchical chain of command and information. This transformation marked a decisive step.

Second, the methods and instruments of administrative action also changed. As offices grew in size, many tasks became anonymous, and there were infinitely more opportunities for interventions, surveys, collection of statistics, and correspondence. A more functional organization was established in Parisian and provincial bureaus: fixed hours were imposed, standards of qualification were established, responsibilities were clearly delineated, and disciplinary measures were specified. In 1774, for example, the Ministry of Foreign Affairs employed some fifty people, and the work was divided among seven bureaus, each headed by a chief clerk who presided over a staff of secretaries, clerks, translators, and scribes. The chief clerks, men with embassy experience, served for long periods: thirty years for Abbé de La Ville, twenty-five years for Pecquet.[17] Beyond a certain age administrative staff personnel became eligible for royal pensions. As work in the bureaucracy became a recognized estate, it began to arouse jealousy and criticism because of the relatively large number of people to whom it offered power and stable employment. The article entitled "Burocratie" [sic] in the *Encyclopédie méthodique* (1789) defined the term as meaning government, administration, or "command by bureau" and condemned the bureaucratic system as absurd, a source of countless woes that created "a harmful division between the administration and the state." The new procedures of government, as well as the protected officials who carried them out, were the very embodiment of so-called ministerial despotism, which was widely denounced in times of crisis, despite the fact that those same procedures and officials were what enabled the state to manage things efficiently on both the local and central levels. The new agents of government were well trained, highly efficient, and motivated by a sense of duty to the state.

Finally, the increase in the number of interventions by ministers and *intendants* led not just to an increase in the number of administrative personnel (which cannot be stated precisely owing to lack of data) but also to a change in attitude: clerks were now treated as functionaries. In areas where the monarchy was particularly active, administrative confusion therefore tended to decrease. Two examples will help to make this point clear: the Ferme Générale and the Ponts et Chaussées.

The Ferme Générale existed because of the old practice of using tax farmers to collect royal taxes, most of them indirect, in order to spare the already complex financial administration the need to do so. By transferring this task to private subcontractors, the state gained in two ways: it filled its coffers more quickly, because private lenders and subcontractors paid up front for the privilege of making a handsome profit later in the collection of tax revenues, and because the costs of collection were shifted to the tax farmers. After 1726 the contract was regularly renewed, so that the farmers-general, usually forty in number, became typical functionaries—private, to be sure, yet all but permanently tenured in their positions.

The position of tax farmer became a regular profession. A tax farmer's career began with his nomination, which required the consent of the other farmers-general, the approval of the Contrôle Général, patronage in high places, and possibly even under-the-table payments. Then came a period of probation as an adjunct. For elderly tax farmers there was even an "emeritus" status. The tendency to create veritable dynasties of tax farmers reinforced the solidarity of the group, which had a specific function to perform. Most learned the trade by traveling through the provinces for years on so-called *tournées* (rounds). Later they might join one of the committees (on the salt tax, tobacco tax, or other excise duties, for example) in which the decisions of the Ferme Générale were made. The *tournées* were thus a form of apprenticeship in which young tax farmers learned about the people and places they would have to deal with later on. This was what Jacques Paulze told his son when he sent him to observe Tronchin's survey in southern France and the Lyons region. This study of cities, customs, manufacturing, commerce, population, and land revolved around the idea of rational management of people and their skills, "for the revenues of the [tax] farms are based on consumption, and consumption is always proportionate to the number and wealth of consumers, [hence] no farmer-general can afford to ignore any fact that may contribute to those two results."[18]

This empirical education was a feature of a career that could take a fortunate, talented clerk to the very top of the Ferme Générale. As Philippe Savoie has shown, the Ferme was essential to the work of the administration at the local level, and its employees were carefully groomed. The reports submitted by roving inspectors were expected to assess the talents (and shortcomings) of local administrators and tax collectors. Their managerial and organizational skills were assessed in accordance with precise criteria of accuracy and honesty. Subordinate employees were also evaluated, and efforts were made to improve recruitment and training of personnel. Suggestions for improving the operations and image of the Ferme were also heard, including the implementation of retirement benefits and the payment of performance bonuses.

As for the Ponts et Chaussées, we saw earlier how it evolved into a solid, hierarchical *corps* with its own independent powers. A competitive examination was established as the basis for recruitment of new administrators. An *intendant de finance* reporting directly to the *contrôleur général des finances* was assigned to supervise the department, whose training school, the Ecole des Ponts et Chaussées, eventually became a model for all of Europe. The way the agency functioned on the local level can be understood only if we understand how this school worked to promote a policy of innovation. Micromanagement and centralization were two aspects of a single approach based on a carefully designed institutional organization.[19]

On the eve of 1789, the *corps des Ponts et Chaussées* was headed by Chaumont de La Millière, who had replaced Trudaine de Montigny. It included a chief engineer, 28 regular engineers, 60 assistant engineers, and more than 120 inspectors, who supervised clerks, site managers, surveyors, and roadmen. In the *pays d'Etats* the corps of engineers and technicians were organized in the same way as in the *généralités*. Talented men could move ahead, just as in the Ferme. The goal was to rationalize the process of designing and building highways, bridges, and other installations by describing and evaluating local conditions and then planning how to cope with them in a rational manner.

It would be an exaggeration to describe the monarchy's administrative institutions as a graveyard of outmoded functions. To be sure, contemporaries often saw the administration as a way of organizing the solution to nonexistent problems in ways that caused very real chaos. Clinging to old habits, confused administrators only compounded new problems. The monarchy's institutions, however, often served as test beds for bold experiments and sometimes proved to be efficient instruments for change.[20] Indeed, what proved most traumatic may have been the combination of innovation with efficiency, for everyone was in one way or another attached to the survival of the old culture.

The *Intendants* at Home: A *Corps* between Two Worlds

Built into this very unsystematic system was the possibility of operating simultaneously in many different time frames. When a new administrative agency was created, older ones were not necessarily eliminated even if their jurisdictions partially overlapped. It is crucial to recall that every agency included a judicial instance of some sort: the Mint dealt with cases of counterfeiting, the Admiralty with maritime cases; provosts heard cases brought by the *maréchaussée;* and officeholders of one sort or another dealt with matters within their purview. Hence the King's Council, that emanation of the royal person, played an important role in harmonizing this hodgepodge, not so much by establishing principles as by creating exceptions. The complexity of the apparatus ensured that the king, through his representatives and delegates, maintained control. The trick of administering was perpetually to take back authority that had been alienated, farmed out, or deputed to others.

It was here that the *intendant* played a central role. Others were commissioned by the king to fill the highest posts in the provincial administration, the governorships and *premières présidences* of the sovereign courts, and diplomatic posts, as well as lower-level posts such as "commissaires des guerres, de la marine, des fortifications, du Châtelet de Paris." The stability of these jobs depended on the king and, increasingly, on the needs of the administration, which sometimes relied on *commissaires* for temporary investigative or judicial functions. The position of *intendant* stood somewhere between stability and instability: although it was a regular appointment, it was not necessarily renewed when the *intendant*'s term was up. The post was seen as the successor to the investigator-reformers of the late seventeenth century, who had been assigned to evaluate the kingdom's strength and resources. Hence it was clear that the central government was going to rely on the *intendants* as a primary source of information. Each *intendant* received strict instructions when nominated. His role was primarily to carry out orders, to serve as an agent of the central government in the realms of taxation and justice (in the latter instance by removing cases from the courts that normally had jurisdiction over them). Nevertheless, because he worked so far away from the central authority, the *intendant* had to be granted a certain initiative. Even though his role was to promote unity, in practice he often ended up translating decisions of the central government into the local patois, as it were, in such a way as to respect local privileges so long as they did not contradict the needs of absolutism. Over time, therefore, as Tocqueville pointed out, the *intendants* opened up new avenues of action for the central authorities.

Sometimes *intendants* came into conflict with the local authorities. Compared with a princely governor such as Condé in Burgundy or Richelieu in Bordeaux, the *intendant* was an insignificant personage, even if he controlled most government action and usually reduced the governor to a ceremonial role. He might intervene with financial or judicial institutions, but disagreements were generally settled by negotiation rather than out-and-out conflict. In the *pays d'Etats,* confrontation was rare (with the exception of the so-called *affaire de Bretagne*). The *intendants* began to exercise tighter control over cities, moreover, but not without making due allowance for the existence of oligarchies with important interests. In short, if the *intendants* took control everywhere, it was because their responsibilities were so broad, covering law, order, and finance, and because they maintained large offices staffed by clerks and subdelegates recruited from among the local magistracy in accordance with the rule of using co-optation to expand one's network of information. In the eighteenth century these local recruits played an essential role as intermediaries between the *intendance* and the populace.

The *intendants* of the eighteenth century were the beneficiaries of a tradition of homogeneous social and cultural recruitment coupled with time-tested means of intervention. A study of a hundred *intendants* by Vivian R. Gruder (1968) confirms that they were recruited from the same background as the King's Council under which they served. The vast majority were Parisians, although the proportion from the capital decreased somewhat under Louis XVI. Including both heirs of the old *noblesse de robe* and increasing numbers of the recently ennobled (four-fifths in the eighteenth century), the *corps* boasted many members who had spent time working in the sovereign courts and a small number who had worked in finance, including the Dupleix and the Calonnes. They constituted a true administrative nobility, in which distinctions were blurred sufficiently that talented men could get ahead.

Intendants began their careers quite young: most obtained law degrees *(licences)* and became *conseillers* in *parlement* or elsewhere before the age of twenty-two. All gained rapid advancement in the sovereign courts of Paris or, increasingly, in the provinces. On the whole, they had a broad understanding of the kingdom's problems, obtained in part through study but above all through service as *maîtres des requêtes*. Before 1715 the average *intendant* served five years as a *maître des requêtes* before receiving his first nomination; by 1780 the average period of service had increased to eight years. By the age of thirty or thirty-five the typical *intendant* was a mature, seasoned individual capable of overcoming the most difficult hurdles. As a group, the *intendants* drew strength from a shared spirit that harmonized with the spirit of the monarchy; their financial independence and broad yet concrete political vision also helped. Parisianism, social as well as intellectual, was their chief weakness. As an *intendant* grew older, his career tended to progress from lesser *intendances* to more important ones. As the century wore on, however, the average tenure in a given post tended to increase from four or five years to around ten years by 1780. With their fingers in everything, *intendants* were at once the king's men and men of the people, and it is easy to see how, on the eve of the Revolution, they could have been accused simultaneously of laxity in Versailles and authoritarianism in the provinces. Although they were the very embodiment of central government intervention, they were also bulwarks against arbitrary rule and influential and powerful local coteries.

Jean Egret and F.-X. Emmanuelli have shown how authority could circumvent provincialism and the powers newly claimed by communities and *parlements*.[21] The *intendants* were obliged to set and hold a steady course despite the uncertainties and hesitations of royal policy and the animosity of Necker (though they did enjoy the support of his successors as *contrôleur général*, Joly de Fleury and d'Ormesson). In doing so they invoked the "public good" and often availed themselves of the language of philosophes and economists. As proponents of moderate interventionism, they gradually moved closer to the camp of reform and development. They inspired the policy of reducing taxes: Turgot in Limousin, Le Pelletier in Châlons, and Bertier de Sauvigny in Ile-de-France called for reform of the *taille* and the *corvée*. At times they found themselves siding with Parlement and the provincial Estates: such was the case with Molleville in Brittany in 1780 and 1788, Sénac in Hanault in 1787, and Caze de La Bove in Grenoble in 1788. In all areas of the economy they backed improvement, publicized the results of surveys, popularized new methods, patronized agronomic societies, encouraged manufacturing, distributed subsidies, reduced duties, protected commerce, and promoted communications policies designed to facilitate trade.

There can be no doubt that, in the final twenty years of the Ancien Régime, the policy of the central government aimed to end isolation, promote interaction, and improve communications. Coupled with this economic policy was a new social and cultural policy: the *intendants* backed philanthropic initiatives even as they attempted to reform charitable institutions and prisons. They encouraged the new city planning and promoted cultural societies nearly everywhere. This took some adroit maneuvering because they had to conciliate the provincial authorities while conveying the king's message, which they knew how to defend when necessary. In Brittany, for example, Bertrand de Molleville, whom Calonne had sent to mollify provincial officials, dug in his heels when they demanded that the central government relinquish certain important prerogatives (such as stud farms, customs duties, and highways).

With respect to culture, enlightened *intendants* were part traditionalists, part innovators. Devoted to promoting the interests of their *généralités* and sensitive to the arguments of local elites, they were less authoritarian than their seventeenth-century counterparts yet still representative of the King's Council, whose charisma had diminished. As such, they may have been the perfect embodiment of the utilitarian approach to government that became popular in the eighteenth century. Their empirical methods made them the preferred target of two groups of critics diametrically opposed to each other: they were accused of ministerial despotism in the provinces and of antiabsolutism by those who believed that the monarchy should take a more decentralized approach to government. When the government decided to experiment with "provincial assemblies" (in Berry in 1778, Haute-Guyenne in 1779, Dauphiné in 1780, and more broadly in 1787), the *intendants* were expected to work with assembly speakers and "intermediate commissions" that had no budgets of their own. As intermediaries between the center and the provinces, the *intendants* had to cope with the principal conflict of the Ancien Régime: between the world of *corps* and *privilèges* and the world of exchange and openness. As a group, they embraced the imperative for change but were unable to give up their role as mediators for the common good. Their modernity consisted perhaps not so much in the impossible choice they were asked to make as in their ability to adapt to circumstances.

Bertrand René Pallu in Lyons, Jacques Turgot in Limoges

The *intendant* of Lyons in 1740 was Bertrand René Pallu. As such he was in charge of a *généralité* that included the immense city of Lyons as well as the provinces of Lyonnais, Forez, and Beaujolais. No local corporation had authority to rival that of the *intendant*, a traditionally important post in this industrial and commercial area (the region of Saint-Etienne became France's leading industrial center). Pallu left Lyons only to appear before the King's Council or the Contrôle Général. At home he benefited from the absence of the governor, Louis de Neuville, but was obliged to compromise with the *cour des monnaies* and above all with the *consulat*. To support him in his work he depended on a staff that included both people from outside the province and local notables.

Pallu was a Parisian, with relatives in the courts, the Grand Conseil, and Parlement. He became a *conseiller* in 1718 at the age of twenty-five and a *maître des requêtes* at thirty-three. In 1734 he was named *intendant* of Moulins, and in 1739 he was appointed to the post in Lyons. In short, his career followed a standard pattern that included the support of a family with important ties to the King's Council, the Rouillés. He was also a man at home in his times: he loved the theater, gambling, dining, and other of life's pleasures and was passionate about literature and science. He corresponded with Voltaire, received Rousseau, and took delight in meetings of the Académie.

To assist him Pallu had a *subdélégué général*, a lawyer and alderman from Lyons by the name of Claude Gillet, whom Pallu eventually replaced with his own man, Etienne Le Camus. Le Camus filled in when Pallu was absent, and the correspondence between the two men shows that they trusted each other implicitly. Besides Le Camus, who reported directly to the *intendant*, there was also Deville, the local director of Ponts et Chaussées, who, like Pallu, was a member of the Académie. A dozen or so clerks, secretaries, and errand boys rounded out the staff of the *intendant*, in addition to which the engineer Deville had a staff of his own. These lower-ranking bureaucrats lived as members of the Lyons bourgeoisie and could aspire to a post as high as *subdélégué*. Their status was intermediate between public and private: on the one hand they were personal servants of the *intendant* and served the state only through him, but on the other hand they were members of the nascent public bureaucracy. They did not own their offices and could be replaced at will.

Pallu delegated some of his responsibilities to a series of *subdélégués* in Villefranche, Roanne, Saint-Etienne, Montbrison, Bourg-Argental, Saint-Chamond, and Condrieu. These locations were also centers of local authority (seats of *élections* or *bailliages*), as well as communications, industrial, or agricultural marketing centers. The *intendance* in this region was able to adapt to economic changes. It relied on the support of a group of notables, magistrates, and *bailliage* officers who derived prestige and authority from this additional function. The *intendant* was in close touch with his *subdélégués*, through whom he acted in ways that were mostly traditional, except perhaps in regard to stimulating the economy: here, the *intendance* had de facto control over all innovation. Relations between the *intendant* and his staff and between the staff and the local population were guided by experience rather than theory.[22]

The headquarters of the *intendance* was located in the center of Lyons, on place Louis-le-Grand. This was both a workplace and a reception hall for meeting local notables and representing the royal presence in Lyons. Most of the work involved correspondence, either active or passive, which clerks sorted for the attention of either Le Camus or Deville. They in turn prepared responses and assigned tasks. The *subdélégué général* organized Pallu's activities. Pallu was a model of nonabsenteeism: he left Lyons only once a year for Paris and occasionally for fall rounds of work sites in the districts as well as when the time came to assess the distribution of the *taille*. Toward the end of his tenure (1749–1750), however, he lived in Paris, and the bulk of the work fell on Le Camus, but business was dispatched almost as efficiently as when he was present on the scene. We can see this in two episodes involving a single case but separated by an interval of ten years: it took forty-nine days to deal with the matter in 1740 when the *intendant* was present and seventy-seven days in 1750 when he was not (though part of the difference can be attributed to the Easter holiday).

The *intendant* was at the heart of the communications system between Paris and the provinces, which was constantly being improved. He also played a key role in surveys whose purpose was to keep the Contrôle Général and secretaries of state informed about various matters. Some were specific and almost confidential, such as the Blumenstein succession; others were routine and involved gathering information from local specialists. For this the *intendance* relied on its network of *subdélégués*, who constantly submitted progress reports, copies of letters of reprimand sent out to recalcitrant correspondents, and reports on the courts and on inspections of mines and factories. The *subdélégué* served as the eyes of the *intendant* and frequently acted in his stead in gathering information or issuing orders. The veracity of that information and compliance with those orders were not always verified.

Pallu's function came down to serving as an intermediary between the Contrôle Général or Chancellery and local parties; to arbitrating disputes between private individuals; to settling conflicts with local officeholders; and to representing the government in negotiations with workers and repression of violence such as the silk workers' rebellion of 1744. Pallu was essentially an arbitrator, but an arbitrator who always had the joint interests of the state and province in mind. He worked within the framework of a centralized government that made allowances for the decentralized reality. His policies were guided by the need to break down barriers between provinces, build major new roads, and encourage development of industry and mining. His influence grew at the expense of weaker officials (such as the governor), and in negotiations with powerful institutions such as the *consulat* he could muster up considerable authority when necessary.

We may compare Pallu's efforts with those of a man of markedly greater intellectual prowess and ambition: Jacques Turgot. Turgot's career resembled those of his counterpart in Lyons and others who became *intendants* via the same route: a background in the magistracy, a cultivated milieu, and familiarity with enlightened Paris. But he began life at a higher station, as the son of a *conseiller d'Etat;* partook of a different culture, as a graduate of the Sorbonne, an "abbé," steeped in scholastic subtleties; and enjoyed advantages of rank, since his family could claim a century more of nobility, and no doubt of wealth, than Pallu's. In the 1750s he took an active part in the intellectual movement of his time: he "secretly" contributed to the *Encyclopédie* (starting with an article on "Existence," soon followed by several others, including one on "Fairs"). He was a habitué of several salons and knew Physiocrats such as Quesnay and liberals such as Gournay. He read widely: his library attests to the broad range of his curiosity, dominated by his interest in economics and study of languages and history. A correspondent of Voltaire and friend of the philosophes, he was a man of the Enlightenment in the very heart of the state, with no compunctions about the exercise of power so long as he could express himself freely, though of course with due respect for the circumstances. Family tradition, esprit de corps, intelligence, and personal talent: such was the baggage of the man whom the *contrôleur général* sent to Limoges in 1761. He had wanted the Dauphiné or Burgundy but got the Limousin instead.[23]

The newly appointed *intendant* found himself at the end of the world. Limoges was a small, rather sleepy country town in the heart of rural France. Although it was a fairly important administrative center, mail from Paris arrived only twice a week. The tempo of life in Limoges was that of the old agrarian society. Life in the region was complicated by the fact that two *parlements* vied for jurisdiction over it. The boundaries of the *généralité* had been drawn in such a way as to encourage unification, without which the *intendant* would have faced impossible odds. Turgot enlisted the support of local urban worthies: bourgeois, officeholders, and merchants—in other words, the backbone of the local elite, men who held offices, served the state, and enjoyed major and/or minor privileges. In Limoges he negotiated with the fifty-six leading merchants. From their number he recruited the recently ennobled François Ardant, who became his trusted adviser. Turgot involved the merchants in his programs and surveys and inundated them with correspondence that he either prepared himself or delegated to a team of secretaries headed by M. de Baulieu, engineers such as Barbier and Trésaguet, inspectors such as Desmarets, and clerks such as Desnaux. For administrative tasks he relied, like Pallu, on a network of notables and *subdélégués*.

Turgot's activities were concentrated in three main areas: mastering space, gaining the support of privileged notables, and civilizing the populace by means of economic development. He was constantly active in all three areas from the beginning of his tenure. He learned about his territory on horseback. To get a better handle on it, he had a map drawn up by the engineer Cornuau, and in furtherance of his plan to modernize Limoges he had an engineer from the Ponts et Chaussées prepare an invaluable street map of the city. His road-building policy revolved around a plan to unify the region and link its isolated villages with a network of major roads. The goal of his communications policy was similar: he organized a foot-courier service and arranged with village curés to gather necessary information. He fought just as hard to modern-

234

ize the semirural town of Limoges, where he had his headquarters—a town remarkable for its poverty, filth, unpaved streets, fanatical beliefs, and prejudices. His successor put it succinctly: "The mere sight of the Limousin is enough to dispel any idea of elegance." Commerce had barely touched the place, much less progressive forms of social intercourse: there were no cultural societies or academies. Turgot had little knowledge of the baroque, Occitanian south of France, whose festive prejudices, idle ways, and local patois he despised. Even worse, the region had none of what Physiocrats considered the hallmarks of a healthy agricultural economy. Hedgerows and pastures were nothing compared to vast plains of wheat, nor could chestnut and walnut trees take the place of the beech and oak that filled the parks of the Ile-de-France. For Turgot the Limousin was a land of exile, and for thirteen years his only thought was to flee; adaptation came slowly.

Though seriously hampered by a lack of resources, he nevertheless set out to do what he could. Two things had a tremendous impact on the young economist. First, he discovered the backwardness of at least one rural region and learned about local rivalries and conflicts of interest. He witnessed the clash between the ideal of freedom and old habits of monopoly and privilege. And he measured the prospects for change in the paper and kaolin industries and in agriculture and husbandry—all subjects of study by the agronomists of the local agricultural society. Second, the fact that the results of Turgot's plans can be termed a qualified failure led him to embark on a more general reflection on the means and ends of reform and on the state's capacity for transforming the economy and society. Even his efforts to resolve the crisis of 1769, which pointed up certain shortcomings in his theory of the grain trade, led him to broaden his perspective. In the winter of 1773–74 Diderot had this to say in his memoir for Catherine II.

> Our leading public men, the *intendants*, attend a permanent seminar. Upon assuming the *intendance* an intelligent man promptly becomes a shrewd man. A mediocre man takes longer. The *intendant* is never a genius, but he learns. Unfortunately, the good men perish on the job and almost never reach the ministries. M. Turgot is one of the best men in the kingdom and perhaps one of the shrewdest in every area. He will never get out of Limoges, and if he does get out, I shall jump for joy,

for it will mean that the spirit of our ministry will have changed utterly and that the present state of affairs will have been altered for the better in an almost miraculous fashion.[24]

Here we see a hopeful new figure coming into the limelight after conducting an experiment that has become widely known and been abundantly commented on: a man who actually experienced the old agricultural kingdom that paternalistic reformers had dreamed of improving. We also witness the passing of the generation that grew up under Louis XV and operated on the assumption that reform of the Ancien Régime was possible. It would soon be replaced by another generation whose frame of reference lay outside the old norms, which had proved incapable of resolving the tensions of traditional society. It is therefore a matter of some interest, as we come to the end of this second look at the relations between Paris and the provinces, to find the *intendance,* as both a parcel of territory and an instrument of power, at the center of a system of instruction in the possibilities of change yet severely limited by the ambiguity of the traditional representation and the practical impossibility of choice.

Provincials and Provinces

In the relationship between Paris and the provinces—a relationship of unity as well as opposition—there is one important dimension that cannot be neglected because it played such an important role in establishing the hierarchy of spaces and representations, namely, culture.

In the cultural realm the triumph of the capital is clear. The keys to cultural power were all in Paris: in the abundance of illustrious institutions, in the munificence of public and private investment, and in the combined interventions of the Church, which controlled the educational system, and the state, which funded such prestigious new institutions as the Collège Royal and the Jardin du Roi, the Ecole des Ponts et Chaussées, and the Ecole des Mines, all in Paris, and which influenced, through its selections and rejections, the agencies that controlled and censored intellectual life. Paris enjoyed incomparable resources because it could draw on the entire kingdom to supply its cultural needs and market its cultural wares.

The predominance of Paris did not, however, imply that the provinces were turned into a cultural desert, as scholars have been all too wont to repeat in the wake of Lavisse and others. On the contrary, what is interesting about the eighteenth century is that it was possible for provincials, while clinging to distinctive old customs that discredited them in Parisian eyes, to adopt new attitudes. Heightened contempt went hand in hand with tightened control, while provincials both embraced the new culture and were wary of it. It would take another book to compare the cultural resources of the capital with those of the provinces. For now, let us simply examine how the image of the disconsolate provincial was related to centralization and how the reinvigoration of provincialism was related to the spread of both new ideas and new hopes of decentralizing reform. The debate over decentralization—a crucial factor in both the crisis of the Ancien Régime and the evolution of French society to this day—was thus a central feature of salon conversation and academic debate as well as an everyday concern of ordinary Frenchmen no less than a preoccupation of intellectuals.

Provincial Unhappiness and Intellectual Centralization

In classical culture the provincial was criticized for his behavior, which was deemed backward relative to the norms of the court and city, and for his "linguistic deficit." The two phenomena were of unequal weight: the first was by nature already a distinctive object within literary and scholarly circulation; the second raised far-reaching questions about the structure of social and political relations, the gap between ordinary people and notables, and the homogenization of cultural space (because provincial patois had impeded standardization of customs and other reforms since the sixteenth century).

The eighteenth century inherited a fund of images and stereotypes deeply etched into the landscape of prejudice. When, for example, Voltaire wrote to congratulate Turgot on his appointment to Limoges, he could not restrain himself: "So, you are off to win the purses and the hearts of the Limousins and to oblige M. de Pourceaugnac's entire family to pay the third *vingtième*." Clearly, Molière's creation was still in people's minds, and it was easy for respectable folk to express horror at the very thought of the Limousin or some other provincial "Siberia," as Turgot himself put it. The force of classical absolutist culture was twofold: provincials felt inferior to Parisians, and the intellectual values of the capital were taken to be absolute.

To one degree or another, these rural images and stereotypes conveyed representations of the thought and behavior of different provincial groups. Different types of socialization left their mark on the imagination. These images were not pure fantasies: they bore some relation to concrete realities and in fact expressed different ways of perceiving those very realities. Interestingly, this sort of ethnic characterology developed at the same time as the modern state and grew increasingly sophisticated as the state extended its control. The way in which different groups of people lived was contrasted with the ethos of the dominant classes. Ethnic stereotyping (which was atemporal, intolerant of contradiction, and as repetitive as a code) served to regulate relations between groups. Real conflicts of class and identity could sometimes be avoided. The ultimate question is whether a true history of "otherness" is possible.

The code by which the provincial was identified can be deciphered in any number of texts: plays, novels, travel accounts, administrative reports, observations by physicians and scientists, and geographic treatises. All reveal elements of a common language with four primary keys: the political, having to do with loyalty to the prince and in many cases the antithesis between rebellion and unity, quickness of temper and readiness to serve (the Breton was reputedly bellicose, the Tourangeau tranquil); the religious, reflecting a need for a unified faith (the Norman is naturally inclined to piety, but the man from the Gévaudan is a Calvinized savage); the economic (there are industrious groups, good housekeepers, sober provincials); and finally the social, which includes manners and morals, intellectual qualities and achievements. On the basis of these principles, prizes were distributed in accordance with historical loyalty to the center and geographic distance from Paris and the sun of the court.

On the eve of the Revolution, Nicolas Restif de la Bretonne, a Burgundian and ardent champion of nature and of provincial peasant culture as against the corrupting city, as well as a creator of fantasies and a man fascinated by masks, wrote his *Histoire du ménage parisien*. The Parisian Déliée, daughter of Jean Joseph Cocu and Sophie de Gallanville, is to marry Jean Joseph's partner Placide Sotentot, a textile merchant. The need to choose a wet nurse ends with several physicians being asked for their opinion about what part of France is most likely to produce the desired rare pearl: Dr. Têtechaudinot favors Picardy, Dr. Brutentout prefers Provence, Dr. Baudetinat the Berry, while Dr. Crassenpoch likes Lorraine, and Dr. Goupipète opts for the Limousin: "They took the advice of Dr. Trognerouge [the Burgundian], who shouted the loudest and who criticized the Norman's penchant for cider, the Picard's petulance, the Breton's choleric humor, the stupidity of the Champenois, Berrichon, and Tourangeau, the Lorrain's baseness, and the Poitevin for the colic to which people in the provinces are subject."

In other parts of this text one can easily decipher three mythologies: first, a mythological hierarchy of morals and behavior, symbolized by names (Niouininon, "neither yes nor no," for the Norman; Toutenvent, "all in wind," for the Gascon); second, a mythology of food and drink, which indicates diversity and competence; and third, a mythology of social behavior, brutality, stupidity, and clumsiness, which supposedly distinguished provincials from the uniformly more polished Parisians. Other texts carried similar implications: the plays of Molière, which were still performed at the Comédie Française et Royale *(George Dandin, Monsieur de Pourceaugnac, La Comtesse d'Escarbagnac);* the novels of the bourgeois realist tradition from Furetière to Marivaux; anthologies of wit; Montfort's *Vasconia;* and of course almanacs. The general aim was to use laughter to discriminate: by putting everyone in his place, laughter reinforced social roles while at the same time releasing tension (derision briefly stood order on its head, thus providing the barest glimpse of other possibilities) and administering a critique in the form of satire. Thus the dividing line between provincial and Parisian behavior was firmly established.

No objection could be made to the influence of language through political and cultural institutions and the circulation of books. The king's language was French, and its use defined two boundaries: one between the vulgar and the respectable, the other between Paris and the provinces. Access to the language explained both collective and individual backwardness. Bear in mind that Picard was spoken just thirty miles from Paris and that two-thirds of French subjects routinely spoke a language other than French. This was how things stood on the eve of the Revolution: the *langue d'oïl* was spoken by 16 million people in the north of France, but some of them habitually spoke the Picard, Norman, or Burgundian dialects; 7 or 8 million people expressed themselves in one of the variants of the *langue d'oc* (Auvergnat, Provençal, Gascon, Limousin, Franco-Lyonnais). The rest spoke Flemish, Breton, Basque, Catalan, or

Alsatian (or some other Germanic dialect). The linguistic map was highly complex, but the important point is that in the eighteenth century, learned people began to think of these dialects and patois in terms of Parisian linguistic superiority: these impure tongues spoken by peasants and others threatened the purity of Paris.

To be sure, these developments were the results of a campaign launched two centuries earlier, which had dislodged Latin from its administrative and judicial positions and discredited the various dialects. Since the middle of the seventeenth century, French accounted for four-fifths of all printed materials. It was the language of notables and of the ruling class. The state shrewdly tolerated and confirmed provincial customs and thus gained the support of elites everywhere, who were the first to feel the attraction of Paris, thereby winning converts to French while making them feel inferior owing to the prestige of French literature, which was a model not only for France but for all of Europe, and to the growing use of French in administrative dealings and public affairs. The accelerated distribution of news and improvements in transportation further reduced the areas in which local dialects were spoken. Villagers who traveled regularly or for long periods spoke only French: these included soldiers, domestics, and migrant workers. Those who remained behind stayed with the more familiar dialect and spoke the official language poorly if at all.

Although there was no language policy per se, as there was after the Revolution, contacts with the dominant culture worked against dialect, as did a dynamic local economy. For a while, the language spoken depended on the sphere in which a person moved: the Church, which published sermons and catechisms in Breton and Provençal, tolerated patois; a notary might use a Frenchified Occitanian dialect, in which the vocabulary was *oc* but the syntax French; a judge might interrogate a witness in dialect and have the clerk record the questions and answers in French; insults, whether in Morlaix or Toulouse, were in dialect so as to wound all the more. But as soon as social or economic commerce came into the picture—any form of exchange from love to trade—French won out, even in the south, though not without compromise or error. People still spoke dialect at home and in the country. They learned it before they learned French, and notables needed facility in the local tongue. The few who learned two or three languages (do not forget Latin) reaped social and cultural rewards: they could serve as intermediaries. In 1755 Boissier de Sauvages discussed this spontaneous bilingualism and its role in separating Paris from the provinces:

> The *langue d'oc* is the language of the people and even of respectable folk brought up in this province. It is the first language that comes to mind, and people speak it freely when, liberated from the respect due to a superior or from the embarrassment caused by the presence of a stranger, they have to converse with a friend or chat familiarly with a servant. French, which they deem inappropriate in all but the most serious situations, becomes for them a foreign language, a language for ceremonious occasions, and they do violence to their own natures when they speak it.

In this trickle-down process, books and other printed matter played an essential role. The influence of Paris, coupled with the fact that what the provinces produced was either trivial and routine or else a clandestine or counterfeit version of materials destined primarily for Paris, confirmed the triumph of the capital, the victory of its language and values. This did not change even after the Enlightenment rehabilitated nature and the countryside. Enlightened thinkers looked at the lay of the land with a new social physics in mind, so that at last intervention seemed compatible with the laws of nature and reconciliation of the "two Frances" seemed possible. The focus of attention shifted to the relation between nature and morality in an urban-versus-rustic context. Apart from the many moralists who followed Rousseau's lead, there was also an economic critique of the city as corrupting consumer, as well as liberal praise for the city as a force for change. Neither did justice to the cultural inequality revealed by the provincial debate.

Peevish, Satisfied, and Discontented Provincials

Provincial self-consciousness was divided. Although provincials saw themselves as inferior (because the provinces could give only what they had, and the best people were leaving), they remained proud (it was possible to lead a quiet and happy life in the provinces, which were beginning to rediscover their past and take pride in their present splendors). Between inferiority and superiority certain "defining drives" manifested themselves. The old basis of inequality began to change. Once, the majority had lived in obedience and subordination to the authorities, while the privileged minority inherited the right to rule. In the first phase of change, from the seventeenth century to the 1750s, people adhered uncritically to the new values of the capital. Then came the prerevolutionary crisis, and in a climate of abortive reform and provocative debate there can be no doubt that there was a revival of provincial pride and political demands.

The academic movement through which we learn of this evolution should not be thought of as an expression of a policy conceived in Paris and implemented in the provinces. There was no clear-cut opposition between a totally absolutist phase and a decentralizing phase. In this area the transition from the seventeenth to the eighteenth century exhibited neither continuity nor rupture but a shift or transformation brought about by the embrace of new values. Learned societies were founded in the provinces as early as the beginning of the seventeenth century, and the movement picked up steam as the century progressed.[25] Academies proliferated everywhere. In Paris there were the great institutions created under royal patronage such as the Académie Française, the Académie des Sciences, the Académie des Inscriptions, and the Académie de Peinture, but the provinces also contributed; in the end, some forty learned societies functioned with varying degrees of success.

The institutional model that prevailed from the end of the reign of Louis XIV to the Regency succeeded first of all because its circles brought together not just men of letters but scholars of all sorts. The capital could afford to offer its intelligentsia five different societies, but a provincial metropolis had to make do with just one circle for all its intellectuals. A second reason for the model's success was its explicit and implicit embrace of Parisian norms, codes, and values. The uniformity of practice that created a bond between the Parisian and provincial administrations had the same effect in this cultural sphere. If we study the history of the foundation of provincial learned societies, we see the importance of royal patronage and the material dependency on the absolutist administration. The academies could never have been founded without the support, protection, and intervention of men on the scene: *intendants*, governors, and bishops worked hand in hand with veritable provincial pressure groups in Paris to get things done. And finally, when it came to organizational formalities, provincial academies received help along with promises of material and symbolic support from the fine gentlemen in Paris.

Readers interested in further details may wish to consult earlier work of mine.[26] The location of provincial academies was not fortuitous. Although they flourished everywhere, they were particularly numerous in the south of France and on the country's periphery. Toulouse, Marseilles, Montpellier, Arles, Nîmes, Bordeaux, Lyons, Villefranche, Caen, and Soissons are illustrative of the first stage of development, in which the provinces tried to compensate for their cultural backwardness and learn the language and customs of the court and capital. Although the movement may have slowed at times, its energy came from its connection with two forms of elite sociability: formal gatherings that placed a premium on politeness and manners, and less formal fraternal gatherings of people bound by age and friendship. Gradually these gatherings became more regular and organized, paving the way for the realization of a common cultural project.

The provincial academies were closed and selective. Because membership carried with it social distinction as well as the promise of contributing intellectually to the process of change, the new institutions drew support from the administrative, ecclesiastical, and political networks, from the provinces to the court and the city to the antechambers of the Council. The first wave of academic foundations, which by 1715 had spent its force, opened up two avenues for further development. Because the new institutions were allied with the academies in Paris, they found a role to play in the development of the absolute monarchy, demonstrating the alliance between knowledge and power. Societies in both the north and south were united by the common goal of spreading the new learning as widely as possible, but they were torn between dependence on Paris and independence and between the allure of the capital and the vitality of the provinces, just as they were caught between the pressure of local elites loyal to the Ancien Régime and the influence of royal agents such as the *intendants* Basville, Foucault, and Pallu, who "temporarily" took up the provincial cause.

From the 1720s until the 1790s, the movement grew until its magnitude raised a question for the Republic of Letters as a whole: "Just how far should the proliferation of learned societies be allowed to go?" the Académie Française asked in a question posed to competitors in its annual

essay competition for 1750. The factors that had encouraged this proliferation were still at work, indeed more potent than ever. Bishops everywhere were determined to have their say about the need for religious
orthodoxy among neo-Immortals. Provincial governors saw an opportunity to refurbish escutcheons somewhat tarnished by the offensive of the
intendants: among them were Villeroy in Lyons, Villars in Provence,
Luxembourg (a friend of Cideville's and Voltaire's) in Rouen, Belle-Isle
in Metz. *Intendants* saw provincial academies as another means of curry-
ing favor with local notables and of solving administrative problems
informally, hence were willing to become members: Pallu, Bertin, and La
Michodière would all court the academicians of Lyons. And Parisian
academicians (among them Bignon, Montesquieu, Réaumur, Chicoyneau,
La Peyronnie, and Mairan) continued to offer patronage and guidance. In
Paris as in the provinces, no one doubted that the *intendants* and others
could hasten or slow academic development at will.

The insistence on intervention by the local authorities, who in most
cases willingly complied, coincided with the emergence of a new type of
provincial consciousness. The fascination with Paris that was obvious in
so much of the writing about provincial academies began to give way to
suspicion or even indifference. The provinces dreamed of liberation from
Paris and insisted on a rather implausible equality with the capital. To be
sure, references to Paris and its scholars and institutions continued
throughout the century, and allowances were made for the influence of
this group or that group, but questions began to be raised. Doubts were
evident, for example, in Marseilles, whose academy did not claim to rival
Paris for genius but insisted on recognition all the same—an insistence
for which Chalamond de La Visclède, its perpetual secretary, became the
butt of everyone's ridicule, including that of Voltaire. The decline of
beaux esprits and the rise of science, coupled with local utilitarianism and
a certain resentment of specialists by amateurs, led to demands that the
spirit of "equality" be extended to the Republic of Letters. "If the capital
retains a proper superiority over the provinces, it can be said in general
that the provinces honor the capital and lend glory to its primacy," or so
Querriau set out to prove in Clermont-Ferrand in 1747. If Paris continued to exert its fascination on the provinces, provincial complaints about
the capital were now the other side of the coin. Cultural inequalities were
no longer acceptable, especially since provincial academics were nearly
always on the side of change and ready to promote it wherever possible.

As the founding of new academies slowed, other kinds of societies sprang up to fill the gaps, as it were. Not only did the scale change, as in the case of Freemasonry, but a new competition developed, a competition that favored local autonomy by fostering a larger number of small, self-sufficient cenacles. A more flexible administrative oversight facilitated this proliferation of new groups capable of satisfying both the old need for social intercourse and the new need for information from the outside world. Such information circulated in abundance at all levels thanks to networks of correspondence as well as the Parisian and provincial press. Federation plans show how the provincial movement saw itself in relation to the capital. The petitions for federation that were addressed to Abbé Yart of Rouen and Condorcet, perpetual secretary of the Académie des Sciences, met with open reluctance. When Condorcet proposed to coordinate activities at the center, circulate news of new discoveries, and thereby turn the work of the academy into "a branch of the general administration," certain provincials opposed the idea that association leads to servitude and that acceptance of the government's principles was incompatible with intellectual freedom. This debate led nowhere, but it did point up the contrast between two different ways of looking at things, two contradictory sensibilities: on one side the men of the Parisian Enlightenment linked the fate of reform and philosophy to the idea of a virtuous liberal monarchy committed to development through cultural homogenization; while on the other side the men of the provincial Enlightenment capped a century of work and reflection by arguing in favor of the autonomy of intellectuals, the equality of academies, and parity between Paris and the provinces.

No one in the provinces doubted that the capital boasted a larger number of men of "talent," not to say "genius." Yet some of these men sprang from provincial soil, which replenished the ranks of the great academies. The provinces were ready to heed their lessons, but only in a relation of parity. They had a number of reasons on their side: one could write as well in a provincial city as in Paris, because the Muses liked silence, and quiet was good for thinking. Everywhere the demand for products of the mind brought forth a new supply. During a stay in Lyons, Grimod de La Reynière noted the progress of the local intelligentsia, and his remarks probably hold true for other cities as well. A new provincial sensibility was emerging in response to the Parisian conception of reason: "Here as in Paris scholars are friendly, studious, and communicative, but the academy has neither the haughtiness nor the charlatanism that can be found in some of your literary societies. If the Enlightenment and learning have made as much progress here as among you, I can assure you that the spirit of tolerance, amenity, and true philosophy has made even more."

Provincials contrasted the divided culture of the capital to the unity and harmony of regional circles. Of course the reality differed markedly from this dream, but one should not underestimate the importance of the dream, for it shows that the provinces and the capital did not manage to live at the same tempo. Indeed, when the tempo accelerated in Paris, it slowed in the provinces, where the Enlightenment took on a distinctive cast. We have an excellent witness to all of this in the person of Roland de La Platière. As an inspector of manufacturing, he was a servant of the state, but as an academician in Villefranche, Amiens, and Lyons, he was a man of the provinces. Consider a brief text of his entitled *De l'influence des lettres dans les provinces comparée à leur influence dans les capitales* (Lyons, 1785). In it he makes the case that the utilitarian Enlightenment of the provinces reconciled *otium*, or the leisure of the rich, with *negotium*, or the activity of the enterprising. Furthermore, the provincial Enlightenment refused any divorce between culture and nature, because the study of "nature elevates the soul by way of the truths one discovers by contemplating it." This takes us back to the debates on space, the economy, and stability versus change: on one side one has abstraction, idleness, and study, and on the other the concrete, the need to live, and the desire to get rich by making others rich.[27]

Here, then, the intellectual expansion made possible by urban power reached its limits. Residents of provincial metropolises and mediocre *chefs-lieux* were aware of the extraordinary force that had gathered on the banks of the Seine, but they also knew that there was a price to be paid for that glory: it abetted inequality and countenanced indifference; it isolated individuals from contact with others and thus led to a loss of feeling for concrete reality; and it represented a risk for both individuals and society. Pre-romantic ideas about the pain of living (admirably analyzed by André Monglond and Pierre Trahard)[28] developed with the new provincial consciousness; they gave rise to critiques of the city and apologias for nature. The masters of the new sensibility were provincials who kept faith with their roots: Diderot from Langres, Rousseau from Geneva, Germaine de Staël, also from Switzerland, Laclos from Amiens,

Bernardin de Saint-Pierre from Le Havre, and Restif de la Bretonne from Burgundy. From Paris they plucked the strings of sensitive provincial hearts and fueled the debate on the virtues of a life close to nature versus the urban style of life, yet again raising the issue of stability versus development. The Enlightenment was forever hesitating on the road to progress.

PART TWO

Powers and Conflicts

8

⚜ ⚜ ⚜

The King and His Subjects

IT IS OFTEN DIFFICULT for historians to understand how institutions think, even if we accept the notion that, while lacking brains and ideas of their own, they do think because they establish what is remembered and what is forgotten, distinguish between good and evil, and determine the very conditions under which intellectual work takes place, and hence the lives of those without whom they would indeed not think. In the foregoing studies of geography and economics and of the social and cultural factors that encouraged or hindered change, we have observed the process of institutional thinking in the classificatory schemes developed by the institutions of the Ancien Régime as well as the surveys that supported those schemes and the administrative logic that inspired those surveys. This is what anthropologists mean by institutional thinking.[1]

What bound the inhabitants of eighteenth-century France together in a community? What were the sources of solidarity and cooperation, and what gave rise to splits, rejections, and mistrust? These are the crucial questions. The period marked a shift from one concept of community to another: from a strong concept based on a society of customs and traditions, on the monarchy, and on religion, in which individual identities were entirely determined by the community, to a weak concept, more fragmentary and utilitarian—a reflection or intrinsic component of the individualistic society of exchange—in which the community is the result of utilitarian cooperation among members seeking to further their own particular interests. In the new conception the community may be external to the individual, but the individual still discovers himself in the community: this is what links the old way of looking at things to the new. No matter which pole is emphasized, "for better or for worse, individuals really share their thoughts and to a certain extent harmonize their preferences, and they cannot make major decisions except within the institutional framework they construct for themselves."[2]

By looking at how authorities and subjects interacted in both harmony and conflict, we hope to discover how legitimate the new view of the world seemed to contemporaries and how the cultural system preserved its institutional arrangements while dealing with matters of justice and injustice, equality and inequality. This was the ground on which the philosophes based their reflection. To understand their thinking, as well as the clash between Physiocrats and liberals over geography and economics, we need a guide. Montesquieu fills the bill because his thinking (as Louis Althusser once showed, not without a certain distortion of Montesquieu's ideas) was situated between politics and history, between observation of the present and explanation through reflection on customs and other patterns that allowed him to interpret modernity in terms of the triumph of commercial capitalism. The question that arises at this point is: What chance did the absolute monarchy have of reforming itself sufficiently to cope with the accelerated pace of historical change?[3]

The Monarchy between Two Ages: Montesquieu

Montesquieu's intellectual physiognomy is surely one of the most interesting of the period, as well as one of the best known.[4] His work, serene and prudent, belongs to a tradition of nondoctrinaire thought. He did not sweep away all facts with the back of his hand, as Rousseau did in his *Discours*. For Montesquieu, politics was the product of history and geography. He knew the world. Though a provincial, he had traveled Europe from north to south, from England to Italy. As a magistrate, he knew the law, whose philosophy he had plumbed in the classics (Cicero, Tacitus, the Stoics) as well as the moderns (Bossuet, Malebranche, and Hobbes, whose work he refuted). His politics was a science of the real.[5]

His personal experience of power (echoes of which can be heard in the *Lettres persanes*); his judgment of events and of the bankruptcy of the Regency, which led him to worry about the potential despotism of the Regent and his henchmen; his likely (though not proven) participation in the discussions of France's first political club, the Club de l'Entresol (to which he supposedly read the *Dialogue de Sylla et d'Eucrate* on tyranny); his interests as an important member of *parlement* and major wine producer well informed about the price of Bordeaux in London and Amsterdam; his involvement in academies along with other magistrate-intellectuals; and above all his aloofness from factional dispute and his keen interest in events—all these things made Montesquieu an authentic witness to his times, a man capable of analyzing the politics of the day and making sense of its apparent incoherence. Montesquieu saw the monarchy both as it was and as it should have been. We may therefore turn to his texts for a better understanding of the political problems of the age of absolutism.

Montesquieu's analysis of the three types of government is well known: republic (aristocratic or democratic), despotism, and monarchy. His classification replaced one that political science had used since the time of Aristotle: monarchy, aristocracy, democracy. To each regime he assigned a corresponding mode of government, along with historical and moral principles to explain its development. His entire argument, especially the contrast, based more on experience than scholarly investigation, between despotism and monarchy, was intended not simply as an assessment of reality but as a value judgment and justification of political choices. Montesquieu favored what he called a *monarchie à la française*, which he hoped to reinforce by borrowing a few new ideas from the English, since moderate states had the biggest impact on history. Monarchy survived as a tolerable regime that allowed some room for freedom in civil society because its fundamental institutions prevented abuses of power. Here, political practice confirmed the spirit and thought of the institutions that governed relations between the sovereign and his people.

Montesquieu's essential argument is contained in Books 2 through 5 of *De l'esprit des lois*. In reading this text, one should keep in mind the idea that Montesquieu's basic goal was to understand the reasons for certain practices:

> They [i.e., practices] should be appropriate to the nature of the country; to the climate, whether frozen, scorching, or temperate; to the quality of the land, its situation and grandeur; to the way of life of its people, whether farmers, hunters, or shepherds; they should also accord with the degree of freedom that the constitution can tolerate; with the religion of the inhabitants as well as with their inclinations, wealth,

number, commerce, customs, and manners. Finally, they stand in relation to other things: to their origins, to the objectives of the legislators, and to the order of things on which they are established.[6]

This theory of the nature of government is thus both rationalist and relativist. The nature of monarchy, its defining characteristic, is that it is government by one person, but that person's power is not despotic because it is limited by fundamental laws. Its principle is "honor," that is, "the judgment of each person and each condition." Honor was more important than the virtue of princes (which was essential for both doctrinaire absolutists like Bossuet and aristocratic reformers like Fénelon) or citizens. Montesquieu stood at the crossroads between the old idea of the French monarchy as based on the *consilium* and sacred authority and the new absolutism, vanquisher of the aristocracy. The unity that joined nature to principle and the power of one individual to honor was fundamental; these were not two separate concepts but two terms of a vital and necessary relation.

The fundamental laws of the kingdom and the role of the famous *corps intermédiaires* made the French monarchy the model of a moderate state inimical to despotism. Denis Richet has shown that, by making the *corps intermédiaires* an element of the unwritten constitution and acknowledging the need to guard against the possible degeneration of the monarchy into despotism (a charge that had been leveled against Louis XIV), Montesquieu took a crucial step with implications that extended beyond the aristocracy: at stake was the liberty of all, which only a composite elite could guarantee. Henceforth the contrast between despotism and liberty would be central to all political debate: not only did this distinction justify criticism of the monarchy (which the *parlements* undertook to provide) and permit hope of reform (administrative, judicial, penal, fiscal, and religious), but also, what was even more important, it made it possible to think about the heritage of the past, the weight of tradition, and the still vital forces that existed within the old landed kingdom while simultaneously doing justice to the new society in which there was room for trade, wealth, and talent.

Montesquieu's social and political analysis was not divorced from his vision of the economy: he sensed changes and wanted to incorporate them into his thinking. When he insisted that merchants be socially integrated into the definition of the monarchy, he echoed Voltaire: Montesquieu's statements were less bold but partook of the same ideology.[7] The old liberties and exemptions granted to municipalities, provinces, *parlementaires,* ecclesiastics, and nobles were no more anachronistic in his eyes than in the eyes of most of his contemporaries: they preserved the structure of society from the king on down to the lowliest of his subjects and from Paris to the remotest provinces, all the more so because they guaranteed the social virtues of competitive liberty and labor. Thus, "there may be unity in a state where one sees nothing but trouble, that is, a harmony that gives rise to prosperity, which is the only true peace. The parts of a state are like the parts of the universe, eternally bound together by the actions of some and the reactions of others."[8]

Monarchy, Montesquieu, argued, was the state for modern times for reasons deriving from the principle of honor and the judgments of people of different ranks, possibly coupled with the dynamic of social passions stemming from the birth of liberalism. Any political society is a sum of differences plus a whole.[9] This was the conclusion that emerged from the interaction of the monarchy with its constituent populations, churches, and social groups. Hierarchies of status and wealth divided society; nascent public opinion judged the actions of the state; and the rise of new powers disrupted harmony and made reform impossible. A whole capable of unifying these parts was therefore essential.

King and Subjects: Elements of the Relationship

Montesquieu showed what a regime that respected its fundamental laws could be expected to provide: a stable government, greater security for those who governed, and protection against despotism. This vision of monarchy presupposed that, though one person ruled, power was in fact shared with a whole milieu and with various pressure groups while at the same time limited by a veritable mystique of Christian justification implicit in the dogma of the union of king and kingdom. At the beginning of the eighteenth century Chancellor d'Aguesseau stated that "the king and the kingdom constitute but a single object." Fifty years later, in his flagellation speech, Louis XV made the same point: "The rights and prohibitions of the nation, which some would dare construe as a body separate from the monarch, are necessarily conjoined with mine and reside in my hands alone . . . Public order in its entirety emanates from me."

Behind this assertion, which can be read on its face as a rebuke to would-be challengers and an expression of authoritarian attitudes incompatible with France's fundamental laws, one senses two important changes: first, the king is justifying his power only in his own sphere, which is that of a function associated with the public weal; and second, respect for the constitutionalism of the *corps* is implicit in the king's admonition. The organic metaphor of the state—the king as head, the people as trunk and members—served as a kind of constitution, which intermediate powers could invoke. The king's role included three distinct parts: the first was enacted at court, where the royal individual encountered the world of practical power; the second was enacted in anointment, where religion came into contact with theories of the state; and the third was enacted in the political sphere, where by midcentury the waning of the political charisma of the absolutist religion was already detectable.

King and Court

The power structure and the pressures of the moment came together in the consciousness of the monarch. What good are royal biographies? They can be useful not if they celebrate some secret, nostalgic cult, but if they help us to understand the resources available to the king and the limits imposed on his action; not if they try to interpret events by psychology, but if they help us to weigh in the balance such disparate factors as the king's abilities, the factions that swirled around him, the importance of personality clashes in relation to the issues of the day, and the selection of personnel in accordance with antagonistic conceptions of royal power, social order, the economic regime, and foreign policy. Ambitious efforts in this direction were inaugurated by Hans Lüthy in the 1960s, but despite a huge amount of work the surface has as yet only been scratched.[10] The crucial goals are to distinguish between the person and the personage, the political role and the effects of circumstance, as well as to gain a better understanding of court society, the driving force behind all social and political organization.

The King's Contribution: Louis XV and Louis XVI

In the *Lettres de Xénocrate à Phères* (1724), Montesquieu expressed a hope:

The monarch who reigns at present in Sicyona is a young prince who makes every Sicyonian hope for happy times. He has a charming face and the most natural manners, he likes to see good done and to right wrongs, and he takes pleasure in the truth . . . May he bring his subjects not just wealth and plenty but the peace of mind that people savor only under good princes, that security in one's estate and inner peace that are always due to honor and virtue.

Here we have the king as model and symbol of hope, security, and prosperity, God's instrument for rewarding virtuous nations but "the scourge of nations He wishes to punish." Similar portraits of good kings can be found in *Arsace et Isménie* (written in 1742 and published in 1783): necessary royal qualities include a sharp mind, a kind heart, and a sincere soul in order to ensure probity in administration, equity in justice, and respect for the law. These were the standards, and the beginning of each new reign offered an opportunity to reiterate one's hopes. In 1774 Louis XV died, Louis XVI took the throne, and people sang this song in the streets of Paris to the tune of the *Air des pendus:*

> Or, écoutez petits et grands
> l'histoire d'un roi de vingt ans
> qui va nous ramener en France
> les bonnes moeurs et l'abondance:
> D'après ce plan que deviendront
> et les catins et les fripons?

> Listen, people great and small
> To the story of a king, aged twenty,
> Who will soon bring healthy customs
> And plenty back to France.
> Under this plan, what will become
> Of the trollops and the scoundrels?

The words of this song express the very real connection that the people felt with their young king. When the monarch was young, the kingdom was also young: youth betokened the new sovereign's good will, his capacity for change, and his role as arbiter among the coalitions of interests that surrounded him. It is easy to imagine the importance of the prince's personality, the influence of his upbringing, and the power of his entourage.

"Who was the king?" Today, when we paint a royal portrait in response to this question, it is apt to be a metaphorical or metaphysical portrait. In describing the king's symbolic body, we reinterpret sovereignty and power as elements of a system of political representation. We distinguish between the physical body (historical and perishable), the juridical and political body (the king as embodiment of the kingdom and sovereignty), and the sacred body (the priest-king representing God on earth); yet all were in fact combined in a single organism in proportions that varied with the historical status of the political and the sacred. Representations of the king took many forms: medals, festivals, paintings, eulogies, histories, and coronations that enacted the "transubstantiation" of individual into monarch. These signs of power became absolute, legitimating the power they represented: "Caesar's portrait is Caesar," said the logicians of Port-Royal. Louis Marin has shown how this system of signs functioned in the case of Louis XIV. In the eighteenth century, historians agree, the sacred dimension of power dwindled and questions were raised about the "political body" as well. Yet even as absolutism tottered, the king's historical body—his person and habits—continued to play a significant role, one whose history has yet to be written. Louis XV was an ambiguous figure, and Louis XVI was weak.[11]

My problem is not to do justice in weighing pros and cons, virtues and vices, capabilities and shortcomings, but to understand the interaction of character, milieu, influence, and statecraft. The *métier de roi*, or royal statecraft, was the heart of the French administrative monarchy. The king's habits and character are interesting because they influenced the sovereign's relationship to the kingdom by way of his personal relations with powerful men close to him and with other powers more distant, relations that were reflected in representations of society's respect for the king, hence of the respect that the state, the society, and the people who constituted it felt for themselves. This is not an easy exercise, because the psychology of people of the past is no easier to fathom than that of our contemporaries. By what gauge are we to measure character through surviving testimony? By what theoretical compass are we to pinpoint complexes and sensibilities? We cannot resort to the maxims of ordinary psychology, which are no truer than their opposites, as Marc Bloch pointed out in his *Apologie pour l'histoire*. Hence we shall try to avoid pointless anecdotes.[12]

Michel Antoine has tried his hand at this task, and succeeded, in the case of Louis XV. He has made his way through the literature of slander by sleazy pamphleteers (whose work, incidentally, can be read differently from the way Antoine reads it) as well as the writings of more respectable authors. Louis XV himself wrote a great deal, but his personal files have disappeared. The king's confessor, Abbé Mandoux, also wrote a lot, following the lead of Jean Héroard, but he burned all twenty-two cartons of his texts: "I spoke too truly in them," he explained later. Hence it is difficult to use the person to explain the personage. Certain traits stand out nonetheless.

Louis XV acceded early to the throne. He was born in 1710, and his father died that same year. The Grand Dauphin, his grandfather, died in 1711, his mother in 1712, and his uncle Berry in 1714. Hence Louis was thrust as a child into a playground for adults—a child without emotional fiber, subjected to the instruction of a majestic cretin, the duc de Villeroy, who taught him two things: the look, the bearing of majesty and, as a result of too many obligatory formal appearances, a horror of crowds. The king was a timid man, torn between the public figure, who used his elaborate manners as a mask yet exploded at times with gibes that were interpreted as marks of cynicism or cruelty but were in fact signs of solitude, and the private man, who was charming and hungry for affection and intimacy. These qualities won the heart of Fleury, his tutor. The discrepancy between the public and private man presaged the way in which affairs of state would later both bore him and, when they gave him an opportunity to overcome his perpetual inhibitions, engage his active interest (the so-called *secret du roi* referred to matters that received the king's personal attention).

Any number of contemporaries, not all of them courtiers, recognized the king's intelligence, clarity of vision, and memory. An excellent education left him with a remarkable knowledge of Europe and the world, in which geography played a central role. François Chevallier, who taught at the Collège Royal, made a good student of him and introduced him to the mathematical empiricism of the day. He had a good grasp of terrain and forces and understood the principles of military architecture. The young king took an interest in Bélidor's "hydraulic architecture." He could draw, and with his curious mind he liked to spend time alone with Gabriel reconstructing Versailles or with Quesnay discussing rural economics. He became patron to Buffon, Nollet, and the surgeon La Peyronnie. He was a man who preferred his study to the world and whose action was in many ways the perverse outcome of a style of government that he neither invented nor modified and of a character which, unlike that of Louis XIV, was more hesitant than theatrical.

Two facts will suffice to show how difficult it is to understand how power functioned in this period.[13] The first has to do with the odd combination of libertinage and religion. To the horror of the Church, which overlooked its own sins in this regard, the king enjoyed the company of the favorites placed in his bed by one faction or another. He had two sorts of affairs. There were first of all the open, acknowledged mistresses: Mailly, Châteauroux, Pompadour, who deserves a special place all her own (intelligent and philosophical, Mme de Pompadour intervened in affairs of state only to stiffen Louis's resolve), and, last of the line, Du Barry. But there were also the *petites maîtresses,* the temporary favorites, shadowy figures in the Deer Park, who were the subject of endless rumors. The acknowledged mistresses were a part of court society, whereas the unacknowledged ones lived in obscurity. They were protected, married off, and kept in secret with their bastard offspring (Antoine counts eight of them), which proves that illegitimacy was no longer seen with the same eye as in the past, when the natural sons of monarchs were displayed publicly.

Despite his transgressions of the Sixth Commandment, Louis XV "had religion." He scrupulously observed its rites. "He has piety in the heart," witnesses testified, and, more important, he took an interest in theology and religious dispute: "I grant bishoprics," he said, "not to names or favorites but to people who in my estimation will do the most good for religion and for peace in the kingdom." And he added, "But I am far from infallible." Because he was tormented by his own divagations from the straight and narrow as well as by theological quarrels and debates over the Church's place in the kingdom, he moved to uphold the principles of monarchical virtue and refused to give in to the opinion of philosophical intellectuals.

He therefore took his work seriously. Although he worked hard, he did not toil like a peasant. From 1723 on he presided over all councils of government and met regularly with his ministers. The political agenda carried on the pattern of the previous regime (and would continue to do so under Louis XVI). It was as well regulated as the court calendar: "Councils (almost every day), work with ministers, hunting, supper in the study every day—these, more or less, were the amusements of His

Majesty," the duc de Luynes noted in 1743. The way in which the governmental machine was reconstructed made it impossible for the king to be lazy.[14] This permanence, this predilection for doing things by habit, was the very essence of this government by council and committee, in which ministers met and compared their points of view with one another and with the king's. Favor was bestowed on those with the talent to overcome the monarch's scruples and doubts.

A man given to pondering files and reports in the privacy of his study, Louis XV worked alone (without a secretary) in a large corner office on the first floor of the Cour de Marbre, annotating and criticizing official correspondence and drafting large numbers of unofficial letters that he did not like to hear talked about. The king's isolation confirmed and encouraged the evolution of the bureaucratic apparatus toward greater autonomy. His choice of councilors had the same effect, moreover. In making appointments, the king had to balance tradition (these posts were *offices*), pressure from coteries who pushed their own *créatures* (the Choiseul faction is the best example), and his own documented judgments. He weighed the possibilities, but the likelihood of his escaping intrigues and cabals varied from case to case: Bertin versus Choiseul, d'Argenson (the count) versus Machault, whom he admired. His crucial influence was perhaps to have appreciated and encouraged the professionals of the Council, whereas aristocrats and *parlementaires* irritated him. He admired d'Aguesseau and backed Machault, d'Ormesson, Bertin, Gaumont, and Trudaine, in other words, the hard core of top administrators who encouraged the development of the bureaucratic spirit, the role of finance, and tight central control of the nation's representative bodies. The growth of the royal state to the point where the king could no longer control it threatened to smother the king himself.

Louis XVI, young if not handsome, was like Louis XV a timid, solitary man, but he at least had the benefit of a solicitous family. His father, Louis Ferdinand, was a devout man who hoped to expiate his father's libertinage by his own austerity. He berated his mother, the timorous Polish princess Marie Leszcynska, and called Mme de Pompadour "Maman-Putain," Mama-Whore. A large baby (people were ecstatic about his weight), Louis grew into a plump child. He became heir to the throne after his elder brother Burgundy died in 1761 and his father the dauphin also succumbed. These caprices of fate created a strange climate in which much ado was made about the supremely gifted Burgundy, who had been confined to his *chaise longue* by cancer and whose death afflicted his younger brother with a sense of himself as usurper.[15]

Berry studied to be king with an extremely pedantic but effective, intelligent, and ostentatiously devout tutor, La Vauguyon, and other excellent teachers. These studies were dominated by the royal paternalism he discovered through Domat, Duguet, and Fénelon's *Telemachus,* and also by an introduction to science and the Enlightenment. The education he received could not have produced the dunderhead that he is often believed to have been. His teachers made extraordinary demands: he read Latin at sight, knew more than the ordinary amount of mathematics, and assimilated the political theorists of past and present; Louis XV introduced him to the details of practical administration, including financial matters. Unfortunately the prince, though well prepared and sensitive if complex-ridden, was twice cursed. In the first place, times had changed, and the public now felt entitled to judge kings on the basis of partial, often biased information. As dauphin and later king, Louis XVI was supposed to have a few rough virtues, little wit, no knowledge, no reading, and no taste; he was known as a hunter and a glutton. Rumors to that effect circulated, at any rate, in diplomatic correspondence, notes passed around Paris, and private conversations. They added up to a negative image because the times were such as to require a thoroughgoing critique of authority. Louis XVI's weakness was the need for political reform, and the new portrait of the king as neither a soldier nor an administrator, uncertain of his role, was a key element.

Louis's second curse was of course Marie Antoinette, about whom everything that can be said has been said. Like him, she was a focus of the critical anxiety that it would henceforth be the lot of princes to endure. A gracious queen who took pleasure in living and, after 1774, in ruling, she was probably a fairly empty-headed woman. She was defended by contemporaries, however, on the grounds that she had married a boor, even though she never read a word and exasperated the men and women who tried to read to her with her frivolous impatience. France's last queen had two defects: in the tradition of enlightened absolutism, there was no place for female interference, except on the left hand, as it were; and the interventions of Marie Antoinette and her clan proved disastrous because of the king's weakness. "An unsatisfactory husband, an unsatisfied wife": such was Edgar Faure's cruel conclusion to his incisive portrait of the royal couple. Here we see how power may interact with physical faculties in a certain context.

Turgot's disgrace came about not because of the young queen's capricious rancor but because of her heedless nature and meddling entourage. The "airhead" (as she was called by her brother Joseph II) was a pawn in a domestic and foreign conflict between Choiseul's heirs (the queen embodied the alliance with Austria to the bitter end), adversaries of peace and proponents of revenge against England (even if it meant bankrupting France—that was for Necker to take care of), and the champions of legal despotism, economists and philosophes (as some styled themselves) hostile to the triumphal reaction of the privileged and the rodomontade of the reestablished sovereign courts, which Turgot—this was his major error—tolerated. Here we touch the heart of the crisis as well as the heart of court society and the complex relationship that existed between the old court and the monarch on the one hand and the nascent society of vigorous, critical, often mistaken public opinion on the other. The dismissal of one minister and the arrival of another can be analyzed in two ways: in terms of the remote and proximate forces that kept such individuals in orbit around the central star, and in terms of interpersonal relationships in a society whose perfidy and violence no delicacy of expression, no flowery and lacy epistolary style, was sufficient to mask.

Challenges to Court Society

When the king became an instrument of propaganda against himself, obviously something was seriously amiss in the political system. In his book *Des notions claires sur les gouvernements*, Louis-Sébastien Mercier showed what was happening—the formation of public space as seen from below:

> In all governments I see nothing but action and reaction, elasticity, coiled energy, impulse, and resistance. Govern me well and I will trust in your action. If you make errors harmful to our property, we will be on our guard, for the law of politics is based only on reciprocity, on mutual interest. If the laws of equilibrium between the part that governs and the part that is governed are disrupted, there will be intestine agitation until equilibrium is restored.[16]

In Newtonian, mechanistic terms instead of the usual organic images, the publicist, journalist, moral observer, and philosophe noted the failure of arbitration associated with the rise of bureaucratic government and conflict among coteries brought about by the eclipse of the royal person and personage.

On the checkerboard of social and political relations, the rules of the game changed. The original rules had endured for two centuries. During that time the court as social formation imposed certain reciprocal obligations on its members, obligations that gave rise to a distinctive code of behavior; the court had also set the pattern for the organization of society as a whole. Norbert Elias has examined the process, common to all west European societies, whereby the "curialization" of warriors (that is, the transformation of a military aristocracy into a court nobility) pacified conduct and induced emotional self-control.[17] This "civilizing process" was inextricably intertwined with the fate of absolutism because it relied on the king's monopoly of military violence, which became the only legitimate form of violence and which put the king in charge of the pacified social space, and because it also relied on the king's fiscal monopoly, which centralized tax collection and allowed the monarch to pay for war and reward his loyal servants with cash rather than land.

The strong central government imposed its authority on the social antagonists: between the aristocracy of sword and robe, for example. The court became the focal point of politics because it enabled all parties to keep an eye on one another under the ultimate control of the monarch. Ambitious men exchanged obedience for favor. The court perpetuated the king's personal power while reshaping the social hierarchy and individual psychology in distinctive ways. At court, wide social disparities were exhibited in close spatial proximity: the social status of an individual at Versailles came to coincide with the representation of that status by himself or others. The "culture of appearances" was a matter of politics as well as behavior. Even though Elias did not bolster his model with all the arguments that the works of Michel Antoine could have provided, it is clear how the incorporation of the King's Council into the mechanisms of court society shifted the very foundations of the state: the king retained his traditional side, defined his reign, maintained equilibrium among the various *corps*, and served as arbiter in disputes over rights and privileges, but he was also a centralizing, statist, homogenizing, interventionist force.

In the late eighteenth century the mechanisms of court society broke down as a result of a deep social crisis: the equilibrium that had been established during the reign of Louis XIV made the king and the *corps,* primarily the *parlements,* the chief centers of power, in relation to which the *noblesse d'épée* and court aristocracy were always in an awkward position, for the mechanism of domination was frozen and, unable to integrate new social partners, could only repeat old conflicts. Outside the court, French society was reshaped by the forces of change, by the simultaneous rise of new strata—bourgeoisies—excluded from political power, by the advent of a new economic system, and by the transformation of a segment of traditional society, all leading to rupture.[18] Hence the king could not play the card of the rising bourgeoisie or the declining nobility and had instead to play that of the old society in which the two were allies as well as rivals against the trump card of a new, unprecedented social formation with its own new set of equilibria. One sign of this was the widespread denunciation of the rising bureaucracy: the administration that was winning out over the king was also an instrument, perhaps perfectible, of tight state control and a guarantor of wealth, the most potent factor in favor of stability and agent of greater openness. The crisis of the royal person and his relation to the world reflected not only the impossibility of reform but also the fact that reforms would have signified a third way led by the monarchy, which thus missed yet another opportunity.

The Royal Celebration

These signs of change should not be allowed to obscure the persistence of conformism and stability. In both theory and practice one finds royal power at odds with society in a different way, leading ultimately to signs of an irrevocable split.

A chapter in any traditional description of absolutism contrasts the principles of the juridical tradition to the inadequacy of social institutions, the theoretical achievement with the practical collapse into contradictory realities. One thing that made royal power so effective was the cult of the monarch. Studying it offers two advantages: first, it takes us into the heart of a difference that is difficult to imagine because of the extent to which the rhetoric of legitimation ascribed an archaic and sacred dimension to royal actions; second, the elements of the absolutist lit-

urgy—coronation, ceremony, and aesthetic and equestrian metaphors—
provide us with an index to the erosion of the image of perfection that
classical France liked to present of itself even at the height of the Enlightenment. This is one of the lessons of *Le Siècle de Louis XIV,* a work
in which the influence of politics on mores is total: even minor duties are
a matter of moral significance, and service takes precedence over titles in
a courtly ideal of uniformity through function. Louis XIV was the equal
of Augustus: at the time this meant something, even if it no longer means
much to us. No detail that enters into the identity of a civilization and
determines its form of political expression is insignificant.

The Twilight of the Miracle-Working Kings

The doctrinal construction and symbolic construction of the French
monarchy were inseparable. Bossuet expressed this in the most eloquent,
if not for a modern the most convincing, fashion in his *Politique tirée des
propres paroles de l'Ecriture sainte:* "God establishes kings as his ministers
and through them reigns over peoples . . . The king's person is sacred . . .
One must obey princes for reasons of religion and conscience . . . Kings
most respect their own power and use it only for the public good."[19] This
pact or contract distinguishes the king's person utterly from all others but
at the same time makes him responsible before God, the only moral limit
on absolutism. To be sure, Bossuet was not the only writer who was read,
and the heirs of Gallicanism, jurists, historians, *parlementaires,* and functionaries did not have to be great intellectuals to be aware of other
authorities: Saint Thomas and contractualist scholasticism had come back
into favor with religious debates over the crisis of conscience. There can
be no doubt, however, that Louis XV and Louis XVI inherited a myth
and a mythology (that for the majority, faith and obedience are one and
the same) as well as a legal legitimacy that was gradually eroded by
criticism and questioning. *Mystique* degenerated into *politique* when the
parallel decline of royal ritual and state symbolism began; indifference to
both was the result. In the eighteenth century the Bourbon monarchs who
had inherited the miraculous power to cure scrofula (also known as "the
king's evil," no doubt tuberculous adenitis affecting the lymphatic gan-
glia) continued the sacred post-coronation ritual: on the day after his
anointment, the newly crowned king touched the sick ("The king touches
you, God heals you"). Louis XV touched 2,000 suffering people on

October 9, 1722, while Louis XVI touched 2,400 on June 14, 1775. The duc de Croÿ, frightened but not skeptical, remarked:

> Because of the heat, the place stank and was quite obviously infected, so that it took great courage and strength for the king to complete the entire ceremony, which I would not have believed to be so crude and revolting had I not seen it with my own eyes. The faith of those good people was truly remarkable: they knelt down, hands joined, with a warm and truly touching look of faith and trust on their faces, so that I would not be surprised if several of them were cured.

Marc Bloch wrote a history of the royal miracle.[20] His thesis corroborates the idea that "public opinion" and the collective psychology of oral narrative, legend, and myth depend on phenomena of diffusion in which the irrational plays a part. Was the connection between the concept of sacred royalty and the belief in the king's miraculous power to cure scrofula the "result of a collective error"? In order to understand a belief of this type, Bloch turned to texts, lists of patients, images, medical folklore, and anthropological studies of the Anglo-French phenomenon.[21] Guided by his own rationalism, he collected information about royal healing in order to show how a cultural practice worked. Belief encountered skepticism: people flocked to Reims for the ceremony, while the *intendant* Rouillé noted the number healed, but the boundary line between miracle and reason was shifting even as the king qua historical individual was beginning to question his symbolic body. The function of the rite was not personal; it was linked to the role of the sovereign. It signaled the completion of the ceremony that made the king a bishop, an anointed cleric, thereby authenticating his bond with God and legitimating his action. Anointment made the royal person sacred and in a sense sacerdotal: the touch was one of a set of shared beliefs reinforced by royal propaganda, beliefs that established a conception of royalty as natural and popular.

After 1722 things changed. The ancient formula "The king touches you, God heals you" left no room for doubt: God would inevitably grant the king's wish. This now gave way to a new formula in the subjunctive, essentially converting the king's action and its necessary consequence into a prayer that might or might not bring results: "The king touches you, may God heal you." The miracle was thus questioned at its very source. Louis XV frequently abstained from touching scrofula victims on major holidays, a decision that caused a scandal but called attention to the change in the king's own thinking about his power: for Louis XV, the efficacy of his action depended on his personal disposition (he was not in a state of grace) and not on his sacred character. People began to make light of the king's power: Montesquieu in *Les Lettres persanes* spoke of the "magician king." Voltaire mocked the dynasty's miraculous powers in his *Essai sur les moeurs* (1756), *Dictionnaire philosophique* (1764), and *Questions sur l'Encyclopédie* (1770–1772). About the ritual itself there was silence: it was not mentioned in the newspapers. In Paris, among the enlightened classes, the time may have come when, as Voltaire said, reason abolished custom.

There are two ways of explaining this change. First of all, the state symbolism in the surviving royal rites diminished: the coronation continued as in the past, but not state funerals, royal entries, or the *lits de justice* that regulated relations between royal authority and the representations of the officeholding class who embodied the old kingdom. The *lits de justice* lost their ritual prestige and became dramatic theater. Here, politics became spectacle, and the king no longer negotiated his power but imposed it. Even the weak Louis XVI, in a *lit de justice* held at Versailles on November 19, 1789, said, "It is legal because I wish it," sending a shiver down the spine of anyone who still believed in fundamental laws. Justice was humiliated by the "Etat-roi" of finance.

Amid the hesitation and the remorse one can also read the strange mixture of skeptical irony with the new rationalism (which affected the touch of scrofula as it did all other effects of the imagination and psychotherapeutic prejudice) and the effort to dispel confusion from the medical clinic—in short with anything that attempted to clarify the boundary between error and truth as now conceived. Waning religious belief allied itself with latent rationalism, uniting Protestants for whom the sacraments were not effective by themselves; Jansenist Augustinians who believed that the theology of grace did not sit well with the idea of a divine and absolute king, a sinner exempt from the common law; and relativist Stoics who placed their faith in mechanism and observation. The possibility of miraculous intervention in the world diminished, mysticism receded, yet faith survived—and paradoxically, the Revolution and Counterrevolution would help to sustain it. Kings could no longer heal their scrofulous subjects.

Expressions of the Cult: Te Deum

Various mechanisms and forms of intervention promoted a conception of royalty and the state that was in effect a belief. What rooted that belief in society was not so much propaganda in the form of spectacles publicly honoring the sovereign and his representatives (such as coronations and official visits) or publicity through images, diaries, pamphlets, and books (magnified by the power of the press) as the way in which news and information were distributed. "The publication of royal decisions is an area in which the state reveals its requirements day after day, in which it discovers its own weaknesses, recognizes the geographic limits of its reach, and runs up against social and local opposition."[22] To shift our attention from royal propaganda to the ceremonies of information is to acknowledge that rulers and ruled shared unspoken beliefs and doubts that made propaganda and indoctrination possible.

From the seventeenth century on, public criers and posters in Paris and the provinces spread the news of important celebrations, decisions, judgments, sentences, and edicts, some or all of which might be repeated in periodicals and pamphlets (as was the case with monetary edicts). Posters bearing official seals manifested the royal will, but no one could be sure how many people read them or to what degree they were criticized. The police therefore kept posters and print shops under surveillance and also kept an eye on readers and commentators. A good portion of the news reached rural France through the channels of the Church. Parish priests made announcements of general interest during sermons even though they were required to read only edicts pertaining to ecclesiastical affairs.

In the late seventeenth and early eighteenth centuries an important change took place in Paris and probably in the provinces as well. The ritual of posting edicts at major crossroads to the accompaniment of trumpets began to give way to commercial publication, which, though supervised by the authorities, had the potential to cover a much wider area. A new system of information began to develop: the hawkers who sold broadsheets no longer read out loud the contents of decisions that attracted potential readers. Society was divided into two groups: thousands of printed copies of royal decrees and edicts were sent out to all administrators and officeholders responsible for enforcing the law and passed on to notables in the cities, while the general public interested in such matters had either to wait for mass or the posting of a poster or else pay for the news if curiosity could not wait. The establishment of new relations, partly based on market exchange, between the state and its subjects reduced the latter to passivity, whereas a small segment of the public, defined by its social and political status, was integrated into the management of affairs. This integration united the nobilities and bourgeoisies and effectively slowed the development of any rift between them and the monarchy because it bolstered the prevailing social order. Court society was held up as a model of political participation for regulating differences between the state and its constitutive *corps*.

The evolution of the Te Deum ceremony reveals a parallel transformation. The celebration was part of a larger ceremonial complex: publication of the peace treaty to the sound of trumpets, Te Deum mass at the cathedral, fireworks, distributions of wine and bread, and possibly a procession. The point of all this was to show that governing was the exclusive business of the king and God. The very excess of the proclamation of peace carved out a space in which the will of the king to publicize his actions could encounter the expectations of his people. The absolute monarchy chose the occasions for the Te Deum as a way of confirming the political order. It outlived the other major rituals of the seventeenth century such as *lits de justice* and royal entries and coexisted with the cult of Saint Louis, which was an important fact of eighteenth-century urban life. More than other ceremonies, the Te Deum sustained the dynastic idea, along with celebrations of royal births, marriages, and funerals; it publicized the triumphs of absolutism, the battles won and treaties signed; and it confirmed the power of the king at the top of the social hierarchy.

The Te Deum was an instrument of political instruction by means of ritualized information. We can gauge its impact by looking at the distribution of letters of celebration sent out during the War of the Austrian Succession (1744–1748). The Te Deum filled three main functions. First, it called attention to major events, distinguished by the king's presence, such as the Te Deum of Fontenoy; it marked historical commemorations which confirmed the importance of military and dynastic aims; and it played a diplomatic role by speaking to allies and enemies as well as Frenchmen. Second, it indicated the king's intention to dominate all of French territory from the palace of Versailles to the most remote diocese. Contemporaries could measure how quickly royal orders were obeyed and how far the king's wishes traveled. Finally, the ceremony ritualized magnificence in a brief burst of consumption (of food, wood, candles, and fireworks), as if pressing a claim against nature and scarcity while at the same time upholding the established order.

The accounts of victories that resounded within church vaults and were posted on church doors were couched in a rhetoric all their own. Such narratives broadened the horizons of small towns and villages by bringing them news of the outside world. Written in French, they popularized the use of that language. And they made the king seem heroic—heroism being the hallmark of the political in this society of representation. In the eighteenth century, representation structured the political sphere more than communication. Rituals separated people as much as they drew people together. They fostered admiration for and belief in a power inaccessible to the majority and contested by notables and owners of delegated public authority. "In order for the public to grasp the image of itself that was first held out to it and then snatched away, people had not only to renounce their love of the sovereign but also to reject the codified blandishments of rhetoric and cease to believe in the permanent presence of God as well as in the actions of kings and men." Here, then, was another gap that would widen as politics shifted from the old realm to the new public definition.[23]

The Monarchy and Its Cult in Representation

The many manifestations of the cult of the monarchy are worth attending to in some detail, because this was a form of political expression. Medallions, with their figures and devices over which the members of the Académie des Inscriptions et Belles-Lettres argued, were aimed at a relatively limited audience of sovereigns, courtiers, and men of letters. *Places royales*, or royal squares, involved more people, because they required deliberations, debates over financing, and elaborate planning. They were a sign, moreover, of urban obedience to royal authority and admiration for the glory of the monarchy. Such monuments were an aspect of urban planning and as such a political matter of great interest to notables, but the support of the majority was passive at best and difficult to interpret. Some royal squares figured in discussions of the relation between architectural aesthetics and politics, such as Abbé Laugier's *Observations sur l'architecture* (1765).

Laugier, a prolific writer, hailed originally from Manosque but moved to Paris, studied with the Jesuits, became eminent as a preacher to the king, was dismissed for carrying audacity a bit too far, and thereafter eked out a living as a man of letters in the thick of contemporary debate. His texts reveal his knowledge of both classical aesthetic principles and the politics of urban improvement. His goal in the book was to reconcile the two through concrete, pragmatic reflection touching on the rational organization of space and the improvement of traffic flow, not for purposes of representation but for economic and utilitarian reasons. Yet political thinking was not absent from the work, which saw the ideal city not with the palace at its center as a reflection of obedience to the prince, but rather as a place of autonomous accessibility and industriousness built around a network of roads and other useful facilities.

In Laugier's writing, which calls upon the authorities to restore order to the chaos of the cities, royal celebration has its place. Nevertheless, in Part 5 of the *Observations*, "On Monuments to the Glory of Great Men," the erudite abbé writes in a way that reveals a major change in the nature of the royal cult. His recognition of royal actions comes only in the context of admiration for illustrious men in general, and the proposal to construct monuments in honor of great men, "the noblest [use] that can be made of the arts," combined celebration of the monarchy with homage to "virtue," "generosity," and "talent." Laugier called upon artists to imagine new forms for such celebration: "We have kings so worthy of our love, our hearts are so pleased to demonstrate their tender, respectful feelings for them, that the whole nation is eager to erect monuments to their glory. But must we limit ourselves to this type of monument alone? Can we imagine nothing better than a state in the middle of a great square? Let us avoid too much uniformity in our homages."

Paris had three great royal squares; Montpellier had its statue of Louis XIV; Lyons and Dijon also honored the great king; Bordeaux, Nancy, Rennes, and Reims all had monuments to Louis XV. But these examples also point up the limitations of the idea: for want of space, it was difficult to build royal squares inside existing cities. Difficulties about real estate, crowding, and expense ruled out initiatives that loyalist sentiments might have inspired.

Hence other kinds of monuments were required to celebrate— efficiently, economically, yet in suitable splendor—the cult of the monarchy. One such was the "arch of triumph," the entablature of which was eminently suitable for showing the king in "a Roman-style chariot, dressed as a warrior with a crown of laurels, trotting proudly," a representation apt "to arouse a different kind of interest from a cold equestrian statue" and suitable for the display of more highly embellished symbols of virtue. Public fountains and isolated columns like those of the Antonines or Trajan also made it possible to represent the love that bound the sovereign and his people. Meanwhile, the permissible symbolism changed: it became possible to portray the king as other than a triumphant warrior or heroic *imperator:* he could be depicted as Apollo, protector of the Muses; or as protector of justice, handing Themis her sword and scales; or in proximity to a church, "granting the protection of the scepter to religion, which recognizes him as protector of the faith"; or in proximity to the marketplace as a symbol of plenty and generosity. Bas-reliefs and columns could also depict the major events of a king's reign, combining effigy and history in a single monument.

The abbé's program was thus in a way more revealing than the rare and limited projects undertaken by artists at the behest of municipal governments or notables. It shows how the absolutist Enlightenment sought to inspire both admiration and belief through acts that were at once obedient and utilitarian, indicating a willingness to submit to royal authority as well as a desire to improve urban space. It also reveals the erosion of the royal cult: city dwellers were asked to honor the king's actions, but only as part of a hierarchy of civic virtues associated with "illustrious men" in general, "lesser stars whose light shines not quite so brightly and illuminates fewer objects" but whose lessons formed part of the same general pedagogy, honoring energy in utilitarian service to a kingdom in transformation.

The Royal Portrait and Equestrian Statue

The evolution in painted portraiture of the monarch suggests that a similar inflection took place there. The royal portrait stood at the summit of a hierarchy of genres of celebration, but it was not much appreciated by theorists, who assigned it a historical function "below history painting; below a canvas depicting any scene from Antiquity or mythology."[24] Lebrun disposed of this paradox by developing a new type of royal portrait that confirmed the hierarchy of genres: he portrayed the king as a legendary, historical, or mythological hero. Painting and sculpture made it possible to magnify the king's own qualities, thereby proving his superiority over the ancient image and casting events as entirely subordinate to his will and grandeur. The royal portrait that transformed the sovereign into Alexander, Hercules, or Apollo was still a celebration of the king's reign. One sees this in the Hall of Mirrors at Versailles, and visitors to Versailles before the Revolution did not fail to grasp the point.

Meanwhile, however, academicians established other rules of formal portraiture that survived the eighteenth century. Rigaud applied his talent in this area in response to the king's desire to "fix for all eternity an image of the royal person that indicates the grandeur of his reign and represents his power": "His grand and majestic air, always serene face, and natural graces evident throughout his person and down to the least significant of his actions, as well as his gentle and pleasing aspect and august physiognomy—all these things indicate to those who see him that he is born to please and to command."

In his 1702 portrait of Louis XIV and various portraits of Louis XV, Rigaud illustrated the idea of representation developed by François de Callières in his *Essay d'un portrait du roi:* the king-hero not only commands but also seduces. The portrait should confirm that the king both *has* power and *is* power. The signs of his power—robe covered with fleurs-de-lis and royal insignia such as the crown and hand of Justice—won allies, while his physiognomy gave pleasure. That is why royal portraits were copied, sent to foreign courts, and given to ambassadors. M. T. Dremière has counted some forty exhibits of royal portraits in salons from 1737 to 1775 and fifteen more under Louis XVI. Some of these works recycled existing images, placing Louis XVI's head on Louis XV's body.

The ideal thus evolved into a convention, and it was this convention that Diderot reproached in Van Loo's *Louis XV,* a portrait that was painted according to the rules but made the king rather too short and gave him more dignity than majesty: it might have been of any magistrate, an important personage but not the most important of all. In other words, the attention to the king's historical person, to a plausible resemblance, had drained some of the meaning from the symbolism of power. This diminution struck the critic even in history paintings such as Dumont's *Publication de la paix en 1749* and Roslin's *Roi reçu à l'Hôtel de Ville,* on which Diderot commented in 1761: behind the monarch we see the man, and Louis XV permitted the circulation of images that showed not his passion for government but his weariness of it. The same could be said of his portrait by Drouais in 1774. The focus of interest had shifted from the image of the monarch to that of the individual. The expectation of the public—to see the very idea of royalty in each royal portrait—was disappointed, the ideal betrayed, and the pedagogy of the culture of representations derailed. In the traditional discourse, the original and its double coincided in the pictorial eulogy. In the new discourse criticism showed through, and the image no longer coincided with the original: what was done and seen outweighed what was said and expressed by the old symbolism of state and sovereign.

In this shift, the royal square and equestrian statue, a type of space and form of expression characteristic of the cult of monarchy, deserve ample analysis. In regard to space, note the ideological significance. The square, with its official program, introduced a uniformity, an affirmation of urban order designed to represent power rather than to enhance utility. The royal statue, with its attributes, hauteur, and decorative embellishment, translated the assertion of the king's power as hero and soldier into the Roman and Renaissance tradition. For the reign of Louis XIV, Michel Martin has shown the extent to which these structures were specified by official commission, which often referred to models such as Girardon's statue of Louis on the place des Victoires. In this area Paris and the provinces worked together: in major cities, especially in the *pays d'Etats*, the royal image confirmed the authority and magnificence of the state. During the eighteenth century, statues were placed in Rennes, Bordeaux, and Reims (where the king was on foot, a rare occurrence). Plans were also developed for Nantes, Strasbourg, Toulouse, Lyons, Metz, Rouen, and Valenciennes, but in these cities urban planning for increased traffic flow took precedence over considerations of grandeur, as Laugier had advocated. Thus there was a growing gap between self-management of urban space and a continued program of royal celebration.

The style and monumental size of these works, which in Paris bordered on the colossal, magnified the regime and its heroic king. Embellishments included both bellicose themes, which exalted the victorious monarch, and peaceful themes, which evoked commerce and economic growth, as in Rennes, Bordeaux, and Lyons, where the sculptural background featured allegories of the Saône and Rhône rivers. A concept of authority was on display: the rider astride his steed sits erect, suggesting a balanced, harmonious, and triumphal pace, demonstrating his cultural superiority to the spectator. The king appears as the master of his realm, natural and ideal, wearing a wig and breastplate in the ancient style, always himself, depersonalized and timeless. This representation amplified the messages of traditional politics in a language comprehensible if not by everyone, then at least by those who were familiar with horses.

Boucharddon, who worked on the living model, placed Louis XV on horseback to decorate the *place-écrin* (jewel-case square) that the city set up outside its walls. Calm, gentle, and peaceful rather than triumphant, the king trots nobly into his capital. The artist managed a tour de force by carving horse and rider as one, thereby symbolizing serene peace, because the horse's movements determine the attitude of its rider and vice versa. The king was portrayed in a naturalistic manner, which individualized the figure of the monarch in the same way that portraits did. On the pedestal, the king is supported in his peaceful works by four Virtues: Charity, Clemency, Dignity, and Discretion.[25] This masterpiece was unfortunately destroyed; we know it only from dozens of preparatory drawings and reduced models such as Vassi's in the Louvre. In choosing a calm horse rather than a rearing, fiery one, Boucharddon surely had aesthetic reasons, but these were reinforced by his knowledge of horsemanship.

Equestrian manuals had ideas of their own about politics. Until the seventeenth century men dominated horses by force alone, without any concession to the horse. But in the seventeenth and eighteenth centuries they learned to control their mounts by intelligence rather than brutality. The animal, made more docile, freely submitted to its rider's will, conveyed through his body. The rider searched for just the right "seat" to harmonize his will with his mount's. Absolutism revealed the political character of the equestrian art by teaching an "art of government." The king managed his horses in the same way he dealt with his entourage. When a man learned to ride, he learned to judge the world and to control it. Theory and practice taught that the way to dominate was to be upright. Now we are in a position to understand why the king's stables aroused such interest under Louis XIV and Louis XV: the royal breeders and trainers produced fine, handsome horses, whose value was symbolic as well as utilitarian. In their search for more perfect rules of horsemanship, eighteenth-century trainers such as La Guérinière and Dupaty were contributing in their own way to the art of leadership. Their program also had something in common with the natural sciences and the new human relationships they promised to establish.

If one grants that bodily techniques [*techniques du corps*] constitute a living language, then it will be clear how the equestrian art (the rational-ized training of man's finest conquest) became a metaphor for the politi-cal. Lest anyone doubt that this was the case, I cite three pieces of evidence. First, growing numbers of people wished to learn how to ride. Second, after 1792, because they were symbols of royal power, equestrian statues became a favorite target of symbolic vigilance, and many were knocked down. And third, irreverent comments were commonplace, as when a statue of Louis XV was unveiled in Paris in 1763, and an anony-mous seditious writer marked its pedestal with the words, "Grotesque monument, shameful pedestal! Virtues go barefoot, while vice rides horseback." Shortly thereafter, Louis XV was portrayed in a standing statue in Reims—another sign of the times.

The Political Space of the Ancien Régime

In looking successively at the role of the king, at court society, and at monarchical celebration, we have learned about the logic and relation-ships that defined absolutist political culture, which should be understood not narrowly in terms of institutions and events but rather as a way of understanding how individuals and groups were able to overcome their diversity, define their positions, and attain their goals. Within this culture old theories and practices confronted new ones. We have already seen this confrontation at work in the de-sacralization of royal authority and change in the nature of celebration. We turn now to Enlightenment-tem-pered absolutist policy, which we shall study by looking at contemporary discourse and identifying key turning points.[26]

Absolutism and Enlightenment

Denis Richet remarks that the monarchy was at once *one* and *divisible*. *Divisible* because it unified without eliminating the plural entities of which it was composed: *corps,* communities, provinces, and regions. *One* because it combined those entities into a unique organism of which the king was the sole arbiter and administrator. Hence the king's power was first of all judicial, intended to bring about social equilibrium. Moreover, the king was not a despot, since he was obliged to respect the customs and "fundamental laws" through which particularism expressed itself. And finally, his rule was absolute, because his power could not legally be

277

challenged by any other power; there was no room for debate. All his actions were justified by reference to the "common good."

The monarchy, Montesquieu showed, functioned with the help of *corps intermédiaires*. Many later defenders of the Ancien Régime, some enlightened, some not, borrowed his arguments: Réal in the *Science du gouvernement* (8 volumes, 1751–1764), Guyot in the *Traité des offices* (1787), and historiographer Jacob Nicolas Moreau in his *Devoirs du prince réduits à un seul principe* (1775) and *Maximes fondamentales du gouvernement français* (1789). For all of these writers power could be absolute because there were "tempering forces" everywhere. The monarchy survived all the crises and abortive reforms attempted before 1789 because the adversaries of "ministerial despotism" had found no formula capable of uniting them.

In fact, two attitudes were prevalent among the political notables influenced in one way or another by the Enlightenment—French, English, or otherwise—when it came to renegotiating the implicit political contract. "Some, especially in the *parlements*, who were more faithful to the letter of the law than to Montesquieu's spirit, used the distinction between monarchy and despotism to mount ever more bitter criticism of the regime. Others, more numerous, rejected that distinction." As Voltaire wrote to Gin (the author of the *Vrais Principes des gouvernements français*, 1777): "I begin by acknowledging that despotism and monarchism are just about the same thing in the hearts of all men and all sensitive beings."[27]

The first group was attached to traditional representations of the *société des corps*. For them, in other words, three principles governed all social relations and matters of public law. First, whenever power was delegated, the chosen delegate (deputy, notable, or city councilor) represented a group, *corps*, or corporation. Second, the chosen delegate was never independent but always bound by an imperative mandate and by the influence of the electors he represented. And third, his power derived from custom and therefore history, not from the constitution. As Carré de Malberg (*Contribution à la théorie générale de l'Etat*, 1791) and Roederer (*De la députation aux Etats généraux*, 1788) showed, true representation did exist under the Ancien Régime in the form of delegates sent by various social groups to advise the king. Even if the modern idea of representation excludes the notions of customary dependency and transfer of will that the Strasbourg jurist, a critic of the Revolution, considered indispensable and that Roederer challenged in the name of national sovereignty, these were nevertheless the principles that governed the political sphere of the Ancien Régime. Because of these principles, the sovereign courts after 1761 and the *cour des aides* of Paris, led by M. Lamoignon de Malesherbes (one of the greatest magistrates of the century and, significantly, as head of censorship and regulation of the book trade, one of the most important officials of the royal administration), were able to mount increasingly vehement attacks on the power of the administration and indeed on the whole apparatus of state that had been constructed since the seventeenth century. Royal authority was thus compromised by the *sanior pars* itself.

The second group—which at times included members of the first and vice versa—was on the side of court society, which was just another name for "despotism." The most important political forces in the kingdom were gathered around the king in Versailles. The court was a microsociety, with its own economy, its own hierarchy, its own pressure groups, and its own culture. Two principles governed its organization. First, proximity to the king established a hierarchy, from the pure to the impure, from the royal family to the princes of the blood to the dukes and peers, to the courtiers, on down to the nobles who did not reside at court but who conveyed the eloquence of the model to the depths of their provinces by virtue of having at least once approached the throne and participated in the royal hunt, as was the case, for instance, with the chevalier de Chateaubriand. The second principle was the division between the sacred offices and the profane: prelates, chancellors, ministers, high crown officers, the grand chamberlain, the grand master of ceremonies, the grand huntsman, the officers of the guard, various officeholders, and domestics constituted a huge entourage, military and civilian, lay and religious. The size of this entourage reflected the magnificence of the prince and the extent of his influence. A complex system of signs and codes, protocol and ceremony, assigned each person a place and determined who had the stature to be invited to the royal retreat at Marly or share in the king's pleasures or receive certain honors. Because the relations between people of different ranks, backgrounds, and functions depended solely on the will of the prince, the king became an isolated figure at the center of a complex liturgy and the ritual of the Council. An immense distance, real as well as symbolic, was created between the monarch and his subjects. In theory the administration was supposed to remedy this, but in practice it only widened the gap more and more. At stake was the very essence of power, which began as judicial but increasingly revolved around finance, utility, and economics rather than justice.

The politics of the Enlightenment played itself out between these two models: that of the *sanior pars,* within which took place an undeniable form of political debate and social interaction associated with the continuous process of negotiation with ministerial authority, and that of the isolated monarch, who based his power on the whole system of privilege (as is evident in the king's attitude toward his officeholders, whose position allowed them to rise moderately in social status and to amass considerable resources) even as he undermined that system through his intervention in fiscal matters and litigation. This conflict was apparent both at the center and at the periphery, for example, in cities in which oligarchies of officeholders benefited from the power conferred by their offices and represented the society of *corps* while implementing the king's fiscal policy, which heightened antagonisms on both sides of the dividing line between privileged and nonprivileged.

The difficulty lies in understanding why there was no void between the political speculations of the intellectuals and political agitation of the people. And the answer is that the potential vacuum was filled by a variety of things. The *parlements* claimed to occupy this space and, invoking Montesquieu, England, and the Roman Senate, arrogated to themselves the right to defend "citizens against arbitrary government." But they were not alone. Between Paris and the provinces a crucial contest was waged, a contest in which the terms were as follows: everywhere there was a fundamental insistence on opening up the *sanior pars* to people who had learned the rules of political intercourse, but the *sanior pars* could invoke the "liberties" of the "privileged corps" to call for political reforms that would give them greater control over the political process. D'Holbach himself, though hostile to the corps, was willing to see the *parlements* as "an always necessary rampart between the supreme authority and the liberty of its subjects." Mably and many others shared the same attitude. Some were exempt, however: the Physiocrats and the defenders of ministerial despotism (Gin, Moreau), as well as the Rousseauists, whose demands were made on grounds of sovereignty more than equality.[28]

Political Academicism, Opinion, and Critique

What we have to understand is how exclusion could have coexisted with participation and demands for allegiance with the rise of critical opinion. Paradoxically, the way to understand this distinctive feature of the political sphere is to study learned institutions. In the past as much as today, people all too often thought that politics ended at their doorstep or that its claims were identical with those of the Enlightenment. In fact, the exclusion of politics, which was a statutory requirement of Parisian as well as provincial learned societies (where discussion of "God, the king, and custom" was prohibited), was tantamount if not to a definition of concrete policy then at least to an ideology of public affairs that justified the principles of state action and the conformism indispensable to an inegalitarian state. The conjunction of knowledge and power instituted by the great Parisian academies and transmitted to the provinces immediately created a political image proclaiming the union of monarchy with culture under the aegis of linguistic purism, which unified as well as distinguished—and all this was done "with the seal of public authority," as Pellisson said in 1660, and under the banner of expertise and learned arbitration.

The Académie Française, mistress of eloquence, the Académie des Sciences, which reigned over the natural world, and the Académie des Inscriptions, which scrutinized history on behalf of the state, created a tradition which was first of all one of political approbation—a cultural program that gained the allegiance of most provincial neo-Immortals. Academic rules established norms intended to guarantee the integrity of societies based on reputation, high moral standards, and wit. Royal letters patent defined the aims of each learned society, the ultimate goal of which was to provide useful service from which enlightened absolutism derived much of its ideological justification, simultaneously conservative and progressive. The new is made from the old.

In practice the academies developed the art of praising the grandeur of the monarch and applauding his designs well beyond their own closed forums. They honored the prince and his family with a veritable cult, whose high point came every year on August 25, the day of Saint Louis. To say that this cult groveled in obedience is to forget the new capacity for ceremonial celebration and the needs of the notables who found reconciliation therein. There were countless opportunities for men of letters to proclaim their attachment to the dynasty while at the same time demonstrating their competence. Illnesses of the sovereign, successful operations, felicitous births, deaths in the family, peace treaties, and victories all offered occasions to celebrate the monarchy, whether in the joy of a Te Deum or the tears of a funeral.

The model for this type of discourse was Parisian. In Paris it was customary for new members of an academy to be welcomed by a *discours de réception*, a practice which was adopted in the provinces as well. The themes of these speeches varied little; generally they applauded the Most Christian King, triumphant over heresy, magnanimous in victory, heroic and peaceful, patron of the arts, and noble gentleman. Eloquence was an art of persuasion, an incantatory apologia. On the eve of the Revolution it may have taken on a certain physiocratic and pastoral tinge, with familial and paternal overtones, but the pattern remained the same: the monarchy was portrayed as if not a cloud were visible on the horizon. In regard to royal power the academies remained an ideal venue, a place where the word retained the ability to reunite the body politic by invoking social utility and the progress of reason.

For Pierre Rosanvallon, this rhetoric represents "a disturbing way of avoiding the use of modern language to think about philosophical and political modernity."[29] It was indeed equivocal about change, since the concept of utility also implied a distinction between the state and the king's person. Consider Helvétius's *De l'esprit*, in which the public discovers that its indispensable role is to criticize "ministerial despotism" along with the utility of action by the state and its representatives, thereby reconciling the holistic notion of the "public good" with the new "English" concept of the "general interest." The academies were not insignificant: not only do they provide us with a response to Tocqueville's criticism of the Ancien Régime, but also in practice they helped to establish the new political sociability on which the modern idea of public space depends—public space with its objective of royal intervention that was simultaneously conformist, reformist, and administrative.

The academies laid bare the contradictions of monarchy, which could not free itself from an order that it was their purpose to uphold. The basis of the academic compromise lay in the idea of an acceptable social mobility: men of wealth and talent were reconciled to the rules of rank, privilege, and birth. This reconciliation defined the elite of the Ancien Régime. But internal equality of privilege, or "academic liberties," did not determine the elite's ability to control the government, for the elite was divided on the question of real equality versus real privilege. Classes with their diverse interests were just around the corner. When change stalled, the government proved incapable of pursuing reform, and the political goals of the Enlightenment dissolved into a multitude of contradictory ends, the ensuing social crisis did not spare either the state or the enclaves of egalitarianism. How could the crisis unfold without calling the very image of the king into question?

Reading and Believing

We have seen how the nature and perception of the king's image gradually changed as the royal cult evolved. Even greater erosion was apparent in certain common practices. Take the widely shared ability to judge the king, the focal point of his subjects' expectations. The commonly voiced opinions that we can glean from the testimony of police spies, from reactions to broadsheets, from the charges against suspects imprisoned for sedition, and from the writings of such chroniclers as Buvat, a copyist in the Royal Library, the lawyer Marais, the bookseller Hardy, or, once again, Barbier do not permit us to say that there was such a thing as "popular public opinion"; but there did exist a certain basic political capacity whose tentative expression constituted a kind of opposition to the actions of the king and his government.[30] This capacity grew out of everyday life and social contacts in conditions under which people observed one another at close quarters and came to believe that they could interpret other people's thoughts and analyze their conduct. The king, more humanized and less sacred than in the past, was not immune from such scrutiny. The Jansenist crisis, which shook bedrock religious beliefs, played an important role in persuading the public of its competence and its right to criticize, to insist on reforms, and perhaps to disobey. During this crisis, a clandestinely printed newspaper called *Les Nouvelles ecclésiastiques* achieved wide circulation despite repeated police efforts to suppress it. The paper summoned laymen to action and emphasized the importance of their critical opinion in challenging decisions of the king and pope. The desacralization of the monarch and monarchy accelerated as the Enlightenment reached its apogee, but much of the work had already been done. The Damiens affair made the authorities aware that opposition persisted: "The attempt to murder Louis XV occurred at a time when critical public opinion had already been crystallized. It revealed a mechanism of the monarchy more than a novel shift in popular views." In seeking the origins of the public's political capacity, we must look to an earlier time. Here we are looking only at a major transformation in the relation of the people to the king, a transformation also apparent in rumors of riot and rebellion.

The popular representation of the monarchy wavered. It is of course possible to cite any number of positive judgments, and historians infatuated with the monarchy, such as Pierre Gaxotte, Octave Aubry, and François Bluche, have done just that. Around the time of Louis XVI's coronation in particular, there was indeed a sort of "honeymoon period," an interlude of hope and anticipation, but we must bear in mind that this was a recurrent phenomenon, something that happened at the beginning of each new reign and that was matched only by the disparagement of the end. Every coronation brought with it an outpouring of propaganda (invariably involving the academies and the press) and a revival of age-old hopes of royal intercession, fostered by penny tracts and almanacs and further reinvigorated by preachers from their pulpits.[31] This mythology tended to deflect anger from its chief target, the king, onto his representatives, usually the bureaucracy but sometimes the traditional notables. With these facts in mind it behooves us to take a fresh look at the discourse of rebellion. It becomes clear that the disenchantment with the monarchy was not a steady process that accelerated after 1750 and inevitably culminated in 1789; what we find, rather, is a distinctive logic that developed around specific events or conjunctures.

At this point we also encounter a second process that infused the opposition with energy and eroded the royal image: the circulation of the printed word. It is traditional to ask whether books caused the Revolution. The tradition is based on the extensive sales of *livres philosophiques*, that is, "naughty" works of political pornography mingled with social criticism that attacked the aristocracy, the court, and ultimately the king. In a series of studies based on the archives of the Société Typographique de Neuchâtel (STN) and corroborated by police documents, Robert Darnton has demonstrated that such works were indeed widely read.

The STN's secret catalog featured three types of works, and these same three types are mentioned in the *Pilon de la Bastille*. Licentious works (including *Thérèse philosophe, Arétin, Vénus dans le cloître, Histoire de dom Bougre portier des chartreux,* and *Tourière des carmélites*) accounted for 15 of the 110 leading titles. These were joined by seditious pamphlets and political broadsides such as the *Mémoires authentiques de la comtesse du Barry* and the *Gazetier cuirassé ou Anecdotes scandaleuses de la cour de France,* attributed to Théveneau de Morande. Finally, there were political chronicles such as *L'Espion chinois* and the *Journal historique de la Révolution opérée dans la constitution de la monarchie française par Monsieur de Maupeou,* by Pidansat de Mairobert and Mouffle d'Angerville. In book catalogs and orders, works such as these figured alongside works by authentic philosophes and political thinkers from Bayle to Rousseau, Fontenelle to Abbé Raynal—moderates and extremists, Deists and materialists, great writers such as Voltaire and "les Rousseau du ruisseau," Rousseaus of the gutter, "wretches of the sort who write in order to live."

In the eyes of both potential buyers and law enforcement officials, these profitable lines of books were linked because they responded to a demand for irreverence, transgression, and subversion. Can we infer, however, from the proliferation of seditious texts that reading was translated into belief and belief into action? The argument has its merits, since the increased circulation of broadsheets undoubtedly helped to desacralize symbols and erode mythologies.[32] These prohibited, corrosive, and sacrilegious works made deep inroads into society (although the question of precisely where remains open) and may have helped to destroy the belief system that had previously assured the king of the love and respect of his people.

Nevertheless, because this line of reasoning may well attribute a power to reading that it does not actually possess, the argument needs to be limited in two ways. The first of these has to do with the demographics of reading and the way in which these works were received. Reading may elicit temporary interest without resulting in definitive conversion and need not result in a unique choice. Any message can be received in different ways. The Rousseauism of Jacques-Louis Ménétra was not the same as the Rousseauism of the prince de Conti or of M. de Malesherbes. Finally, and perhaps most crucially, the increased distribution of texts may reflect nothing other than that such a thing was now possible. The fading of such monarchical symbols as the king's body and the court left those symbols open to criticism, which texts provided. The "disenchantment" of the monarchy took place well before the reign of Louis XVI in ordinary representations and practices generally well removed from "philosophical" discourse. It reflected two processes at work in society from top to bottom: the metamorphosis of remonstrances into rational critique aimed at reform, and the transformation of majority (and not just popular) opinion, not by a gradual linear process of reading one text after another, but by a greatly expanded capacity to learn about and understand public affairs.[33]

Comparing these two hypotheses does not tell us which one is true. In fact, both are partly true. Both presuppose a common conception of history in which it is possible for interpretive emphases to change. What matters is how key activities were internalized and what principles governed them. In other words, the "reign of criticism" affected humble folk whenever the actions of the authorities impinged on such fundamental matters as belief, faith, and the sacred. Sharp changes of attitude could result, but so could compromises, divergent interpretations, divisions, and regressions. That is why historians never get to the bottom of people's ideas and representations. The same movement that gave rise to exuberant enthusiasm could also result in rage, both being frequently the consequence of unsatisfied desire or unrequited love. This was the dilemma that united the king and his subjects, his people.

9

❧ ❧ ❧

The King and the People

IN THE FOREGOING chapters we have seen evidence of two distinct tendencies in the evolution of the king's relation to his subjects. On the one hand, the ancient idea of the bond between king and people was reinforced, namely, the idea that it was based on the royal functions of leadership and coordination, functions that were in fact accentuated even if the direct administration never totally dominated the part of the administration that was assigned to the farmers-general or sold to office-holders. Behind the king, in other words, loomed the state, or, more precisely, the bureaucracy. On the other hand, there was the royal cult with its age-old rites and customs, which were the monarchy's way of expressing its own idea of its relation to the people, and the way in which that cult was increasingly questioned by people and elites alike shows that the French no longer believed in, understood, or loved the monarchy as they had in the past. A major symbolic crisis affected the organic structure of the Ancien Régime state.

Bear in mind that the old monarchy, which was defined by the notion of universal obedience to the will of a single individual (even though the institutions of the monarchy ensured that real power was never concentrated in one man's hands), was based on conceptions of society, politics, and religion totally different from our own, which are the product of the individualistic, egalitarian period that followed the Revolution. A simple idea served as the basis of the social pact between king and people: the king as "father" of his people. This justified the monarch's power, his right to tax, and his responsibility to dispense justice. From this it followed that the relation between state and people was not one of blind bureaucracy to a totally passive and oppressed population. Both king and people had duties defined not by a constitution but by practices and the texts that described or constructed them.

What the American historian Stephen Kaplan has shown about the *police des subsistances* and the king's duty to provide for the subsistence of his people shows that the king's subjects were not just a nation in the economic sense in which one nation trades with another. Since the king was by nature the ultimate food supplier, his noblest duty was to guarantee his children not just their daily bread (the most material and at the same time most symbolic expression of the relation between politics and religion) but everything that was important in life. This was what people expected of the king in exchange for their allegiance, and they measured the sovereign in terms of his paternal efficacy. Royal paternalism, administrative, financial, judicial, and police policy, and the social order were inextricably intertwined. The people's rights coexisted with constraints; the government's obligations coexisted with prerogatives. To be sure, the medieval and Renaissance image of the prince as succoring hero did not survive without change into the Enlightenment. But it was still associated with the theocratic discourse of Bossuet, which spokesmen for the aristocratic opposition such as Fénelon shared, but with altered emphases, in their heart of hearts. Even eighteenth-century theorists did not dismiss that image outright.[1]

Montesquieu, for example, asserted that the state must provide for its citizens. Radical critics of absolutism such as Mably and Linguet made the sovereign responsible for man's ultimate right: to exist. The crown's sacred duty was to ensure "public prosperity": subsistence, security, and justice. This crucial notion had survived the ages to become the fundamental characteristic of the "well-ordered state," that is, the state whose institutions successfully maintained the common good, established order, and secured domestic tranquillity. To contemporaries, the role of the state as regulator and mobilizer of national forces and resources was comprehensible only in terms of this primary function, in relation to which it is easy to see how conflicts arose between the forces of conservation and the forces of change. Once again, the eighteenth century is interesting because it was situated between two worlds, two far-reaching conceptions of politics.

Contemporaries lived, in other words, according to ancient rhythms, which rural, agricultural France kept alive. State and society were conceived as an organic whole: social and political unity derived from communal rights and from the ancient association of religious and civil powers. The national identity was defined collectively and, as Louis Dumont has shown, expressed in terms of natural law. Paramount in this conception of the nation was the concept of "holism," the assertion of an essential *universitas* and inequality, according to which society was a whole of which individual human beings were merely parts. At the summit of the hierarchy was the priest-king, the supreme political leader in relation to whom men were both means and end, who embodied the unity of the whole. As mediator, the king reconciled all differences in one universal.[2]

At the same time, however, modern society, with its increasing complexity and new forces of labor, exchange, and the post-Renaissance royal state, invoked not a sacred, natural order but an autonomous human order. If, according to the new theories, the state was simply composed of individuals, and if the business of government was to reconcile those individuals with one another—that is, if individualism prevailed over holism—then the relation of each individual to the government had to change. If the individual was the measure of all things, the inegalitarian principle could no longer serve as the basis of all social rationality. If the egalitarian principle replaced it, the justification of the old form of government, the duties of the monarchy, the nature of enlightened absolutism, and the attitudes of the king's subjects (no longer children of a paternal king) were all called into question and reconceptualized in theory and practice. What we must try to grasp, in other words, is how, in terms of the regulatory and mobilizing functions that continued to define the role of the monarchy (tax collection, justice, security), this transition was conceptualized. If we can understand this, we can perhaps reinterpret the traditional conflict between innovation and conservation, change and continuity.

Tax or Gift?

Among the resources mobilized for the public good and required by the growth in the state apparatus, taxes surely provoked the most discussion. Taxation was central to all debates about the economy, as is clear from the figures on works of economics published between 1700 and 1789: *La Dîme royale* went through eleven editions, the marquis de Mirabeau's *Théorie de l'impôt* went through eighteen, and Necker's *Compte rendu au roi* seventeen, not counting foreign editions. Behind these best-sellers advanced an army of essayists and other writers with things to say about state finances, taxes, and money. Their works were widely circulated.

Taxes were a central concern of humble people because the level of taxation determined the ability of small households to invest, and because tax policy met with constant, violent hostility on the part of the people. Antifiscal themes survived the tax revolts of the seventeenth century. The old slogan "Vive le roi sans gabelle!" (Long live the king, without the salt tax!) vividly expressed society's attitude toward the king and his heartless, therefore oppressive administration. In order to understand French attitudes toward taxation, we must first answer three questions: How heavy were taxes in reality? (Of course this has to be looked at in terms of the channels through which wealth flowed.) How heavy were state expenditures? (This question is of course related to the legitimacy of taxation.) Finally, what about representations that portrayed the king as capable, and the state as incapable, of securing the public good?

The Inexorability of Taxes

Few people were capable of understanding the technicalities, legalities, and rules of the tax system.[3] About the laws governing indirect taxes, Necker said: "They are so confused that scarcely one or two men per generation has managed to understand them, and reform is impossible if one begins with details. The only solution, if there is one, is to destroy everything." Here, once again, the prestige of privilege and the tenacity of custom made destruction impossible: the new was superimposed on the old, and confusion reigned from one end to the other of the chain along which the state, through its receipts and expenditures, simply passed along a portion of the national revenue, that is, of the labor of all.

What the ordinary subject—whether peasant or, somewhat less vulnerable in this regard, city dweller—knew was how much he had to pay every year and how he had to pay it. The old idea that taxation was not quite "normal" and that the king would do better to live on the income from his "estate" was still commonplace; "ordinary" taxes were thus always "extraordinary," that is, justified by unusual circumstances. Whatever the king's reasons for seeking additional resources, it had been some time since he had last made do with the income from his estate, yet people still believed that he should invoke some temporary necessity such as war or debt to explain his request for increased "aid" from his people. Taxpayers were bitter that so many "temporary" imposts had been transformed into permanent taxes. Was there no end in sight?

Several factors made the financial burden still heavier. The fiscal sedimentation accumulated on top of direct dues, which, though present everywhere and everywhere denounced, were unevenly distributed geographically and therefore unevenly resented: included under this head were seigneurial dues and tithes as well as ground rents. Thus the royal tax collector claimed his share of an already reduced income, and his exactions introduced unpredictability into the stable world of the peasant. The arrival of a new tax collector could spell ruin, or at the very least administrative difficulties associated with the revision of the tax rolls. The fiscal archives bulged, largely because of new taxes added to existing ones: the *capitation* to the *taille*, the *vingtième* and the *dixième* to the foregoing, and the *ustensiles* and quartering of troops to earlier levies. Under the circumstances it is easy to see why people in villages and towns saw a direct connection between census taking and revision of the tax rolls, and their understandable fears in this regard made them wary of the central government.

What is more, taxes were rarely debated or approved by the public. They were imposed from above, generally by assessments made without consultation. The king (and his Council) set the amount of the *taille* or *capitation*, and this amount was divided up and passed down the chain of command from the *intendants de finance* to the *commissaires des généralités* to the *collecteurs*, *trésoriers*, and *élus*, and finally to the parish assemblies. There, individuals, groups, and families developed their own small-scale fiscal strategies. They selected a person—generally the richest, but sometimes the poorest (with nothing to lose)—to be responsible for apportioning shares and assisting the tax collector. Communities sometimes banded together and petitioned their lord for an abatement. There was a certain amount of power in passive resistance. Rural notables and curés filled in where there was a shortage of local administrators. Although the *pays d'Etats* had the right to debate taxes, this was a privilege limited to notables, and the burden that fell on the general population was roughly the same as elsewhere. The central government got less, but the difference went to the province. The (limited) right to consent did not reduce the actual tax burden.

There were also inequalities between subjects and between different types of taxes, the one sometimes reinforcing the other. As complex as the fiscal machinery was, the inequality of taxation was glaring. Peasants paid the bulk of both direct taxes (*tailles, capitations,* and related levies) and indirect taxes *(aides, traites, gabelles)*. Furthermore, the urban bourgeoisie, officeholders, clergymen, and nobles were assessed unequally: the cities and the higher orders of society paid *corps* dues and commutations, made free-will gifts to the government, and received privileged abatements. Thus the tax system maintained the gap between the beneficiaries of the surplus product, who kept the merchant economy going, and the peasant society, which was somewhat insulated from the cash economy. But taxes played a double role: while accentuating differences by introducing the cash economy into a stable society, they also encouraged development aimed at improving the productivity of agricultural labor.

The institution of the *capitation* and *vingtième* did little to correct inequalities in direct taxation, which were reinforced by the ability of the cities and the privileged to negotiate reductions favorable to themselves. Direct taxes, whether real or personal, remained inegalitarian to the end, although the king did manage to wring taxes out of non-*taillable* nobles and officeholders, whose *capitation* doubled and even tripled in the period 1760–1763. Taxes assessed against particular sources of revenue, such as the *dixième* of 1733 and the variations on the *vingtième* proposed by Machault d'Arnouville on income from land, industry, and offices in order to reduce state debt, were unequal by their very nature. After a period of rigor, the clergy was again exempted from taxation, the Estates were allowed to subscribe, and municipal taxes were increasingly combined with royal taxes. Louis XV again succeeded in levying taxes on nobles, officeholders, and communities, but technical problems of assessment remained to be solved. In France, despite Bertin's projects, there was no cadastral survey, hence the interest in tax schedules linking assessment to property; and because there was no control of tax declarations, underestimation was common.

The fiscal burden also varied geographically. In the *élection* of Sens alone, the ratio of tax to income varied from 5 to 53 percent; the corrected average was 18 percent, with no account taken of the value of the land or its actual productivity. Inequality was built into the system. There were also variations between localities and provinces: Auvergne was overtaxed at eighteen livres sixteen sols per head in 1784 (this figure represents the total of both direct and indirect taxes on the average individual), whereas in Flanders the average was just five to seven livres. Geographic inequalities reflected the local history of fiscal privileges and customs: in one place nobles paid a small amount, in another place they paid nothing; indirect taxes were heavy in one place, light in another. The variation in indirect taxes makes it difficult to gauge their actual burden. For the *gabelle,* or salt tax, depending on whether one was subject to the *grande gabelle* or the *petite gabelle,* the cost ranged from five livres in some places to two in others, or from five days of work in Ile-de-France to a few days in some places and a few hours in Brittany and Franche-Comté and of course nothing at all in exempt regions such as Flanders, Artois, Hainault, and Béarn. Apart from the fact that an essential item such as salt was everywhere overpriced, this diversity of the salt tax encouraged fraud and provoked opposition. Most consumption taxes (the *aides* on drinks and tobacco, entry duties, taxes on weights and measures) varied from place to place. Along with *traites* on merchandise such as cloth, soap, ironware, and spices, these taxes raised the cost of living considerably, perhaps as much as 200 percent. The fiscal chain from producer to consumer exacerbated inequalities, all the more so in that the quid pro quo for taxes paid was less visible in the countryside than in the city.

Nearly everyone paid taxes in one form or another. Exemptions depended on personal as well as territorial privileges, but the decisive factor was the fact that some people received only abatements while others who advanced the state money in the form of loans or through the purchase of offices received regular interest payments. This was the real privilege: to share in the redistribution of the fiscal product, whether directly in the form of pensions, salaries, bonuses, or indemnities or indirectly in the form of interest and rent.

Throughout the eighteenth century the sale of offices was used as a regular device for government borrowing. A disguised form of taxation when it involved increased capitalization of existing investments, and much more when offices proliferated under Louis XIV, the venality of office was completely integrated with the organic system of *corps* and privileges. It regularly provided cash at low cost and on terms favorable to the state, and reinforced *corps* solidarity. Although various forms of oversight were instituted, the tax exemption remained, and the *corps* were well aware of their interests and zealous in defending them. They also played another crucial role by familiarizing their members with solidarity in the choice of objectives and procedures. Given the close interconnection between credit and taxation, egalitarian discussion among officeholders served to define a version of the "general will." The corps of officeholders could thus lighten their burden through negotiation, thereby maintaining harmony and helping the king through a network of lenders shored up by privilege: in 1788 this accounted for a quarter to a third of the total state debt, some 700 to 800 million livres. Thus, within the society of fiscal privilege we find mechanisms that would later be extended to society as a whole.[4]

From Receipt to Expenditure

If fiscal mobilization demanded more of the poor than of the rich, the reason was that it was easier to increase the amount of a tax than to alter its apportionment. In the realm of taxes, therefore, order was preserved, even though the royal government was driven by its own internal processes toward innovation. Battle was waged repeatedly on the tax reform front, but without success. When stability prevailed, however, the government turned its attention to expenditures. Increasing tax revenue was implicit in the very dynamic of development, whereas to economize was to opt for stability. The apportionment of budgetary posts is ultimately a sign of the relation of state to society.

Receipts did indeed increase: from 180 million in 1715, or less than ten livres per head, to 470 million in 1788, just under twenty livres. The state's fiscal revenue thus nearly tripled, whereas the tax burden on the average individual certainly did not double. In fact, according to calculations by Peter Mathias and Patrick O'Brien, the individual tax burden did not increase as much in France as in England. Taxes as a percentage of income were probably lower in the eighteenth century than they are today, perhaps 5 to 10 percent of gross income. Why, then, the persistent belief that the tax burden was intolerable? There was no dramatic increase in the eighteenth century to compare with that of the seventeenth century, when taxes spiraled rapidly upward. From Law to Fleury the *taille* diminished: that of 1743 was the lowest of the century. Afterward, however, regular increases resumed. Tax revenues reached 207 million livres in 1750, 318 million in 1770, and 419 million in 1780, but in view of rising prices and incomes the inflation-adjusted tax level may have remained stable.[5] Two facts cast doubt on this hypothesis, however: the uncertainty of tax receipts and the widening gap between receipts and expenditures owing to the growth of the state.

For contemporaries, from the *contrôleur général* on down to the peasantry, two things made tax increases seem less tolerable than they should have been.[6] First, there was the nightmare of seasonal treasury shortfalls, to which the only possible response was to suspend payments and rely on cash advances from tax collectors who later repaid themselves out of what they took in. These "treasury bankers" obviously pocketed a portion of what taxpayers paid in—a banker's dream. There was one such treasury banker per *généralité,* and this handful of individuals enjoyed an ideal set of circumstances of the sort that most bankers can only dream of.[7] Until the Revolution and even beyond, these men enjoyed considerable privileges, such as exemption from the *taille* and a guaranteed 8 percent return on moneys advanced. There were two reasons for this: first to avoid costly shipments of cash, and second to reserve gold for situations in which it was needed to pay crown creditors or might be useful in local commerce. Here the state played an important role in economic development.

A second problem affected the entire system: the fear of irregular tax revenues owing to the irregularities of an economy based largely on agricultural incomes. Crop failures meant fiscal failures, while good years meant lower prices, which were scarcely better news from the standpoint of the state. Given fixed family needs, the severe ups and downs of the rural economy thus hindered development and made increased state exactions seem intolerable. Crisis years only exacerbated the needs of the state, which had to maintain order and feed the hungry. The low tax rate was dictated by the economy itself and the impossibility of exceeding a level determined by the conditions of production and judgments about the legitimacy or illegitimacy of particular tax proposals, judgments influenced by the use of the prospective revenues and the image of the monarchy itself.

According to Morineau's calculations, two factors largely determined the tax requirements of eighteenth-century governments. Warfare accounted for 25 to 42 percent of government expenditure: 35 percent in 1726, 25 percent in 1788. The other major item was service on the public debt: 33 percent in 1726, 41 percent in 1788 (in the wake of the American Revolution). Expenditures almost always exceeded receipts: 182 million livres after the Regency, 633 million under Louis XVI. Military operations were financed by debt, and long wars could not be contemplated without a willingness to incur still more debt. The monarchy met its needs by borrowing. Expenditures for civilian purposes remained more or less constant: 23 percent in 1788 (5.7 percent for the court and pensions; 3 percent for the administration, courts, police, and roads; 3 percent for poor relief; less than 2 percent for education and public assistance; and 3.7 percent for public savings). The growing gap between ordinary income and ordinary expenditures was more than the economy could support and left the monarchy more beholden than ever to its creditors.

There were two types of creditors. The majority were figures of traditional society: *rentiers* with bonds on the Hôtel de Ville, the Church, and the communes, as well as officeholders and privileged underwriters of tax farming contracts. Everyone with a share in what the Physiocrats called the "net product" thus had a hand in the gargantuan state debt, accounting for 82 percent of total receipts in 1789. In addition, toward the end of the Ancien Régime, money changers and international bankers were increasingly invited to share in the growing state debt as well as in credit generally.

Borrow more in order to spend more while encouraging the whirlwind of development: that, in a nutshell, was the essence of a financial policy aimed at circumventing the need for reform. In the monarchy's final budget, the king and state were cast in a strange light: the king was portrayed as a modest monarch at the head of an impoverished state, despite all the literature attacking the lavish expenditure on luxuries for the court.[8] The state was said to be poor in the midst of a country that was rich (with a gross national product estimated at 4 billion francs). The level of taxation was tolerable at 10 percent, but 80 percent of tax revenues went to service the accumulated debt. This income redistribution favored nobles and others who already benefited from the increase in ground rents and profits. In other words, the fiscal system was transferring income from the pockets of the poor to the pockets of the rich: eight of every ten livres that came in went to bondholders and bankers. The system that people rejected was thus a system that had gone awry, but its failures were probably less apparent than was a certain change in the idea of what taxes were for.

Taxes: Given or Coerced

According to the traditional image of the king as father, he was supposed to be generous with his favor.[9] "Eager to win the hearts of his new subjects and dazzle his neighbors," Voltaire wrote, "the king handed out favors on all sides: gold and gems were lavished on anyone with the slightest pretext to talk to him."[10] The monarch, moreover, set an example for the nobility and the whole of court society. Splendor, luxury, and openhandedness confirmed a man's rank and status and gave evidence of friendship between states.

In the wake of criticism from economists and philosophes, however, this calculated display of wealth was no longer seen in the same way: the tax question came to outweigh the importance, real as well as symbolic, of income redistribution. The increased prominence of financiers in the administrative apparatus accentuated this change, for they insisted that expenditures be trimmed to match revenues, whereas the king had always spent whatever he needed to spend without worrying about how much he had. The king's gifts and court expenditures accordingly became a focal point of protest that bore little relation to reality. The criticism pointed up the precariousness of the monarch's position as lord of lords and head of state. For the majority of his subjects the state was simply an obstacle, a screen between the father-king and his people. For them the state meant not the king but taxes, which the government no longer requested but demanded. People still remembered a time when consent outweighed authority, which had triumphed in the form of absolutism. But permanent taxes were possible only if the king's subjects were prosperous. The economic aspect of politics outweighed everything else: exchange took precedence over gifts. What mattered was perhaps not so much the actual burden of taxes as the various forms of parasitism that taxation encouraged.

The entire fiscal hierarchy of local notables, tax collectors, sheriffs responsible for seizing assets, and others was suspected, rightly or wrongly, of prevarication. Tax farmers, always detested, had since 1726 been grouped together in a permanent institution recognized as being indispensable to the monarchy, the Ferme Générale.[11] Their extensive powers made them and their employees extremely unpopular. The tax system was criticized on two grounds: first, the private nature of tax collection generated huge profits for tax farmers, and second, the methods of tax collection and inspection generated hostility. These two criticisms fueled the myth of the *laquais financier,* or financial lackey.

Feared by the king's subjects for his coercive powers, the *financier* was suspected by the monarchy of embezzling funds destined for the royal treasury. Yet his role was indispensable. In the *Tableau de Paris,* Mercier attacked the Pâris brothers, whose extraordinary success drew frequent criticism:

> Four brothers, blessed with a distinct sort of intelligence and clever enough to recognize it, threw in their lot together early on, and much to their advantage, for no great fortune was ever amassed without mutual assistance. At their first meeting, one of the brothers addressed the eldest in these terms: "You have genius and imagination but no common sense. You're always thinking up new ideas at the drop of a hat. God has given me a logical mind but no genius, so I will correct your errors and see to it that your plans remain within the bounds of possibility. And you, little brother, have no ideas but are gifted with a golden tongue, so you will haunt the waiting rooms of the ministries and explain our plans to the ministers, who are susceptible to glibness. And you," he said to the remaining brother, "you will be the banker, the steady guardian. We have powerful passions, whereas you have none, so you will be the tight-fisted cashier who manages our expenses. On these four wheels, brothers, our carriage will roll quite nicely."

Similarly, the Montmartels, wrongly thought to be the sons of an innkeeper from the Dauphiné, were widely believed to have amassed a huge fortune.[12] Mercier's critique reflects the image of financiers as blood-suckers and lackeys, which Daniel Dessert has shown to be inaccurate.[13] The portrait he draws was still valid on the eve of 1789: financiers came from a cohesive milieu of wealthy families, with fortunes on the order of several million livres, but were more notable for the rapidity of their rise than for the magnitude of their wealth. Most were nobles who owned offices. Their unflattering reputation did not reflect reality, but it does point up how ambiguous the position of financier was in the traditional hierarchy and how much social advancement owing to wealth was re-sented. This was a useful myth, "a ruling-class ideological image that amazingly enough accredited the idea that the rabble could be fleeced only by their own kind,"[14] which made scapegoats of financiers and left them vulnerable to public opinion. Consensus was restored by excluding the financier, as in the time of John Law and the *chambre de justice*, and leaving the whole system, tied as it was to the monarchy and inegalitarian society, exposed to criticism.

Between 1780 and 1789 the fiscal system was at the center of a dispute in which the traditional image of the financier no longer worked because financiers were even more powerful than they had been at the beginning of the century and in a better position to withstand attack. There was no *chambre de justice* in the eighteenth century, and financiers were more fully integrated into the second order. They had left their mark on society and culture: think of Lavoisier and Ledoux. In 1789 the monarchy was unable to hold society together by using them as scapegoats. "That role [i.e., the role of scapegoat] would be filled by the monarchy itself."[15] The king was no longer the father of his people. That was no longer possible.

From Glory to Peace

A change similar to the one in the fiscal and financial system of the old monarchy can be observed in one of the principal functions of royal power, a function to which Louis XIV had attached considerable importance: the glory of the warrior king. In the monarchic ritual of Versailles, the sword played an essential role, as did the ancient-style apologia for disciplined violence, for both grew out of the imperative to maintain order, to ensure a *bonne police,* through strength in war and firmness at home. State control of the armed forces had evolved in the seventeenth century. The technical and administrative means of controlling both land and naval forces that had been developed in the 1700s continued to be effective in the 1800s. War, together with its instruments, was a fundamental ingredient of state power, institutionally and legally identical with sovereignty. War was also the supreme affair of state, as well as the justification for increased state power. Yet thinking about warfare changed during the Enlightenment, as did the relationship between military society and civil society.[16]

In the ceremonial of information, the celebration of victory occupied a fundamental place. Royal letters alerted people in the parishes to the king's intentions, calling them to arms and justifying the king's decisions. Alexandre Dubois, curé of Rumegies from 1686 to 1739, kept a diary in which he noted how people living along France's northern boundary reacted to these royal messages.[17] As is well known, Louis XV boosted his popularity by personally taking part in the War of the Austrian Succession (1743–1748). Yet it was difficult to persuade people to swallow defeat, humiliation, and peace treaties concluded on terms unfavorable to France even when they included certain benefits. The issue was not an implausible patriotism but the political importance of the charismatic image of the warrior king.[18] The importance of the protective function diminished as the nature of warfare changed, and along with it the role of the army and its relation to society.

The Ideology of Peace

In the final years of Louis XIV's reign, at the end of a long period of international hostilities, the European public embraced an ideology of peace expressed most strikingly in the abbé de Saint-Pierre's *Projet pour rendre la paix perpétuelle.* Over the course of the eighteenth century, this work, which offered historical arguments to show why the great powers should work together to negotiate a lasting peace, drew wide comment in places ranging from the discussions of the Club de l'Entresol to the works of Voltaire and Rousseau, and thus served as a kind of model. It was solidly grounded in the diplomatic realities of the day and offered a model of arbitration based on a mythical vision of the Holy Empire. The abbé argued for toleration (especially in the realm of religious affairs), condemned warfare (which he likened to gambling), and offered a critique of the notions of "equilibrium" and "balance" among nations based on the idea that the balance of power was difficult to assess because it depended on the hierarchy of international relations and the intangibles of military might. He also compared international relations with relations existing within civil society, an idea that Rousseau would strongly challenge in the work that grew out of his reading of the abbé.

One can interpret this evolution as marking a stage in which the idea of the state began to overshadow the waning concepts of the sovereign and his dynasty, and when the reputation of a prince began to depend not so much on his martial virtues as on his talents as diplomat and peacemaker. There are echoes here of Fénelon's values and of the widely shared aspiration for a new order based on economic rather than military realities. The "system of war" inevitably led to tyranny, whereas the "system of peace" allowed for moderate governments and a better way of life, as Montesquieu recognized when he called for economic development. It comes as no surprise that Hardion, the royal censor, refused to grant a privilege for publication of Montesquieu's *Projet* in 1728 because the work played down territorial claims and proposed a freeze on international borders. Saint-Pierre called for preaching morality to nations and for rationalizing conflict, which he discussed without invoking the judgment of God. What he proposed was a diplomatic utopia based on concepts used by contemporary negotiators, concepts that implied a repudiation of Europe's religious underpinnings and of the sovereign's function as protector of the nation. He called for peace rather than war.[19]

International relations in the eighteenth century directly reflected what can be interpreted as a crisis of traditional representations fueled by criticism of military society. Three elements of this criticism stand out: France was safe from invasion, the realities of military conflict were changing, and the role of the army was evolving.

French territory had been secure since 1715, and walls and ramparts were being demolished nearly everywhere. The regular system of border fortifications pioneered by Vauban provided all the defense that was necessary. The attacks on Alsace in June 1744 and Provence in 1746 and the landings in Brittany and Normandy in 1758 and 1760 had been inconsequential raids and nothing more. Frenchmen were still fighting on land and sea but outside France, and all current treatises on strategy dealt with the realities of the day: invasion was scarcely mentioned except as a case study in the art of warfare. The civic rhetoric of Rousseau in his *Considérations sur le gouvernement de Pologne* (1772) and Guibert in the *Essai général de tactique* (1772) should not be allowed to deceive: it was intended to warn people of the vulnerability of a nation that could not be mobilized because it lacked patriotism and of the dangers of an army unprepared to do its mission because it failed to institute reforms made necessary by the awakening or reawakening of national sentiment.[20]

Indeed, the reality of warfare in eighteenth-century Europe had changed. War became less frequent as negotiation headed off armed conflict in the 1720s and 1730s and even in the 1740s. The grounds for conflict were less clear, and many people were incapable of seeing any reason beyond shifting dynastic interests why French soldiers should be sent to "die for the king of Prussia" on German battlefields. French engagements were limited because mercantile France was divided over the issue of defending colonies and failed to persuade the government of the need for a concerted policy of imperialist expansion like Britain's:

Canada and India held less appeal than islands with sugar plantations. In short, France mobilized for Europe, entered into disconcertingly ephemeral treaties, and switched allegiances without entirely convincing people that Choiseul's decision to ally with Austria and abandon the traditional Protestant unions was the right choice. Yet even though people paid with their hides for every armed adventure, the nation as a whole did not suffer greatly up to the time of the American Revolution. Expenses rose, and some sectors of the economy, such as the ports, did suffer, but at no time did the country plumb the depths of misery as in the time of the Sun King, and recovery was quick after each crisis. Output was not hindered unduly by heavy taxation, and domestic trade picked up considerably.[21] The bellicose periods of the Enlightenment were dark interludes during which the state ran up considerable debts, but those very debts proved profitable to *rentiers* and did not alter the structure of the economy. The catastrophic wars of the past gave way to the parenthetic wars of the present, wars that could be withstood without disaster and were perhaps conducive to development in the medium to long run.

These changes of course made it possible to use the army for new tasks. Domestic order was rarely disturbed (I will come back to this point), and this calm can be related to the progress made in mastering the territory. Royal authority was firmed up, and in the 1720s the reorganization of the *maréchaussée* and a series of reforms in the urban police forces (the *guet*, or watch, *robe courte*, and *prévôté de Paris*) bestowed military status on security activities. In the countryside several thousand mounted police, organized in brigades and efficient because of their mobility, knew the terrain and the people well and provided security on highways, kept order at fairs and markets, and guarded royal funds in transit. They not only upheld order but also promoted conditions favorable to development. No one complained about their presence. On the contrary, there were regrets that such an efficient militarized service was not larger than it was: the state repurchased some offices, and noncommissioned officers and troops were shifted from the army to tightly disciplined police brigades. In the cities, especially Paris, the army patrolled regularly and also cooperated in special police activities, such as the arrest of an important nobleman or action against members of *parlement* opposed to reform. And of course the army was also called in whenever the regular police forces proved incapable of restoring order: in Paris in 1775, in Lyons in 1786, and elsewhere on frequent occasions. In the course of such service, the army, especially the Royal Household Regiments and the French Guards, was transformed. It acquired a conscience, which it repressed, and proved susceptible to philosophical and political debate. Misunderstood, the army began to speak.

Military Men and Civilians: Critique and Rehabilitation

Two developments combined to alter the relation between military society and civil society. The armed forces changed profoundly, as did the demands civil society placed on them. The prestige of the uniform declined early in the century. A new state of mind was apparent not only in critiques of war but also in attitudes toward the revival of bourgeois militias. The recruitment of militiamen forced many families and communities to bear additional charges for the support of mobilized troops and to buy their way out of service. Conscription by lot provoked riots, especially when the authorities tried to force guild members to participate, as in Bordeaux when Jacques Ménétra visited there in 1757. Along with opposition to the militia there was also hostility toward restrictions on mobility imposed in wartime in order to keep tabs on potential recruits. The militia was deactivated in 1763, except for a brief period during the last war of the Ancien Régime (1778–1783).

The appeal of military life waned for officers as well as enlisted men, even though many nobles continued to respect tradition, and fascination with the military kept recruitment up. Still, the unpredictability of military careers exhausted the patience of many and reduced the number of people who made the military their calling. Furthermore, study of military records has revealed a decline in traditional forms of recruitment, in which a lord formed a company of vassals and other subordinates; in the old society such practices had seemed "natural," but this was no longer the case. Captains no longer found men in their villages willing to fill slots in their companies. Military service therefore tended to take men out of their native provinces and send them to garrisons in border towns or, increasingly, in Paris. The city and its attractions determined who joined up and who did not: it tended to attract those who were without property or depressed as well as adventurers and of course delinquents. It is by no means certain that recruitment to the navy was any more effective, despite the influence of the class system on the coastal population. Shortages of manpower were constant on land and sea, and the problem was not resolved by calling on foreign mercenaries, who made up some 20 percent of the armed forces in wartime, or from 200,000 to 300,000 men.

Malaise in the military reached its apogee in defeat: the Rossbach syndrome (named for the German village where Frederick II defeated the French in 1757) was a form of discouragement, a failure of emulation. Guibert and others criticized urban recruitment, which resulted in an army consisting of "the most contemptible dregs of society," a rabble of the poor and down-and-out: the middle classes shunned the ranks and were replaced by the lower strata of the urban and rural population. Further criticism greeted the mischief of the military, including libertinage and scandalous behavior as well as thievery and other criminal activity in peacetime.

Two things strengthened the military in its isolation. The Choiseul and Saint-Germain reforms professionalized the army by requiring soldiers to serve for longer periods and increasing discipline in order to restore a "community" of interest between commanders and troops. Yet the odious aspects of these reforms, the "slavery" they imposed, outraged part of the army itself, to say nothing of enlightened thinkers hostile to the Prussianization of the French military. Meanwhile, the army was afflicted with the caste spirit. It blamed its failures on incompetent officers of common birth who had procured commissions through money or favor. It extolled the chivalrous virtues of honor and courage, which impure blood could not provide. The chevalier d'Arc urged king and state to respond to the needs of poor and impoverished nobles in his *Noblesse militaire ou le Patriote français* (1756). The army, once a non-uniformed "civil service,"[22] was stripped of high dignitaries by the absolute monarchy, controlled from Versailles by the *secrétaires d'Etat à la Guerre* and their civilian clerks, dominated by men of noble blood who were not career soldiers because their military service was brief and irregular, and subjected to the ideals of obedience and economy. It dreamed of ultimate militarization as a way of solving both a social problem and the problem of its own relation to the rest of society, whose contradictions it embodied.

The chevalier d'Arc, descended from a Bourbon bastard, was in fact participating in a fundamental debate initiated by Abbé Coyer's discussion of luxury and commerce in *La Noblesse commerçante* (1756), a work whose central idea was to reconcile trade with nobility, the new economy with the old kingdom. The response of the "French patriot" reveals the opposition of a faction of the nobility to any form of mercantile economy: the patriot denies the virtues of commerce, denounces the social mobility made possible by money, and ends with the difficulty of reconciling talent with birth. The "profit economy" is condemned, and moral conversion is urged:

> Why do we often find the favors of the sovereign insufficient? Might it be that they are not adequate to maintain a level of luxury whose cost is increasing day by day? Before complaining about this, however, let us measure what decency requires, and let us do so without exaggeration. Then our only complaint will be about the luxury that is blowing everything out of proportion. Let nobles deserve merit, then, let them serve, and let them fear not that under a government as just as it is enlightened their services may go unrewarded. They need nothing but courage and resignation to bear the wait.[23]

The appeal to the "value of prejudice" was heeded and can be seen at work in various reforms, including the Saint-Germain reform of 1776 and the edict of 1781 barring ennobled or wealthy commoners from receiving commissions in the military. The requirement of "four degrees of nobility" did not solve the problems of impecunious noblemen or meet the need for a more professional military, but it did anger members of the second order whose nobility was of recent date and sons of the bourgeoisie whose hopes of military careers were dashed.

From the Philosophical Military to the Educational Army

In the final years of the Ancien Régime, the isolation of the military was reduced by a new form of integration. This was achieved partly through culture, which gave military men a new role in society, and partly through pedagogy and its effects on behavior.

Military officers took part in the arts, science, and literature. In Paris and the provinces they accounted for a significant proportion of the membership of the academies: 10 to 20 percent on average, and even higher in garrison cities such as Metz, Grenoble, Brest, and Valence, but less in cities with *parlements,* because "the army always despises the Senate," which dominated learned institutions wherever it was present. For men such as Laclos, the academies provided an entrée into local society (in his case that of La Rochelle). For Carnot, they offered a way to participate in intellectual life. Groups affirmed their collective existence by joining academies, as the "Messieurs du Grand Corps" did in joining the Académie de Marine in Brest, or as the "Chevaliers des Galères" did in Marseilles. If culture was not incompatible with the profession of arms—and many officers corresponded with Voltaire and Rousseau, while many more participated in the life of the mind (36 percent of the *pensionnaires* of the Académic des Sciences were military men, including Vauban, Bélidor, Chabert, La Gallissonnière, Borda, Admiral d'Estrées, the duc de Castries, Richelieu, and Maillebois)—military men were even more at home in societies of Freemasons. Many belonged to military lodges (53 percent of the officers of the regiment of Penthièvre and 20 percent of the Royal Household Regiment); half of the 2,500 Masons in Paris were from the military. In these social circles military tradition, based on service and honor, melded with the ideal of social utility, good works, and reform sponsored by the academies and the Masonic lodges. Military men thus became philosophes. They wrote, thought about re-forming the military and society, defended humane warfare, and painted an image of the soldier as a useful and beneficial member of society. The army hoped that participation in civilian life would bring it closer to society: it fought against the plague in Provence (1720–1723) and helped with canals and other public works projects. In Paris the French Guards played a variety of roles, and the press reported on their contributions to the public good. But the army was divided in the same way as Enlighten-ment society itself; hence it was not easy to reconcile the old royal roles of seeking glory in war while protecting the people.

Military recruitment and education policies also contributed to change. The army's internal rationalization of its administration, organization, and doctrine subjected the behavior of soldiers to rational controls and evaluation. Artillery and supply services became standardized. The army of the Enlightenment era helped to pioneer new manufacturing tech-niques. Navy arsenals in Brest, Rochefort, Lorient, and Cherbourg had set standards for urban planning and rationalized shipbuilding procedures since the seventeenth century—a triumph of naval engineering mobilized for war. In addition, the corps of royal engineers at the Ecole de Mézières made science a part of military training.[24] Among the faculty were distin-guished scientists such as Monge, Ferry, and Abbé Bossut. The school's instruction had a profound impact, even if its 542 students devoted them-selves primarily to martial labors. In the royal military schools the army experimented with new educational techniques whose influence extended well beyond the barracks walls. Young men from mercantile families attended these schools alongside the sons of military officers.

In addition, the army spurred economic activity throughout the kingdom: it bought goats, food supplies, cloth, and weapons that kept men at work in forges and factories. The military budget generated substantial profits, and expenditures were increasingly monitored by the war ministry through its *commissaires* and *trésoriers*. The billeting of troops and the management of military hospitals changed the way people behaved. Simply wearing the uniform changed men's aspirations. The army also taught many people to read and write and encouraged social and geographic mobility; hence even as it instilled discipline it was also a force for liberation.

The relationship between the sovereign and the military changed. Reformed, influenced by the Enlightenment, but divided sociologically and ideologically, the army was seen less as an instrument of the king to be used in whatever way he wished than as a disputed asset whose support for the monarch could no longer be taken for granted.

Justice, Security, Assistance

Since Michel Foucault published *Discipline and Punish,* we have known that the history of punitive techniques (whether directed toward body or soul) must be seen in the context of the history of the body politic, that is, the structure of power relations among subjects.[25] The history of judicial procedures and tortures thus parallels the political theory of the monarchy as perceived through legal discourse, whose purpose was to assign people accused and convicted of crimes a place in the sociopolitical sphere. The judicial system involved the whole legal heritage, which was social as well as cultural. It was the result of a delicate balance between "custom," the law of the social group, and "law," the legal code of the king and state. The judicial system tended to unify standards and actions. It was the place where jurisprudence and judicial institutions interacted.

The legal system involved all segments of society. It dealt with private matters as well as public, civil cases as well as criminal ones. In it the king occupied a central position. René Louis de Voyer d'Argenson contrasted the duties of the king as lord to those of the king as magistrate: "Monarchy strictly speaking means a government in which the monarch assumes responsibility for everything by virtue of his property rights in the states he governs . . . Royalty [*royauté*] is government by one man in view not of his property rights but of the good of the state of which he regards himself as simply the first magistrate."[26]

The relation between the monarch as lord and the monarch as magistrate still influenced the exercise of power in the eighteenth century. Its roots lay in the notion of the common good and the role of the modern state as an arbiter of conflict yet bound to respect its contracts with its servants. The modernization of the judiciary was slow and perilous because it implied a reappropriation by the monarch of power shared with others: Was the king a lord, that is, a judge among other judges, or was he the supreme magistrate? This ancient cultural conflict persisted in the minds of jurists and lords, and any resolution promised to have profound implications for the very idea of justice.

With the concentration of the judicial hierarchy in the eighteenth century, the idea of justice changed. Philosophical criticism did not spare the courts: the philosophes insisted on milder punishments and an end to abuses of power. Changes in attitudes toward the poor led to questioning of a whole aspect of the judicial and law enforcement apparatus (confinement of paupers and use of *lettres de cachet*), as reforms raised new moral and legal challenges to traditional practices. The origins of this struggle can be traced all the way back to the thirteenth century, and the eighteenth did not put an end to it; the persistent criticism did considerable damage to the image of the king as the "source of all justice."

Royal Justice and Judicial Justice

The conflict I have alluded to was apparent in the organization of the judicial system itself. Here I shall limit myself to the main features of that system.[27] The state did not have an absolute monopoly over justice. "Ordinary" judicial functions were dispersed among a pyramid of courts and hierarchical yet at the same time competitive institutions. The king could intervene in this tangled web of competencies and jurisdictions by virtue of his role as suzerain lord and magistrate and thereby moderate certain excesses. Above all, royal intervention made it possible to take certain general steps and to arbitrate disputed matters for the sake of public tranquillity. In the realm of what was called *la justice concédée*, or the delegation of judicial powers, as conceptualized in the theories of regalian jurists, the king was a prisoner of an ancient devolution of rights upon which monarchs had been trying to impose limits since the Middle Ages. By the eighteenth century, however, there were several competing judicial systems in France. Of these the most important was seigneurial justice, but there were also ecclesiastical courts (the so-called *officialités*), urban courts, and consular courts that intervened in mercantile matters.

The seigneurial courts played a ubiquitous, tenacious, and crucial role in everyday life and basic social relations. In the Paris basin there was one such court for every two or three parishes; some had jurisdiction over a tiny area at most. In the Dore Mountains, the fiefs of Murat and Le Planchat, *seigneuries* of La Tour d'Auvergne, incorporated several parishes and transgressed boundaries with abandon. This was not always as much of a problem as we with our tidy logical minds like to think, however, because the older jurisdictional lines remained indelibly etched in people's minds: everyone knew perfectly well which judges had jurisdiction over them.[28] Royal intervention helped to unify this mosaic by setting standards for the recruitment of judges, declaring a growing number of matters to be "royal cases," establishing appellate jurisdiction over the seigneurial courts, and, in 1772, assuming responsibility for court costs in cases transferred to royal judges. The king was unable to get rid of the seigneurial courts entirely, for to have done so would have further diminished the powers of the nobility while destroying an entrenched and vital institution. Seigneurial judges may, as their critics charged, have been biased and incompetent, but they served a useful if modest purpose by dealing with the kind of local, internal conflicts that were the staple of justice in a stable society.

The royal-delegated common law courts (*prévôtés, bailliages,* and *parlements,* except in Paris, where there was no *bailliage*) served a different world entirely. They formed the backbone of urban society, and the magistrates—*grands et petits robins*—constituted a subculture within the larger culture. There were probably more than two thousand *prévôtés* and *viguiers,* more than a hundred *bailliages,* some sixty of which fell into the more prestigious category of *présidiaux,* and thirteen *parlements,* of which the Parlement of Paris was the largest and most extensive but not necessarily the most representative, along with thirteen sovereign councils. All told, these courts employed several thousand magistrates and thousands more court officers and attorneys. To round out our survey, let us mention as well the twenty or so financial tribunals, the Grand Conseil, the *tribunaux des eaux et forêts,* the admiralty courts, the military tribunals, the constabularies, and the *prévôtés des maréchaux.*

The mere enumeration of these many kinds of tribunals is enough to suggest their influence on society and the complexity of the maze in which litigants often lost their way. The problem was that these judicial institutions sprang from three different sources. Some were inherited from the past, from history, from the way in which France was constructed, and these could not be reformed without challenging the deep attachment that people in various localities felt to their customary laws. Others formed part of the system of privileges and offices and reflected the need for specialized administrative courts and for a credible monarchical presence. Still others were associated with the growth of the royal administration, in the course of which each new department was granted jurisdiction over litigation in its area of responsibility. Caught between venality and tradition, the courts were not the most favorable target for the kind of rationalization called for by some and opposed by others on grounds of liberty and privilege. Listen to Montesquieu: "In despotic states, the prince can judge by himself. He cannot do so in a monarchy: the constitution would be destroyed, and consequent intermediate powers would be demolished. All formalities of judgment would cease, and fear would take hold of people's minds. Their faces would turn pale: without confidence, love, and security, there can be no monarchy."

What better way to describe the conflict between royal justice and judicial government over the issues of who should judge and whether or not reform was possible?[29] Here again we see the close relationship between feudal complexity and venality, with Montesquieu defending both. Who should judge and how to judge: everything was in question.

Before we look at the principles of the king's justice, however, two factors that reinforced the power of judges need to be pointed out: the defense of particularism and the cultural role of the magistracy. Despite the standardization of judicial practices and the sense that a unique legal code was becoming more and more indispensable (an idea that influenced leading jurists such as Guyot, Merlin, and Boucher d'Argis), the idea of an independent, pluralist judicial system clearly won out. It was impossible to limit or eliminate the sovereignty of magistrates in the exercise of their power, even if this led, as Voltaire charged, to "contradiction, uncertainty, and arbitrariness." Two things followed from this. First, each court and tribunal had a specific function and kept a watch over certain local interests, and the restiveness of judges varied widely from place to place. The example of Paris was not universally followed. Second, and perhaps more serious, the lower courts proved insubordinate, and their lack of discipline in matters of appeal or enforcement of general decrees destroyed the image of a hierarchical judicial system and undermined the authority of magistrates generally. This insubordination provided the authorities with an additional argument to justify their efforts toward greater centralization. Robert Mandrou has studied these tensions in relation to witchcraft trials.[30] In the final witchcraft trials of the seventeenth and eighteenth centuries, where the issues were less clear-cut than they might seem, *intendants* sometimes favored innovation while at other times they defended custom, depending on the king's interests at the moment.

Changes in the courts were important because they revealed the cultural influence of magistrates over the rest of society. By "magistrates" I mean not just *conseillers* and *présidents* of the sovereign courts but also *avocats, procureurs,* and other court officers of all levels, including lesser officials overshadowed by the great judges who presided over the courtroom ceremony and led the way in urban processions. Magistrates were less isolated in provincial capitals than in the seats of minor jurisdictions. They belonged to the intellectual elite and to the privileged ranks of the wealthy and ennobled. In the practice of their profession they lived up to society's expectations of them, which we must be careful not to judge with today's prejudices. Magistrates were in contact with the leading figures of Enlightenment culture: in Bordeaux with the Secondats, in Toulouse, and in Dijon with Bouhier and de Brosses. Everywhere, academic magistrates helped to build the intellectual framework within which the social and cultural elite generated its innovative ideas for reform. Magistrates accounted for 48 percent of academic memberships and communicated news of the academies to family members and professional associates. All owned libraries. What effect did this vibrant extrajudicial intellectual life have on their judicial activity? Mandrou has answered this question for the seventeenth and early eighteenth centuries: the courts' slowness to adopt a new jurisprudence was due not simply to ignorance and prejudice but also to a certain intellectual fastidiousness. New ideas did take hold after arduous debate, as rationalism and scientific thinking gradually spread. The world of the law was not divorced from the world of the intellect or the world of politics, but communication was more intense at some times than at others.

Royal Justice: Surveillance and Punishment

From Louis XIV to Louis XVI the monarchy justified its intervention in the courts with the slogan: "But for God and me [that is, the king] and the courts there is no law." In cases of *justice retenue* (that is, not delegated to the courts), the king acted as sovereign judge through his Council or *commissaires. Evocations* (assumptions of jurisdiction) and *cassations* (quashing of verdicts) allowed the king to arbitrate in all sorts of conflicts. And then there were the various administrative procedures that enabled the bureaucracy, and behind it the king, to intervene in the judicial system: judgments by *commissaire; chambres de justice* as in 1717; provincial commissions to punish smuggling in Valence (where the notorious thief Mandrin was tried); Reims, Saumur, Paris, and Caen from 1733 to 1785; and ordinary commissions temporarily empowered by letters from the Council or an *intendant*.

Montesquieu denounced all this in Book 6 of *L'Esprit des lois:* "Judgments rendered by the prince may be an endless source of injustice and abuse." The symbol of such abuse was the *lettre de cachet*, the principal instrument of *la justice retenue* and of disciplinary and political intervention. The government, acting on its own authority, could use this instrument to imprison opponents for sedition. *Lettres de cachet* were also used as a police tool both to promote the public interest and to prevent "disorder in families." The fact that this "extraordinary procedure" could be used for so many different purposes reflects a situation in which social conditions and family relations were very different from what they are today. The *lettre de cachet* was the last remnant of a patriarchal system of justice in which the king was every family's guardian as well as the guarantor of public order in a society where anything likely to disrupt stability, corrupt morals, or question the majesty of God or the king was out of bounds. These same imperatives governed the Chancellery in its censorship of printed matter, and "supreme justice," whose decrees were enforceable throughout the kingdom by the police (primarily the Paris police), without regard to the jurisdictional boundaries of the ordinary courts or to provincial borders. The dysfunction of the ordinary justice system coupled with the real but ambiguous growth of the extraordinary system provoked challenges to the system of trial and punishment and ultimately led to a judicial crisis.

The history of criminality, on which a great deal of work has been done in the last forty years, points up some of the complexities of the issue by showing how norms, the economics of law, and criminal habits all varied simultaneously, though of course not in precise harmony. Interestingly, relatively few cases went to court: Nicole Castan's study of appeals to the *parlement* of Toulouse shows that in a jurisdiction with a population of 3 million, appellate judges dealt with one hundred to three hundred criminal cases per year, "a modest number even if one adds sentences handed down by the *prévôtés* from which no appeal was possible."[31] In this same period British justice was undeniably more repressive: two hundred capital crimes compared with just one hundred in France, and ten death sentences in Surrey with its population of just eighty thousand, as many as in all twenty-two dioceses of the province of Languedoc. On the local level, privileged notables shared responsibility for justice with officials of the monarchy. The monarch provided the backup, but law enforcement was left to local officials, including both seigneurial and royal magistrates. There was no regular police force, and investigative techniques were primitive. The *maréchaussée* was limited to surveillance duties, and prosecutions depended on local witnesses.

The courts managed to contain the worst forms of crime at low cost; because of the large number of civil cases that had to be heard, they deliberately limited the number of criminal prosecutions. Not that there were no criminals, but apart from pathological cases, deviants, and impulsive criminals, who could be understood and therefore "tolerated," most were charged with routine crimes of theft, assault, and battery, crimes that anyone might commit. The courts could therefore choose to intervene on occasion to make an example of someone charged with a crime: the regular courts usually chose foreigners, loners, and deviants, while the special courts concentrated on separating the wheat from the chaff. When urban growth, geographic mobility, and demographic changes disrupted customary social relations, people of certain age groups or with certain lifestyles were particularly susceptible to criminal behavior. As the "dangerous classes" swelled because of increased poverty and social mobility, judicial reform became necessary because the only alternative envisioned by the old system was too stark: either execute the accused or release them into the community. Better investigative techniques were also needed.

The study of court records reveals another process at work: as crimes became less violent, punishments lost some of their intensity. Crimes against persons (murder, mayhem, assault and battery) decreased, while crimes against property (theft, fraud) increased. Common delinquency moved out of the limelight; not that it disappeared, just that it was punished by other means, and in any case two centuries of joint efforts by the Church and the police to "civilize customs" had diminished the frequency of delinquent behavior. The nature of organized crime changed over the course of the eighteenth century: gangs led by such notorious criminals as Cartouche, Raffiat, and Mandrin were hunted down and destroyed, only to be replaced by a more fluid, more individual form of criminality. As society became wealthier, there was greater opportunity for crimes against property rather than persons. Communal lawbreaking, a form of collective protest, was transformed into fringe-group deviancy. The crime rate did not diminish, but the target of the authorities changed.[32] Calls for reforms in sentencing reflect a desire for a more effective judicial system. More than three-quarters of the cases judged by the Parlement of Paris from 1775 to 1786 involved crimes against property. In Toulouse from 1750 to 1789 half the cases fit that description, and in Dijon in 1760 nearly two-thirds. Punishments varied accordingly: the number of death sentences declined, but more criminals were sentenced to the galleys, and the change occurred more rapidly at the top *(parlements)* than at the bottom *(bailliages)* of the judicial system. Urbanization and "civilization of morals" were primarily responsible for these changes, just as they also spurred thinking about reforms and new ways to prevent crime and provide assistance in hard times.

From Reform to Social Control

Jurists and philosophes denounced the sovereign's claim that it was his absolute right and duty to punish and avenge by means of exemplary torture. Public opinion turned against the excesses and failures of the judicial system. Indignation was aroused by a new literary genre, the essay on the cause célèbre, which brought to reports of tragic criminal cases a new style of writing quite different from that of contemporary "gallows literature," with its tough, moralistic attitude.[33] These essays provided a new vehicle for the discussion of reform and a new conception of the economy of power. They also revealed the cultural ambiguities that were central to certain notorious cases, most notably the Calas affair, which David Bien has studied.

A broad consensus gradually emerged about the need for a penal code to redefine crimes and punishments and limit the powers of judges so as to guarantee the rights of defendants while respecting the need for public security. Literary and legal works addressed to professional magistrates and other officials reached a much broader audience, reflecting a strong current of opinion in favor of penal reform. Reformist thinking was encouraged by the government: in the preamble to the edict of May 1788, Lamoignon asked people to send reform proposals to him. Voltaire's brilliant pamphlets on the Calas, Sirven, and chevalier de La Barre affairs fueled the reform movement, which also drew inspiration from the writings of Montesquieu and Rousseau. Meanwhile, in Livorno in 1764, Beccaria published his extremely influential treatise *Dei delitti e delle penne,* which was translated by Abbé Morellet in 1766.

The character of the reform movement changed over time. Voltaire had taken up his pen in response to certain notorious scandals, which had revealed the intolerance of certain magistrates in a way that justified criticism on religious and political as well as legal grounds. Later analyses, however, were spurred by a dozen cases of no particular religious or political significance, cases involving ordinary people—domestic servants, poor peasants, horse traders, soldiers—with whom others could easily identify. These new scandals proved devastating because they led to public demonstrations; they destroyed confidence not in the principles of the law but in the judicial system and its procedures. Furthermore, much of the early criticism came from amateurs such as Voltaire and Beccaria, joined on occasion by magistrates such as Montesquieu, Servan, and Elie de Beaumont and lawyers such as Linguet. Later, however, a large segment of the judiciary itself became involved: dozens of essays were produced by magistrates such as Muyart de Vouglans, *parlementaires* such as Dupaty, and attorneys such as Lacretelle, joined by nonspecialists, including Jean-Paul Marat and the marquis de Condorcet. In fact, this criticism emanated from the academies, many of which organized competitions on judicial themes (Châlons, Arras, and Marseilles among them), drawing entries from reformers such as Brissot, Dupaty, Robespierre, and Le Trosne.[34]

Reformers from Beccaria to the writers of the prerevolutionary period insisted on a number of themes. Some wanted to overturn the entire judicial system and replace it with a new conception of penal law based on individual freedom, personal responsibility, and rationalism. Robespierre, for example, won the Metz Academy's prize in 1784 for a dissertation on *peines infamantes,* or penalties involving a loss of civil rights; Marat's *Plan de législation* and Brissot's submissions to the academies of Châlons and Berne were in a similar vein. Others were content simply to transform the existing system and took their inspiration from the efforts of reform-minded ministers of justice such as Miromesnil (1774–1787) and Lamoignon (1787–1788), who asserted tighter control over courts and arrests, abolished torture as an investigative tool, and encouraged thinkers ranging from the philosophes to Turgot and Malesherbes. This group included Lacretelle, Philpin de Piéappe, the young Boucher d'Argis, Jean Blondel, Pastoret, and François Marie Vermeil.

The reformers' goals were to decriminalize intent as opposed to action, to secularize punishment, and to sharpen the distinction between crime and sin. All the reformers more or less shared Voltaire's utilitarian concept of sentencing: the punishment should serve the interests of society. The range of crimes for which capital punishment was prescribed was to be reduced, as Beccaria had recommended and as many magistrates in the *parlements* had come to recognize as a wise course. Still, while nearly everyone called for less severe punishments, no one in France was yet ready to follow the lead of the Italians, who had abolished the death penalty in 1787. The reformers were most cautious in the area of procedure. Only a few of them were willing to allow persons accused of crimes to be represented by attorneys, and the concept of proof received little scrutiny except from those who advocated trial by jury, such as Dupaty.

Broadly speaking, French writing in this area was attentive to legal criticism from throughout Europe but not as innovative as the work of leading judicial reformers such as the Italian Filangieri or the Englishman Jeremy Bentham.[35] The French did not confront the fundamental dilemma of whether society must be reformed before the judicial system or vice versa and limited themselves to two main goals: to establish a more reliable, more moderate criminal justice system, and to reform society so as to reduce recidivism and the spread of criminal behavior. Reform could thus focus on the internal workings of the judicial system, aiming at a redistribution of power and more efficient operation. In the end, what the critics sought was a system in which the power to judge stemmed not from discrete local privileges of delegated justice but from the "continuous distribution of public authority."[36] Since the target of reform was so widely dispersed throughout society, reformers had to refocus their attacks and adjust their scale in order to preserve the jeopardized social contract.

This internal criticism sometimes had undesired effects. Take the Calas affair. The Protestant Jean Calas, a prosperous cloth merchant, was accused of having murdered his son Marc-Antoine, who in fact probably committed suicide. Through a series of misfortunes, Jean Calas was convicted of this crime and condemned to being broken on the wheel. The authorities and the majority of the public were convinced, without much evidence, that the father's fear or knowledge that his son was either about to renounce, or had already renounced, the Protestant faith led to murder. Jean Calas denied this to the end.

The case was a difficult one for two reasons. First, the city of Toulouse had been gripped with fanatical and irrational fears in the waning days of a wave of anti-Protestant repression. The *capitouls* (aldermen) treated Marc-Antoine as a martyr for the Catholic faith, and the clergy, followed by a large crowd, had marched in solemn procession behind his body. Calas's alleged crime had provoked fear in the Catholic community, which suddenly felt itself to be the target of violence in a city where implicit tolerance had prevailed (and would prevail again once the crisis was over). The upper echelons of Toulouse society had absorbed the Enlightenment through the city's academies, lodges, and museum, and Loménie de Brienne preached de facto if not de jure tolerance.

The very anachronism of the Calas affair had a galvanizing effect on circles of the enlightened. That was the second reason for the difficulty of the case. Far from being fanatically anti-Protestant, the *parlementaires* of Toulouse reacted irrationally owing to the threat of war with England as well as to the Rochette affair of 1761, which had raised fears of an uprising of Protestant peasants. By indicting Jean Calas alone for the murder, they actually resisted the more delirious calls for vengeance against the entire Calas family and against Calvinists generally. As in the time of the witchcraft trials, the magistrates did not believe fully in the myth, but it is by no means impossible that, being ordinary judges in both senses of the word, they saw France in jeopardy and acted in order to forestall any outbreak of religious fanaticism. Catholics in Toulouse blamed *parlement* for being too lenient, while the magistrates themselves thought they were doing battle against religious crime. The Calas and Sirven affairs brought about a shift from passive tolerance to active tolerance. The nascent civil society insisted on religious coexistence: civic unity required it. Public opinion took the place of the king as judge. If, as Voltaire said in his *Remarques pour servir de supplément à l'Essai sur les moeurs* (1765), public opinion did not make the laws, it did accept or reject them. Enlightened circles feared the tumultuous tyranny of anarchy more than the reformed oppression of the authorities.

The idea that all violence is fanatical reminds us of a key feature of the final decades of the Ancien Régime: the growing sense of insecurity, which reflects the failure of the *grand renfermement* (locking-up of paupers and criminals), the disintegration of communities by the forces of the new economy, and the decline of internal regulatory processes. The king was responsible for protecting his subjects, but protection, as Beccaria insisted, was also a matter of prevention and education. Although criminality remained a marginal phenomenon, the acceleration of all trends in the crisis years led to new thinking about misery and poverty. The general hospitals and *dépôts de mendicité* could no longer handle the growing influx of paupers left to fend for themselves.[37] The sources of poverty are apparent when we compare resources with needs: the gap widened, with 37 percent of men earning less than three quarters of the minimum required for subsistence. Anyone born poor was bound to die poor, and it took resourcefulness to survive. Criminality was just another stage in coping with mounting necessities. The boundary between illegality and deviancy became blurred, as the records of the *maréchaussées* reveal. Charity and exclusion were no longer enough to contain the flow of paupers. Poverty became a source of fear and a threat to the well-to-do.

The tightening of controls on the poor went hand in hand with a secularization of public assistance. The *brigades* and *prévôts* assumed responsibility for eliminating the most visible delinquents. Assistance to the poor became a public service, increasingly managed by royal and urban bureaucracies. In Paris, high society took up the cause of philanthropic reform. Resources were lacking, however, and people began to wonder about the purpose of the tithe. The authorities in charge of the poor did not distinguish between poverty and misery, repression and assistance, moral preaching and remedial efforts. Public assistance became a function of government because the organic religious society, which the king headed, had ceased to do its job. The failures of the courts and of public assistance revealed the same void that people were beginning to discover in the other principal royal functions.

10

❧❧❧

The End of Rebellion

IN POWER RELATIONS and social conflicts, the king and his agents stand out more vividly than his subjects do. We learn about the king's subjects through comparison, negatively, as it were, because the classical period witnessed the emergence of a new discourse of difference, along with new social concepts and classifications. We see this especially in religious and administrative discourse.

The elite and the people were of course linked both at and below the surface, for example, through reflection on the treatment of poverty. The secularization of assistance noted in the previous chapter reflected a slow change in the way the relation of the poor to the social order was understood. The discovery of mass misery disrupted the religious discourse of the Counter-Reformation. The "people" were differentiated from the elite by cultural and behavioral as well as other criteria. Such distinctions are important if one believes that the politics of the Ancien Régime cannot be reduced to the thought and action of the dominant elite. Continuity and change must be seen in this context.[1]

The eighteenth century is fertile ground for studying the relations between the elite and the people. The bleakness and violence of the seventeenth century provided an excellent rhetorical battleground on which historians who believed in the class struggle, such as Boris Porchnev, could square off with those who believed in the society of orders, such as Roland Mousnier (to name only the two most prominent participants in this debate). Once the dust of historical confrontation had settled, what remained was the fact that from the sixteenth to the eighteenth century, France was shaken by repeated refusals to submit to royal and social authority. Major rebellions, triggered by various combinations of political, military, economic, and religious factors, showed that the people of both the cities and the countryside were capable of rising in protest against the conditions of their existence, especially taxes (taxes—generally new taxes—were directly at issue in two-thirds of these uprisings). Owing to the very nature of the Ancien Régime, nearly all these protest movements shifted their ground from economic to social objectives.[2] As an *intendant* in the Dauphiné remarked at the time, most disorders began with "the people's misery" but continued because of divisions among the "powerful persons" who might have been expected to oppose popular movements of any kind.

After 1715 major rebellions seemed a thing of the past, but throughout the country diffuse, sporadic, and scattered protest movements erupted in rural areas and, less often, in the cities. These popular protests revealed changes in social consciousness: the dominant elites were more in unison with the authorities than in the past, and previously explosive and/or subversive critiques of society had lost some of their punch. Various factors fueled these "riots," and they tell us something about the state of the popular mind and the masses' capacity for political thinking. Social class and economic role are keys for understanding these clashes and their interpretation.

The new protests no longer expressed the views of the old community of orders, status, and custom but instead embodied the grievances of specific groups of peasants and city dwellers. Their evolution can be studied alongside changes in religious practice. In studying both protest movements and religious practice, we are interested in the social roots of group behavior.[3] Often this behavior took the form of oral (and less often written) expression, and it was seen as deviant with respect to the triumphant cultural norms of court society. In this realm social status and level of consciousness are all but indistinguishable; times of crisis differed from ordinary times only in that the former revealed what the latter kept hidden. Similar questions were asked about popular religion and popular social behavior: contemporary descriptions employ a standard rhetoric despite the confusion, opacity, and excess of the phenomena they describe—phenomena that are particular as opposed to universal, irrational as opposed to rational. The formation of public consciousness thus needs to be linked directly to the customs and practices that stood in its way. The administration launched surveys such as that of Orry on the "faculties of the people." The Société Royale de Médecine and the academies also sponsored investigations whose purpose was both to understand reality and to suggest ways to change it. Writing about difference revealed the various ways in which people of distinct social status used the term "popular." This is what we will look at first. We then turn to forms of popular political expression in the traditional political context in the hope of shedding light on the relation between protest and "moral economy."

"The People" and Its Representations

The many studies of "the people" undertaken over the past twenty years or so invariably point up the ambiguity of the word and the thing. By focusing on the kinds of facts one can find in archival documents, demographic and fiscal analyses, and studies of the economy and of material culture, historians have made a place in the history books for the silent majority excluded from the political histories of earlier generations. Meanwhile, however, it has become clear that studying the popular classes presents many problems—problems that force us to reconsider the definition of social history and its methods.

"The people": the concept once played a unifying role in histories by men such as Jules Michelet and Jean Jaurès and even in the work of men contemptuous of the popular, such as Adolphe Thiers and Hyppolite Taine. What it has since lost in unifying power it has gained in taxonomic precision, however. The frontier between people and elite that I mentioned earlier is not fixed; neither is the relation between the people and the norm or marginality or poverty or criminal deviance. Nowadays, studying the people is not so much a matter of discovering an amorphous yet supposedly homogeneous reality as one of attempting to understand why the concept was so important in eighteenth-century social debate. We must first explore the history of a basic mental representation, a representation that was controversial, versatile, and energizing. Words and images that express the diversity of the people are as precious as the documents produced by the administration and police. Beyond the variety of expression we detect a common language and therefore a common relation to historical reality. What the speech habits of the lower classes reveal is a system of social perceptions that evolved from the classic period to the Enlightenment. The classical system of representation diverged from that of the people in the clash of ideas, the words in which those ideas were couched, and the metaphors that made them palpable. As the old society changed, economic, social, and cultural innovations began to make their way into the language of the people.

Classical Images, Exclusion, and Integration

The eighteenth century proclaimed, as it ended, the sovereignty of the people. But outside of political theory, in terms of everyday acts, what did this mean if not a fundamental rupture of the bond between the people and the monarchy? The people, qua historical actor, had staked their claim to their new majesty, yet the consequences of this move were by no means clear to either the rural or urban masses or to those who claimed either to represent or oppose the new sovereign as conflict began to proliferate. That is why it is important to consider the remote antecedents of popular sovereignty and the cultural split that divided both the old society and the new one, a split between the knowledge of the learned and the experience of the unlettered, between political ideas and concepts on the one hand and general mental representations on the other. The people were of course silent, which is to say that they did not speak the language of their betters. Nevertheless, they played a central role at all levels of production of the written word, from the catechism to the theological treatise, from the dictionary to the code of law, from the harangue to the memoir, from novels to theatrical plays. The reason for this, surely, is that the idea of "the people" was the key to social understanding, an influential if untheorized theme. In classical, absolutist society, and in the learning and culture of that society as transmitted by the *collèges*, academies, and salons, the people existed fully. The confused nature of this discourse, which has made it impossible for historians to reduce its exuberant polyphony to a single theme, probably reflects the reality of the time: the people were a strange monster, bearing all the paradoxical characteristics of difference, not to say exoticism. When it came to interpreting the world, however, they occupied an essential place.[4]

The words commonly used to refer to the people *(roturier, canaille, vulgaire, mendiant, pauvre, rustre, badaud, plèbe, populace)* and the images commonly used to portray them indicate an exclusion from the world of their betters, a position of inferiority with respect to people of higher station: nobles, clerics, the well-to-do and well-born, and the educated. A boundary line divided rulers from ruled and educated from uneducated. The people were perceived as lacking in dignity and being under an obligation to work, especially in degrading manual labor; they were politically dependent and in danger of pauperization. The imprisonment of the poor and expulsion of dangerous outcasts were made possible by a decline of religious feeling, which allowed the well-off to attempt to resolve social problems by sending the poor to school and putting them to work. Genuine and false paupers were treated the same way under policies designed to preserve security and order.[5]

Whether portrayed positively (because utilitarian values were stressed in discussions of the economy, and the wealth of nations was said to be the product of the labor of all) or negatively (in portraits of the forces of sedition, which drew on the reality of brutally suppressed rebellions that provoked fears of the multitude), the people defied precise social analysis, particularly in legal constructs based on the idea of "three orders." The Greco-Latin and Christian heritages seemed to be in contradiction: the manifest dignity of the pauper was recognized, to be sure, but only in its proper time and place, when it was necessary to remind the monarch and his faithful servants of their duty of charity. The same duty justified both the punishment of malingerers and relief for the genuine poor: "use the useless," as the slogan went. Here, the economy of the gift and the economy of exchange were not at odds. A major feature of mercantilist theory was its emphasis on the regenerative power of work and its ability to reintegrate the excluded into society. It was possible for exclusion on the basis of denigration of manual labor to coexist with integration on the basis of the idea that "all republics depend on" a positive assessment of the value of popular labor. The work of the people, and especially of the peasant, thus became exemplary, a fundamental moral value. The good farmer and the ideal worker figured in the utopian and moralistic writings of Fénelon and La Bruyère as ideal representatives of their estate and condition, while at the same time they were classified under the headings of oppression and servitude.

This was noted in the middle of the eighteenth century by Abbé Coyer in his *Dissertation sur la nature du peuple,* which the chevalier de Jaucourt copied for the *Encyclopédie:* "In olden times, in France, the people were regarded as the most useful, most virtuous, and therefore most respectable part of the nation."[6] This was followed by the traditional evocation of the Greek and Roman peoples, which established two things: that the people could take part in their own government, but they were not undifferentiated. That is, Livy's *turba forensis* (rabble) was not the same as the people. Though blessed with reason, the people worked; hence self-interest guided their actions:

> Things went so far that the people began to raise questions about their state: Are we animals? One hears this question in public work sites: Are we animals? People! So they may be. Weigh yourselves down like the beasts of burden, turn over the earth along with the animals, and be happy if you are not allowed to die in misery: that is all that politics owes you, and philosophy assigns you the same rank. Urge a philosopher of the court or of Parnassus to believe in our mysteries. What response will you receive? Tell your myths to the people, that is, to creatures human in face only.

The enlightened abbé's slap at philosophy and its contempt for religion as good for the people serves here to highlight the continuity of the Christian reference and the religious virtue of labor. This old pact was in the process of falling apart, however.

The political theory of the absolute monarchy (even when modified to take account of utilitarian, mercantilist goals) assigned the people the same role and importance as did Christian political economy. No matter how one explained the origins of social division, whether in historical or racial terms involving Gauls, Franks, and Germans, the people were seen as having lost or given up their freedom. The social contract was based on a transfer of sovereignty according to God's plan, as Bossuet explained it in his *Politique tirée de l'Ecriture sainte*. From this fundamental principle, which made the king God's representative on earth, stemmed the king's political, religious, and economic responsibility toward "his peoples": the use of the plural transformed the homogeneous social collectivity into diverse political subjects linked by custom. It also reflected an obsession with possible political opposition to the sovereign: from "people" to "peoples" was more than a single step, because a corollary of the same principle was that the people—each of the peoples constituting the kingdom—must be obedient and submissive to the king. Kings are made for peoples and not the other way around, or so the boldest thinkers believed.

Such ideas were shared by readers of Grotius, Bossuet, Bayle, and even Hobbes.

Hence all political debate and definitions inevitably drew a contrast between *le peuple* and *la populace,* the well-behaved, obedient subject on the one hand and the rebellious rabble on the other. Drawing on organic metaphors for society borrowed from Plato and Aristotle and revised by medieval theologians such as Boniface, John of Salisbury, and Thomas Aquinas, the political theorists of the early eighteenth century conceived of society on the model of the human body. Regardless of whether social functions were explained in biological or mechanical terms, the organic metaphor implied a certain hierarchy (head and members) and imposed mutual obligations on the various parts of the organic whole. Accordingly, popular uprisings and outbursts were interpreted as maladies inflicted by God as punishments.

This conception was bolstered by images of the inferiority of the people. Sometimes they were identified with primordial bestiality, at the mercy of pure instincts and uncontrolled passions. At other times they were compared to Cicero's hydra or to various domesticated animals such as asses, mules, horses (less frequent because horses were relatively well treated), camels, oxen, sheep, and occasionally even pigs and other barnyard animals. Or they might be likened to more rapacious beasts such as the wolf or fox or even to forces of nature such as storms and earthquakes. In this system the fear of violence, which was used to justify royal interventions, played a powerful role. There was also a need to hierarchize appearances through the expressive use of clothing and anthropomorphic discrimination, a need that found abundant expression in literature and iconography: the people were portrayed as ugly, heavy, dark, clumsy, and thick, wearing crude, filthy, patched clothing. Social, political, and religious imagery depicted everyone as accepting his place in a changeless society and as being afraid or suspicious of social mobility, which was always denounced as a form of usurpation (as in the myth of the lackey financiers). At the same time, popular forms of speech and behavior were discredited and taken as evidence of inferiority, which thereby came to seem self-evident, an irrational consensus that could nevertheless be invoked in rational argument.[7]

This view of the people carried with it its own corrective, which we glimpsed earlier in my discussion of politics: the idea of a "moral economy" or a "Christian political economy." The organic link between the sovereign and his people implied mutual obligations. The king's "good government" was supposed to enable the people to live; social inequality and poverty were tolerable only if wealth was redistributed through giving. The misery of the people pointed up the failure of Christian political economy.

Bossuet, Fénelon, Vauban, and Giraud de Villethierry gave voice to these fears and questions, whose practical implications were developed by Delamare in his *Traité de la police,* which, though published at the turn of the eighteenth century, remained relevant well into the reign of Louis XVI. In order to forestall the popular protests that the government found so frightening, it had a duty to make sure that provisions reached the marketplace in a timely fashion. In a world in which the fear of bread shortages was confirmed by frequent crises, the "tyranny of grain" dictated the mechanisms by which the sovereign had to intervene—a fatal paternalism, if you will.

A set of rules, beliefs, and myths united people and authorities on the issue of distributing bread through a monopolistic price-fixing system. The interests of society as a whole took precedence over the interests of individuals, dictating protective policies and surveillance of the production and sale of bread. Equity consisted in giving each person not the same thing but what he was due according to who he was. Because the people had no dignity and were required to work, they were entitled to a compensatory gift, since the economic responsibility of the prince was based on a circuit of gift giving. The people invariably behaved like children, whose weakness, credulity, foolishness, and fears they shared: "They are persuaded only by what they see. They judge with the eyes of their body rather than with the eyes of understanding, and they have some difficulty accepting reasons that go against appearances."[8] Hence the education of the people is best understood as a way of inculcating submission and its principles in a form that was essentially religious.[9]

The People of the Enlightenment

The Age of Enlightenment did not immediately change these fundamental representations of the people. The great cultural divisions did not disappear, and popular lifestyles, customs, and ideas about work, leisure, and time were at the core of certain reformist obsessions. The Church hoped to Christianize morals. The police wanted tighter controls and more effective surveillance as well as guarantees of a steady supply of food (see Guillauté or Commissaire Lemaire). The philosophes, moralists, and economists hoped to rationalize the productive process in which the people participated. For the ruling elite, the vulgarity and cultural inferiority of the people were consequences of their baseness: physically, intrinsically vile, the people would always incarnate wastefulness, materialism, and libertinage. Like the ancient followers of Bacchus and Pan, the people had no conception of time, work, or money. Suspicion of the poor, coupled with religious and political justification of social and economic inequality, was widely shared: one cannot distinguish philosophes from antiphilosophes on the basis of these attitudes, with the exception of a few special cases such as Rousseau, whose imitators, such as Rétif and Mercier, were already less convinced than he was. Yet this deep unanimity began to break down; contempt for and anxiety about the poor became more subtle; and more and more questions were raised about the "image of the people" and the actual state of relations between the poor and the elite. Boundaries became clearer even as they proliferated. Yet the people remained, and there were still certain things they were not and could not become.

For eighteenth-century writers, the distinctive feature of the people was still work, or the need to participate in a productive process whose means they did not control.[10] As Boisguilbert showed, moreover, the people also played a central role in consumption. The chevalier de Jaucourt, who wrote in the *Encyclopédie*, Abbé Coyer, and countless lesser writers from Barbier the memoirist to the marquis d'Argenson, the lawyer Marais, and the curé Meslier, all agreed in this respect with Rousseau. Late eighteenth-century moralists and physicians were mindful of the criteria that distinguished an active, hardworking, quiet people from their lazy, indifferent counterparts who needed to rediscover the virtues of nature in order to return to the straight and narrow. The utilitarian program of imprisoning the poor continued and after 1775 began to gather momentum from the food crisis itself. The heroes of bourgeois and populist dramas and of tearful comedies in the manner of Nivelle de La Chaussée or Louis-Sébastien Mercier always raised themselves by their bootstraps. The fact that these men owed their rise to hard work was a mark of their social inferiority but also of their social ascent.

Administrators and *intendants* did not speak a different language: they noted the existence of misery and familiarized intellectuals with the idea that poverty was not the same thing as marginality: the working poor were people who paid taxes and for whom the king bore responsibility.[11] The shock of misery and the new aspirations toward prosperity gave rise to pressure for the integration of the poor; instead of correcting the poor, people now began to think of ways to abolish misery and its causes. The major disorder was no longer the fact that there were poor people who failed to obey the law but the very coexistence of the less fortunate (virtuous workers in other respects so close to nature) with the well-to-do. Charity and imprisonment were no longer satisfactory responses to a poverty whose relation to utility and labor had changed. The state was forced to intervene in a new way. The political power of the people coincided with a new political consciousness: the oppression of the majority by the minority was also the oppression of virtue by vice.

Labor was not only a healthful social condition but also a positive value associated with economic advancement. Boisguilbert and Cantillon pointed to a link between self-interest and individuality, to a role for the people as producer of wealth and satisfier of new needs in a society driven by the circulation of money and commodities. Meslier and others such as Mably, d'Holbach, and Raynal—men who saw the rich exploiting the poor—shared the sense that the time had come for the people to demonstrate their power: "Keep all those riches in your own hands, hold on to all the goods that you so abundantly produce with the sweat of your bodies, keep them for yourselves and your own kind, and give nothing to proud and useless nations, nothing to the proud and idle rich, and nothing to proud and haughty tyrants or those who serve them."[12]

Even if economists did not agree about essential matters (such as the definition of value or the function of luxury and consumption), their ideas encouraged study of the social division of wealth, the clash between rich and poor, and the effects of social class on the hierarchy of the society of orders. Social distinctions could no longer be based solely on social utility. Labor was no longer a sign of inferiority but an indispensable social value. Turgot and Rousseau were in agreement on this point and many others.[13] The rupture would soon extend to social practices and relations.

At this point in the debate, a second central issue arose. Recognizing the independent functional utility of the people, reviving social assistance by seeking work for everyone, and thus restoring the active role of the state did not solve all the problems of the day. There were "the people" and the rest of the populace, the *people* and the *rabble*. This distinction was not new: it had fueled the fears of the classical era. But whereas classical thought had tolerated a certain ambiguity as indispensable to a pejorative notion of the people, the Enlightenment saw itself as more rigorous. The use of such interchangeable terms as "rabble," "riffraff," and "canaille" was intended to justify the exclusion of a segment of the population that could be plunged into turmoil and driven to destructive folly on the slightest pretext. From the time of Louis XV to that of Louis XVI, the boundary line was reinforced between those who, though excluded from power and status, nevertheless remained loyal, reasonable, useful workers and the hordes of useless, unemployed failures, living proof of the deficiencies of the correctional system: this "underground of the Enlightenment" was prone to trouble and violence.

This sharp distinction between people and rabble became a feature of the political culture, as is clear from the dictionaries and from the work of writers such as Condorcet, Turgot, and Diderot as well as from press reports on events in 1774–75 and 1787–88. Society will never be free, happy, and good so long as the rabble outnumber the people, proclaimed the newspaper *Révolutions de Paris*: "Under despotism, there is no people; there is only rabble. Under the fasces of liberty, there is only the people; there is no rabble. The latter word should be stricken from the idiom of a free nation." This incantation of a revolutionary journalist reveals two major shifts in Enlightenment thinking: toward control of violence through education and toward popular sovereignty.[14]

As the monarchy declined, a new question began to emerge outside the realms of economics and philosophy. Novels and narrative paintings demonstrated an intense need to display the reality of ordinary people's lives. Take the series of images known as "Cris de Paris." Prints from this series outnumber all others (63 percent are from the eighteenth century). They reflect a growing taste for a variety of urban types represented in various ways dictated by the visual codes of the time: in fine prints, crude images on paper, decorative motifs for fine china and ceramic pieces, images for children's games, and so on. In short, there was incontestably a vogue for a widely available set of images intended to enrich the study of the bibliophile and collector as well as to decorate the walls of ordinary households and taverns. The *crieurs populaires* embodied changes in the way in which the people of the city and urban life itself were perceived.

It is apparent that the earliest images in this series were based on old stereotypes: burlesque hawkers, common tradesmen, "difficulties of the city." These images tended to disappear at the end of the seventeenth century, however, although they remained as collector's items and in popular literature. Another set of images caught on: these featured the domestication of the body and the aesthetics of symmetrical figures and were attentive to the rules of self-presentation. The taste of the Bonnarts idealized the bodies of common people and made them an acceptable artistic motif. Greater attention was paid to the urban background and to careful painting of details of clothing, yielding something like a social typology of working-class Paris. At the same time, popular prints emphasized the animation of city streets and featured textual comments on the pictorial images.[15]

These two categories of prints cannot be identified with high and popular modes of consumption or representation, because the circulation of models relied on borrowings and adaptations of both engravings by masters and commonplace images. The notoriety of "Cris de Paris" engraved by such major artists as Boucher, Bouchardon, Cochin, and Saint-Aubin reflects the idealization of the people, who furnished subject matter for fashionable engravings, amorous iconography (Boucher, Fragonard), and licentious imagery. There were frequent literary correspondences with fairground plays, aristocratic skits, and works by Vadé, Cailleau, the comte de Caylus, and the actor Taconnet. This art of social representation was aimed at a varied audience, a public with its sensibilities attuned to a certain form of exoticism.

Perhaps the people became a motif in these reproductions all the more readily because their representation was neither accurate nor concrete. Images of filthy ragpickers and foul-mouthed fishwives revived old fears of the rabble as uncivilized savages apt to erupt into violence at any moment. By contrast, images of birth, wealth, education, decorum, and savoir-faire bolstered confidence in the established social order. These images reflected the uncertainties of a civilization no longer clear about its values. The very ambiguities in the depiction of work made it possible to present popular figures in various disguises and masks that wealthy collectors coveted.

The theatricalization of popular behavior depended on a typology of characters, physiognomies, customs, and feelings that reflected a knowledge of reality available to artists and men of letters, moralists and social reformers, but not to the upper classes in general. By using realistic effects drawn from the physical and material life of the people, this social theater made a place for the popular in social representations as well as in the hierarchy of artistic and literary genres. With distance and condescension the elite were able to regard the people as an aesthetic object. Paradoxically, however, the same vulgar images caught on with the people themselves, thereby making social conflict a feature of the imagination. In this way the theatricalization of the poor reinforced the intellectual processes that invoked the misery and utility of the poor as arguments for change. It offered a nonviolent resolution of the new conflict between the wealthy and the miserable stemming from the state's inability to transform the old charity into "public debt" and thus exchange obedience for assistance. This important change was reflected not only in the relationship between the people and their representatives but also in violent protests against authority.

The People and Their Representatives

As political, economic, and cultural representations evolved from the classical age to the Age of Enlightenment, they preserved a legacy of condescension and hostility, familiarity and fear—a legacy that suggests how difficult it was to read the word *people* as anything other than an "indistinct name." We must not, however, be too hasty to conclude from this state of affairs, which persisted long after the Revolution, that the people had no capacity for political representation whatsoever.

Indeed, we must take into account the specific ways in which society in earlier periods dealt with the problem of popular representation. It opposed any individualist conception of representation and relied instead on intermediate groups based on legitimate interests recognized by the sovereign and sanctioned by custom.[16] As the French monarchy evolved, some of these intermediate organizations were bypassed: the assemblies of orders, for example. Only the assemblies of the clergy survived under the modus vivendi accepted by the Gallican state in the seventeenth century, and this was primarily for financial reasons that required an independent clergy. In the eighteenth century the nobility and Third Estate were no longer *persona representata*. Their actions were scattered and depended on local privileges in the *pays d'Etats* or in particular peasant and urban communities. The major changes in older forms of representation occurred at the local level (city or village). We must look at these before coming back to the question, adumbrated earlier, of the change in the people's image: What political capacity did people have? Was education capable of inspiring new directions compatible or incompatible with stability and tradition? The ability of any society to generate the conditions necessary for change depends on the political faculties of its people.

The *Sanior Pars*

In older representations of society, some people had the right to govern, others the right to obey. Village communities and urban *corps* discharged their basic duty in different ways.[17]

Social relations in the village were organized around three structures, which sometimes reinforced one another and at other times worked in competition. The first of these was the parish, which defined its territory, reinforced the authority of its priests, and confirmed its property. The assembly of residents was called to meet in the church by the local priests and churchwardens, notables who managed the vestry and temporal possessions of the church. At these meetings news circulated, the operations of the parish school were discussed, and changes in religious practice were considered. The second structure of local authority was the seigneury, which supervised various activities, though more in the north of France than in the south. The seigneur was the "eminent landlord": he collected dues, supervised the courts, and intervened constantly in daily life. The so-called community of inhabitants *(communauté des habitants)* fell between the seigneurial and spiritual authorities. It grew out of the parish assembly and imposed limits on the powers of the lord. In the eighteenth century this community, once nameless, was recognized as a collective individual on a par with the vestry council, with which it was in practice identified in the north of France. Taxes and wars were the two driving forces behind these communities, which banded together to face insecurity and to negotiate when necessary over the size of the fiscal "gift" to be given to the king. The community enabled villagers to be represented by proxies.

Three questions arise. First, how independent was the community with respect to lords, priests, and representatives of royal authority such as *élus, subdélégués,* and *intendants?* The first two powers sat in the assemblies, and the royal authorities everywhere tightened their control in order to restore order to communal finances and liquidate debts. Reimbursement often led to the sale of communal property (woods, pastureland, stream banks), and it was local notables such as landlords and prosperous farmers who profited. The cohesiveness and power of the community were thereby weakened. Its most important functions were still to nominate the people responsible for assessing and collecting the *taille* and to monitor the activities of the rural police. This evolution was more pronounced, however, in northern and western France than in the south, where community representatives were more numerous, privileges were better established, and community powers over both land and people were more extensive. Persistent southern styles of sociability also helped to sustain the communal spirit there.

The second question concerns the effectiveness of the community as an institution. Because the village community controlled its own expenditures, assessed taxes, and managed all sorts of local matters, it undeniably provided many useful services. Above all, it stood for solidarity against outside forces. Its fundamental vitality is evident in any number of indispensable activities: collective responsibility vis-à-vis the state, defense against thieves, struggle against calamities. The community served as mediator in many legal and criminal matters, as Yves and Nicole Castan have demonstrated in the case of Languedoc. Accommodation involved negotiation, arbitration, and evaluation and relied on the authority of traditional mediators such as lords (who played less of a role in the eighteenth century than in the past, however, either because they were absentees or because they were unconvinced of the validity of local grievances) and priests (as part of their pastoral duties and in accordance with the recommendations of the post-Reformation Church).[18]

This brings us to a third question, more fundamental than the previous two: How effectively did rural communities represent the people? It is not always easy to know who was excluded from communities that ideally were supposed to function like small agrarian republics as envisioned by Rousseau. In theory, anyone who headed a family was eligible for membership in the community, but in reality this was not the case. Households headed by women (that is, by widows) were the first to be excluded from decision-making councils. Men who did not own land or who were too dependent on other men—the vast majority of sharecroppers, vineyard laborers, orchard workers, and farmhands—were not considered "inhabitants" and were therefore not eligible to sit in the "community of inhabitants." This left the *sanior pars* of the village population: prosperous peasants, local notables, large-scale farmers, and rural bourgeois, who arrogated all power to themselves. Some assemblies consisted of no more than a dozen members, the *général de la paroisse.* The village community was indeed a *persona* but not a *persona representata.* It represented only a part of itself, yet its role was in principle to defend the interests of all.

Jean-Pierre Guitton has shown how important the so-called rural bourgeoisie was in fostering village sociability. We find typical examples of the rural bourgeoisie as early as the seventeenth century in Ile-de-France, Burgundy,[19] the Lyonnais, Provence, and Languedoc. Its powers depended not only on rank and wealth but also in many cases on culture (the king's French was spoken in courts of law) as well as on usurpation of seigneurial authority. Only in the Pyrenees and the Alps, where notables exerted power in other ways, in particular by controlling credit,[20] did things evolve differently, allowing village communities to play a more representative role. These regions managed to avoid some aspects of central government control for a longer period of time. Indeed, the central government encouraged recognition of the power of the *sanior pars:* the Physiocrat Dupont de Nemours did so in his *Mémoire sur les municipalités* in 1775, and this was the goal of the edict of 1787, which gave official status to the communities of inhabitants and defined their legal place in relation to the seigneuries and parishes. The community then became the agent of the central government. Although this reform was not implemented for lack of time and spurred conflict everywhere it was proposed, it does indicate the direction in which things had evolved and confirmed the power of local notables (which we know about from analyses of *élections* in Lorraine, Alsace, Touraine, and Forez). It also suggests that aldermen and councilors did have genuine political experience, even if civic life in the villages moved at a different pace from that of the central administration.

All other things being equal, municipal liberties in various ways reflected a similar state of affairs. For all its variety, the communal heritage implied the existence of a municipal government built around the functions of finance and police and controlled by an oligarchy representing the city's bourgeoisie and nobility. The general assemblies of residents no longer included the lower classes or petite bourgeoisie. The royal authorities' suspicion of commerce helped to consolidate the power of the urban *sanior pars*. The number of notables was prescribed nearly everywhere by regulations, which the oligarchy approved and maintained: this was the case in Flanders, Angers, the Dauphiné, and Brittany. The "freedom of election" proclaimed by edict in 1704 and 1765 for all cities of more than 4,500 inhabitants solidified this state of affairs. The old customs prevailed and made reform difficult. The existence of offices for sale and resale further complicated matters.

Thus, municipal government provided an opportunity for political action, but of increasingly limited scope, while at the same time excluding the majority. This was the setting in which the debate between conservation and change took place. In the cities, as we have seen, this debate pitted innovators against those unwilling to contemplate possible improvements. In the countryside it triggered the opposition of the majority, necessarily attached to custom, to economic changes advocated by a handful of notables and lords. There is no point in looking at such debates as reflecting a search for some form of mythical peasant or urban republic based on an idealized egalitarianism. They were mainly a way of seeking a new role for individuals and institutions divided by status and self-interest in the face of action by the state, the *intendants,* and/or local lords—in other words, a search for political resources and a necessary education.

From Politics to Education

Political capacity in traditional communities took a different form than one might expect: not class conflict or outright rebellion but certain persistent forms of behavior whose interpretation is not always clear, whether because the realm of the political is broader than we tend to assume (in periods of crisis, traditional folkways became spontaneously political and holidays were transformed into protests)[21] or because the use of the term "popular" leads to debate about the social origins of a particular movement or the cultural roots of certain practices. It is all too easy to dismiss popular politics as "archaic rage" even when people acted in ways that revealed a capacity for reflection and organization as valid as that of the elite but disorganized and undifferentiated and therefore more difficult to perceive.

One way of studying the political capacity of the people is to look at how communities related to the courts. The "need for justice" was fundamental. People turned to the courts to regulate their private relations. The lost honor of an accused chicken thief, the prestige of a cuckold, the reputation of a snobbish woman or of a man overdue on his debts: all these were matters in which the courts were asked to intervene. All sorts of petty problems brought people to court and thereby revealed their capacity for using institutions to regulate social relations.[22] Going to court was also a way of challenging authority. Country folk and city dwellers found ways of challenging seigneurial and municipal justice. In the seigneuries of suburban Paris, people protested alleged abuses by local officeholders by calling in the Paris police and courts. More and more they decried scandal and called for rebellion while denouncing the mischief of the government's agents (that is, their failure to respect the representative pact).

Peasants stood in a complex relation to the law: some sought redress in the courts frequently, while others, in Auvergne for example, settled their conflicts among themselves. Elsewhere royal tribunals were asked to arbitrate disputes between lords and peasant communities, especially in areas where rights of common pasturage, gleaning, and use of communal lands were important (eastern France, Burgundy, Lorraine, Franche-Comté, and Alsace). In Burgundy, royal edicts authorized the *intendant* to intervene in ways that gave villagers an additional ally in opposing the actions of certain lords. When called upon by a community, the *intendant* might dissuade a landlord from going to court against his villagers. Conflicts of this sort were common after 1756, and landlords were invariably forced to bow to the king's wishes. Seigneury was driven to defend itself against the alliance of peasants and administrative monarchy. Peasants frequently demonstrated a talent for exploiting divisions in the opposition, while the administration imposed its taxes as well as its arbitration.[23] The integration of village assemblies into political structures gave peasants the capacity at least to formulate political options. Royal intervention in local administration disrupted the politics of isolation and gave the peasantry the means to seek fairer treatment by the courts, in contrast to the sovereign courts' reinforcement of seigneurial rights. "The growth of the state gave the peasantry the ability to protest as well as new reasons to avail themselves of that ability," since peasants could now hope for change arbitrated by the monarchy rather than dictated by self-interested landlords.

Through the disturbances that continued to erupt in Enlightenment

France, we thus glimpse a political reality that had as much to do with practical matters as with ideology. It was characterized by concern with everyday, routine worries such as food and work. This political activity reflected not just a desire for survival but a veritable social demand. Until the middle of the eighteenth century, the *police des grains,* or regulation of grain distribution, was thus seen as a political issue, for it grew out of a belief in the role of the monarchy as ultimate food supplier. Here, in a sense, politics was all but transformed into mysticism. This transformation explains why the "general will of the people" drove the laissez-faire reformers onto the defensive. Anti-tax protests tended to proliferate whenever the standard of living declined. Places where ideas could be passed on through conversation also became important: among these were inns, workshops, fairs, bakehouses, and mills. Rebellions sometimes resembled popular festivals, and people therefore naturally turned their folk traditions to political purposes.

Popular political activity took place within a local setting, close to home in terms of space and time: a village, neighborhood, or parish. People liked to keep negotiations short and keep an eye on what their representatives and notables were up to. Custom lived on in the popular mind, with its old fund of folk wisdom, and people were well aware of the endless delays that occurred when they turned to the courts or the administration to settle conflicts. The only way to get quick results was to strike while the iron was hot. The Christian tradition stressed equality and fraternity, and these values were sometimes invoked defensively: "In a climate in which written texts were not absent, to be sure, but oral communication was crucial, and in which innovation was not automatically valued and was always suspected of posing a threat to daily life, tradition played a conservative role, more so, no doubt, than among the elite, which was more open to change. Memory was an active force, sustained by families, trades, and villages."[24] Although popular politics took place in the framework of traditional protest, it could nevertheless be aimed at achieving innovative change, but this depended on the education that people at various levels received. And of course change raises the issue of violence, which was always possible when the "rabble" and "riffraff" got into the act—not that the rabble were to be confused with the "people," the general public, that is, the people for whom education and new social norms were intended.

Should the People Be Educated?

Any movement or event could trigger a violent explosion in a minority of the populace. It was common in the Ancien Régime to try to explain these explosions as maladies of the will, proof that the regime itself was not culpable. A rebel could always be hanged, but he was still just one molecule among many. For legal as well as philosophical reasons, riots were always seen as forms of social rebellion. In order for the people not to behave as rabble, some sort of transfer of sovereignty was necessary.

The whole century lived in hope that education would somehow prove effective, that the people could somehow enter into a different culture. The people needed enlightenment. Condorcet argued that before ordinary people could become citizens, laws were needed to combat their degradation and to promote freedom through education. For most French (and European) intellectuals, the moral and cultural backwardness of the majority meant that the threat of a regression to plebeian disorder was constant. The people—ignorant, inarticulate, and systematically deceived ("coddled with myths")—lived in prejudice and were lulled by preaching that kept superstition alive. Oppressed by work, they had no opportunity to learn. For the thinkers of the Enlightenment, Voltaire included, the people lived in a world of unreason, caprice, passion, excitability, and misplaced energy. Without education they would never find their way out of darkness. In 1780, at the behest of Frederick II and d'Alembert, the Academy of Berlin organized a competition around the question whether or not it was useful to deceive the people. The entries were divided: some answered in the affirmative, others in the negative. But the contradiction was insurmountable. The Enlightenment sought to liberate the human spirit through education based on rational values and prudently supported by enlightened rulers; it had no intention of giving the people the means to express their sovereignty. Rousseau was virtually alone in proposing a different solution to the problem. The question remained open throughout the last three decades of the eighteenth century.

In the minds of many Enlightenment thinkers, belief in the power of education was justified on three grounds.[25] The first was the general intellectual climate, which stemmed from the ideas of John Locke and the philosophy of empiricism. If human nature was infinitely malleable, then "education makes man," according to Philippon de La Madeleine, an indefatigable candidate for academic honors on this question. Second, the importance attached to education stemmed from an extraordinary desire to understand and reform the world. In 1746, at the Academy of Rouen, Abbé Terrisse argued the opposite of the usual thesis according to which "knowledge of reading and writing, which is today so common among rural people, is an abuse that a political philosopher should repress, and anyone whose profession is agriculture should be denied a faculty that may disincline him to perform the hard labor that his estate requires." This was an old argument, which can be traced back to any number of seventeenth-century political thinkers, yet for the members of societies that prided themselves on "dispelling ignorance and developing useful arts and sciences," it was more important to develop the rudiments of culture. Not only would religion benefit, but also "practicing these exercises keeps people from committing crimes and injustices that trouble the social order. Hence reading contributes to the good of the state." What advantages does reading offer? First, through reading the peasant and artisan gain access to the printed word, which communicates the principle of change. Second, they enter the egalitarian sphere of talent and utility. And finally, the opportunity for emulation is increased for everyone, from the humblest to the most gifted. In other words, society has everything to gain from the point of view of moral order, religion, politics, well-being, and development if it follows the advice set forth in the *Examen de la question s'il est utile ou préjudiciable au bien de l'Etat que les gens da la campagne sachent lire et écrire* (Rouen, 1743).

This debate would continue for forty years, until everyone was familiar with the reservations and compromises expressed in turn by the proponents of exclusion, the champions of a slow diffusion of enlightenment, such as Voltaire, and the partisans of rapid education. Positions across the spectrum were dictated in part by considerations other than utilitarianism, especially the need to link the struggle against ignorance to the struggle against religion. On this point as on many others, Voltaire differed from Rousseau. In general, however, when intellectuals faced a crisis that was often blamed on a general perversion of morals, they tended to seek a remedy that combined moral with educational reform. Furthermore, for men of letters, academicians, Masons, and educated Frenchmen generally, a belief in the power of education was essential because such a belief made it possible to imagine a future without abrupt or untoward changes, a future without a revolution.

Growing economic demand, coupled with the philosophical and political rehabilitation of the toiling masses, combined to create a situation in which the education of the people regained its proper place. People tried to preserve the equilibrium between the newly formed political society and a new politics based on a more just, more equal, more mobile population as well as respect for older customs and beliefs, while making room for hierarchies based on merit. Enlightenment thinkers were divided as to the legitimacy of the demand for equality of condition and the ability of societies to remedy poverty. The education of the people must be contained within just boundaries: it was designed not so much to liberate the lower classes as to make them more efficient economically and more docile socially. The only philosophe who followed the logic of the Enlightenment all the way to the end on this point was surely Condorcet, who said this in his *Esquisse d'un tableau des progrès de l'esprit humain:*

> One can instruct the entire mass of a people in everything that each man needs to know about household economics, the administration of his affairs, the free development of his industry and faculties, the defense and exercise of his rights, the extent of his duties and how best to fulfill them; and about how to judge his actions and those of others according to his own lights, and how not to be a stranger to any of the noble or delicate sentiments that honor human nature . . . in order to defend himself against prejudices with the sole force of his reason.

This debate has yet to be resolved even today. In the eighteenth century, perhaps, it could not be resolved, because the emergence of an autonomous political sphere implied if not that the people be eliminated from politics, at least that they remain in their place. In order to overcome this contradiction, the people first had to get beyond older representations of themselves and of the nature of power. But those representations still held sway over men's minds.

Popular Protest and Moral Economy

The king's image was conveyed to the people by means whose variety has yet to be catalogued and whose impact remains to be understood.[26] As we have seen, monarchical rituals were still important, despite their decline. Certain indirect representations of power were capable of overcoming resistance. As late as 1788, Etienne Garnier of Troyes was still selling thousands of copies of *Le Jargon ou langage de l'argot réformé*, an old hawker's pamphlet about phony beggars and their fraudulent stratagems. These beggars were said to be organized in a manner that aped the old corporatist society. The pamphlet affected a noble style to treat a vulgar subject in the carnivalesque tradition of linguistic parody. It was not a political tract (we find none in the Troyes library), yet the text expresses joy about Louis XIII's capture of La Rochelle and gives thanks to God for "dapper Louis's" success and asks him "always to preserve the noble fleur-de-lis." Texts like this, along with quantities of other objects, images, and tales, informed the daily lives of countless individuals, affecting the way people prayed and shaping their love for the monarch, whose authority they bolstered. Such loyalty was not so very different from that of the academic elite. The pamphlet was designed to bestow praise on the king's majesty. It was a passive and obedient form of political expression. The *Dictionnaire de Trévoux* put it well in 1771: "The French people love their sovereign, and the sovereign is occupied with the happiness of his people(s). To call the king the father of his people is not so much to praise him as to call him by his name."

Yet images of the rebellious rabble, of protest and fury, point toward a different reality. A repressed underground current of violence threatened to undermine the whole system, and the threat was only compounded by the fact that celebratory violence could so easily be transformed into rebellious violence. In such moments the community rejected the law and turned its fury on symbols; familiar actions took on new meanings.[27] Two historical figures can help us to understand the linkage between violence and politics, the weakening of social controls and the transition from traditional protest to the expression of a new demand for freedom. The first of those two figures grappled with the principles of moral economy as embodied in the youth organizations known as *compagnonnages* (associations of journeymen). The second discovered the new political violence in local antiseigneurial protests associated with fraud and smuggling.

Compagnonnages: Authority and Violence

Jacques-Louis Ménétra has left us an autobiography that offers unique and essential information about the old form of workmen's association known as the *compagnonnage*.[28] A glazier who belonged to the large class of Parisian tradesmen involved in urban renovation and construction work, Ménétra spent the seven years from 1757 to 1764 traveling in France as a young *compagnon,* or journeyman. He describes the way in which traveling journeymen were received wherever they went in workshops ruled by a master craftsman and his *bourgeoise,* or wife. Ménétra was initiated into his trade in Tours. He gives a brief account of the initiation rites, spelled out in a handwritten text that invoked the name of the mythical founder of the guild, Maître Jacques, who supposedly helped build the Temple in Jerusalem. After initiation, Ménétra was known by the secret talismanic name Parisien le Bienvenu. Such rituals are one reason for scholarly interest in the *compagnonnages.* Of course, many scholars simply repeat the criticisms of these archaic rituals first formulated by eighteenth-century notables and later reiterated by nineteenth-century labor unions. But others are fascinated by the idea of a "golden age" in which working-class social relations drew strength from secret, "esoteric" rituals. Another reason for studying these organizations is that they can teach us a great deal about a transitional stage of political practice between the older communal traditions and the modern politics of free citizens.

The *compagnonnages* were clandestine organizations of young workers that were tolerated by the guilds and the police, which kept a close eye on all meetings and on travel by individual members. The *compagnonnages* defended the interests of younger journeymen in each profession, or *vacation,* and offered them protection and assistance. They drew their strength not so much from secrecy as from their ability to meet the needs of journeymen making their "tour of France" and to trace their origins back to earlier professional youth societies and religious confraternities. Similar groups existed even in professions that had no organized "tour of France," such as the typographers.[29] Symbolic customs and powerful myths drawn from a variety of sources reflected a general conception of work and of the world that unified traditional sensibilities and proved attractive to young workingmen. The *compagnonnages* transmitted the values of the political hierarchy to the organic world of local communities, and they kept a lid on violence: these were their two chief roles.

The world of *compagnonnage* was not a world of protest. Each *compagnonnage* defended what it saw as the interests of the profession in accordance with tradition. The clandestinity of the movement, made necessary originally by the suspicion of religious authorities, police, and employers, was maintained even after the *compagnonnages* were accepted as de facto institutions. Measures that had once served as defensive precautions became signs of distinction and ways of asserting cultural difference. The *compagnonnages* served an economic function above all: they organized the movements of tens of thousands of workingmen and linked them to the labor market in places where there was work to be had; in this way they reconciled mobility with stability. At the same time, they reinforced the power of the guilds and their hierarchical traditions, accepting a holistic vision of society in which each body consists of a head and members, master craftsmen and journeymen, workers and apprentices, as well as a patriarchal vision in which the father's authority extended to the workshop as well as the household. A Christian understanding of privilege and authority underpinned the whole system. To be sure, the fraternal solidarity of the *compagnons* developed at a time when corporate solidarities were being eroded by conflicts of interest and increasing competition. The *compagnonnage* system was a form of self-regulation of labor that reinforced authority within the trades while providing training and social mobility (made easier by the fact that a marriage market developed in parallel with the labor market).

By the end of his journey, the journeyman had internalized the rules of his profession as social values governing professional negotiations and fraternal solidarity. Ménétra's story is interesting for a variety of reasons. It shows how a skilled craftsman evolved by stages from aspirant to initiate to journeyman to "captain" of a trade to "first journeyman" to owner of his own business. The defense of tradition was also a guarantee of a certain ideal of life and work, indeed of a form of politics. Finally, institutional solidarity depended on the acceptance of hierarchy and discipline. Because of that hierarchy and discipline, employers and police could tolerate the excesses of young workingmen: in normal times, the workmen's own organizations guaranteed that things would run smoothly.

Historians are wont to express surprise at the violence of revolutionary crowds. In fact, what this violence reveals is the limits of social, judicial, and educational pedagogy as well as the circumvention of social controls. Violent behavior was omnipresent in eighteenth-century society. Violence was a part of everyday travel, activity, and leisure; it occurred in private conflicts as well as in public disputes, as Arlette Frage has shown in the case of Paris. Ménétra corroborates evidence from the rural courts that violence was associated with youth and mobility. He shows that the "mild manners" sought by the elite were far from being achieved despite the existence of methods for inculcating them.

Brawling had a dual function, just as celebration did: it reinforced the solidarity of the *compagnonnage* by celebrating violence, but at the same time it confined that violence within relatively narrow bounds. Ménétra's narrative is notable not for the veracity of its details but for the significance of its overall pattern. Huge brawls did take place: he mentions a dozen or so, and police archives record hundreds of similar occurrences. These skirmishes were a collective, ritualized way of settling conflicts between hotheaded members of rival groups. The fratricidal battles of the tour were also a way of asserting the existence of a countersociety vis-à-vis the official order. The benefits outweighed the costs. Townspeople, police, and constables watched these outbursts with a wary eye, while mounted policemen pursued victors and vanquished alike. Priests buried the dead whenever they could find them, but the *compagnons* often took their dead and wounded with them and tried to hide them from the authorities. In recounting his exploits, Ménétra displays a concern with organization that was probably more imaginary than real but that nevertheless points toward an ideal: a need to control the violence of one's adversaries. In a more peaceful vein, celebrations and bacchanals served a similar function of reinforcing solidarity. Workmen toasted the employers and authorities, who saw to it that they had what they needed in abundance.

The proliferation of *compagnonnages* in the eighteenth century is revealing of the changes that were shaking the family-centered "Christian" economy and making profit the day's watchword. The *compagnonnage* was a kind of substitute for the family, which provided mutual aid and a gendered division of labor, and subjected violence to discipline. It constituted an autonomous political space of collective responsibilities, whose commitments were not unlike those that existed within families and universities. But it existed in a transitional period between the future of capitalist free enterprise and the past of restrictive privilege. The journeyman's dream was similar to that of the entrepreneur: to reconcile freedom with security.

It is a mistake to think that the typical journeyman's education produced individuals incapable of independent choice. Ménétra's journal shows that, even though he moved in a world firmly rooted in tradition, he had largely abandoned the traditional values of the past. He could think critically and envision a new politics. A loyal subject of the king, respectful toward old ideals, Ménétra was also a man stubbornly suspicious of authority, whether of the government or the courts, the guilds or the Church. "For many people, the sense of an insuperable gap between their own daily lives and the world of the powerful was colored by a stubborn desire for independence."[30] Ménétra wrote his memoirs for such people. Despite his loyalty and passive conformism, whose sincerity is not in question, he expresses constant distrust of those who discipline and punish, make the rules and enforce the laws, and seek to make people thrifty and well behaved. His life is proof that one could cheat, avoid, and resist. His was a moral politics for the century, emancipated from old loyalties and guided by concern for himself and his own interests, which served to justify strikes and conspiracies within the workaday world.

Ménétra was fond of the theme of the "Three Harlequins," which reflected his suspicion of and skepticism toward the authorities as well as his confidence in his own judgment and in the equality of those considered inferior by their betters. A symbol of popular freedom in the culture of the public sphere, Harlequin, the masked incarnation of crudeness and provocation, became a manipulator of men. The first Harlequin was the executioner, who carried out the decisions of courts that were quick to arrest the down-and-out along with the truly guilty. The second was the archbishop of Paris, who symbolized the Church and its ability to dupe people (and in this connection it hardly matters that the pious Christophe de Beaumont was not guilty of the offenses that Ménétra in his anticlerical verve was all too ready to credit). The third was Carlin, an itinerant actor who showed how easy it was to amuse the people. The "Three Harlequins" showed how one could be a conformist without being a fool. And that lesson was already a step toward a political existence.

Riots and Contraband

Rebellion was one expression of political capability, but at no point in the seventeenth and eighteenth centuries was it the only one. Nearly all the insurrections of the seventeenth century were fiscal protests of one sort or another. Their nature was evident from their targets: tax officials. They also gave expression to the solidarity of the people of a locality or region, mobilizing whole communities without regard to social class:

priests, nobles, and officeholders protested alongside ordinary townsfolk and peasants against violations of what they took to be their ancestral rights. Finally, the tax revolts were scattered throughout the areas of France newly conquered between the fifteenth and seventeenth centuries: they spared the old Capetian territories but struck the kingdom of *pays*, privileges, exemptions, and "public liberties."

After the turn of the eighteenth century, these major anti-tax movements subsided. Limited local insurrections, provoked by hostility to taxation and food shortages, persisted. Above all, protest found a new target, moved to new territory, and adopted new means: it was directed against local landlords, was prevalent in formerly unrebellious eastern France, and availed itself of official mechanisms and legal avenues before resorting to violence. Villages were politicized against an order in which the old solidarities (which had not always been effective in any case) no longer worked. Against a new order that was at once state-centered and economic, villages, cities, and *corps* invented new forms of political action. People mobilized against actions that revealed the new order of things: peasants rose up against seigneurial innovations, Parisian workers rose up against entrepreneurial innovations, and communities of tradesmen rose up against the "useful liberties" of the faubourg Saint-Antoine—liberties that encouraged competition and market segmentation. In the face of insubordination and cabals, master craftsmen joined together in defensive solidarity to reaffirm the guild system which defined their social identity. The crisis revealed the disintegration of social relations in Paris: "the rings necessary for commercial work and prosperity" no longer interlocked. The imagined golden age may never have existed, but in a time of crisis it was possible to generate considerable nostalgia for the way things supposedly had been. By the end of the eighteenth century, the people of France were no longer what they thought they ought to be.[31]

Limited insurrection and restrained riot: this was what one had in 1750 in Paris, when children were supposedly being abducted from the streets by the police, as well as in the "flour war" crisis and the "armed masks" protest in Vivarais—which demonstrated a clear change of behavior and an astonishing legalism, without social inversion or millenarianism or violence against persons (only property was attacked)[32]—and in the forest clashes of Burgundy and upper Normandy and the seditions of Provence and Franche-Comté. All of these disturbances demonstrated the existence of social tensions, but they were short-lived and more exclusively popular than were previous uprisings. In looking at a wide variety of incidents, we discover that people protested when they had difficulty finding a place for themselves in society that accorded with their principles. Insurrections and riots were ways for crowds of people to debate the issue of order versus disorder and to remind the authorities of the rules of the game. Sometimes, as in the case of the alleged abduction of children in Paris, they succeeded in gaining a hearing for their point of view.

Riots occurred when emotions ran high, when pent-up resentments were released, or for no reason at all, as when a rumor circulated in Paris that children were being snatched from the streets so that their blood could be used to treat an ailing but unidentified prince. When things like this happened, young and old, masters and journeymen, petits bourgeois and domestic servants poured into the streets to protest. Crowds acting in accordance with their own conception of power sometimes clashed with authorities imbued with new ideas of order. The riot of 1750 revealed the distance that had grown up between the monarchy and its subjects. The people no longer loved their kings as they had in the past. What they condemned was the monarchy's repressive policies, and they attacked the policemen responsible for enforcing those policies. The rumors of abductions made sense of the crowd's actions. These new uprisings were not led by notables, who no longer believed the rumors and no longer confronted the central authorities. For the time being, the people were on their own.

That solitude explains why smuggling played such an important role in rural and urban France. Smuggling developed as both an individual and a collective response to heavy excise taxes: individual because people acted for reasons of self-interest, but also collective because smuggling was so common and geographically widespread. Eighteenth-century France was full of boundaries: between *généralités*, *pays d'Etats*, salt tax regions, excise tax districts *(circonscriptions des aides)*, seigneuries, provinces, city limits.[33] In Paris the wall erected by the farmers-general did not end tax cheating but exacerbated it: in 1787 and 1788 alone, incidents and riots at the wall's gates were too numerous to count.

Salt and tobacco were the most frequently smuggled commodities. The records of commissions in Saumur, Reims, and Valence give us some idea of the magnitude of the practice.[34] *Faux-saunage*, or breaking of the salt laws, was a daily occurrence in the *pays de grande gabelle*, where the salt tax was highest. Cheating on salt and tobacco taxes was a target of action by the Ferme Générale along the borders between Picardy, the Soissonais, and Champagne and the *pays francs* of Artois, Cambrésis, Flanders, and Hainault to the north, together with Lorraine, Franche-Comté, and Trois-Evêchés to the east. When summoned to action by the Ferme Générale, the commissions judged hundreds of delinquents every year. The worst offenders were sentenced to the king's galleys: between 1777 and 1789 the judges of Saumur sent a thousand men to the galleys, while the judges of Reims sent three hundred men between 1740 and 1742 and another four hundred between 1786 and 1789. Everywhere the majority of people convicted of salt tax violations were men, and two-thirds were adults under the age of forty.

Smuggling was mainly a business for semiprofessionals, but everyone was involved to one degree or another. It was not a full-time activity but a supplement to other work.[35] Even the few professional smugglers did not live solely on the sale of contraband. They spent months doing ordinary chores around the village and enjoyed the support of their communities. Many major smugglers were caught, but small-scale smugglers often escaped capture in western, eastern, and southeastern parts of France, where smuggling was common. All segments of the peasantry participated: smugglers were less often marginals than poor country folk (in Saumur 20 percent were beggars, in Reims and the wealthier provinces only 1 percent). Everywhere the smuggling trade was dominated by day laborers, small farmers, village artisans, and people involved in one way or another in merchandising and trade. Ultimately, of course, the world of smuggling was the world in which taxed salt and tobacco were consumed (the "bourgeois" of the cities did not have to pay). The far-flung clientele explains why smuggling was so widespread, and the needs and capabilities of that clientele account for the rhythm of the illicit trade. Salt smuggling was a seasonal activity. In hard times the pace picked up: when demand flagged, in part because of a shortage of cash, supply tended to increase.

The problem for the Ferme was thus to combat the clandestine competition for marginal consumers, since official consumption was compulsory and guaranteed. Surveillance depended on control of the territory and on a rationalized, disciplined administrative organization not subject to the influence of the local population. The strategy of the Ferme, which relied on the efficiency of the special tribunals, aimed at limiting the extent of smuggling by meting out heavy sentences and at recouping losses by imposing heavy fines on relatively minor offenders. Enforcement was brutal because of the insistence on exemplary punishment, which far outstripped the offense. The fines were levied because of the need to keep cash flowing in and because of standardization of law enforcement across the country. Rural society approved of salt smuggling but did not always look favorably on bandits who failed to share their spoils with the local populace. Passive complicity was the general rule, since everyone disliked stringent customs inspections, home visits, and searches. In a broader sense, smuggling was a state of mind: it represented the local versus the central, a culture of custom versus the state, and a morality of marginal redistribution versus profit. This was where the myth of Mandrin derived its force.

Louis Mandrin, who was put to death on the wheel in 1755, had little involvement in salt smuggling, but he was a notorious participant in the smuggling of tobacco and fabric over a region that stretched from Auvergne to Provence and Savoy to Burgundy. He was a true "social bandit," in the sense that he organized gangs capable of holding out against constables and army troops, taking advantage of ill-guarded borders, occupying cities, and enlisting the enthusiastic support of the poor against the rich. The people, in any case, preferred the *mandrins* (Mandrin's gang members) to the *gabelous* (tax collectors): the former, apart from police spies, left them alone, whereas the latter got under their skin. Mandrin was widely known and imitated (the chevalier de Caumont, sentenced for similar crimes in Saumur in 1754, vanished into thin air). Mandrin's activities were notable for their geographic extent and diversity. His smuggling, moreover, was plain for everyone to see: usually the *gabelous* and other authorities looked the other way. The only protection that Mandrin and his men had was the power of violence. By terrorizing a few they obtained the complicity of many. But Mandrin was only the tip of an iceberg: there were thousands upon thousands of small-time smugglers, whose invisible exploits made the struggle between smugglers and tax collectors an important chapter in the literature of criminality.[36]

In the history of social banditry, Mandrin occupies a place all his own. He was celebrated, along with Cartouche and a few others, in burlesque dialogues, poetry, and song, so that his fame reached a large audience of pulp fiction readers and became a fixture of French collective memory. His story appeared in anti-crime "scaffold literature," but more often than not he was portrayed as an exceptional and fascinating character. This fascination with transgression was certainly a form of political expression, and in French society it took on a subversive character.[37]

Contemporaries attentive to the social seismography of the period, such as the marquis d'Argenson, attentively followed the major episodes in Mandrin's life and remarked on his ability to sow disorder: "Unfortunately the people are all for these rebels because they make war on the farmers-general, who are reputed to be excessively rich, and bring people goods at lower cost. Hence the officers who must fight in this war do so reluctantly and speak of nothing but their woes." The gang's exploits were viewed as episodes in a domestic war. Because Mandrin was seen as a sort of Robin Hood, a righter of wrongs, he gained the sympathy of the people: "The whole country is for the smugglers." At the time of his execution, his memory was popularized by books and newspapers that portrayed him as an admired hero as well as a controversial target of government propaganda. *L'Histoire de Louis Mandrin depuis sa naissance jusqu'à sa mort; avec un détail de ses cruautés, de ses brigandages, de son supplice* (140 pages, octavo, 1755, with nine known editions, three of which appeared in the "Bibliothèque bleue") took the side of the champions of law and order, for whom Mandrin was guilty of lèse-majesté:

> Bandits should not enjoy a place in history. People criticize Sallust for teaching us that Rome had a Catilina. Apparently every robber chieftain since then has sought glory by walking in his footsteps. Yet the ordeal that lay in store for them should have put an end to their crimes. Cartouche died on the wheel, as did Mandrin. That is how all thieves, murderers, and arsonists end up. No guilty man has ever enjoyed his crime with impunity.

L'Histoire de Louis Mandrin also shows us the isolation of his gang and offers proverbial wisdom in justification of his punishment despite countless other texts that took a favorable view of the notorious bandit.

Among the latter were the *Oraison funèbre de Louis Mandrin,* the *Testament politique de Louis Mandrin, généralissime des troupes de contrebandiers, écrit par lui-même dans sa prison,* the *Mandrinade, en vers héroïques, adressée aux partisans de Mandrin,* the tragicomedy *La Mort de Mandrin,* and a host of popular songs, all of which transformed the criminal into a "beloved hero" of a somewhat ambiguous sort. These texts oscillate between portraying his crimes as a form of social protest and shaking a finger at them, between praising Mandrin for his honesty and denouncing him for his crimes, between admiring him as an avenger of the people and shuddering with terror at his utter contempt for the law. Other texts go so far as to portray Mandrin as a rival of history's greatest conquerors, as in the *Dialogue entre Charles XII, roi de Suède, et Mandrin contrebandier*, by Mme de Baumer, the *Epigramme sur le roi de Prusse*, and the *Memoires pour servir à l'histoire de notre temps* by François Chevrier.

The ideology surrounding the Mandrin myth shows that he had already become a figure of legend. These texts respected certain rules and were conservative in their political pronouncements yet promoted social protest by challenging the representatives of authority and retracing the boundary between criminality and honest conduct. The social construction of Mandrin's image reveals the gap that existed between the expectations of the people and the culture of the elite. Current events were virtually absent from the high literature of the day, apart from a few allusions in correspondence and memoirs. This silence is indicative of how difficult it was for the Enlightenment to incorporate the doings of ordinary people into its battles. Peasants and members of the urban lower classes could identify with heroes who challenged authority: this was a form of political statement which indicated a wish not so much to rebel as to claim justice from a sanctified body politic or a society controlled by a rational state.

The king had diminished in people's minds along with the *sanior pars*. But did this not leave notables in control of things everywhere? What happened in the provincial capitals of Provence is a good example.[38] Was not the real danger that the old system of political representation would persist because the only right it granted to the people was the right to delegate authority, thereby sanctioning a passive rather than an active politics?

11

❦ ❦ ❦

God, the King, and
the Churches

THE RELATIONSHIP between the French monarchy and the sacred is fundamental to understanding the society of the Ancien Régime. That relationship was not identical with the relationship between church and state. The Catholic Church was always both a powerful institution and a community of believers, but religious structures were subject to new social movements, influenced by social and cultural changes, and buffeted by political and social currents.[1] The state, for its part, enlisted the support of believers. To govern is also to inspire belief, and for that the state relied on the Church, whose leaders it had selected and supervised ever since reforms initiated in the sixteenth century and finally completed under Louis XIV. The whole system depended on striking a proper balance between protection and control, a balance typical of Ancien Régime society in general: a well-understood exchange of influence and services guaranteed the continued vitality of the "two powers." Like the Church, however, the state had to contend with the growing influence of the Enlightenment and the need to strike a new balance with religion, a more utilitarian balance determined in large part by its own political rationalization. The coronation ritual reflected this slow evolutionary process.

The age-old ritual of anointment and coronation of the king proved that even in the middle of the eighteenth century, royal power still rested on a profound union of two sources of legitimacy; one was political, based on the king's acceptance by his human subjects, while the other was religious, based on a transcendent ideal. The enthronement ceremony demonstrated this alliance to its spectators and, through newspapers and images, to the public at large. Two elements combined to make the king a symbolic figure, an inviolable, sacred personage: a plainly religious liturgy was coupled with ritual manifestations of the more political aspects of the monarchy. The latter took on particular importance in the coronation of Louis XVI.

On the religious side, to judge by the rigorous descriptions in Ménin's *Traité historique du sacre et couronnement des rois et reines de France* (1723) or Guyot's *Traité des droits et franchises*, based on the *Sacre et couronnement de Louis XVI* published in 1775, one had the miraculous ceremony of the Holy Ampulla; the role of the archbishop of Reims, who received and anointed the king and heard his solemn oath; the anointing with the precious oil of myth; the blessing of the king's gloves, scepter, hand of justice, and royal ring; the role of the ecclesiastical peers; the proclamation of the monarchy in eternity ("Vivat rex in aeternum"); the Te Deum; and, over the next few days, the touching of scrofula victims. The liturgy of the coronation was clearly religious.

On the political side, other aspects of the ceremony showed the old importance of the bond between king and kingdom: the presence of the lay peers (in 1775 these were princes of the blood, proof of the honor of the royal family), the gestures that served as a reminder of the king's election, the deputation of peers sent to fetch the king, the pre-coronation ritual of the king's awakening, the solar symbolism inherited from Louis XIV, the presentation of the king to the Assembly between the promise to the Church and the oath to the kingdom, the bestowal of the royal ring, and, following the enthronement, the admission of the public to the cathedral.

Commentators such as Pidansat de Mairobert in *L'Espion anglais* and the anonymous author of the *Sacre royal ou les Droits de la nation française reconnus et confirmés* now tacked on explanations that reduced the significance of the religious portion of the ceremony and stressed the secular aspects in order to prove that the inaugural ritual was far more a political act than a ceremony linking the king and the Church and intended to demonstrate to the people that the person of the king was sacred and inviolable. In this ceremony the sovereign of the nation ratified a contract with his people making him the organic embodiment of a power based on morality. The image of the king was adapted to the new language of

Enlightenment. It lost some of its mystical charge but, echoing the traditional analogy between the relation of subjects to monarch and that of body to soul, implied the notion of an accord, a sovereignty of all, whose nature was not that of abstract, impersonal representation. Accounts of the coronation such as the one that appeared in the *Journal encyclopédique* confirmed this alliance of the old and the new. The coronation, a ritual of the inegalitarian society of orders, was presented as a "family holiday" connoting the opposite values of equality, private individual relationships, and transparency: "Every man has his rank, but all are citizens."[2]

In this mutual exchange between religious, sacred values on the one hand and political, secular values on the other, we see how difficulties had begun to emerge in a relationship that throughout the Ancien Régime had existed on two levels. In the first place, the king's ties to the Church were governed by the "theory of the two powers," which Bossuet had set forth in his *Politique tirée de l'Ecriture sainte, Sermon sur l'unité de l'Eglise,* and *Déclaration des quatre articles de 1682:* the king was master of the temporal realm, while the Church under his protection ruled the spiritual realm. Furthermore, the Church constituted the first order of the state, and in exchange for its "free gift," the king promised to respect its immunities and privileges. The boundaries were thus clearly laid down. But, like everything else, they moved, and in that movement the clergy was reduced to a choice between, on the one hand, solemnly affirming principles without influence on the actions of the king and his agents and, on the other hand, acting as an agent of the state and further formalizing the relations between the "two powers" and the practices of the faithful.

The Church thus presented a new face to society: the Church in the monarchy and the monarchy in the Church still demonstrated the truth of the old adage, "Une foi, un roi, une loi." But various issues, the Jansenist problem foremost among them, had plunged orthodox Catholicism into a controversy that faithfully reflected the political and economic aspects of the continuing social debate. In addition, the confrontation between the Church and the Enlightenment, between religion and the new values of the age, led to changes in clerical culture and Christian thought.

Before examining the signs of an ambiguous de-Christianization, which may have been merely one aspect of a much older process of secularization, we must try to understand how, in a uniformly Catholic France in which the Church enjoyed exorbitant privileges and officially unanimous theoretical support, institutional and political decline were nevertheless perceptible—signs of internal intellectual and spiritual decay in the wake of French Catholicism's failure to adapt to the Enlightenment.

Religious Power and Exclusion

The theory of the two powers governed the relationship between the monarchy and the Church. It stood at the heart of seventeenth-century Gallican doctrine and of eighteenth-century ecclesiology as taught in the seminaries through such works as Tournely's *Praelectiones Theologicus de Ecclesia Christi* (1726). Let us pause for a moment to recall its essential features.

Kings derived their authority directly from God and stood immediately below him in rank. In temporal matters the king of France did not have to answer to any ecclesiastical authority, and certainly not, as Ultramontanists insisted, to the pope. Accordingly, all clerics and laymen were subject to the authority of the king. Even if he abused his authority, they still had a duty to remain loyal; rebellion was damnable. In return, the Church was made paramount in spiritual matters, and the king, who was considered to be a "bishop outside the Church" (that is, not ordained), had a duty to defend the Church while abstaining from intervention in matters of doctrine and ecclesiastical discipline. Although the king could not "prevent" the judgment of the Church, he was obliged to carry out its instructions. According to Gallican ecclesiology, neither power was subordinate to the other. Each was "sovereign, independent, and absolute in matters within its purview, [and] each finds in itself the power appropriate to its institution. The two powers have a duty to assist each other but in concertation and correspondence, not in subordination and dependence."[3]

This equilibrium, established at a time of major conflict between the monarchy and the papacy, fixed the political relationship between church and state as one in which each maintained a presence in the other but the king had the power to appoint the bishops of the so-called Gallican Church. The bishops, by defending their order against the claims of the Roman Curia and the regular clergy and asserting their power over other clerics, essentially confirmed the royal conception of the Church's role as utilitarian and administrative. In the meantime, both the political establishment and the religious establishment had to face challenges from those excluded from this arrangement: heterodox Catholics, Protestants, and

Jews. In the ensuing debates the representatives of the Church became targets of both the internal and external opposition, adversaries of episcopalism and critics of the "Christian religious system." Religion became both a social issue and an object of study.[4]

The State in the Church and the Church in the State

The selection of bishops and control of benefices were the main items of exchange between the two powers. After 1516 the king used his religious prerogatives as a political weapon to secure the loyalty of powerful nobles and regulate court society. The monarchy's policy was to award nearly all of France's episcopal sees to the nobility. The revenues of the great monasteries and abbeys went to a few distinguished families whose names appeared regularly in the *Almanach royal:* the Rohans, the d'Estrées, the La Rochefoucaulds, the Montesquious, the Bouillés, the Chabannes, and the Vintimilles, all of whom enjoyed the king's favor. Apart from loyalty bought and paid for (bishops received not only the revenues of their diocese but income from various abbeys as well), the king relied on his bishops to control the sometimes troublesome activities of the lower and regular clergy, in addition to the lives of ordinary parishioners, who received spiritual guidance and charitable assistance from the Church.

Episcopal authority over the clergy and discipline of the faithful were the heart of Gallican policy, which was implemented through clerical training, regulation, and supervision. Another purpose of this policy was to defend orthodoxy against various challenges. In practice, religion served to support the established order. In this respect, there was no difference between Catholics and Protestants, both being subject to the same repressive laws. The two opposed religions coexisted within a political space constructed by the monarchy and evolved in similar ways. Evidence of this includes the growing interference of royal judges in religious cases, state intervention in doctrinal matters, and royal measures to discipline the regular clergy by bolstering episcopal power over them and establishing a "Commission des réguliers."

Between 1766 and 1781, this commission attempted to restore order to the checkered world of abbeys and convents (more often by combination than by elimination) and to re-regulate monastic life. It symbolized the clergy's submission to royal authority. In the words of Jean Georges

Lefranc de Pompignan, archbishop of Vienne, the bishops who sat on the commission "did not act as successors of the apostles, as religious leaders granted authority by Jesus Christ; they exercised only the power delegated to them by the king." In saying this, Lefranc de Pompignan, an enlightened enemy of the Enlightenment, recognized the rise of social utilitarianism in the religious realm as well as the continued alliance of the two powers. The protection that the king extended to the Church justified his encroachment on its territory by offering enormous advantages to the bishops, masters of the regular clergy, who no longer had to worry about intervention by the *parlements*. Although this arrangement made the Church subordinate to the state, it also transformed the very rule of monastic life, the conception of spiritual vows, and the idea of spiritual authority. Decadence was merely a pretext for rescinding exemptions and reinforcing hierarchical authority within the Church.

One thing at stake in the matter of subordination versus independence was respect for the immunities and riches of the Church. The state had long been tempted by the vast real estate holdings (perhaps 10 percent of all land) that the Church had accumulated over the years not only through the tithe but also through countless long-forgotten bequests and foundations. In this realm the first order had always defended its privileges: "Our immunities originate in the consecration, purpose, and original emancipation of our properties. They have always been held to stand outside of commerce and to form an inalienable sacred domain," the assembly of the clergy still insisted. The monarchy naturally took a different view of the matter. A compromise was struck as the result of a bargain over the manner in which the Church would contribute financially to the monarchy. Claude Michaud has described the social mechanisms involved in this bargain from the sixteenth to the eighteenth centuries: the clergy made a "free-will offering" *(don gratuit)* to the monarchy of 3 to 4 million livres a year, or 1 to 3 percent of its income.[5] It also provided services whose cost, though high, is difficult to measure: schooling, hospitals, public assistance. In return, it insisted that the monarchy respect the voluntary nature of its gift. The gift was administered by a substantial independent administration, the Recette Générale du Clergé, and overseen by general assemblies held at regular intervals.

The clergy was the only order to dispose of such a forum, of which it availed itself to defend its liberties in a struggle that grew increasingly bitter as time passed and as the size of the state's debt to the Church increased. The first order also used the assembly to reaffirm its exemption from normal forms of taxation. Witness what happened in 1750, when the king attempted to subject it to the *vingtième*. "Our conscience and our honor will not permit us to suffer the transformation into a compulsory tribute of what can only be an offering of our love": such were the proud words of the representatives of the clergy under the Ancien Régime, who opposed any change in the traditional arrangement. Similar words could be heard in assemblies of notables in the 1780s, in reactions to the proposals of Calonne and Brienne, and in the protests of the assembly of 1788. The new/old threat of confiscation still hovered over the clergy. The example of Holy Roman Emperor Joseph II was still fresh in their minds. The last assembly of the clergy offered the smallest gift of the century (1.8 million livres) and flatly rejected all proposals for reform. After a century of church-state alliance and resistance, the conflict over the Church's temporal goods, finances, and contributions to the state had become one element in a far broader struggle. The assemblies were not, as the *parlements* insisted, merely groups that met to discuss economic matters but forums for the clergy as a body, capable of negotiating with the king, reaffirming the old organic relationship between church and state, and dealing with all religious, social, and political matters as well as with the debates that agitated the public sphere in a different way.

The assemblies of the clergy thus became a cog in the administrative machinery of the monarchy, an effective center of government, of circulation of wishes, news, and orders totally controlled by the episcopacy, and a place for discussion at regular intervals of the sacred and the secular and the participation of the clergy in the establishment of new economic, social, and political relations. The assemblies were therefore omnipresent as an independent force, but an independent force whose effectiveness depended on royal backing. They could not act on their own.[6] The theory of the two powers ceased to be operational after 1750, and the religious cohesion that bound the two partners dissolved.

As a first example, consider the educational policy of the monarchy, which was elaborated over the objections of the clergy. In 1762, after the expulsion of the Jesuits left the educational terrain vacant, the bishops asserted their right to be the primary agents of educational reform. They opposed the royal edict of 1763, which entrusted the reorganization of the schools to local notables working in bureaus in which the bishop had a voice equal to that of other members. Two different conceptions of educational policy thus came into conflict. On the one hand, the central and local administration, together with the *parlements*, wanted to entrust control of secondary education to the secular authorities, granting the bishops no more than the power to review the religious curriculum. On the other hand, the bishops demanded that the edict be revoked in view of their privilege to exercise "primary inspection over the education of the young." The bishops were reduced to a choice between protesting against royal policy by refusing to participate in the work of the bureaus and attempting to assert their influence over them (an influence that would still have fallen short of total control).

As a second example, consider royal policy concerning the circulation of "wicked books." With each new assembly the clergy reiterated its alarm, in response to which the king adopted delaying tactics: although he shared the bishops' worries, he saw no point in promulgating new laws, and everyone knew that his agents in their own way offered protection to various controlled publishing enterprises. After 1780 the clergy, its patience exhausted, proposed a law to halt licentiousness: "The lessons of philosophy reverberate in the workshop of the artisan and in the humble home of the farmer." In order to put an end to this, the bishops proposed reinstating theological censorship and tightening controls on the book trade, print shops, and lending libraries. In fact, however, the royal authorities had long held serious doubts about the effectiveness of any such measures, and the clergy received no response.

The king's support for the clergy was limited, as a series of crises showed. Among those crises were the refusal of sacraments and the rise of parliamentary interference from 1752 to 1754 and the expulsion of the Jesuits from 1761 to 1764. In each instance the monarchy abandoned its traditional role as arbitrator between competing *corps* and came down in favor of utilitarian secularization. In so doing, it reinforced the tendency of the assemblies to regard themselves as the bearers of a "conciliar function" needed to remedy religious woes that the king refused to recognize, in part because he did not wish to compromise the monarchy's generally positive relationship with a papacy prepared to accept a quiet, unassertive royal Gallicanism (the king needed the pope's support in his struggle with Jansenism), and in part because the monarchy was pleased to look upon the clergy as one of its agents—an agent particularly effective in dealing with the people.

The abdication of the clergy brought to the fore a new logic not defined by it: the logic of utilitarianism. The Church took its place in a new social and political order, but to the detriment of age-old sacred attachments. It credited the state with what had previously been its own role: social mediation of common salvation and distribution of the public wealth. Political ethics carried the day: "Religion alone shapes the true virtues and renders them useful, and the courage of the virtuous citizen gives strength to the State," Lefranc de Pompignan wrote in his *Lettre à un évêque* (published in 1802).[7] The role of the episcopacy in the dioceses and clerical assemblies proved to be an essential key to this evolution, for everything depended on what was given up in exchange for powerless bishops and on acceptance of the sovereign's religious policy.

Power and the Bishops: The Political Utility of the Episcopacy

Although the seventeenth-century reform of the episcopacy did not ensure that every bishop was an edifying personality, it did establish institutions in the dioceses that made it possible to change the behavior of the clergy and the religious life of the faithful.[8] Such was the power of one form of enlightened despotism. We know its social and cultural physiognomy thanks to the work of Michel Perronnet[9] and Abbé Sicard.[10] The bishops of the Gallican Church (176 in number, 166 of whom played an active role) formed a hierarchy defined by the age of their sees (archbishops and bishops), their rank (some were cardinals—in 1789 there were five), and the extent, population, and income of their dioceses (there were *évêchés crottés*, or "muddy bishoprics," especially in the south of France, as in Senez and Glandèves, as well as in prestigious metropolises such as Paris, Lyons, Strasbourg, Besançon, Rouen, Bordeaux, Aix, and Toulouse).

At this point bishops were recruited among the nobility, but the king, advised by the Conseil de Conscience, the "ministre de la Feuille" (the pressures upon whom are easy to imagine), and his confessor, made his choice on the basis of two alternative principles linked to quality of bloodlines. The first principle was that bishops should come from a group of thirty families that had divided the cathedrals of France among themselves throughout the century: the Rohans (who monopolized Strasbourg), the Choiseuls, the Cicés, and so on. Bishoprics were passed from uncle to nephew or cousin to cousin under a system of nepotism influenced by favor at court. The second principle was that at least some bishoprics should go to sons of the lesser nobility who rose through the ranks of the clergy. In other words, some bishops owed everything they had to birth, while others earned their station through talent and the patronage of influential prelates, such as the *grands aumôniers* and archbishops of Aix from the Boisgelin family. Family strategies and luck took care of the rest, as can be seen in the careers of men such as La Fare and Talleyrand-Périgord.

The gentleman bishops, who were often proud of their rank, were nevertheless for the most part capable and cultivated men, promoted generally in their forties (and rarely under thirty) after years of experience. The majority had done well in school. In 1788 the average bishop was sixty years old; the more active bishops were between forty and fifty. They were educated for the priesthood over a period of many years, generally progressing from Saint-Sulpice to the Sorbonne as recounted in the memoirs of Abbé Baston and Abbé Morellet. Broadly speaking, the bishops formed a coherent group in which traditional vices such as commendam, nonresidence, and confusion of ecclesiastic and seigneurial powers were not absent but, owing to strict controls, were less prevalent than in the past. Continuity is evident in pastoral discipline and training, seminaries, ecclesiastical conferences, oversight by vicars-general and deans, and pastoral visits by the prelate or his proxy, and long episcopal tenures only reinforced this: thirty-seven bishops were transferred two or three times, but the majority remained in place for fifteen to twenty years and fully a third for at least twenty-five years. In short, talent for the job could help a clergyman get ahead, as could favor, fervor, and friends in high places. Bishops adopted various lifestyles, but all were distinguished, carefully cultivated the art of hospitality, and participated in local celebrations and scholarly institutions. Hence they enjoyed all the privileges of birth, wealth, and culture combined.

Bishops were responsible for both the spiritual and temporal administration of their dioceses. Enlightened prelates organized veritable socioeconomic pressure groups. On the one hand they demanded that the monarchy restore the old order, while on the other hand they heeded the call of the Enlightenment and worked to change society by intervening in public affairs and advertising secular concerns. When Loménie de Brienne became a bishop, for example, Abbé Morellet said that he "aspired to one of those bishoprics which are coupled to some administration as in the sees of Languedoc, and he sought to learn all there was to learn about government." In the *pays d'Etats* bishops were therefore among the most active officials, and some were reformers who encouraged public works and debated tax reforms and agricultural improvements. A full sixty or more bishops thus played an active political role, most notably Dillon in Languedoc, Boisgelin in Aix, Barreau de Girac in Rennes, and Marbeuf, bishop of Autun and "*élu* of the Estates of Burgundy." Nearly all bishops took an interest in economic activities, creative charity, and utilitarian assistance, as well as in education, the purpose of which was for them to create good Christians but which, despite their wishes, changed the way in which people related to the world. As administrators of church property, as landlords, and as members of the assembly of the clergy responsible for their subordinates, these were clearly men challenged by change. Many joined learned societies, in which we find fifty-eight prelate patrons and honorary members and fifty-six regular active members along with twenty associate members, accounting for roughly 10 percent of the more than 1,300 academic clergymen.

The power of their sacred role meant that bishops as a body weighed in on the side of tradition, but culturally and politically they were often on the side of change. It is not wrong to think of the episcopacy as divided into two camps, even if it is easy to see some overlap and crossing back and forth: think of La Fare and his friend and rival Talleyrand. From 1781 to 1783, the *Lettres secrètes sur l'état de la religion et du clergé à Monsieur le Marquis de* . . . , a pamphlet circulated both within church circles and beyond and attributed to Maury or Boismont or at any rate an adversary of the triumvirate of political prelates consisting of Brienne, Marbeuf, and Boisgelin, made this opposition manifest: "The disease of statesmanship has ruined the best minds; episcopal concerns are today tinged with politics; apparently our prelates are no longer familiar with the sources of the gospel." The triumvirate stood on one side, Lefranc de Pompignan, Christophe de Beaumont, and Leclerc de Juigné on the other. The triumvirate wanted to involve the Church in change, while their opponents were wary of "economic fervor" and called on the clergy to concern itself "more with the saving of souls."

If there was a conflict between the two traditions, that of the "administrators of provinces" and that of the "administrators of the sacraments," the future and the past came together in relation to the king. The high clergy had done a great deal to popularize the royal cult and was deeply involved in court intrigue (this was essential to the system of the administrative monarchy). Some bishops, such as Rohan, Dillon, and Boisgelin, aspired to compete in the political arena, and some others triumphed there, including Dubois, Fleury, Tencin, Bernis, and, toward the end, Brienne. Thus the principal characteristic of the episcopacy was perhaps its inability to choose between corporate intransigence, defense of privilege, and utilitarian politics. At this point in history, a bishop's management of secular affairs was governed by the same logic as his ecclesiastical administration: the logic of utility and service to the monarchy. In this respect, as Dominique Julia has shown, the solemn warnings issued to the faithful by the assemblies of the clergy in 1770 and 1775 are significant: their intent was not to prove the truth of religion to the incredulous but to offer a truthful exposition of the advantages offered by the Christian religion, an "amiable gospel," an education in matters useful and proper for building a public order in civil society.[11]

The Frontiers of Exclusion Recede

The Church could not oppose the gradual increase of religious tolerance toward Protestants and Jews, which the royal authorities supported. For Protestants, the eighteenth century was a period of clandestinity made necessary by the revocation of the Edict of Nantes in 1685, a period of persecution and sincere or feigned submission. The "so-called reformed religion" benefited from a relative calm in the state of permanent threat maintained by the laws of exclusion, which did not lapse until quite late, in the 1770s. Until then, persecutions and prosecutions disrupted Protestant congregations and caused notorious difficulties. The most common form of persecution came from overzealous Catholic clergy and laymen, who provoked any number of local incidents in northern France. Periodically, the royal government initiated anti-Protestant operations on a wider scale. In 1717, 1726, 1745, 1748, and 1756 such operations struck at areas where Protestant communities were numerous and active, where "prayers in the desert" maintained the fervor of the faithful, and pastors from Geneva risked their lives to sustain the faith of their flocks. Each phase saw its share of repression, arrests, and executions, although such measures met with increasing hostility from both Protestants and the enlightened public.

Protestants called on all their resources to resist, relying primarily on family support and individual piety. They adapted to circumstances and maintained congregational allegiances. Pastors ceased to travel from place to place and settled instead in one spot. Passive resistance bore fruit: the proportion of the population that was Protestant held steady at 2 percent, and traditional Protestant bastions in the south were less affected by persecution than regions in the north. Meanwhile, the enlightened public called for tolerance and action against clerical oppression and sought to mobilize pressure for reform of the relation between church and state. Voltaire pleaded for humane, natural tolerance. The Calas affair, the ambiguities of which I discussed earlier, served as his springboard. In the *Traité sur la tolérance*, published in 1763, he attacked the iniquity of anti-Protestant legislation: the death penalty for ministers found preaching the reformed religion, and the galleys, loss of civil rights, and other punishments for anyone who took part in Protestant religious services. Voltaire did not go so far as to demand equal rights for all; he asked only for tolerance. But his modest request in 1763 was the only conceivable possibility under the regime that then united church and state:

> We know that several family heads who earned vast fortunes in foreign countries are ready to return home. They ask only the protection of natural law, recognition of the validity of their marriage, certainty as to the state of their children, the right to inherit from their fathers, and freedom for their persons; not public temples or the right to hold municipal office or other honors . . . It is no longer a matter of granting vast privileges and secure places to a faction [as the Edict of Nantes did] but rather of letting a people live in peace and of softening edicts that, while they may once have been necessary, no longer are.

The campaign led eventually to the edict of 1787, which recognized not religious pluralism but the first form of civil marriage.

The process of state secularization was not slowed by protests from the episcopacy and assemblies of the clergy, which until 1770 called for enforcement of repressive religious legislation. Episcopal intransigence ran up against increasing administrative tolerance. In the eyes of the administration, it was no longer up to the Catholic Church to decide the status of citizens. The Church's reasoning was incompatible with the state's despite the king's oath of anointment, because the monarchy had entered into a de facto understanding with religious reformers. The Catholic clergy's critique of Protestantism therefore shifted to political ground: religious diversity, it was argued, is a source of dissension. But this very shift confirmed the withering of the old principle "Une foi, une loi, un roi." The same change can also be seen in the evolution of official and public attitudes toward the "Jewish nations."

In discussing this topic, one must stress the force of the hostile prejudice against Jews, a prejudice rooted in memory and custom, encouraged by the attitude of the Church and the devout, and reinforced by penny pamphlets that spread the image of the "wandering Jew" and taught contempt for Jews despite the absence of any palpable Jewish community. There were perhaps some forty thousand Jews in all of France, but scattered across the country from Alsace and Lorraine to the southwestern and southeastern corners of France. Moreover, this Jewish community was itself divided in terms of origins and customs. What defined the Jew was an idea in the minds of those who reviled them, such as Ménétra before his arrival in Carpentras (anti-Jewish sentiment was traditional in the trades) and Voltaire, who denounced the fanaticism of the biblical people. The enlightened were as divided about Judaism as the rest of the population because no one was able to rise above reductionism and prejudice. Academies such as the one in Metz discussed the possibility of regenerating and thereby emancipating the Jews. Late in 1787, after the edict granting civil status to Protestants, Louis XVI assigned Malesherbes to study the situation of France's Jews. The academy of Metz had contributed to a movement that would eventually lead from emancipation to assimilation; another breach was about to be opened in the venerable and sacred relationship between the monarchy and the Church.

The rise of tolerance—the prelude to religious freedom—and the end of fundamental discrimination can be interpreted as the culmination of the state's emergence as the sovereign civil and administrative power and the decline of an old order which, though still enshrined in law, was increasingly precarious. This disjunction pointed up the shattering of the old religious unity, the replacement of the old organic religion of salvation, shared by the king and his people, by new forms of individual salvation, of singular commerce between man and God. This shattered unity is also evident in Jansenism, with its attendant divisions and conflicts and assumed transformation of man.

Jansenism and the Decline of the Common Good

As a result of several decades of controversy and protest in the seventeenth century, the spiritual thought of the Jansenists came to be seen as a structural feature of the French religious mentality. Although the eighteenth century inherited this influence, it is difficult to understand the magnitude of the conflict that erupted over the final stages of papal intervention (with the bulls *Vineam Domini* in 1705 and *Unigenitus* in 1713) and royal intervention designed to put an end to a conflict within both church and state, in which the Jansenists ultimately emerged as a group with many of the characteristics of a political "party." Yet at no time in the seventeenth or eighteenth century was there a single Jansenism; rather, there were several forces which expressed themselves at different times.

By 1715, however, the theological movement that had originated at Port-Royal in association with such illustrious names as Arnauld, Pascal, Sacy, Racine, and Mère Angélique and that had gone on to turn French intellectual and religious life upside down was past its peak. The eighteenth century inherited this legacy as though it corresponded to some fundamental need, animated by the legend, history, and perpetuated memory of a common movement identified with certain spiritual and temporal choices. What we see is the transformation of a meditation on various Augustinian theses concerning the predestination of certain individuals to salvation—ideas that had aroused the passions of a small elite of clerics and their followers—into a form of political protest. Obstinate Jansenists who flouted the laws of the kingdom and the Church out of conviction showed how new fissures could develop in the monolithic unity of traditional society. A veritable opposition to the monarchy and its religious policy thus emerged, and this opposition was more powerful and influential than had been the Jansenists who clashed with royal authority in the Great Century. Between the episcopal Jansenism of the first third of the eighteenth century and the Jansensism of parlementary jurists, priests, and ordinary people, there was a change of accent or tone with respect to doctrinal principles, which, make no mistake, were perceived as essential by everyone involved. Indeed, a major feature of the movement was that it proposed a different ecclesiology and a preaching of conviction that were in a sense more democratic than the tradition and in any case more conducive to the involvement of the faithful.

From History to Action: Episcopal Jansenism

In 1715 Jansenism seemed definitively doomed as a result of the combined action of Louis XIV and the pope. With the destruction of Port-
Royal and the issuance of the bull *Unigenitus*, it seemed that Louis XIV
and Clement XI had achieved their common goal, namely, to restore
religious unity and peace through unanimity of the Gallican episcopate
and the Roman pontiff. With its adherents being persecuted and its doctrine condemned by the two powers, Jansenism did not seem likely to
survive this ultimate crisis. In fact, however, the bishops were not unanimous—eight dared to demand an explanation from the Holy Father—
and the king, who had ordered the registration of the papal bull in 1714,
died without having been able to force the *parlements* to order the bishops
to publish the bull and receive it in the assembly, and without having been
able to depose Monsignor de Noailles, the archbishop of Paris and a
notorious opponent of *Unigenitus*. Hence the reaction surprised no one.
But what was at stake? And how did the opposition proceed?

In condemning Pasquier Quesnel's *Nouveau Testament en français avec
des réflexions morales sur chaque verset pour en rendre la lecture et la médita-
tion plus faciles à ceux qui commencent à s'y appliquer,* the bull sought both
to quash the theological opposition and to reaffirm the pedagogical principles of the Counter-Reformation. In extracting 101 "heretical" propositions from the 1712 reissue of a forty-year-old approved work, the Roman censors intended to offer a succinct statement of condemned
doctrines and ideas concerning grace, predestination, justification by
works and faith, knowledge of Scripture, the action of the Church, and
its morality and sacramental practices. The scope of the debate stemmed
from the fact that by fabricating a unified heretical doctrine, the censors
gave prominence to certain ideas deemed unacceptable by the Church,
such as Quesnel's extreme view of the efficacy of grace, which for him
was so great as to negate individual free will, along with his Gallican
hostility to the infallibility claimed by Rome and his fondness for Richer-
ism (that is, the doctrine that parish priests should have a role in governing their dioceses, which flew in the face of triumphant episcopalism),
while at the same time condemning moral and sacramental propositions
accepted by all Augustinians, not just Jansenists. The Jansenists' austerity
and rigorism, their shunning the world for the sake of spiritual perfection,

and their consciousness of election made them a strange subculture within a society of orders in which religious ways of life were strictly defined and delineated. The history and memory of the Jansenist movement rapidly transformed these religious principles into reservations about, if not outright opposition to, triumphant absolutism.

The crisis over the bull proved that there was indeed deep opposition to political and religious absolutism, an opposition in which Gallicanism and Jansenism joined in reaction against the joint success of divine right and ultramontane infallibilism. The very ambiguity of Jansenism thus reveals the stakes hidden behind the violence of crisis. Jansenism stood at the crossroads between two worlds: it belonged to the old order, which saw a profound link between the natural and the supernatural, whereas in the long run the theory of the two powers justified the separation of the temporal and spiritual; yet it introduced into organic society a right of conscientious opposition, along with a fierce individualism which, in search of the truth in God, sought its own criteria—primarily reason and nature—in man.[12]

The crisis that lasted from 1715 to 1730 reflected the results of the intellectual and spiritual efforts of the previous century, which had made questions of doctrine accessible to better-educated clerics as well as to a lay elite of nobles and officeholders and, through preaching and works of piety, to an even larger audience in the shops and workshops. After the destruction of Port-Royal, the Jansenists gathered in Paris, whose suspect parishes harbored (according to the papal nuncio Lercari, who studied them in 1739) "heretical" relics, clergy, and faithful. Saint-Jacques-du-Haut-Pas held the body of Saint-Cyran, Saint-Etienne-du-Mont the bodies of Pascal, Racine, and Lemaistre de Sacy, and Saint-Médard the body of Nicole. Before long these centers were filling the role that Port-Royal had played in the seventeenth century. The Jansenists were not isolated, because many who did not adhere to their doctrinal teachings were nevertheless Gallicans who could not accept the idea that the pope alone could decide important matters of religion. These people called for a church council, for which the assembly of the clergy was no substitute. Such Gallicans, close to the parliamentary nobility, were numerous among the lower ranks of the clergy, the loyal bourgeoisie, and the people. They applauded the Jansenist effort to broaden if not democratize religion. Religious debate in this period reached an unusually wide audience thanks to the distribution of tracts by hawkers, broadsheets, and booksellers, and to the indefatigable efforts of agents who favored one party or the other. Propaganda was spread by agents of both parties in the form of brochures and pastoral letters, legal briefs, theological notes, images, engravings, and songs. In 1714 no fewer than 180 works were devoted to the bull, and some 60 percent of the works condemned and sought by the police were Jansenist publications. Jansenist theologians opted for a pedagogy of vulgarization by publishing works that would help people defend the cause and tracts that would rally the faithful by proving the orthodoxy of Quesnel and pointing out factual errors in Rome's condemnation.[13]

Two ideas are essential here. The first is the matter of acknowledging an ecclesiology that granted the second-order clergy the right to teach the truth, as Nicolas Le Gros, canon of Reims, advocated in *Du renversement des libertés de l'Eglise gallicane* (1716). Here, "liberty" meant giving back the right to speak freely to priests and canons, who had forfeited that right to the bishops; it also meant accepting the authority of particular churches against the hardening of Roman doctrine. The second idea has to do with the use of "figuralist" theology, which saw the Old Testament as the type or figure of the New; this transferred authority to those designated by signs and symbols. The perpetuity of the faith belonged to a small phalanx of priests and adepts who bore witness to the truth. "The small number is in itself, excepting a miracle, the natural and visible sign of the throne," wrote the director of the seminary of Saint-Magloire in *Le Témoignage de la vérité*, published in 1714. To hold this view was to take yet another step in opposition to the bishops, a step that was all the more forceful because these ideas drew on an eschatological vision of history and were justified by a symbolic reading of Scripture. Persecution was aimed at the elect, who were in possession of the truth. Resistance was legitimate: it was modeled on a revival of the "primitive church," which played a fundamental role in polemics. The opposition thus identified with a tradition, but this was a source of weakness as well as strength: if Gallicans and Jansenists joined in appealing to a broad public, they differed over the possibility of compromise with Rome. Truth itself was at issue.

Initially, when the Regent appointed Noailles to the Conseil de Conscience, there was hope for reconciliation and appeasement. Paris could sing:

La grâce efficace a pris le dessus;
les enfants d'Ignace ne confessent plus;
ils sont chus dans la rivière,
laire lairelanla,
ils sont chus dans la rivière,
ah qu'ils sont bien là!

Efficacious grace has taken the upper hand.
Loyola's children no longer preach:
they have fallen in the river,
laire lairelanla,
they have fallen in the river—
ah, such a good place for them!

The bishops' appeal to the council stirred up public opinion and gave visibility to the Gallican coalition. The number of appellants increased, but at no time between 1717 and 1728 were there more than seven thousand. This was a small minority of the priesthood, perhaps 5 percent, and no doubt as divided as the episcopate itself. The movement was geographically limited: it included Paris, the refuge dioceses of the Paris basin, Tours and Auxerre, and a very few places in the south despite the presence there of active bishops such as Colbert in Montpellier and Soanen. Finally, Jansenist clerical ranks were swelled by theology faculty graduates and recruits among the regular clergy, who accounted for 35 percent of all signatures, including many members of the Benedictine, Genevievan, and Oratorian orders. The Jansenist movement, which supported the appellant bishops, was a small clerical elite, which, because of its intellectual role, its connections, and its social relations with magistrates, lower court officials, and the people, wielded considerable influence. That influence was gradually lost, however, after the authorities clamped down on the faculties of theology (beginning with the Sorbonne in 1729), the religious orders were compelled to give their allegiance to the king, the bishops exerted pressure on curés and canons, and everyone got older.

Governmental action paralleled the action of the episcopate. Fleury was hostile to Jansenism not so much on religious as on political grounds: Jansenism created disorder, and the minister wanted peace at home as well as abroad. He went after individuals rather than the movement as a whole. He isolated Noailles with the defection of his troops, intimidated him by condemning Soanen at the Council of Ebrun, and, with the help of age, induced him to surrender. The *brigandage d'Embrun* that gave the cause a martyr in 1727, together with the archbishop's renunciation, sounded the death knell of episcopal Jansenism. The episcopate accepted the bull, and all the vital elements of the Jansenist party were repressed. The royal declaration of March 24, 1730, supported the bishops' local action, and *Unigenitus* became the law of the land. All recalcitrant ecclesiastics were excluded, the *parlements* could no longer intervene, and the purge of the dioceses moved ahead rapidly. By 1740 Jansenism had lost the battle within the clergy.

The joint victory of the royal authorities and the episcopate was won, however, without any real understanding of the degree to which the religious debate had affected the hearts and minds of ordinary Christians. Rumor had magnified the controversy, and the sympathy that people felt for their own pastors had added further fuel to the fire. The persecution of the clerical elite confirmed many people in the belief that Louis XV was the modern Nero, a ruler who had forsaken the common good invoked by the theologians of the "primitive Church."[14] Pierre Barral took this position in his *Maximes sur le devoir des rois* and *Manuel de souverain* (1754): "Love of the people, the public good, and the general interest of society therefore define the immutable and universal law of sovereigns. That law is prior to any contract. It is based on nature itself."

No sovereign could resort to tyrannical despotism to restore religious discipline, for to do so was to violate the pact that made him the father of the great family whose happiness God had placed in his hands. Even as Jansenism went awry politically, it still drew strength from Christian ideas of economic policy.[15]

Parlementary Jansenism, Popular Jansenism: Politics and Miracles

Fleury defeated episcopal Jansenism, but the movement that the bishops had launched now garnered the support of the previously timid magistracy, whose Gallican proclivities had been reawakened by the imposition of *Unigenitus* as the law of the land. Meanwhile, a notable shift in the nature of the movement came about as a result of miraculous happenings first in the faubourg Saint-Antoine of Paris in 1725 and later in the faubourg Saint-Marcel. In the capital Monsignor de Vintimille took Noailles's place: he was celebrated for his gourmandise, so that wags

nicknamed him "Ventremille" (Thousand Stomachs). On his door someone placed a sign saying that Saint-Antoine (Monsignor de Noailles) had
been replaced by his companion, the legendary pig. Vintimille was an
amiable and moderate prelate, but he carried on the policies of Fleury,
which his successor as manager of the bishops' newsletter, Boyer, bishop
of Mirepoix, pursued with excessive zeal and lack of caution after 1743.
Parlement, led by the *conseiller* Pucelle, protested the registration of the
edict of March 24, 1730. This gave rise to a well-known ditty:

> Le cardinal Fleury avec sa séquelle
> fit exiler de Paris l'bon abbé Pucelle,
> le peuple se mit à crier,
> les demoiselles à chanter:
> rendez-nous Pucelle au gué,
> rendez-nous Pucelle.

> Cardinal Fleury with his sequel
> had the good Abbé Pucelle exiled from Paris.
> The people began to weep,
> and the young ladies began to sing:
> Give us back Pucelle,
> Give us back Pucelle.

A song like this tells us something about the popularity of the robe,
which earned the opposition a new round of harsh measures, a flurry of
lettres de cachet, and exile to the provinces, although none of these steps
materially changed the situation. Enforcement of decrees bogged down in
a round of remonstrances. Indeed, from 1730 on, the Jansenists were well
aware of their isolation and addressed themselves to the public at large.
The *lettres de cachet* sustained a spirit of martyrdom and persecution
within the party, especially when the harsh repression ensured that purges
of the congregations would receive unprecedented publicity. Countless
incidents affected all the regular orders, the robe, and the clergy. If this
policy weakened the party, it paradoxically also strengthened it, because
the core of the faithful saw the persecution and miracles as signs of
God's favor for the appellants' cause.

In 1727 miracles were reported at the grave of a Jansenist, Gérard
Rousse, canon of Avenay, in the diocese of Reims. A polemic erupted
between Languet de Gergy and Monsignor Colbert. The latter published
his letter of February 5, 1727, on the *Pensées de Pascal sur les miracles*

373

demeurées jusque-là inédites. In 1730 miracles were again reported at the grave of Deacon Pâris in the Saint-Médard cemetery. Pâris was a pure Jansenist, retired from the world of the robe into which he was born, who became a deacon and was recognized as a saint owing to the strictness of his morals and a charitable spirit "more admirable than imitable." Pâris was venerated by the poor and by the Jansenist clergy. Even at his funeral there was already talk of miraculous cures: Noailles inquired about these reports, and people came to pray in the cemetery.

Saint-Médard was located in a miserable section of Paris, far from the center and quite disreputable—a dark, muddy part of the city where carriages bogged down by autumn, a working-class neighborhood of breweries and dye houses. Situated between the rue Mouffetard and the *collèges* of the Montagne Sainte-Geneviève, it was a district in which workers mingled with clergymen, students, and bourgeois. When miracles began to happen among the graves, the lame and halt rushed to the scene, and spectators followed. Slivers of a chestnut tree that once shaded the cemetery were sold as relics, and packets of the graveyard's soil were hawked as remedies to onlookers who rented chairs as at the opera.[16] The clergy was quick to react: on August 13, 1731, twenty-four curés from the diocese called for an investigation. The influx of the lame and halt had drawn pilgrims who came to pray as well as libertines who came to amuse themselves at the sight of ecstatic believers in the throes of convulsion. The police observed these scandalous proceedings and took the names of participants and onlookers. The Jansenist propaganda mill churned out countless lives of Pâris. Thirty peddlers of pamphlets and pious images were locked up. The extent of the frenzy is apparent from the catalogs of miracles compiled by Catherine Maire and C. Mabillat.[17] By the time the king and Fleury decided to close the cemetery, it had become a notorious theater of scandal: "By order of the king, the performance of miracles in this place is prohibited," read a sign posted by an anonymous individual on January 30, 1732.

The convulsions moved elsewhere, and the Jansenist public closeted itself away in private meetings, where by our lights things got even more out of hand. In garrets and cellars convulsions became more common than ever. In order to loosen up their stiff bodies and alleviate suffering through even greater suffering, the afflicted contrived strange torture devices and called upon spectators to "help" them in increasingly violent ways: by clubbing them with sticks and truncheons, piercing their flesh with swords, squeezing their skin and tongues with pincers, sewing their ears shut, giving them hot coals to swallow and broths of urine and excrement to drink—such were the astonishing torture remedies that ghoulish nurses administered while indulgent spectators looked on. Out of the public eye, these dramatic demonstrations of faith escalated, culminating in simulated crucifixions, which became the specialty of certain *convulsionnaires*. Many women were drawn to these graphic displays of faith in "God's cause." In effect these people were enacting martyrdom for the truth. Beatings and arrests only proved their "election" and the rightness of their cause.

In the wake of repression, the movement disappeared from public view and disintegrated into sectarian groups that survived long thereafter, yet its impact remained considerable. Both the monarchy and the Church perceived the scope of the movement as a real threat. Barbier estimated that five thousand people were involved in various related cabals in 1734, and d'Argenson put the number at two thousand in 1750. The police locked up three hundred people, 70 percent of whom were women (mainly from the lower classes), 30 percent in religious orders, 40 percent nobles and *robins*, and 30 percent bourgeois (counting only identified suspects). The dissidence was not marginal but located within the very urban and institutional core of the monarchy and Church. It was all the more worrisome because the *convulsionnaires* were receptive to egalitarian ideas and forms of sociability. "Brothers and sisters" renounced social distinctions and imagined themselves to be reconstituting the community of the primitive Church, the church of the elect. Hence the phenomenon cannot be marginalized. It showed that, in clandestine conditions of the sort apt to foster apocalyptic movements, some people were able to seize on a deep strain within Jansenism that used austerity and metaphysical abstraction as a mask for a profound belief in miracles: a series of miracles (going back to the miracle of Sainte-Epine in 1656), each with its harvest of relics, proved that Jansenist doctrine had God's support. The death of Port-Royal's saints gave rise to emotional outbursts that generated a need for the interpretation of signs, for which existing cultural practices proved inescapable.

Saint-Médard and its convulsions should be seen in the context of a more general popular exaltation encouraged by word and image. In 1743 Adrien Le Paige counted 358 "Bleeding Christs" in his entourage. The "Bleeding Christ" was a widely circulated engraving depicting Deacon

Pâris and his brother the *conseiller* at the foot of the Cross miraculously covered with blood. In this we see an explosion of repressed popular piety, which remained highly emotive and obsessed with death. Such tendencies were incomprehensible to the clerical and philosophical elite, who, led by physicians, attended at the bedsides of the *convulsionnaires* and read accounts of miracles. They were aware of witnessing a final outburst, the last scene of a long play in which politics and religion came together and split apart in the language of the humble. The episode speaks of the deep pain inflicted by the repression of Jansenism, which deprived the people of their pastors. As traditional guides vanished, a rage to persuade gained the upper hand. The ensuing debate pitted people such as Louis Carré de Montgeron, who claimed that the majority could not be wrong, against those who denounced popular delusion and madness. The crucial point, no doubt, is that so many people could have been mobilized in defense of obscure principles condemned by equally obscure propositions, and that they followed Jansenists who had appealed to the king, the bishops, and the council. Witness the crisis over the *billets de confession* provoked by Christophe de Beaumont, the new archbishop of Paris, whose intransigence became the butt of ridicule:

> Dieu lui donna la bienfaisance;
> le diable en fit un entêté;
> il couvrit par la charité
> les maux de son intolérance.

> God made him benevolent,
> the devil made him stubborn.
> He heaped charity
> upon the woes caused by his intolerance.

Beaumont ordered priests to refuse the sacraments to anyone who failed to present a *billet de confession* proving that his or her confession had been heard by a non-Jansenist priest. Reacting to this glaring outrage, *parlement* summoned the archbishop to judgment. When Christophe de Beaumont invoked his conscience, the duc de Richelieu replied: "Your conscience is a hooded lantern that illuminates no one but you." The king exiled both the *parlement* and the archbishop.

The affair was important for two reasons. First, the breakdown of the marriage between the two powers was once again underscored. Although the clergy expected disobedience to the bull to be punished, the king was prepared only to make promises while tolerating the parlementary actions initiated by the *appel comme d'abus*. The stakes became apparent in the great crisis of 1761–1764: when the *parlements* launched their attack on the Society of Jesus, the debate was immediately and permanently transformed into a political controversy. The king intervened of his own accord or allowed others to do so. Examination of the Jesuit constitutions might have been a prelude to examination of Church immunities. Hence in 1765 the Church published a stinging declaration of the rights of the spiritual power, which condemned the works of Rousseau and the *Encyclopédie* and reaffirmed the infallibility of the Church in moral as well as doctrinal matters. The king applauded its zeal but did not subscribe to its appeal. Cut off from the Church, he exposed himself to the possibility that the reign of criticism would turn against himself and his actions.

Second, that risk was compounded by the fact that the Jansenist movement had demonstrated the power of clandestine ideas. In proscribing works that mentioned *Unigenitus*, the royal authorities drove part of Jansenist thought underground, where it survived among networks of initiates who adopted false names and communicated with secret codes. Via this underground network, exchanges took place between writers in different locations and of diverse social backgrounds. The history of the *Nouvelles ecclésiastiques*, which was under constant threat from 1728 to 1789 but never seized, proves that propaganda could be published with impunity. And the history of Jansenism in Lorraine demonstrates the existence of a network of relations connecting Paris, the provinces, the United Provinces, the great abbeys and modest convents, and certain *châteaux* and *hôtels* belonging to members of the robe.[18] Part of the richness of Jansenism stemmed from this extensive network of communications, although as time went by there was increasing compromise with political and temporal authorities. The underground press and clandestine communications helped to shape critical opinion and spread opposition to a despotism that presumed to dictate to people's consciences, along with a certain anticlericalism. At a time when papal moderation, changes in the recruitment of bishops, and the progress of the secularizing Enlightenment were pushing Jansenism out of the spotlight, it survived in the sectarian movement and among the Richerists, who were numerous in the lower ranks of the clergy. Their concerns were spelled out in Maultrot's *Code des curés* and the works of the Gallican secular canonists. The canonical rights of the lower clergy and the people became well known to men of ideas and even began to influence practice.[19]

Enlightenment and Catholicism: Religion and Society

A third party intruded upon the relationship between Church and king: the Enlightenment. Criticism of prejudice was one of the Enlightenment's goals, a reflection of its drive for free, unfettered scrutiny. As Leo Strauss observed, "The word 'prejudice' was the unambiguous polemical correlate of the word 'freedom,' which was still too fraught with significance." Prejudice meant unfounded judgment and was thus central to the questioning of religion and its authority. The distinctive radicalism of the *Aufklärung* was to challenge the dogmatic interpretation of the Bible by the various churches. Written tradition was no longer absolutely authoritative; its truth depended on its credibility in the light of reason. Theology and, as we saw earlier, history had absorbed this dictum from seventeenth-century ideas and practice. In the eighteenth century, reason was directly associated with the power to organize practices. Its job was to filter opinion, ideology, superstition, and prejudice out of the realm of rationality and efficiency. Society and government attempted to set limits on religious expression in the name of utility, efficient management, and productivity. This effort created new cultural divisions: an urban civilization with its new learned authorities sought to distinguish itself from a savage and superstitious populace and a superstitious and fanatical clergy.[20]

Questions remain, however. Why was the criticism of prejudice not pursued everywhere with the same zeal, with the same extreme consequences of freethinking and atheism, which were common among French intellectuals, less common in Great Britain, and still less common in conservative Germany, which recognized the "true prejudices" of the Christian religion and developed a different philosophy of history on the same intellectual premises? The critique of prejudice can also be seen in certain elements of preromantic thought, which began at the same place as the critique of religion but ended up in a different place because pursued under the sign of "rehabilitation of the old as old": the simplicity of peasant life, the return to nature, the social hierarchy, the Christian association of states, the Middle Ages. Why did French clerics not follow this line instead of allowing themselves to become contaminated with an idea that Montesquieu set forth in the eighty-sixth of his *Lettres persanes:* "All religions contain principles useful to societies"? The process is best analyzed on three levels: in terms of the relation between critique and religion; in terms of the strength of the new clerical model; and in terms of the failure of religious apologias.[21]

Reason and Religion: The Ambiguities of Utility

If philosophical reason questioned religious beliefs and institutions, it did not attack all aspects of religious culture in the same way. The theological construct dominated by scholasticism bore the full brunt of the Enlightenment critique in France; elsewhere it was better able to resist. In order to gauge the effectiveness of criticism, I shall focus on three themes: the application of critical reason to religion, the attempt to define a rational religion, and finally the rejection of criticism of religion in certain quarters, widening differences and perpetuating conflict.

The philosophes, as heirs to *libertinage érudit* and readers of Bayle, no longer drew the traditional distinction between "superstitions," or beliefs characteristic of false religions and indicating exclusion through divisive particularism (the Catholic Counter-Reformation was a form of universalism), and the "mysteries" of the revealed religions. Initially there was no overt opposition between belief and criticism. Believers—faithful Christians and scrupulous priests—honed the weapons used by such doubting rationalists as Abbé Thiers, the illustrious confounder of pseudo-pagan beliefs and author of the *Traité des superstitions.* "The purge of knowledge in the name of reason corresponds to the will to scrutinize texts, dogma, and reason itself in order to rid the faith of the blemish of superstition."[22] It was for the benefit of religion as well as science that people sought to expose the mechanisms of error, an effort that made relativism a topos of critical analysis and authorized doubt. "God dead of the ultimate torture? An idea worthy of Punch!" Voltaire would exclaim. This skepticism was shared by those naive yet perspicacious characters, Montesquieu's Persians, Voltaire's Ingénu, and Diderot's Jacques le Fataliste. These were all men in search of a truth of their own, emancipated from ordinary beliefs, and persuaded of the futility of arguing about the unknowable. Criticism at the time derived its power from religious policy itself, from conflicts of religion such as the Jansenist-Jesuit quarrel and the revocation of the Edict of Nantes, the persecution of reformers and heretics, and a real overheating of theological thought after a century of triumphalist, assimilating Reformation. On the whole, the Enlightenment condemned intolerance, rejected mystery, and distinguished between spirituality and religious ethics. As Voltaire wrote in his *Essai sur les moeurs:* "Scaffolds dripped with blood because of theological arguments, now in one country, now in another, for five hundred years, nearly without interruption. And this scourge lasted so long only because people always neglected morality for dogma."

Philosophes and Christians found common ground with respect to socially useful "formal practices." The ethics of the Enlightenment were rooted in an old distinction between, on the one hand, the acts of civil and political society and, on the other hand, religious life, linked as it was to state or utilitarian culture. On the lost battlefield of Christianity transformed into morality it was possible to experiment in various ways with the relation to the sacred and the accommodation to negation. All these experiments were more or less suffused with the "disenchantment of the world."

Consider first of all the various forms of deism, which drew their strength from an anti-Christianity in which the natural and organic order was set over against the sacred. Although the term "deism" was never precisely defined, its various interpretations include a common set of core beliefs. Foremost among them was the belief that a rational religion was possible. In the place of historical Christianity, deism posited a religion of space and a universal set of "common human" beliefs. It also assumed the possibility of a natural religion free of mysteries and rituals, a desacralized religion whose divinity was identical with the laws of nature. These views, developed early on by three English deists who taught Voltaire—Toland, Collins, and Tindal—attached a higher priority to social relations than to spirituality and affirmed the right of laymen to discuss matters of faith. Propositions such as these redrew the boundary between political and religious authorities. God vanished or withdrew from the world, and with him went rituals and churches. For Voltaire, God was the eternal geometer, the basis of all human communion, and deism was a form of religion based on a collective ethic. As René Pomeau has shown, these views led to a form of "theism," an abortive religious reform but also a clear-sighted attempt to ensure that life and human society would not be drained of religious feeling. Theism was a public promise that was echoed everywhere, especially in the founding of Masonic temples, where

Christianity was reduced to essentials. It became a social cement, a means not of salvation but of necessary recognition and explanation, respectful of established beliefs as well as of adventurous, esoteric explorations. The Masons' insistence on fraternity and morality and universalist teachings fit well with the general religious conformism of the day.

At the opposite extreme from the theists stood the atheists and materialists, whose critique of established beliefs was radical. Leave aside Spinoza, who influenced everyone and was secretly interpreted in a bewildering variety of ways. As Paul Vernières has shown, Spinoza's pantheism, which identified God with nature and did without revelation or creation, served as an initiation for many other thinkers.[23] Condemned by the Church and read in secret, he turned unbelief into a social force. The materialists claimed him, thereby giving proof that they were not as crude as has been alleged. Between deism and atheism, which both gave the clergy chills, there was a connection involving the rejection of evil as a negative argument justifying religion and of the need for a creator, who was replaced by the laws of matter. Here there was nothing particularly original, nothing that one could not have read long before; but in the transition from atheism to materialism there emerged a new conception of man as the product of education and society, along with an exaltation of the morality of the human spirit, which had a profound impact. Modern materialism has its roots here, because d'Holbach, Helvétius, La Mettrie, and Diderot all argued for the autonomy of human activity. If man could shape himself, he could dominate nature.

Here, the rationalism of the Enlightenment aroused all the old forces of opposition: the only solutions were either sarcasm ("fat baron d'Holbach and his materialism") or silence (to prevent bold theories from gaining a hearing). The major works of philosophy were not widely read: we will encounter this problem again when we analyze the deep social transformations of the period. For now, however, the question is the relationship between Enlightenment rationality and its opposite. Political ethics carried the day: it required accommodation with the world denounced by the Church, which had its own laws and imperatives. The Church defended itself along the boundaries of the sacred, symbolized by the priest and his isolation in difference. Throughout the century, moreover, it sought to keep its own language, the language of tradition, alive, but in a confrontation with the enemy, that is, in combat beyond its frontiers.[24] The wall of religious language still stood: formalism in practice and debate left the religious terrain divided up among ethics and apologetics, religion, belief, and spirituality. The crisis of sensibility of 1760–1790 revealed the persistence of prelogical, irrational forces, forces repressed as much by clerical reason as by philosophical reason. Rousseau, interrogated by the Church, showed his share of unbelief: he was a revealer of consciences, the emblem of truthful discourse.

The Good Priest in the Eighteenth Century: Theology and Institutions

Dominique Julia has shown how theological representations influenced historical institutions and, conversely, how the cultural and political situation of the clergy changed theological culture. The question is important because, from the seventeenth century on, reform of the Church depended on reform of its pastors, from the episcopate on down to the curés and the rest of the clergy, which was now defined by exclusion.[25] Three sacred signs differentiated the clergy from the profane: the habit (the black cassock was a mark of rigor, indicating a concern with appearances), comportment (clerics avoided scandal and behaved differently from other people), and celibacy. These requirements reflected society's expectations of theology. Two representations of the clergyman were involved: the "good priest" was motivated by an ideal of spiritual perfection, religious imperatives, and worldly action, whereas the cleric as agent of the Church was also socialized to be a social notable who performed a useful public service.

The reform movement, which linked Christian policy to state action, gradually imposed a sacramental theology that placed the accent on the sacrificial character of the priesthood and on the acknowledgment of hierarchies and defined the church as a separate clerical sphere vis-à-vis an increasingly civil society. It was the priest who established the boundary between the sacred and the profane and who, by his virtue and his example, held out a model of holiness to the faithful. The transformation from profane recruit to sacred priest did not take place overnight, and the theory ran up against a variety of temporal realities. For example, the priesthood was still a career in the eighteenth century owing to the system of benefices and the principle of *beneficium propter officium*. This career had its own selection criteria (including the expectations of graduates) and other rules (such as *resignation ad favorem* and lateral exchange of position) that hindered actions by bishops and reformers. There were regional differences in the recruitment and density of the clergy. For example, Brittany, where the proletarian priesthood survived, and Rouergue, where there were still presbyterian fraternities, differed profoundly from the reformed dioceses in which we find that a purely ministerial clergy of deans, curés, and vicars had enormous appeal. Books such as F. H. Sevoy's *Devoirs ecclésiastiques* (1763) show how the very definition of the requirements suggests an ultimate goal that was not always achieved. Similarly, the teacher training provided by the seminars varied widely in time and space. Only gradually did the idea of prolonged studies and tighter moral controls catch on.[26]

Priests were seen as men in possession of a kind of knowledge. They were increasingly selected for promotion on the basis of intellectual attainment. Although there was still a vast difference between the instruction received in a modest seminary such as Manosque in Provence or Gimont in the diocese of Auch and the teaching available at Saint-Sulpice or Saint-Magloire in Paris, training was standardized. It consisted of reading the Bible for spiritual and moral edification and practice preaching. Historical criticism as practiced by scholars and philosophers was entirely neglected. The doctrine was Gallican and rigorist but increasingly anti-Jansenist; moral theology dominated everything else. The ministry placed increasing demands on good priests, who extended their studies with "ecclesiastical conferences" in which group consciousness was reinforced through sociability (see the memoirs of Bernard). Priests became active readers, but solely for professional purposes (except in the cities): in urban western France their libraries consisted of 80 percent religious books. Selected by practical theology, conditioned by isolation, priests lived in a cultural ghetto from which profane subjects were proscribed. These were exclusively for the scholars of the order or else for the abbés of court and alcove, common in Paris but rare elsewhere and who in any case were not very ecclesiastical in their outlook. Ordinary priests were the prisoners of a uniform discourse that turned them into functionaries serving a religious ideology, with one foot in the state, the other in the Church. Accordingly, they suffered the fallout of every conflict, and their cultural isolation had other damaging effects as well.

Limited to administrative tasks and reduced to silence on matters of faith, the clergy found itself among the notables who hoped to change society by changing the way people lived. Priests enforced orders prohib-

iting certain festivals and proscribed "indecent" and "superstitious" practices. Pastoral visits were ambivalent. The priest gave his flock no cause
for complaint, because he was different and set himself apart, yet he
assiduously served the community as an intermediary, carrying messages
to notables and lords, acting as a teacher, assisting the health authorities,
and arbitrating minor conflicts (in Languedoc, for example). In so doing,
however, priests and bishops made religious observance a practical affair;
official visibility, uniformity of doctrine and mores, and Christian experience were all one. To be a parish priest was to stand at the beginning of a
professional career: the assembly of the clergy discussed this in 1775,
weighing the advantages of merit versus favor. It was no accident, finally,
that the clergy found itself tempted once again by Richerist ideas. The
theory masked egalitarian political demands and assumed an increased
secularization of the priest's role. Is there any need to point out that for
Voltaire, Turgot, and Rousseau, the good curé was a social as well as a
religious necessity? The "insurrection of the curés" grew out of the
Jansenist conflict, the priest's spiritual authority (all the greater because
priests refrained from interfering in temporal affairs of their parishioners,
about which there was no unanimity), and perhaps the susceptibility of
the religious enclave to the ideas of the Enlightenment. In this connection
it is of some interest to note that Jean Meslier, curé of Etrepagny in the
Ardennes, a graduate of one of France's best seminaries, kept silent
about his beliefs all his life but left a vehement profession of his atheism
that was discovered only after his death. The withdrawal of the clergy
from intellectual debate, the paralysis that kept the intellectual revolution
of the Enlightenment from thawing frozen theological discourse, led to
silence and clandestine violence.[27]

The Pedagogy of the Church: The Limits of Apologetics

God proposes, man listens. The teachings of the Church, conveyed
through works of theology and preaching, imposed constraints on
change. The Church was involved in two struggles. One was a struggle
against itself, symbolized by the conflict with the proponents of rigorist
Augustinianism, and not just the Jansenists. The other was a struggle
against the world, symbolized by the battle with philosophy. We are now
well informed about the social influence of rigorist preaching, whose

rejection was a key factor in the secularization of the West.[28] The correspondence between Abbé Bergier, a Franc-Comtois exiled to Versailles, where he taught catechism to the royal family, and Joseph Trouillet, curé of Ornans, proves that doctrine could be challenged and Augustinianism questioned at the very heart of the Church. Trouillet's panicky reaction reveals the solitude in which the apologist for the true faith found himself isolated "out of fear of stirring up trouble in the Church." Two sorts of values were questioned: those of the economy and those of the powers of the word.

The Church and Economic Values

Religious thinking about labor and wealth was afflicted with a sort of congenital curse, since the former was thought of fundamentally as a penance and the latter as a means of charitable redistribution. These ideas defined the human condition: work was a form of holy discipline, and accumulation made sense only if the fruits of accumulation were rejected. Actual behavior departed from these principles in two ways, however.

First, as Bernard Groethuysen showed in a book that is insufficiently well known, *Les Origines de l'esprit bourgeois en France* (1927), the values of labor isolated the productive or popular strata of society, subject to the need to earn their daily bread and the necessity of discipline, from the privileged world of the nobility and clergy, governed by the virtues of *otium*, which was rebaptized by the Church, an institution more attentive to form—that is, to regularity, to the opportunity to shun the temptations of idleness—than to the results: money and power. Ecclesiastical discourse required a dual interpretation of the world and of concrete existence, one based on the opposition of inferior and superior, the other on the opposition between rich and poor. Certain tensions between the two dictated rights and duties, responsibility and charity. Between power and wealth, the ideal of a stable world made room for the idea of equality by accepting that "a rich man qua rich is merely a dispenser of God's bounty," with investment in the hereafter compensating for worldly success. Charity basked in the light of benevolence. Wealth was thus directly linked to the status and freedom it bestowed: the wealth of great nobles was legitimate, while that of traders, usurers, banks, and merchants was still to some degree suspect. Confessors' manuals vilified the pursuit of lucre and as late as the eighteenth century continued to condemn competition in its many forms, rejected the idea of money as a productive resource, and forced merchants to resort to technical subterfuge so as to avoid Church prohibitions of usury. The ideal merchant was the one who settled for "respectable mediocrity." The values of labor and wealth were invoked not in opposition to the social order but as a means to maintain it.[29]

Second, the change in religious discourse can also be related to the increased role of money and the increased power of wealth in society. Traders, shippers, bankers, and tax farmers had acquired nobility. They sponsored economic development and invested the results in both business and culture. Their financial power gave them access to the "net social product." The new spirit threatened to transform the whole social fabric, as Abbé Prigent noted in his *Observations sur le prêt à intérêt* (1783): "Respectable and happy mediocrity can be found in a nation of farmers, but one would look in vain for it in our commercial cities. What do we find in them? For every rich man, overburdened with plenty, we find a host of artisans crowded, indeed virtually squeezed, into a workshop, pressed, and covered with rags."

How, under the circumstances, could the Church be reconciled with development? Commerce was merely a sign of an evolutionary process that was shifting the balance of power between urban France and the old agricultural kingdom in favor of the former. For the sake of the public interest, the theologians were forced to modify their positions: "The real reason why the profits of bankers are legitimate is that they are fulfilling the duties of an estate and that estate is useful and authorized. Any establishment of a utility recognized by society is also a licit establishment, because supreme wisdom would not have set the order of things in opposition to the rules of morality."[30]

Despite this approval, a deep misunderstanding persisted between development-oriented capitalists and the Church. Too many voices proclaimed the legitimacy of profit, the utility of labor, and the necessity of accumulation, which were grounded in reason and progress. In this as in other respects, the Church as institution had facilitated the new utilitarian ethic. A new man could oppose the Church on this ground because he had already proved his mettle, deployed his forces, and built a new world in the very shadow of the old.

Church, Authority, and the Cure of Souls

Economics is only one example of the closed nature of religious language, which we also find in apologetics. To defend the faith the Church had to venture onto foreign ground and engage in combat with outsiders, with bizarre materialists and atheists of limited intellect and utterly without morality. Religious spokesmen attacked these outsiders mercilessly, but without trying to understand what motivated them. Deists were not taken seriously; their behavior contradicted their words, and their abstract God had nothing to do with the living God. The Church was in many ways close to its fiercest adversaries.[31] The impious individual was therefore an obligatory polemical trope, and preachers used unbelief as a symbol of evil. Christians were exhorted to fear the power of "wicked books." Apology itself could be dangerous: it diverted attention from things Christian and penetrated the heart of the unbeliever, who risked being burned. The unbeliever was not an interlocutor for the apologist but rather the antihero of a discourse internal to the Church. One did not speak to him except to condemn and censure him: so the bishops requested of the king, and so, too, did the faculty of theology decree in defense of orthodoxy. As time went by, the assemblies of the clergy turned up the rhetorical heat in response to storms stirred up by powerful books, the books of the Jansenists, the Protestants, and the philosophes, who from 1760 on seemed to be joined in a conspiracy against the Church: "A host of writers appear to have conspired against the Lord and his Christ; they have declared war." In this respect the Church expected great things from the king; it was inevitably disappointed.

When the royal authorities rejected repressive measures, the Church therefore hardened its position, and in the last quarter of the century apologetic discourse developed in the space between interdict and pastoral preaching. Preachers first had to be provided with arguments to refute unbelief on its own ground. Then the language of authority and collective judicial action had to be replaced by interdict: pastoral rhetoric required persuasive argument. Civil interdict would prove that the old relationship between the royal government and the Church was still working, and it would nullify the apologias. Ecclesiastical interdict made apologias necessary: as the statements issued by the assembly of the clergy made clear, it was through apologias that the Church hoped to reach the faithful. A myriad of authors were employed at the task: more than five hundred titles rolled off the presses. Their task was to use exegetical scholarship, theological rationalism, and stories of conversion to exhort and persuade. For his "accuracy, clarity, profundity, and precision," Abbé Bergier, the author of *Déisme réfuté par lui-même*, received a pension. His gift was to have refuted Rousseau, the best reasoner and most eloquent of the unbelievers. Apologists were in great demand, for among the educated the Church was in the position of having to win back its faithful. One read the texts of the enemy only to reach the true audience of Christians and "return to the calm place of religion." Rousseau was a distinguished adversary because his *Emile* and *Social Contract* prescribed action and change in what the Church perceived to be the very realm of religion and "representation." More than anyone else, Rousseau was able to enter into the internal quarrels of the Church because he was interrogating belief.

If novelty was a priori impiety, then apologetics could only reaffirm the stability, certainty, and truth that eluded the philosophes. Thus the Church could not do without unbelief, but it did not address itself to the unbeliever. Its arguments could therefore incorporate any and all utilitarian values. Take, for example, Monsignor Jean-Georges Lefranc de Pompignan, a typical prelate of the Enlightenment Church and yet an adversary of episcopal enthusiasm for "public affairs," a moderate conciliator in practice and yet a zealous defender of the threatened faith. His work is not, *pace* A. Monod,[32] that of a "mediocre reasoner" and "poorly educated scholar." It tells us what the bishops thought of their adversaries and serves as an example of a utilitarian ideological apologia.[33] Its focus changes between *Questions diverses sur l'incrédulité* (1751) and the *Traité de la religion vengée de l'incrédulité* (1773): an apology that began as a rational exposition of Christian truths and the logic behind them ended as an attempt to demonstrate their utility. This fundamental change of emphasis was made necessary by philosophical discourse itself. By adopting a comparative method, the apologist in a sense incorporated the new discourse and made himself dependent on it, to Rivarol's dismay: "For what demented reasons I do not know, the philosophes insisted on proofs of religion, and the priests fell into the trap. The philosophers demanded proofs, and the priests supplied them. The scandal, the madness were at their height when the Revolution began. The priests and the philosophers were treating religion as a problem, whereas what was needed was for the former to preach it and the latter to respect it."[34]

And so the Catholic Enlightenment failed in France, as the ancient alliance of the "two powers" fell apart and the Church refused a change that nothing—neither proof nor preaching—had the power to prevent.

12

❧❧❧

Elites and Nobilities

THE ABSOLUTIST STATE was able to extend the range of its intervention and expand its personnel of servants and administrators only by containing and altering existing social forces. Fiscal pressure and administrative action revealed the state's two facets, the repressive and the progressive. Continued protest against monarchical expansion shows that the state did not succeed in totally destroying the existing *corps* and communities.

Thirty years ago historians were seriously divided about the nature of eighteenth-century society and the reasons for its evolution. Was it a "society of orders" or a "society of classes"? The debate, as one might expect, was not purely academic. The issue was to understand how a society's conception of itself affected its capacity for change. Eighteenth-century society could be interpreted in such a way as to reflect our own political debate, the social choices that we ourselves faced. This led to a clash between those who saw social classes and their conflicts as a means of establishing a more just and egalitarian society and those who saw a society of orders and communities as a source of necessary stability, freedom from turmoil, and even respect for God's commandments.[1] This debate no longer has the heuristic value, not to say the ideological asperity, it once possessed. Its focal point has shifted to give it a new lease on life, however, and it remains important as a means of understanding the interaction between the social and the political, the influence of social relations on a society governed by principles of stability and hierarchy but under stress owing to change and mobility.

The question is not whether French society in the eighteenth century was "really" a society of orders or a society of classes: there is no denying the fact that the social theorists of the time (jurists, theologians, notaries, experts in protocol) thought in terms of orders and that their ideas were capable of shaping a common worldview and therefore of influencing social behavior and relations. The real question is why societies need to reflect on their own nature and why at certain times they feel compelled to change the rules that govern such reflection. The time has now come to replace a single explanatory principle with a more wide-ranging interrogation, for both theoretical and historical reasons. Social groups are what they think they are, but not just that: they are also what they are not aware of being. To study the categories in terms of which contemporaries deciphered their society is therefore strictly complementary to doing social analysis with categories of our own; there is no opposition between the two. Furthermore, eighteenth-century French society interpreted itself in different ways: some analysts focused on distinctions between orders, others on the hierarchy of wealth or the distribution of economic roles or the variety of forms of social behavior. Hence no single historical classification can yield the key to the social structure. In order to grasp the full complexity of any society, one has to look at the whole range of contemporary classifications and compare these with quantitative demographic analyses.

These considerations do not simplify the work of the historian, who must now investigate the why of these various social classifications. If many social classifications existed, we need to understand why they came into being and disappeared. What was the nature of each? How long did a particular classification remain useful? For what purposes were social classifications used, and where: in the cities or the countryside, for tax collection or the Church, for the lord or the peasant? In what spirit were they conceived, and what impact did they have or might they have had? The eighteenth century was particularly fertile in such social classifications because there was a new need for social description and understanding. Society had become opaque, made so by accumulating wealth, new forms of behavior, the transformation of urban space, increased social mobility, and other changes that disrupted traditional vertical allegiances and solidarities.

Orders, classes, categories, and groups can therefore be examined either together or separately, provided we keep quality distinct from quantity. The latter could have a greater impact than the former in an old hierarchical order in which subtle differences of status were paramount. We can look at the principal social actors, especially the nobility and bourgeoisie, in the light of contemporary data and traditional definitions of the political and social order, with special attention to how the social vocabulary helped to shape social models and dictate behavior. We can also reinterpret the distinction between a traditional society and a modern society in which orders and classes coexisted, and in which social interactions were sometimes accompanied by conflicts that revealed the persistence of old inequalities. Equally interesting were attempts to transform a novel social ethos into the basis of a new social bond.

Elite or nobility? The question is not meaningless, for contemporaries did in fact debate the issue of how much emphasis to place on birth and privilege and how much on talent and fortune. The essence of the debate is clear: to understand the process of social mobility and its implications for the legitimacy of the established order.

Orders and Privileges: The Reality of the Imaginary

Louis Dumont taught us not to limit our thinking about society to the social stratification model, which makes sense only in relation to present-day values and to an egalitarian culture.[2] This lesson must be heeded if we are to avoid creating an artificial distinction between the concrete on the one hand and the symbolic and imaginary on the other: "Man does not merely think; he also acts. He has ideas, but he also has values. To adopt a value is to establish a hierarchy, and a certain consensus about values, a certain hierarchy of ideas, things, and people, is indispensable to social life. This is entirely independent of natural inequalities and the distribution of power."[3]

Eighteenth-century French society must first be interpreted in terms of the "mother ideology" that animated it, and in full recognition of the value hierarchies built into the system of orders and privileges. This is particularly true because the society embraced a new vision according to which the world was defined in relation to the individual, and in terms of an individualism that rapidly gained support until it ultimately became the dominant worldview in the Age of Romanticism.

The Three Orders of Enlightened Absolutism

The values of the society of orders were passed on from the seventeenth to the eighteenth century through the writings of jurists. The concept of estates or orders was based on the idea that society is composed of distinct social groups defined by their social function. The order, derived from the medieval *universitas,* encompassed its individual members; each person had a place in a particular order and thus a means of contributing to the global order. "Justice consists in apportioning social functions in relation to the whole." Clergy, nobility, and Third Estate: those who pray, those who fight, and those who work. These were the "three orders" or, as Charles Loyseau put it in his *Traité des ordres et simples dignités* (1610), "three estates of the kingdom," which, in this world, between heaven and earth, defined a vision of equilibrium and perfection, an ideal of social function. Everything must be "assigned its proper rank," because the order of the terrestrial world was part of the cosmic order.

Some may object that these old principles no longer exactly fit the actual social hierarchy of the time, which is obviously true; yet they did fulfill a purpose in the social constitution. They could serve as a reference point to mark historical change, or else they could justify certain types of behavior and concrete realities. The beating administered to Voltaire by his "betters" is evidence of this, as are the important as well as silly conflicts over priority. Social esteem, dignity, status, and individual and group honor confirmed a hierarchy that was maintained by endogamy and made manifest by specific symbols: the cleric's habit and tonsure, the noble's sword and coat of arms, the prerogatives of honor and privilege. In this respect the Third Estate was special, since it was defined negatively by that from which it was excluded: not privileges to be sure (since it had acquired a range of privileges of its own), but blue blood, birth, and the service of God.[4] To the end of the Ancien Régime there persisted a gap between the real and symbolic representativity of the Third Estate and that of the other two estates. One suspects that the explanatory value and concrete force of the old schemes were more accentuated in the village, where the social pyramid was clearly visible, than in the city, where the social division of labor and the complexity of social relations gave rise to more flexible rules and created new problems.

The traditional tripartite scheme remained alive, although doubts had been raised as far back as the seventeenth century about its ability to explain adequately a society that had changed considerably. This coexistence of old and new ideas allows us to speak about orders and classes at the same time, depending on which principles of stratification we wish to invoke.[5] The overtones of old words were still present in the dictionaries. Open Furetière's dictionary, for example, and note the constellation of meanings that still revolved around the word "order" at the beginning of the eighteenth century: "The situation of things in accordance with the estate, place, and rank appropriate to their nature or their functions. The creator placed all the parts of the universe in a suitable order. The chain of secondary causes is an order established by Providence. When the order or economy of the human body is disrupted, man dies."

Thus, the natural notion of order was also functional: it corresponded to a regularization, a direction, a necessary submission. It was an arrangement that governed things on earth as well as in heaven, the hierarchy of angels as well as of men. It also offered a method for organizing things where confusion reigned: it was both a principle and a method. The principle regulated

> the distinction of persons and *corps* in a state for both assemblies and ceremonies. The estates of France are composed of "three orders," the Church, the nobility, and the Third Estate. The clergy is composed of two orders: the first comprises the cardinals, archbishops, and bishops, the second the abbés, deans, canons, and other ecclesiastics. Among the Romans, there was the order of senators, the order of equestrians, and the people.

The method made it possible to create order when natural precedence did not apply to men or things: "Councilors will be seated in order of seniority," that is, in accordance with the date of their appointment, an accidental consequence of age and merit.

Beyond the usually emphasized legal aspect of the word "order" lay two implicit interpretations of the world. An order was part of an organic series willed by Providence, and it revealed man's freedom to define the framework of his action, the interconnections between things that assured his mastery. From "order" to "orders" there was a unity of principles and effects that could not be modified without recourse to violence. This unity dictated its discipline (Loyseau already saw this as an essential effect of social division), defined its subdivisions (each order had its categories), and legitimated the use of symbols and marks. In this way boundaries were drawn, and with them the possibility of usurpation, derogation, and exception that enabled the order of orders to regulate disorder without violence.

In the *Encyclopédie*, the chevalier de Jaucourt followed the same meta-physical line of argument from the order of things to the physics of social arrangements. He introduced a profuse diversity with his lengthy analysis of canonical jurisprudence, which established the law of the "sacred orders" and regulated "the sixth sacrament of the Church." He demonstrated his virtuosity as a jurist by examining civil jurisprudence and customary practice. And he showed himself to be a historian of the "religious and military orders" and even a student of "orders of battle." In other words, he studied all the various orderings, natural as well as cultural, that put things in their place. From *ordonnance* to *ordonnée* to *ordovice* to Orduña (a city in Spain) and *ordure*, "order"—the word and the things it organized—is the subject of fifteen dense pages under the capacious rubric of "Political Justice":

> Order in a state, different classes and assemblies of men, with their different powers and privileges. It is not possible to destroy or essen-tially change the orders of a state so long as the spirit and character of the people remain as pure and vigorous as at their inception; but they would be essentially altered if the spirit and the character of the people were lost: this alteration of the orders would lead more certainly to loss of liberty than if the orders were destroyed.[6]

The old society survived, but certain forces obliged it to evolve. Be-hind the alteration of the old orders, one diagnosed a loss of liberties owing to the process of aging, the flourishing of cities and trade, and the rise of the state.

The Reality of Orders and the Diversity of Classifications

The orders possessed a certain measure of reality, but they had lost their universal political power: there were no more assemblies of corps (except for the clergy), no more representation of notables (except in those Estates and *corps de ville* where the *sanior pars* was influential), and no more Estates General until the promises of 1788 and the debate of 1789. From Louis XIV to Louis XVI, the strength of the orders lay in their equivocal ability to embody "liberties" and to exemplify hierarchy. Listen to the remonstrances of the Parlement of Paris on March 2, 1776:

> Sire, the French monarchy, by its constitution, is composed of several distinct, separate estates. This distinction of conditions and persons arises from the origin of the nation; it was born with its mores; it is the precious chain that links the sovereign to his subjects. If the estates of persons were not distinguished, there would be nothing but disorder and confusion, says one of our most enlightened authors. We cannot live in equality of condition; it is essential that some command and that others obey. Sovereign lords command everyone in their states; they issue their commands to the greatest of their subjects, the greatest to the middling, and the middling to the small. In the assembly composed of these various orders, all the men of your kingdom are your subjects; all are obliged to contribute to the needs of state. But in that very contribution order and harmony still have their place.

After this eloquent preamble, with its traditional definition of the three functions justifying rights and duties and services and therefore privileges, Parlement refused to register a fiscal edict regarding compulsory labor *(corvée)* because it abolished the ancient heritage. In short, "who could even tell the nobles that, after subjecting them to the *corvée*, no one had any intention of subjecting them to the *taille?*"[7] With reference to Loyseau, the author went on to say that while the members of the Paris Parlement might claim to be defending the "common good," they actually favored division of the society into distinct orders, which made them defenders of privilege and thus of the feudal constitution and the seigneurial dues that the administrative monarchy had claimed for itself. From top to bottom, the fundamental social hierarchy had not changed. The rich were allowed to rise to a precarious status within the seigneurial class.[8] This mobility became a feature of the social structure, the potency of which would be revealed in the conflicts of the 1780s.

It was even more apparent in urban celebrations. A description of the city of Montpellier in 1768, which Robert Darnton interprets as an index of bourgeois culture, may be nothing more than a response to an administrative inquiry initiated by an *intendant*.[9] For the author of that description, the city is a congregation of orders and estates. He first depicts the bishop and the clergy, then the municipal authorities, then the magistrates of the *cour des aides*, the governor of the province who preceded them, the officers of the presidial court, and then a host of more modest dignitaries, a group of administrators, representatives of guilds and corporations, and finally the undifferentiated "people." The description emphasizes the growing complexity beneath the appearance of order. By attending to the visible discrepancies between power, status, and wealth, he shows how a processional vision of society exaggerated the fundamental traits of the hierarchy of orders but neglected or excluded certain other criteria that organized reality in just as powerful a way. For example, the *trésoriers de France,* whose offices cost more than those of *conseillers* of the *cour des aides,* nevertheless enjoyed less consideration and marched behind the *conseillers.* Monks led the procession, but the author does not hide the fact that they have little dignity in his eyes. Montpellier was a commercial city whose citizens had a healthy respect for wealth, yet traders, merchants, manufacturers, artisans, shopkeepers, and tradesmen did not enjoy a place of honor in processions. By contrast, the numerous poor did enjoy a place of honor.

Thus the description was not a reflection of the social structure but an expression of the dominant values of the day: a person's quality was determined by his rank and function, not by his individual skills or talents. Next, the spectator notes how the three traditional estates joined together at the heart of the procession, where the dais holding the Holy Sacrament was carried by six consuls representing the city and *corps.* Around Christ's living presence the clergy and its highest representatives, the bishopric and cathedral chapter, joined the *sanior pars* of nobles, rentiers, and guild officials. The social order revealed itself to spectators as a graduated succession of dignities organized by rank and wealth (from which certain groups were omitted). When the author resumes his description of the city's institutions and categories, he therefore modifies the order of estates and places the nobility first, indicating its various components, followed by the official bourgeoisie and then the bourgeoisie of affairs. Money and social utility, of fundamental importance, thus modify the description of dignities.

This text emphasizes three characteristic elements: politics was a matter of negotiation involving representation by *corps;* social mobility and ennoblement ensured that the whole system kept working; and the most worrisome boundary was that between the Third Estate and an impoverished, wild, undisciplined, and dangerous "Fourth Estate." The author's chief concern was to find a way to include all the necessary distinctions.

Cultural habits and symbolic markers such as clothing were essential descriptive elements, lending a harmonious unity to the whole, an effect of wealth and education. Dignities of the orders, wealth and faculty of the estates, theater of daily life: these were three ways of interpreting the social structure, a traditional idiom, a functional and utilitarian language, a style made harmonious by the way of life of the urban elite, the notables.

Three modes of classification were most common: by orders, still, and primarily for the essential distinction between common birth *(roture)* and nobility; by estate and resources; and by occupation. Nobility was primarily inherited but could also be purchased or obtained by administrative devolution or "ennoblement by letters." Background investigations of prospective nobles show what was expected of them. It was generally agreed that ennoblement recognized not so much the excellence of a particular individual as that of a whole milieu, the gentlemen of the entire *généralité*, whose consensus the *intendant* interpreted. It could also recognize excellence in a profession, a reward to a leading merchant or renowned magistrate. Finally, ennoblement crowned the marriage of birth with fortune. Many things went into the making of an order. As Jean-Claude Perrot admirably puts it, "Nobility was a precipitate that epitomized a social judgment: it was a trace, the past remembered by the present." It was a symbol that gave substance to a family's history. Its significance was ampler when it commemorated the immemorial, the night of time, the grandiose genealogy, but its essence was the same for the recently ennobled: "It always addressed the society's memory and culture."[10]

The administrative monarchy developed new systems of classification to aid in the collection of taxes. From 1695 on, the society was divided into classes according to the supposed resources of its subjects; the old orders were temporarily forgotten. The first *capitation* came after jurists had written about fiscal equity and economists such as Domat and Vauban had examined ways in which the system might be repaired. Domat represents a milestone in the conceptualization of the social system because he saw society in terms of spiritual and temporal needs under the aegis of the state. His "orders" reflected his utilitarian ideas and presaged a new hierarchy of ability. The new tax, from which only the clergy was exempt, laid the groundwork for a variety of experiments designed to distribute the tax burden in a more equitable fashion: Law's *denier royal*,

Pâris-Duverney's *dîme royale,* the various *dixièmes* and *vingtièmes,* and the *taille,* whether *proportionnelle* or *tarifée.* Implicit in all these schemes was a weakening of the fiscal privileges of the first and second orders.

Nevertheless, despite what some scholars have said, the tax schedule of 1695 does not reveal "the true social hierarchy of old France."[11] It shows how the royal administration thought about the tax problem and attempted to solve it in a utilitarian manner. It was an imaginary classification with real consequences. It proposed one of the first occupational classifications in history in a manner that made wealth a primary factor. But this revolution was empirical. It depended on the evaluation of visible, seizable assets. The first twenty classes corresponded to charges and offices and to income, which was difficult to evaluate, as opposed to wealth. Within each class, it was rank and position (and to a lesser extent industriousness and labor, which were harder to take into account) that determined the hierarchy: 22 classes, 569 ranks. In each class the ternary order remained: the warriors, the administrators, the producers of wealth; various forms of nobility and common birth tended to overlap. Administrative and fiscal considerations came together, and the social structure was interpreted in terms of proximity to the state in the case of military men, administrators, and judges. The old social order was not altered but diverted to new ends, and the state was cast in the role of unifier of society. Within each class, utilitarianism dictated that the highest rank be given to those most closely associated with the state in terms of occupation, estate, quality, and wealth. Those whose importance in society as organized by the state was clear were precisely identified, while others were assigned to more fluid categories. What is more, classification gave rise to certain adjustments, extension to other areas (such as the schedule of indirect taxes between 1722 and 1749), and even debates over corrections to the tax tables and creation of new ones (for example, in 1781 by Necker and Joly de Fleury).

To propose a social classification is of course to have a political conception of society, but it is also to generalize abstract, rational methods for obtaining social knowledge.[12] In its search for tax revenues, the royal administration organized society without imposing any unique criterion because its vision of the social world prevented it. At the same time, it constructed an interpretive scheme in terms of which social transformations could be deciphered.

Such transformations were implicit in speculation about economic classification, which implicitly or explicitly recognized the imperialism of wealth. Turgot, in his *Réflexions sur la formation et la distribution des richesses* (1788), proposed dividing men into three classes: producers (farmers), the industrious class (merchants and artisans), and men of leisure *(gens disponibles)*, or capitalists. Although the terms are different, the scheme is the same as that of Quesnay in the *Tableau* or of the marquis de Mirabeau in the seventh part of *L'Ami des hommes*. These categories made it possible to understand production and exchange and the circulation of wealth, but difficulties remained: the imprecision of these definitions led Turgot to introduce finer discriminations (for example, a series of types of merchants ranging from the street peddler to the large wholesale trader), and there were overlaps (for example, a capitalist could be classified differently depending on the use of his property or the origins of his wealth). "In short, the economists excelled above all at defining the manual laborer, the ancestor of Marx's proletarian, who contributed nothing but his working day to the circuits of production and received only a wage equivalent to what was needed to keep him alive."[13]

These various attempts at classification revealed needs for further social description and comprehension. They not only yielded new knowledge but established new social symbols as well. They took their place among countless other social taxonomies that attempted to reconcile new and old criteria, traditions and proprieties, observation of customs and hierarchies of occupation or estate. The jurist Dareau proposed one such taxonomy in his *Traité des injures dans l'ordre judiciaire* (1775): appropriate reparations for an insult depended on the combined effect of the words used, blows struck, and slaps administered, *ratione materiae et ratione personae*. Louis-Sébastien Mercier said that eight classes were necessary to undersand the population of Paris in terms of social utility, degree of parasitism, and cultural behavior.[14] In *Contemporaines par gradation* (1783–1785), Rétif de La Bretonne proposed an order of precedence based on nuance. Titled women preceded all commoners, among whom there were subtle distinctions within the magistracy, business and finance, and even "parasitic beauties": he carefully distinguished the "mistress of an important personage" from the "procuress, bachelor's housekeeper, kept woman, and prostitute."

In every scheme of orders or classes there was an element of truth. Orders, enshrined in law, always advanced openly; classes, designated by wealth (according to Karl Marx) or status (according to Max Weber), advanced masked. Hence we must investigate not only social classifications but also social conflicts and disputes, effects of the concealment of reality that appear, inextricably intertwined, in both texts and events. They tell us about both social groups and the mobility that determined their composition, about shared representations and fundamental divisions.

Nobilities and Liberties

The Remonstrance of 1776 declared:

> To subject nobles to a tax in lieu of compulsory labor *(corvée)*, in defiance of the maxim that no one is subject to the *corvée* who is not also subject to the *taille*, is to declare them to be subject to the *corvée* like commoners . . . Thus the descendants of those ancient knights who placed the crown upon the heads of Your Majesty's forebears, the poor and virtuous lineages which for so many centuries have given their blood for the defense and increase of the monarchy, neglected and often consumed their fortunes in order to give themselves entirely to the public good, pure-bred nobles whose income is limited to the modest product of what they inherited from their forefathers, which they cultivate with their hands and often without help from any servant other than their children—gentlemen, in a word, could be exposed to the humiliation of being dragged off to the *corvée*.

Every word in the Remonstrance was carefully weighed. The purpose of the text was to thwart the "unjust proposals" and "novelties" that were taking the monarchy down a road whose end was unknown but which certainly spelled the end of fiscal privilege. To that end, the document evoked the dynasty's origins and history (about which intellectuals argued), as well as the history of the nobility itself, identified by its devotion to the "public good": the latter expression was well chosen, for it reminded the king of his duty to maintain a balance among the three orders. The text also constructed a myth: that of a poor, hardworking nobility ruined by service to the king. Historians have had a difficult time finding any group fitting this description, because with few exceptions no nobles were truly poor by the standards of poverty that applied to commoners.

History, law, and myth were thus pressed into service at a crucial moment in connection with a fundamental issue—the policy of road building, the very symbol of change and the source of the need for additional revenue—in order to put an end to disruptive policies. The occasion provided an opportunity to state a theme of fundamental importance: to interfere with the privileges of the nobility was to question the "unwritten constitution." The liberties of the nobility were the liberties of all. The diversity of the nobility in terms of seniority, function, wealth, and culture was suddenly transformed into unity. Conflict disappeared: conflict across the noble-common boundary as well as conflict within the noble order itself.

From Nobilities to Nobility

We must therefore understand what was distinctive about a controversial group if we wish to clarify the century's crucial social change: the transition from a world in which the nobility claimed and was granted clear superiority to an egalitarian society in which the claim of nobility was nothing more than a sign of vanity.

The social power of the nobility derived from its privileges, which broadly speaking can be grouped under four heads: fiscal exemptions, feudal profits (which no longer belonged exclusively to the nobility and had not for some time), ego-flattering insignia of power (some of which were taken up by new lords), and restricted employments. Contemporary controversies highlight the fact that not all nobles had equal access to these privileges. The debate revolved mainly around inequality in the face of taxation, because here the threat was real. Nobles were not supposed to have to pay taxes, which were a sign of common birth. There were three exceptions to this rule, however: it did not apply to the south of France, where the *taille* was attached to lands rather than persons, so that nobles had to pay tax on their *terres roturières;* from 1695 on the king subjected the nobility to the *capitation;* and the nobility (like the clergy) was by no means the only group exempt from taxation. There was also the anachronism of restricted employments: in the army and the navy, where belated regulation put a definitive stop to careers for commoners; in the Church, where the highest charges and most desirable benefices were reserved by the king for the old families; and finally at court, where the king, noblest of all nobles, awarded the best offices to his faithful nobles. To be a page one had to prove a nobility of 200 years. The same was true of places in prestigious educational institutions: a young lady who wished to be admitted to Saint-Cyr had to prove 140 years of nobility, while the military schools of artillery and engineering required proof of four degrees of nobility.

The enumeration of privileges underscores the variety of cases. While all nobles shared certain privileges in common, the idea that all nobles were equal was a convenient fiction that concealed a contentious reality. It was a defensive claim, which allowed the most rustic aristocrat and the most recently ennobled commoner to believe that they shared an old cultural heritage with the greatest of lords. "The unity of the nobility is a claim based on opposing principles: some make the claim in the name of tradition, others in the name of Enlightenment, of philosophy."[15] This specious unity masked the profound inequality within the second order and reflected the contamination of its ideology by the assertion of equality and by questioning, if not rejection, of the idea of hierarchy based on birth and blood, and by the transformation and standardization of high-society manners. The nobility could not remain what it had been. The conflicts that arose revealed two things: disparity of origins cast doubt on the presumption of "pure blood"; and some nobles began to insist that the boundaries of the second order be defined in terms of manners and merit.

Prejudice of Breeding, Conflicts of Rank

The older lineages generally supported the principle of immemoriality and the heredity of "pure blood." These were ideally embodied in the typical *grands*—the dukes and peers, princes of the blood, and great prelates—a few hundred men belonging to a small number of families. The *grands* enjoyed considerable wealth, which depended on the king's favor, since at least part of their income came from charges and pensions. This was true of the Condés, Contis, and Penthièvres as well as the dukes and peers. In the eighteenth century that wealth was increased by soaring ground rents and in many cases by judicious investments, yet much of it was squandered on a way of life. The indebtedness of the high nobility made it dependent on creditors, and scandalous bankruptcies such as that of the Rohan-Guéménées sapped the prestige of the court nobility. Meanwhile, in accordance with the principles of *consilium*, the high nobility pressed its political claims. The *grands* never accepted the king's absolute power, the omnipotence of his ministers, or the rise of the bureaucracy.

Invoking the ancient ideal of *consilium,* they insisted on being admitted to the king's councils (their right to do so was not challenged in the eighteenth century), on being granted important positions (generally as provincial governors) through which they could exercise patronage, and on control over military commands (which they were almost never denied even on account of unfitness or old age), and they rejected any proposal to alleviate the tax burden of the many at their expense. Because they enjoyed all the privileges and all the advantages that society had to offer, they were centrally involved in all the major debates, in which their undeniable cultural capacities were an important asset.

The country gentlemen and titled nobility of the provinces, whose wealth varied, subscribed to the same principles. Their local superiority had much more to do with their role than with their number: they stimulated a flow of goods and services between country and city, in which many now maintained temporary or permanent residences. In the best of circumstances, as in Brittany[16] and the Midi,[17] they were integrated into urban civilization and, as "good managers" of their land, they assisted in development by encouraging commerce in wine, grains, textiles, and leather, but behind the scenes. They resisted the temptations of Versailles yet remained as attentive to their privileges as to the management of their estates. Arthur Young recognized these French nobles as distant cousins of the British gentry. For them, the things that mattered most were good bookkeeping and good marriages, for it was through careful stewardship of one's property and careful attention to matrimonial strategy that one maintained one's station in life and secured the future of one's children; sons were free to choose careers in the army, the courts, or the Church. But not all nobles lived in the best of circumstances. Guy Chaussinand-Nogaret has found that below an income of four thousand livres (corresponding to a *capitation* of a few dozen livres), some 50 to 60 percent of the French nobility lived in straitened circumstances, in danger of sliding still further back into the ranks of the peasantry. Nobles ran into difficulty for any number of reasons, including debt, unfitness, and a customary fondness for large families. Difficulties gave rise to a tradition of resistance to change and a cult of arms. In the heart of the kingdom, these rural and urban nobles contributed less to change, of which they were wary, than to opposing it. Their rigorous and often ill-tempered insistence on their rights cast them in the role of social reactionaries, and they became the focal point of various passions.

Between these two worlds, a tenacious legend places a group generally characterized as the "parliamentary bourgeoisie." Now, in the eighteenth century, in the majority of provinces, it was the old and high nobility that sat in the courts. Jean Meyer has shown this to be the case in Brittany,[18] Monique Cubells in Provence,[19] François Bluche in Paris,[20] William Doyle in Bordeaux,[21] Maurice Gresset in Besançon,[22] and Jean Egret in Grenoble.[23] The robe-sword opposition no longer made sense: judicial power everywhere was captured by a minority faction of the nobility—a faction of high rank. In Paris, before 1771, out of 590 magistrate families, we find a majority of lineages ennobled before 1715 and a mere 13 percent commoners. In Brittany no commoner was received after 1660. In Aix, aristocratization was clear-cut: 42 percent of magistrates were gentlemen (with four degrees of nobility) in 1715, and 61 percent in 1789. The aging of noble magistrates was due to the natural succession of generations and to a growing intransigence that was softened only by family and professional allegiances among robe dynasties. Throughout France, the noble magistrates formed a highly endogamous milieu; they enjoyed substantial wealth, largely feudal in origin, seigneurial, based on land, and consolidated by tough, efficient, avaricious management, which produced sufficient income to subsidize urban investments, a sumptuous lifestyle, fine furnishings, and culture. Although Rennes was not Paris, it does show that the robe was jealous of its privileges and prepared to defend them, and that its attitudes were ambivalent, tolerant of profit and of the change that profit required but only as needed to defend its own status, and suspicious of innovations, especially those that were sponsored by the state and threatened that status.

What made this possible was the fact that, three centuries earlier, the monarchy had introduced a new definition of nobility, a definition that initially benefited certain old lineages but eventually became a subject of controversy. The principle according to which "the king and the king alone can make new nobles" gave rise to a series of conflicts and demands within noble society, which countered that "the king can make nobles but not gentlemen." At stake was the monarchy's control over its judicial, administrative, and even military personnel, for which it relied on the aspiration of wealthy commoners to enter the circle of the wellborn. Birth remained the vital heart of the institution of nobility, because the recently ennobled person was legally "noble" and thus entitled to engender new nobles: "Nobility is seminal fluid." Within the noble order, however, the crucial distinction remained the date at which the seminal fluid acquired its virtue. This explains the keen interest in genealogy and the need to push the date of one's family's ennoblement as far as possible into the past. Defending the boundaries of the order therefore depended on criteria of dating and control over the means of authentication. The king offered two passports to candidates for social promotion: "ennoblement by office," which was the most common route, leading to fairly rapid integration into the second order by way of court, judicial, financial, or municipal office; and "ennoblement by letter," which rewarded perhaps a thousand individuals in a century and was rarely gratuitous. A sample of 500 cases registered by the *cour des aides* of Paris in the eighteenth century shows that letters of nobility went to important traders and financiers (67), administrative agents (40), decorated military officers (76), and various magistrates and intellectuals. Gradually, ennoblement became a reward for talent, but only if backed by court favor and sustained by wealth and local prestige.

References to traditional values were supplanted by praise for economic activity, industrial relations, and works of scholarship, art, and literature. After 1760 ennoblements rewarded people possessing "the virtue and feeling that constitute the character and source of nobility." This was a way of making room for talent alongside birth, but without eliminating heredity as the dominant principle. To have done that would have required a more energetic monarchy, a monarchy capable of overcoming its contradictions sufficiently to impose new principles of social distinction, to reconcile merit and fortune, and to ensure the victory of a new form of equality in a context of continued inequality. In fact, driven in part by fiscal needs and in part by pressure from commoners hungry for recognition, the king simply knuckled under to "bourgeois treason" and its hierarchical notion of order. Wealth had always guided the nobility, which could not do without it. The social escalator continued without interruption, demonstrating once again the prestige of the noble ideal: nobility, as Pierre Goubert said, was "the ultimate stage of the bourgeoisie." But the monarchy also kept a close watch on the frontiers of nobility. Its *recherches de noblesse* no doubt encouraged a part of the bourgeoisie to reflect on its status, because these investigative procedures were designed to impede if not prevent merchants, lowborn officeholders, jurists, non-noble military officers, and men of talent from entering the highest lay order. Ultimately, we can say that if the bourgeoisie became more noble, the nobility became more bourgeois. The question that then arises is why these mechanisms failed to create a uniform, harmonious ruling class.

Noble Ideology and Enlightenment

A "cascade of contempt" ruled the second order. The high nobility reigned supreme, but within it there was perpetual wrangling about rank: princes of the blood versus dukes and peers, *gentilshommes* versus dukes, the "political nobility" of the Councils versus those excluded from membership, the party of the court versus the rest. At any moment royal favor could disrupt the stable hierarchy defined by seniority, distinction, service, and position. The robe found it difficult to live with its inferiority to the sword; nobles of the robe could not present their wives at court, or could do so only with special dispensation. In 1701 Fréauville, a *conseiller* in Parlement, published *Les Prérogatives de la robe,* in which he put forth the robe's case for superiority, for a Roman-style priority over arms *(cedant arma togae),* and for excellence of virtue as the distinctive unifying principle of nobility. This argument was repeated in articles on "Nobility" and "Estates" written by jurists of the second order for the *Encyclopédie méthodique* (1784–1786). Unity, in other words, became a necessity, and indeed had been a necessity ever since Louis XIV whenever the nobility wished to challenge the power of the monarchy. The Grand Roi had broken the tacit contract on which the monarchy was founded: he had excluded the *grands* from the Council by interpreting the representative *consilium* in a restrictive manner. It was possible to contest the king's power on these grounds, and the session of Parlement at which the Regent had allowed Louis XIV's last wishes to be overturned authorized a rethinking of tradition and of the relation between nobility and monarchy. The nobility was henceforth counted as one among many elements of the state. In return, it fulfilled its role in the great spectacle of the court, and its most eminent members, those closest to royal favor, had everything they could wish for. The state was obliged to guarantee adequate employment for its nobles and perpetuation of the privileges of nobility.

The political thought of the day was enriched by the writings of a first group of theorists of the nobility, including Fénelon and his circle, Chevreuse, Beauvillier, and Saint-Simon. These writers called for an aristocratic monarchy, in which the king would share power with the "best" of his subjects. Nobility deserved preference when it combined dignity with merit; such preference offered a rampart against arbitrary rule. The law was simply the principle of power, for it limited the arbitrariness of the sovereign while restraining his subjects from audacity. This theory, set forth in Fénelon's *Plan de gouvernement* in 1711, promoted the idea that the nobility had a necessary role to play in the construction of the nation; it defined the rights and liberties that the philosophes would later revive. If, as Boulainvilliers put it, "the nobility owes neither its position nor its rights to the monarchy," it could, for a time at any rate, embody a new form of legitimacy based on the assertion of autonomous rights rooted in history.

A second group of writers, associated with Montesquieu, synthesized the thinking of seventeenth- and eighteenth-century jurists such as Chancellor d'Aguesseau. In their writings, the condemnation of absolutism was not encumbered by historical references of the sort favored by Boulainvilliers, who insisted that commoners were descendants of the defeated Gauls, whereas nobles were descended from the victorious Franks. Instead, this second group of writers tended to emphasize the importance of intermediary powers and bodies: "In order to prevent the abuse of power, power must be organized in such a way as to impede power." The power of intermediary bodies had historical roots going back to the assemblies of the Franks. Under the law, the *parlements* shared the power of the expanded Council. But the intermediate powers were also rooted in dignity, since nobles and *corps* were independent, free of servitude. Montesquieu offered harsh criticism of the court: "Ambition in idleness, baseness in pride, desire for wealth without labor, aversion to truth, flattery, treason, perfidy, violation of all commitments, contempt for the duties of the citizen, fear of the virtue of the prince, hope for his weakness, and most of all ridicule aimed at virtue form, I believe, the minds of the majority of courtiers."[24]

He defended aristocratic equality and unity as a foundation of the rights of the nobility vis-à-vis the government, and this defense later served as a source for criticism of both absolutism and aristocratic privilege, of both the monarchical and feudal usurpations of sovereignty, for example, in the work of Mably *(Observations sur l'histoire de France)*, René Louis de Voyer d'Argenson, and still later Rousseau. In seeking to define its identity and justify its difference, aristocratic political thought helped to redefine "despotism" in the name of ancient liberties, but it also revealed internal disagreement over the question whether to include the principles of merit and equal opportunity among its values. To do so, aristocratic thinkers would have had to do what Rousseau urged them to do in his *Considérations sur le gouvernement de Pologne*, namely, renounce "the feudal barbarism that is responsible for severing from the body of the state its most numerous and sometimes healthiest portion," that is, its identity. In social policy, therefore, the nobility remained caught between corporate society and individual society. It favored the latter only to the extent that its values implied a leveling of disparities within the nobility on grounds of merit. Without compromising itself, the nobility was able to call for recognition of the liberties of individuals without accepting the principle of equal rights for all.[25]

Nobility and Wealth, Nobility and Elite

Thus, far from constituting the core of an elite society, the nobility clung to the idea that, if an autonomous society of notables were to exist, the enlargement of that ideal elite should be controlled by aristocratic principles. The central political debate was not over orders versus classes, and it was not between an aristocratic, historical faction, a bourgeois, rationalist faction, and a democratic, plebeian faction. Rather, as Denis Richet has shown, it took place within the aristocracy itself.[26] Should the aristocracy cling to an ideal based on privilege accorded to breeding? Or should it admit bourgeois notables of talent, property, and wealth, men respectful of hierarchy and eager to join the magic circle of the nobility?

Boundaries did exist, and over them bourgeois and nobility became involved in conflicts of interest intensified by clashes of ego. At the same time, there was a common cultural community in the academic societies and Masonic lodges where members of the second order could mingle with the notable elite of the Third Estate. Here there was little sign of conflict or of an obsessive concern with a supposed gap between aristocratic and bourgeois ideology. Indeed, nobles and bourgeois shared a common ideology of efficiency and utility, which justified their concern with civilizing action. The academies symbolize this common concern: they defined a sphere of equality in which talent and merit reigned supreme. Social relations in these institutions were shaped by a conciliatory cultural model. Modernity and tradition were continually linked, and the very way in which the academies functioned tended to promote a kind of equilibrium.

The ideology that they promoted was anything but orthodox: it was a "school of suspicion." The primacy of experience and observation, justified by a pedagogy of vulgarization, resulted in an esoteric body of learning. It was a culture of distinction, reserved for men of established power, a culture of transmission, perhaps, more than a culture of creation, and a culture of leisure, of exemption from the need to work, and thus a possession of authentically free citizens. The monarchy availed itself of this elite culture to preserve the support of notables, but it did so from the standpoint of intellectual administration. In other words, stability depended on compromise. To those outside, the sticking point in this compromise was the idea of privilege based on birth, which restricted access to the elite. In *Qu'est-ce que le tiers état?* (1789), Sieyès said:

> It does not astonish me that the first defenders of justice and humanity came from the first two orders. Talents stem from the exclusive use of intelligence and long habit. Members of the Third Estate should excel in talent for a thousand reasons, but enlightened ideas about public morality must first appear among the men best placed to grasp the great social relations, among whom the original motor is less commonly broken: for there are forms of knowledge that depend as much on the soul as on the intelligence.

If the text offers a fine illustration of the constant tendency to form an open elite respectful of the hierarchy of nobility but making room for property, wealth, and talent, it also implies that ultimately privilege must be eliminated and equality redefined. "The drama came when a part of the nobility flatly refused to expand the elite."[27] We can grasp the gap that existed between cultural capacity and political action by examining the nobility's attitude toward wealth and its understanding of the prospects for economic development. Here a decisive transformation took place, because the nobility, with its contradictory unity (legal class/social class), harbored a variety of positions on the economy and attitudes toward bourgeois advancement. Hence the nobility cannot be identified in any simple way with traditional agricultural France and with the purely ostentatious use of the nation's "net product." Still, although the nobility was not the feudal class that some writers have accused it of being, neither was it the paragon of capitalism that other scholars have seen in it.

Nobility, Wealth, Property

"Money governs the social evolution of families. Wealth hastens that evolution, while indigence hinders it," wrote Gaston Roupnel in his unsurpassable book on the countryside around Dijon in the seventeenth century.[28] In speaking of the nobility of the Paris Parlement, François Bluche flatly states that "the first condition to be met was that of wealth and influence." This is just another way of stating the correspondence of nobility and wealth. Wealthy bourgeois in a hurry to achieve nobility could purchase royal secretaryships for 60,000, 100,000 or 200,000 livres, but such subterfuges fooled no one. Jean Meyer has calculated that from 1715 to 1790, the market provided some 10,000 to 11,000 opportunities for ennoblement, but not all of these could be used by members of the bourgeoisie because some posts were available for sale only to existing nobles. Some posts turned over rapidly, as on the Grand Conseil (533 real changes as against 280 in theory), while others turned over slowly, as in the Parlement of Paris.

Two facts stand out. First, most of the eighteenth-century nobility consisted of families ennobled in the modern era. Second, the promotion of new families to the nobility was slower from the reign of Louis XIV to that of Louis XVI than it had been earlier. According to difficult calculations made by Guy Chaussinand-Nogaret and Jean Meyer, of 100,000 to 120,000 individual nobles from some 25,000 to 30,000 families, individual ennoblement accounted for less than half the total (perhaps one in three) in the eighteenth century.[29] The nobility was not closed: the eighteenth-century nobility was in part an ennobled bourgeoisie that chose to invest its wealth in status either through the purchase of offices or through matrimonial alliances. Thanks to its economic strength, the second order absorbed much of the country's wealth through a variety of channels.

The mechanics of ennoblement transferred real and movable capital from one side of the boundary to the other. In Beauvais on the eve of 1789, of fifty-eight participants in the assembly of the nobility, twenty-seven came from ennobled families, nearly all ennobled by purchases of royal secretaryships; five bore the name Regnonval, five the name Danse, and six the name Michel, while all were descended from illustrious families of seventeenth-century merchants and drapers. They owned land and seigneuries, but their social ascent was based on commerce and trade with the colonies. In Brittany, a majority of the three hundred persons ennobled in the eighteenth century came from either the world of trade or the navy. In Saint-Malo the entire nobility came from the bourgeoisie of merchants, privateers, and smugglers and from the monopolies of the Compagnie des Indes; some had amassed enormous fortunes. Yet the vast majority of shippers was not admitted to the second order. The Saint-Malo oligarchy melted into the Breton nobility.[30] In mercantile, maritime France, nobility was the ultimate honor bestowed on successful families. This had been going on for some time, however, and was not specific to the eighteenth century. In the Parlement of Paris, only 6 percent of families could claim to possess nobility prior to 1500. The other five hundred ennobled families came from the worlds of commerce and above all finance in its various forms. All the leading families had a farmer-general, a munitions dealer, or a financier of provincial estates in their past. In short, these were men who had contributed to the construction of the monarchy by advancing, collecting, or investing the revenue from direct and indirect taxes. The dealings of *les grands,* the clergy, and the king brought new blood to the nobility of France and through alliances and marriages sustained the old families and the highest feudal aristocracy.

What happened once the frontier was crossed, when the ennobled individual gave up his original business activities so as not to derogate from nobility and in order to live quietly on his income from land, pensions, and state charges? The question is important because of its implications for the conception of society itself. Did these customs favor the society of privilege, or did they in some ways at least promote economic innovation and capitalist development?

One can only assent to the second question while acknowledging that the first demands a careful response. For a majority of the nobility, those who counted on the local level, in the seigneuries, most of their economic power derived from seigneurial property: land, with all the rights, privileges, and powers associated with it, was, as we have seen, still the principal social symbol. The noble was always a landlord (all the regional studies—on Brittany, the Toulousain, and Paris—with variations, confirm this), but there was no equality of property. A minority of major landowners coexisted with a majority of minor lords. There were transfers of property between different segments of the nobility: in Brittany, for example, the *parlement* and the ennobled were winners, while the court nobility were losers. Agricultural dynamism and social capacity for action to concentrate properties and launch initiatives varied with farming ability and income. There were prestige properties and income-producing properties, many of the latter being estates cultivated by modern farmers who served as models of agricultural capitalism which peasants either imitated or opposed. Landownership did not unify the nobility, even though it remained fundamental: no landlord ever renounced his rights. For the bourgeoisie, the purchase of land went along with social mobility. The seigneurial reaction as well as the passion for agronomy were also responses—different but sometimes associated—to the times, ways of overcoming difficulties and facing up to needs. Those needs grew most rapidly for nobles with social connections in the cities or at court; such connections exerted strong pressures. On the whole, however, the landed nobility, like the bourgeoisie and peasants with land to sell, benefited from the rise in prices that favored all landowners; in addition, along with the owners of seigneuries, they were entitled to dues that were rising faster than prices.

With respect to the new economic forms, then, the nobility was not united in either rejection or participation. A majority of noble families that were barely able to maintain their rank had neither the means nor the training nor the intellectual or psychological incentive to immerse themselves in business. The rest, however, were subject to a variety of pressures ranging from a background in affairs to sufficient revenues to expenses rising fast enough to require still greater income. How did such people become involved in the development of capitalism? Going into business or launching an enterprise did not require a conversion: profits could of course be obtained indirectly through intermediaries or investments. We have seen how this worked in the case of royal finance. Someday scholars will have to take a fresh look at how luxury consumption stimulated trade and industry. In some cases, nobles, either by themselves or in conjunction with bourgeois merchants, traders, bankers, and financiers, played a large part in promoting commercial capitalism. To begin with, those who were ennobled by purchase of a royal secretaryship (of whom there were more than three thousand in the eighteenth century) were under no moral obligation to cease their business activities: no ennobled Nantes shipper closed his business upon assuming his title. Furthermore, nobles almost everywhere were involved in local commerce. The grain and wine producers of the Toulousain are a case in point, as are the wine producers of the Bordeaux region. For such men it was easy to expand from local to international trade, as Montesquieu showed, as well as to large-scale transoceanic commerce.

The high nobility invested in all sorts of businesses ranging from maritime commerce to colonial companies, plantations, and the slave trade. After 1770 one finds prominent nobles in trading companies such as the Compagnie du Sénégal, the Compagnie du Nord, the Compagnie de la Correspondance Maritime, and the Compagnie de Cayenne. In Brittany, the Luynes, the d'Espevients, and the Chateaubriands—families belonging to the *noblesse dormante,* or "sleeping nobility"—went into shipping and the slave trade to refurbish their escutcheons. The *noblesse débarquée,* or "immigrant nobility" from England and Ireland, controlled a substantial proportion of the trade in ports such as Nantes and Saint-Malo. Along with the ennobled, they formed a milieu that, while not exactly a commercial nobility, was closely tied to commerce. In Paris, Yves Durand has shown that the profession of finance was no longer compatible with common birth: all the farmers-general sought ennoblement, and we find traces of their involvement in colonial and maritime ventures. Voltaire, comte de Ferney, took an interest in and encouraged modern farming techniques. In short, "derogation" could be overcome—the state played a fundamental role here—and commerce could lead to ennoblement.

Similarly, a segment of the nobility took a hand directly or indirectly in manufacturing and mining industries. Here, the old nobility gave no gifts to the new: using straw men, it invested in joint stock companies, whose anonymity served as a screen. It also used its rights of domain to exploit, or pay others to exploit, mines, quarries, and forests. When coupled with an interest in science, the quest for profit produced some very lucky businessmen, among them Buffon, who was involved in any number of business ventures. In 1787 his income was 110,000 livres, 40 percent of which came from government pensions, charges, and bonds and 60 percent from land and industrial ventures in glass-making, coal, metalworking, and publishing. He was the very type of the Ancien Régime capitalist, "not so much a great businessman as a great man in business," at once seigneur and entrepreneur, rational calculator and amateur, free marketeer and protégé of the state.[31] There were similar men throughout France: in Brittany, for example, where *parlementaires* vied with *les grands* (the Condés, Rohans, Villeroys, and Chaulnes) for forges, as well as in Dauphiné, the Nord, Champagne, central France, Le

Creusot, Lorraine, Franche-Comté, and Burgundy. In Anzin, the duc de Croÿ and the marquis de Coeuvres poured seigneurial and domainial rights as well as capital into coal until they controlled the majority of French production. From Hayange in Lorraine, the ennobled de Wendels speculated on protected state business and naval supply contracts. They set up a factory in Indret to manufacture cannons, then another in Ruelle, and finally in Le Creusot.

Countless nobles joined in advanced technological and industrial ventures, as well as in speculation in real estate and stocks. In short, much of the nobility took part in the new economic regime while clinging to political ideas and social myths that justified its superiority, perhaps because its "liberties," which is to say, its deep identity, defined by battle with the state and defended on the frontier of privilege, was at stake in the struggle over "liberty." Between "liberties" and "liberty" the gap was huge. Do not let the words deceive: they did not resonate with the same meaning for all. As in the *cahiers de doléance* (declarations of grievances), most nobles could accept at least some of the new ideas without the slightest thought of giving up their fundamental privileges. For some nobles the goal was to save the monarchy from despotism, while for others the very existence of their class or order was at stake. The "controversy over the commercial nobility" demonstrated in the intellectual realm how a change of estate and occupation could raise questions about the whole organization of society.

The Controversy over the Commercial Nobility

Two markers staked out the ideological terrain over which a controversy erupted in 1757 when Abbé Gabriel François Coyer published a brochure entitled "La Noblesse commerçante." The first was the monarchy's policy of creating a hybrid state that would have combined the prestige and privileges of the nobility with the lucrative activities of the bourgeoisie, either by abolishing the principle of derogation or by granting letters of nobility to merchants or allowing ennobled individuals to continue to engage in commerce. The other was the existence of a segment of the nobility which, while not poor, was at least relatively impoverished and whose prospects were limited by lack of resources to purchase military or administrative commissions or live in a manner commensurate with its rank.

The derogation issue was first of all a legal matter, and there were, as we have seen, many ways to get around it if one had the necessary economic wherewithal or social or political influence. But it was perhaps even more a cultural issue, for although a segment of the noble order took part in "commerce" (the word referred to both trade and industry), a larger segment disapproved. Living within the restricted horizons of their estates, and deeply attached to the ethic of "good stewardship," many nobles were not ready for the sirens of profit and consumption. Furthermore, the representatives of the Third Estate, of the mercantile and manufacturing guilds, had always quietly opposed the edicts which, from the time of Colbert to that of Moreau de Séchelles (*contrôleur général des finances* in 1757), had sought to allow the nobility to engage in commerce without derogation. The Conseil du Commerce received complaints from bourgeois opposed to allowing nobles into the guilds: nobles already had enough privileges without allowing them to enrich themselves without paying taxes. The struggle proceeded on two fronts: within the nobility, where either local custom triumphed (derogation was still prohibited in Brittany and Marseilles) or else some subterfuge was adopted (nobles engaged in business by way of straw men or intermediaries); and between the nobility and commoners, where exclusion from the guilds prevailed except where the royal government used its monopoly to encourage essential enterprises. In any case, prejudice and tradition coupled with lack of economic know-how and resources discouraged derogation for most nobles.

The controversy revealed a real conflict of opinion among administrators and economists concerned over the need to do something about the discrepancy between the necessity of commerce and the discredit that attached to it. Everyone agreed that commerce was an indispensable ingredient of state power and of a prosperous economy: "It is the life of the people and the health of the state," said Abbé de Saint-Pierre. "If agriculture is the basis of a state, commerce is the soul of agriculture. Therefore let no one reproach me for neglecting agriculture [in favor of commerce]," wrote Abbé Coyer. But the scorn for merchandise was still palpable, as was appreciation for the value of land and courage in battle; commerce was criticized on moral grounds for encouraging luxury and for sowing the seeds of decomposition in an organic society with a Christian economy. For Montesquieu, commerce was a necessity; yet at the same time the nobility should be forbidden to engage in it because of the need to preserve the liberties of the *corps intermédiaires:*

> It is contrary to the spirit of commerce that the nobility should engage in it in a monarchy; it is contrary to the spirit of monarchy that nobles should engage in commerce in it . . . The practice in this country is very wise: merchants are not nobles, but they can become nobles . . . They have no more certain way out of their profession than to do well or prosper in it, as people generally do who are self-sufficient.

Political and social wisdom thus reinforced the agrarian values imposed by the success of Physiocracy. Agriculture, the most honorable as well as the most debased profession, was the "soul of commerce," and commerce sustained various prejudices with perverse consequences for development.

The profusion of texts produced in response to Coyer's brochure reveals what was at stake in the polemic: Should the nobility be encouraged to take part in commerce and become involved in other forms of economic activity? Should impoverished nobles be urged to share in the progress of the economy in their own interest and in the interest of France, but at the risk of being absorbed into the other classes of society?[32] The Jesuit's work often borrowed ideas for productive development that were passed on from mercantilism to liberalism, but its provocative, paradoxical tone distinguished it from the work of many other economists. Coyer had a knack for boldly associating antinomic terms. He challenged the idea of derogation and opposed those who wanted to limit the nobility to waging war and managing its estates. His work met with immediate success. The press took an interest in it, and twenty or so books appeared either in support or in opposition. The chevalier d'Arc scored a notable success by defending the military role of the nobility, preserving the distinction of orders, and maintaining the concept of honor. Adversaries of Coyer's book praised Arc's. The marquis d'Argenson backed Coyer, as did Pinezon du Sel, a gentleman manufacturer from Brittany, and Sera, the author of *Commerce ennobli*. Billardon de Sauvigny *(L'Une ou l'autre ou la Noblesse commerçante et militaire)*, a soldier, man of letters, and royal censor, tried to reconcile the opposing views. The government fretted; the *parlement* of Grenoble published an attack on "the confusion of ranks," and Forbonnais published a response. Additional texts continued to roll off the presses. Things calmed down somewhat after 1759, but until 1789 some additional number of pamphlets or articles on the controversy were published each year. The whole controversy is evidence of the way in which economic thought influenced public opinion.[33]

Coyer acknowledged the indigence of some nobles and criticized the listlessness of French commerce. His proposed remedy implied an end to derogation, something that was already happening out in the countryside. Attacking the concept of aristocratic honor as he did, Coyer turned the monarchy on its head, substituting the honor and glory of business for the preeminence of arms and blood and hereditary courage. His critics charged that this led to a confusion of estates, that Coyer, in abolishing derogation, had destroyed the equilibrium that the state maintained between commoners and nobles. Neither the Third Estate nor the nobility accepted this idea. Coyer had no intention of making a revolution, since he proposed reinforcing the powers of the privileged; the question of fiscal privileges loomed behind the elimination of derogation. The *parlements*, consulted on the subject of a proposed edict intended to facilitate the involvement of nobles in commerce by exempting them from the requirement to register with consular authorities, approved this idea; the *intendants* and *députés de commerce* were also in favor, but opposition from the six *corps* and many urban guilds doomed the proposal. The controversy forced the government to draw back. There would be additional "commercial nobles" but no "commercial nobility," for to have created such an entity would have made it necessary to compensate those subjects who worked and paid taxes by eliminating the fiscal privileges of the commercial nobility, assigning equal rights and obligations to all.

Thanks to the controversy over the "commercial nobility," we are now in a position to answer the question of orders versus classes, nobility versus elites, posed at the outset. The controversy reveals a society in which the highest levels of the bourgeoisie and the highest levels of the aristocracy tended, in terms of economic practice and social relations, to break the legal framework of orders and classes in such a way as to form a single existential group that can be seen as the predecessor of the notables in nineteenth-century bourgeois society. At the same time, however, a substantial segment of the society was unwilling to give up its existing privileges. The compromise around the "commercial nobility" was like the academic compromise: it was based on an idea of "acceptable" social mobility that gained the support of men of wealth and talent prepared to accept the rules of privilege. And it ran up against the same obstacles: the existence of a group of people excluded from the benefits of such a compromise, debarred from entry, together with the contradictions of a monarchy unable to free itself from an order it was pledged to protect. Every crisis and every failed reform proved the reality of these obstacles.

13

<hr/>

Public Space

WE HAVE GRADUALLY begun to focus on an issue that was fundamental to the future of traditional French society. Criticism of all aspects of human action, including political action, had begun to be heard. The symbols of monarchy had lost their transcendent power over men's minds and were being called into question. The preconditions for a profound social transformation were in place. But how could a space be created for politics in a society whose nature and traditions were apparently inimical to such a thing? In the nineteenth century, Alexis de Tocqueville was the first to raise this question, which has continued to preoccupy historians ever since.[1] The eighteenth century witnessed the birth of a realm of public opinion, situated apart from the real society, the royal government, and the practical, efficient action of the centralized monarchical administration and led by "men of letters" interested in an "abstract and literary politics." Listen to Tocqueville:

> When we remember also that the French nation, excluded as it was from the conduct of its own affairs, lacking in political experience, shackled by ancient institutions and powerless to reform them—when we remember that this was the most literary-minded of all nations and intellectually quickest in the uptake, it is easy to understand why our authors became a power in the land and ended up as its political leaders.
>
> In England writers on the theory of government and those who

actually governed co-operated with each other, the former setting forth
their new theories, the latter amending or circumscribing these in the
light of practical experience. In France, however, precept and practice
were kept quite distinct and remained in the hands of two quite independent groups. One of these carried on the actual administration
while the other set forth the abstract principles on which good government should, they said, be based; one took the routine measures appropriate to the needs of the moment, the other propounded general laws
without a thought for their practical application; one group shaped the
course of public affairs, the other that of public opinion.

Thus alongside the traditional and confused, not to say chaotic social
system of the day there was gradually built up in men's minds an
imaginary ideal society in which all was simple, uniform, coherent,
equitable, and rational in the full sense of the term. It was this vision
of the perfect state that fired the imagination of the masses and little by
little estranged them from the here and now.[2]

This fundamental conceptual text,[3] shaped in part by a new concern
with interpreting the facts—facts that Tocqueville, a noble of ancient
stock, had to face in the upheavals of the early nineteenth century—and
in part by the need to strike a balance between aristocratic liberties and
democracy, combined political and social interpretations without reducing
one to the other. The development of the centralized state caused civil
society to disintegrate and thus contributed to the rise of new ideologies.
As François Furet has pointed out, it was the historical process of the
development of the monarchy that created the conditions under which the
monarchy could be challenged. The royal administration juxtaposed
seigneurial loyalties, local and customary forces, bureaucratic rationality,
and programs of modernization. It was an unstable compromise between
a modern state and principles of social organization inherited from feudal
times, a power at once modern and archaic.[4] Caught in this contradiction,
it inevitably alienated society's elites and lost its legitimacy, which was
transferred to the intellectuals. Genuine authority was thus severed from
power as the administration was cut off from politics. Debate was possible only outside the government.

Tocqueville's explanation highlights two changes. First, there was a
breakdown of communication between theory and practice, general ideas
and experience, imagination and reality, the ideal city and the actual city.

Second, men of letters became not a ruling class but the aristocracy of a substitute government, at once omnipotent and powerless. Society was deprived of its real weight by the Ancien Régime's lack of true representative institutions; everyone excluded from participation in public affairs was drawn to the new elite. Tocqueville's critique of the monarchy emphasizes three key factors: that the new political thought grew out of a process of unification of classes and spaces (the Enlightenment was not limited to the bourgeoisie or to Paris); that intellectual politics meshed perfectly with the actions of the centralized administrative government; and that the monarchy was shaped by a new cultural unity despite the persistence of certain disparities arising out of old rights and privileges. In this interpretation the opposition between government and "literary politics" is central. Indeed, it may be characteristic of the political structure of the Ancien Régime.[5]

To understand this culture, then, we must first criticize two clichés: first, the certitude that the action of the centralized monarchy was monolithic and inexorable, and second, that intellectuals had an abstract concept of action totally unrelated to the world of practice. In regard to the monarchy, one has to recognize the existence of modes of representation characteristic of an inegalitarian society, the primary purpose of which was to produce unanimity in favor of the status quo yet which were also capable of playing a fundamental role in the opposition to despotism: included under this head are the parlementary crises of the second half of the eighteenth century, as well as the political debate that developed around the Jansenist issue, as we saw earlier. The intellectual agitation and fermentation of the period exposed to public view the state's private mysteries and their influence on thinking, but more than that, the burgeoning debate began to focus on the very nature of the monarchy and its fundamental principles.[6]

As for the intellectuals, the idea that they had a totally abstract and unreal conception of politics runs up against the reality of the Enlightenment and the impossibility of drawing an artificial boundary between realms of elaboration, areas of practice, and the philosophies themselves. There was no single "philosophy of the Enlightenment" but a number of distinct currents of thought. The innovation of the century lay in the multiplicity of practices and theories that developed in response to utilitarian demands and concrete questions. A new cultural sociability developed, a sociability rooted in the need to manage space and people in an efficient manner. The nature of that sociability, and the institutions and ideas that supported it, indicated a profound need for new types of social organization and representation. The state, an active agent of reform, served the Enlightenment as a cultural intermediary. What we need to understand, then, is why the state failed to achieve its goals, for if, as Tocqueville said, it contributed to the "revolutionary education" of the people, this was not to its own advantage.[7]

Our goal, then, is to understand how public opinion or public space emerged without destroying the continuity between the state and the divided civil society. Historians in recent years have borrowed the ideas of "public opinion" and "public space" from the work of the German philosopher Jürgen Habermas, who showed how "a bourgeois political sphere" developed in the eighteenth century as a space for debate free from state control and critical of the state itself.[8] If he characterized the new sphere as essentially "bourgeois," it was not so much because it coincided with the interests and ideas of the triumphant bourgeoisie as because it formed outside the traditional spaces for debate and information associated with the public authorities and court society. It was defined first of all as a place in which private individuals could make public use of their reason. It coincided with the constitution of a civil society based on trade and labor as well as with an increase in individual autonomy created by a process of privatization within the family itself. Communication was now assumed to take place between equals. As old *corps* and customs broke down, the spheres of thought and action expanded without limit; nothing was now exempt from critical judgment. The formation of a public space marked a departure from traditional modes of representation involving the king, the state and its administration, and the traditional *corps*.[9] Men of the Enlightenment now assumed this role.

This major innovation can be looked at in two ways: either ideologically, in terms of ideas and the responses to them, or in terms of the development of practices that paved the way for the reign of criticism. Although I will take the latter, social and cultural, approach, other approaches may be just as interesting. In any case, the approach I will take sheds a different light on the invention of public opinion and on the ways in which criticism emanating from civil society began the process of dissolution of the Ancien Régime. In addition, we will discover some of the limits of a process that, in spite of appearances, did not proceed toward an obvious goal because parts of society were left out.

Progress can be measured along three fronts: educational sociability, cultural sociability, and—closely related to these as both cause and effect—the sociability associated with reading and seeing. In these three areas one can pinpoint simultaneous changes in the scale of phenomena and inequalities of opportunity and note high and low points in a realm in which cities had a clear advantage. Schools, learned societies, and booksellers—elements of the cultural apparatus of any modern society—depended on economic and social conditions. They developed where administrative and financial efforts created a milieu prepared to embrace the new cultural outlook, and the rules of access were different from what we might think.[10] It was a phenomenon of scarcity more than abundance—of scarcity linked to the economy, which limited investment opportunities and ascribed a particular role to private financing of schools, theaters, and libraries. Scarcity was also linked to exclusion on grounds of manners or ability: access to culture was governed by rules that, although generally elitist and selective, varied from place to place and group to group. Finally, there was scarcity due to the small number of people involved in cultural activities, a group that could hope to achieve stability only at the end of a controversial process of expansion. Thus, throughout the century there were clashes between those who favored a broadening of cultural opportunities (hence capacity for change) and those who favored limiting such opportunities.

From Education to Sociability

Access to public space, the influence of which became apparent during the revolutionary decade, required the right background and education. Most people were excluded. Now that everyone goes to school for a relatively long period of time, it is hard to imagine an era when things were different. In this respect a great change took place in the eighteenth century: going to school became the norm, and the purpose of education changed in the process.

Schooling made inroads everywhere. Education without schooling—which once took place mainly in the family and on the job, for a period of time that depended on social position—now became education in addition to school coupled with apprenticeship. Here, the family had a distinctive role to play, private circumstances were important, and attitudes toward childhood were crucial. Over the long run, the interplay between formal schooling and education at home determined the boundary between the private sphere and the public, for the public sphere was no longer governed by general acceptance of the representations of power and its signs, while the private sphere emancipated itself by promoting the values of intimacy and freedom of self-representation. The state defined its own educational goals at the same time, and these figured in debates over reform.

Older ways of learning lost their preeminence in the eighteenth century. The new society believed in pedagogy, the ultimate arbiter: for the philosophes, this was a key to human liberation. All men were by nature capable of thinking, but their ability had been sapped by priests and kings; education would liberate them. This controversial conception of the role of education reflects a mastery of intellectual process (the textbook came into being at this time), a turn away from rote learning and memorization, an appeal to the intelligence, and a transition from education for the few for the purpose of social reproduction and control to education for social mobility, spiritual and intellectual freedom, and social transformation. The school therefore became the focal point of battles between church and state, nation and family. It was obliged to choose between producing perpetual students and producing citizens, between reproduction and liberation. Access to culture and, in the long run, to the public sphere was thus accompanied by social diversification. Differences of access reflected specific social divisions, which can be mapped and measured and which reflected inequalities in access to education.

School, Government, Education

Make no mistake: for the majority the family remained the primary place where knowledge was acquired. To their offspring families transmitted a culture, a style of dress, and specific skills as well as roles, norms, and disciplines. The father and mother, *patron* and *bourgeoise*, were professional and spiritual educators who created a patriarchal economy. Apprenticeship was designed to impart the "secrets" of a trade as well as respect for master craftsmen—"as if they were our fathers," Jacques Savary says in the *Parfait Négociant*. As children grew older and reached adolescence, they gained greater freedom to spend their leisure time as they wished, and joined groups in which they would remain until they married and had their first children. These groups defended the interests of the youth cohort. They preserved society's memory even as they represented its future. The Church was continually called upon to mediate between families and youth groups by imposing its own norms. Everywhere, youth groups helped to create social bonds across classes, creating a network of solidarities and a space within which young people could learn the ways of the world. The strength of such groups vis-à-vis the authorities should not be overlooked, and here by authorities I mean both the hierarchy of notables and the patriarchy. These early experiences of social life, which had the power to shape a civilization, were strongly influenced by schooling.[11]

In this respect, the eighteenth century repeated the legacy of developments that can be traced back to the Reformation. A key moment in the Counter-Reformation came when the bishops turned their attention from the clergy, which was now much better educated than in the past, to the people and the "prodigious ignorance found in the countryside." The need to win converts through Christian education continued from the seventeenth century into the eighteenth. Education was a battle against ignorance of religious truths. In the clash between the oral culture of the people and the written culture of the clergy, the clergy sought to teach first a catechism and morality and later the rudiments of culture: reading and writing. Episcopal texts emphasized the need for schools, and the assemblies of the clergy agreed. The bishops stressed the need for teaching religious practice through regular spiritual exercises; reading and writing were secondary. Content was more important than method, and the conception of the child as a passive receptacle for precepts was more important than any pedagogical technique. An obsession with morality required separate instruction for boys and girls.

The schools of the Counter-Reformation thus emphasized Christianity and culture, but their real mission was to combat heresy. This is where the monarchy had a legislative role to play, a role reflected in the ordinances of 1698 and 1724. The idea of making schooling compulsory and of requiring every community to support a school can be interpreted in two ways: it was motivated by a desire either to drive out the Protestant minority or to impart universal education, since the ordinances required *all children,* even "former Catholics," to attend school. The terms of the law suggest a desire for universal schooling and indicate how students were to be recruited and how teachers were to be paid. Implementation of this legislation was left to the *intendants,* who noticed a decline of the

Protestant threat over time and who "added to the king's silence" (there was no royal legislation on schools after 1724) their own hostility to rural schooling. There is considerable evidence of a desire to reduce the number of schools, and the issue led to a new conflict between the Church and the administration and further opportunities for both rural and urban communities to mobilize in order to save their schools.

The results of these confrontations are evident in two areas: the location of schools and the acquisition of sufficient cultural skills to take a first step into the world of information and exchange. Access to schooling was quite unevenly distributed until the nineteenth century. North of the Loire, schools were quite dense. In some provinces, such as Champagne, education was seen as a virtual right. In the south, however, schooling was much harder to come by. Only towns with populations above 1,500 or 2,000—practically small cities—maintained regular and permanent schools. Cities had always enjoyed an advantage over rural areas in this respect, and that advantage did not diminish despite increased school construction in the countryside. Many local factors influenced the location of schools: wealth, concentration of the population (a scattered population was nearly always a disadvantage), ease of travel, and proximity of Protestant areas coupled with the intensity of religious conflict. In general, it was the demand for education that made the difference, and that demand depended on people's attitudes (some preferred training outside the classroom). Educational problems could be solved if the community became involved: typical problems included recruiting teachers, finding money to pay them, and designating classrooms in which they could teach. Education was something that people clearly desired.

That desire is manifest in the success of literacy training, which can be taken as an index of cultural level and measured (not without difficulty) in terms of statistics regarding signatures. Although the available data do not allow us to distinguish clearly between people who had fully mastered writing and those who may only have been able to write their own names in a stumbling hand, we do get a clearer picture of what was at stake in the transition from oral culture to written culture. Writing opened up a new world in which what counted was the ability to manipulate signs. The ability to read and write offered access to lists, accounts, notes, manuscripts, and printed texts and thus the ability to acquire knowledge, organize one's thoughts in various ways, and augment one's memory. In the long run, everyone was supposed to learn to read and write: this was the intent of the law. But some people, such as Rousseau, saw this as a source of decadence. In the *Essai sur l'origine des langues,* he argued that education increased alienation. Perhaps; but it was far more surely an instrument of profound liberation. To master reading and writing was to reconcile three worlds: the world of things, the world of sounds that designated those things, and the world of letters that mimicked and therefore recalled those sounds. The century's measurable progress on a variety of fronts had prepared people to accept change.

Illiteracy declined from 71 percent in 1700 to 63 percent in 1790. The north maintained a considerable advantage, but the south had begun to catch up, while Brittany, Auvergne, and the Basque region stagnated. The gap between city and countryside persisted everywhere, but urban advances were strongly influenced by regional differences. Because internal migration was considerable, the increase of literacy was not linear, and its pattern varied from place to place. Finally, literacy among women increased sharply, and at a faster pace in the north than in the south. Social differences diminished but did not disappear. Gender differences were less marked in the cities, not only among the more prosperous commoners such as artisans and shopkeepers but also in peripheral and working-class populations. Social status, occupation, and type of work were more important than geographic differences in determining literacy rates.

In general, elementary education imposed a basic discipline of body, soul, and manners on rural as well as urban populations. The little savage ignorant of the ways of the world went to school and came out an educated, disciplined Christian subject. More regular schooling and better organized instruction inculcated the same principles everywhere, even if there was greater resistance to the lessons taught in some areas than in others. Economic imperatives also dictated greater homogeneity, as did new utilitarian needs. Ultimately it became possible to divorce the fundamental religious purpose of education from the practical methods that had long since formed the basis of instruction.[12]

Elite Strategies and New Aspirations

Liberation through education became the destiny of many individuals: the apprentice, whose job was to learn; the soldier, generally better educated than the rest of the population; the domestic servant, who was deemed clever and therefore worthy of a better wage if able to write; and the clerk, tax collector, and other state officials.

Four levels of cultural hierarchy stand out, although the boundaries between them were fluid and there were local variations. The illiterate, at the bottom of the ladder, were all too apt to fall prey to the shrewdly literate one rung up: the businessman, the landlord, the lender, the tithe owner, the landlord's agent, and sometimes even the curé. Even the wary were obliged to sign documents, and increasingly they had to deal with papers from the tax authorities, the Church, and even the police. Their strength lay in solidarity and in the advice of people in the know. They had a capacity for resistance derived from their everyday experience and age-old tradition. Neither totally alienated from the outside world nor totally free in their own world, they became the focal point of the combat between the Church and the school and the struggle over whether the role of the state should be one of social control or liberation.

The next level of the hierarchy included those who could read, write, and do sums: the artisan who owned his own business, the shopkeeper, the foreman, the shopgirl, the lord's steward, the prosperous farmer with ambitions, the postmaster. For them, reading and writing were matters of daily necessity but not constant practice. They needed to check the terms of leases and orders, write letters, discuss estimates, and keep accounts. The law made literacy essential. Many of the barely literate wrote with difficulty and found reading laborious, but they could do accurate sums and use their arithmetic to justify demands for higher salaries and bigger budgets, as in the factories of Lyons. For these people, literacy was a workaday tool and had little effect on social attitudes, yet this was the milieu in which change was most dramatic. While the more prosperous farmers were still rooted in the culture of the countryside, they also heeded the rumblings of the market and speculated on price fluctuations. People in the towns were strongly influenced by the spillover from the Enlightenment in the larger cities, and some saw themselves as writers in the rough called upon to attest to the changes affecting their fellow citizens. This fermentation, though frightening to many notables, gave the towns an advantage when it came to political action.

At a still higher level of the cultural hierarchy we find the entrepreneur and wealthy merchant, who could dispense with Latin but did need to write French—increasingly so as time went by. Businessmen, concerned mainly with profits, planning, and the balance sheet, read account books, price lists, advertisements, and memos more than anything else. Commercial correspondence was a daily necessity. Local judges acquired a veneer of cultivation from their legal studies, while rentiers and landlords were not obliged to do much reading beyond what was required for business. Studies of libraries do show a slow transformation in the reading matter of merchants over the course of the eighteenth century, however.

Finally, at the summit of the cultural hierarchy were the men of letters, who could read and write both Latin and French. These were men confident in themselves and their ability to lead others. Those whose educational strategies earned them this privileged status gained access to the theater of knowledge and power. The educational changes made in the curricula of the *collèges* in the seventeenth century had a profound impact on the elite. Three-quarters of these institutions were located in cities with populations over five thousand. They were sustained by private and local public initiatives sponsored by bishops, *bailliages*, *parlements*, provincial estates, and municipal governments as well as by the teaching congregations, each of which had its own educational policy. The Jesuits, with more than 100 of the 350 *collèges* in operation in 1760, had solid roots throughout the country. So did the Oratorians, but their schools were concentrated in the north and west as well as in Champagne and Burgundy; in Ile-de-France they had only two schools, the most celebrated of which, Juilly, enjoyed a national reputation: Montesquieu studied there. The Doctrinaires' schools were mainly in the southwest and south. Small schools could be found in even the humblest cities, reflecting the success of an eighteenth-century ideal of which most people approved: instruction in the humanities should be made available to as many people as possible and as close to home as possible. As many as one in fifty French children attended *collèges*, and in some cities the figure was as high as one in ten or even one in five.

The number of children in *collèges* rose to just below fifty thousand in 1789, but a growing number of students chose new institutions, and the sons of the wealthiest families were able to experiment with tutors, boarding schools, and riding academies, for which the demand was increasing. Educational mobility, which accompanied social mobility, enabled students to broaden their horizons. Privilege was reinforced, the nobility having established itself in the *collèges* in the eighteenth century; but students of all social classes were admitted in theory and, to judge by registration lists, in practice, though most came from the bourgeoisie or privileged classes, with a sprinkling of sons of well-to-do shopkeepers and artisans and a few bright young peasants. The privileged students stood out in two ways: wealthier families could afford to send several children to the *collège* and leave them there throughout their adolescence; and less wealthy students (and a few poor ones) generally started later and left earlier, except in unusual cases. Between two-thirds and three-quarters of the students came from the elite, and they invariably jumped all the hurdles; many good students from outside the elite had to leave school after a year or two even though they passed all their courses. Adaptation to the culture of the educational institution was of no avail against economic necessity, but it did sometimes produce students capable of overcoming all obstacles, proving not only the virtues of talent but also the merits of the institution that was clever enough to recognize them. The whole educational system was based on this inegalitarian process, for its purpose was to train future lawyers, judges, and bureaucrats. An even smaller minority went on to the universities.

There was no sharp distinction between the old institutions and the *collèges*. Students moved back and forth between them, and some schools offered teaching by the congregations without the usual degrees. Before Cahors was combined with Toulouse, there were twenty-four universities in France. They faced competition from the *collèges* and seminaries, however, and their student bodies did not grow rapidly. Academic circulation was reduced, and recruitment was regionalized. The job market stabilized. All told there were perhaps ten to twelve thousand students in the universities. Recruitment rates varied from discipline to discipline: for theologians and even jurists it was stable, while for physicians it increased in Montpellier and especially in Paris. Growth in all faculties was modest. As usual, the big universities were the winners: Paris, Montpellier, Toulouse. Turncoats fled the theological sanctuary for the classes of Aesculapius and Themis. Yet fewer than one young man in a hundred reached the universities, which limited their role to turning out professionals in an efficient manner. Paris was already enticing the provincial elite to the Sorbonne, where future bishops were trained, and to the law courts, where future magistrates and administrators apprenticed. In the universities the sons of the privileged and children of officeholders dominated the social hierarchy, which made room for a few new men. Sons succeeded their fathers. A few talented students stood out: as in the *collèges,* they served as justification for the entire system. Women were totally excluded. Their fate remained unchanged, and only a few people, generally urban and wealthy, took any interest in the education of women beyond elementary school. Only a few feminists, Condorcet among them, called for equal education for men and women.

What was taught in the *collèges* fortified the stronger sex. In the closed, idealized world of the Latin-based curriculum, students learned to think of the age, the world, and themselves by looking at the past, Christian tradition, and pagan authors. The *collège* trained orators to exercise the *magisterium* of the word in churches and councils; it produced masters of the "art of eloquence" and guardians of established norms. Little time was devoted to science, which was postponed until the end of the curriculum and therefore available only to a minority, who enjoyed hearing about the remarkable curiosities of nature from Jesuit physicists and Oratorian scholars. Above all, students learned to be what they were supposed to be: they were taught how to groom themselves, to dance, and to act on stage, which improved bearing as well as morals. In short, they were taught to conform. The educational ideal was not one of advancement. If a few of the disadvantaged were admitted along with the elite, it was to subject them to the common mold. This process of cultural unification was not questioned until after 1750. Two developments cast the system in a new light: the clash over schooling and the impossibility of reforming the *collège*.

The administrative and political elites were hostile to any large-scale schooling throughout the century, increasingly so as time went by. In part this hostility expressed the old mercantilist fear that wealth and production would decline and social parasitism increase if the labor force were diminished. Hence expanded educational opportunity would mean decreased tax revenues: the Physiocrats, agronomists, and Voltaire himself accepted this argument. The *procureur général* Le Chalotais declared that "the good of society demands that the people have no more knowledge than their occupations require." Most Enlightenment thinkers opposed teaching peasants how to read and write, while the Church and especially the lower clergy favored it, not without contradiction, for although there was good reason to be wary of impious books, the needs of the community had to be taken into account. Therein lay the first difficulty in moving from subject to citizen by way of education. On this point even Rousseau was much more conservative than his own political theory. His argument was not economic but moral: he justified not educating peasants

432

on the grounds of a distinction between nature and culture. As he wrote in *La Nouvelle Héloïse:* "Those who are destined to live in bucolic simplicity do not need to develop their faculties in order to be happy, and their hidden talents are like the gold mines of the Valais, which for the sake of the public good cannot be exploited . . . Do not educate the peasant's child, because education does not suit him." A passage like this shows that the motives of obscurantists can be hard to fathom, but clearly there were limits to extending public space and the freedom to criticize to lower levels of society.

At the upper levels, by contrast, the real battle was not joined until after the expulsion of the Jesuits, but before that d'Alembert published an article entitled "Collège" in the third volume of the *Encyclopédie* in 1753. In it he made two major points: he attacked the primacy of Latin and useless philosophy and argued in favor of basing secondary education on useful modern knowledge such as logic, science, history, and geometry in order to respond to society's diverse utilitarian demands. The void left by the departure of the Jesuits gave currency to the Encyclopedists' proposals and triggered a series of debates, projects for educational reform, and academic contests. In both Paris and the provinces active notables, bishops, administrators, and members of municipal *corps* mobilized on behalf of an "impossible reform."[13] But no new consensus was achieved, and the Encyclopedists did not supplant the humanists.

In the 1770s and 1780s the educational world divided. The universities and *collèges* remained fortresses of stability, yet even here the desire for change made itself heard. Meanwhile, countless innovative experiments were launched in a variety of institutions receptive to modernity: drawing schools, boarding schools, royal military schools, Christian Brothers' schools, academic courses, lycées, atheneums, museums, public chairs assigned to various faculties, hydrographic institutes—a whole range of institutions within which the sciences, arts, and technology figured in the curriculum. This proliferation of new educational opportunities accounts for the decline in the enrollment of the *collèges*. It tells us something about new expectations and new educational strategies in a society concerned about development and mobility—concerns that the old institutions failed to meet. Increased access to elementary education slowly shifted the social demand for education in a direction that coincided with the needs of development. As literacy increased, the schools became the central focus of philosophical and political debate, the ultimate result of which was equal secular education for all. The new secular, utilitarian spirit was not yet dominant, however: ignorance might hinder growth and maintain prejudices, but education posed a threat to the established order. When forced to choose, philosophes and anti-philosophes did not always make the choices one might expect. The expansion of public space was thus contained, or at any rate delayed.

From Cultural Sociability to the New Political Culture

When we try to analyze how likely it was that increased access to education could have produced an expanded public sphere—a larger number of people capable of formalizing their thoughts about their present and future status and applying it to their practice—we discover instead how few people were directly engaged in innovative work. The class within which a rudimentary political culture had begun to develop was quite small. If we assume that everyone who could sign his name could also read, there were perhaps 10 million potential readers in France, at least half of whom resided in the cities. The number who attended the *collèges* and universities was less than 100,000, and we know from urban statistics that notables constituted less than 10 percent of the population of the cities. These figures measure the limits of public-spirited France, demonstrating once again the decisive importance of small numbers in periods of upheaval, when social and intellectual elites come to the fore, all the more so because they are capable of acting independently of the state to form an autonomous cultural sphere.

Change came in two primary areas. First, the judgments and decisions of the public were no longer dictated solely by the norms of court society or filtered through monarchical intellectual institutions bound by privilege and monopoly. Second, a market developed in cultural goods and values, a market whose logic was based on principles of liberty and equality. For that reason it is essential that we take another look at the problems of sociability, whose importance we have already glimpsed. The chief difficulty in answering the question of how critical opinion formed has to do with the fact that it developed in old spaces subject to old values and yet speculated on the possibility of innovation and of the simultaneous transformation of thought and practice.

In recent years the concept of sociability has become a useful tool of historical analysis. From the definition proposed by Maurice Agulhon in

434

1968—"sociability is defined as the human aptitude for intense public relationships"—it is clear that we have here a concept capable of explaining not only associative behavior but also the way in which such behavior can give rise to a new political dimension.[14] We must take care, however, not to extend the concept unduly to include every sort of encounter, participation, and private or family connection. What is important is the way in which sociability can create enclaves of independence and liberty within an inegalitarian society, enclaves that according to organicist logic should not exist. Overgeneralization deprives the concept of its force and precludes understanding of the way in which a public space is constructed in relation to the private sphere and vice versa. Sociability is not to be confused with social relations in general: in society at large, necessity and chance do not play the same role as in the more restricted realm of sociability.

If we limit the application of the term to the range of social practices that occur in the interval between the family and the state, we can use it to think about what was distinctive about eighteenth-century politics.[15] Of course the problem is fundamental for understanding the emergence of new democratic forms and the formation of the political arena, especially if we wish to avoid the imputation that the *sociétés de pensée* were rigid, disciplined organizations that manipulated the thinking of their members, as Augustin Cochin has argued and, following him, François Furet.[16] The "history of association" provides a way of thinking about the question in a longer historical perspective and of interpreting public opinion in relation to intellectual developments and social practices that were intimately intertwined.[17] It is best to proceed by looking at concrete organizations, structures, relational processes, and forms of communication.

Four principles organized the new space: voluntary association, meaning association not due to social constraint or a search for profit but on behalf of an abstract general interest; rejection of social exclusiveness; a need for differentiation, which on occasion contradicted the principle of nonexclusiveness and could lead to closing of membership; and finally, some combination of egalitarian demands with references to traditional hierarchies. Clearly, the idea of sociability described here is one that was peculiar to the dominant classes in the Age of Enlightenment. Much work remains to be done to describe the characteristics and proliferation of the popular versions of sociability that began to appear in the era of political revolution.

This study will proceed in two directions. I will look first of all at voluntary associations from a political and anthropological point of view. My goal will be to understand how, in places where men and women came together in ways governed either by unwritten rules or by written regulations, in more or less public circumstances, and with some capacity for action, a major social and cultural change took place. Having done that, I will turn to the sociology of knowledge and the idea that to study a cultural class, one must study its concrete forms of existence, practice, and recruitment in order to interpret its production and promulgation of norms. What makes such a social construct coherent is not just the internal rationality of its content but also the community of shared gestures and tastes and pleasures that produced that content: social behavior counts as much as, if not more than, ideas. The social milieu I have in mind is best described by looking at four specific examples, through which we will discover the new ideology in a concrete and accessible form: first, various types of Masonic lodges; second, academies and literary societies licensed and recognized by the state; third, salons; and fourth, free voluntary societies without official status.

Freemasons and Political Consciousness

Freemasonry played a particularly important role in the transformation of political behavior through association. One reason for this was its substantial recruitment: in 1789 there were probably between 50,000 and 100,000 Masons. Another was that Masonic lodges existed almost everywhere. The first lodges, in Paris, Bordeaux, and Marseilles, were founded in the 1730s, and despite internal dissension and conflict, the movement grew steadily thereafter. Through its network of a thousand or so groups, both civilian and military, Freemasonry taught the value of egalitarian association, spreading its lesson from the major provincial cities to the humblest towns. By 1750 it had affected all urban classes, and its further spread was influenced by a variety of factors, including the geography of circulation, expansion through addition of affiliated groups, and rivalry between competing lodges. It was not the policy of the Grand Orient de France, reconstituted in 1773, that resulted in the spread of Freemasonry but the existence of a widespread desire to join the movement. Its growth was unrivaled by any other Enlightenment society, salon, club, or academy. Within the society of orders, the Masonic lodges carved out a vast space in which individuals were not distinguished by legal status or estate and in which recruitment and promotion were based solely on merit. This zone of democratic sociability was essentially based on equality, although that ideal was sometimes contradicted by inegalitarian social realities that obtruded on this egalitarian enclave.[18]

Freemasonry was without a doubt more open than any other institution of cultural sociability. Membership was largely dominated by representatives of the Third Estate, who accounted for 74 percent of Parisian Masons and 80 percent of provincial affiliates in academic cities. To varying degrees the lodges admitted social groups all but banished from other gatherings: merchants, shopkeepers, and artisans.[19] Still, Freemasonry had rejects of its own: those whose "vile and mechanical" occupations deprived them of the freedom and wealth necessary for participating in the lodges' works and charities. Various speakers made the point that the lodges should not accept people with whom one would not associate in civil life because they lacked education, financial resources, and manners. The real equality of the lodges was elitist, if not aristocratic, because it was based on the fact that associations drew men of similar social background and did not recruit on the basis of real, universal equality. Not without tension and conflict, Masonic society reconciled equality with ostracism: it respected social differences but not distinctions of order.

It owed its success, perhaps, to the conjunction of two contradictory aspirations: on the one hand, the appropriation, by groups excluded from more scholarly forms of sociability, of a less intellectually demanding mode of association, hospitable to a form of ersatz sacred ritual, a secularized form of Christian values and actions that appealed to bourgeois notables; and on the other hand, the spread, well beyond the aristocracy, of a form of equality that included people with money, education, and leisure in a trans-European network of useful relationships. Casanova joined the Masons in Holland when he was there negotiating a loan. Over time, these two aspirations were unified by the critical function.[20]

Masonic society was based on a code of ethics and regulated by freedom of conscience; hence it set itself up as a judge of the state. Although the lodges claimed unfailing loyalty to the monarchy, in practice they undermined the system of traditional values: "Apparently without affecting the state, the bourgeois were creating in the lodges, their inner sanctum within the state, a place where civil liberty could develop under the

437

protection of secrecy. Liberty in secret became the secret of politics."[21] The spirit of the lodges was not so much a spirit of achieved democratic equality as of heightened "political consciousness."

Institutions of Cultural Sociability

Unlike the lodges, the other institutions of the "Republic of Letters" were chiefly interested in discussion, reflection, production, and circulation of knowledge, and consumption of books and manuscripts. Among the participants in these institutions we find people from a variety of intellectual domains, whose engagement varied with their place in society. Age and sex invariably played a role. Academies and philosophical societies were largely masculine; women were invited only to the most public meetings, and their presence on such occasions was the exception that justified the rule. The young were excluded, but exceptions were made for genius, which has no age. This was a critical barrier: the most disciplined and selective societies had crowds of young people knocking on their doors, and from 1770 to 1789 one of the key problems faced by the cultivated class was what to do about them. At the Museum of Bordeaux, for example, a majority of members were under forty, a good third were under thirty, and all the men who would become the political leaders of the city during the Revolution were represented. The gerontocracy of the academies stood in sharp contrast to the youth of the philosophical societies. The salons, for their part, recruited and received without regard to age or discrimination by sex: women were present and active, and this was long seen as an essential aspect of the period's *douceur de vivre*. But the freedom of the salons was not incompatible with ostracism for social or demographic reasons: each coterie tended to age along with the person at its center, and change gave rise to fierce rivalries to retain star attractions and draw new talent. The lifetime of a salon was brief, no longer than the social life of the individual at its center, and short indeed when compared with the ongoing existence of academies and societies.

In the academies the new critical spirit vied with political conformism. There is nothing paradoxical about the idea that the provincial as well as Parisian academies were schools of politics. Here I want to consider how the sociability of the academies established an effective network for transmitting not only scholarly results but a new political culture as well. This network was primarily an urban phenomenon. Two-thirds of academic cities had populations above twenty thousand, and three-quarters of cities with populations that large had academies. This pattern reflects the prevalence of urban occupations among academy members: the roughly forty cities in this group were distinguished by the presence of spiritual, legal, and administrative personnel. On the benches of the academies, representatives of the urban nobility sat alongside bourgeois whose talents made them eligible for social ascent via traditional routes. The clergy were less well represented: their influence had fallen victim to a secularizing reaction that allowed other social groups to move ahead. The academies were not sites of conflict or reaction; they were in fact one of the principal agents of social compromise, a testing ground for efforts to fuse bourgeois *savoir-faire* with aristocratic *savoir-vivre* in a conciliatory ideology of service and efficiency directly related to the unifying conception of monarchical action.

The association of power and knowledge proved decisive: it dictated the way in which cultural responsibilities were divided among various institutions. Operating under the aegis of public authority, the great Parisian academies confirmed the establishment of a fundamentally political order. The Académie Française set the writers whom it honored the task of defining linguistic norms and defending the hierarchy of genres. The Académie des Inscriptions celebrated the great achievements of the monarchy and set standards for commemoration and historiography. The Académie de Peinture et de Sculpture and the Académie d'Architecture rewarded the true artists (as distinct from the mere daubers and chiselers) whose responsibility it was to designate models worthy of emulation while enhancing the legitimacy of the monarchy. This academic edifice dominated intellectual life and set standards. Yet the academies were adroit enough to admit representatives of the heirs to the great philosophes, and the Parisian model was emulated in the provinces, where the academic movement had always enjoyed the protection and support of local authorities. Academies everywhere saw their link to the monarchy as the justification for their existence. It scarcely mattered that philosophical minds were inwardly ironic about this relationship to the monarchy and often yearned to take a more critical stance toward authority; they depended on it, and as public figures they contributed to its legitimacy.

Yet matters were too complex to leave it simply at that. Even as monarchical authority was displayed in theatrical fashion in the academies, other dynamics were at work. Academic power was concentrated in a few hands: under the scrutiny of the established authorities, a small number of sages presided over the cultural destiny of France. But at the same time, within the academies, an autonomous organization developed with an internal hierarchy of its own, an organization whose basic rule was equality of talent and merit. Academic society is not to be confused with the larger society: it had its own brand of liberty. The new order of things meant that social rank as such carried no weight inside the academies; members voted on rules, and posts were assigned either by election or by lot. As Poncet de La Rivière said in Dijon: "The freedom to vote is guaranteed to produce sound decisions. The common interest is the point at which special interests converge, and esprit de corps will banish any foreign spirit."[22]

In everyday practice within this enclave there was no shortage of conflicts, to be sure, but strict observance of the rules often sufficed to resolve differences. Without idealizing or overestimating the value of the academic model, one has to admit that throughout the century the prestige of the academies was real. Some six thousand individuals were involved in these literary cenacles, including many of the greatest names of the day: Montesquieu, d'Alembert, Condorcet. New categories of thought and political action thus became familiar. Within the academies, men of letters and of the world slowly became accustomed to the idea of equality, of a will superior to the wills of individual members who, from the weakest to the most powerful, were free to express themselves on any issue. In the 1790s this new cultural experience would be shared with a much larger audience.

Because the academic system operated behind closed doors, it did not directly threaten the principles of the old society. But the academies also defined new roles, whose influence was less internal and therefore more directly innovative. The mission of the academician, it was repeatedly stated, was to work for the public good, to establish a reciprocal "commerce" between society and enlightenment. Men such as d'Alembert, Condorcet, and Vicq d'Azir made this point in academic speeches, and countless provincial academicians followed suit. Academic meetings were supposed to produce programs of wise reforms motivated by social utility and publicized by urban ceremonies. Academicians thus established a right to intervene critically in public affairs, and their efforts in this regard coincided with steps toward administrative rationalization. By initiating scientific and historical investigations and introducing a new rhetoric and new forms of behavior, the cultural societies gave certain dominant social groups an entrée into politics: public opinion had been born.

The Development of Literary Societies

Between 1770 and 1789 a broad movement reshaped the cultural landscape in Paris and the provinces, partly in competition with the Masonic lodges. This movement has not yet been fully studied, but already it is possible to describe its main features and geographic contours. Doing so is important because it allows us to measure the gradual spread of the model of cultivated sociability and its adaptation to new milieus. Four main centers of the movement can be distinguished.

The first was in Paris, where various new groups sought to compensate for the weaknesses of the universities and spread the Enlightenment through new forms of teaching while expanding the concept of cultivated sociability to accommodate people excluded from the academies. The Société des Neuf Soeurs (or Société Apollonienne) was founded in 1780 at the behest of Freemasons interested in sponsoring public readings. In 1781 the Musée de Monsieur opened its doors under the leadership of Pilâtre de Rozier. In 1782 Court de Gebelin created the Musée de Paris, and in 1783 a third museum joined these two. In 1780 or 1781 Pahin de La Blancherie dreamed up the Correspondance des Arts, an organization whose purpose was to promote communication among scholars, writers, and artists and which published the *Nouvelles de la République des lettres et des arts.* In 1788 the Musée des Dames completed the circuit, which was notable for its expanded recruitment, encouragement of public activities, and critical spirit.

In the provinces, three regions were affected by the movement. In the southwest and Provence, most of the newly founded institutions were in smaller cities. These were in contact with academic cities such as Bordeaux and Toulouse, where museums were established on the Parisian model. There were similar developments on a smaller scale in Picardy, Flanders, and Artois. By contrast, in Brittany the new institutions filled a void and led to a veritable transformation of the regional culture. In all these places, two types of sociability coexisted: one was relatively informal, consisting of circles, study groups, book clubs, and the like, the other more formal, with regular organizational by-laws. In every case, however, reading was a central activity: reading of books and especially newspapers was combined with recreation and refreshments. A "select class of citizens" found these meetings an opportunity for free expression, despite close surveillance of these cultural organizations by the police. In 1769 *France littéraire* offered a fairly clear picture of the new style:

> In Millau, the Société holds meetings every day except Sundays and holidays; newspapers provide the substance of these sessions. When there is nothing more to be read in the papers, the group turns to the best books of the day. Upon entering the hall, each academician chooses a book that he finds interesting. If, in the course of his reading, he finds a subject worthy of notice, he shares it with his colleagues. Private reading thus turns immediately into general conversation. When the academician's observations have been thoroughly discussed, everyone returns to reading.

Do not be misled by the use of the word "academician." The book club operated in a very different way, a mélange of the public reading room, lecture hall, and open conversation on any topic. Ladies were welcome, and manners reflected their presence. In this atmosphere, part library, part salon, news and recent books could be circulated, and the actions of the government could be judged on the basis of reports in the press. It was possible for a hierarchy of organizations to develop, with new groups opening their membership to ever wider circles. In Nantes, Arthur Young saw the cultural societies as an opportunity for the merchant class to broaden its horizons. The city had six reading rooms with roughly a hundred subscribers, all "leading citizens." The new museums also played a crucial role.

The movement, which began in Paris, spread to regions such as Brittany in which academies had yet to develop. An example is the Société Patriotique Bretonne, studied by Auguste Cochin. In Amiens a museum was founded by Roland de la Platière, who was hostile to the academy and keen to encourage his friends to occupy themselves with "civil reflections." In Toulouse the academies themselves opened their doors to leading citizens for intellectual, artistic, and social gatherings. In Bordeaux lawyers and merchants organized meetings, committees, concerts, and exhibitions. Young and old, men and women, writers and artists, amateurs and specialists were all welcome. Recruitment was broad and discussion wide-ranging. Museums and other liberal institutions played a crucial role in educating the "Rousseau du ruisseau," or Rousseaus of the gutter, as enlightened men of the people were disparagingly called. These circles broadened the sense of a public right to judge works of all kinds and to express independent opinions. One sees this in the mesmerist movement and in the arts, for example. The meaning of the terms "public" and "opinion" was still limited by the conditions of social practice, but their breadth increased as they came to denote an anonymous but plainly visible tribunal authorized to pass judgment on any subject in the name of "love of the public." Such a conception clearly falls, as Mona Ozouf has pointed out,[23] within the political mind-set of the Ancien Régime, where public opinion shared with older forms of political participation the characteristics of infallibility, exteriority, and unity; but it was also consonant with the future, for people began to see the need for individual consent and rational consensus. The cultural societies did not manufacture public opinion any more than the academies did: they began a process of cultural diffusion and standardization of practice. Through them critical thinking gained a concrete location and a sensibility.

Salons and Conversation

Salons played a crucial role in the politicization of the learned and literary public sphere by reducing the degree of dependency on the state. In the salons, where men and women of the world met with men and women of letters, the art of discussion reigned. People were attracted by a shared interest in common pastimes: dining, gambling, reading, and debating. Recalling his youth and reflecting, thirty years before Tocqueville, on a certain homogenization of good manners in French society, the comte de Ségur saw the salons as a major feature of the period. Social intercourse on a regular basis depended chiefly on "conversation, the mother of good manners." In the salons discussion was calm and argument virtually nonexistent. Polite manners and *bon ton* were prized in a setting in which a spirit of equality reigned, a spirit "born of constant interchange and mutual association," although to be sure relations between bourgeois and nobles were characterized more by familiarity than true equality. Tocqueville speaks of a difference of rights.

Salon society is not easy to catch hold of, for it was a changing, fugitive environment in which certain relationships were stable and others not, always vulnerable to the caprices of unpredictable individuals. There is no doubt that the salons were one of the primary places for aristocrats and men of letters to mingle, as talented writers such as Duclos and d'Alembert observed, but it is difficult to see how the inorganic and unorganized, fluctuating, and fleeting sociability of the salons could have created anything as solid as *l'opinion*. Indeed, there were salons and salons: each defined itself by the people it excluded, and to frequent one or many was in itself a kind of statement. Each salon defined a circle, and the various circles in a city such as Paris or a provincial town did not coincide. Salon society was riven by battles for preeminence in which the prize was control of social life and hence of intellectual life. Opinion was therefore not unified but fragmented among various circles. Those who attended Mme Geoffrin's salon did not necessarily go to Mme du Deffand's, and those who dined with Mme de Lespinasse did not always visit Mme du Deffand, her aunt and erstwhile patron. Between different salons there was a kind of warfare, with rivalries, alliances, truces, and conflicts whose language neophytes had to learn to decipher. The young man or woman with "entrée to good society" quickly learned to read the signs. Would-be writers had no choice but to find their footing here because there was no other way to pursue a literary career: salons were the source of pensions, posts, and success in academic elections. The progress of the candidates for available chairs was followed closely in the salons, as each coterie sought to advance the fortunes of its candidate in contests that were also occasions for ideological confrontation. Mme du Deffand triumphed by arranging for d'Alembert's election to the Académie Française and in so doing enabled the philosophes to conquer that bastion of intellectual legitimacy.

The dynamics of sociability suggest, however, that the activity in the salons had other consequences. As an ongoing institution, the salons served as a kind of model in the "art of living," whose lesson, while not directly political, had clear civic implications: the salon was where appearances reigned supreme, the realm "of the mask and fine words"— hence an organ of social control. The sociology of this process has yet to be studied and can be studied only in relation to an analysis of practice. Here, the mingling of the sexes was paramount: in the salons women were able to exercise power directly, and salons in which men dominated were quite rare (one such was the "d'Holbach coterie," whose loyal core and occasional visitors were bound by philosophical loyalties and open atheism). The salons brought people from different social milieus together on a regular basis: court and city, robe and sword, Paris and provinces, French and foreigners, and of course the world of letters and high society. The sumptuousness of the reception depended on the wealth of the mistress of the house—and her husband, who remained in the background. Amusement sustained social intercourse and cosmopolitanism. Foreigners joined in the fun: every visitor had to see a salon or two, and some, such as the brothers Grimm and Horace Walpole, succumbed to the blandishments and stayed. Adventurers like Casanova came to seek their fortunes.

Against this social background, two factors contributed to the political impact of salon sociability. First, the salons made it possible to extend the sociability of the court to a wider audience. Second, habitués were expected to hinge their conversation to an ideal, egalitarian world, which resulted in a sort of sublimation of intellectual intercourse. The urbanity of the salon was one manifestation of the effects of the civilizing process that diminished the degree of violence in human relations and promoted the internalization of social constraints.[24] From the moment when physical confrontation gave way to cabals and discussions and when calculation supplanted instinct, a veritable social psychology came into being. People began to observe one another and to explain behavior in social terms, since they needed to regulate their behavior in relation to that of others. The centralization of power and the complete recasting of social relations led to changes in the structure of the psyche. Internalization of tensions that could no longer be resolved by violence resulted in increased emphasis on good manners, dress, and respect for social taboos. As heir to the *cercles* of the seventeenth century, the eighteenth-century salons disciplined high society and provided a new avenue for the expression of social tensions. Distinct models of society confronted one another, and different social groups could mix without losing their identity, even if it took a connoisseur to distinguish one from another. Sophisticated pleasures and intellectual games typified this esoteric world. Comedies, dialogues, romances, pastoral poetry, and mysterious rituals such as those of the regiment of la Calotte or the Lanturlus were the diversions of a minority that preferred its amusements to be frivolous and often pointless. Everything concrete was avoided; material and social interests were unmentionable. Salon sociability acquired an intrinsic value of no practical use.

Yet that very same artificiality drew those who frequented the salons

445

into the realm of public opinion and critical debate. The playful atmosphere of the salons, which depended on good manners and conversational skill and a code of behavior that excluded any spontaneous expression of feeling, required reserve and self-control, and these qualities helped to unify a diverse and shifting cast of characters. In such a setting ideas took on a certain sophistication, for what Mme de Staël called the "need to talk" was the soul of good company; conversation defined the aesthetic of the salons and their idea of virtuosity. The exigencies of conversation were responsible for a certain vacuity of style: the need to demonstrate wit forced all ideas into a common mold, limiting genuine debate and excluding any discussion of technical issues. Yet men who came to the salons mainly to listen became increasingly involved in the discussion. The talk turned to matters of economics, philosophy, major controversies in the world of letters and the arts, and choices affecting the future of society. The need to sparkle meant that conventional or showy topics often dominated the conversation, however. In this Helvétius rightly saw the "spirit of the century": "In order to please in company, one must never delve into any subject in depth but dance constantly from one topic to another. One's knowledge must be highly varied and therefore quite superficial. The ideal is to know everything without wasting one's time fully mastering anything in order to give an impression of breadth rather than profundity."

Rousseau was of course quite resistant to social relations of this type. The debate over "the mask and fine words" was one of the century's central controversies. By adopting the tactics of the salon, intellectuals gained knowledge of man in society, skill in analyzing human relations in terms of social intercourse, and a way of penetrating an adversary's defenses that would prove useful in political confrontation. As Philippe Stewart shrewdly observes, the issue was not to unmask others: "Self-defense required that one be wary of others while taking care to prevent others from penetrating one's disguise. It was essential to train the eye and the understanding . . . but to unmask was to destroy sociability."[25]

Thus the eighteenth-century salon taught a political lesson by offering instruction in the analysis of social and psychological forces. In addition, the salons spread not only news but also a certain critical spirit that helped society to pick out a path between conformism and innovation. Their independence from the government created a modest space for political discussion before 1770 and a larger space thereafter. There was more discussion of current events than of doctrine, but the important thing was the spirited nature of the conversation. Expression was particularly free in the circle that gathered around the baron d'Holbach. "In order to find this door open, it is not enough to have credentials and learning. You also have to be good, because goodness ensures communication and sufficient esteem to contradict one another." This remark suggests a change in the rules to accommodate greater originality and reminds us that the real influence of a salon stemmed not so much from social and ideological coherence as from the way in which the shared sentiments of some habitués interacted with the easy social intercourse of others. On rue Saint-Honoré, Diderot rubbed shoulders with the pallid Marmontel and audacious Naigeon, with pampered rich men and poor devils, and with recognized scholars as well as provincials still out to establish their reputations. Unity grew out of a common search for social success, tolerance for differences, and agreement about the need to discuss all kinds of reforms. It was possible to conform outwardly and still think bold thoughts. Under Louis XVI society changed: "Our manners became less frivolous," the comte de Ségur recalled, "but also less polished . . . In this, politics gained, society lost." His view is corroborated by the history of Necker's salon and to a lesser degree by that of the cenacle of Mme de Genlis, where practical philosophy, economics, and politics were openly discussed. Necker's Friday salon, inaugurated in 1770 between Mme Geoffrin's Mondays and Wednesdays, Helvétius's Tuesdays, and d'Holbach's Thursdays and Sundays, bore its host's stamp. The Swiss Protestant banker and businessman was a true original in Ancien Régime society, and his salon served as a sounding board with which to further his ambitions. A place where financial, intellectual, and political capital was managed shrewdly, it was the forerunner of later political assemblies and orchestrated propaganda campaigns. Ostentatious virtue dethroned the frivolity of earlier years.

In the institutions of sociability, behavior was playful and politics rhetorical and theatrical. The undeniable cultural proximity fostered by these institutions did not eliminate differences of rank and status. Opinion formed in social interaction before it became a clear and distinct force in action and reflection. The salons, philosophical and debating societies, academies, and lodges formed a world unto themselves, governed by laws of their own, and their impact was not immediately felt outside the "Republic of Letters." But the movement was not totally isolated: it linked up with other forms of political education in the cities and countryside, and the triumph of print culture expanded its influence as new teaching methods took hold. The press contributed to the diversification and clash of opinion: the number of newspapers rose sharply after 1750, and the frequency of publication increased. Manuscript and published correspondence familiarized the larger society with the rules of behavior developed for the restricted world of the salons. In the last quarter of the eighteenth century attitudes were changing in a thousand ways, and the spread of this new type of social relation contributed to the crisis of traditional society as group and individual relationships evolved simultaneously. The concept of sociability is useful because it brings together material and intellectual aspects of culture and makes it possible to draw parallels between social conditions and practices and ideologies of social change. Kant recognized the importance of this in his *Anthropology from a Pragmatic Point of View:* "As insignificant as these laws of sophisticated humanity may seem, especially when compared with the laws of pure ethics, anything that encourages sociability, even in the simple form of maxims and pleasant manners, is nonetheless to be commended as an advantageous raiment for virtue."[26]

14

❦ ❦ ❦

Crises in State and Society

I BEGAN BY illustrating the various conflicts that animated France in the
years 1715–1789 through a series of portraits: of the king, his subjects,
the state and its people, the Catholic and Protestant churches, the nobles
and other elites, and public opinion. To some extent I have thus far
deliberately ignored what was at the end of the line because I did not
want to give a teleological account. Meanwhile, I have emphasized the
way in which long-term rhythms (and variations in those rhythms) interacted with a variety of intersecting and overlapping phenomena to reveal
changes in social and political attitudes: in other words, I have shown how
structures impinged on events without discussing events per se. Events
cannot be disposed of altogether, however, not because they were for so
long the very matrix of historical memory but because they offer a
different kind of insight into the construction of reality over time.

One goal of this book is to help us understand how a world of politics,
with all its associated ideas, practices, and symbolic correlates, was able to
develop within the very bosom of the Ancien Régime—a political culture, in short, that cannot be reduced to anything else because we have
access to it only through the surviving discourses produced by groups and
individuals whose projects grew out of the interaction between the "surface agitation" of the short term and the deeper currents of the long run.
In the eighteenth century, a series of crises punctuated the evolution of
the conditions under which news circulated, negotiations were conducted,
and confrontations occurred. As those conditions changed, the relation

between society, religion, and custom was transformed, and a new capacity emerged, a capacity to criticize "the nature and foundations of French collective identity, in which public opinion gradually took the place of the royal authorities as the court of last resort."[1]

Social and political protest erupted over old issues, dating back to seventeenth-century religious conflicts, tax matters, and questions of law, administration, military force, and foreign policy. Little by little, these issues, and ways of responding to them, became a systematic rather than an intermittent feature of the political culture. They helped to shape public opinion even as public opinion defined them (by way of allusion, memory, and logic).

A crisis can be analyzed on two levels: first, it creates a temporal space in which signs, symptoms, a whole pathology can emerge and remedies can be brought to bear; second, it points up contradictions in reality and shows how well the actors involved are able to measure and understand the social significance of events. When historians use the word "crisis," they are treating an event as a symptom that reveals an underlying structure, a point of observation. A crisis tells us how a system functions, be it political, economic, social, or cultural, and in return it helps to modify that system. There is no going backward.

In this connection, it is not without interest to note that the eighteenth century marked an important shift in vocabulary, an extension of the use of organic metaphors to understand social facts. We would do well to avoid artificial distinctions between intellectual and political history, say, or the history of ideas and the history of practice. The very word "crisis" had connotations arising from medical discourse, on which thinkers in other disciplines drew: think of Quesnay, himself a physician as well as an economist and a disciple of Boerhave (and it makes no sense to separate the physician from the economist); or Diderot, who audited Bordeu's lectures and wrote the article entitled "Crisis" for the *Encyclopédie;* or Forbonnais, who, when he wrote a discourse on method for a new liberal political economy that would stand the economy of the Physiocrats on its head, spoke of "a conjecturable [sic] science like medicine."

For economists and political thinkers, the problem was to accommodate the accidental to the logic of history. Rousseau used the word "crisis" in his project for a government in Poland: "Any free state that fails to foresee a major crisis is at great risk of perishing in every storm."[2] The term came naturally to a period that favored organic theories of society and the "body politic." Again Rousseau offers an example in his article "Political Economy" in the *Encyclopédie:* "The body politic taken individually can be considered to be an organized body, a living thing similar to the human body."[3] Hence it was legitimate to speak of change in terms of crisis, of a turning point in the life of the political organism, because "analogical usage" suggested that both the human body and society were to be understood as "totalities," or organic wholes. The metaphor of a body politic gave rise to an idea of disease as a sociopolitical category.

Broadly speaking, contemporaries explained the origins of social pathology in three ways. The first was theological: in the assemblies of the clergy, the bishops of France opted for religious conformism by denouncing the new political philosophy as impious. The second was intellectual: one sees this in the shift of the idea of revolution from the medical to the political, as people began to search for causes and historical discourse began to explain political change in terms of errors by the administration and the "public spirit." And the third was natural: political life was seen as subject to the same ills that threaten all life, as the national organism rebelled against actions that attempted to alter its natural course of development. Here, the interaction of the organs of the body politic defined its unity and suggested a logic of change through trial and error marked by alternating phases of stability and instability.[4]

When things went awry, new voices arose to express awareness of change. People confronting the difficulties of the moment spoke out about how to end the troubles. An example of this is Enlightenment commentary on the historiography of the "English revolutions" of the seventeenth century. In a roundabout way this literature was meant to affirm faith in the future of the French monarchy despite threats to its existence. Similar ideas can be found in a variety of works analyzing a wide range of historical accidents: among the Turks as well as in Siam, Sweden, Rome, the Netherlands, Morocco, Japan, and Spain. Discussion of revolution served a pedagogical function: it explained what a political crisis was, examined the future of absolutism, and offered ideological responses to concrete situations and political changes.[5] The authors of these treatises played the role that Diderot's friend Bordeu, author of the *Ency-*

clopédie's article "Crisis," attributed "to the philosophical physician who began as a witness, developed from practitioner into keen observer, and, transcending the usual boundaries, rose above his condition. Open up the riches of medicine, count the legislators." Just as physiological crises revealed the great doctors, political crises revealed the true philosophers and correct opinions.

In a letter from Diderot to Necker dated June 10, 1775, after Diderot had read the *Traité de la législation et du commerce des grains* attacking Turgot and free trade, the philosopher, who had seen a spate of revolts triggered by food shortages and who, though a supporter of Turgot, worried that such disorder demonstrated the validity of the book's objections to liberalism, alluded not so much to the current situation as to the work's theoretical and political consequences. In the passage that follows, what we see taking shape is a definition of public opinion and of the role of intellectuals in a time of crisis:

> Opinion, that vehicle whose force for good and evil you know full well, is at bottom only the effect of a small number of men who speak after having thought and who continually congregate at various places in society, from which reasoned errors and truths spread gradually to the outermost reaches of the city, where they establish themselves as articles of faith: there, all the apparatus of our discussions has evaporated; only the last word remains. Our writings affect only a certain class of citizens, while our speeches affect all classes. These are like a mirror upon which someone has breathed. People know that wheat must be cheap, because they earn little and are very hungry. But they do not know, and will never know, how difficult it is to reconcile the vicissitudes of the harvest with the need for grain, which never wavers.

When crisis came and a remedy was needed at once, neither statesmen nor people nor men of the world nor businessmen could hear the lessons taught by philosophical writers. Hence thinking men were obliged to "argue publicly," to publicize their political palliatives, and enlighten opinion.

Three moments stand out as times of profound change in French political culture and society: the astonishing eight years of the Regency,[6] the parlementary crisis of 1750–1775, and the crisis of absolutism from Calonne to the return of Necker. We will examine the events of these periods, which put men and ideas to the test.

The Ruptures of the Regency

The Regency was not an intermezzo but the beginning of a period of "conservative transition," in which the authoritarian political system of the reign of Louis XIV, destabilized by war and economic difficulties, sought to regain its equilibrium and to eliminate the various rigidities that had developed in the great king's final years. Political responsibility was transferred to a new team, including newcomers such as Dubois and Law, which, while audacious as well as experienced, nevertheless faced a difficult domestic and international situation.

The crisis was both diplomatic and military in nature. France remained isolated in Europe owing to the triumph of the maritime powers and the division of the continent between Hapsburgs and Bourbons. The crisis was also economic and social: rentiers as well as peasants were suffering, the court nobility was divided, and the *parlements* were ready to reassert themselves. The Regent had to contend with all these conflicting pressures. Finally, the crisis was also religious, a *crise de la conscience*. Although many Protestants had converted or left France, thereby reducing religious tensions, Protestant agitation was still worrisome because it was seen as a reflection of the influence of "Huguenot" powers and the danger of the "republican spirit." Protestantism was viewed as a threat to political and religious unity. And Jansenism was still a force and a potential source of conflict. Winds of protest emanated from both the Protestant regions of the country and the Augustinian bastions. Meanwhile, England was redrawing the political map of Europe, offering philosophes and other critics a new model. Things that had previously been tolerated at best and more often than not proscribed now became forces for change. In three areas—diplomacy, economics, and ideas—the Regency marked a new beginning: people saw that, while it was impossible to turn back the clock, it was also impossible to leap ahead. Such was the background against which decisive changes occurred in a time of intense cultural creativity and intellectual reflection.

Change and the Impossibility of Turning Back

On September 1, 1715, when the duc d'Anjou became Louis XV, it seemed inevitable that he would continue the political system put in place by the late king and described for the benefit of his successor in his *testament.* But the Regent, Philippe d'Orléans, nephew of Louis XIV, dismantled that system and in so doing demonstrated not only his determination to rule but also his insistence on putting his own men into key positions. His strength came from his ability to enlist the support of two groups at odds with the old system: a *camarilla* of Orleanists, libertines, and adventurous spirits who took an ironic attitude toward a Versailles grown stiff with age in the last years of the great king's rule, dominated by Mme de Maintenon; and the heirs of the late reformers Fénelon, Beauvilliers, and Chevreuse, of whom the most active was no doubt the young duc de Saint-Simon. Both groups were hostile to the "old court," the aristocrats, ministers, generals, and prelates who had surrounded the Sun King and intrigued with the king's legitimated bastards and the royal favorite. In a *lit de justice* held on September 12, 1715, the Regent got rid of the bastard princes and assumed sole responsibility for government: "I wish to be free to do good, but I consent to be bound so as not to do ill." In order to secure his hold on power, the Regent restored the *parlements'* "right of remonstrance," which Mazarin had abolished. He thereby lodged a political contradiction in the very heart of the monarchy.

A brilliant and courageous man, the Regent had demonstrated his abilities in the final years of the War of the Spanish Succession. He was also an artist and, as was often said at the time and frequently repeated later, a libertine not only in his private life but also to some extent in his thinking, for he was not a man stifled by religious devotion. The devout Louis XIV of the final years did not trust him and kept him out of public affairs, which was easy to do because the carefree duc d'Orléans was more interested in his own pleasures. His true colors emerged only in action. As Pierre Narbonnes, the *commissaire de police* of Versailles, put it, the duke "became Regent by being a fox and survived by being a shrewd politician." An improviser, he lived from day to day and governed as a flexible opportunist, according to Voltaire, "all too keen on pleasures and novelties." If the private morals of political men have any importance in politics, it is not so much because of the moral value judgments they elicit as because of the choices they permit and the symbolism they inspire. The Regent was undeniably a libertine, but this matters for only three reasons: first, he moved the center of government from Versailles to Paris, bringing the monarchy closer to the city and the forces within it; second, he created a free atmosphere in which the man in power divorced his private life totally from his public life, inevitably affecting the very image of the monarchy; and finally, the Regent's private life became a political issue.

If the *petits soupers* of the Palais-Royal were portrayed as orgies (with considerable exaggeration, as Saint-Simon makes clear), it was because a new kind of literature had begun to appear, a literature "infected at its very source."[7] Opposition to the court was couched in the form of political pornography such as *L'Histoire du prince Papyrus, Les Amusements de la princesse Amélie, Les Aventures de Pomponius, Les Phillippiques* of La Grange-Chancel, and a host of bawdy street songs duly reported by police informers. Whatever basis such works may have had in fact, they reveal the existence of a certain political imagery embodying a persistent critique of certain individuals, practices, and institutions of government. The success of this new genre owed a great deal to the fact that this pamphlet literature was concerned with the great issues of the day: it attacked the *testament* of Louis XIV, was critical of dishonest financiers, and revived a certain form of religious polemic. The Regent's libertinage was a key feature of a multilayered, anarchic, self-contradictory discourse, which touched on a wide range of subjects while on occasion stating demands and proposing innovations. Power was a relative thing, not an absolute, according to the pamphleteers, who also believed that public opinion should play a role in decision making, although no one yet went so far as to propose a transfer of sovereignty from the monarch to the public.[8] Hence this body of literature can be consulted for clues to the political and religious preferences of the people, couched in the form of images, allegories, interpretations, and parodies which adapted the symbols of political criticism to a variety of audiences, including the very humblest strata of the population. Here it was the Regent as individual as much as ruler who served as a catalyst.

The elimination of holdovers from Louis XIV's reign secured the succession against the return of Philip V of Spain in case the young king died (which was not beyond the realm of possibility), because it enabled the Regent to secure the support of influential factions by offering them important positions and favors: the high nobility obtained places on various councils, the *parlements* were only too pleased to have their former rights restored, the Jansenists and Gallicans were delighted to be allowed for a time to rail against the pope's bull, and bondholders and others were glad to see financiers and other financial manipulators prosecuted.

The power formerly wielded by ministers was transferred to a series of councils: the Conseil de Régence, Conseil du Dedans, Conseil des Affaires Etrangères, Conseil des Finances, Conseil de la Guerre. This "polysynody" was inspired by the ideas of the abbé de Saint-Pierre, ideas suggested by his friend Saint-Simon. The Regent's maneuver gave the great aristocrats, the "Gotha of the old court," and the men who had been powerful under the absolutist regime the illusion of power, whereas the reality was that most power was still in the hands of the *maîtres des requêtes* and *conseillers d'Etat*. Among those included in this polysynodic rule were the royal bastards Maine and Toulouse; the dukes Saint-Simon, Noailles, La Force, and d'Antin (another legitimated bastard); the marshals, many of whom were also dukes, including Villars, Harcourt, and the duc de Bourbon, who brought the support of the Condé clan; and former ministers such as Voisin and Phélypeaux. In short, this was a maneuver apparently designed to reduce affairs of state to a domestic matter: gradually everything devolved into arguments over personalities and protocol, into foolishness and impotence. These great lords, most of them cultivated and intelligent men, were prisoners of their own prejudices and victims of their exclusion by Louis XIV. Who would be allowed to sit during council sessions? Who had the right not to remove his hat? What rank should be accorded to *conseillers, maîtres des requêtes, parlementaires,* and specialists summoned to give reports? There were endless controversies over protocol and hierarchy. No government could function under such conditions. The experiment was therefore ended on September 25, 1718, when the Regent abolished the councils and reverted to the earlier form of government, but not before he had succeeded in disarming the potential aristocratic opposition, giving certain segments of society—oppressed notables, Jansenists, *parlements*, Gallicans—the means to express themselves, and paving the way for a diplomatic and foreign policy offensive by modifying the system of alliances and entering into negotiations with the Hanovers. Domestically, the powerless councils had provided the cover for a rout of the anachronistic aristocratic insurrection and paved the way for a return to traditional politics.

That return was the triumph of Abbé Dubois, the Regent's chief adviser, who by a somewhat irregular route had joined the Council of Foreign Affairs in 1716. The abbé, who was the duc d'Orléans' former tutor, pressed for a restoration of the *secrétariats d'Etat*. In September 1718 he became secretary of foreign affairs, in which position he managed to maintain the "European equilibrium" by way of a shrewd compromise between the old and new diplomatic systems. Following a brief war and the failure of the Cellamare conspiracy, in which the duchesse du Maine compromised herself, Philip V renounced his claims to the French throne, and France gave its support to the Hanovers against the House of Stuart. Foreign policy highlighted the need for a restoration of authority. After Parlement rejected the Franco-British treaty of August 1, 1718, Dubois arranged for a *lit de justice* that stymied the opposition of *parlementaires* and bastard princes. The return to authoritarianism had consequences across the board.[9] It affected diplomacy, the dynastic issue, the structure of the entire state apparatus, religion (because it triggered a resumption of anti-Jansenist persecution), and economics and finance (because it set in motion the decisive Law experiment). With respect to political culture, two important changes occurred: England became a model—the Regent himself turned to Dubois for lessons on the workings of the House of Commons—and, even more important, there was a shift from the ideal of aristocratic reform in the spirit of Fénelon to that of philosophical criticism in the spirit of Montesquieu.

The Impossibility of Leaping Ahead: Law's Anticipation

The Law experiment of 1716–1720 remains, in its anticipation of the future, the chief symbol of the Regency and its failure. The consequences of the experiment proved decisive, and in the short run the "Law System" and its contradictions contributed to the return to authoritarian absolutism. The financial situation of the monarchy made Law's risky venture seem reasonable. War had emptied France's coffers: in 1715 the country's debt stood at 2.5 billion livres, with interest close to 140 million and an unconsolidated floating debt of 800 million. The annual income of 70 million was clearly insufficient. Even with various expedients such as reduction of interest payments on bonds, a reduction of part of the floating debt through a disguised form of bankruptcy, reminting of coins, elimination of offices, and trial of financiers, the duc de Noailles still failed to solve the problem. He did encourage new thinking about the *taille*, however: on August 26, 1716, a *lit de justice* banned any further discussion of fiscal edicts. The inflation of all paper financial instruments—of the state, church, private lenders, and so on—was serious enough to threaten both the credit of the state and the economic recovery that had been under way since 1713 or 1714. Dubois needed money for his foreign policy. Medicine having failed, it was time to call in the surgeons, that is, to cut expenses, which peace made possible, and consider deflation. The prosecutions of financiers (which involved some four thousand people and recovered some 50 to 60 million livres out of an anticipated total of 200 million) were aimed at reducing their grip on the state. The Regent hoped that after an initial deflationary phase he could accelerate the pace of economic growth. For that he turned to John Law.[10]

A Scottish adventurer, gambler, traveler, and economist (or at any rate author of books on wealth), John Law came to Paris in 1706 and was expelled by d'Argenson's police as a "too lucky gambler." In 1714 he returned after traveling throughout Europe, whose financial strengths and weaknesses he knew from Holland to Venice. He was a man full of plans, with a remedy for every ailment, and somehow he was able to gain the ear of Desmaretz and the Regent. His *Mémoire sur l'acquittement de la dette publique* (May 1715) attracted attention, and his *Mémoire sur la banque* drew even more. The new government was willing to listen to anyone with a reasonable chance of putting the country's finances back in order, and "the Regent had a liking for new ideas." Dubois shared his views, and Law was not proposing anything in the way of institutional or political reform but simply promising to fill the nation's coffers and pay off its debt. Why not listen to what he had to say?

In order to restore the state's credit, monetary circulation had to be increased and commerce and industry revived. A bank that withdrew metal from circulation and issued paper instead stood a chance of hastening the recovery, especially a bank that enjoyed the advantage of receiving state revenues with which to back its paper. The state could then use this paper to pay off its creditors and diminish its debt. The bank also took over the monopoly on commerce with France's North American colony and created a commercial company. Shares in this company could be purchased for either hard cash or "notes of credit" (shares in the debt), thereby helping to revive commerce while retiring the debt, which would gradually be converted into stock certificates. Ultimately, all financial institutions would be reformed and a single tax on land would become possible. As early as 1705 (as proved by *Trade and Money* and other brochures), Law had dreamed of a currency based on something other than gold or silver, a territorial currency linking public power to land power. Unfortunately, the conditions under which he embarked on his venture both limited its scope and increased its risks.

Law's bold theoretical and practical step was to combine the machinery of public finance, currency creation, and private capital formation in a single entity.[11] He saw a financial obstacle to economic development in a system that funneled money from the state treasury to bondholders rather than into productive investment and credit to fuel the economy. Law hoped to create a system of credit in order to channel cash instead into commerce and industry, whose profits would be assured by the circulation of paper. Law took the economic and financial realities of the Ancien Régime into account but subverted the existing system in order to substitute another.

The first phase of Law's System was a success. His private bank, established on May 20, 1716, and converted to a royal bank on December 4, 1718, did well. It was at once a repository for deposits, a clearinghouse, a discount bank, and an issuer of currency, but it did not engage in commerce. Parisians, other bankers, and bondholders had confidence in Law's paper money. The difficulties began when the concern was expanded, speculation began on shares of the Compagnie d'Occident, or "Mississippi," and the affairs of the bank became enmeshed with those of the trading company; these difficulties ultimately led to failure. From 1719 on, the bank was both a commercial company and a fiscal administration. In 1720 Law headed the Contrôle des Finances. The collapse resulted from confusion of company shares with banknotes, which became caught up in the speculative fever. When interest dropped, confidence in the bank waned, and when the rate fell to 2 percent, investors fled. The shrewder shareholders and people in the know converted their paper to hard currency; princes of the blood—Conti and Bourbon—set a bad example for others. Despite an attempt to shore up the value of Law's banknotes by fiat, the bottom fell out. The System ran afoul of the devaluation of revenue resulting from the accelerated circulation and ended in a collapse of public credit as interest rates began to fluctuate, triggering rage among bondholders. The *parlementaires* who denounced "the Scotchman's inflationary madness" were not wrong. Law was obliged to flee France and died in poverty in Venice in 1729. There were winners and losers in every segment of society. A return to the previous financial policy was envisioned, and the Pâris brothers took the task upon themselves.

The collapse of Law's System came at a time when mercantilism was at its height, toward the end of a long and difficult period. The shock was too much for the economy and financial system to absorb. Long afterward

459

Necker offered this assessment: "Monsieur Law sacrificed the progressive advantages that the state might have derived from a duly constituted bank for the fleeting splendor of a grand illusion."[12] The consequences were considerable, some short-term, others long-term. The financial system was patched up with the help of the "visa," but Paris, which had been integrated into the financial circuit, reverted to its former isolation and dependence. Older financial methods were reinstated, severing France from the rest of the world and ensuring that cash would flow to safe state bonds rather than speculative but productive investments. Law's failure marked the failure of a certain form of capitalism and the triumph of closed-circuit state financing. "Except for armaments and maritime expeditions, the private economy, which in any case was subject to administrative controls, offered few opportunities for investment." Economic activity was concentrated elsewhere: in agriculture, which Quesnay would analyze, and finance, which divided its revenues with the king, as well as in opportunities for trade with Spain and the colonies. A major storm had briefly roiled the economy, triggering impressive transfers of wealth that left a lasting impression and enriched the high nobility, which saw its debts reduced, its speculations encouraged, and its revenues increased with inflation. Law's System probably stimulated a recovery in agriculture and manufacturing; increased demand spurred trade. It may have alleviated the general distress by reducing debt and decreasing the relative tax burden.

In any event, the Law experiment leaves a major historical problem unsolved: that of the relation between Law's various schemes for encouraging speculation and the popularity of those schemes with both commoners and aristocrats. This was an interesting moment in the development of public perceptions: attitudes toward finance and credit need to be investigated by way of careful study of advertisements and songs, posters and memoirs. Buvat, Marais, the chevalier de Piossens, and Marmont Du Haut-Champ, the first historian of the System, all need to be reread with these issues in mind. Chroniclers retailed scurrilous anecdotes and sage commentary linking the widespread and cynical libertinage of high society to Law's bankruptcy, and in so doing reflected a shift in moral and spiritual values. Law's schemes temporarily united all segments of society in speculative equality and the quest for riches. Some, like the marquis de Mirabeau, emerged from the experience with a lasting hatred of money and profit. Others, who made money, attacked the ensuing social instability; their criticisms served as a mask for their own upward mobility. In retrospect, the Regency was a brief period of experimentation and questioning; its pain marked the birth trauma of a new society.

Society and Criticism

The Regency also embodied a tone, a style, a moment in the history of civilization that is perhaps all too easily symbolized by *fêtes galantes* and much better represented by Montesquieu. The salons of Regency Paris— Mme de Lambert's, Mme Dacier's, the duc de Sully's—were open to the timorous as well as the free-spirited. Intense intellectual fervor coincided with speculative excitement and superficial changes in manners. A new philosophical curiosity was evident in the *sociétés de pensée* and other places where intelligent minds assembled. At the home of the duc de Noailles, a broad-minded man who hired Fréret to tutor his son and played host to critical historians such as Boindin, Mirabaud, and Dumarsais, one could listen to the conversation of the duke's friend Boulainvilliers, a noted free spirit. And the président de Maisons hosted a circle which, according to Grimm, included only atheists: "There people indulged in some fine impieties!" It was at this time that the first cafés were born: by 1723 there were 380 of them, and within fifty years the number had grown to nearly 2,000. Café conversation did not lack for audacity, as the *lieutenant de police* was duly apprised by informers. The criticism was aimed not so much at the government, as was the case in London, as at religion, whose teaching certain clever abbés tried to reconcile with the spirit of the times. At the Procope, Abbé Bouchard expressed doubts about Christ's divinity, Abbé Butier mocked the Assumption, and the philosophe Boindin openly preached atheism, which earned him the nickname "Boindin the impious." In general, tolerance was the rule, despite the surveillance of police and religious authorities. After 1723, however, the authorities took a harder line in the face of renewed Jansenist protest. The Code de la Librairie (1723), the imprisonment of dissidents, and the censorship of publishing showed, as Voltaire said, that the "Holy Inquisition" had come to French letters.

In a different way Montesquieu's *Lettres persanes* revealed the conjunction of the satirical and philosophical spirit with changed manners and renewed intellectual curiosity. A provincial honored by the Académie Française in 1716, Montesquieu achieved quick success through his use of a traditional literary genre: he described his own civilization through the eyes of a foreigner. The *Lettres* had countless precursors, including Marana's *Espion turc* and any number of travel books. What the correspondence between Uzbek and Rica showed, with its satirical look at French customs, government, religion, and society, was that the world could be interpreted as a place of "universal facticity." If the Persians asked why French institutions and customs were as they were, it was not because they expected a satisfactory answer but because the question was a necessary one. It pointed up the absurdity and relativity of all customs and beliefs and affirmed the power of the mind to free itself from traditional values by saying no to the status quo. Montesquieu's critical powers knew no limits, and he proposed a lesson in liberty that presaged a revision of French laws. In the *Lettres persanes* he explored a host of ideas and inaugurated lines of inquiry to which he returned in later theoretical works such as *L'Esprit des lois*. His criticism went down all the more easily because it availed itself of the resources of fiction, treating passion, psychology, and the erotic in a novelistic way. The Regency, having reverted to absolutism, was nearing its end, but the changes it had wrought in manners and ideas were irreversible. Culture inevitably becomes political.

The Courts and the King

During the eighteenth century, the *parlements* figured centrally in a recurrent crisis which made them the monarchy's most dangerous oppositional force. The sovereign courts, backed in many instances by royal office-holders as a group, saw themselves as traditionally entitled by the so-called *droit du conseil* to offer the king their observations on government policy in the form of "remonstrances" that could be issued whenever royal decisions were promulgated. All royal edicts were supposed to be registered by the courts before they could be enforced, and if the courts refused, the monarch could compel them to do so. The procedures involved, which have been amply studied from a legal point of view, took on new significance in the eighteenth century. Previously, under Louis XIV, the *parlements*, while not totally denied the right to make observations to the king, had lost the power of "repeated remonstrance" ending in refusal to register royal edicts. The Regent, acting precipitously, restored the courts' former prerogatives on September 15, 1715. Bear in mind that it was the social position of magistrates that made the right of remonstrance so significant. The *parlements* and other sovereign courts formed a world apart, distinguished by its functions (to dispense justice and deal with matters that would today be dealt with by the bureaucracy or police), numbers (more than 2,300 *officiers*), close association with royal power (embodied in the magistrate's official contract), social influence (a large number of other professions and *officiers*, to say nothing of plaintiffs and dependents, were dependent on the robe), and finally the magistrates' cultural prestige.

Judges who could not under any circumstances be removed from office thus wielded considerable influence over public policy while also enjoying such basic privileges as the right to bequeath their offices to their heirs. Every attempt to attack the magistracy ran up against a double obstacle: judges owned their offices, and the only way the king could get rid of a magistrate was to buy back his charge. Dismissal was thus impossible, and reform costly. The courts were therefore powerful institutions. They wielded the traditional right to register or refuse to register the king's edicts. In addition, administrative tradition allowed them to issue *arrêts de règlement,* or local regulations applicable to their districts, as well as to intervene in all sorts of matters from censorship of books to price-fixing, from municipal ordinances to urban planning and traffic regulation. This brought *parlementaires* into conflict on many fronts with royal *gouverneurs* and *intendants.* To be sure, the magnitude of these conflicts should not be exaggerated. Because of the vigor of their opposition, however, the magistrates often seemed strong while the government seemed weak. What is more, the sovereign courts were forever extending the scope of their protest, and their challenges to royal authority, printed and circulated either with the approval of the judges themselves or by others less discreet, were increasingly cast in the form of veritable appeals to public opinion, which people thought of as the arbiter between the king and the courts. Furthermore, the provincial *parlements* were increasingly active and effective, thus extending a role that in the seventeenth century had been filled mainly by the Parlement of Paris.

Of course, these ongoing conflicts were in no sense similar to the political party battles and debates of our democratic age. They were sporadic, of dubious legality in the eyes of some, and lacking any true organization. Yet from one crisis to the next they sustained a dynamic of protest, fueled by the political contradiction at the very heart of the monarchy.[13] The universalist logic intrinsic to the administrative and development-oriented worldview was at odds with the local, traditionalistic, particularistic logic of the social order that formed the basis of judicial government. In every conflict, moreover, the parlementary opposition opportunistically mixed recurrent issues (such as the complaints against royal interference in the judicial process, the activity of the *commissaires,* and the role of the Grand Conseil) with new demands for legislative powers, "national rights," control over taxes, and various "liberties."

Parlementary protest can be divided into three phases. While all three dealt with a variety of issues, the central focus moved from religious conflict to complaints about the administrative monarchy to protests against authoritarian absolutism, which temporarily triumphed at the end of the reign of Louis XV only to collapse in the coalition that formed against Turgot.

The Religious and Administrative Crisis (1715–1763)

The first enactment of a scenario that would be repeated many times over—examination of a royal edict by the *parlements,* remonstrances, *lit de justice* to force registration—came in connection with a crisis that erupted in Paris between June and September 1718 concerning certain of Law's financial measures. On August 26 the Garde des Sceaux, Voyer d'Argenson, who had replaced the disgraced chancellor d'Aguesseau, issued a stern warning to the magistrates, reminding them of the king's authority and refusing to allow the Parlement of Paris to proclaim itself the "necessary legislator of the kingdom." When certain magistrates refused to give in, the Regent had the ringleaders arrested; once the furor subsided, he set them free. The pattern thus established would persist long thereafter.

Until 1760, however, it was religious controversy that dominated the conflict between king and *parlements.* As was mentioned earlier, the main issue was Jansenism and the attempt by the king and Church to impose silence on both proponents and adversaries of the papal bull *Unigenitus.* The declaration that Abbé Dubois, an eager aspirant to a cardinal's miter, obtained from the Regent on August 4, 1720, was duly registered despite criticism from Jansenist magistrates and restrictions that would have a crucial impact later on: the decree preserved the right of appeal and the rights of the appellants. Fleury returned to the offensive, and on March 24, 1730, a declaration confirming that of 1720 was registered in a *lit de justice*. The Parlement of Paris opposed its enforcement through a series of decrees, which were quashed one after another by the King's Council. This led to remonstrances, resignations from the council, strikes by magistrates, and the banishment of 139 *parlementaires* on September 7, 1732, for opposing measures imposed by *lit de justice* on September 3. All this caught the attention of the public, especially in Paris. As early as 1730, some forty *avocats* from Parlement had submitted petitions whose substance was incorporated in the official remonstrances. At least one *avocat*, Barbier, did not approve of Parlement's tactics, "because when one mutinies against one's master, no matter what the justification, one forces the sovereign to go to extremes." He also feared the potential for violence, given the "Jansenist fanaticism" of the people. Hence he describes events in such a way that one can see what was really at stake: the fusion of popular protest with the critical spirit in a new public space between court and city.

The issue came up again in a more serious way in 1750. When Bouettin, the curé of Saint-Etienne-du-Mont, refused the sacraments to M. Coffin, a *conseiller* of the Châtelet, Parlement summoned him, issued a reprimand, yet justified his action in a remonstrance issued on March 4, 1751. On August 30 another remonstrance was filed against Christophe de Beaumont's intervention in the affair of the Hôpital Général. Whenever a Parisian parish was involved, Parlement intervened. The crisis culminated in the *grandes remontrances* of April 9, 1753, the result of lengthy deliberation and mature reflection by the leaders of the Gallican opposition, Durey de Meinières, Robert de Saint-Vincent, Lambert, and Abbé Chauvelin. The king refused to receive them, jailed four opposition ringleaders, and dispersed the remaining magistrates to seven different cities: Angoulême, Bourges, Châlons, Clermont-Ferrand, Montbrison, Poitiers, and Vendôme. The magistrates' strike, coupled with widespread publication of the remonstrances, support from the *parlements* of Rennes, Rouen, and Aix and to a lesser degree Bordeaux and Toulouse, and subsequent debate finally forced the court to capitulate. Henceforth the "law of silence" reigned in religious affairs, but, as d'Argenson declared, both the court and the *parlementaires* emerged with honor intact.

The controversy over the sacraments helped to clarify public opinion and launch a wave of anticlericalism to which Voltaire contributed. It revealed the weakness of the monarchy to the *parlementaires,* who saw that the royal government was powerless to deal with the many manifestations of a divisive issue. It was a prelude to the courts' triumphant campaign against the Society of Jesus. Victory did not come at once, because the Jesuits had friends in the provincial *parlements.* Of twelve *réquisitoires* (bills of charges) presented by various *procureurs généraux,* six were for the Society and six against. Councilors were often divided, as careful study of local deliberations reveals. On the whole, however, the position of the Parlement of Paris was ratified, and the court resigned itself to confirming the decrees of the majority. The alliance between the Parlement of Paris and the proponents of Jansenism gave rise to a political rhetoric in which the monarchy was characterized as despotic and the Gallican clergy was criticized for acting as a political instrument of the regime. What gave the movement its strength, however, was surely its religious aspect and its appeal to individual consciences. Jansenism receded from the limelight, but its struggle in alliance with the *parlements* left a legacy of protest that became a permanent feature of French public opinion and helped to establish the right to debate not only religious policy but many other matters as well.[14]

Tax Protests and Antireformist Sentiment

Conflicts in all areas proliferated in the 1740s, culminating at some point after 1750. Montesquieu's prudent theory, worked out at the time of the first remonstrances, expressed the idea that it was in the best interest of the public for a harmony to exist between the government and the courts:

> The bodies that hold the laws in trust are never more obedient than when, late in the day, they lay before the prince reflections upon the laws of the state of a sort scarcely to be expected from the insufficiently enlightened court or the ever-pressed royal councils. What would have become of the finest monarchy in the world if its magistrates, by dint of dawdling, disgruntlement, and prayer, had not thwarted the very virtues of its kings when those same monarchs, consulting only their own vast souls, wished to reward services ren-

dered with boundless courage and fidelity with equally limitless compensation?[15]

The king's sovereignty was protected, while the influence of the courts was maintained. Such moderation gave way to a more active determination to respond to each new crisis by any means available. Increasingly, the chief sticking points were administrative and fiscal rather than religious, and the impact of discord was even greater as a result.

In 1725 the Parlement of Paris protested against the *cinquantième*. In 1741 it renewed its protest against the *dixième*, in 1748 against the *centième denier*, in 1750 against the new *vingtième*, and in 1756 and 1759 against the third *vingtième*. From then on protest was constant. It focused on the initiatives of the *contrôleur général*, Machault, who worried about paying for the expenses and debts of war and sought to develop the resources necessary for a more rational fiscal and administrative system. To that end, he proposed taxing the privileged. One after another, all the *corps* protested, and remonstrance after remonstrance was submitted to the king. In 1763 Bertin eliminated the third *vingtième* and the increase of the *capitation*, but he extended the second *vingtième* for six years, widened the application of the *droits de mutation*, and initiated property assessments. The Parlement of Paris expressed its outrage but under compulsion registered the fiscal edicts, only to have the king back down, thereby confirming the power of the courts.

The tax question gave rise to countless pamphlets and broadsides as well as treatises and other theoretical works: in 1760 Mirabeau proposed universal taxation in his *Théorie de l'impôt;* Roussel de La Tour, a *conseiller* of the Paris Parlement, advocated a modification of the *capitation* in his *Richesse de l'Etat;* the *avocat* Darigrand argued against the Ferme Générale in his *Antifinancier* (1763). The debate heated up: twenty-two pamphlets were published in support of Roussel, whom Jacob Nicolas Moreau, writing on behalf of the government, attacked in his *Quelques Doutes su la richesse de l'Etat*. Roussel and Darigrand urgently called upon public opinion to back the fiscal policy of the courts against that of the court. The court, for its part, sought the "trusting collaboration" of the magistrates, but in vain, although this effort, backed by Malesherbes and pursued by L'Averdy, gave rise to a variety of texts proposing ways to harmonize taxes, develop the national wealth, and introduce needed reforms. Protest erupted everywhere, and reform edicts were greeted with a hail of remonstrances. "These," the magistrates of Rouen proclaimed, "solidify public opinion. They sustain the courage of the downtrodden, which so easily evaporates when their champions desert them."

Encouraged by local opinion, spurred on by clan and family rivalries within each court, galvanized by success, and increasingly aware of playing a "representative role," the sovereign courts found it possible to attack, almost with impunity, the regular tax hikes, the *commissaires'* administration, and the omnipotence of the Ferme Générale. They could now plausibly aspire to the role of proposing needed changes, a voice in opposition to all who favored higher taxes. This opposition unified the protest movement, which reflected both privileged interests and segments of a divided public. The protest had popular backing everywhere, and it led to a major crisis that raised questions about authoritarian monarchy itself. All this had an immense impact on the political culture.

From Protest to Principle

The court, the king, the Council, and a series of principal ministers criticized the restiveness of the sovereign courts and the Roman-style rhetoric of their "senators." Louis XV, Malesherbes observed in 1772, "has a great attachment to despotism and a great aversion for the *parlements* and the affairs they occasion." In the conflict that would become the greatest "affair" of his reign, the king bet on the Council, to which he assigned the task of preparing the answer to the *parlements* that would eventually find its place in the declaration of March 3, 1766. Everything was spelled out in black and white: the *parlements* did not constitute a single body whose parts were distributed among physically separate locations; they were in no sense an intermediary power between king and people; they had no right to resist the king's will and on no account were they authorized to constrain the sovereign. Remonstrances were part of the game, but the winner was foreordained by the rules of absolutism, about which Président de Brosses had this to say: "Here is the heavy artillery: oriental despotism and naked tyranny!" All the king's ministers supported this reinforcement of his authority: the comte de Saint-Florentin, who headed the Royal Household; Bertin, a reformer and authoritarian; L'Averdy, who replaced Bertin at the Contrôle Général and abandoned the parliamentary cause for the absolutist camp; and Choiseul himself, who negotiated with the *parlementaires* but was irritated by their resistance: "Will the king suffer the Constitution to be changed by mad whims and a resistance senseless in both form and substance? . . . Like Monsieur le Prince [i.e., Condé during the Fronde], I daresay that I have little skill at chamber-pot warfare, and the king should not waste more than a hundred of his troops on it. That number, with one gun and four pounds of cannonballs, should suffice to silence the *parlements'* big guns."[16]

But the conflagration was spreading. The Parlement of Paris fanned the flames by issuing a series of remonstrances in 1756 protesting the king's treatment of the *parlements* of Guyenne and Normandy. In 1758 and 1759 it unleashed its fury against the *intendant* of Besançon, Bourgeois de Boyne, who had ordered the banishment of refractory *conseillers*. Nearly all the sovereign courts joined in the attack on the king, his *lettres de cachet*, and his disciplinary orders. Only three remained silent: the *parlements* of Douai, Metz, and Pau. In 1763 the courts spoke out in defense of the *parlements* of Rouen and Grenoble, and again in 1765 in defense of the *parlements* of Pau and Rennes. In the latter, the conflict involved a clash between two powerful personalities: M. d'Aiguillon, the *commandant* of the province, and La Chalotais, the *procureur général*. As positions hardened, prosecution of the irascible La Chalotais bogged down, and the remonstrances of the Paris Parlement grew more vehement, the king intervened personally. On March 3, 1766, at a *séance royale*, a *discours de la flagellation* was read, condemning parliamentary claims of legislative power as well as the principle of one *parlement*. Yet nothing— not royal discipline or the appointment of Maupeou, formerly *premier président* of the Paris Parlement, as chancellor—could quell the magistrates' wrath. The Brittany affair and the Paris Parlement's attempt to prosecute the duc d'Aiguillon triggered another royal intervention: Louis XV halted the proceedings, suspended the magistrates, and ordered Maupeou to reform the system of justice. This time, and until his death, the king stuck to his guns; what is more, he made two crucial innovations, ending both the sale of offices (with a plan to reimburse current officeholders) and charges for use of the courts. Malesherbes drafted a remonstrance for the Cour des Aides protesting the high-handed treatment of existing magistrates and calling on the public to support them and block their replacement; he also called for a convocation of the Estates General. But this move elicited little support from the other courts, and for three years authoritarianism reigned unopposed.

The consequences of this did not become fully apparent until after Louis XVI had reinstated the *parlements*. Within the government there were administrators and others for whom the future of the monarchy depended on the ability of "enlightened despotism" to make necessary reforms. Their failure marked the failure not only of absolutism but also of the administrative reorganization promoted by the triumvirate consisting of Terray, Maupeou, and La Vrillière. The vehemence of the opposition revealed the depths of the crisis in the privileged *corps* and the impact of that crisis on the cities. It also showed the strength of the antiabsolutist movement and marked a shift toward "national" principles. The parlementary opposition developed four themes, which resonated with the political criticism of the Enlightenment (common to the heirs of Montesquieu, the readers of Mably, and the audiences that attended the plays of Beaumarchais): the right of the sovereign courts to represent the nation; the nation's right to accept or reject new taxes; individual rights; and the separation of powers.

After 1750, when the *parlements* refused to register a royal edict, they also insisted on the right to review all legislative texts: the law, it was asserted, was not the expression of the will of the monarch alone but the result of a decision. In the course of debate it became clear that the opposition case rested on three main points. First, the *parlementaires* insisted that the law was above the king and that the purpose of remonstrance was to point out contradictions between royal edicts and the fundamental laws of the kingdom: the law, the sovereign, and the state were all one. Second, the Parlement of Paris argued that the purpose of the courts as a body was to safeguard the law; in keeping with the theory of intermediary bodies, it was up to the courts to ensure the rule of law, if necessary even against the will or whim of a misguided or misinformed monarch. Finally, a distinction was made between the king and the nation: if the king represented the state, he no longer represented the public. The *parlementaires* dispelled the "mystery of the monarchy." In place of the traditional vocabulary of "subjects" and "peoples," they used the vocabulary of "nation." They bolstered that vocabulary by borrowing from natural-rights theorists the idea of a "contract," an idea that some critics associated—wrongly—with the oath of anointment, which in fact obligated the king not to the nation but only in the eyes of God. As F.-O. Martin has shown, the notion that the courts' remonstrances were also the nation's, indeed that the courts represented the nation, was based on the principle of a "union of classes," a principle derived from a "historical fiction," the supposed general assembly of Frankish warriors, which was in fact a convenient figment of the *parlementaires*' imagination.

From reasoning such as this came the idea that the courts had a right to intervene in the legislative process, and in particular to consent or refuse to consent to any tax. Here, the *parlementaires* moved beyond the traditional view that their responsibility was to inform the king when his subjects were in distress, call for reductions in spending, and demand the abolition of taxes made necessary by war; they adopted the more radical position that they had a right to resist if the fiscal rights of the nation were flouted. This responsibility was invoked in the 1759 remonstrances against the third *vingtième*, which ultimately led to calls for a convocation of the Estates General by the *parlement* of Rouen in 1760 and the *cour des aides* of Paris in 1771, calls supported by nearly all the provincial courts.[17] Such demands were based on the idea that the lawful rights of the people could be invoked even against the king, an idea whose full consequences would not become apparent for some time.

The *parlementaires* did not conceive of individual rights in the same sense as the philosophes. They were interested not in freedom of expression or conscience but in defending the rights of individuals against arbitrary acts of absolute authority. In religious matters, in the use of *lettres de cachet* to exile appellants, and in repressive measures intended to compel their obedience, they saw opportunities to assert their rights as magistrates. The remonstrances of April 4, 1759, asserted that according to the ordinances of the kingdom, they could not be hindered or thwarted in the exercise of their functions by *lettres de cachet* or any other means, nor could they be removed from their positions for any reason other than death, voluntary resignation, or proven abuse of authority. In other words, there could be no liberty without respect for regular judicial procedures. When Voltaire attacked the *lettre de cachet* in *Le Huron* (1767), he was simply harping on the persistent idea that the infamous *lettres* were nothing but an instrument of despotism, which of course was not entirely accurate. The *parlementaires*' criticisms were consonant with the views of proponents of natural rights as expressed in the *Maximes du droit français* (1772). At the time such arguments were more important than the defense of equality, which was not of concern to many magistrates or philosophes before the 1780s. Taken together, these various causes gave rise to the suggestion, still very cautiously expressed, that the courts should be independent of the executive, that the laws should define a boundary between justice and administration.

Taken together, the various crises that agitated the sovereign courts had two important consequences: they sharpened the conflict between the particularist spirit and the logic of reform and administrative expansion of the monarchy, and they contributed to the formation of a public spirit or public opinion stimulated by government harassment, professed in the common interest, and defended in pamphlets and brochures. The temporary defeat of the *parlements* in 1771 brought an important phase of the old political culture to an end. In any event, the monarchy, as it lurched from one compulsory registration and ostentatious remonstrance to another, had provided a space for negotiation that allowed for the peaceful expression of fiscal and religious discontent. The *coup de majesté* caused the whole ancient legal system to unravel. In self-defense, the sovereign courts sought the support of a different coalition of opinions, which led to the emergence of a group of people who already were being called *patriotes*, people prepared to challenge the society of orders and *corps*. In trying to defend their own interests, the sovereign courts, which were historically a royal creation, had given voice to critical opinion. First muzzled and then restored, that opinion could not backtrack when the final crisis came; the only option was to move forward.

The King and Public Opinion

The crisis of the Ancien Régime began much as a mirror breaks: a sharp blow cracked the surface in many directions at once, revealing lines of weakness and strength. Over a fifteen-year period we witness a series of attempts to save the monarchy, and at each stage the consensus on which the regime was based disintegrated a little more. The institutional crisis pointed up the deficiencies of each new government. None of these enjoyed the backing of supreme authority, which was embodied in a king too scrupulous and too listless to do what was necessary, or the insight of the traditional dominant classes, who remained too absorbed in their own affairs to measure the ways in which political relations had changed. France was thus afflicted with both a crisis of government and a crisis of authority, compounded by financial difficulties. The depth of these crises became apparent only gradually, as the country proceeded through a series of political experiments and expedients.

As we saw at the outset, Louis XVI's accession to the throne was taken as a sign of hope. Before the reign was very old, however, uncertainties about the future began to reemerge. The triumvirate was deposed despite its successes, and the new government, with the conspiratorial Maurepas pulling the strings, was divided between *choiseulistes* like Miromesnil, who was named Garde des Sceaux in place of Maupeou, and philosophes like Turgot. What the public saw was a government weakened by uncertainty and personal animosity, tension between the various functions of the Council and the "ministries," and maneuvering on the part of outsiders scheming in the shadows to get back in, such as Choiseul, who returned to Paris after the death of Louis XV, and Necker after his first ministry. The period can be divided into four phases, each associated with the name of a principal minister: Turgot (1774–1776), Necker (1776–1781), Calonne (1783–1787), and Loménie de Brienne (1787–88). With each new government, the monarchy's inability to reform itself became increasingly clear, and the collapse of the Ancien Régime as a political system became apparent.

Turgot's Experiment

Turgot's brief tenure marked the fact that the new thinking had reached the Contrôle Général. Jacques Turgot brought with him a feel for government that he got from his family, experience acquired in the field, and a belief in reformist principles. His work, from the *Eloge de Gournay* (1756) to the *Essai sur la formation et la distribution des richesses* (1766), proves that he had thought about the problems of the day. He was a moderate Physiocrat who believed in a natural social order that reason could comprehend and governments ought to promote. His thinking was, in its origins, the polar opposite of the *parlementaires'*.[18] Turgot was also a liberal who believed in the power of free trade to breathe life into the economy. The strong point of his policy, as set forth in the *Mémoire sur les municipalités*, written by his friend and adviser Dupont de Nemours, was to combine fiscal reform with a reform of representation so as to offer a greater voice to landowners, people with shares in the "net product" of the nation, and people in a position to encourage economic development.

473

His vision embodied the dream of a monarchy in which self-interest would be regulated by reason, state intervention would be harmonized with free economic initiative, sovereignty and power would be shared by the king and property owners, and all decisions would be underwritten by intelligence.

More concretely, Turgot concentrated his efforts in four main areas. The first, though crucial, is difficult to interpret. On October 20, 1774, the reinstatement of the *parlements* seemed to subject the crown to supervision by the robe. In any case, it negated the work of Maupeou, who had achieved a political revolution by breaking the power of a single social group to paralyze reform. Turgot did not oppose this move, either because he saw it as a necessary concession to his enemies (Maurepas and the queen) or because he, along with Malesherbes, acknowledged that the *parlementaires* represented a valid segment of public opinion, a truth that the abbé de Véri and Condorcet denied. In any case, remonstrances were no obstacle to Turgot's reform experiments, for the *parlements* were no longer as militant after 1774, and the king's minister was able to overcome their resistance. While Turgot's willingness to compromise helped initially, it caused difficulties later on when he lost the confidence of both the king and the *hommes de privilège*. In the area of budget and finance—the second area on which Turgot concentrated—he sought to slow the rate of tax increase, to apportion taxes more equitably, and to reduce the state debt, and in so doing encountered few obstacles. He counted on his economic policy to increase tax revenues as a result of higher prices. Third, as a commercial liberal, he called a halt to Abbé Terray's earlier experiment with regulation (it, too, a source of dissension). Turgot's edict of September 13, 1774, abolished Terray's regulations. In its preamble Turgot forcefully affirmed his belief in progress against prejudice, but the results for 1775 did not bear him out. Fourth and last, he proposed a series of physiocratic social measures, two of which were of fundamental importance: the reform of *corvées* and the elimination of the *jurandes* and *maîtrises* that controlled employment in certain occupations organized by guilds.

The failure of the grain policy, the "flour war," and the remonstrances of the courts attest to the coalition of various opposition groups. At the bottom of the social hierarchy was the *populace*, which lived in terror of "dear bread," an affliction that people were inclined to "impute not to the nature of things but to the wickedness of men."[19] They wanted a regulated market. Meanwhile, at the top of the hierarchy, the elites of court and city joined in wariness of innovations that threatened their privileges. This led to the paradox of 1775–76: a minister who had put down riots and sought to pursue progressive policies found himself isolated by the opposition of monopolists and men of privilege. In April 1775 Necker published a large tome, *Sur la législation et le commerce des grains,* which caused a sensation and presaged a return to a managed economy. Turgot's disgrace marked the failure of the alliance of philosophy with absolutism, the defeat of enlightened despotism in France, and the impossibility of overcoming entrenched privilege. It also demonstrated the strength of antiabsolutist sentiment, the disintegration of central authority, the power of the *corps,* and the pervasive ambiguity of their opposition, which sought to defend inherited privilege while promoting certain aspects of Enlightenment philosophy.

The Necker Interlude

Turgot was dismissed on May 12, 1776. "Good is impossible, Turgot has been toppled, and I weep for France," the abbé de Véri noted in his diary. Along with Necker came a policy that Choiseul inflected toward war with England and a return to a state-managed economy. The two were linked, because military intervention aggravated France's chronic ailment, namely, shortage of finance. The war cost a minimum of a billion livres, and the Genevan banker's preference for borrowing over fiscal reform— "He waged war without taxes," Mirabeau exclaimed, "he is a god!"—dramatically increased the public debt. His appointment to the Council with the title of director of the treasury and, later, of finance, alongside Taboureau, who nominally held the title *contrôleur général* but wielded no power, marked two fundamental changes in the policy of the monarchy.

The first of these changes came at Turgot's expense when Necker and his advisers began their campaign to seize power. The scion of a family belonging to the Genevan oligarchy, Jacques Necker was an experienced banker who had made his fortune through lucrative loans that shored up the tottering Compagnie des Indes. By the time he gave up speculating, his wealth stood between 7 and 8 million livres.[20] There was no mystery about where it came from: his bank. He learned the ropes of government while serving under Terray in negotiations between the state and the Compagnie des Indes. In 1772 the banker became a diplomat; in pursuit of office he also launched a publicity campaign, doubtless among the first of its kind. Three factors proved decisive: the role of his wife and of the salon on the chaussée d'Antin, where Abbé Morellet, Abbé Raynal, Marmontel, Grimm, Diderot himself, and Buffon until his death provided the banker with a solid intellectual cover; the maneuvering for academic chairs, which extended Necker's influence to all of Parisian society and various provincial institutions; and Necker's own work in economics. When the *Eloge de Colbert* was selected for a prize by the Académie Française and read to that body by d'Alembert on August 25, 1773, Necker earned philosophical consecration for his political ambitions. As is well known, the *Eloge* was in effect a declaration of candidacy cast in the hollow, superficial elegance typical of the academic eulogy. In it, Necker affirmed certain moral principles and praised conjugal virtue in terms apt to provoke laughter at court and among libertines but also to appeal to adepts of lachrymose philosophy in the city. His *Essai sur la législation* (1775) hammered the point home: Necker was a thinker who despised the theories of the physiocratic sect; he also had thoughts, destined to become influential later on, about the "iron law" of wages. In the end, his strength was perhaps to represent middle-range opinion, confused, easily frightened, afraid of reform and the problems it created. His success was not in presenting new ideas but in orchestrating existing ones in a favorable climate: he created an image.

This brings us to the second change. Necker stood for banking and international credit. He was a man who knew how to arrange large loans and feed the state's growing appetite for cash. His position on the fringes of the King's Council symbolized the reason for his appointment: not to direct policy but to bolster public confidence and finance war with a minimum of pain. He came to power as a man who knew where to find money, who understood the secrets of finance, and he would keep the royal treasury afloat the same way he had revived the Compagnie des Indes, by measures that turned out to be precarious and ultimately ruinous.[21] Rentiers of every stripe applauded. The public, temporarily won over, offered its support. The court and the pro-war faction were divided because the banker talked out of both sides of his mouth. The privileged grumbled.

With respect to finances, Necker managed the deficit: he negotiated short-term loans, attracted money from Geneva and Holland at 8.5 and 10 percent, and meanwhile tried to impose savings that no one wanted.

With respect to reform, he tried to circumvent obstacles by modernizing the apparatus of government, especially in the area of finances. He modified the structure of the Council itself and eliminated the *intendants des finances* and *du commerce*. He initiated political reforms, following Turgot's lead by replacing the *intendants* with assemblies which were granted local administrative powers and in which landowners (half from the Third Estate, a quarter each from the clergy and the nobility) were represented and voted by head. The experiment was tried in Berry, Guyenne, Dauphiné, and the Nivernais. It was a partial success and marked an important step toward improved circulation of information. But it had the effect of uniting the opposition: courtiers, *intendants*, magistrates from the Council, the queen, the *parlements*, and the clergy. Necker's response was a testimonial to his genius: in February 1781 he published the *Compte rendu au roi*, which presumably summed up the state of the king's finances but actually discussed only the regular budget (*l'ordinaire*) while saying nothing about the deficit in the special or war budget (*l'extraordinaire*), where a billion and a half in military expenditures were hidden; add to that a further deficit of 90 million livres in the regular budget, concealed by sleight of hand. In fact, Necker's report was neither a budget nor a balance sheet but a publicity stunt. Yet it earned him an undeserved reputation as the man who ended secrecy in the regime's finances and established a limited monarchy on the English model, with a responsible head of government. Four months later, however, his government fell, opening the way to further years of uncertainty and inconclusive experiments.

From Calonne to Brienne and Brienne to Necker

From 1783 to 1787 the reins of government were entrusted to Charles de Calonne, the last in a line of financiers and *parlementaires* from Douai, who had served in the *parlement* of Flanders and as a *maître des requêtes*, an opponent of the sovereign courts in the Brittany affair, and *intendant* in Metz and Lille. He had experience at all levels of government and had formed advantageous connections at court with the Condés, Polignacs, and Luynes. He came to the "Hôtel des Déménagements," as the headquarters of the Contrôle Général was known, with substantial experience under his belt, but his role in opposing La Chalotais and perhaps also the drafting of the remonstrances of March 3, 1766, had earned him the lasting enmity of the *parlements*. His two-pronged program unfolded in two stages.

First, he tried to revive the economy in order to maintain the state's creditworthiness, so that he could borrow abroad. A series of initiatives was designed to create a climate of confidence: these included an agreement with the Ferme Générale, public works projects, rescue of the Compagnie des Indes, and an Anglo-French commercial treaty. Well advised by the future Talleyrand, Dupont de Nemours, and Vergennes's secretary Gérard de Rayneval, Calonne made France a showcase for change and Paris the capital of speculation. Swiss bankers such as Perrégaux, Clavière, Scheitzer, and Panchaud made the most of this opportunity, betting that the market would rise or fall on the basis of the best information they could muster. It was the heyday of the "money manipulators," financial companies, and currency and stock speculators, but the collusion between the high society of the Ancien Régime and profit-hungry speculators was exposed to the harsh light of day, as was the excessive indebtedness of the wealthiest landowners. Calonne's economic policy had the effect of generating funds needed for the development of manufacturing and industry at a time when income from land was heavily mortgaged and enormous bankruptcies were shaking the aristocracy; yet much of the cash set in circulation by taxation and borrowing failed to reach its intended destination. On the whole, indebtedness increased the circulation of paper, and credit transformed real estate debts and *rentes* into negotiable securities, but the scope of these changes was limited to specific sectors. The public saw a disparity between the amounts of money squandered by the state and court, which were living beyond their means, and the real resources available. It was perhaps the first time in history that such a disparity was noticed.

By 1786 Calonne found it impossible to borrow additional funds and was obliged to acknowledge the growth of the deficit, the failure of his reinvestment policy, and the need for emergency measures. Already in December 1785 the Parlement of Paris had condemned the latest loans in new remonstrances. In a work entitled *Précis d'amélioration des finances*, Calonne proposed a revolution in three areas: fiscal, comprising a reduction of the oldest imposts *(taille, aides, corvées)* and replacement of the *vingtième* by a territorial subsidy assessed on all landowners; economic, with free trade in grain, elimination of internal tariffs, and unification of the national market; and political, entrusting management responsibilities to representative assemblies and submitting proposed legislation for ratification not to the *parlements*, as was traditional, but to an assembly of notables which convened in December 1786. In February 1787 this last maneuver ended in failure when the assembly, while accepting all of Calonne's other proposals, rejected the proportional, egalitarian tax on all landowners if not duly approved in the traditional manner. Thus administrative reforms worked out by high-level functionaries, *conseillers d'Etat,* and economists ran up against a coalition of privilege and enlightened opinion. Nobility, magistracy, and clergy (and the clergy in particular, keen to protect its prerogatives and immunities, played a decisive role) formed the heart of an opposition that began to call for a convocation of the Estates General. Calonne's initiative thus triggered the machinery of consultation. Like Necker, the *contrôleur général* appealed to public opinion, which did not back him. His *Avertissement,* a warning shot fired over the heads of the notables, led supporters of Necker and Brienne to join forces; intrigues multiplied. Calonne was dismissed.

The new *contrôleur général,* Loménie de Brienne, epitomized the administrative talents of the clergy. An ambitious, intelligent, and enlightened prelate as well as a rather libertine *philosophe,* clear-sighted and ready for compromise, Brienne followed the same paths, encountered the same obstacles, and suffered the same setbacks as his predecessor. His efforts revealed the growing resistance to reforms imposed from above. Political change was impossible because it required the consent of people who benefited from and therefore supported the Ancien Régime, as well as the approval of public opinion, whose demands grew more insistent with each new crisis. This final phase of political conflict (1787–88) can be characterized as a noble reaction, an aristocratic revolution, or a revolution of notables. Then, in 1788, came the socioeconomic shock that drove the people into the arena. Hence Brienne, the archbishop of Toulouse, assisted by competent advisers (he recalled Malesherbes and appointed Nivernais, both well-known *philosophes*), had only sixteen months to overcome a legacy of accumulated and growing difficulties. He reformed the Council, reduced the bureaus, and made massive cuts in the court budget, by now a symbol of waste. The notables, who had agreed to the idea of equal taxation, rejected the first fiscal edicts in the absence of any means of national consent or control. The king dissolved the assembly on May 25, 1787. Brienne revived the project of English-style provincial assemblies together with a doubling of the representation of the Third Estate. Some twenty of these regional assemblies were successfully launched with enthusiastic support from a segment of the provincial nobility and considerable participation by the legal profession. On the local level the administrative monarchy thus enjoyed a brief period of success, but not long enough to resolve the deficit problem.

Brienne was thus obliged to confront the *parlements*. The year 1788 marked the climax of the old conflict between the absolutist administration and the robe. In July 1787 the Parlement of Paris, though divided between patriots and moderates, called for a convocation of the Estates General and recognition of the principle of no taxation without consent. On August 4 the king ordered his edicts registered. On August 7 and 13, on a motion by Duval d'Epremesnil, the *parlementaires* voted to disobey the king's order. They were exiled to Troyes, then recalled under pressure from the Chambre des Comptes and the Cour des Aides bolstered by major popular demonstrations. Louis XVI thus found himself backed into a corner where he had no choice but to bring matters to a head, as he had clumsily attempted to do in 1774 only to reverse himself. He ordered Lamoignon to begin a reform of the magistracy, which triggered a revolt by the magistrates of the high courts, supported by the local nobility and clergy. In the political debates, speeches, and literature of the day, three main issues were discussed: the rights of man, a theme introduced by the patriot wing of the Paris *parlementaires* (Fréteau, Duport, and Duval) and given resonance by the success of the young American republic; the defense of "liberties," whose powerful appeal stemmed from a certain confusion between the singular and plural senses of the term; and the idea of convoking the Estates General, which meant that the *parlementaires* had ceased to pose as the representatives of the nation. Thus the old monarchy faced rebellion by both the traditionalists and the modernists, a coalition of disparate interests and privileges on the one hand and political abstractions on the other. The provinces were in turmoil: the *pays d'Etat* were demanding reinstatement of their rights as well as of their assemblies where applicable, and the movement garnered support from the people, especially in Rennes and Grenoble, where the protest turned violent. On August 8, 1788, Brienne and the king gave in to the pressure and convoked the Estates General for May 1, 1789. Brienne stepped aside in favor of Necker. With these two acts the divine right monarchy acknowledged its helplessness. It put itself in the hands of the public and its financial wizard.

This narrative of the series of crises that beset the monarchy shows how the practices of political struggle and the principles of a political culture simultaneously crystallized around two main conflicts: a conflict over the best way to solve the kingdom's financial problems and a conflict about whether representation should take a traditional or a new form. This ever more ambiguous conjunction of two conflicts became increasingly explosive with each new crisis and each new attempt at reform. At the time there were of course no political parties in the modern sense, only factions, which were at once pressure groups, movements of public opinion, and networks of patronage, solidarity, and sociability that sparked political alliances and oppositions. Perhaps 2 million people became actively involved in politics, although they still lacked any clear sense of the vicissitudes of political life. In the capital, as well as in the major parlementary cities and a few active centers of capitalism, an extensive and heterogeneous group of people felt concerned with problems of state and government, with fiscal and financial policy, because these things had an impact on the very basis of the power of the traditional nobility, to say nothing of people's daily lives. Philosophical societies, newspapers, and publishers (covert as well as overt) relayed news of events in Paris to the tiniest villages via networks of intermediaries. Until 1787–88 the public opinion thus engendered nursed two hopes, two major political tendencies.

In this sense one can say that there were two parties, a party of reform and a party of monarchy, but with the caveat that the two were sometimes allied and sometimes at odds, because it was possible for the hope of reform to be invested in the monarchy. Indeed, the ablest defenders of the monarchy as a global political organism, a social and political system, were not always monarchists. The most striking feature of the new political culture was that it developed not outside the monarchy on the basis of abstract philosophical speculation but inside the orderly structure of monarchical institutions. In this insidious conquest the *parlements* played a central role, and it was Maupeou's reform that finally transformed the opposition movement into a mobilization against "despotism." Michelet rightly saw this moment as the death of the monarchy. In the ensuing crises, practices had a chance to define themselves, while ideas remained confused. The vocabulary of protest unified the opposition all the more easily because its key terms were ambiguous: nation, fundamental rights, constitution of the kingdom, sacred and inviolable laws, liberty/liberties. Each of these notions cut more than one way, but taken together they allowed the opposition to coalesce. It was in the course of the long struggle against absolutism that the final confrontation emerged, the insoluble opposition between inegalitarian society and egalitarian society, which rendered any compromise among elites useless: events would decide the outcome.[22] We turn next to the question of how discussion within Enlightenment society created the underlying conditions for this final transformation.

PART THREE

Enlightenment and Society

15

Life Triumphant

UNABLE TO REFORM, incapable of choosing between the past and the future, the monarchy was sick. The past could be measured and understood; history and philosophy could shed light on its nature. About the future nothing was known, for no prognostication had ever proved effective, but people imagined it, constructed it, and tried to clear a path for it. Prophetic ideas and projects poured forth. A few were tried, with varying degrees of success. Hundreds of utopian thinkers braved immutable traditions and principles and tried to invent the new society of the future. Nobody knew what would emerge from all the crises, from the many difficulties that the regime in the past had somehow always overcome. The state had survived because it had always managed to find exceptionally able servants, who analyzed its ills and proposed effective, or potentially effective, reforms. Yet in each case, after Machault and Turgot, and even Necker, Calonne, and Brienne, the troubles always returned.

In two areas in particular, tax reform and reform of the *parlements*, the desire for change went unfulfilled because it ran counter to the very nature of society, to the very principles on which society was based. Ever since the time of Louis XIV, it had been obvious to great administrators and countless reformers that the state had no choice but to expand its tax base, which meant reducing the privileges of those exempt from taxation or limiting their ability to avoid certain taxes. The increase in the deficit only reinforced the egalitarian challenge: it mobilized *liberties* against *liberty*. The fact that first the *parlements* and later the notables regularly exerted such a powerful influence on the opposition to "despotism" points up one of the regime's fundamental contradictions: the venality and heritability of office made the leading *parlementaires* the most prominent defenders of the social privileges and political customs that defined their status within the monarchical state. The reform proposed by Maupeou, who was working on the grand project of a unified judicial code for the entire kingdom, went to the political and social heart of the matter. Lamoignon's ultimate reform added insult to injury, but too late and with less audacity than Maupeou's, for venality was left intact. By recalling Necker in 1788, Louis XVI and his advisers condemned the monarchy to follow public opinion and thus set policy on a day-by-day basis. By offering a possible solution to the financial and fiscal problem, the Estates General might indeed have saved the Ancien Régime. We know that this did not happen, but the idea that it might have is not absurd.

Still, the main phenomenon was undoubtedly the introduction of public opinion into the traditional conflict between the monarch and the *parlements*. Political debate became more serious. The nature of the discussion was transformed by its extraordinary publicity, as newspapers, pamphlets, and brochures carried the news to the "little people." Scholars have counted 312 such publications for the period 1774–1786, while the number rose to more than a thousand in 1787–88 and to 3,305 in 1789.[1] Because pamphlets could be produced cheaply, many aimed to reach the lower strata of society. They relied on the tried and true formulas of other mass market publications: political catechisms, almanacs, comic texts, and ribald parodies. A kind of dialogue developed between readers, whose numbers were growing, and authors (many of whom were anonymous, a fact that makes it difficult to study them as a group). This literature has much to teach us about the conventional wisdom of the time, the underlying tensions, and the catchphrases that people picked up in the course of their daily activities or learned from elders who had witnessed the clash between the forces of tradition and the forces of change. As deep-seated currents reshaped society and transformed individuals, a popular political memory and culture emerged. Age-old practices began to be questioned as large numbers of people discovered new ideas and possibilities: "What sort of man is not a scholar nowadays? What footman, tailor, or fruit vendor does not wish to be a philosopher? The rage to learn has become a national disease." This opinion, voiced in Paris by Olympe de Gouges and corroborated by many others (such as the bookseller Hardy), needs to be examined carefully, but it does suggest that the path that people followed to "the invention of liberty" and to the "construction," at all levels of society, of forward-looking individuals deserves close study. We need to consider the experience of the Enlightenment in terms other than confrontation with the political system.

If we are to understand how the new world developed, we must not isolate changes in consciousness from material change: this fundamental theme is what unifies the various approaches I have taken in this book. The fortunes of a society can be assessed in terms of improvements in living conditions, both physical and spiritual, and the emergence of new social personalities. If it is still possible to interpret Enlightenment politics as an attempt to organize collective coexistence and secure the happiness of individuals, it is because it was during this period that society discovered that its fate was in its own hands rather than in the hands of God and was able to mobilize a variety of forces galvanized by the new belief in progress and science. People began to trust in the power of the will with an optimism born of the triumph of intelligence, and they began to live and talk and look at things in new ways that questioned the whole of existence. What had been a fundamentally religious, backward-looking society now began to look to the future and at the same time became increasingly secular.

The Triumph of Life

In the second half of the eighteenth century the population of France grew rapidly.[2] This growth, which needs to be measured and understood, increased the country's ability to confront nature, take stock of its situation, and channel forces that had previously lain beyond human control. A new belief in science and progress encouraged innovative thinking and experiments in fields such as agronomy. Various institutions promoted new ideas and spurred discoveries. Theory and practice reinforced each other across the land, changing man's relation to nature.

Situated at the intersection of biology, the environment, and human consciousness, the "theory of climate" is a good example of the influence of man's changing relationship with nature. Theorists argued that man, while subject to the laws of climate, is capable of modifying those laws. Consciousness is partly shaped by the world but is also partly independent of it. In order to conceptualize climate, one needs a certain frame of reference, a way of integrating man into the structure of the living. In a study of "nostalgia," a concept that physicians and other thinkers derived from the theory of climate, Jean Starobinski has shown how homesickness was understood as an affliction of wandering, disoriented minds: the nostalgic individual was a displaced person, who could be cured only by returning home and recovering home's associated certainties.[3] Man was thus a creature whose life was intimately intertwined with all ambient forms of life. This sentimental attachment to nature affected the development of science and technology, which in turn altered the "human dimension" and man's attitude toward life itself.

The Lesson of the Graphs: Demographic Growth

The royal administration sponsored numerous surveys to determine the number of households and measure local and national populations as well as to assess the tax base. From 1724 to 1726, for example, salt tax inspectors and collectors in the Paris basin surveyed the people in their districts. After 1740 new methods were employed in gathering statistics on both the national and regional level. Traces of these methods are common, but it is difficult to lay hands on the results. A novel way of studying population changes was developed. Instead of counting heads, one could take the number of births in a given year and multiply it by a calculated coefficient. In 1757 the *intendant* La Michodière and his secretary Messance proposed a "universal multiplier" close to 25. The administration ordered all *intendants* to apply this method of calculation to annual birth statistics in order to gauge the growth of the population. From Terray to Turgot to Necker, administrators were required to fill in tables with a variable number of columns indicating sex, marital status, approximate age, and in some cases social rank of persons in their districts. The use of the universal multiplier introduced certain distortions and discrepancies, of which men such as Moheau, Montyon, and Necker were aware.

Historians now argue about population figures based on parish registers, whose quality improved over time and with progress in clerical education. From this debate it has emerged that eighteenth-century Frenchmen mistakenly believed that the population of their country was declining. Although this error led to better theoretical understanding of economic and demographic phenomena, the fact is that the French population increased. The loosening of the demographic vise proved vital and rejuvenating.

Population equals wealth: the eighteenth century inherited this important principle from the mercantilists. In the late seventeenth century, however, population losses owing to war, repeated economic hardship, famine, and disease led to a reconsideration of the role of population. For the reformers of the early eighteenth century, an abundant population was no longer the primary cause of wealth; instead, wealth was said to have a decisive influence on demography. For Vauban, Boisguilbert, and their successors, production and consumption were the key factors in economic development, determining the link between supply and demand, needs and resources. Population still played a role, however, since productive effort was impossible without a sufficient number of citizens. The specter of depopulation, which haunted the ancient empires and toppled Rome, had influenced everyone's thinking since Montesquieu.

People believed that the population of France was falling. This belief became a weapon of enlightened philosophy; it fueled the debate over agriculture; and it was a central hypothesis of the Physiocrats and others who attacked reform. The idea of decline figured in all economic thinking. Population depended on customs, as Cantillon demonstrated with his fable of the "man-eating horse": a coach required four to six horses, each of which required twice as much land to support it as a farmworker. A flourishing population was a consequence of economic circulation, not a cause; population increased in proportion to wealth and income, hence a growing population was in the national interest. The only remedy for demographic decline was economic growth: so believed the liberals as well as the proponents of a state-managed economy, the moderate reformers as well as the utopians. Conversely, adversaries of growth such as Rousseau and Mably were obliged to take a regenerative line, advocating a return to nature and condemning cities and their superfluous consumption. Could economic expansion and populationism be prerequisites of prosperity?

As the debate came to a close, people began to take a more sophisticated view of what to expect from demography. As we saw with respect to urban populations, Moheau and Montyon expounded the need for scientific knowledge, arguing that mathematics was the only way to achieve sound rules for collective progress. Underlying the period's thinking was an imperative need, evident in the descriptive approach taken by the Encyclopedists and their pupils, to understand the relation between natural phenomena and social facts, as well as man's relationship to space and the constraints imposed by economy and society.[4]

Today, of course, we can compare the calculations of the demographic pessimists and the estimates of the political arithmeticians and others with data from selected samples. We find that eighteenth-century experts believed strongly that the population of France was declining despite their own data to the contrary (in works published in the last two decades of the century). For instance, Brion de La Tour's *Tableau de la population de la France avec les citations des auteurs au nombre de soixante-douze, qui ont écrit sur cette partie de la statistique* (1789) tabulates all available data, yet his discussion of the multiplier factor often yields implausible results. In fact, the second half of the eighteenth century was a period of almost steady population growth: Expilly counted fewer than 21 million Frenchmen in his *Dictionnaire* of 1765 and just under 23 million in his *Mémoire au roi* of 1783. With the authority of Laplace and Condorcet, the Académie des Sciences proposed a figure of 25 million in that same year, and Lavoisier offered the same figure a year later. All estimates proposed in the period 1787–1789 fell somewhere between 24 and 27 million.

When I was a student, estimates put the population of France at the end of the Ancien Régime at approximately 25 million. More recent estimates by the French national demographic institute (INED), based on careful study of parish registers (presumed to give a complete record of births) and certain auxiliary hypotheses (that the number of people entering France equaled the number of people leaving and that discrepancies in birth and death figures for each generation are accounted for by missing statistics for deaths of children under five), place the population of the kingdom in 1789 at very nearly 28 million. In all probability the population in 1740 stood at 24.6 million and in 1700 at 22 million (if we count the territory within France's present boundaries). These figures indicate a growth of 13.4 percent in fifty years, as compared with 38.8 percent for England. For earlier periods, the best we can do is to compare high and low estimates based on interpretations of various demographic trends, especially in the birthrate, and on the rate of recovery from crisis.

Until the reign of Louis XV, the French demographic system was fragile, and scholars for a long time explained this fragility in terms of the "Malthusian scissors." Changes in population, Malthus argued, are regulated by mortality: when the population increases, living conditions deteriorate as the subsistence level dwindles. Famine and epidemic are therefore able to cut a swath through a weakened population. There are major problems with this argument as applied to the eighteenth century, however. For one thing, eighteenth-century demographic growth did not result in the expected increase in mortality. For another, crises were not limited to the most populous regions: population changes varied from region to region, and cities had a dynamic of their own, some gaining and some losing citizens. If we are to understand the relation between mortality and fertility, mortality and natality, we must acknowledge marriage as an additional regulating factor. The age of marriage was the "veritable contraceptive weapon" of seventeenth-century Europe: a high average age of marriage yielded a birthrate almost 25 percent below what was theoretically possible. This was necessary to maintain the equilibrium of the system: a peasant could not start a family without land, and there was a one-to-one correspondence of families to farms almost everywhere. The difficulty of supporting a family limited the marriage rate in the cities as well, and growth was possible only through geographic mobility and consequent social *déclassement* or even proletarianization. After each crisis, the recovery process entailed an increase in marriages and births. Society maintained its own level, which was not determined by the subsistence level so much as it was the very condition of subsistence.

Fewer Crises, Vital Growth

The eighteenth century's demographic growth highlights the fact that, in comparison with the previous period, crises were now relatively infrequent. In a sign of major progress, the mortality rate declined, and the number of births consistently exceeded the number of deaths. The explosions of mortality that had disrupted the natural demographic cycle in the "classical period" diminished in intensity, frequency, and impact. The years 1709–10 marked a turning point: this last severe demographic crisis of the Ancien Régime had the virulence of an epidemic decimating an undernourished population. It left traces everywhere and struck everyone's imagination. We do find subsequent periods of heightened mortality (1740–1743, 1747, 1772–1775, 1779–80), but these were of relatively limited scope. The crisis of 1743 actually began as early as 1738 in the north and subsequently invaded Brittany, the east, and the south. Mortality preceded rising prices; epidemic diseases were the leading cause of death. In 1747 and 1748 the southwestern and southeastern parts of France were affected, from the Lyonnais to Guyenne. In 1772–1775 and 1779–80 it was mainly the west of France that suffered. The last major plague epidemic, 1720, was mainly confined to Marseilles, where the bacillus arrived from Syria aboard the *Grand-Saint-Antoine*, but the disease did extend into upper Provence and the southern Massif Central. It claimed some 120,000 victims in all. This ultimate outbreak of plague put an end to centuries of terror and showed that, even in the absence of an effective medical treatment for the plague, quarantines and *cordons sanitaires* did pay off. Although the new practices marked a great improvement over the past, it was clear that the south of France, which had to a degree been spared by the deadly scourges of the Grand Siècle, was vulnerable to a new threat.

The great Anjou epidemics of the decade from 1775 to 1785 illustrate the way in which disease first attacked poor regions in times of famine.[5] The dysentery epidemic of 1779 ravaged Anjou from summer through autumn. People looked on in amazement as the malady laid waste to entire cantons, and for the first time in a long time the number of deaths exceeded the number of births. This would be the last year in which that happened until the 1790s. The Anjou example also demonstrates the inequality before death that characterized these final shudders of the old regime of mortality. Everywhere the small number of the privileged and well-to-do—better housed, better clothed, and better fed than others—survived more readily than the vast army of the wretched, for whom disease was a child of poverty. The scourge mobilized the administration, led by the *intendant,* du Cluzel, and his *subdélégués.* These late epidemics encouraged people to think about matters of public health, including not only the question of how to treat the afflicted but even more how to prevent future disasters by keeping a close watch on the health of the population and encouraging economic development.

The diminished frequency of lethal epidemics would not have sufficed to ensure vital growth if the normal mortality rate had not also decreased somewhat, but the precise extent of this decrease is still controversial. Yves Blayo maintains that the French birthrate did not change much: from 39.9 per 10,000 in 1740, it rose to 41 in 1750 but declined again to 39 in the 1760s and later dropped still further to 37 or 38. The mortality rate, which remained almost stable at 40 per 10,000 in the early 1760s, slowly decreased: between 1775 and 1789 it wavered, hitting 30.6, 37.1, and 35.5

in selected years. There was no return to the high level of the 1740s and 1750s.[6] Not until the decade 1780–1789 do the experts find any noticeable change in the mortality rate for children from one to five years of age, half of whom failed to survive. The decrease in infant mortality did not come until after 1790, and even that date may be too early, since there was a temporary degradation in the quality of record keeping. The shift may not have occurred until the turn of the nineteenth century.

Two yet-to-be-confirmed hypotheses are worth singling out for special mention: first, that childhood mortality may have declined to one degree or another at certain points in the eighteenth century; and second, that life expectancy remained low because adult mortality also did not improve much after the major victories won over the plague. If life expectancy is calculated at age five (in order to eliminate the effect of the very high infant mortality rate), we find that it was 40.25 years before 1750 and 44.5 before 1789. For women, the change was similar: from 41.2 to 44.3. These gains are not remarkable, but something had begun to change. Infants continued to die in large numbers, but there was progress: the well-off lived longer, and it is not impossible that other adults had also begun to enjoy longer life spans.

The difficulty of achieving firm answers to these important questions divides the optimists among demographic historians (Pierre Chaunu, J.-P. Bardet, J.-P. Poussou) from the pessimists (Jacques Dupâquier, Blayo). Both groups are apt to interpret rates in a manner that justifies their longer-range interpretations of demographic change. The optimists think that there was a clear improvement in the mortality rate in the eighteenth century, while the pessimists see only a few preliminary signs of progress that would not be confirmed until the nineteenth century, with further changes in the economic sphere and accelerated progress in medicine. In any case, we can be sure of one thing: after 1750 the population did begin to grow, and once it did there was no subsequent downturn, such as occurred in the fourteenth and seventeenth centuries.

Understanding sustained growth requires attention to social and economic as well as demographic factors. Progress depended on many little things, and when we examine these we begin to see why age-old attitudes toward life and death also began to change. For one thing, the narrow victory over death was won in part by commonsensical methods that anyone could put into practice. With help from the state in making these known, a new state of mind, conducive to long-range transformations, began to develop even before nineteenth-century medical advances dramatically accelerated the pace of change.

Growth and Medicalization

Actual demographic expansion posed a threat to the equilibrium of the demographic system (population increases were supposed to lead to land shortages, which in turn were supposed to limit further expansion of the population), and hence on the ability of supply to keep up with demand. Until the nineteenth century, demand exceeded supply. Population growth, by increasing the supply of labor, led to a transformation of rural society. Some sectors of the economy thrived, such as large farms, which consumed massive amounts of labor, and rural industry, which provided work and allowed higher population densities, as in the Valenciennois. People worked more than one job, each complementing the other, and increased use was made of female and child labor. Meanwhile, however, there existed a vast reservoir of labor, consisting of people who had neither new jobs nor expectations of inheriting land. Rural proletarianization fed migration and urban growth, which in turn enabled the countryside to sustain an increased population. The new dynamic equilibrium was fragile, however, as the crisis of 1775–1790 revealed. Nevertheless, it did not reverse the trend.[7]

Growth undeniably permitted a transformation of the rural economy, the nature of which is still a matter of historical controversy. In turn, this transformation had a major impact on the industrial sector. Some scholars have challenged the idea that there was an "agricultural revolution" in the eighteenth century and have argued that the signs of an "economic takeoff" are misleading.[8] Output appears to have increased less rapidly than population. Still, the population growth was real and has to be explained. Three explanations have been proposed.

The first involves several factors: the intensification of labor, the introduction of more frequent and more complex crop rotation systems, and the consequent planting (or extension to wider areas) of new crops such as corn, potatoes, and, in poor regions, chestnuts. In proto-industrial zones, part-time industrial work, coupled with subdivision of farm plots, sustained an increased population. Hence growth did not necessarily depend solely on higher yields, which in any event have been questioned in the case of wheat and rye, the two major grains used in bread making.

Higher yields were not the only element of the supposed "agricultural revolution" and should not blind us to other changes.[9] Improved yields and more extensive cultivation of wheat, technical improvements in the preservation of grain and in milling, and undeniable innovations in the use of clover and alfalfa for pasturing, in fertilizers, in plowing and soil conditioning methods: taken together, these things show that in large-farm regions, in areas close to cities, a breath of modernity allowed for both demographic growth and the initial stages of agricultural expansion. Marc Bloch and Ernest Labrousse were not altogether wrong.

Indeed, the second explanation extends the scope of progress still further. Where the environment allowed, various initiatives increased the intensity of cultivation, for which the availability of labor was indispensable. Small regions thus began to specialize in commercial agriculture. This was true of the vine-growing regions of Alsace and Beaujolais, for example. Wine was exchanged for wheat, something that could not have been done without complementarity of regional production and a flourishing grain distribution network such as existed in the Paris region and in southwestern France. Large farmers served as examples to others and helped to spread knowledge of new techniques.

Finally, the third explanation is that at least part of the growth can be attributed to improvements in the road network, which made for better distribution of agricultural products as well as easier circulation of men and information. Growth was not linear and did not benefit everyone: economic and social blockages left many people unemployed and turned some into vagabonds: 10 percent of the population was reduced to permanent begging. But the effects of growth on urban and industrial sectors were crucial as trade began to have an impact on the structure of demand. Certain areas of production, such as livestock rearing (whose cultural system was more elastic than that of grain growing), adapted more rapidly than others. The existence of grain shortages and social instability should not blind us to the fact that experimentation with new methods did take place.[10] Life became easier in unexpected ways, and this made demographic growth possible.

On the farm as well as in the cities, such growth was intimately intertwined with a noticeable shift in attitudes toward death and disease and a willingness to seek medical help. Of course, it does not follow that disease necessarily declined as a result (although the frequency of plague outbreaks surely did). We need to know more about the precise nature of many endemics and epidemics before we can say why they became less prevalent. Mortality diminished in many key areas, as rough and ready methods yielded many small victories.

Smallpox was one front on which progress occurred. The "red death," a contagious disease that was at once endemic and epidemic, wreaked havoc everywhere: La Condamine proposed a figure of 50,000 to 80,000 deaths from smallpox in France in 1754, with a particularly high rate of morbidity among children. The struggle against this familiar disease began in England, and Voltaire took up the battle cry in the eleventh of his *Lettres philosophiques*. French physicians were divided over the wisdom of inoculation (and the pro-vaccination faction would not win a clear victory until the early twentieth century). The battle was waged locally by enlightened physicians and with the encouragement of the authorities, as in Franche-Comté, where Girod became the "apostle" of inoculation. The royal family and other high nobles set an example: Louis XVI and his brothers were inoculated in 1774, and inoculation became fashionable. Tronchin and Gatti inoculated the elite, while country doctors attempted a more general prophylaxis. Behind all these initiatives lay a state-sponsored expansion of medical intervention, the expression of a new, and zealous, belief in life.[11]

Another important area of change, by now well known, was obstetrics. The shift was fundamental. In both countryside and city, childbirth had been enveloped in a symbolic realm in which fertility rites, magical beliefs, and birthing techniques served to calm fears and overcome insoluble difficulties. The key figure in this dominant culture was the midwife, a woman of moral authority in whom the secrets of childbirth were vested. Her ministrations affected not only the mother but also the newborn, whose very shape was hers to mold. All the powers that be were jealous of her role: the Church, the state, and, in the eighteenth century, the medical establishment. The midwife was condemned for her failings, her untheoretical methods, and her ignorance. The *accoucheuse* of old was forced out in favor of the *sage-femme*, the professionally trained midwife over whom the authorities exerted a tight control. This made it possible to instill basic principles of obstetrical hygiene: boiled water and Marseilles soap became the indispensable accompaniments of childbirth. The training of professional midwives gave rise to a novel form of royal intervention. Rather than send her midwives to school, France sent a teacher into local communities: for twenty-five years the celebrated Mme

Du Coudray crisscrossed the kingdom. Using a realistic "dummy," she gave courses in midwifery that amazed rural and urban students alike. Out of these classes came cohorts of excellent midwives.

At this point pressure for further changes came from obstetrical physicians and surgeons. As their knowledge of anatomy and useful nostrums increased, they pushed for additional courses for midwives and expanded their propaganda campaign. The doctors triumphed: they won in part because people saw the results and asked for their services, in part because mothers were more aware of the potential complications of childbirth, and in part because royal, municipal, and religious authorities were on their side. The authorities encouraged midwives to serve as emissaries from the cities to the countryside and soldiers in the war against "prejudice and superstition." They also encouraged physicians to expand their services into rural areas.

Two tendencies thus converged. The naturalistic worldview, which had linked living and dead in a fragile community held together by various rituals and symbols, was rapidly disappearing. Meanwhile, the transformation of religious and urban, scientific and medical, administrative and utilitarian culture dissolved old family solidarities. Fatalism gave way to hope: people began to seek medical care from doctors and midwives. The medical community had state backing, symbolized by the Royal Society of Medicine, founded in 1776—an institution typical of the enlightened state.[12]

The creation of this society, sponsored by Turgot and led by Vicq d'Azir, one of the leading figures of Enlightenment medicine, had a profound impact on both the medical world and the government. It was proposed that physicians should end their isolation by entering into correspondence with one another and investigating the causes and symptoms of disease. By publishing "topographies" of sickness, the society hoped to speed up medical training and improve therapy. Underlying this agenda was the idea that epidemics were linked to the seasons and that it might therefore be possible to map pathologies and identify pathogenic social sites. Hospitals, prisons, barracks, camps, and ships became, along with cities, observation posts for studying the causes of disease and experimenting with cures. The object of all this was the "public good," an old ideal that neo-Hippocratic medicine turned into a positive goal to be pursued with all the resources of government. From the Contrôle Général to *intendants, subdélégués,* and physicians involved in the study of epidemics, observations and information were passed around and shared, statistics collected, and effective remedies publicized. The Royal Society, with help from local learned societies, overcame obstacles and collected thousands of facts and a torrent of statistics.

The medicalization of French society after 1750 shows two things: first, people had changed their thinking about nature, so that their goal was no longer to unveil nature's secrets as much as it was to understand its mechanisms; and second, progress would have been impossible without specialization and professionalization.[13] The Royal Society of Medicine may not have done much to push back the frontiers of mortality, but it did bring about a fundamental change in attitude, a change similar to that which we will encounter when we look at the evolution of religious beliefs. People began to question stability, to reject scandalous situations they had once accepted, and to believe in progress. We can try to measure the extent of that belief by looking at two places where science and nature converged: in agronomy and in academies of science.

The Triumph over Nature

If the scientific and philosophical elite now found it possible to look upon death and disease as "redoubtable enemies," it was because scientific discoveries had made it possible to believe in life: it might just be possible to loosen death's viselike grip on the living. "The physician is the only philosopher who deserves to be honored by his country," La Mettrie proclaimed in *L'Homme machine,* which he dedicated to Haller, a professor of medicine at Göttingen. The statement is but one reflection of a general increase in esteem for creative individuals who generated useful knowledge. Two of these, the agronomist and the scientist, directly contributed to man's mastery over his world.

All of society depended on agriculture, yet agriculture remained a simple business of cultivating fields using old-fashioned techniques that produced mediocre results. Few innovators were thinking about how to increase yields. New editions of Olivier de Serres's *Théâtre d'agriculture* appeared all the time, and each reprinting of Estienne and Liébault's *Maison rustique* incorporated scattered signs of change.[14] Before agronomy, innovators were mainly interested in such marginal matters as flower and herb gardens and vineyards; new methods and formulas such as pruning and grafting, training and tillering, forcing and bell-glassing were constantly compared. Florists and gardeners familiarized others with the idea that living things could be understood and improved.[15]

Agrarian science marked a sharper departure from past practices. The keys were experimentation and quantitative measurement. In 1787 Lavoisier published his *Statistiques agricoles et les projets de réforme*, which answered a question that obsessed Europe at the time and still obsesses historians today: "Why is agriculture less advanced in France than in England? The [French] nation is no less hardworking or industrious than the English nation."[16] The mobilization of agronomists and the theoretical, if not practical, triumph of agronomy demonstrates the joint role of science and government, the pressure of increased social needs, and the importance of ensuring adequate supplies of grain and wood. Economists showed how markets ought to be organized. Indeed, organization was initially more critical than productive science. This did not change until the eighteenth century, when scientific agronomy became an indispensable component of a new agriculture that made men and animals less dependent on the elements. The experiment was not successful everywhere, however: the "agronomic revolution" depended on prior legal and social reforms to make it work.

Reform through Agronomy

In the preface to his *Eléments d'agriculture* (1762), Duhamel du Monceau writes:

> Broadly speaking, what is the mechanism of vegetation? What are the best ways to clear land for cultivation? In what does good plowing consist, and what may it hope to achieve? What are the different fertilizers, how are they obtained, and in what ways are they best used? How should seeds be selected and prepared? In what different ways may seed be sown? What care is required of grain while it is in the ground? How should it be harvested, threshed, cleaned, and stored? What are the best tools for plowing? Is natural pasture preferable to artificial pasture? How should pastureland be prepared? What special methods are required for growing certain useful plants? Finally, what are some of the abuses that stand in the way of agricultural progress? Broadly speaking, these are the subjects that will be treated in the two volumes I am presenting to the public.

This catalog of subject matter shows the state in which the new science arrived on the scene. A proponent of the "new agriculture," Duhamel stressed the connection between needs, theory, practice, and reforms. He and his colleagues in the Académie des Sciences were present on all the fronts where the battle of growth was being waged: in the forests, which provided fuel and building materials for everyone, in the workshops and factories, on construction sites, and wherever useful instruments—from spoons to shoes to spinning wheels to looms—were made.

The expansion of manufacturing and construction of new forges, coupled with urban growth, left forest resources in short supply, cutting into both capital and revenue and overwhelming attempts to regulate woodland use. The incompatible needs of different communities gave rise to conflicts, which the administration tried to resolve. All this led to reflection on ways to improve the wood supply, perfect furnaces and heating systems, and save fuel. Duhamel consulted charcoal burners: "To save wood, burn charcoal." Réaumur thought about forest management. Buffon investigated the physics of trees. It was a time to economize by using resources wisely while planning for future woodland expansion.

The threat to the land was better understood. Wheat—a "necessary evil"—exhausted the soil and forced farmers to clear new land. Solving the problem required introducing new plants in order to make continuous planting possible. French farmers turned to their English counterparts for a model, which they then adapted to local conditions. This was possible because France had "discovered" England, which had been experimenting with new techniques since the time of Francis Bacon. England was a prosperous rural nation with its eye on the future, but it was not until 1715 that the French noticed the flourishing English countryside—a veritable earthly paradise whose orchards, plowed land, and hedgerows made a beautiful landscape where grass grew in abundance, farmers loved to plant, aristocrats loved to farm, and everyone ate roast beef. Britain served as a "lesson" and an "example." Pioneering agronomists studied British methods. By 1750, Duhamel du Monceau's *Traité de la culture des terres* popularized the "new system." To list only its essential features: the extension of pastureland limited the expansion of wheat fields, allowing rural space to "breathe." Forests did not have to be cut down. But in order for the system to work, the land had to produce more per acre. The British system linked livestock rearing to wheat farming through a new foddering system: herds could thus grow and produce manure to fertilize the land. English agronomy posed a challenge to French farmers, who did not understand that the logic of the English system was to place a premium on grassland, meat, butter, and cheese. France remained loyal to grains because grains had made England rich; but the French failed to see that England was abandoning grain in order to bet on the international market. In France, only a few regions felt the influence of urban markets: in Normandy, for example, peasants grasped the advantages of selling to Paris consumers. Change may have been slow because most people viewed the new system through the lens of the old grain-based system. Lavoisier's calculations demonstrate this.

How could improvements be made perceptible, and how could the capacity for change be measured so as to convince skeptics and doubting adversaries? As the great chemist, landowner, and experimenter wrote: "One cannot hope for immediate changes. One can only lay the ground-work for a series of slow revolutions, because in order to increase the amount of hay, one has to use more fertilizer, and in order to produce more fertilizer, one needs more hay. Clearly, these two linked goals can be achieved only gradually." In order to make improvements concrete, farm-ers needed to keep accurate records and compare the results of old and new methods. Lavoisier's recommendations are reminiscent of the early empirical work of the Physiocrats, which Quesnay and his disciples later abandoned in favor of the abstraction of the *Tableau* and normative economics. The key concepts were already present in their early efforts to establish agricultural accounting, a realistic microeconomics based on measurement of output, recording of costs, and comparison of results. Ultimately agronomists hoped to observe regional differences and iden-tify the effects of disparate agricultural customs.[17]

Lavoisier borrowed certain aspects of physiocratic microanalysis and applied them to agricultural chemistry: "There is an equation, an equality, between what is produced and what is consumed. Hence in order to know what is produced, it suffices to know what is consumed, and vice versa." Instead of calculating what the soil yielded, he proposed starting with what each individual animal consumed. Lavoisier's approach was quanti-tative: "Everything that goes into the barn is counted or weighed . . . All the quantities that come out are likewise numbered and weighed." Output could then be related to the quantity of ingredients required to produce it. He also measured "territorial wealth" using similar quantitative tech-niques, designed to leave no room for illusion. Lavoisier substituted science for common sense, statistics for mere observation and description. Once perfected, however, the method had to be taught to farmers: this was the ultimate, and almost insurmountable, obstacle.

In fact, agronomy in general took a somewhat different path. It defined itself as a science, and its influence was extended not so much through systematic teaching as through controversy, especially the controversy over Physiocracy. Agronomy was not an exclusive doctrine or an abstract science; it did not rely on soil physics or chemistry. It was essentially descriptive and explanatory in its coverage of all aspects of the rural economy. It was a place where various sciences came together, thereby drawing farmers and scientists together as well. Agronomy eventually gained recognition as an independent discipline. In 1753 it was accepted as a legitimate specialty by the Academy of Sciences. At the time it was associated with "English-style agriculture," although it maintained its own distinctive identity.

Because agronomists saw themselves as enunciating laws that farmers ought to obey, they challenged tradition and called the very organization of rural society into question. Agronomy questioned routine, interrogated everything from the shapes of fields to the role of landlords, and attempted to measure poverty. It not only told men how they ought to behave but also, because the ultimate goal was to improve the agricultural system in general, developed new techniques and methods and more ambitious theories, investigated the pathology of animals, plants, and soils, and proposed therapies for the maladies of each. Vicq d'Azir and Bourgelat pioneered in veterinary medicine; Du Tillet worked on phytopathology; and Puvis, a reader of Bergman, specialized in pedology, soil treatment, and marling techniques, while others investigated methods of storage. Information was disseminated both by agronomic journals and by travelers. The English traveler Arthur Young was an agricultural observer and a reader of the agronomic press. Traveling naturalists like him familiarized the people they visited with new techniques and new crops and pointed out the dangers of dependency on a single crop and the advantages of rotation and diversification.

As this new theoretical and practical discipline developed, and as its proponents engaged in debates and exchanges with others, many new voices made themselves heard. The agronomic movement was by no means identical with physiocratic agriculture. Quesnay's agro-social system was based on the notion of cultural individualism; it assumed a curtailment of traditional usages and assigned a leading role to landlords. Thus, as A.-J. Bourde points out, it was in effect a technological gloss on the principles of "la grande et riche agriculture," that is, a style of large-scale farming that was extremely hard on smallholders. Not all agronomists shared Quesnay's assumptions, however, and some dreamed of legal and social changes to accompany the "agronomic revolution." "Philosophical economists" developed the idea that politics could and should promote the new agriculture as the basis of economic development. Thinking about the reorganization of space and property pointed toward the wisdom of homogenization and, beyond that, to the need for a national market. Gradually agriculture was suffused with a new spirit: farmers began weighing their harvests and calculating their profits, while a group of bourgeois and noble improvers, "distinguished men of the common class" (in the words of Arthur Young), encouraged the ferment that was opening agriculture up to the influence of capitalism. Turgot gave one section of his *Réflexions sur la formation et la distribution des richesses* this title: "The Deficiency of Capitalist Entrepreneurs Limits the Exploitation of Small Farms." We thus come back to a question posed earlier: Was the agronomic movement limited to a small number of primarily noble landlords, or did it have an impact on its immediate environment?[18]

The Improvers Revisited

Improvements did occur despite the absence of a complete program. They occurred mainly within a restricted milieu of readers of agronomic texts, a milieu whose extent will be more clearly understood when scholars have finished inventorying the quality and size of collections of books on agronomy. J.-M. Moriceau has pertinently identified three types of individuals who contributed to the dissemination of this literature. First were the administrators. Among them were ministers, such as Bertin, whose influence extended well beyond his work at the Contrôle Général (1759–1763), since he remained an active, economically oriented, and influential *secrétaire d'Etat* until 1780; his staff engaged in vigorous discussions up to the time of Necker's resignation. There were also *intendants* such as Turgot and Limousin and d'Etigny in Auch, as well as *subdélégués* and numerous other officeholders. The second group consisted of men whom Moriceau calls "initiators": aristocrats such as La Rochefoucauld, royal officeholders who kept a close watch on their estates, and gentleman agronomists such as the marquis de Turbilly, who promoted land clearing in Anjou and whose work interested Arthur Young. Many of these men set up model farms in accordance with the precepts of Lavoisier and Duhamel: they documented their activity, read books, and subscribed to journals. It may be that not all of them succeeded, but this remains to be seen. Locally, they created tensions necessary for change. Finally, a third group of improvers consisted of bourgeois property holders, noble land-lords, and educated farmers. Although this was the largest of the three groups, it is the least well known. Its members served as intermediaries between the city and the countryside and set an example for more modest peasants. Some well-informed farmers read to keep abreast of the latest developments and were prepared to adopt profitable new techniques, while others belonged to the elite and were members of royal agricultural societies.[19]

These royal societies partially supplanted the academies; they enjoyed the direct protection of the administration as long as Bertin was in office, although Bertin, who took advice from Turbilly, saw to it that the new societies did not offend the older institutions. Between 1757 and 1763, sixteen royal agricultural societies were created: in Rennes, Tours, Paris, Limoges, Lyons, Orléans, Riom, Rouen, Soissons, Alençon, Bourges, Auch, La Rochelle, Montauban, Caen, and Valenciennes. Four others were added before 1789: in Poitiers, Aix, Perpignan, and Moulins. The geographic distribution of these institutions shows that they could not exist unless the local *intendant* was in favor and local notables were interested. Their density, which is higher to the north of a line drawn from La Rochelle to Soissons than to the south, suggests the importance of possible relations with England and above all the influence of large-scale farming on agronomic thinking. The further influence of Paris and of the capital's great landlords may also have created conditions favorable to agronomy. Finally, in areas where there were no royal agricultural societies, there were sometimes other centers of discussion, such as the Estates of Béarn, Languedoc, and Burgundy as well as academies that may have continued to take an interest in rural matters, as in Montpellier, Nancy, Bordeaux, Arras, Amiens, and Besançon. Elsewhere, academicians often played a key role: interests, goals, social representation, and a belief in progress based on the spread of knowledge were the same in both networks. Bertin, Abeille, and the marquis de Turbilly were all active in the academies. The goal in every case was to disseminate new agronomic knowledge based on research, experiment, and debate, following the example of England's "agronomic bureaus." Both farmers and scholars were invited to participate in the societies, whose membership was less restrictive than that of the academies.

Many agronomic bureaus were located in fairly small towns, where the members of the agronomic society represented the "party of Enlightenment." The dream was to create an organism "in which farmers would become philosophers and philosophers would learn to be farmers." Some thirty local committees included more than six hundred members, of whom the nobility accounted for 35 percent, the clergy for 18 percent, and the Third Estate for 36 percent. The social origins of the remaining 11 percent are not clear, but many undoubtedly sprang from the "rural bourgeoisie." Interestingly, participation by the upper nobility and country gentlemen was high, and the clergy was also represented, as were administrators, *subdélégués,* officeholders, a few surgeons and notaries, and even ordinary farmers and a few postmasters.

The Paris agricultural society included a number of recognized scientists among its members: Abbé Rozier, Tessier, Commerelle, Parmentier, Valmont de Bomare, Fourcroy, Cadet de Vaux, Vicq d'Azir, and Chaptal. Rural members were specialists: the gardener Pépin, farmers such as Etienne Charlemagne and Cretté de Pallel, Charlemagne's son-in-law Bernier, a seigneurial farmer, the farmers Mouron and Opereix, the *engagistes* Delporte and Lormy, and the postmaster Petit. Everywhere farmers, administrators, and people in a position to disseminate information played a key role. Because papers were published anonymously, it is likely that less important farmers also participated. J.-M. Moriceau has shown that new techniques were often emulated by neighbors and relatives of better-known modernizers. The great improvers—Lavoisier, the duc de La Rochefoucauld, Malesherbes, the duc de Charrost, the marquis de Guerchy—not only served as patrons of the movement but also set an example for others. New methods were put to the test and debated. Old agronomic classics were reprinted and sometimes updated in accordance with changing tastes: such works included *La Nouvelle Maison rustique* (1783) as well as more popular texts such as *Le Parfait Maréchal* and *Le Médecin des pauvres.*

It would be misleading to say that the new agronomy triumphed over all obstacles, but its influence should not be underestimated. Its importance is measurable in a large-farm region such as Ile-de-France, where the introduction of artificial pastureland, fertilizer, and other technical innovations made possible a first "green revolution." Here, no doubt, agronomy merely accelerated a trend initiated by the proximity of Paris and the development of a true rural capitalism. Elsewhere, as in Beaujolais, a small group of oenologists stocked libraries on the subject and experimented with nontraditional techniques in their own vineyards. The Royal Agricultural Society of Beaujolais invented "Beaujolais nouveau" and *soutirage*, a technique for clarifying wine by drawing off a portion of a barrel. People began to look at problems in new ways. The risks of innovation, which at first only a few people were ready to confront, diminished. "Farmers do not learn from books. We learn from our successes, our mistakes, our trials and errors, because the facts are obvious and provide the only documentation we need," wrote Abbé Rozier, who believed in the power of example. Rural modernization, regardless of whether it came through intensification of human labor or investment in new techniques, could not occur if peasants opposed it but would come only with their support, and this required teaching. Hence we come back to the issue with which we began: that of the number of people living on the land and the beginnings of social conflict. When peasants became too numerous, the land became their enemy, and the cities turned against the countryside. But literacy also began to spread.

Enlightenment agronomy responded to challenges of two kinds. It focused attention on the economic obstacles that made it difficult to meet the needs of a growing population. Turgot made this clear with his law of "nonproportional yields," or diminishing returns: "If inputs are increased, the output also increases, but to a smaller and smaller degree, until, at such time as the fertility of the land is exhausted and no amount of art can increase it, a further input would add absolutely nothing to the output." This was one difference between capital and land. Furthermore, agronomic science posed a challenge to tradition, if only by accentuating some of its inequities and provoking peasant mistrust: enthusiasm for agronomy sowed trouble. Believers in progress squared off against partisans of the status quo. Significant and sudden change is never acceptable to more than a minority. When change threatens the traditional way of life of the majority, it can come about only through trial and error; experiments must prove their worth over the long term. This may have been true not only of agricultural change but of a broader transformation of which innovations in farming practice were just one aspect: the conversion to a new mentality that placed its hopes not in custom or providence but in the possibility of transforming nature and controlling its forces, including biological forces, the latter being the major obstacle to progress in a world still ruled entirely by the net agricultural product.

The Hope in Science

How are we to write the history of science?[20] Obviously it is not easy to answer in a few pages: much ink has already been spilled, and will continue to be spilled, over the matter. To simplify a complex subject, the problem is to get beyond the debate between "internalists," who want to explain changes in science from within, and "externalists," who invoke sociological considerations and the historical context. This debate is far from over. It is difficult for historians, as opposed to historians of science, to intervene, because their "natural" tendency is to take the side of the "externalists" simply because most historians are not well versed in the internal conceptual logic of specific scientific disciplines.[21] But there is a real danger in reducing theoretical concepts to their simplest common denominator or in using extrascientific social factors to articulate them. This is a serious problem for the cultural historian who would like to explain the relation between science and Enlightenment, science and the ambient mentality of the age.

Two ideas may be helpful in this regard. First, we can look on science as an "institution" which defines and displays certain objects, encourages invention and innovation, and for a time establishes the validity of and teaches a body of doctrine and technique, a feat that would not be possible without a relatively homogeneous scientific community. Hence there must be some kind of dialogue between conceptual matters and matters of a social and political order. Second, in addition to measuring the distance between the content of science and its context, the historian must look at the social issues that influence scientific work in order to show the ways in which science is a cultural construct.[22]

Science produces reality by the way in which it organizes research and through the methods, instruments, practices, and interpretive systems it adopts. "But for the science that men build upon it, nature is silent."[23] These remarks are intended to encourage historians to change their attitude toward science and adopt a less superficial approach to the subject.

Here, I can do no more than mention some of the issues at stake in the encounter between the Enlightenment and science; more specifically, I will show how certain values became part of man's common capital. The dissemination of books and education and the proliferation of scientific academies encouraged belief in both science and progress, utility and knowledge, or, rather, in the utility of knowledge. To say this is already to indicate certain limits: the appeal of science could not extend beyond the literate and learned, whose ignorance was only partly alleviated by the vulgarization of science that was the most important intellectual phenomenon of the time, as a glance at the bibliography of the period quickly reveals.

From Reading to Social Dissemination

As the number of published books increased, from fewer than a thousand titles per year in 1715 to four thousand by the end of the century, so did the number of scientific books. The growing number of books on science and the arts came at the expense of religious publication—a sign of increased interest in man's relation to nature and society. Scientific publishing had not increased in the seventeenth century; the scientific revolution that, from Galileo to Newton, had sought to translate the world into the language of mathematics and physics had yet to have an impact on the world of publishing. The growing power of scientific works in the eighteenth century is yet another instance of the way in which innovations occur first on the margins only to win broad acceptance later on. All aspects of science and the arts gained in popularity, suggesting an encyclopedic ambition to classify the things of this world and master a desacralized universe.

This shift in interest has not yet been fully studied. The nature of scientific books themselves changed, and this change affected both scientific thought and the relation of science to society.[24] For example, Latin and Greek, already abandoned by some scientific writers in the seventeenth century, were used less and less. The switch to the vernacular increased the potential audience and initiated a brisk market in translations. "The scientific book will always have an international dimension because science is international." Books circulated not only among individuals but also among institutions. The example of agronomy illustrates this, but we see it also in chemistry (Lavoisier knew Priestley and

Cavendish), physics and mathematics (think of the role of the Bernoullis), and medicine (Boerhaave). Translations were also opportunities for translators to debate with their authors, as when Buffon translated Stephen Hales's *Vegetable Staticks* in 1735 and altered that work's providentialist explanations, or when Lavoisier and his wife translated Kirwan's *Essay on Phlogisticon* and published it together with Lavoisier's refutation in 1787.

Scientific production itself changed. The disciplines gradually became more independent, and there was notable progress in the natural and experimental sciences. Meanwhile, notorious controversies and enthusiasms triggered brief flurries of interest in certain subjects. One sees this in debates over the nature of comets, the measurement of the earth, and the wisdom of inoculation. Such moments came when the needs and interests of the public coincided with the work of specialists. Further evidence of the tendency to publicize useful scientific discoveries can be seen in the number of books devoted to subjects such as venereal disease (on which five hundred titles appeared between 1670 and 1815), electricity, magnetism, and of course agronomy. The decline of Latin and Greek, the availability of translations, the adoption of new ways (including conversational dialogue) of presenting scientific discoveries, and the publication of scientific textbooks made scientific subjects available to growing numbers of bourgeois and noble readers. Scientists and amateurs alike needed periodic updates to keep abreast of the latest developments and enjoyed playing "games with physics" and "mathematical recreations." Abbé Pluche's eight-volume *Spectacle de la nature* went through twenty editions between 1732 and 1770; a best-seller, it was purchased by twenty thousand people and may have reached as many as a hundred thousand readers. The work was a veritable compendium of scientific subjects from the natural sciences to the study of man in society. It was cast in the form of a conversation involving an aristocratic couple living in the country, an ecclesiastic, a scientist, and a young knight eager to complete his education in this rural setting.

People enjoyed the facile side of science, and bibliophiles snapped up illustrated books in abundance. Many of these were official works, published in installments. The most striking example was Buffon's *Histoire naturelle,* whose six hundred books in thirty-eight volumes were financed by the state and published over a forty-year period from 1749 to 1789, with immediate reprints as well as counterfeits—all the ingredients necessary for a huge success. The popularity of travel books (3,540 titles published in the eighteenth century compared with 1,566 in the seventeenth and 456 in the sixteenth) shows how scientific interests could converge with the desires of the public and the needs of the state. Travel literature, which depended on careful geographic observation and investigation, became the traveler's indispensable companion. Readers followed the progress of discovery in texts of various kinds: imaginary voyages, expedition reports, and descriptions of other civilizations that became the basis of the new anthropology.

The increased publication of science books and works of scientific vulgarization was directly linked to the expansion of science teaching. Instruction was available in three complementary forms: through schools, scientific institutions, and circles of amateurs.

Jesuit and Oratorian schools were quick to offer formal scientific instruction. In 1700, eighty of eighty-eight Jesuit *collèges* offered courses in physics; by 1761, the number had risen to eighty-five out of ninety. The study of mathematics and hydrography was encouraged by grants from local authorities. Teachers specialized as curricula and teaching methods grew more diverse while eschewing abstraction and metaphysics. *Collèges* equipped themselves with laboratories and collections of specimens. Large audiences possessed enough eclectic knowledge to follow scientific controversies in various fields. Meanwhile, the Oratorians continued a tradition begun in the seventeenth century by scientists such as Malebranche and Lamy; only a minority of the Oratorians' students took courses in "philosophy." Some twenty *collèges* offered regular scientific instruction to their pupils, and similar syllabi were later adopted by secularized *collèges* and schools founded or revived by the teaching congregations. It was partly for this reason that in 1776 the royal government chose a Benedictine school as the nucleus of the Royal Military School.

The steady expansion of science teaching in the *collèges* contrasts sharply with the difficulties that science faced in the universities, where tradition persisted and a series of reforms had failed to resolve problems stemming from the complex structure of the old faculties of arts. By contrast, the teaching of medicine and surgery appears to have been more open to innovation. The medical faculties welcomed the thinking that led to the clinical revolution, for example, and disease ultimately came to be defined by the clinical gaze; students learned at the patient's bedside to decipher the signs and symptoms of disease and classify them in accordance with accepted nosologies.

Apart from the schools, various public and private institutions took part in the teaching of science. The Jardin du Roi, or Royal Garden, founded in the seventeenth century, created new professorial chairs and added equipment and staff as it broadened its teaching to include chemistry, botany, and anatomy. Its prestige grew still more under Buffon, who died in 1788. Technical schools such as the Ecole des Ponts et Chaussées (founded in 1747) also offered courses (including the first classes in mineralogy, given here until the Ecole des Mines was founded in 1783); chairs in hydrography were created in many port cities; and drawing schools answered the technical and aesthetic needs of Parisian and provincial society. In those days drawing was an instrument for setting things down in a fixed form in order to act on them in one way or another, as well as a tool for teaching others to perform similar operations.[25] Further instruction was available from the Engineering School at Mézières and from various academies, museums, and lycées. The navy offered courses in health. Private courses in mathematics, physics, and medicine could be had in Paris and the provinces at boarding schools and scientific laboratories. Scientific experiments became fashionable, as did collecting and astronomy and meteorology. People began to invoke the authority of science. Lavoisier in Paris and Guyton de Morveau in Dijon were among the many wealthy amateurs and curious individuals to whom science appealed.

It is a mistake to see this appeal as simply a result of the triumph of natural science, which Diderot heralded as early as 1754 in his *De l'interprétation de la nature,* and the end of the reign of mathematics. It would be more accurate to see it as a reflection of the success of a movement that was interested more in the concrete than in the abstract. Apart from d'Alembert, the best minds of the century were not particularly good at mathematics, yet calculation played a major part in many of the new practical techniques. As Buffon wrote in his *Essai d'arithmétique morale* (1777), there are truths of different types, certainties of different orders, probabilities of different degrees. Clearly he had an inkling of the importance of the new language that encompassed all the sciences and their approaches to natural and human phenomena.

Academicism and the Values of Science

The Academy of Sciences set the tone. It can be seen as a reflection of the reshaping of science and culture, of a change in the hierarchy of scientific disciplines, ideologies, and cultural norms and values. The academy, which was subject to the influence of various individuals and groups, translated abstract principles into concrete roles and assignments. It focused attention on the relations between the scientific community, the society, and the government and between scientific and philosophical thought. By looking at the work of the academy, we can see how truth was constructed through controversy and practice.[26]

The creation of the Academy of Sciences in 1666 inaugurated a tradition. It was founded because of the need to disseminate information and resources. But unlike the Royal Society of London, the French academy was from the outset a monarchical institution that served as an umbrella for various private initiatives. It helped shape a corps of professional scientists with a utilitarian mission. The reign of words was over, Fontenelle said, and the reign of things had begun. Science was judged by its ability to transform the world. The institution succeeded because it linked the aspirations of the scientific community to the utilitarian concerns of the Colbertist administration, which created not a Baconian society open to all comers and all disciplines but a closed academy limited to Parisian scholars. The tension between open and closed models was resolved only in Paris; in the provinces it remained, because there the boundaries between recognized scientists, useful technicians, and distinguished amateurs were not as firmly drawn as in the capital. The academy was conceived as a technical adviser to the monarchy, as an instrument of glory to be judged by its fruits.

Three things made it a success. First, different categories of membership—*honoraires, pensionnaires, associés adjoints,* and *correspondants*—acknowledged different levels of competence and made room for wealthy amateurs. Second, systematic metaphysics was rejected. The academy did not try to decide between Cartesians and Newtonians; it laid down no dogma and insisted only on respect for observation, basing the progress of science on the accumulation of facts, on investigation before interpretation. Finally, the royal institution set itself up as an arbiter of individual discoveries rather than a sponsor of collective research. Its collective achievements are evident only from its publications. In the continually expanding realm of science and technology, including social science, it recognized achievement and rewarded success. Hence it emerged as the place where "normal science" was defined and disseminated and where challenges to normal science could be raised in temperate controversy. Innovation had to contend with inertia within its ranks, as theories became enmeshed in human and social complexities. The academy performed two crucial functions: it gave visibility and purpose to emergent disciplines, and it trained new scientists. The nascent sciences represented in the academy were comfortable with these two roles, functional and reproductive, which gave the institution the same duality that one finds in living organisms.[27]

The construction of science could not have occurred without an enhancement of the social status of scientists, whose role the academy praised. Scientists were described as teachers of mankind, the most useful of all citizens. They were of course members of the scientific community, a department of the Republic of Letters, and their freedom was secured by the academy's regulations. As members of a *corps,* academic scientists enjoyed certain privileges. These were more akin to communal liberties recognized by the state than to the economic liberties claimed by the members of guilds. Scientists were also men of ability and talent, exemplars of the mobility and freedom essential to any progressive society, even though they still operated within the shadow of the administration. Finally, scientists were also "functionaries" in the service of the monarchy. Men of science themselves defined the criteria for entering the Republic of Science, barring the door to the half-educated. This social model was powerful because it coincided with the designs of the reformist state. Science and scientists were a part of the state; their role was one of intellectual guidance. They gave the government support in exchange for independence. Their modest salaries and pensions liberated rather than alienated them. Eulogies delivered throughout the century by academic secretaries such as Fontenelle, Mairan, Fouchy, and Condorcet developed the image of the model scientist and thus established the norms of the scientific order, the principles of scientific practice, and the ideal of bureaucratic service.

The academy succeeded in integrating science into the apparatus of absolutism. The institution ensured its role in a variety of ways: through its printing privilege, patent privilege for the protection of inventions, and competitions whose renown increased apace with the range of subjects proposed. In this respect Paris imitated the provinces. Scientific intervention in the realm of technology, which was so important to the administration, should not be neglected; the academy did experiments for the Bureau du Commerce, offered expert opinions to the Contrôle Général, did consultations for the city of Paris, and evaluated industrial processes. Its prestige, which was linked to its monopoly, was further reinforced by the rewards available only to members: professorships, managerial positions, and bureaucratic posts. When Turgot created a commission to look into the building of canals, he appointed Condorcet, d'Alembert, and Abbé Bossut. When he perceived a growing danger of epidemic, he turned to the scientific community for advice: Condorcet, Duhamel, Trudaine (a member of the academy), Lenoir, Tenon, Daubenton, Chabert the veterinarian, and Vicq d'Azir. It was in academic circles that Condorcet and Laplace worked out their ideas on constitutional reform in accordance with the mathematics of probability, ideas that were published in the *Essai sur l'application de l'analyse à la probabilité des décisions rendues à la pluralité des voix* (1785) and the *Essais pour connaître la population du royaume* (1783–1788). The Academy of Sciences managed to strike a delicate balance between recognition of Ancien Régime values and the autonomy of science, between service and independence.

A breakdown of the membership of the Academy of Sciences reveals the secularization of science (only 13 percent of its members were clerics). The nobility was represented by military men, specialists, and *anoblis;* there were few magistrates. The bulk of the membership consisted of bourgeois with administrative posts, professorial chairs, or bureaucratic sinecures. The academy, totally identified with the Parisian elite and its compromises, was not exempt from challenges to that elite. The pressures that I have noted in the world of letters also existed in the world of science. Followers of Rousseau were critical of academies in general, as were some liberal economists and "Anglophiles." Such opposition resulted in the creation of new societies for the dissemination of scientific information.

In fact, the whole academic system was attacked. Hence, it is important to remember the role of provincial societies in the dissemination of science. Many provincial institutions welcomed the Parisian academy's programs and played a similar role on a local level. But the provincial movement remained open to amateurs and nonspecialists. These local societies were generally allied with local authorities, which recognized the utilitarian value of science. Cideville, the president of the Rouen society and a friend of Voltaire's, gave voice to this ideal:

> How many unknown treasures does this beautiful province still hide in its bosom or display on its surface? How many important facts will its history yet reveal? How many branches of industry remain to be developed or created here? How many new methods will prove useful in agriculture, in the rearing of domestic animals, and in the expansion of commerce? It is within your purview to answer these questions. The more you explore this province, the broader your career path will become. Through your efforts the sciences will lend letters their methods and their precision, in exchange for which letters will bestow upon science that purity of language, that clarity of construction that give luster to the dogmatic style. From the volumes of your dissertations on a range of subjects that I can here do no more than indicate will come one day a majestic edifice, a complete corpus of the civic, physical, and political history of this province. What an abundant treasure for the state if the various parts of France contribute similarly to the public weal.

This ideal, to which Cideville gave voice as early as 1745, was eventually embodied in concrete works and studies: 60 percent of these dealt with science and the arts. Not all provincial academies were equally involved in this movement, to which booksellers and publishers also contributed. Some societies held back, while others, in Montpellier, Bordeaux, Brest, Dijon, Metz, Valence, and Toulouse, were deeply involved. Science was widely discussed, especially after 1760, and some occupational groups, including military men, engineers, architects, physicians (who accounted for 25 percent of the membership of the provincial academies), and functionaries, were more active than the high magistrates, traditionally noted for their curiosity. Public meetings and competitions made scientific subjects more familiar. The academies saw themselves as "interpreters of the sciences for the people," but to the broader public they nevertheless looked like privileged institutions, hence ripe for protest. In the 1770s and 1780s the social role of science in the academies became an object of discussion along with the cultural system in general. The phenomenon of mesmerism—part pseudoscience, part occultism, and sharply criticized by academicians everywhere—nevertheless elicited a fantastic degree of enthusiasm on the part of the social elite, indicating the extent to which hopes were invested in the miraculous possibilities of science and the profound resonance of debates that aroused the passions of a politicized and critical public.

It is not surprising that this movement gradually transformed itself, broadening its concerns and expanding its interests until it took on a radical coloration. The debate turned toward political denunciation of academic institutions. Roberger de Vaussenville, Carra, Bergasse, Brissot, Marat, Mesmer, Soulavie, and Bernardin de Saint-Pierre all cast themselves as martyrs of "intellectual despotism." "Unrecognized genius," "misunderstood sensibility," "rejected talent," and "direct communion with nature" were among the favorite themes of a widely read pamphlet literature. The academies remained unmoved, loyal to their ideal of compromise and service.

The criticism of the academies reveals two salient features of contemporary science: the importance of controversies over counterfeit science, and the degree to which the scientific academies were associated with state utilitarianism, which had a profound effect on the scientific worldview. In critiques of false science we find affirmations of the "reign of things," a reign established by experiment and spread by language. Science was still seen as a well-made language. It makes no sense to look for a typical or average notion of scientific truth; what we can see are specific forms of behavior and investigative practices, in short, technologies which, taken together, constituted science. These included material technologies, such as instruments, herbariums, and analytical apparatus. They also included social technologies: academic meetings, competitions, debates, and techniques for publicizing proofs and corroborating findings (experiments relied mainly on sight). In addition there were physical "technologies" or disciplines: scientists worked and exchanged views in various environments, and different disciplines governed the classroom, the study, the laboratory, and the observatory. Last but not least were the intellectual "technologies," including such methodological practices as keeping notebooks, writing reports, presenting papers, and composing books and instructional manuals. All of these technologies went into the construction of science.

The history of scientific travel is a convenient index of science's cognitive capacity. Science saw space as homogeneous. Classifications (including that triumph over worldly variety, the botany of Linnaeus) and catalogs recorded results which, it was hoped, would yield mastery over the world of the living. The world was objectified in practice through a combination of materiality and intellectuality. Man redis-covered his vocation as master and possessor of nature and along with it the meaning of life, which the blue periwinkle revealed to the botanist Rousseau. Nature became a theater in which man no longer enjoyed a privileged status among the facts of nature, but he recouped his loss by developing an awareness of himself as the creator of values which he imposed on the physical world in the form of civilization. This dream of man's creative potential was summed up in two key words: utility and progress.

The goal of science, as well as the purpose of the academies, was the promotion of utilitarian optimism. Contempt for the human condition gave way to praise for man's ability to create wealth and values. "To look at the universe as a prison and at all men as criminals awaiting execution is the idea of a fanatic," wrote Voltaire in a well-known chapter of his *Lettres philosophiques* on Pascal's *Pensées*. Human relations must be recon-structed for the benefit of all. In this respect the eighteenth century was the student of Locke—physician, teacher, traveler, chemist, and political adviser—who said that "true knowledge is that which leads to some new and useful invention, which learns to do things better, more quickly, and more easily than in the past." The *Encyclopédie* gave wide currency to this aspiration. Economism, with its scientific offspring demographics and agronomy, publicized it further. "The greatest good of the greatest num-ber": Bentham's formula was put into circulation as early as 1726 by Hutcheson, whom the French philosophes read. It was the social expres-sion of a eudaemonic philosophy that held itself out as a principle of government whose realization would require not only a new political order but also a new economic structure. Individualism would later draw its own conclusions from this. Meanwhile, the utilitarian values implicit in science encouraged a belief in progress.[28] The word "progress" came into use relatively late, but the idea, with its implication of improvement in the human condition and success for human enterprise, was already spreading its influence. Henceforth humanity would be admonished to live under the sign of change rather than eternal order. And history was a way of measuring change, as Voltaire noted in his *Essai sur les moeurs:* the meaning of man's presence in the world was questioned; in the future the order of nature and the order of culture would no longer be one. Turgot put it this way in 1750:

Natural phenomena, subject to constant laws, are confined within a circle of unvarying revolutions; everything is born again, everything dies . . . By contrast, the succession of human generations offers, century after century, a constantly varying spectacle . . . All ages are linked to one another by a series of causes and effects, which connect the present state of the world to previous ones. By giving men the means to take possession of their ideas and communicate them to others, the arbitrary signs of language and writing have shaped all specialized knowledge into a common treasure, which one generation transmits to the next, a heritage augmented by the discoveries of each century, so that the human race, encompassed from the beginning within the gaze of the philosopher, looks like one vast whole, which, like any individual, has its childhood and its periods of progress.[29]

Writing forty years after Turgot, Condorcet did not improve on this, but he did focus his philosophy on the future of the human race, which he saw as the agent of its own liberation. Accordingly, some philosophers began to worry about man's estrangement from nature, about the value of civilization and the possibility of stabilizing the course of history. Rousseau dreamed of a social state that would set just limits to progress. Perhaps the uncertainty about the future had yet to be fully dissipated.[30]

16

᪾ᬠ᪾ᬠ᪾ᬠ

The Liberties of Individuals

FROM BIRTH TO DEATH, people in Ancien Régime society were caught up in a chain of obligations and instructed by a series of traditions, customs, and practices that bound them to their community. Because of religion primarily, along with other important forms of social organization in which equality and liberty had no part, a collective idea of man dominated. As in Plato's *Republic*, the ideal social structure was defined in terms of ends rather than of individual happiness or progress.

Over the long run, the emergence of a new conception of man can be seen in the gradual replacement of the concept of *universitas*, of which living men were merely parts, by *societas*, which simply referred to an association of individuals. Louis Dumont has recounted the stages of this evolution and shown that there was a connection between, on the one hand, the birth of modern individualistic ideology and the realm of politics and, on the other hand, the emergence of the economic sphere.[1] Religious ideology, such as that of Saint Thomas, for instance, was fundamentally holistic in its attitude toward the earthly community, but there was also an (otherworldly) Christian individualism associated with ultimate ends; a whole current of Christian thought culminated in Calvin's decision to place the individual at the center of the world. The Enlightenment inherited this aspect of Calvin's thinking. At the same time, the state, which rivaled and to a certain extent supplanted the Church as a "global society" (a development whose full implications would not become apparent until the nineteenth century), had been engaged since the late Middle Ages in the creation of a new sphere of politics. Out of this twofold differentiation within the religious realm came an autonomous political sphere and with it the idea of equality as a fundamental social value. It was Rousseau who gave the most vivid expression to the ideal of the individual: there must, he argued, be some rational way to combine equality with liberty. The future of modern society depended on some moderation of the egalitarian political norm, which alone could mitigate the historical effects of inequality.[2] For Rousseau, the political individual was above all a "social being opposed to the abstract individual man of nature." His was perhaps one of the last attempts to base radical change on a reconciliation of individual rights with necessary communal forces.

After the political sphere differentiated itself from the religious, Dumont further argued, the economic sphere differentiated itself from the political. Economic ideology then developed as a new way of explaining human phenomena.[3] Emblematic of this development was the publication in 1776 of Adam Smith's *Enquiry into the Nature and Causes of the Wealth of Nations.* Henceforth the economic realm enjoyed a separate existence, emancipated from the political in which mercantilist thinkers and moralists still sought to confine it.

The differentiation of the economic sphere occurred in two stages. Quesnay of course already believed in the autonomy of the economic. He argued that production could be analyzed as a rational process governed by a hierarchy of factors, land foremost among them. Though an individualist, he was still influenced by earlier ways of thinking, for he also believed in wealth as the paramount value. His system was dominated by custom and morality rather than exchange. Rousseau, a critic of the Physiocrats, put his finger on a central feature of their thought: Can one separate the political from the economic?

The second stage was almost simultaneous with the first: Could one separate the economic from the moral? Yes, answered Mandeville in his *Fable of the Bees:* "We do not count on the benevolence of the butcher, brewer, and baker to supply our dinner, but rather on their self-interest." "Private vices, public benefits," as the saying goes. In other words, individual liberties could not exist without a sphere of freedom distinct from the religious and moral sphere; the emergence of individual liberties therefore coincided with the appearance of the political sphere and over time became linked to economic capacity in one form or another.

In order to develop a fuller picture of the confrontation out of which modern society was born, I propose to explore three distinct areas. First, the family: of the various ways in which individuals relate to society, many revolve around the family. Every change in values affects the family. Holistic and inegalitarian when the religious and political ideal of the age demanded, the family evolved as values changed and a new parental philosophy emerged. Second, we can look at how individualism and the profit motive produced new types of people and patterns of behavior. And finally, we can examine the advent of new "liberties" in both theory and practice (which of course were closely related).

Family, Authority, and the Individual

The family is special: it is the "common solution" to both the problem of "filiation" (for the family is above all continuous in time, linking generation to generation, shaping individual personalities while simultaneously constituting the social fabric) and the problem of "mobility" (marriage being the fundamental form of social exchange).[4] Like the family of today, the family of the eighteenth century was first and foremost a response to biological necessity; as such, it was subject to social constraints. It represented a specific compromise between nature and culture, with its own unique structure and distinctive relation to the larger society.[5]

Families are of course of great interest to social and cultural historians. To the horizontal and vertical relations described by anthropologists, they add a complex network of contextual relations, with implications for demographics, kinship structures, sociology, and religious and political history. Individualism impinged on family structure in two ways: it influenced the norms governing the choice of a spouse, which came to be dominated by free will, consensus, *affectio*, and even love;[6] and it altered the notion of authority and the relationship between parents and children.

In the eighteenth century a new conception of the family took hold along with new attitudes toward affectivity, sexuality, norms, and society. But historians remain divided about the family's true role. Two groups are in contention. One is resolutely pessimistic and negative: it sees the family as the institution in which behavior was normalized, an instrument of social control and discipline. The other is more positive and optimistic: it treats the modern family as the place where the individual came into his own, where the personality as opposed to the personage developed, and where affective and sexual liberation occurred. "Families, I hate you," André Gide famously said. One set of historians would agree with him, another would disagree. Both are partly right.

Eighteenth-century family history has been extensively studied. Abundant sources—marriage contracts, legislation and other legal documents, and literature, both high and low, some of it garrulous, some luminously pithy—tell us much about the diversity of life throughout France. The rules of the game changed somewhat, and with them images of ancestors, parents, and children—a whole range of representations and relationships. Family structures were slow to evolve because their very purpose was to transmit and reproduce, to control change. Meanwhile, the emergence of the individual reflected everything that was most vital in the intellectual and religious climate. Evidence of this can be seen in the introduction of new forms of sentiment in literary texts, forms that also manifested themselves in physical and symbolic relationships: attitudes toward children became more positive, and love found new champions.

Love—whether parental love for children or love between husband and wife—did not originate in the eighteenth century, but its manner, expression, and meaning did change. The changes initially affected the top of the social hierarchy: the wealthy, noble, and cultivated people of the towns, the disciplined and enlightened *sanior pars.* The majority continued much as they always had, sometimes affectionate, sometimes violent. Yet married life was no longer as subject to traditional social influences and representations as in the past. The authority of the extended family over its members diminished. The transfer of control over marriage to the Church imposed a familiar discipline (marital matters came under the jurisdiction of the *officialités,* which were closer to the people than secular institutions were) and a putative equality between marriage partners, as well as a crucial individualization of marital obligations. Old traditions and laws were reinterpreted.

Families and Power over Individuals

The monarchy saw each individual as subject to the discipline of the *corps* and family to which he or she belonged. As the great dynasties and lesser clans were subjected to monarchical control, paternal power was reinforced in what has been called the "Romanization of family authority." Although broader solidarities still counterbalanced this influence of the law in practice, two other forces became fixtures of the scene during the Enlightenment: *la police fiscale,* or fiscal authority, which established the *feu,* or hearth—in essence, the nuclear family—as the basis of taxation and enumeration; and *la police des moeurs,* or moral authority, which imposed discipline on marital and parental practices. Head counts reflected the preconceptions and purposes of the counters: whether drawing up lists of workers for compulsory labor or estimating the tax base, census takers flattened out differences in a way that misrepresented reality. Administrators began to think in terms of nuclear families, whereas the reality was that households still varied widely in size depending on their ability to support parents, children, and servants. Differences of wealth and other resources created inequalities, even though mortality still claimed "surplus" births everywhere.

Records of the activities of the *lieutenants de police, commissaires,* and judges show how new norms and social expectations were internalized. Families requested *lettres de cachet* to deal with their problems. Philosophes denounced these *lettres* as an instrument of arbitrary power, but they were also a weapon that families could use to defend their integrity. Private life and state authority were thus linked by free choice as well as fiat. The king's agents penetrated family secrets, punished deviant behavior, and imposed on marriage and the family a private order consistent with the principles of society. The mechanism of power dealt with threatening tensions and allowed people to internalize social norms.

This transformation, which assumed the existence of harmonious nuclear families, coincided with an identification of the state with patriarchal authority in legal and political discourse. The social compact which linked families to the monarch and made regicide the most heinous of crimes—at once patricide and sacrilege (as reflected in the torture of Louis XV's would-be assassin Damiens)—had as its quid pro quo the king's responsibility toward his "children," or subjects. This responsibility was what justified the imposition of social controls: the image of the paternal king was of course influenced by the very powerful association of biological reproduction with political authority. Add to that the government's instinctive natalism and economists' calls for policies to increase population and it becomes clear why families were seen as a fundamental source of power in the service of the state as well as an instrument for inculcating norms and integrating individuals into the traditional cycle of life. The individual who was subordinate to God, nature, and his family was also obedient to political authority. In view of this convergence of interests, the culture of both clergy and administrators had to evolve in complementary ways before change was possible.

The traditional clerical vision was not inegalitarian: for centuries the Church had championed the idea of mutual consent in marriage, individual freedom to make wills, conjugal morality based on indissolubility, parental control over children, and disciplined sexuality. The clergy saw individuals as responsible for their own actions. In the early modern period, however, the lay and monarchical view triumphed, and that view imposed limits on individual choice. This triumph was a victory for the king's agents and royal jurists. The Church's monopoly over marriage was broken in order to defend parental discipline against willful children who married in secret. Civil law guaranteed the integrity of the family against any irregularities. In the eighteenth century the state won a final victory: there could be no legitimate marriage without parental consent, which in practice meant without paternal consent. In exchange for this transformation of marriage from pure sacrament into civil contract, however, the Church gained the power to regulate sexuality and ban disapproved prenuptial practices through parish priests backed by civil authorities. Procreation became the essential purpose of marriage. The cornerstone of the whole edifice was the father.

The Golden Age of Sovereignty: The Paterfamilias

Until the turn of the eighteenth century, both the Reformation and Counter-Reformation reinforced the image of the paternal monarchy at the head of the society of orders. The authority of the father—or, rather, the mother's lawful spouse—was recognized by law; fathers of illegitimate children had no rights. Paternal authority, based on French interpretations of Roman and canon law, inspired respect. Hence in the "classical age" any advice intended to allow the paterfamilias to play his assigned role was welcome. It was a man's duty and justification to perpetuate his line by engendering offspring. He did not marry solely for his own sake but, as Montaigne put it, for the sake of "our race in the far-distant future." A man assumed the rights and duties of fatherhood the moment he ceased to be a bachelor. (In France, 7 percent of males born in the 1730s did not marry or died before marrying. Four percent of the population remained permanently celibate, but the percentage was higher in cities than in rural areas. Some 80 to 95 percent of males of marriageable age were either married or widowed.)

In this society impotence and sterility were a source of dishonor and a butt of mockery. Few cases achieved notoriety, however. Men dealt with problems of this sort by consulting a magician, priest, or physician. A vast literature offered advice on procreation—"unraveling the braid of Venus" and overcoming other curses that prevented conception—designed to produce vigorous, healthy, handsome offspring. Contemporary science confirmed the fecundating omnipotence of paternal semen, but not without controversy. In 1673 Stenon and De Graaf discovered the female ovaries. "Fertility is wholly vested in the female," Maupertuis asserted. But the roughly contemporary observation of spermatozoa by Ham, Leeuwenhoek, and Hartsoeker reinstated the male virtue. It would be a century more before the necessity of both egg and sperm was demonstrated. Procreation meanwhile remained a teachable art with its own psychology, dietetics, gymnastics, and even meteorology. In this golden age, paternity was a struggle.

It also entailed responsibilities. The principal obligations were enumerated in law, which habit and custom corrected: "Whoever makes a child must feed it," rear it, educate it, and bequeath it a patrimony. Catholics and Protestants agreed on the father's role as teacher, a duty obviously linked to the division of labor within the family. There the father's authority reigned supreme and children learned to behave as individuals; the quality of the relationship between husband and wife and between parents and children determined the quality of family life. Rationality and utility vied with love and emotion. The sources reflect the importance of custom and contract: family and property were intimately associated. Still, we are free to imagine more specific features of family life, forms of sensibility appropriate to the period. Love did exist, but it was very different from what we call love. We must be careful not to oppose individual choice and social constraint, heart and reason, because society was no more rational than its individual members, and no less passionate. The choice of a spouse depended on perceived attractiveness as well as calculated interests, to say nothing of taboos and norms (which could be accepted or rejected). While transgression was not impossible, there were customary sanctions for infractions of the rules, including laughter, derision, and cruelty. Youths assumed the role of punishing violators.

Broadly speaking, premarital relations were tolerated: the Church tried to impose a strict discipline, while families were traditionally more lax. Pregnancy outside marriage became the exception rather than the rule, and couples probably abstained from sexual relations before marriage, although not all historians agree on this. The sacrament of marriage changed the couple's status: sexual intercourse became permissible, and the couple could settle down to the business of earning a living and raising a family. Urban or rural, the family, regardless of type (and we know that the nuclear family was henceforth the most common), enforced the rules of morality. The authority of husbands and fathers was total: it conformed to the patriarchal and monarchical model and was reflected in traditional marriage rituals, proverbial sayings, and prognostications. *Bachelleries,* or bands of youths, made sure that it was obeyed, for household discipline was a community affair. The oppression of women was thus perpetuated: mothers were above all reproductive instruments and servants of family interests, responsible primarily for nursing and early child rearing. The vast majority of women nursed their own babies; only the well-off and some urban mothers put their babies out to nurse. Until the child was at least seven, the mother was responsible for its upbringing; the exaltation in religious literature of the woman's role as teacher and housekeeper may have been no more than a reaction to persistent antifemale attitudes. These fed on male fantasies that we find in both learned tomes and pulp literature *(Le Miroir des femmes, La Grande Querelle des ménages)* as well as popular images.

Representations of femininity were of two types: wicked (women were shown as authoritarian, rebellious, complaining, diabolical, evil, and illtempered) or good (hardworking, enterprising, thrifty, virtuous, excellent as mother and wife). Rétif de La Bretonne celebrated women as subjects of paternal authority in *La Femme de laboureur* (1783) and *La Vie de mon père* (1778). Rural virtues were contrasted with urban corruption in the portrayal of both women and family relations. Rétif, for example, described the patriarch gathering children and servants around him in front of a huge fireplace: "The father assumed the leading role. He talked, told stories, gave instructions. He was listened to with avid interest, his wife setting an example for the others." As the first subject of his little kingdom, "she looked upon her husband as her leader, guide, master, and father. She had nothing whatever to do with the dangerous and criminal system of equality, which only urban libertines favor. She thought of herself as a dependent, and she obeyed not as a slave but as a daughter."

The Church also exalted the paternal role. It compared priests to fathers who engendered Christ in the souls of the faithful—the true fathers of nations ("pères des peuples"), in the words of Jean Eudes—and preached the superiority of spiritual paternity over biological paternity: for the Church, "the best of fathers" was Saint Joseph. While Protestant preaching did not avail itself of the same devices (for it did not emanate from a Church governed by "celibate fathers" and took cognizance only of "fathers" in the literal sense), it achieved the same results. Despite the absence of a sacramental conception of marriage, Protestants stressed conjugal union as the vocation of both men and women. The notion of universal priesthood further reinforced the father's religious role: the home was also a temple.[7]

For both Catholics and Protestants, the image of paternal authority and majesty was joined by another association, of the father with kindness and tenderness. Theology underscored his gentleness and patience: "The father has the right to command, but he is obliged to love." Memoirs, journals, and diaries of the classical period reveal the influence of these images and models, as fathers expressed themselves with paternal tenderness. Of course, bad fathers did exist: a certain level of violence still persisted in family relations, as judicial archives and contemporary pamphlets reveal. Nevertheless, a shift in sensibility had begun, and it would accelerate dramatically in the Age of Enlightenment.

Criticism of Fathers and Individual Freedom

After paternal authority was shaken by the reign of Louis XIV, other factors confirmed a shift of equilibrium within the family, and writers and philosophes gave currency to a new image of the family based on a new image of politics. As I just mentioned, Protestants and Catholics alike identified the father with the king: every man was a king in his own castle, his power subordinate only to the power of God and tempered by love. The anti-Protestant edicts of the 1680s, which continued to be enforced for years to come, undermined paternal authority: an edict of 1681, for example, authorized children to renounce their father's religion; edicts of 1683, 1685, and 1686 increasingly emancipated children from parental and paternal authority; the need for parental authorization to marry was abolished in 1724; and fathers of the "so-called reformed religion," stripped of civil status until 1787, were never certain of being allowed to bequeath their property to their children. Although it is true that compromise on all these points made for a precarious truce, the unintended effects of royal legislation must also be taken into account: it provoked indignation on the part of the pastors of the Refuge, and this in turn encouraged political thinkers to begin advocating individual rights over the paternalistic monarchy of Bossuet.

The impact of the English Revolution and the Puritan struggle against the British monarchy led political thinkers in other directions. John Locke, whose *Treatise on Civil Government* (1681) all the philosophes would read, demolished the notion that paternal authority is original and absolute. As paternal power tottered, so, too, did monarchical power. In its place Jurieu proposed the idea of reciprocal obligations guaranteed by "contract." For Locke and the theorists of natural rights, if the monarchy was not based on the idea of family, it was not based on anything. The way was clear for the advent of the individual as citizen. Thus, Protestant versions of paternity had an influence even on non-Protestants: the Protestant vision was incorporated into political thought, casting doubt on the origin and extent of paternal authority just as other factors were transforming relations within the family unit. Norms and sensibilities began to shift.

As for women, although it is true that the hour of liberation had not yet struck—women continued to be watched closely and oppressed, and husbands still ruled the roost—the winds of emancipation had begun to blow. A few writers discerned signs of progress, including such prominent figures as Marivaux and Diderot and, later, Beaumarchais and Condorcet. Some urban guilds accepted women, affording them work and access to the public sphere. A very small number of women wielded influence as *salonnières* or journalists and boldly made their voices heard in a world where information was in the hands of men. Women also scored advances in the area of education, although limits were placed on what they were allowed to learn on the grounds that their destiny was motherhood. Nevertheless, literacy increased more rapidly among women than among men, and more rapidly in the cities than in the countryside.

A debate developed over sex roles and authority in the family. The issue was still whether reason could harmoniously coexist with sexuality. Several factors changed the terms of the debate, however. The educated elite began to admit that if men were free and equal, women ought to be as well. Lower down the social scale, people exalted the idea of maternity, idealized the Christian couple, honored marriage, paid homage to the Holy Family, and repressed natural instincts, perhaps to an excessive degree; all this coexisted with traditional authoritarian patterns. Marital relations were no longer incompatible with pleasure, thanks to greater self-control and new social norms. In the cities standards were undeniably more lax, to the consternation of the police and religious authorities. Meanwhile, new attitudes toward children contributed to the change in climate. Children were treated more kindly and gently, and, though they were becoming better educated, responsibility for that education was delegated. Young people left home as a natural part of the life cycle to work as domestic servants or journeymen on the "tour of France." This put greater distance between fathers and sons, even as other trends brought husbands and wives closer together. Domestic life was restructured. Medical advances and an increasingly youthful population played a part. Greater freedom of body and mind shaped a new kind of individual, more rapidly in the cities, where family surveillance and constraints were not as strong, less so in the country, where there was less freedom of choice. Everywhere the boundary between public and private shifted, closely watched by fathers of a new breed.

Here the literature teaches us to understand the association of the real with the symbolic, the lived with the imaginary: myth inspires existence. The countless father figures we find in books allow us to measure the militant function of a craze: the image of the father had implications not just for private life but for the collective future as well.[8] The very rich literature on fatherhood—from Voltaire's *Oedipe* (1714), portraying the murder of a father by his innocent, rebellious, and heroic son, to Rétif de La Bretonne's *Monsieur Nicolas* and *La Vie de mon père*, which staged the life of Edme Rétif and offered a complex portrait of the father as incarnation of authority—is full of ungrateful sons and unscrupulous fathers. Painting, too, dramatized paternal power: Greuze did so in several works of the 1760s *(L'Accordée de village, Le Fils ingrat)*. All of these fathers illustrated the intensification of emotions in the family, as well as a questioning of authority in the name of historical relativism and philosophical individualism. In Rousseau, family society has all the voluntaristic characteristics of the new political societies. In Diderot, paternalism is an essential element of monarchy. According to the *Encyclopédie*, "political authority" is modeled on "paternal authority" and based solely on consent. This generalization of individual experience borrowed from the sphere of domestic relations to create the new image of the collective father.

A more tranquil, more familiar image here supplanted the "Gothic tyrant" of old. Through the father figure, a new social morality abolished distinctions and opened up the prospect of an egalitarian world. The father was featured in the imagery of "illustrious lives" and in countless academic eulogies, as well as in stereotypes of the educator and citizen of talent. Until 1789 the monarchy also toyed with the image. The cult of Henri IV depended on it, and even Louis XVI benefited from the new sentimental aura surrounding fatherhood, which was not without implications for the future political history of the nation. Necker as father was celebrated by his amanuenses and by his daughter, Germaine de Staël. Solemn and affectionate, he was the very opposite of a despot, a good and sensitive man. The way was clear for the parallel proclamation of civic paternity and the private heroization of the paternal role. Parental relations, like marriage, were a compromise between social constraints and ever more strongly articulated individual aspirations.

Profit Affirmed: The Individual Liberated

Social relations, including the possibility of individual expression, cannot be isolated from economic changes, nor, for that matter, can theoretical individualism. The industrialization of the countryside, which accompanied or even accelerated demographic growth, probably contributed to the decline of the extended family. The nuclear family helped to establish a certain model of economic growth with simultaneous promotion of individualism and profit. In France, however, as opposed to England, the family unit was immersed in the rural community. What changed in the eighteenth century in response to various kinds of pressure was the internal coherence of this system, its level of stability, and its ability to put children to work.

As time went by, it became increasingly necessary to find places for young people to work outside the home. Families at all levels of society—prosperous peasants, artisans, merchants, magistrates, and nobles—exchanged children. This displacement of formative experience had a decisive impact on the development of the affective and social personality. The system became a veritable school for individualism, in which young people learned to be independent, to live without the authoritarianism and affection of the family unit, and to distinguish between kinship relations and work relations. Because people had to adapt to the changed economic conditions defined by demographic growth, the nuclear family became the seed around which the spirit of enterprise crystallized. Open and unstable structures—those that encouraged mobility and circulation of information, commerce, and exchange—facilitated change. In this, entrepreneurial behavior played a crucial role. So, to a lesser extent, did the liberating circulation of money. Out of all this came a new economic ideology.

Enterprise and Entrepreneurs

The development of business enterprise in eighteenth-century France marked a crucial transformation (which one suspects began much earlier). Economic historians have demonstrated this beyond any doubt. They have investigated the factors that accelerated the growth of enterprise and analyzed its diverse forms and modalities. The pace of change was different in rural and urban areas, and the density of development varied from region to region. Beyond the economic statistics was the drama of men in action, to which they committed themselves wholeheartedly: their mission was to gain respect for a view of the world different from the traditional one. Indeed, they waged war on tradition, a war that was in part physical, in part intellectual, "involving nothing less than the very conception of action."[9] The history of vocabulary can help us to understand what their goals were and how their thinking moved from concrete practices to concepts, from the informal to the formal, from the nonexplicit to the explicit. The various meanings that clustered around the idea of "enterprise" shed light on both the economy of ideas and ideas of the economy.[10]

If we look up the words *entrepreneur* and *entreprise* in the great classical dictionaries, from Furetière's to the Académie's, from Richelet to Savary, from Trévoux to the *Encyclopédie*, we find three principal meanings. The first of these belonged to the realm of military strategy: it placed "enterprise" in a context of organized confrontation of risk and linked economic activity to the tradition of dangerous, adventurous action. The second stressed the calculation of risk and the way in which acquired knowledge could increase confidence about the future. The third sense belonged to the realm of economic thought and had to do with the need to expand capital through profit.

According to the dictionaries, *entreprise* referred to "something that is to be done." The primary sense was that of a "bold resolution" to bring something to a conclusion. This was of course the responsibility of the entrepreneur, who took it upon himself to steer the project toward the desired end. Initially that end was associated with war. One "undertook" *(entreprendre)* a campaign; one thwarted the enemy's "enterprises"; the French were "enterprising" to the extent that they disciplined their boldness and courage in order to win a victory. For Vauban and other theorists of war who followed his lead, it was the soldier's valor, his disciplined courage and "brave spirit," that allowed a commander's "enterprises" to be concluded successfully. Ancient heroes and chivalrous knights were once models of men who made themselves by facing ordeals and embarking on adventures. In the eighteenth century, however, they were discredited, sometimes because reason condemned the choice to engage in warfare for nothing more than the sake of honor, sometimes because the ideology of monarchy preferred to draw a veil over the bellicosity of feudal lords and impose rules on the use of force. War had long provided a field for individual exploits, but individuality gave way to the logic of statecraft, where the state represented the structure of society and acted as arbiter among the classes. Why shouldn't individuality arise solely from rational conduct directed not at achieving personal perfection but at creating an order? Given a choice between Alexander, the chivalrous hero, and Caesar, the model of the entrepreneurial monarch, Montesquieu chose the law and order of reason. He rejected the pleasure of risk as contrary to the art of war and condemned the chaotic character of feudal ambitions. One meaning of enterprise that survived in spite of social transformation was mentioned by Descartes in his *Traité des passions,* in which he discusses the pleasure that young people often take in attempting difficult enterprises: here enterprise is a therapy for the soul, a palliative for disgust, an end in itself. Success mattered more for itself than for any profits it might bring.

Nevertheless, calculated profit became the principal new dimension of enterprise even as money, as medium of exchange, became the focal point of entrepreneurial activity. Earlier I described this process as an opposition between two "spaces": that of traditional peasant France and that of commerce, circulation, and urbanization. Enterprise defined itself as a form of engagement in which victory was rewarded by profit. The ability to earn a profit depended on the cleverness of the entrepreneur, who was driven by the pleasure of winning to make the best possible use of the mechanisms of demand determined by the ancestral rights of landlords and desires of consumers. Enterprise increased the difference between supply and demand by multiplication, just as it widened the gap between production prices and market values, thereby inducing mobility of capital. Availing itself of possibilities inherent in the old system of production, enterprise encouraged the development of new social relations and modified traditional modes of production and distribution involving farmer-entrepreneurs, merchant-manufacturers, financiers, and traders. Within the economic sphere the word "enterprise" took on a new meaning, drawing on aspects of warfare, politics, and justice: directed toward the future, enterprise was always a form of encroachment, subversion, and coercion designed to produce a calculated new order. The entrepreneur was an effective agent for reducing uncertainty about the future. Estimates, calculated prices, business plans, and accounting techniques all served the same purpose: investing capital was risky, and earning a profit required acceptance of risk, as in gambling, coupled with rational estimation and skill.

An entrepreneur could therefore be "credible," could enjoy "credit." The "confidence that one places in an entrepreneur depends on the consciousness one ascribes to him, that is, on his ability to carry out a series of complex operations in a rational manner. This in turn depends on his ability to evaluate gains and losses, expenses and investments. The entrepreneur operates in a competitive market."[11]

People did not begin thinking about the relationship between entrepreneurial activity and profit until after a systematic manufacturing economy had developed. Profit, theorists argued, was the reward for risk. It depended on both exogenous factors (such as wages, determined by food costs, and rents, determined by farm costs) as well as endogenous ones (competition among entrepreneurs). Enterprise undermined the price structure; it showed that prices were the result of social practice and that the introduction of money into traditional society was a form of subversion. Cantillon defined the entrepreneur as an economic subject. His *Essai sur la nature du commerce en général*, which was probably written around 1720, was published posthumously in 1755. The author, an Irishman, was a businessman who prospered in banking in the days of John

Law, from whose System he profited handsomely. A reader of the English political arithmeticians, Cantillon set himself apart by his use of inductive methods and "systematic analyses" of observable market mechanisms and price systems. The entrepreneur, he argued, played his role in the interstices between production and consumption, values and prices. By anticipating the demand for commodities and therefore their prices, he reaped profit as his reward:

> The farmer is an entrepreneur. So are wholesale dealers in wool and grain, bakers, butchers, manufacturers, and merchants of every variety . . . Still others concern themselves with mines, theaters, buildings, and the like, or with trade on sea and land. There are roasters, pastry makers, innkeepers, and so on. And there are entrepreneurs of their own labor, who need no funds to set themselves up in business, such as journeyman artisans, kettle makers, menders, chimney sweeps, water carriers . . . master artisans such as cobblers, tailors, carpenters, wig makers, and so forth, and entrepreneurs of their own labor in the arts and sciences, such as painters, lawyers, and so forth, and even beggars and thieves are entrepreneurs of a certain class.[12]

This celebrated passage indicates what made it possible to subsume so much economic and social diversity under one concept: all entrepreneurs lived with uncertainty, for they had to adjust their demands to the desires of the client. The appearance of the entrepreneur, or the "third man," as Jean-Baptiste Say called him, was associated with the realm of chance and the dissolution of old social bonds. In another passage Cantillon gives an impressive account of the uncertainty faced by the entrepreneur:

> The farmer is an entrepreneur who promises to pay a landlord a fixed sum of money for a farm or piece of land (ordinarily assumed to be equal in value to one-third the product of the land) without being certain of the benefit he will derive from the enterprise. He uses part of this land to feed his livestock, produce grain, wine, hay, and so forth, without being able to predict which kinds of product will bring the best price. Prices will depend in part on the seasons and in part on consumption. If wheat is abundant relative to consumption, it will sell for a low price; if it is scarce, it will be dear. Who can predict the number of births and deaths in the state in any given year? Who can predict whether families will increase or decrease their expenditures? Yet the

prices of the farmers' products naturally depend on these events, which he cannot predict, and he therefore runs the farm enterprise with certainty.[13]

Among those who capitalized on chance, we find, interestingly enough, large-scale farmers, who profited from the long-term increase in prices and took advantage of the development of an organized market for grain made possible by the speculations of entrepreneurs willing to gamble on total demand. Decision making was distributed throughout society, and Cantillon's *Essai* was a theoretical tour de force because it went beyond the visible social hierarchy to divine an entrepreneurial order invisible even to those involved in its daily workings.[14] The concept of enterprise arose not so much in opposition to the corporate order with its regulations and privileges as in response to the emergence of a new economic space, in which the entrepreneur was able to subvert traditional forms, bringing cash into the circuit of exchange and linking production to capital in new ways. Hence, enterprise helped to transform the social and economic system by directing cash into a secondary system where it played a fundamental role. Enterprise thus produced individualization; cash helped to engender individualism.

Money and Individual Freedom

Enterprise extended the scope of commercial exchange, multiplied the number of circuits through which commodities and monetary instruments (cash, promissory notes, letters of exchange) could flow. The rhythms of simple commodity circulation, which still dominated in most of agricultural France, were overlaid by the more complex temporal patterns of merchant France. Much of entrepreneurial activity was taken up with dealing with the unequal distribution of people, products, and money. Money was invested, accumulated, and mobilized in a variety of forms.[15] If we hope to understand what, beyond the materiality of things, indeed beyond historical materialism itself, linked the realities of the day to the intellectual imperatives, and if we wish to see intentions and psychological structures in a proper light, we must restore economic life to a place among the causes of spiritual culture. The study of money offers an ideal opportunity for this, assuming that we can agree that exchanges among men, together with production, or man's exchange with nature, should be classified as "values." In both types of exchange, "the goal is to give up something in exchange for something else of greater value. In this process, an object closely associated with the desiring and pleasure-experiencing self is alienated from it; only then does it become value."[16] Exchange and value determine each other reciprocally, and the economy is a special case of life, which is itself exchange, that is, giving up something in return for some benefit—in other words, a sacrifice necessary to obtain some object or satisfy some need. Where there is no obstacle, there can be no value. Money comes to symbolize the economy because it stands for the values in objects and freedom of choice. It comes into play as an instrument for enhancing individual freedom, overcoming customary obligations, and instilling a desire for change.

Spinoza called money the "omnia rerum compendium," an epitome of the world or universal agent. The eighteenth century showed how skill and talent could be exchanged for cash. From the entrepreneurial farmer to the author liberated by his rights, earnings, and capacity for abstraction, money drove a wedge between having and being and made it possible for an idea of freedom to become a reality. Through taxation, it initiated serious thinking about equality and the possibility of social change. The *capitation* and fiscal theory called attention to the relation between taxation and personal situation, and the extension of the cash economy brought greater individual freedom than was possible under earlier forms of taxation linked to land or real estate. This marked a stage on the road toward greater individualization, as did the decline of payments in kind. The monetary economy helped to separate personality from possession; owners became more autonomous. Money wages afforded workers more freedom than did wages in kind. They distributed risk. For the worker, bread and housing were absolute values. Under the old system, fluctuations in their monetary values were absorbed by the employer. Under the new system of cash wages, workers had to pay when prices increased, but in return they enjoyed greater freedom. The complexity of the old wage structure needs to be reinterpreted in this perspective, as do struggles over the control of guild labor by master craftsmen. The same can be said about seigneurial dues in kind, which the *censitaire* paid directly to the lord. Capons, chickens, barrels of wine, and sacks of grain established powerful personal ties. The recipient had a direct interest in the quality of the goods received: he personally would consume what the other person provided. Monetary payments reduced the personal investment on both sides. Even if this led to harsher relations, it also established a certain level of objectivity.

Georg Simmel has given countless examples of this process: hourly wages as opposed to piece wages, for instance, or mechanical printing, which made price independent of quality. One paid almost as much for pulp fiction as for a great masterpiece. The specific connection between buyer and producer or individual and obligation was destroyed. Money gave rise to distinctive new processes. It also enabled individuals to free themselves from organic ties and customary forms of sociability. People thus became free to join with others for chosen purposes of their own. They could pay dues, for instance, to Masonic lodges or literary societies and thus join in the Masonic movement or the Republic of Letters. They could participate without giving up their personal freedom or private preserve. In the economic sphere, the joint stock company allowed people to invest without any concrete shared interest or sense of community; their only common interest was in making money. Even big investors did not need to take the slightest interest in what a company produced.

All in all, then, the expansion of the monetary economy accentuated the interrelation of individuals, the integration of personality with action, the enlargement of the social sphere, the break with nature, and the march toward abstraction. Monetary value was even attached to some individuals: neither dowries nor wages for prostitution were exempt from the effects of scarcity. More important, money played an objective role in the acquisition of lifestyles, as we see in the increasingly forceful way in which social differences were expressed.[17] All these symptoms of the cash nexus are real, but one thing still needs to be looked at: How much money was actually in circulation, and what forms did that circulation take?

It is impossible to answer these questions here, but I do want to make a few comments to indicate why they are interesting. The monetary mass undoubtedly increased in the eighteenth century, but not all forms of money were equal. Metal currency was fine for some purposes, but paper and credit were essential for others. Some of France's metal currency came from America by way of Spain. Still, as Pierre Vilar has noted, the century's monetary stability lends particular clarity to the movements of precious metals.[18] Conversion was no longer allowed, and people no longer speculated on abrupt changes in exchange rates; it was the trade balance that counted, and an influx of metal remained a sign of economic superiority. Yet money was nothing without the market: the scarcity of coin mattered less in the fairgrounds than the quantity of merchandise. Producers who did not ship were not paid.

As commerce developed, increasing use was made of monetary instruments. The problem of credit was not limited to the sphere of commerce: it came up wherever taxes had to be paid, goods purchased, or production financed. We need to know more about the devices that allowed demand to increase. Estate inventories show that humble folk generally kept very little cash on hand and relied largely on credit. Producers and consumers were both likely to be in debt, and the spiraling debt structure weakened the economy, as is evident from the frequency of bankruptcy. Copper and nickel coins played an important role in daily life. Urban workers and farm laborers were rarely paid in silver and never in gold. Wages were paid in copper sols, which went to pay the butcher, baker, and grocer. Speculation in copper coin led to inflation and reduced purchasing power.[19] In 1792 the amount of gold and silver coin minted in the period 1726–1792 was estimated at 2.674 million, copper coin at 10 million, and nickel at 12 million. The difference is striking, but any shortage or inflation of small coin was a serious matter because it affected the most precarious strata of the population. Mention should also be made, finally, of institutions that made credit available to the humble: these were late to arrive in France, despite ubiquitous plans to establish them, as in Lyons as early as the sixteenth century and again in the seventeenth century. When a *mont-de-piété*, or municipal pawnshop, was at last set up in Paris, plans were revived in many other places as well. These shops were not only a response to pauperism but also a source of credit for artisans.[20] They illustrate the backward state of French banking.

How important was metal coin to the economy? The question is controversial, but notarial records provide a fuller answer than is sometimes thought.[21] Estate inventories and other records are full of receipts for cash payments; prosperous farmers accumulated substantial reserves of hard currency; and small sums were not necessarily reserved for productive purposes. In short, cash could be present even where there were no profits, and it could begin its work of liberation without being invested in for-profit ventures. Cash played a role at various moments in family life: it was used for dowries, interest payments on debts whose nature and purpose are unknown, and expenses incurred in the course of village or neighborhood life. Much work remains to be done before we can say how much increased reliance on promissory notes, letters of credit, and more complex forms of payment eased the difficulties caused by shortages of cash.[22] It seems likely, however, that the easing of monetary scarcity contributed to the triumph of economic individualism. One has to imagine a continuum linking the modest activities of the majority to the ideas and values of the few who read Adam Smith and Quesnay. From all this comes another way of looking at the genesis of the individual out of the collective, another way of understanding freedom and dependency.

Liberty and Equality: From Ideas to Realities

The social history of the categories of the human spirit remains to be written. In the evolution of the family and the expansion of enterprise and monetary circulation we have seen the strength of a new "ideological configuration," which attached new value to the individual, subordinated the totality, emphasized the relation between man and things (objects, nature) rather than between man and man, and witnessed the emergence of the economic as an autonomous category. A new creed, liberalism, was born and accepted. What is more, liberal discourse had practical consequences: ideas influenced social relations, intellectual concerns affected daily innovation, and vice versa.

Equality and Liberty

France in the late eighteenth century was as passionate about equality as about liberty. The passion for equality was linked to the national history and psychology, and therefore to the history of the monarchy, which had encouraged men of talent. Equality won the battle of public opinion even before events made it a reality. The passion for it stemmed in part from the Christian idea of equality as promoted by various preachers, including Bossuet. This was an otherworldly ideal, based on the belief that men need no intermediary in their relationship to God, that everyone is equal in the face of death. The worldly inequality justified by God's plan exists only during the short span of human life: "Death confounds prince and subject, between whom there is but a fragile distinction, too superficial and fleeting to be taken into account." In this world, however, merit was unequally distributed by the will of God—the very antithesis of individual equality. As Mona Ozouf writes, "It is easy to see that this notion of equality, despite having played a formidable subversive role in undermining the established powers, was not the one cherished by the men of the eighteenth century: that century's hedonistic penchant took it a long way from an anthropology of destitution."[23]

The equality of the Enlightenment was ushered in by reason, along with universality of moral judgment and insistence on rational argument. The rise of utilitarianism and the struggle against prejudice emphasized an equality proportionate to the service a given individual rendered to society, a meritocratic equality. Academic encomia offer a good illustration of this shift in emphasis: the encomium, which supplanted the funeral oration as a literary genre, stressed the merits of the social man. What counted was no longer conversion and an exemplary death but a good life and services rendered to mankind: "By insisting on eulogizing all their members, the academies hope that modest scholars will find their reward and that unrecognized merit will cease to go unrecognized. Illustrious men who have lived full enough lives to establish their glory on a firm footing are not the people whom these institutions are most keen to honor with this kind of tribute."

M. de Ratte, the perpetual secretary of the Academy of Montpellier, delivered this proclamation on behalf of his colleagues. What he hoped to see established was a truly egalitarian system, a system whose norms the encomia would justify and propagate. He thus opposed leading Parisian scholars such as d'Alembert, Duclos, and Condorcet, for whom academic egalitarianism was not incompatible with hierarchy.[24] Inequality could develop within a context of equality because the different services offered by different individuals could give rise to new distinctions. This was also the view of Montesquieu: "Thus distributions are born of equality, even as they seem to be eliminated by successful service or superior talent." The eulogy of the great was supposed to teach people not only how to live but also how to recognize talent, thereby inspiring emulation in both public and private life. Meritocratic equality encouraged criticism of hereditary privilege and of the prerogatives of birth.

A second debate soon extended the first: meritocracy, it was argued, was not enough to put an end to inequality, because it did not deal with real needs, with the "equal distribution of happiness among citizens." A new egalitarianism therefore attacked not inequality of birth but inequality of wealth, which leads men into perdition and nations into decadence and which destroys social bonds. The primary task of good government is to restore equality in this regard. This view of equality was of course incompatible with the organic conception of society, which was replaced by a homogeneous conception of a society composed of individuals with equal rights and duties. Obviously this raised the sticky issue of property and the redistribution of wealth. Inequality of condition was a much easier problem to solve than inequality of wealth. Utility could be invoked as grounds for certain distinctions, as in the first article of the Declaration of Rights, more readily than for de facto equality. In this respect, Rousseau's "social contract" can be seen as an ambiguous expression of the century's yearnings. It instituted a form of politics in which individuals justified themselves and thought of themselves as individuals, and one can see it as a step toward the curtailment of liberty by the general will derived from the constituent wills included as parties. This was perhaps a way of reconciling the abstract ideal of *societas*, derived from the idea of natural freedoms and cleansed of the blemishes of ill-governed political society, with *universitas*, the mother of all thinking beings—in other words, a way of reconciling holism with the new social and political individual.[25]

"The word *liberty* is by itself a whole political catechism for a lot of people." Liberty was the touchstone of good government, of government with the consent of its citizens. It was supposed to put an end to old servitudes. What the political struggles of the eighteenth century showed was how absolutism's attacks on "liberties" (plural) gave rise to the idea of "liberty" (singular). The older idea of "liberties," guaranteed by *corps* and reflecting the nature of the society of orders, applied only to flesh-and-blood communities; it was compatible with inequality and hierarchy. The new idea of "liberty" was based not on an equilibrium of powers in a system of checks and balances but on a guarantee of independence for equal individuals. For economists, the homogeneity of the market spelled the end of the diversity of privileges and monopolies. For political thinkers such as Mably and Rousseau, the citizen's liberty derived from identical rights for all and from the harmony of a singular will. Man realized his freedom by obeying the law: "A free people obeys," Rousseau said, "but it does not serve. It has leaders, not masters. It obeys laws, but only laws. And it is by virtue of the law that it does not obey men." For Rousseau, the idea of liberty was not associated with property, as it was with Locke and the Physiocrats. Liberty was not so much a possession to be protected or a consciousness of individuality as it was a form of solidarity and a potential to be fulfilled in the general will. Hence good government was not a matter of guaranteeing a neutral space for individual independence but a question of achieving the ends of the community through social cohesion. This resulted in a heroic, positive idea of liberty.

Between "liberties" and "liberty," liberty born of complexity and liberty born of unity, Mona Ozouf has shown that there were constant exchanges and reversals. The Enlightenment did not settle the question of the best form of government or the ideal form of society: the discussion remained open in both theory and practice. Everyone, including the privileged, could find a satisfactory definition of unity. The political liberty of the citizen was that "tranquillity of spirit that results from each person's belief in his security," according to Jaucourt's article on liberty for the *Encyclopédie*. The article on equality asserted that the principle of natural equality was "the principle of all liberty," because naturally free men are subject only to the pursuit of their own happiness; because historical differences of birth, power, and wealth disappear in the face of common humanity; because each person must grant to others the rights he claims for himself; because property is subject to law and equity; and because, as the judicious Hooker argued, these principles can be derived from natural charity. This litany of beliefs resolved the tensions between the old law and the new natural rights, between liberties and liberty, between the abstract and the social individual.[26]

Manifestations of the Individual

In the invention of liberties, it is important to look closely at what, apart from principles and ideas, contributed to the advent of the individual. How did the idea of citizenship develop in the minds of people who were still subjects of an absolutist regime? Did recent developments such as the vogue for portrait painting and the newfound ability to sign documents and write letters lead to a shift in sensibility that created new tensions and thus contributed to change?

Paramount among those recent developments was of course the fashion for, not to say the very inception of, autobiography. Compared with other kinds of writing that tell the story of a person's life (memoirs, histories, novels), the autobiographical narrative was defined by the commitment of the principal narrator to reconstructing his relationship to others as it really was. The genre was related in complex ways to other forms of "writing" such as the intimate diary, the autobiographical novel, and the self-portrait. Its subject was its author, and in particular the author's individual life and the genesis of his personality. The autobiography was the most elaborate manifestation of the *discours du moi,* or ego discourse.[27]

If the analysts of the Ancien Régime—legists, clerics, and administrators—saw men only as members of a group, and most found the isolated individual inconceivable or at least difficult to conceptualize, then autobiography and other forms of the literature of individuality represented a revolution. Order was no longer self-evident: it came from within and had to be sought out and constituted; it was established through conflict. Ultimately the self ceased to be "hateful" (as Pascal had termed it) and became an object of veneration.

Personal life became a source of values, which fiction could express and successful novels could propagate. In *L'Histoire de Cleveland* (1731), Abbé Prévost wrote: "As one who has always professed to believe that the good or evil in an action must be judged on the basis of the principle behind it and hence that only a bad motive makes an action dishonorable, I am not ashamed to allow myself to be seen as I am in public or to confess my faults in all candor." Part of the power of this assertion comes from its spiritual dimension, a legacy of the literature of edification: self-scrutiny was a form of the examination of conscience. The practice therefore began to flourish wherever religious freedom flourished, in places where the religious consciousness refused to identify with the institutionalized Church. The Enlightenment self was schooled by the Puritan schism and the Augustinian, Jansenist, and Pietist quests, all being movements driven by the need for the inner self to confront God directly in the hope of revelation. For Lavater, the theorist of physiognomy, the Pietist autobiography evolved into the secular secret diary. With Rousseau's *Confessions,* a writer of acknowledged genius confided his private secrets to the world. The work's success opened up a new cultural space and served as a model for others, but it was also a response to a need. In Rétif de La Bretonne's *Coeur humain dévoilé* we find a substantial belief in the efficacy of witness. A student of Rousseau, Rétif believed even more than his teacher that confession was instructive. Moral anatomy taught lessons to the human race—not without laying down moral challenges as well. In the writings of Jacques-Louis Ménétra, who knew Jean-Jacques, quoted him, and no doubt learned from him, we find not only the Jansenist influence but also signs of growing social tension in the form of challenges to old urban hierarchies. With Ménétra as with Rousseau, the citizen began to develop behind the mask of the subject.

What distinguished the Parisian glazier from the Genevan and other celebrated autobiographers such as Marmontel and Jamerey Duval was not so much his desire to show how overcoming adversity shapes the personality, or to prove that all experience is liberating, as it was to argue that change could be reconciled with continuity at a deeper level of being. Ménétra's goal was not to explain the road he had traveled but to show the fatality of immobility and the disruption of working-class tradition by historical change. Writing an autobiography enabled him to resolve the contradiction; remembering was a way of affirming his ability to be himself in spite of everything, and despite the passage of time. One can thus read Ménétra's memoir as the expression of a political will that has its counterpart in the work of Rousseau. The glazier needed social rules and political principles, which he found in his aptitude for assessing hierarchies and his ability to imagine new forms of solidarity (among workers united by shared experiences of work and play or among individuals united by mutual esteem, sympathy, and transparency). In opposition to various forms of authority, he asserted his faith in individual freedom and opposition to fate, even though compromise with the established order was often unavoidable.

In both respects the Genevan aligned himself with the same political ideology. First, the theory of the contract, whether social or pedagogical, assumed some sort of emotional exchange. Autobiography showed that appearance and reality did not coincide, that men were at war and that transparency and obstruction were locked in struggle. Second, Rousseau, a "rebellious intellectual," critical of what he saw as a society based on lies, proposed to live in material independence in order to guarantee his intellectual independence. What gave the politics of Ménétra and Rousseau its power was the ability to preach resistance to illusion. Only by understanding this, Rousseau wrote to Archbishop Christophe de Beaumont, can one "be free and good in irons." He thereby expressed his fundamental faith in equality and liberty, a faith that he lived and preached in his own way.

Other forms of expression help us to understand how, if not why, statements of this sort were apprehended and reproduced. The wave of individualism engulfed other areas besides literature, including the fine arts. Painters, abetted by art critics, used portraits to express the idea that men could be free and that free individuals need not be isolated in their singularity. Freedom could be savored only if it was communicated, only if the individual asserted his presence in the world, which his portrait helped him to do.[28]

Portrait art was a minor genre. According to the academic canon it ranked below history painting. But it liberated itself in the time of David through the acquisition of new rules and new techniques. One could be a portraitist without being a history painter and still be acknowledged to be great, as the example of Quentin de La Tour illustrates. Although the idea of portrait painting as a minor genre remained just below the surface, portraiture shared with history painting ("a higher genre because it portrays heroes in action") an ability to portray men and their passions. Portraitists were accordingly numerous, and their works often found favor in the Académie's Salons. Portrait painters preserved the faces of the great, including the greatest of all, the king, for posterity and displayed the signs and symbols of power. For a long time to come, the personality of the model would remain inseparable from his social standing, for everything—not least the social order—insisted on it.

Nevertheless, a new idea of portraiture gained favor with artists and spectators alike. The *Encyclopédie*'s definition of the portrait suggests a shift from a social to an individual logic: a portrait "is a likeness according to nature." This definition did not constitute a total break with classicism (already in the work of Roger de Piles the principle of individuality was coupled with idealization), but it did accentuate the need for combining exact resemblance, or the "character [and] physiognomic appearance of the persons represented," with moral description. The purpose of imitating a person's features was not simply to permit physical identification but to reveal the model's spirit and temperament. A portrait was always a "painting of the soul," a quest for the elusive, a translation of psychology into paint, a demand for truth. It was an opportunity to reconcile the aesthetic ideal with the individual nature: resemblance and beauty could no longer be separated. "What made the eighteenth century the great century of portraiture was the intuition that nature was inexhaustible, never repetitious, and never satisfied until she had created difference. It was also the conviction that certainty arises only out of the effort of a singular consciousness and always originates in an individual action, that is, in a living presence granted the privilege of organizing the world with itself at the center."[29]

With painters such as Quentin de La Tour, Chardin, and Liotard, what the subject of a portrait represented was the multiplicity of being, the myriad of different states, faces, and secrets, the variety of individuals, and yet at the same time the capacity of sociability to unify human relations: individualism perceived but also an instrument of perception. It is not surprising that aesthetic theory, preoccupied as it was with expressiveness and individuality, found common ground with the grammar of character and feeling as an essential tool for deciphering the language of action, as in Lavater. The rhetoric of passion shifted from the ideal nature, the ideal character, to the individual and social condition of the subject.[30]

Individuality was increasingly expressed through letters. For various reasons—administrative, communal, familial—the volume of correspondence grew for everyone. Improvements in roads and in the royal postal service helped. Publication of the letters of great writers contributed to the creation of a public space. Letters repeated what was said in conversation and spread the sociability of the salons far and wide. Painting lent itself to the portrayal of this lively form of social intercourse. At first letters merely added ambiance to portraits, evoking scholarly or literary activity without any necessary connection with psychology. The influence of Dutch genre painting had introduced the theme of the young woman reading in an opulent setting. Chardin, Fragonard, Boucher, and Liotard worked many variations on this theme, which epitomized the acme of social life, the success of a society of "words and masks," of personality construction through epistolary commerce.

Meanwhile, the epistolary novel dealt with the same theme and psychology in a different key: the *Lettres persanes* (1721), *Lettres anglaises* (1734), and *Lettres familières écrites d'Italie* (1740) marked the growing authority of individualized forms of expression. These works mimicked the randomness of reality, and Montesquieu, Voltaire, and De Brosses used the effect in a masterly way. Rousseau's *Nouvelle Héloïse* (1761) and Laclos's *Liaisons dangereuses* (1782) developed the genre to perfection. Both taught readers to understand characters from within in terms of psychological and poetic verisimilitude and social conditions. In both the epistolary novel and actual correspondence, what appealed to people was the possibility of using an instrument with which they could fashion themselves for the purpose of persuasion or seduction. The expression of individuals who existed only because they told their stories was the expression of a society that existed only through commerce, which taught people to know themselves.[31]

Was it only the cultivated and wealthy who engaged in correspondence? Not at all. There were no unbreachable boundaries in this or any other area. Humble folk knew how to write and did write letters for utilitarian purposes. What was to prevent them from achieving a degree of introspectiveness, an ability to analyze their feelings? Evidence of this can be seen in Parisian estate inventories: papers, letters, and writing implements became increasingly common as the century progressed, despite the fact that such things tended to be overlooked by indifferent notaries. The autobiographies of Ménétra and Duval reveal customs that are no less worthy of our attention just because they were commonplace. Ordinary people exchanged letters, infrequently to be sure, but that only made them and the people who wrote them that much more important. Letter writing was a communal activity, involving public writers, circumstantial intermediaries, and collective readings. It was not an easy thing to do, even when paid agents were used.

Before the eighteenth century writing was a rare skill, so those who practiced it stood out all the more. We still do not fully understand the relationship that developed between public space and private space.[32] The interconnections between the two probably increased over time. Writing and signatures took on symbolic significance through religious and administrative documents, and letter writing only enhanced this. By the end of the eighteenth century, the letter had become a mark of identity, the touchstone of a person capable of writing, expressing himself, and signing contracts: individual man met *Homo economicus*. Writing was a natural act: after a long history of symbolism and icons, it became a trace, an equivocal imprint.[33] Signatures served to classify: they identified individuals and validated documents and thus contributed to the security of civil society, as Abbé Lanzi remarked late in the century. Sometimes a man could be recognized simply by his handwriting. People collected autographs as tokens of personality.[34]

That the self was a relatively new category is clear from the evolution of the family, entrepreneurship, and individualism. It was left to Kant to show how practical reason grew out of the condition of the individual, the sacred character of the human person.[35]

17

❧❦❧❦❧❦

Consumption and Appearance

SIGNS OF INDIVIDUALITY proliferated, and with them we find a change in attitudes toward the world and things. Growing numbers of people—first men and then women, too—acquired new social skills and developed a new perception of vital social forces.

Consider another sign of change: if we look closely at statements given by witnesses in court concerning their age, we find that around 1760 attitudes changed. Previously, most people were vague about their age and generally misrepresented it in court. They envisioned the life cycle in terms of "stages of life"—youth, maturity, old age—and few were lucky enough to live their full measure of years. But after the middle of the eighteenth century, the precision of witnesses increased, reflecting a new emphasis on exactitude in many areas and a belief, fostered by educational advances, in the value of quantitative measurement. Farmers, merchants, artisans, and rural as well as urban elites quickly acquired new reflexes; urban workers and farmhands took longer. In general, however, attitudes toward time changed.[1]

In studying such changes, the historian must confront not only the image of the eighteenth century but also, as Jean Starobinski has shown, its mythology.[2] The nineteenth century dreamed of an elegant and frivolous eighteenth century, a lost age of sweetness and light for history's vanquished and a moral justification or alibi for the victors. Out of this image of pleasure came the idea that "the invention of liberty" altered the relation between man and things. Not just the elite but the entire society was affected by a new profusion of objects given wide distribution by nascent industry and even more by urbanization. New ideas about the ethics of consumption appeared not only in high art and philosophical theorizing but also in everyday attitudes. Indeed, it was because artists and philosophers perceived changes in daily behavior that they sought to influence the course of history and protect individual liberty from both archaic constraints and the threat of alienation that they saw in the proliferation of material goods.

The change was apparent in two areas. In the economic sphere, it marked a shift away from a preindustrial demand structure. And in the social and cultural sphere, it revealed a change in social attitudes as well as a new relationship between intellectual culture and material culture, subject and object.

In a preindustrial economy, demand for consumer goods depends on mechanisms of economic circulation. In eighteenth-century France, agriculture still drove incomes and budgets; hence agricultural output influenced prices in other sectors of the economy. Variations in demand for discretionary consumer goods had a major impact on total demand. There were several reasons for this. Most consumers still lived at the basic subsistence level and supplied their own needs. Consumer goods were in short supply, yet social functions were as diversified as they are in an industrial society. Finally, different sectors of the economy were not hermetically isolated from one another: in a monetary economy with global income constraints, everything was interconnected. Commodities complemented one another in a hierarchy of consumption ranging from subsistence goods to luxury goods and articles of display. In other words, demand for essentials was relatively constant, while demand for other kinds of consumer goods varied.

Economic facts also had social implications. Extreme hierarchical differentiation made some people especially keen to diminish or mask social distances. Low incomes kept luxury goods and display articles beyond the reach of many consumers. The growth of the cash economy enhanced the social and cultural significance of consumption. The three markets—subsistence, luxury, and display—came together, as J.-Y. Grenier has shown, and at each level demand and prices obeyed a distinctive rationale.[3] The amount of income spent on each type of commodity—wheat, meat, clothing—varied over time and with social status.

Consider two broad but related issues. Did the burden of obtaining necessities lessen for large numbers of people? And if so, did this increase their consumption of luxury goods? For the vast rural majority we cannot answer these questions. We know even less about how different sorts of consumption were related: people ate bread every day but could do without meat. Some display items, such as clothing, were virtual necessities, but old clothes could be mended and reused; consumption patterns therefore depended on whether the economy was one of scarcity, where people tried to keep their possessions serviceable for as long as possible, or a more dynamic consumer economy. Cities hastened the shift to an economy of consumption, simultaneously accelerating supply and demand.

On the social and cultural side, it is important to recognize that, despite a deeply entrenched intellectual tradition, commodities did not necessarily foster alienation; in fact, they generally meant liberation. Material culture involves commodities, technology, art, and anthropology. All too aware of a vertiginous growth in the number of commodities, eighteenth-century thinkers inaugurated a philosophical tradition that deplored material alienation and consumption. But the expansion of consumption was not purely negative and did not lead only to passive imitation. Acquisitiveness was a way of broadening one's range of knowledge, as Legrand d'Aussy recognized in his *Histoire de la vie privée des Français* (1783; reprinted 1815):

> Yet if our graybeards are to be believed, luxurious clothing, sumptuous dining, and debauched morals are recent developments. To hear them tell it, they witnessed the beginnings of these things. Yet when we look back at different stages of the monarchy, we find the same complaints being voiced by the writers of every period. The voluptuaries of the reign of Louis XV extolled the purity of morals and innocence of the centuries of Louis XIV and Francis I.

Change itself became a subject of investigation. People studied the evolution of "mores" and the "national spirit." Each generation asked itself how commodities figured in the construction of social and individual identities. How did market changes affect the classification of goods? How was nostalgia to be avoided? How did the proliferation and circulation of commodities impinge on the authenticity of the individual?

For the eighteenth century this kind of analysis is not easy to do. France combined aspects of traditional (or what anthropologists call "segmentary") society, which is inegalitarian, hierarchical, and not totally market-oriented, with aspects of modern (or "fragmentary") society, which is egalitarian, individualistic, and market-centered. We need to approach all these questions, moreover, without undue simplification. Ultimately, the question we have to address is how subjectivity was constructed.

I suggest that the answer lies in consumption and exchange, the source of all value. As we shall see, the abstract, impersonal power of money established new kinds of social relations. In social terms, men no longer differentiated themselves on the basis of essential qualities; the social hierarchy was instead based on the possession of goods and the wherewithal to buy them. Money and commodities circulated, creating equality and inequality and justifying ever more abstract notions of identity. The crux of the matter was still a person's ability to command part of the nation's surplus production: therein lay what Georg Simmel has called the "tragedy of culture,"[4] and the eighteenth century was culturally astute enough to have grasped this tragedy at its inception. I explore the matter by analyzing two aspects of the transformation of consumption: the great "luxury debate," which related moral issues to economic ones, and the *Encyclopédie* as a work emblematic of the new faith in economic growth and technological progress at its acme.

The Progress of Consumption

The vagaries of industrial history are best grasped by looking at production. Growth was undeniable, and foreign trade remained the leading sector.[5] Yet domestic commerce still accounted for the majority of all transactions: three-quarters in the seventeenth century, four-fifths in the eighteenth century. In the marketplace the principal buyer was the peasant, whose demand for commodities drove the economy; urban purchasers came second. Boisguilbert and Cantillon were the first to analyze the mechanisms and circuits appropriate to each.

Industrialists responded to increased demand stemming from demographic growth and increased overall wealth. With urbanization, demand not only increased but also diversified as more exigent customers insisted on a wider range of goods than had been previously available. New problems arose. A shortage of raw wool, cotton, and silk left France a net importer of textiles. A shortage of iron ore and fuel led to an increase in the price of iron and encouraged work on new technologies, importation of British models, and emulation of successful methods. Manufacturers competed for new customers on the basis of quality and creativity.

From Production to Consumption

Let us briefly survey the overall surge in the economy. Consider the growth of domestic trade. At Beaucaire, the average annual rate of increase of fairground sales was 3.1 percent from 1728 to 1749, reaching a peak of 7.8 percent in 1780 as the southern French and international economies picked up speed. The pace also picked up in Guibray and Caen after 1735; it slowed again after 1780 but never dropped back to its original level. This trend is confirmed by other indices: payments of the duty known as the *octroi* after 1745, investments in roads (1749), and port shipments. Toll receipts on the Seine and Rhône also rose. In short, commodity circulation increased.

Growth in production was more complex but equally certain. The industries of the past progressed moderately. Output of wool textiles grew by 61 percent between 1768 and 1789, with considerable variation between regions: growth was 127 percent in Champagne and 143 percent in Languedoc but only 7 percent in the Beauvaisis and Picardy, while output in Burgundy actually declined. In silk the average annual growth was 2 percent after 1730. Production of linen increased more rapidly, despite difficulties in western France. Finally, cotton was still forging ahead after 1730: the rate of growth calculated for the *généralité* of Rouen exceeded 4 percent. Everywhere, the number of textile firms increased, as did the number of items produced. This transformation of the productive apparatus was driven by changes in domestic demand and encouraged by the government. The success of cotton print fabrics reflected complex changes affecting all of society.[6] It triggered an industrial "gold rush" involving technological innovation, social and geographic mobility, and expanded employment opportunities for mechanics and clerks. Other branches of industry such as mining, smelting, and iron manufacturing registered significant growth, although they still accounted for only a small fraction of total output. One finds advances in all the indices: number of plants, volume of output, and quality of production. The result was an annual growth rate estimated at 3.8 percent for coal mining and 1.9 percent for cast iron.

According to Tolozan's data, France's gross national product stood at 2.550 billion livres in 1786. Agricultural production accounted for four-fifths of this. The industrial output of 526 million livres was dominated by textiles (48 percent); smelting rose to 15 percent. As the structure of demand varied over time and from region to region, industry raced to respond, altering the relative proportion of subsistence, luxury, and display goods in total output. But there is still a great deal that we do not understand about the relation between supply and demand.

The magnitude of the change can be appreciated by studying the clothing industry, but much uncertainty remains about specific aspects of the phenomenon, such as retail sales. Many other sectors are worth looking at, including hardware and the building trades in both rural and urban settings. But the textile sector offers a good illustration of the interaction between material aspects of the productive process and socioeconomic factors. The industry straddled the divide between the old society and the new. Textiles—the quintessential commodity—changed the way people behaved. For the first time we witness the emergence of two systems of production, two parallel economies, and two modes of consumption. High-volume mass production increased: the cotton print industry is a good example of this. Yet other firms continued to produce quality textiles. These took many hours of labor to produce. Firms in the quality-goods sector were protected against competition by *privilèges*, and workers were subject to corporate regulation. Traditional cotton and linen production was a paragon of stability, security, and routine. The two sectors of the textile industry were not totally distinct: they interacted in various ways. And there was ambivalence about change, as is evident from the work of the *inspecteurs des manufactures*, caught between defending regulations and embracing liberal ideas spurred by the changing demand structure. One inspector in Picardy had this to say: "New conditions make the old regulations pointless. It is perfectly clear that people nowadays change the way they dress as rapidly as their means allow. Production and sale of these fabrics used to move slowly, but today the market is much more brisk. Consumers must be sought across Europe."

Textile manufacturers and others responded to changes in demand owing to changes in wages and income. Social and geographic disparities existed, of course. Markets did not evolve as rapidly in the countryside as in the cities. In rural villages textile work was ubiquitous, although basic fabric production was now left to specialists, and families turned to the market to fill some of their needs. Women of course did the spinning and sewing. The proto-industrial economy introduced new methods of cloth making; old customs vanished, as is clear from conflicts over the use of waste and other shady practices.

Proto-industrial manufacturing relied on both home workers, mainly women, and professionals, including dealers who provided raw materials and then bought the finished goods for resale. Weavers, tailors, linen makers, and cobblers also played a part. Brie supplied roughly 60 percent of the linen goods consumed in the province. The proportion of locally made clothing was probably lower. As society urbanized, more and more clothing manufacture was put out to home-based seamstresses. As first city and then country girls went to school, they did less and less sewing for their own families. Proverbs and other sources make it clear, however, that clothing continued to be a potent symbol. Dress played a part in all major social rituals from birth to death. Strict rules of civility and propriety applied. Country folk dressed according to the occasion: everyday costumes differed sharply from holiday wear. Regular clothing was loose-fitting, functional, and aesthetically indifferent, while finery for special occasions could emphasize the shape of the wearer's body and use various devices to indicate social status or ritual role.

In the cities, and especially Paris, which was reputed to be the "Mecca of fashion," all sorts of manufacturers helped to change people's habits of dress. The Parisian weavers' guilds were quite active: they controlled more than 10 percent of the city's looms and employed some thirty thousand individuals, including 20 percent of the city's master weavers and 40 percent of textile workers. Women played a key role, both as workers (although their numbers are difficult to gauge) and as a force for change in occupations such as seamstress, linen maker, and fashion retailer.

Paris stands out for two reasons. First, artisans were always important there, and so was the world of fashion. Second, retail sales in Paris had a direct impact on manufacturing. The capital's haberdashers served as intermediaries between clients and suppliers, and leading fashion designers spurred sales with their creations. Fashions changed at a dizzying pace, accelerated by the influence of the media: one innovation was to publish engravings of new designs, and another was the advent of publications for women (which also attracted men as readers and contributors). At once literate, coy, and commercial, the magazines helped to propagate both the values of the new commercial economy and a specifically feminine conception of the Enlightenment. Women discovered equality in individualism and looked forward to a new balance between male and female roles in both public and private life.

On the whole, while occupational specialization by sex continued, corporate competition helped to unify the market and ensure the triumph of Paris fashions. The elegance of Parisian creations induced people to adopt new styles of behavior along with the new styles in clothing. The theatricalization of appearance helped, as did the advent of a consumer economy. The industry's ability to respond quickly to changes in demand was important, as was the ability of designers to generate new fashions. The influence of the capital was felt in the provinces and vice versa; the same can be said of regional centers and the smaller towns and villages they served. Thus, the profits of the land were redirected according to the choices of individual consumers, who determined where jobs would be created, what sectors would be stimulated by increased demand, and where new revenues would flow. Luxury and display goods therefore took on real economic importance.

The Revolution of Appearances in Paris

Estate inventories enable us to see how consumption evolved. Historians have long made use of these inventories but not always in a systematic, comparative way. Many have used them more to illustrate preestablished hierarchies than to elucidate individualized modes of social appropriation. These documents are difficult to interpret, for they are private family records whose content was largely determined by the habitual ways of clerks and notaries. Yet by their very nature, as descriptions of the contents of private homes, they contain a wealth of information about all aspects of everyday life. Their use requires certain precautions, about which I have written elsewhere.[7] With the help of this infinitely rich source, we can try to pinpoint changes in Parisian consumption patterns, looking first at urban society as a whole, then at the lower strata, and finally at a specific aspect of consumption, namely, purchases of clothing.

We have detailed knowledge of various aspects of material life in the seventeenth and eighteenth centuries from a sample of some three thousand Parisian estate inventories representing people of all classes: merchants and master craftsmen account for 49 percent of the sample, while another 20 percent were workers, journeymen, or members of various guilds. The rest belonged to the aristocratic, clerical, or bourgeois elites. My interpretation has been guided by two principles: indicators of social and occupational status must always be cross-checked against material indices, and comparative analysis across a broad time span (in this case, early seventeenth to late eighteenth centuries) is essential.

Over this period we find considerable evolution of domestic interiors. Before the turn of the eighteenth century, living space tended to be arranged vertically; rooms were not assigned specific purposes, and a screen or partition was often the only form of privacy; work space and living space overlapped; the kitchen and hearth area was used for many different purposes; and in homes with more than one room, the bedroom played a key role as the center of living space and focal point of public and private socializing. To be sure, social differences had a major impact: for example, three-quarters of wage earners, or more than a third of the total population, lived in single-room dwellings.

The most important changes occurred among those who lived in the best conditions: the number of rooms per dwelling increased, certain rooms were set aside for specific purposes, privacy increased, and bedrooms became private. New words for rooms indicated new functions. Guests were received in the dining room and salon. Libraries and studies, of a size appropriate to the family's status, existed in the wealthiest homes. At the very top of the hierarchy, women had their· own "boudoirs" for additional privacy. Some homes had dressing rooms and bathrooms. These changes reflected two new values: privacy, which was a consequence of changes in the family and the rise of individualism, and a more rational, functional division of space, which was subdivided for specific purposes.

Moving from rooms to what was in them, we notice two further changes. The first pertains to methods of storage and the furniture associated with them. At the turn of the eighteenth century, most belongings were still stored in chests and trunks. From the poorest to the wealthiest families, utensils, bedding, and personal items were stored in a haphazard yet functional manner. After 1750, fewer than 20 percent of the inventories mention chests. These were replaced by the double-doored armoire, which made for more methodical storage. This was often a quality piece, more costly than a chest and available in several varieties. Increasingly common as well, especially among the rich, were chests of drawers—

commodes, chiffoniers, and the like—which made it easier to put things away and encouraged more orderly storage. In the kitchen two related changes occurred. Well into the eighteenth century, women still knelt, crouched, or sat while cooking. Kitchen utensils were few in number and were either arrayed around the kitchen or stored on shelves. After 1750, however, fireplaces with multiple hearths became common, the tripod replaced the trammel, and stoves and ovens allowed women to cook standing up. China, crockery, and pottery became increasingly common, and storage improved. All in all, the inventories reveal a veritable revolution in household furnishings: new types of furniture, individual beds, greater variety of seating. The well-to-do acquired a wide range of sophisticated new accessories: card tables, writing tables, and dressing tables, for instance, as well as books, clocks, and barometers. Various types of bibelots reflected a taste for the frivolous as well as for new materials and colors, a tribute to the productivity and creativity of many types of craftsmen.

Our understanding of material progress has been hampered by two puzzles. First, the role that privileged groups played in the material revolution is unclear. Second, scholars have characterized the early modern era in general, and the eighteenth century in particular, as a time when people developed new attitudes toward other people and things, yet we are told that there was a price to be paid for material gains and more rational organization: the ransom of progress. Estate inventories clarify two important points. First, the whole city was involved in the proliferation of material things. Of course the rich had many more possessions than the poor; but insofar as production was concerned, the effects of advances in material culture were widespread. Second, beyond the accumulation of objects, we sense certain changes in values: the importance of representation diminished, and the hierarchy of prestige and status was overturned. Like the court, Paris served in this respect as a model to be emulated (although the specifics of this process have yet to be demonstrated in detail).

What about ordinary people as opposed to people of privilege? Three areas of difference need to be kept in mind. First, the relative value of real estate versus other possessions is a key variable. Understanding the choice between use value and exchange value is important for a proper appreciation of access to the enriched world of objects. Among workers, use value outweighed exchange value: in a sample of one hundred workingmen's estates, we find that one-third consisted of no more than a few items of furniture, utensils, and some linen. Yet among domestic servants in the same period, exchange value dominated. In 1700, people with fortunes under five hundred livres owned mainly tangible goods. But for those with fortunes above three thousand livres, tangible goods accounted for less than 5 percent of heritable assets. By 1789, the proportion of essentials relative to items with exchange value had diminished for wage earners; some inventories even included securities, especially promissory notes, which suggests that part of the improvement was based on credit.

Second, not everyone prospered. Some people had no estates to be inventoried, and their number was greater in the 1780s than in earlier decades. Inflation diminished the actual value of estates under five hundred livres; we find both an increase in the number of large fortunes and widespread impoverishment of people without professional skills. The poorest domestic servants no longer bothered to go to a notary. Real progress came at the expense of unskilled workers, the army of those destined to labor at the innumerable thankless jobs without which urban development would have been impossible.

Third, as long ago as 1981 I wrote about advances made by Parisian workers and the relation between the acquisition of material goods and the acquisition of culture. The material revolution, which had its most immediate impact, perhaps, on the lower classes, reached them through cultural intermediaries such as servants and better-paid workers. These cultural agents copied the manners and habits of people of higher station. The poor always looked to their betters for guidance in these matters.[8] Everyday life was not entirely private: work and leisure escaped the "tyranny of intimacy." Changes in lifestyle were reflected in efforts by the administration, clergy, police, and employers to discipline workers, and in the ability of workers to internalize new norms without losing their distinctive identity or giving up their distinctive patterns of behavior.

It is interesting to look at dress in this light. People at all levels of society were spending more on clothing and undergarments: in 1700 the average noble spent 1,800 livres on clothing; by 1789 the figure had risen to 6,000—an increase of 233 percent. For workers, expenditures on clothing rose from 42 to 115 livres, or 215 percent. The increase in this area outpaced all expenditures on necessities and initiated a series of important changes, such as the spread of commercial laundries. Meanwhile, habits of dress became more similar across classes: wardrobes contained the same types of clothing, although differences in quantity and quality ensured that the hierarchy was preserved. A revolution in underclothing marked a major advance in personal hygiene affecting the entire population: whiteness became a symbol of moral purity. Other changes also cut across social divisions: lightweight fabrics supplanted heavier ones (cotton replaced wool, for instance); there was an explosion of color and design; and loose-fitting clothing allowed greater freedom of movement. In other words, sensibilities changed in the eighteenth century even as scarcity diminished. Lower clothing costs made it possible to acquire new clothes more frequently. Here, certain people were more susceptible to the new ways than others: women of all classes headed the list; then came cultural intermediaries such as domestic servants and people in the clothing business; and finally soldiers, who were able, because of the prestige of the uniform, to inculcate new standards of discipline, a favorable attitude toward change, and modern attitudes toward personal hygiene.

Changing fashions of dress—and the broader revolution of appearances—thus reveal a new conception of economy and society, as well as the problems that came with it. Implicit in these changes was a masking of social differences: disparities remained, but they could no longer be recognized in the old ways. People had to learn to interpret subtle nuances and to identify marks of refinement. At the heart of the "culture of appearances" lay the conflict between a society of civility, in which clothing revealed a person's social and moral condition, and a society of consumption, in which emulation undermined hierarchical representations and led to struggles over new ways to symbolize difference. By emphasizing the value of change, the new culture sharply distinguished itself from the tradition of *bienséances*, or protocolary proprieties, which identified appearance with reality, display with the hierarchy of power, and accumulation with a sin against charity. It promoted the values of individualism by way of materialism and established a new hierarchy of needs and abilities.[9]

Two things should be borne in mind. First, Paris and the country that followed its lead still lagged somewhat behind England, and this lag raises questions about the economic and social basis for change and the pace and stability of development. Second, the picture of material change that I have assembled from estate inventories focuses on transformations that occurred at the center; it remains to be seen how rapidly these changes spread to cities other than Paris and to rural areas. The evidence examined so far suggests two hypotheses. First, the changes reached provincial cities such as Meaux, Limoges, Chartres, and Montpellier through their elites and with a certain time lapse. Second, the countryside remained for some time in the world of scarcity and reuse, and rural people continued to make their own thread and cloth. The frontier of luxury became increasingly difficult to cross. In rural Poitou, for example, stability reigned from 1700 to 1800. Possession of objects did not become more common, and no new words were added to the lexicon of clothing. There are, however, signs that regional "micro-costumes" had a certain importance. Color preferences changed: blue gained favor everywhere. These changes were side effects of manufacturing aimed primarily at large-scale colonial commerce. Once again we find peasant France stuck in its ways. In the words of Jean-Baptiste Say early in the century, "Our villagers are a little like Turks." When it came to clothing, peasants remained conservative, thrifty, and rather threadbare. Where circumstances were favorable and urban influence was strong, however, consumption among the better-off did increase, for example, in the countryside around Paris, and in the Ile-de-France and Vexin, among the more prosperous peasants and notables.

We therefore need to pay attention to where and how "redistribution" occurred. Fairs played a fundamental role in unifying the market, integrating local and regional networks into national and international circuits of exchange for luxury goods. Local fairs provided outlets for raw materials and finished products from the region and redistributed manufactured goods including textiles and clothing and imported spices to local retailers and peddlers. The range of products for sale at fairs broadened, and new customers came to the fairgrounds. One clearly sees the primacy of demand, which increased as information, news, and models for emulation spread. Frequently fairs and markets coincided with holidays: in Combourg, for instance, where the young Chateaubriand grew up, as well as in Poitou in western France. The scene was often portrayed in literary works and paintings. Rural people, for whom commerce was never unadulterated, came together to buy and sell and celebrate.

How did people adjust to the advent of consumer society? Fairs were spectacles that anyone could attend, but not everyone could consume in the same way. Emulation was a complex phenomenon, and not without contradiction, but in the long run it resulted in greater homogeneity.

Various agents played a part in the process. Peddlers were mobile enough to bring the new culture to out-of-the-way hamlets and backwaters, introducing not only unheard-of luxury items but also baubles and trinkets to embellish the body, stir the soul, and inspire dreams. Local shopkeepers filled their shelves with wares purchased at fairs. Some people received novelties as gifts, while others stole items that caught their eye. All this was important because it changed people's habits, yet the whole process has to be seen in the context of other symbolic and festive practices. That is why the debate over luxury, which pitted proponents and adversaries of the new culture against one another, was so important.

The Polemic over Luxury and Consumption

The culture of appearances was just one aspect of a profound revolution in behavior. What is particularly interesting about this is that intellectual and material changes proceeded in the same way at the same pace. New social attitudes were learned and communicated to others, with interesting gender differences: men led women in acquiring literacy, for example, whereas women were in the vanguard when it came to adopting new styles of dress and perhaps new personal values generally. The power of the superfluous confronted religious, political, and philosophical authorities with the same question as the new culture of individualism: Just how much was tolerable?

The grip of necessity was gradually loosened, first in the cities, then in the countryside. Economic metaphors began to crop up in moral and economic discourse: "Exchange affects words just as it affects other commodities," Président De Brosses remarked in his *Traité de la formation mécanique des langues* (1765); "the effects of mutual importation are rapidly gaining ground, moving from the individual to the nation and ultimately even from people to people." This linguistic analysis can be applied, *mutatis mutandis*, to material progress in general, because clothing and objects constitute a system of communication, a kind of code. This was where luxury and fashion made their force felt: the language of things ran riot, blurring conventional signs and undermining their meaning as people raced to distinguish themselves from one another. The debate over the immediate and long-term effects of this process shows that it was an essential aspect of both economic and moral change.

The debate over luxury began in the realm of political theology.

Christian political economy favored a stable hierarchy in which consumption was governed by the principle of "to each according to his status." But it did not remain there for long, owing to the importance of the issues. The future of society was at stake, and it was not only France that was involved but also England, where many of the fundamental questions originated, and the rest of Europe from Italy to Holland and Prussia. All the major thinkers were involved, and all the economists of the day were called to testify as men of ideas mobilized in an effort to understand the power of things.

One would like to know how this controversy relates to the history of luxury itself, but this will take further research. For now it is enough to state that the word "luxury" carried several meanings which society fabricated one after another and which, to complicate matters, could coexist. The assumption that representations of luxury simply reflected the ambient realities of the day is too simple; we cannot isolate what was from the way people talked about it any more than we can today isolate what is from the way people talk about it. Luxury does not stand out from necessity as extraordinary events stand out from ordinary ones. We study it in order to understand how the social imagination was constituted along with the realities that shaped it and were in turn shaped by it. Both were constructed simultaneously and must be interpreted in terms of objects, laws regulating the consumption of those objects, and economic norms that circumscribed people's behavior. When we have done this, we will have a better understanding of why the Enlightenment debate about luxury went to the heart of the way the new liberal and individualist society was transforming the old Christian society; we will also have gone some way toward answering questions about the relation between individual freedom and conditions of existence, use and exchange, and desire and need.

Luxury Accepted, Luxury Contested: Religion and Production

In a stable, egalitarian society, luxury could be tolerated: surplus resources were reserved for certain segments of society, primarily the court, the high nobility, and the cities. The contrast between the poverty of the humble and the excessive wealth, indeed absurd wastefulness, of the rich was not incompatible with the social values of the day. In the economy of scarcity, redistribution was accomplished through charitable gifts inspired by the principle that in the next world everyone would be equal. Luxury still had a symbolic character: luxury consumption was worth a great deal in monetary terms, but it was even more a mark of power, a source of respect and charisma. No one challenged the extraordinarily luxurious settings devoted to the service of God, for example. The nouveau riche who tried to cast off his recognized, inherited status had long been a focal point of criticism but became even more so with the beginnings of economic expansion and increased social mobility. Such criticism was a staple of satires attacking the bourgeoisie and its alleged ideology. Its object changed over time as the acquisition of nobility became increasingly rare though not impossible. Regnard's *Turcaret* took up where Molière's *Bourgeois gentilhomme* left off.[10]

The eighteenth century began with this traditional attitude toward luxury but eventually developed a critique based in part on aristocratic fears of social mobility sponsored by the absolutist state and in part on perceptions of poverty. This critique combined two ingredients that we find forcefully expressed in the work of Fénelon, whose *Télémaque* (1699) remained influential long after his death in 1715, as well as in Beauvillier, Boulainvilliers, and Saint-Simon. The first was the need to return to some notion of the "common good," which meant putting an end to the economy of waste and vanity best exemplified by the court. In the second place, aristocratic political criticism made common cause with utilitarian advocates of the "public good," a concept that combined elements of Christian asceticism, alleged Roman and Spartan virtues, and ancient republican austerity as in Fénelon's "Bétique." Such criticism posed a challenge to a civilization based on material expansion. The sovereign, it was argued, must limit the spread of excess in the name of the public interest. The economy demanded nothing less, since expenditures on luxury items threatened to undermine the stability of the currency. Social harmony also depended on it, because luxury was a form of usurpation which contributed to the confusion of ranks; because nobles required to spend ever increasing sums in order to maintain their rank were being led into ruin; and because the legitimacy of luxury encouraged and confirmed the power of the "new men" who became scapegoats for aristocratic and Christian criticism. A complex economic and social reality was interpreted in moral terms as a consequence of the human vanity condemned in Ecclesiastes and as a source of corruption in any civilization.[11] Listen to Fénelon in *Télémaque:*

Just as too much authority poisons kings, luxury poisons an entire
nation. We are told that luxury serves to feed the poor at the expense
of the rich, as if the poor could not earn their livings in more useful
ways by multiplying the fruits of the earth without softening the rich
with voluptuous refinements. The entire nation is becoming accustomed to looking upon life's necessities as superfluous . . . Luxury goes
by the name of good taste, the pinnacle of the nation's arts and
politeness. This vice, which attracts a myriad of others, is praised as a
virtue. It spreads its contagion from the king to the dregs of the
populace . . . The tastes and habits of an entire nation must be
changed; it must be given new laws. Who can do this, if not a philosopher king?[12]

Note how economic morality spontaneously expressed itself in organicist terms and how the critique of the economy led to politics. The
transition from an economy of scarcity to an economy of abundance (still
relative in 1699) thus spurred a call for moral reform inspired by Christianity, the myth of a golden age, and the supposedly frugal beginnings of
the Greeks and Romans.

In Defense of Luxury: The Necessity of the Superfluous

Some time between 1700 and 1730 a turn was taken that would lead to a
rehabilitation of luxury. Three things combined to change people's thinking: a historical lesson based on the personal experience of Pierre Bayle;
the reflections of the "French" economists Boisguilbert, Cantillon, and
Melon; and Mandeville's pathbreaking *Fable of the Bees*, which revealed
the autonomous function of the superfluous.

Bayle's contribution, in his *Réponses aux questions d'un provincial*
(1704–1707), was to refute the myth of ancient frugality by showing that
the idea that Sparta and the Roman Republic were exemplary states
embodying all the moral virtues was based on a misleading historical
reconstruction intended solely to edify the young.[13] In other words, the
ancients had made a virtue of necessity; there can be no moral value
where there is no choice. History itself demonstrated the falsity of the
model: victorious Rome changed its ways and shed its "old sentiments."
But Bayle's critique also drew on his experience as a refugee in Holland,
where economic development and moderate luxury coexisted with civic

pride: "A moderate luxury is of great use in Republics. It causes money to circulate; it keeps humble people alive. If it becomes excessive and worrisome, your descendants will take care of it. So leave worry about the future to those to whom it belongs and think about the opulence of the present."

Bayle demolished a historical case based on nothing more than nostalgia. The economists gave reasons to promote luxury as an economic necessity. In 1704 Boisguilbert demonstrated the function of money in exchange and showed that circulation implied parity of purchase and sale. Luxury goods were not exempt from this rule; they could not be eliminated without injury to the economy. The motor of the economy was no longer supply but demand, or consumption. It was therefore plausible to look upon luxury as an economic barometer. Agriculture remained the cornerstone of the economy, but luxury was essential to growth and the increasing division of labor. If "consumption and income are one and the same," then luxury, or the surplus beyond the necessary and the convenient, was a positive good, for it encouraged growth:

One principle is incontrovertible: all the professions in a given country work for one another and sustain each other mutually, not only by supplying each other's needs but also by making each other's existence possible. No one buys a commodity from his neighbor, or the fruit of his neighbor's work, unless a strict though tacit and unstated condition is met, namely, that the seller also buys from the buyer, either directly, as sometimes happens, or indirectly by way of other hands or professions, which in the end comes to the same thing.

In this endless round of mutual exchange, on which all prosperity depends, luxury and superfluity have their proper place.

Cantillon, mentioned earlier in connection with the birth of city planning, also saw luxury as a factor of growth. Spending by landowners was crucial because it created employment: "The humors, fashions, and habits of the prince and especially of the owners of land determine the uses to which a state's land is put and cause the market prices of all things to fluctuate."[14] Everyone knew the fable of the "man-eating horse," which showed how decisions by the wealthy determined the need for labor. The crucial thing was to find work for people to do: "The state is reputed no less rich for the thousand trinkets that delight ladies and even men or that find their use in sport and recreation than for its useful and practical projects."[15]

J.-F. Melon, the author of the *Essai politique sur le commerce* (1734), was John Law's secretary as well as an *inspecteur général des fermes* and, in Voltaire's words, a "man of intelligence, citizen, and philosopher." Melon justified productive luxury, which he saw as a relative concept:

> What was luxurious for our fathers is nowadays commonplace, and what is luxurious for us will no longer be so for our nephews. Silk stockings were a luxury in the time of Henri II, and porcelain is as much a luxury compared to ordinary earthenware as fine china is compared to porcelain. The peasant finds luxury in a prosperous villager, and the villager finds it in the resident of a nearby city, who in turn sees himself as rustic compared with the denizen of the capital and even more rustic compared with the courtier.

Luxury creates work, and like labor it is the soul of wealth. It is useful to the state, unlike destructive oriental opulence. It encourages emulation and discourages laziness and idleness. Beyond this almost unreserved praise for luxury we detect a new understanding of human effort in an expanding economy.

From 1705 to 1729 Bernard Mandeville, a physician born in Rotterdam and settled in England, worked out a new theory of economic value that justified consumption in all its forms and, in particular, characterized luxury as a source of economic development driven by free individual choice. His allegorical poem, *The Fable of the Bees,* together with commentaries added with each new edition, was translated into French in 1740 and succeeded in attracting a considerable readership. The image of the beehive delivered from vice to virtue illustrated two principles: individual perfection leads to stagnation and is incompatible with social stability, while private vices make for public prosperity. In effect, the opulence and vanity of the few keep thousands of the poor alive. Envy and amour propre are the "ministers of industry." When virtue and justice prevailed, the bees died.

Mandeville's ideas had a powerful impact for two reasons. First, he showed that a purely Christian society was impossible and that morality was a separate matter from social utility. Second, he demystified moral behavior and showed that people who preached the virtue of austerity were frauds. Beyond economic facts Mandeville rediscovered the power of passion. He saw how passions made society work by directing desire into useful channels. His route to the future was not that of the French economists or the optimistic Enlightenment but a new path which, because of its apparent cynicism, was not always understood. Mandeville treated eudaemonism as an intrinsic consequence of human nature and culture as a matter of learning rules of social intercourse. Luxury was obviously a necessity. It was a relative status, and in the society just then coming into being it would be shared by growing numbers of people. The consequences of development could no longer be analyzed in moral terms.

The paradox of *The Fable of the Bees* no doubt lay in the fact that its power derived in part from the Augustinian tradition and from Jansenist and Calvinist moral theology. The power of the passions suggested the ideas of civilizing evil and frivolous amusement. Mandeville discovered that luxury, broadly defined, was an aspect of culture. He saw it as an index of development related to the division of labor, the expansion of commerce, and the growth spiral. He also confronted the problem of the moral costs of development. Mandeville uncovered the true motor of early capitalism and showed how the values on which it was based were rooted in human nature.[16] French optimists would dispute his pessimistic cynicism.

Development Accepted: The Immorality of Growth

Between 1736 and 1789, more than a hundred works were published in response to the issues raised by the debate among Christian economists, expansionist economists, and Mandeville. The academies became involved: in 1770 the Académie Française sponsored a competition on "the advantages and disadvantages of luxury." In 1782 the Académie de Besançon worried that "luxury had ruined empires" and received eighteen papers in response. Voltaire entered the fray in 1736 with his poem *Le Mondain* and his *Observations sur MM. Jean Law, Melon et Dutot, sur le commerce, le luxe, les monnaies, les impôts.* He read Mandeville and defended the boons of civilization. His main argument was that consumption spurs development: either there is no luxury, or luxury is everywhere. Voltaire had this to say in the *Dictionnaire philosophique:* "In a country in which everyone went barefoot, was the first man to make himself a pair of shoes living in luxury? Was he not a very wise and industrious fellow? Can we not say the same thing about the man with the first shirt? And as for the fellow who first thought of having his shirt laundered and ironed, I see him as an endlessly resourceful genius capable of governing a state." To indict luxury was to condemn mankind to stagnation on moral grounds and thus to fly in the face of history.

Diderot said much the same thing in his article on luxury in the *Encyclopédie:* "The principal object of desire is luxury, hence there is luxury in all states; it contributes to the happiness of humankind." As resources and values evolved, it became necessary to distinguish between the "ostentatious luxury" of poor, despotic states and the "pragmatic luxury" of the developed nations. With this distinction it was possible to condemn the wastefulness of the court and the aristocracy by contrasting it with the misery of the poor while at the same time singing the praises of the moderate, utilitarian luxury of the less spendthrift.

Condillac, a theorist of perception, economist of language, and linguist of economics, used a similar argument to refute ascetic values. Utility is the essence of the social, he insisted; hence material culture flourishes when needs increase. "When a society begins to enjoy things of secondary necessity, it begins to choose among food, clothing, housing, and weapons; it has greater needs and greater wealth." Exchange makes consumption a dynamic process, and economic expansion makes luxury a common possession. Nevertheless, the author of the *Essai sur le commerce et le gouvernement* was aware that the new economy had produced imbalances: "It is all too true that the luxury of a great capital is a source of misery and devastation." In other words, the economic logic of consumption based on a concentration of labor, power, consumable objects, urban wealth, luxury, and theatricalized dress could come into conflict with civic and moral values. Society needs wealth but can do without the wealthy.

Luxury, Morality, Politics, Economics

By midcentury, luxury and the flourishing economy that made it possible appeared to have carried the day. Mandeville's ideas had become well known in France through Melon, who passed them on to Montesquieu and Voltaire. The economists had given those ideas a persuasive technical veneer.[17] Hume's *Essay on Luxury* was translated into French in 1752. Hume was in fashion at the time, known in Parisian salons as a historian of England, a liberal, and a philosopher of the understanding and the passions. From 1763 to 1766 he served as secretary to the British ambassador in Paris. His essay rekindled the debate over luxury by advancing three new ideas: first, that ages of luxury are historically the happiest; second, that luxury is useful to society only if it is moderate; and third, that there can be no political progress unless industry is conjoined with liberty.

The revival of controversy marked a fundamental shift in both the intellectual and material situation. While mass consumption remained confined to necessities, consumption of luxury items, both foreign and domestic, reached unprecedented levels in both quantity and quality. This raised new questions about development and its consequences.

Thanks to the Physiocrats' lucid analysis, we can see why controversy flared up at this point rather than dying out. For one thing, the "net product" of agriculture remained the dominant economic factor, and expenditures by landowners still drove both trade and manufacturing. Hence the Physiocrats argued that it was important to avoid squandering agricultural output on "sterile expenditures," and this in turn meant imposing limits on luxury, whether of embellishment or subsistence. What was luxury if not a "superfluity of expenditure prejudicial to reproduction." Behind this definition lurked a conception of value and labor, profit and production, derived from the idea that a society dominated by landowners represented a "natural order," since land was the sole source of all wealth. Once again, consumption was judged from a moral point of view. In *L'Ami des hommes* the marquis de Mirabeau enumerated the consequences of excessive consumption. He imagined a cosseted landowner returning to his estates from the capital and worrying that his country seat might fall short of the standards imposed by the latest fashions:

He arrives only to find that his central avenue is too narrow. Another is needed, with two side paths thirty cubits in width and extending as far as the eye can see. So a perfectly good plot of land is turned into an avenue, product zero. The park, hedges, quincunx, labyrinth, and topiary gardens produce another zero. To set aside three hundred acres for such purposes is not too much. The vegetable garden is too small: it needs borders, partitions, a pump to supply water, greenhouses, and an *orangerie*. The pebbled terraces, the pruning, the upkeep of the gardens whose fresh fruits are packed off to the city, and the trouble of maintaining and raking all the paths in the park, keeping the pumps in working order, and so on—if all that costs no more than 10,000 livres, it's not too much. In the house, the furniture and polished woodwork call for a butler. If such a fellow, with his family and upkeep, costs no more than 100 pistoles, he is a bargain. The land was good for 15,000 livres in rent; it cost 400,000 francs plus expenses. Sixty thousand livres were spent to make the place worthy of its master. The land set aside for decorative purposes reduced the rent by 4,000 livres. Upkeep is 11,000. Nothing is left for my lord.

This picturesque account of the changes imposed by social necessities, which an economist like Cantillon could see as creating employment, amounted to a condemnation on both economic grounds (because luxury expenditures "decrease investment in the land") and moral grounds ("wealth that lies stagnant in corrupt channels or is diverted from its natural course decays or disappears"). Luxury, in other words, is a slippery slope that leads to corruption. Mirabeau expressed the main tenets of the conservative aristocratic critique of development in a new key: he condemned court society while accepting the idea of moderate luxury geared to social rank; and he rejected usurpation of social position by the wealthy. A problem that arose in the course of economic analysis, a problem that Adam Smith addressed only in theory, took on new significance when posed in psychological terms. In reality, what was at stake was the fundamental relationship between consumption and liberty.

Meanwhile, a slow change had begun in the economy of the old society, probably as a result of growing monetarization. As the volume of trade grew, most basic needs continued to be supplied by the domestic economy, while a good proportion of luxury items came from abroad. The two circuits were connected at the top, that is, in the upper reaches of church and state, but changing patterns of consumption gradually influenced the rest of society as well. Opposition to material culture and the spread of luxury increased, as Albert Hirschman has noted,[18] for the increased availability of what Adam Smith called "baubles, trinkets, and notions" raised questions about the very foundations of society. It was no coincidence that a controversy about the commercial nobility erupted at around the same time. The shock of plenty yielded satisfaction and enthusiasm in some quarters but disappointment and even outright hostility in others.[19]

At the heart of the new economy there was a curious ambivalence about the new material prosperity. In *The Wealth of Nations* the liberal theorist Adam Smith justified the expansion of wealth: the enjoyment of useful and pleasant things, he argued, was what distinguished flourishing, civilized nations from poor, savage tribes. But in the fourth chapter of Book 3 of that work, he showed that nobles had bartered ancient feudal ties for material goods, real human bonds for frivolous luxuries. In this text, written in 1776, he took up a theme first broached in 1759 in his *Theory of Moral Sentiments*, in which he used similar language to disparage the kinds of things money could buy. In the same passage in which he used the metaphor of the "invisible hand" to describe the force that regulates the market, Smith described the acquisitive desire as an "illusion that stimulates the industry of mankind and keeps it in perpetual motion." Smith's belief in the necessity of opulence was coupled with a certain animosity toward it, an animosity inspired perhaps by metaphysical reflections and Augustinian ideas about the roots of evil: self-interest was no longer condemned as such, but questions remained about the illusory aspects of man's material and moral situation.[20] The same contradiction can be found in the work of other Enlightenment thinkers, including that of the most famous detractor of material culture, Jean-Jacques Rousseau.

Rousseau's complex position cannot be reduced to the Christian, aristocratic, and feudal traditions that inspired it.[21] It is best understood in relation to three contexts. The first is economic and social: between 1745 and 1755 the intellectual climate was agitated by the consequences of the War of the Austrian Succession and fears of social unrest mentioned by the marquis d'Argenson among others (the thief Mandrin was put to the wheel in 1755). Second, the Physiocrats and liberals had precipitated a general crisis in moral and economic thinking. Rousseau dropped his bombshells before the major physiocratic texts appeared: his two *Discours* appeared in 1750 and 1755, whereas Quesnay's article "Fermier" did not come out until 1756, followed in 1758 by his *Tableau* and in 1767 by Baudeau's essay on luxury. Finally, by the 1750s, the principal signs of change had become apparent, as questions about the "two economies" reveal.

Rousseau's criticisms applied both to England, with whose debates he was familiar, and France, where he would ultimately break with the dominant school of the *Encyclopédie*. At the outset he did not have the animosity toward high society that is often associated with his name. He was an apologist for luxury, as can be seen from his *Epître à M. Bordes* and *Epître à Parisot*. His "illumination" came "on the road to Vincennes," a conversion experience whose symbolism was borrowed from Augustinian tradition. From that point on, Rousseau knew where he stood in the debate that was agitating the world of the intellectuals and academies. There was nothing bold or imprudent about the question on the sciences and the arts that the Académie de Dijon posed in 1749. The relation between civilization and morals was an old rhetorical topic— knowledge does not lead to virtue—but Rousseau stood it on its head: man, he argued, is naturally good, but society, civilization, material production, and luxury plunge him into depravity. Immediately a collective shift in thinking took place, as this table indicates.

Period	No. of academies offering prizes	No. of prizes	No. of subjects	Topics in economics or moral economy	Books on economics
1700–1709	2	40	19	1	35
1710–1719	4	60	30	3	39
1720–1729	6	86	56	9	77
1730–1739	9	122	89	9	67
1740–1749	15	185	133	21	88
1750–1759	21	359	230	35	363
1760–1769	21	360	224	28	558
1770–1779	24	334	216	11	483
1780–1789	29	589	293	4	829

Note that initially the increase in the number of prize competitions on economic topics, which suggests a growing interest in the discipline, was confirmed by a concomitant increase in the number of books on the subject. Note also the connection between events and the heightened interest in economics, a connection that is clear overall if somewhat restrained in the learned societies. The academies had some difficulty adapting to the rules and rigors of the new economic discourse, and the ultimate political debate of the Ancien Régime was conducted more in pamphlets than in prize essays. Rousseau's ringing indictment gained a large audience just when the two graphs (of the numbers of prize competitions and books on economics) crossed. After 1770, academic rhetoric on economy and morality cooled. The focus of the debate shifted to more concrete matters, to the reshaping of society.[22]

The major tenets of Rousseau's critique are well known: the sciences and the arts corrupted man, and other, worse ills followed, among them luxury, the product of idleness and vanity. Mandeville was the target of all this, even if he was not named, and Melon and Voltaire were attacked along with him. The remedies were clear: sumptuary laws, a return to peasant thrift, and idealization of the man of the soil. This line of criticism embodied a double refusal: first to separate economics from morality and politics and second to accept a society driven by development. For several years the public was captivated by efforts to refute Rousseau, whose critics were under no illusions about what he was rejecting. Rousseau's eloquence—his use of "invention," or images, to demonstrate abstract ideas in a powerful way—aroused interest, and his personality injected an emotional note into a great intellectual debate. The polemic played a different role. It moved the traditional economic and moral question onto new social terrain, as is evident from Rousseau's response to Bordes and Stanislas: "Luxury may be necessary to give bread to the poor, but if there were no luxury, there would be no poor."[23]

In the *Discours sur l'inégalité* and subsequent major works, Rousseau developed his major themes: luxury and inequality are related, progress and nature are antagonistic, and politics must settle a debate that is moral and social in nature. He offered a general critique of *Homo economicus* and development, arguing that society must return to a conception of the "public good" and to a morally oriented political economy. He rejected the moral and utilitarian consensus in the academies and dismissed the views of the economists. Rousseau then turned to the task of reconstructing the concept of natural rights, a task made necessary by the catastrophe that had befallen mankind. His solution was not so much a return to nature, to a primitive state of existence which Voltaire and Palissot ridiculed, as it was to overcome the antithesis between nature and culture by constructing a secular "theodicy" designed to combat evil not in man but in society. In other words, he pointed the way toward a new salvation.

One sees this in both the economic utopia of *La Nouvelle Héloïse* and the sociopolitical edifice of *Le Contrat social:* both are concerned with the problem of reconciling wealth with virtue and equality with property and liberty. Social order is created not by the economic but by the political.

Man must be made by man, and so much the worse for luxury. Rousseau did not believe in healthy growth and dizzying progress.[24] Since he chose to live in accordance with his philosophical choices, his message still attracts people who believe that material abundance undermines the theological-political order, as well as those who believe that growth widens the gap between rich and poor. He was thus the father of egalitarian individualism and the first person to speak of material alienation. Two social crises came together in his thinking: the first affected man's relation to himself and his creations, intellectual as well as material, his attitudes toward other people and culture; the second involved man's relation to the environment, which economic growth and technological advancement seemed to disrupt.[25]

If all of Rousseau's thoughts now went toward reconciling appearance with reality, it was because he saw the condemnation of consumption as a way of overcoming the limitations of technology. The new inventions were capable of producing vast quantities of material objects but not of diminishing the tragic side of the human condition: anxiety, disease, death. Nor would the acquisition of things rescue man from distress and ennui. Rousseau did not denounce material goods as foolish or frivolous. Instead, he presented them as a consequence of man's disastrous desire to extend his knowledge without limit.[26] Ultimately, the denunciation of luxury was a response to a sense of disappointment—not a usual category of economic analysis—with the fruits of the scientific and technological vision embodied in Diderot and d'Alembert's *Encyclopédie*.

The *Encyclopédie:* Consumption and Technology

This is not the place for an analysis of the goals and influence of the greatest monument to the thought of the Enlightenment: the *Encyclopédie*. Two points are worth making, however. First, the *Encyclopédie* was not, as has often been claimed, a coherent "war machine" in which the capitalist bourgeoisie, the only class certain of its goals and resources, expressed its vision of its historical role. Second, the work's readership— from the authors themselves, who were its first readers, to the subscribers who purchased the various editions made available to the public—was motivated not by any common social ideology but by a very widespread need to know. If the *Encyclopédie* was able to reach nearly all of society (although it is true that peasants and most of the urban poor had access to the work only indirectly), it was because the project was broadly conceived as a work of popularization, of useful diffusion of knowledge—in short, as a political and educational effort to bring about change through example, argument, demonstration, and image. This goal implied a determination to impose order on abundant but haphazard scholarship handicapped by a neglect of science and technology in favor of matters of history and religion. The *Encyclopédie* drew on the work of mechanicians, geometers, experimental scientists, technicians, artists, and engineers rather than of the dogmatic theologians of the Middle Ages or the humanists of the Renaissance and their followers of the baroque period, caught between ancient thought and modern traditions.

The *Encyclopédie* would have been inconceivable without three things: the confluence of Cartesian analysis with English thought; the utilitarian outlook of a period that sought to identify forms of knowledge useful for social development by combining the approaches of the scientist and the technician; and, finally, the influence of pre-encyclopedic thought in certain institutions of knowledge and power, namely, the academies and other organs of cultural sociability. It is now more than twenty years since the influence of the academies was first recognized.[27] The English contribution is well known: through Locke and Newton, analysis became experimental, and language came to be regarded as an active instrument of knowledge. It no longer defined essences or innate ideas but described reality. The technological aspect of this change deserves emphasis, since the *Encyclopédie* was part of a broad empirical movement in which thought was subordinated to language. The work responded to a need for a key, based on the new conception of science, to understanding the material world and its capacity for change. For twenty years it served as a vast laboratory, a "factory" for ideas and illustrations whose aim was to integrate both science and technology into a coherent information system and thereby "change the common way of thinking," as Diderot put it in his article entitled "Encyclopédie." In short, the *Encyclopédie* was about the hope of achieving prosperity through technological change.[28]

The nature of the technological knowledge proposed by the *Encyclopédie* was strikingly different from that of traditional technical know-how, and so was the way in which the new knowledge was acquired and transmitted. Traditional technical know-how was instinctive, a form of manual dexterity, of habit or "second nature," and more mechanical and physical than intellectual; exclusive, it was acquired through initiation, and its techniques were likely to be secrets, existential skills associated with certain raw materials and objects. This contrasts sharply with the rational, theoretical, scientific, and universal knowledge advocated by Diderot and d'Alembert. "The greatness of the *Encyclopédie* lay in the fundamentally important role assigned to its plates of drawings and models, which paid homage to skilled craftsmen and to rational knowledge of technical operations."[29] These plates were not included solely for documentary purposes; it was hoped that they would contribute to further technical progress. Rational knowledge—rational because it relied on calculation, measurement, and objective analysis—was thus made available to the general public without restriction or secrecy; it gained power through universality. In the world of technology everything was interrelated, yet nothing was jealously guarded by any corporation. By studying this information, a society could manage itself. The technological lessons of the *Encyclopédie* introduced a new force into the world and a new social dynamic: the world of technology discovered its independence when it recognized its unity. It was able to do this because the example of scientific thought liberated technological thought and because the wedding of images to words extended its influence.

Thus the eighteenth century declared the technician's right to exist despite the resistance of society.[30] For the time being, however, technology's liberating potential was limited to the sphere of the individual, since the productive sphere remained hierarchical, organic, and artisanal. Its boundaries had yet to be forced back. The *Encyclopédie* remained silent about major technological innovations (which should not be exaggerated, given the duration of the enterprise). It continued to address its recommendations to artisans and artists and thought of manufacturing as dispersed rather than centralized. Yet these shortcomings merely reflect the culture in which it was conceived, a culture of classical machines and artisans that left the human individual, the technical individual, intact among his tools—tools that sustained him and allowed him to work. Nevertheless, it communicated to large numbers of readers a theoretical ability to overcome inertia through knowledge.

Two further changes would complete the transition from artisanal to "industrial fabrication." "Automatic machines" worked in parallel with laborers, whose role in the work process became less that of actors and more that of spectators. Meanwhile, however, the myth of craftsmanship and the language of corporatism continued to serve as a basis for understanding a mode of production that economic development was about to transform. Luxury and technology had simultaneously inaugurated a debate that set the Enlightenment to arguing with itself. The *Encyclopédie* contributed to this by extolling the genius of the mechanic more than that of the engineer and by stressing the need to protect enterprise with *privilèges.* It thus placed itself between two worlds.

18

Desacralization, Secularization, Illuminism

THE TRIUMPH OF LIFE, belief in progress, expansion of concrete as well as philosophical individualism, a new material independence that changed people's understanding of nature and society—all these things characterized the triumphant, optimistic side of the Enlightenment. The rise of "man"—his "advent," along with unprecedented material prosperity—became a subject not so much for political and social thought, which lagged somewhat, as for religious thought, which had a synthetic function. Ever since the time of Paul Hazard, the history of ideas has pondered this great issue in one form or another. Is it true that at the end of the seventeenth century "the majority of Frenchmen thought as Bossuet did," that is, in terms of hierarchy, order, discipline, obedience, revealed dogma, and subordination of the human to the divine, whereas "in the eighteenth century, the French thought as Voltaire did," that is, in terms of equality, natural rights, freedom from coercion, nonconformism, relativism in religion and morality, and primacy of human reason?[1]

A debate that began before the death of the Sun King revealed a variety of new influences, necessary preludes to the Enlightenment's conquest of liberty. Stability gave way to change. Intellectual exchange and commercial travel made comparative analysis possible. The aesthetic and historical ideals of the "ancients" were supplanted by more "modern" forms of admiration. Erudition and criticism remade the landscape of religious and civil texts. Skepticism gained ground. The present and the future triumphed over the past. The intellectual hegemony of southern Europe was challenged by the new perspectives of the Dutch and English. The spirit of nonconformism gained at the expense of authority. And finally, the rationalists, heirs of the libertines, repudiated Cartesian metaphysics and questioned the core beliefs of religious faith. With Locke, empirical reason inspired new thinking about the foundations of social life. In politics, the divine right of kings was attacked by natural-rights theorists. In ethics, utility supplanted the divinely ordained moral order and, through the concept of tolerance, gave rise to dreams of earthly felicity. In science lay the hope of unending progress and conse-quent human happiness.

After 1715, "a phenomenon of unprecedented breadth" lent consider-able amplitude and force to the movement of ideas. What had begun to germinate in the shade now blossomed in the light of day: the specula-tions of a few select minds began to influence large numbers of people, and timid thoughts grew into provocative ideas.[2]

In the innovators' indictment there was one principal accused: God—the Christian God, the God of the Protestants as well as the Catholics. Suddenly this adversary was attacked from all sides; everywhere there was talk about emancipating the individual from religious belief. And it was not a matter of obscure threats, timid demands, schisms, or heresies. Listen to Paul Hazard: "The eighteenth century was not content with a Reformation. It wanted to topple the Cross. It wanted to eliminate the idea of a revelation, a communication between God and man. It wanted to destroy the religious conception of life." With all due allowance for the unwarranted generality of Hazard's formulation, as well as for the existence of a broad antiphilosophical and apologetic defensive move-ment and for the exaggeration inherent in the tendency of the history of ideas to grant unquestioned primacy to philosophy and thought, it re-mains true that never before had such a forthright message of liberation been so forcefully delivered. To be sure, we now know the social limits of the atheistic materialism of La Mettrie, d'Holbach, Dupuy, and Sylvain Maréchal. We know the extent to which the "Christianity of habit" resisted the various forms of deism and theism. And we have learned not to caricature the "Christianity of grace," in which man turned to God solely for salvation. Still, it remains true that "for many consciences, the rational acquisition of knowledge was superimposed on the Christian notion of revealed knowledge. The rejection of private revelation was an intrinsic tenet of the new faith. The vehemence of the attack on religion in the first half of the eighteenth century had a religious character because the new ideas insinuated themselves into mental structures inherited from the age of Christianity; a substitution occurred."[3] Crucially, it became possible to question man's relation to God, and in the void thus created, in the space thus emptied, other structures were created for the future.

What is surprising about this historical characterization is that, but for a few minor points, all of the major students of the subject agree. For Hazard, the culture can be described using the "metaphor of an individual," so that an entire period can be characterized as having opinions, ideas, and desires. For Ernst Cassirer, the forms of intellectual discourse can be analyzed in abstraction from social and biographical contingencies to reveal the philosophical structure of the Enlightenment.[4] For Bernard Groethuysen, bourgeois consciousness can be reduced to a collective socioeconomic phenomenon involving a fundamental transformation of religious ideas and a profound crisis of faith.[5] And for Pierre Chaunu, the change can be interpreted in terms of the rapid expansion of knowledge resulting from the "multiplier effect of the mechanistic age," the new theory of knowledge elaborated by Kant in response to the need for rational certitude, and the new impossibility of proposing an ontology in the absence of revelation.[6] All agree that what occurred was a fundamental rupture, a basic shift that still defines our world. In Lessing's words, "a horrible, gaping abyss" opened up.

What can one add to these judgments? These various analyses of discourse all suggest a strong coherence, a necessary simultaneity of phenomena that happen to have been contemporary but from which all traces of vanished mentalities and premonitory signs have been eliminated.[7] The power of Christianity was questioned both in depth and on the surface, and with it the domination of tradition, authority, and ancient hierarchies. For the past half-century, historians have tried to locate this rupture in practice, to relate ideas to the anonymous forces that shaped them, and thus to discover the new freedom made possible by the unprecedented belief in the power of man. When the period is approached from this angle, it becomes clear that even as the old faith was discredited, religious references continued to have a function; the very definition of belief conditioned the response. The idea that there was a massive, active de-Christianization of society from the top down assumes that there was once a unique and universal form of Christianization. But as

Jean Delumeau has remarked, "Have we not for too long applied the name 'Christianity' to a grab bag of practices and doctrines which in some cases bore only a distant relation to the message of the gospel? And if that is the case, should we go on talking about de-Christianization?" The decline of the "last things" and the rise of "first things" must be understood against the background of a broader and longer-term transformation of beliefs. History is complex. We therefore need to take a fresh look at religious discourse, taking Voltaire, an anticlerical yet still a religious man, as our witness. We need to examine the pronouncements of all parties for signs of the day's leading ideas: not only prosperity and energy but also anxiety. Only then can we reformulate the question of religion in the Age of Enlightenment in terms not of positive religion but of new forms of religious vitality based on "illumination" other than the clear and distinct light of reason.[8]

Religious Crisis and the New Religious Spirit

The question of de-Christianization needs to be considered in a broader context, for the phenomenon cannot be reduced to a contrast between seventeenth-century fervor and eighteenth-century tepidity. One has to think of "Christianity" as a state in which conformism coexisted with superstition and fear, with fervent, emotional piety and the "religion of grace." De-Christianization involves parameters as distinct and complex as the decline of practice, declericalization, deconfessionalization, the desacralization of the world, changes in moral values, and the secularization of social and individual behavior.

How do we characterize what changed? Signs of change are visible at more than one level. They point toward a weakening of conformism and a reinforcement and transformation of the religion of the enlightened. A comprehensive history of Christianity that wants to avoid oversimplification must explain how two curves crossed in the eighteenth century, one rising, the other falling. The first is a qualitative index of religious intensity, the second a quantitative measure of religious participation. Even as the message of the gospel was more fully grasped by some, conformist religious practice declined as civilization was transformed.[9] Habitual Christians remained in the majority, yet their behavior began to change. A disaffection with traditional practices revealed itself as social pressure declined. Yet as the focus of religious belief shifted from the collective to the individual, some people found new and richer vocations and a basis for new thinking about their faith.

Christianity of Habit and Questions about Religion

The continued centrality of Christianity makes it difficult to gauge accurately the shift from a religion based on social constraint to one based on individual authenticity.

> One is tempted to ask: to what extent were all the inhabitants celebrating the gift of sacramental grace, and to what extent were they merely indulging in a taste for civic pageantry and fairground frolics? That question, however, can never be satisfactorily answered in a society where spiritual and temporal were so closely bound together, and where the general imagination had no conception of the possibility of their separation. All legislation assumed that churchman and citizen were synonymous . . . It is difficult to find criteria to assess the religious life of the common people, who followed the cycle of the Church's calendar in their daily life so automatically as they rose in the morning at the sound of the cathedral bell or interchanged winter and summer clothing at All Saints and Easter.[10]

Let us concentrate on the fundamental changes that preceded the shift in sensibility and crisis of commitment. The uniformity of eighteenth-century religious practice was the result of the Church's constant efforts, from the sixteenth century on, to shape the habits of the faithful. Improved pastoral education, the influence of missionaries and preachers, and careful parochial administration had made religion and the sacraments a part of everyday life. Two things symbolized the triumph of the clergy: participation in Easter communion and regular attendance at mass. Other sacraments also reflected clerical efforts: baptism, confirmation, extreme unction, and confession. But parishioners took Easter communion not so much because they were impressed by the miracle of the host as because it was both a duty and a pious ideal. Compared with previous centuries, in the eighteenth century the practice was virtually universal. The number who did not participate decreased to less than 1 percent of all parishioners (from both ends of the social scale, ranging from those in itinerant occupations such as shepherd, sailor, and soldier to noblemen excommunicated for loose morals). As social pressure increased, so did participation in communion. On pastoral visits parish priests were asked about observance of Easter communion, which was taken as a basic indicator of religious commitment: from 1610 to 1670 the question was asked in 58 percent of all parishes; between 1670 and 1730 the frequency increased to 78 percent; and from 1730 to 1790 it declined to 57 percent, as if the battle had been won almost everywhere. Cities were slower and more reluctant to fall in line, however. With this battle won, the Church's emphasis could now shift to communion at times other than Easter, which also increased owing to efforts by both the secular and regular clergy. After 1750 solemn communion became increasingly common.

Attendance at Sunday mass was similarly reevaluated: what had been a pious habit became a strict obligation. Along with the tightening of discipline went a sanctification of the mass. Reformers banished dogs from the churches and prohibited inappropriate behavior. Catechism classes and pastoral discipline taught the faithful to pay attention and understand what was going on in church and even to participate by reading the ordinary of the mass in French. Although it is difficult to say to what extent the change in behavior was mere passive acquiescence as opposed to active adherence, there can be no doubt that church attendance increased, though partly for social reasons, to be sure, since public and private announcements were often made after the sermon. Basic religious practices created a shared fundamental identity. By performing the same ritual acts over and over, people developed an intimate sense of belonging. Religion provided the fundamental framework with which people made sense of the world, time, and life. Once a week the "Lord's day" renewed the connection to the stable world of the Church. The yearly liturgical cycle implicitly reenacted the dramatic history of redemption.[11] If the seventeenth-century sense of time had a distinctive characteristic, it was the relationship thus established between the quotidian and the sacred.

Yet this uniformity of religious practice did not totally eliminate regional variations, urban-rural differences, or contrasts between more devout areas such as the *bocage* around La Rochelle and less devout areas such as the plains and marshes of Aunis. The clergy Christianized the kingdom by doing battle on two fronts. As we have seen, priests made sure that ordinary ritual actions had spiritual meaning for their parishioners. Religious ritual made the quality of a person's faith palpable, and the Church took careful note of cultural differences in this regard. At the same time the clergy waged war against practices deemed pagan or superstitious: traditional festivals, ancestral cults, miraculous statues, sacred fountains, and dubious pilgrimages all became targets of the new clergy's rigorous determination to sanctify and purify. But these campaigns also divided the clergy from the masses of the faithful. Morality gained, but spiritual experience may have lost in the process, if it did not take refuge in a different, more individualized tradition of moral conscience exemplified by Jean-Jacques Rousseau.

Changes in Behavior and the Crisis of Commitment

Against this background of universal fervor, two important changes occurred, primarily after 1750. Attitudes toward life and death were transformed, and the commitment to religion diminished.

Demographic data reveal a marked change in behavior of the most private sort. The use of contraceptive techniques is inferred when the average age of women at the time of giving birth to their last child is clearly less than their average age at the end of fertility. By this measure we find an increase in the use of contraception nearly everywhere in France: in Rouen before 1730 some 20 to 30 percent of couples took precautions against unintended pregnancy, whereas by the 1780s the figure had risen to 50 percent. A similar increase occurred in the Vexin, at Meulan in Lorraine, at Vic-sur-Seille, and probably in Paris as well. The well-to-do took to contraception earlier than the middle and lower classes. What took place may be termed a contraceptive revolution: henceforth copulation no longer led inevitably to procreation.

These facts are not easy to interpret, however. According to the new ethos of the family, women were to be protected against the risks of multiple childbirth, and children deserved education, the prospect of decent employment, and greater affection than in the past. New Church teachings in favor of women and children undermined traditional precepts. Preachers also denounced sexuality as impure and encouraged delayed marriage, conjugal abstinence, and ultimately control of sexuality through coitus interruptus. The preaching of strict doctrines of austerity made people feel guilty. The maps of early de-Christianization reflect the spread of Jansenism. The increased demands placed on the faithful, resentment over lengthy delays in granting absolution, and the use of religion in partisan battles not only "democratized" theological conflict but also encouraged people to doubt: the politicization of the sacrament of confession had precisely that effect.[12] An increase in premarital births (which accounted for some 10 to 20 percent of all births after 1760) and illegitimacy (from 6 to 10 percent of babies born in the cities were bastards) shows how the Church's teachings were turned against it: freer, more independent, and better educated than ever before, individuals chose to live their lives by other principles. Not all set themselves up as theologians, but everyone learned to understand tradition and religious authority in new ways.

The change in attitudes toward death, no matter how one interprets it, has similar implications.[13] The study of both men's and women's wills from Paris as far as back as 1730, from Provence after 1770, and elsewhere at comparable dates has revealed changes in key indicators: the number of requests for masses for the repose of the soul decreased (in the Midi from an average of 400 per year in 1750 to 150 in 1780), for example, and religious language vanished or was watered down in a sample of wills from Enlightenment Paris as early as the 1730s.[14] To be sure, there was more than one reason for this: notarial conventions changed, and notarial services were used by different social groups; wills were increasingly tailored to individual tastes; other, more profound upheavals affected will-making practices; and the fear of death may have diminished as a result of increased familiarity—people stopped saying what they no longer felt a need to say. Still, these changes were accompanied by a disintegration of Christian discourse itself; "preparations for death" began to refer to the needs of the living; and the terrifying, Christ-centered imagery introduced by seventeenth-century preachers fell out of fashion. Taken together, these signs suggest that the change in wills was more than a matter of internalization of faith; it was due, if not to de-Christianization, then at least to a major shift in worldview, to a crisis in the very idea of death. Groethuysen sums up the change succinctly: contrasting Voltaire and Rousseau's contemporaries with Pascal's, he says that "in speaking of death, they were no longer talking about the same thing." The men of the seventeenth century believed in death as they believed in God; those of the eighteenth century saw death not as a mystery but as a fact. Everything else followed from this.

Other facts corroborate the decline of Christian commitment and religious sociability. Secularized Christians turned away from the Church's rituals, rhetoric, and institutions. The number of ordinations dropped markedly after 1750. The trend was only partly compensated by an increase in peasant vocations toward the end of the Ancien Régime, an increase which, together with urban recruitment and a steady flow of young priests from traditional sources such as Brittany, Lorraine, and Normandy, filled at least some of the Church's need. Regular vocations also declined, reflecting a split between the society's elites and the Church, since the initial reason for the drop was disaffection among the nobility and bourgeoisie. The decline of both types of vocation, secular as well as regular, points up the problematic status of the religious calling in a society increasingly driven by utility. The image of priests and religious changed as the very meaning of a calling was adapted to fit the needs of a more worldly society.

Another sign of religious change can be seen in decreased recruitment by confraternities and Marial congregations. In Provence the sociability once animated by confraternities was transferred to Masonic lodges. Wherever the relevant indices have been studied, we find conformism crumbling, religious fervor cooling, religious activities becoming increasingly secular, and traditional forms of piety waning. In the iconography of devotional objects popular in the south of France, of paintings of souls in Purgatory, and religious painting generally, we can detect a depletion of the deep sources of religious inspiration; as history painting came to the fore and the hierarchy of genres was revamped, religious painting had difficulty finding its place. In some areas, such as Alsace and Lorraine, the old subjects retained their hold on the imagination, but elsewhere the diminished charge of religious imagery is clear.[15]

A question arises: How much of this change was due to internal evolution, to an interrogation of belief by belief, and how much was the result of external factors—"the fault of Voltaire and Rousseau"? The first part of the question can be answered by looking at how Christianity was taught. One approach was to stress the importance of strict orthodoxy and asceticism. Another was to engage in debate and controversy with critics, though this tended to reduce religious belief to one opinion among others. Doctrinal differences and unwillingness to compromise estranged the faithful from the clergy. Paradoxically, the "Christianization" of the clergy could lead to de-Christianization of their flock by heightening the opposition between sacred and profane and substituting control, discipline, and mediation for a more immanent relation to the divine. "The Church's plan to make all Christians share the clerical definition of Christianity was a source of unbearable tension."[16] A certain detachment from the Church that had been acceptable during the Christianizing offensive ceased to be so once the wave of conversions was spent and ecclesiastical authority declined. Social mobility, the end of rural isolation, urbanization, and the uprooting of rural populations undermined discipline and loosened ties of dependency. The city led the way toward secularization. As social utility became the sole beacon of morality guiding the consciences of individuals, the way was cleared for a broad-based secularization that dragged both politics and religion in its wake. Political institutions imposed their own criteria on religious institutions, whose acceptance of political objectives was the price of protection. Religion was thereby politicized.[17]

What role did philosophy play in this major upheaval? The question was of course raised long ago by historians of ideas, but my approach is rather different. What was the role of books? What was the social impact of the separation of philosophy from religion? In the vastly increased output of printed matter, we find a clear secularizing trend: the proportion of religious works among all works granted permission to publish decreased from 35 percent to 10 percent between 1720 and 1780, while the proportion of works on science and the arts rose from 20 to 33 percent. Add to this the fact that the vast majority of clandestinely published works were secular and critical of religion and it becomes clear that the nature of the publishing market changed dramatically in the space of sixty years. This change has been interpreted as a reflection of the triumph of a homogeneous civil society in which "the quintessential social act was publication."[18] The popularization of new ideas undermined the Christian order and robbed readers of their certitudes. This was true even though a significant proportion of book production was still of devout inspiration, as is indicated by the fact that from 1778 to 1779, 63 percent of provincial reprint applications were for religious works compared with just 10 percent for works in science and the arts.

In order to interpret this shift, we need to take a broader look at the indices. After the crisis of 1762–1768, for example, a certain liberalism took hold in the education of adolescents of the elite. News of the world and banned texts began to be read in the *collèges,* and the freer, more rational, more curious minds found their belief in the old values shaken. The secularization of the Parisian worldview spread to the provinces by way of notables who joined learned societies and subscribed to the *Ency-*

clopédie. The political-erotic pamphlets produced by the "Rousseau du ruisseau," or "Rousseaus of the gutter," had as much of an impact on religion as on politics. The convictions of readers were changed not directly but indirectly: it became possible to read and think differently. The diary of Jacques-Louis Ménétra traces a history of religious indifference, then hostility, and finally conversion to secularism, and his case may not have been unusual. Disappointed by priests and their mysteries, and a confirmed adversary of the clerical institution together with its theology and sacraments, the journeyman glazier was like a Voltairean in his denunciation of the prejudices and superstitions that delivered the credulous into the hands of the clergy. Hostile to religious fanaticism and to the terrorism of the "last things" ("the great cauldron doesn't frighten me"), he was able to embrace an individualistic religion whose object of worship was a benevolent and tolerant Supreme Being.

A New Religious Spirit: Pietism and Theism

That the spiritual and profane are inseparable remained a fundamental tenet of the civilization within which the process of secularization and de-Christianization took place. Christianity retained its political status and theoretical unity. The line between belief and unbelief was therefore difficult to draw. The clergy itself was not exempt from the effects of the Enlightenment, and through its participation in cultural sociability it propagated and internalized certain values that tended to reconcile the service of God with the service of men. Hence we would do well to look for signs of change within Christianity itself. As we have seen, enlightened opinion in general must not be confused with the views of the most advanced thinkers of the day, and the conflict over religion must not be reduced to a battle between obscurantists and progressives: in the religious realm, tensions and contradictions are apparent everywhere. Although the ecclesiastical hierarchy, allied as it was with the state, remained strong, its triumph was no longer assured. The consequent doubts caused some Christians to turn inward, to delve deeper into the Christian conscience. "The various confessions, affected by a sort of disestablishment, found themselves in an awkward position in a new realm where they no longer benefited from their familiar certitudes."[19] Significantly, moreover, no one could figure out the meaning of this change overnight.

Contemporary views can be interpreted as echoes of the complex process that was decentering and recentering religious life. Various signs hinted that a different sort of religion might be possible: these included attacks on atheism, remarks on various weaknesses of religion as traditionally organized, and attempts to redefine religion without the support of authority.

Turgot, in his *Seconde Lettre d'un grand vicaire sur la tolérance* (1754), relied entirely on individual choice: "Men can judge the truth of religion, and for that very reason others must not judge for them, because each individual conscience will be called upon to give its own account. Furthermore, in good faith, if anyone could judge for others, it would have to be the princes, and did Louis XIV know any more about the matter than Leclerc or Grotius?"

In this way a liberal position took shape: separate the state from the churches and the churches from their individual members, whose choice was a matter of conscience, of which "God is the sole witness and judge." This was the rule of a form of natural religion to which Rousseau would subscribe in *Le Contrat social* and *Emile*. The *Encyclopédie* itself embodied a similar rejection of spiritual despotism and orthodoxy. Rather than lead to new certitudes, the debate over atheism and free thought gave rise to uncertainty and further questioning. Instead of the risk-free spiritual comfort made possible by submission of the individual conscience, people had to face up to the consequences of a divided conscience: no longer a matter of passively accepting an obligatory truth, faith became a commitment.

Tradition taught that outside the Church there is no salvation. Various thinkers, authentically religious in their own way, tended to assert the opposite and to affirm the possibility of a religion of the mind and heart. Voltaire and Rousseau may serve as touchstones for two different versions of the coexistence of faith with reason under the auspices of a more natural religion. Voltaire's religion was not expressed in philosophical form: it was a provocation, a position carefully staked out between the social and political necessities of "Ecrasons l'infâme" and the metaphysical constraints that led to a rejection of atheism and insistence on the need for a "watchmaker" God, "creator of the universe."[20] It was also a vast meditation on the deist tradition, the tradition of the rationalist libertines of the seventeenth century, of Englishmen such as Woolston, Collins, and

Toland and Frenchmen such as Boulainvilliers and Montesquieu. Its originality, defined by Voltaire's personality, was captured in aphorisms that became well known through the polemics they initiated. Voltaire's ideas exerted a powerful influence on public opinion in the second half of the eighteenth century.

A man of tormented, sickly disposition, moribund from the age of thirty, Voltaire found liberation in the written word. His passionate, total commitment gradually made him aware of an intellectual need for God if not of an actual presence of God in his life. From his youth as the son of an extreme Jansenist father he took a hatred of fanaticism. Pomeau notes that Voltaire came down with a fever on August 24, the anniversary of the Saint Bartholomew's Day massacre, and that as a child he was deeply immersed in religious questions. His education by Jesuits led him to reject religion, however. By the time he was finished with the men of the Society, he was no longer a Catholic, although he would remain a Christian. After he began to associate with libertines, to travel, and to spend time in England, his religious views matured rapidly. Seven of his *Lettres philosophiques* are devoted to religion. They express a belief in the value of religious pluralism, allude to the Quakers as proof of the possible coexistence of reason and faith, and invoke the need for a "purified Christianity." After his retreat to Cirey, this latter idea was deepened by reflections on history and comparative religion, which Voltaire saw as tools for "desacralizing" traditional religion and affirming the common basis of all religious belief. Influenced by Newton's ideas as well as Locke's, and obsessed with the notion of evil, Voltaire, after a final crisis in 1749, began to formulate a definitive position based on two principles: first, that "evil exists, hence so does God," and second, that deism would rise upon the ruins of the Church and the carcass of fanaticism. Until his death in 1778, Voltaire would continue his war on all that was institutional, dogmatic, and intolerant in the dominant religion: he confronted Pompignan, poured scorn on the accusers of Calas and the chevalier de La Barre, sought rehabilitation for Sirven, and turned out provocation after provocation under pseudonyms or for clandestine publication. At the age of eighty he defended his metaphysical position against the more outspoken atheists, including d'Holbach and the Diderot of the *Lettre sur les aveugles,* and confirmed by his own example, as a patriarch integrated into society, the need for a reformed, state-controlled religion. Even his death, "following a long illness," symbolized who he was: he died *in* the Catholic religion but never declared himself to be a Catholic. The Church congratulated itself: he "died alone." This was Pascal's revenge.

Out of this rendezvous of an individual with his century came the principal traits of a deism that combined a conception of the religious with a moral thesis. Voltaire's deism was a deism of rejection: rejection of the God of predestination, pessimism, and the Incarnation and rejection of the cruel and vengeful God of the Jews. Voltaire's God was a good God, diametrically opposed to the God of the Bible—a God liberated from mysteries and rituals. His force was rooted in the tradition of all mankind, in the universality of truth—truth as the ubiquitous recognition of God's existence. The true religion was natural religion, the religion of humanity, and in it Voltaire saw the "principles of the common morality of the human race," the necessity of which he proved by metaphysical argument: human existence and experience implied the existence of God, which is manifest in nature. "If God did not exist, one would have to invent him, but all nature cries out to us that he does exist." Necessary and remote, he was nevertheless present in society governed by the morality or ethics of self-interest and benevolence. After 1750 Voltaire's deism became a theism as he insisted on man's "obligation to worship the deity." His *Profession de foi des théistes* (1768) was a riposte to Rousseau's *Profession de foi du vicaire savoyard* as well as to the rise of atheism in high society. Voltaire portrayed theism as the religion of those who adored God, friend of man—the religion of religions. He gave it a practical cast with a dual commandment: "Pray and be just." Theism can be understood as an abortive reform,[21] but even more as a serene yet desperate attempt to make sure that religion remained within the confines of human society, unattached to any supernatural myth, independent and self-conscious.

Voltaire's religious thought can thus be seen in two lights: it grew out of a reversal of the relation between philosophy and theology, and it aspired to demystify Christianity. It was greatly influenced by the critical rationalism of English freethinkers and their unwillingness to accept the traditional historical basis of Christianity. It incorporated Spinozism's critique of Christianity but also its understanding of religion as worship of the Supreme Being and insistence on an intelligible natural order, as well as its certainty of God's existence.[22] It was also related in some ways to the Masonic belief in a unique Supreme Being and "great architect of the universe," although Voltaire proceeded independently of Freemasonry. It was undeniably the characteristic response—between traditional religion and atheism—of a new mobile society which was eager for rational progress yet socially conservative, a society in which morality could not yet be severed from its religious roots. Voltairean theism even influenced the effort, central to traditional religion at the time, to apply formal moral rules to practical life.[23]

Rousseau's quest in this respect was not so different from Voltaire's. One understands how Voltaire, after summing up his grievances against his old adversary, could have written to Peyrou that "in the end he created the Savoyard vicar, so I forgive everything else." Nevertheless, Rousseau arrived at his religious philosophy via a route very different from Voltaire's: his thinking about religion cannot be divorced from his religious experience and sensibility, which remain fundamental for understanding his philosophical and theoretical choices in general. To begin with, Rousseau was the product of a Protestant education, and he would always carry the Geneva sermon book inside him. From his family and the Reverend Lambercier he imbibed a Christianity that was less dogmatic than affective, charitable, and moderate.[24] The whole climate of Geneva suffused his childhood: the austerity of Calvinism, knowledge of the Bible, the magical chanting of psalms. He fled in 1728, before his first communion and therefore without formally pledging allegiance to the Protestant faith. He subsequently came under the influence of Catholicism in Confignon, Turin (where he stayed at a home for Catholic novices), Annecy, and Chambéry (where he was received by Mme de Warens). Soon converted, he accepted the lesson taught him by Abbé Gaime and his reading at Les Charmettes: that religion is a matter of sincere virtue and morality. Instead of the harsh theology of Geneva and the Jansenists, he passionately embraced the idea of a God discovered in solitude, in nature, by the individual believer. Rousseau had become a Catholic but remained a "Christian," a man opposed to dogma but given to heartfelt prayer. "The essence of the Savoyard vicar's religion can already be found in Rousseau's religion of Les Charmettes."[25]

During his time in Paris and years of celebrity (1742–1756), his beliefs continued to evolve. Rousseau came under the influence of the Encyclopedists and moved away from Catholicism. Subsequently, in the first *Discours*, he rediscovered the values of Christianity, which he set in opposition to the forces of moral laxity. Later he would invoke his

Protestant past and sing, in a new key, the praises of a "Christianity without borders" that united clergymen and men of ideas across northern Europe, from England to Germany and Holland to Switzerland. In 1754 he returned to the Protestant fold and regained his Genevan citizenship. On this journey political enthusiasm definitely outweighed theology, but theology was the point of departure for Rousseau's "reform." His open-air conversion—"When the sun falling on the fields illuminates nature's miraculous scene, I recover my faith and my God"—was surely more important for his later novels and major theoretical works than his outward embrace of Genevan Calvinism. Thereafter, in his life as well as his texts, he championed a sentimental theology as a compromise between the call of the heart and the laws of reason. In the second *Discours* (1754), the *Lettre à Voltaire sur le désastre de Lisbonne* (1756), the *Lettre à d'Alembert* (1758), *La Nouvelle Héloïse* (1761), and *Emile* (1762), he set forth the arguments and principles with which he sought to ease the distress of a life lived on both sides of the border dividing Catholics from Protestants and the difficulty of expressing a philosophy torn between reason and sensibility.[26]

The *Profession de foi du vicaire savoyard*, contained in *Emile*, would resolve Rousseau's crisis and lay down the essential principles of the Rousseauian faith. This is one of the most fundamental expressions of French and European religious consciousness in the eighteenth century. The vicar, a Christian by nature, a Catholic by accident, and of dubious orthodoxy, must solve an important problem: Emile, at age eighteen, has yet to embrace a faith, but his education has put him in a position to "choose the religion to which the best use of reason will lead him." The vicar attacks the materialism of the moderns, proves the existence of God, and justifies natural religion. In the *Profession de foi* we find assembled in a single, coherent argument points made in more contradictory or less assured fashion in other texts such as the dialogue between Saint-Preux and Julie in *La Nouvelle Héloïse*, in which Rousseau advanced two incompatible theses.

The vicar's theology can be reduced to two main propositions: first, that the order of nature proves the existence of a creator God, and second, that evil, which can be blamed on history and man, requires the idea of a reparative God. What distinguishes this doctrine from Voltaire's theism is the role of sensibility, of the heart. The inner light that illuminates the soul, the "infallible consciousness of good and evil" with which man is endowed, acts on a different plane from reason: the order of the universe is not explained by futile systems but felt *in the sight* of such marvels. *Sensible, sentiment, conscience:* these are the words that the Savoyard vicar uses repeatedly, and the free man does well to take them as his true guide. Here we have the key difference that separates Rousseau from the revealed religions, for Rousseau's God reveals himself only through nature and reason, once and for all, and for all mankind.[27] The second part of the *Profession de foi* is therefore devoted to a refutation of dogma and revelation. Rousseau's respectful doubts would earn him official condemnation, while his heartfelt affirmation of the divinity of Jesus Christ (in the famous text in which he compares Christ to Socrates) would draw the ironic barbs of the materialists.

Rousseauian religious doctrine did not end with the profession of faith—a completely liberal theology and for that reason anathema to all orthodoxies and churches. It also held out the hope of personal communion with God, which led to a veritable quest for ecstasy. One sees this in the *Lettres à M. de Malesherbes* and in the "reveries" and "promenades," in which Rousseau borrows from mysticism without losing himself in it. He identifies with God in nature; in solitude he ceases to be conscious of himself and of the passage of time and experiences an eternal instant.[28]

Thus Rousseau's pietism, the influence of which was considerable, worked on two levels: it was a deism that led to an experience of ecstasy, and according to which the conscience causes us to love the order that reason reveals; and it was a theism that also culminated in a civil religion. The Genevan was both a believer and a secularist, the champion of a liberated Christianity that made itself heard in near-silence, in the fervor and anxiety of small groups often linked to Freemasonry. He was a thinker who treated religion as a political problem. In the final chapter of *Le Contrat social* his problem was to give a definitive foundation of citizenship. He therefore considered the relation of religion to society and proposed a true civil religion whose principles he states "without explanation or comment": "existence of God, Providence, sanctity of contract and laws, intolerance only of the intolerant." Nothing else is within the province of the legislator. The "religion of man," the spirituality of the Savoyard vicar, can develop in a state where civil faith is a political requirement for constituting a civic morality: religion begins with the social contract and flourishes because of it.[29]

The examples of Voltaire and Rousseau show how a segment of Enlightenment society sought to deal with its spiritual anxieties outside any established church. Their experiences, at once similar and different (both were theists, but they disagreed about the balance to be struck between reason and the heart), inspired an individualized religion while calling enlightened men to arms against intolerance, dogmatism, and insolent ignorance. Both captured an essential truth about the new society, which required liberation not only from spiritual tradition but also from total explanations (whether cosmic, historical, or supernatural), yet saw religion as a necessary basis of morality. This was the religious expression of a changing society, a consequence of both material progress and individual self-affirmation, and surely bourgeois in that it contested the inegalitarian order and envisioned a different form of social organization. Sentiment replaced spiritual fervor and shaped religious expression in all its forms even as it influenced the whole spectrum of philosophy. It thus accentuated the divorce between the traditional inspiration of Christianity and the emergent culture defined by the new concepts of happiness, energy, and anxiety.

Happiness, Energy, Anxiety

The history of ideas makes us aware of the existence of certain categories of thought characteristic of a given culture. We can then use these as a way of understanding social and intellectual changes. The categories tell us about both advances in thinking and the contradictions they create. Because these categories shape thinking in general, they leave their mark not just on works of literature and philosophy but also on artistic forms and social practices. We must adopt a global view, however, if we hope to understand why these categories were successful. The work done in literary history over the past several decades is useful for this purpose. Three themes stand out, because they underscore the importance and essential continuity of moral rationalism from the classical period to the Enlightenment as well as the break in that continuity brought about by the conflict between mind and heart, the inability of consciousness to penetrate its own secrets. These three themes, to which I devote the remainder of the chapter, are happiness, energy, and anxiety.

Human Happiness and the Decline of Ultimate Ends

As I have stressed repeatedly, the idea of happiness was a new one, especially when set in opposition to the finalities of religion. Yet it had always attracted the attention of philosophers, moralists, and writers. What was distinctive about the eighteenth century was the proliferation of treatises on the subject and their concern with recounting personal experiences—which exasperated Diderot, who complained that "they are never anything more than the stories of the people who wrote them." Happiness became a key concept, invoked by everyone and represented everywhere as a way of linking experience to the structure of the world, the individual to the social. Writers defined it as an element of an *art de vivre* and contrasted it with anxiety and the mythology of woe. Happiness required certain resources: "health, freedom, wealth, the esteem of others." It also required certain conditions, such as the possibility of living in a certain style, between solitude and sociability. In other words, customs and ideas evolved together. Imagined happiness mirrored lived happiness, and lived happiness exulted in the imagination of pleasurable feelings and obedience to the laws of reason. Repose, pleasure, and passion defined the eudaemonic sensibility: nature, society, and virtue defined its social dimension.

Sensualism was at the core of eighteenth-century thought: happiness was said to result when man lived in harmony with his sensations, when soul and body were in tune. Repose and the rejection of extremes served to guarantee the requisite harmony. In poetry and fiction this dream took the form of contempt for the world, reflected in themes of retreat and refuge, leisure and study, and domestic repose. The happy life was a life of immobility. Such tranquillity could mask ennui, however, from which the only escape was to vary one's pleasures. Accordingly, change and diversion were rehabilitated: "What is pleasure? It is virtue by a jollier name," wrote Edward Young in *Night Thoughts*, translated into French by Le Tourneur. This rehabilitation justified a new ethos and new "methods" of hedonism that put technology at the service of happiness. Desire stimulated mechanical inventions and inspired the development of new theatrical accessories and musical effects. Reason was called upon to control the passions, to apply hygienic scrutiny and set legitimate limits to the desire for happiness. Progress brought with it a need to find rational ways of teaching happiness. Natural conditions were not supposed to stand in the way of human felicity; nature, in other words, was supposed to be compatible with human nature. Hence psychological and physiological factors were just as important to understand as social and material ones.

Happiness, it was argued, is a privileged mode of being. It results from an equilibrium of desire and gratification, social and individual well-being, virtue and nature. It is almost always a compromise between a conscience in repose and a soul in motion, hence doubly beneficial. More and more emphasis was placed on the physiological basis of happiness: health, depression, the ills of libertinage, and even death, despite the diminished terror it held, became subjects of reflection. The social realities that fed into the idea of happiness were not immediately perceived. In the *Essais sur divers sujets de littérature et de morale* (1735), Abbé Trublet held that it was possible for people of all conditions to achieve *le bonheur*. Status in itself was no obstacle, since the equilibrium of good and bad equalized the various estates. D'Holbach, Voltaire, and Condorcet all shared this idea. In the end, each individual's capacity to profit from life would depend on many things: his surroundings (nature being more conducive to happiness than culture, the civilized countryside more than the city), the organization of his time, his family life, and above all friendship as embodied in correspondence. Gradually there emerged an ideal of harmonious existence independent of religion. The *Encyclopédie* offered a typical definition of happiness:

> The possession of goods is the basis of our happiness but is not itself happiness, for how would it be if we possessed goods but not the sentiment of possessing them? . . . Therefore our most perfect happiness in this life is merely a tranquil state punctuated here and there by occasional pleasures that brighten our surroundings . . . These pleasures are the pleasures of liberality, temperance, and conscience: pure, noble, spiritual pleasures greatly superior to the pleasures of the senses.

In other words, individual happiness is defined by a state of mind and certain social practices, not by material circumstances. The "philosophical happiness" that was discussed throughout the century stood in contrast to Christian happiness. No matter what form it took, whether in Voltaire, Diderot, Rousseau, or a minor writer such as Levesque de Pouilly, the author of *La Théorie des sentiments agréables* (1747), or again, in a materialist such as La Mettrie, discussions of happiness came in two varieties:

optimistic, emphasizing the goodness of man and his ability to dominate the world, and pessimistic, betraying a fundamental anxiety, namely, that liberated from the supernatural, man might come under the sway of nature and the passions. The optimistic and pessimistic views coexisted throughout the century, at times in authors as different as Voltaire and Rousseau.[30]

In trying to move from happiness defined as a synthesis of individual experiences to a more social view, one finds it difficult to avoid the truism that it was the economic vitality of the eighteenth century that sustained the idea of happiness and that this idea was the expression of a period in history when a vast flood of wealth was transformed into luxury for a small minority and prosperity for a larger number. A closer look at the sources suggests two modifications to this picture, however.

For a small group of administrators and notables, some of noble birth and others celebrated for their talent, the idea of collective happiness took on real force: happiness was no longer the preserve of the select few but the right of all, and it was the work of government to achieve that end through administration, education, and reform. On this foundation rested the triumphant utilitarianism that exerted such a profound influence on the culture as a whole. In 1754 Turgot stated that "the true morality looks at all men with the same eye; it recognizes that all have an equal right to happiness."[31] With this he struck a blow against the "stationary state" and in favor of the "progressive state" that Adam Smith would subsequently describe.

Another typical definition of happiness took the form of what we might call "bourgeois happiness," which was identified with the new social order. On this view, happiness was the result of creative activity and of a way of life based on balance and virtue which shunned the faults of both the common man and the courtier. It was also the product of a philosophy whose fundamental tenets were the *aurea mediocritas* and the need to strike a balance between excess wealth and insufficiency: extremes, in other words, were incompatible with happiness. In this way the activity of the entrepreneur was reconciled with the life of the citizen, and accumulation and enjoyment both received their due. Identifying who read the books that described happiness in these terms is again less important than trying to understand how the various ways in which this important idea was appropriated revealed tensions within the society. If the right to happiness ultimately ended the pact between religion and society, condemnation or compromise was the only possibility for apologists. Social thinkers faced a similar difficulty. One could advocate either frugality and asceticism (the collective form of the ideal of repose) or consumption (symbolizing both abundance and desire): in short, the happiness of inaction or the happiness of movement.

Existence and Action: An Energetic Philosophy

The idea of energy offers a different glimpse of Enlightenment society and reveals conflicts over the definition of the self, the individual, and therefore of individual agency. After 1770, advocates of "energeticism" proposed a series of social reforms and critiques of the social and political order. The very word "energy" was new: the successful neologism first appeared in two distinct fields, science and rhetoric, as a synonym for forceful and effective oratory, for an occult force in the old physics, and gradually for substantial commitment in the conduct of public or private affairs. In a 1779 letter to the duchesse de Choiseul, Mme du Deffand commented on the term's success: "I remember that he [Abbé Barthélemy] once made fun of me for using the word 'energy.' I hope he knows that it has now become fashionable, more so in writing than in conversation."

The enthusiasm of the salons persuaded the public and influenced the evolution of thought and sensibility.[32] Energy became a quality that animated the tongue. In the classical period, which shuddered at the thought of exaggerated expressions of the imagination and senses unchecked by reason, the word had connoted a threat to order and clarity, but the eighteenth century invented the "energetics of communication." A forceful language of action was central to Condillac's sensualist philosophy. In the *Essai sur l'origine des connaissances* he made energy the source of both knowledge and language. The idea became a normative precept for Diderot in *La Lettre sur les aveugles* and *La Lettre sur les sourds-muets*, and Rousseau used it in a similar way. In both language and the arts, energy was praised for its ability to counter the enfeeblement of words and signs arising from the progress of civilization. In France it was used as a weapon against the doctrine of clarity: words were meant to sway by emotion, not just to convince by argument, and for that "primitive energy" was required.[33] Like Homer, poets were exhorted to use new words and imagine new, more natural ways of living. Literature reflected this shift from a linguistics of clarity to a linguistics of expression, from an aesthetic of imitation to an aesthetic of creation. By inverting values in order to rehabilitate the depleted resources of prose, "neology" became an instrument for resurrecting the powers of creation. Louis-Sébastien Mercier and Rétif de La Bretonne saw energy as a force for making the people heard, for retrieving the authenticity essential to the expression of sensibility. Listen to Mercier: "Use the energy of your art to impart majesty to all that the people are supposed to revere . . . Swept along by this great project, the poet may then hit upon images and fictions suitable for animating the oracles of reason, and the law, cloaked in the charms of eloquence, will soon be graven upon every heart."[34]

Energy confirmed the political mission of the writer. In the end, the word caught on because it suggested both a way of understanding the world that was not mechanical and rational (but "dynamic") and a way of changing society. "Energeticism" connoted not only the powerful, troubling presence of nature but also man's role in history and aspiration to grandeur. The problem was to reconcile progress with the poetic energy and primitive politics of a bygone era. Diderot put it this way: "As a nation's violent conflicts wane and recede into the past, spirits calm, thoughts of danger fade, and literature falls silent. Great geniuses are born in difficult times; they flourish immediately thereafter."[35]

The concepts of "individual" and "self" were affected by this shift in the meaning of "energy": "Energy, a word once applied only to God or nature or matter or language, now applied to human beings, whether to integrate them into the cycles of nature or to cast them in the role of bearers of a new spirituality."[36] This development presupposed a connection between physical energy and moral energy. It transcended or subsumed the conflicts of materialism, which Diderot had not escaped, concerning the role of organization, of acquired abilities transmitted through education, and the relation between the physical and the moral. Energy was said to be spiritual; the activity of the soul was contrasted with the inertia of matter. For Mercier and the generation of 1770, it was the justification of creative freedom. For Mme de Staël "internal energy" was to serve as a cornerstone of both a "new philosophy" and a moral renewal whose roots can thus be traced back to a "pre-Romantic" concern with sensibility and human energy.

Energy was both a moral choice and a physical cause, and writers asked how it related to sex and age. Adolescents and women were fired with the energy of youthfulness and hope. Beaumarchais, Chénier, and Laclos portrayed men and women traditionally excluded from power and prestige. People thrilled to the *sentiment de l'existence* in an age of high passion and intense emotion, torn between repose and action, happiness and woe. "Sensitive souls exist more fully than others: goods and ills breed in their vicinity," Duclos wrote in *Considérations sur les moeurs de ce siècle* (1751). Jaucourt borrowed the remark for his article "Sensibilité" in the *Encyclopédie,* and Rousseau echoed it in his *Dialogues* but added a recommendation of moderation. The debate continued in the outpouring of novels toward the end of the century; it pitted "sensitive souls" against libertines, as in the novels of Sade. Rehabilitated human nature came into conflict with the religious ethic of renunciation and the classical ideal of equilibrium and repose.

Powerful passions, it was argued, were good for transforming society and moving history forward. Diderot went so far as to play with dangerous paradoxes in a letter to Sophie Volland: "To bestow an ethos upon a people is to increase its energy for good and evil. It is, if I may put it this way, to encourage great crimes and great virtues." In doing so he nevertheless showed how aesthetic energy could be linked to moral energy and to action. Out of this came an ethic of progress and happiness premised on the conversion of evil into good. Society was stood on its head; its values were overturned, as the virtue of the nobility—"if energy there was, it belonged to the noble"[37]—was supplanted by the energy of the scientist, the merchant, the entrepreneur, the developer. By focusing attention on work, however, the notion of energy raised questions about expenditure and excess, which threatened to undermine the principles of order and regulated production. The concept of energy could be mobilized in support of both the traditional and the new, the aristocratic and religious as well as bourgeois and utilitarian points of view. Its ambivalence points up certain similarities and differences between the triumphant learning of the *Encyclopédie* and the creative imagination of pre-Romanticism. Aesthetic and moral contraries came together; materialism and spiritualism made common cause. This did not resolve their underlying antagonism, but it did show the magnitude of what was possible and allowed the sons of the Enlightenment to see understanding transformed into action. The violence that exists in both individuals and society—a violence that the philosophes had dismissed as "unnatural" and irrational—was enlisted on the side of change. The addition of energy to

Enlightenment marked a decisive turning point, a liberation of new initiatives whose principle was aptly captured by Kant's phrase "Sapere aude."[38]

Enlightenment and Anxiety

Scientific knowledge, belief in progress, and a new feeling for nature rooted in a sense of shared universal energy did not eliminate anxiety from people's lives. Anxiety was either the primary adversary of happiness or else, as Locke and Leibniz would have it, an essential source of felicity in God's creatures. "Daring to know" implied the possibility of an anxiety of consciousness, of the necessity of doubt: in ontology the Enlightenment gave up the supernatural props of human certitude; in epistemology it cut its "mooring to the absolute." Without preestablished truths, everything remained for man to do on his own. For Jean Deprun, "anxiety was a consequence of the Enlightenment."[39] The age was not unaware of certain dissatisfactions, of a void in the heart, a more or less vague aspiration for some good capable of filling the soul. It tried to incorporate these feelings into its rational and natural theories, to bring heaven down to earth. The explanation hinged on the psychic and physical structure of man and on history (and therefore inequality); or else it suggested that anxiety provided the necessary impetus behind the search for happiness and aesthetic pleasure. A "physiocentric" theory of anxiety replaced the "theocentric" theories of the Augustinians. Just as the writers of *sensibilité* used the idea of feeling to overturn accepted beliefs about man and aesthetics—love, art, and life[40]—so the writers of *inquiétude* used the idea of dissatisfaction. Not only in philosophy but also in other important areas of culture, anxiety was a fundamental concept, a bridge between doctrine and representation.

Anxiety grew out of different ways of conceiving subjectivity. The eighteenth century inherited Augustinian anxiety, that mark of sinful human nature that Malebranche saw as related to Cartesian metaphysics and its reconciliation with physics: anxiety, in other words, as an aspect of the search for truth. Thinkers like Boulainvilliers, a reader of Locke and Leibniz, and Vauvenargues brought anxiety down from heaven to earth, into nature and action. Anxiety originated, for example, when an individual felt threatened by the environment; the absence of God had no part in it. Anxiety could also be a positive force, a goad to activity. Condillac and

Helvétius saw it as a life principle, a cornerstone of the "physical sensibility." Diderot also severed all connections between anxiety and God. But Rousseau and his adepts harked back to the Augustinian conception with the view that anxiety was a warning against the dangers of materialism: "A machine does not think. There is no movement or figure that produces reflection. Something in you seeks to break the bonds that contain it. Space is not your measure; the whole universe is not big enough for you. Your sentiments, your desires, your anxiety, even your pride have a source other than this constricted body in which you feel as though bound in chains."

So said the Savoyard vicar in language borrowed from Malebranche and the Augustinians: spirituality was defined by anxiety. The metaphysical battle over anxiety pointed up the central issue in Enlightenment thought: Was man dependent on a supernatural power, God, or was God just another name for a purely natural force, freedom or grace? Deprun's work shows that this was not so much a *mal du siècle* as it was a tension between the belief in happiness and the practical effects of that belief on man's view of the world and the structure of society.

Anxiety affected people in various ways. A physician might find his patient "agitated." Medicine, in other words, desacralized anxiety: the semantics of the word changed when it entered the medical vocabulary. Compare the article "Inquiétude (grammaire morale)," or anxiety as moral grammar, with the article "Inquiétude (médecine)," or anxiety as a medically treatable condition, in the *Encyclopédie*. The latter, written by Dr. Vandenesse, defined anxiety as a symptom of a certain pathology, a defense mechanism adopted by an organism. This position, similar to Locke's, brought anxiety back within the confines of nature. This natural interpretation is also apparent in medical discourse about varieties of anxiety associated with differences of age and sex. Anxiety, it was observed, develops in the turmoil of adolescence: it is one sign of a particular stage of life. It is also found frequently in women and melancholics. This medical analysis helped to naturalize anxiety by portraying it as an aspect of organic life.

Similarly, collective as well as individual anxiety was proposed as a causal factor in history. It was anxiety that drove explorers to adventure, motivated great statesmen, and incapacitated hapless rulers. As a case in point, Voltaire drew a contrast between Peter the Great, the civilizing tsar, and Louis XIII, a king incapable of making decisions. Anxiety shaped civilizations: it figured in Rousseau's argument about false needs and inequality, and it drove the quest for a utopian solution to man's woes in Mably, Dom Deschamps, and Morelly. A mystical theme was transposed into a political key: "By relating man's historical anxiety to the conditions of human history, eighteenth-century French socialism transformed theocentric spirituality into an unwitting tool of secularization." Whether a matter of essence or existence, anxiety informed the Enlightenment's interpretation of history just as it inspired its poetry, music, and architecture. Everywhere the connection between our physical nature and the symbolism of anguish was made apparent.

The gap between the religious interpretation of anxiety and the naturalistic interpretation grew wider as the century progressed. The impact of the Enlightenment was apparent not only in hopes of change but also in the reaction of sensibility to reason, where the tone was set by major works such as *La Nouvelle Héloïse* and *Paul et Virginie,* each of which represented for Michelet "a new era, a moral revolution."[41] On May 5, 1789, when Louis XVI opened the Estates General, he announced that "the general anxiety will be calmed by a canvassing of wise and moderate views." Deprun, who quotes this statement, goes on to remark that "without knowing it, he [the king] had just named what would become the *mal du siècle,* or perhaps its honor."[42] The complaint against the Enlightenment was not just about the abstraction of reason: doubt and anxiety were an inherent aspect of all areas of thought and practice. The heart was always involved, and energy always on call. In short, the discourse of reason had its darker side in the counterdiscourse of sensibility, energy, and anxiety.

Other Enlightenments, Another Society

Diderot borrowed the epigraph to his *Essai sur l'interprétation de la nature* from Lucretius' *De natura rerum:* "E tenebris autemquae sunt in luce tuemur" (From darkness we contemplate the light). What better way to express the difficulty of separating the enlightened mind from the sensitive soul than a rhetorical exercise designed to unravel the contradictions between texts and reality? One does not want to attach too much significance to debates that anticipated later changes, however. Listen, for example, to Diderot criticizing d'Alembert in a letter to Sophie Volland written on August 31, 1760:

D'Alembert closed out the session of the Académie Française with an address on poetry . . . I am told that he described the *Iliad* and the *Odyssey* as boring and insipid works . . . That is what comes of speaking about things one has not studied carefully. It is difficult not to say foolish things. The man does not know a word of Homer's language . . . Let him stick to his equations. That is his bailiwick. I am reminded of the cold geometer who, tired of hearing praise for works of Racine he did not know, finally decided to read him. At the end of the first scene of *Psyche* he asked: "So, what does it prove?" Had I been there, I would have said to him, "That you have no feelings, you tree stump."

The real shift in sensibility came slowly. A new ideal type—the *honnête homme* and philosophe of sensibility, the Romantic soul—emerged slowly. I have drawn the contrast starkly in order to make the change intelligible. But people experienced the shift within the context of a stable culture and a shared anthropology, a basic understanding of the world that included certain inherent contradictions.

Because of this continuity, historians of the eighteenth century have always had a certain difficulty in interpreting the three principal developments of the late Enlightenment: the politicization of public opinion, technological and economic progress, and the rise of the irrational. Yet the forces of science and reason did indeed mingle with dark forces that became secret sources of energy for subsequent developments.[43] By the end of the century the irrational was too powerful to be ignored: thinking was more obedient to the logic of participation than to Galilean reason or the rules of Port-Royal. It relied on "dark lights" and intuitive understanding and lent impetus to the eager, passionate quest for a new society.

The crucial phenomenon was the coming together of the esoteric and the political.[44] A form of knowledge that had apparently disappeared in the sixteenth or seventeenth century was rehabilitated: its explanatory principles were *convenientia, aemulatio, analogia,* and *simpatia*.[45] Similarities, it was argued, made the world intelligible. To know was to unveil the system of resemblances that linked one thing to another and brought them within the ken of human observers. The same approach also worked for language. Within Freemasonry there was speculation about such matters, particularly in the "Scottish rite" and higher degrees, although Masonic sociability in general emphasized utilitarian and rational values.

Esoteric language and symbolic expression of incommunicable experiences established a relationship between reason and irrationality. It hid secrets from noninitiates while imparting to initiates knowledge that reason alone was powerless to convey. In other words, we have entered the territory of the occult, where suprasensible knowledge controls forces on which the material and spiritual well-being of the human race depends. This occultism was driven by a hunger for total knowledge, a will to power embodied in various forms of "theosophy." Some occultists incorporated recent scientific discoveries into their thinking. For example, the "Unknown Philosopher," Claude de Saint-Martin, combined science with cosmic mysticism in his *Tableau naturel des rapports qui existent entre Dieu, l'homme et l'univers* (1782). Masons thus coupled the need for a better, reformed society to a desire for total regeneration. "Martinism" offered a new religious interpretation of the world, a spiritualism outside the established churches, and a critique of the alienation created by the scientific study of matter.

Mesmerism added a radical dimension to occultism.[46] Mesmer and his Société de l'Harmonie taught that the flow of planetary magnetism could be tapped to restore health. People had clearly become intoxicated with the idea of availing themselves of spiritual, astral, and vital forces, which they hoped to use just as the Montgolfier brothers used hot air to fly and Benjamin Franklin used lightning to generate electricity. Mesmer's Société copied the organizational structure of the Masonic lodges: it advocated perfect equality among its members, and its dues were only one hundred louis, less than the dues of the lodges. Mesmerist societies blanketed all of France. In Paris, important aristocrats such as Lauzun, Coigny, and Talleyrand rubbed shoulders with *parlementaires* like Duport, *patriote* writers such as Brissot and Bergasse, and *savants* like Marat. Two intellectual currents came together: a belief in science, repackaged for popular consumption outside the much-criticized scientific institutions, and an obsession with marvels in general and a miraculous regeneration of society in particular. For example, Bergasse and Brissot, inspired by Rousseau, formulated a plan for both moral and political regeneration, the one being inseparable from the other. Rousseauism coupled with the vulgarized science of mesmerism gave rise to hopes of transforming institutions by physical means: "Any change," Bergasse argued, "any alteration in our physical constitution thus produces infallibly a change, an alteration in our moral constitution." Ultimately, Robert Darnton comments, "this moral revolution would transform political institutions."[47]

In mesmerism and other forms of occultism, part of Enlightenment society found in the irrational both a compensation for its dissatisfaction with rational, geometrical theories and an outlet for its emotional needs, literary exaltation of the ego, and energeticist belief in genius. The irrational was embraced all the more readily in that it offered a way to express, on a higher plane, religious needs that had never totally disappeared. A new society in search of identity could thus define itself and imagine its future in terms of a "religion without churches," a secularized pietism, a wedding of the religious and political projects, a convergence of empirical rationalism and pre- or parascientific illuminism. It was, as Jean Fabre has shown in his study of Diderot, the beginning of a crucial cultural shift from the Enlightenment to intellectual Romanticism.

19

⁓❧⁓⁓❧⁓⁓❧⁓

Materializing the Intelligence,
Abstracting Things

In *Candide* (1759), Voltaire writes:

The country was cultivated for pleasure as well as necessity. Every-where the useful was also agreeable. The roads were filled, or rather decorated, with carriages of admirable design and construction, carrying men and women of striking beauty hastened along by huge red sheep capable of driving a carriage faster than the finest horses of Andalusia, Tetuan, and Mequinez. "Surely this," said Candide, "is a finer country than Westphalia" . . . At length they came to the first house in the village. It was built like a European palace. A crowd gathered at the door and an even larger crowd inside. Very pleasant music could be heard, and a delightful fragrance wafted from the kitchen . . . "Let us go inside," [Candide said,] "this is an inn." Imme-diately two boys and two girls of the hostelry, clad in gold and their hair tied up with ribbons, invited the visitors to sit down to dinner. Four soups were served, each garnished with two parrots, a boiled condor weighing two hundred pounds, two flavorful roast monkeys, three hundred *colibris* in one plate, and six hundred hummingbirds in another; along with this went exquisite stews and delicious pastries, all served on crystalline plates. The waiters and waitresses poured various liquors made from cane sugar. The guests were mostly merchants and coachmen, all exquisitely polite.

This passage, from what is probably the most famous tale of the eighteenth century, contains at least three important lessons. First, the economy of abundance combines the necessary with the superfluous: in utopia luxury is "ubiquitous." Second, commerce depends on the circulation of men and things: inns are palaces, and even carriage drivers are polite. Finally, buildings, roads, vehicles, clothing, food, dishes, and table manners all reflect an aesthetic of prodigality.

Eldorado is of course a utopian image, an ideal country to inspire the social-imagination contrast with Westphalia, which serves as a metaphor for traditional civilization. Thus it is not surprising to find that Eldorado is a place where materialism is under control, where things serve men and not the reverse. But it is also a stage of a journey and as such allows us to see significant ways in which it differs from its unacceptable alternatives. Candide leaves the tropical paradise—an exemplary, miraculous, transparent, egalitarian society—because it does not offer solutions to the characteristic evils of the old world, does not provide a key to eliminating old woes. Eldorado occupies an intermediate position between the static world of the golden age and the future world in which commerce, technology, and science are "conceived of apart from profit, in which abundance is a reality for all, in which enrichment takes place without accumulation, and in which the state exercises its power and intervenes in exchange without tyranny. Do not love gold, Eldorado seems to say, and you will be happy. These are empty words whose illusory character is exposed by the text itself, since Candide and Cacambo reject the lesson."[1] Voltaire's Eldorado is the ambiguous paradise of a society in the process of questioning its future, a society facing the fears and hopes of the new world of commodities and change. It exists somewhere between heaven and earth, a model that remains to be transformed into a reality. A follow-up to the *Essai sur les moeurs* (1756) and the *Lettres anglaises* (1734), Voltaire's tale contains the ingredients of a possible earthly paradise based on useful skills and fine arts, exchange and liberty, civility and equality. But the prospect of happiness it holds out is also illusory, because desire creates needs that compel the hero to keep moving forward without rest. The fable became an illustration, a fragile yet optimistic crystallization, of questions about the possibility of progress and its "sufficient reason."

Candide was a success: its Swiss publishers, the Cramers, shipped 1,200 copies to the Paris market. Publishers in the capital reprinted it six times in the two months after it first appeared in Geneva, reaching another 10,000 readers. Presses in London, Liège, Lyons, and Avignon churned out several thousand more copies. In 1760 it was a triumph for an anonymously published book to sell 20,000 copies on what can only be called the black market.[2] *Candide* reached a diverse readership, ranging from hostile *antiphilosophes* (such as Omer Joly de Fleury, the Swiss scientist Haller, who disapproved of the "irony toward Leibniz," and Fréron) to approving philosophes (the Grimms, Pierre Rousseau). There was plenty in the text to please and displease its readers: it dealt gleefully with the most serious of subjects and exuberantly combined smutty jokes with the most elevated of meditations. Voltaire's style allowed him to treat topical matters in a humorous way in order to teach his readers a lesson in active skepticism. It is said that in Paris, people in the street took up the refrain "Let's eat some Jesuits" at a time when hostility to the Society was growing steadily.

The appeal of *Candide* lay in its representation of a key idea of the Enlightenment: the embrace of the concrete, the idea that the spiritual does not exist apart from its manifestations. To a society passionate about happiness the book taught many lessons: about the misery of war, the Lisbon earthquake, colonial hopes, utopian Eldorado, the cultivated garden. The end of *Candide* stood Pascal's reasoning on its head: work and recreation, Voltaire argued, are the only remedies for man's misery. The fact that an important lesson here coincided with a style, an aesthetic, was not without importance, showing once more that the eighteenth century was by no means a frivolous age. It was probably the first time in history that a hedonistic art of living came within reach of large numbers of people, extending far beyond the consumers of luxury goods, mere "decorative declarations of superfluity acquired for the sole purpose of conspicuous consumption."[3] As Montesquieu pointed out, the evolution of politics and society had made it possible for "all interests to become special." Economic change, coupled with social and geographic mobility, gave rise to a new conception of the ideal life. We turn next to an examination of that new ideal in the context of everyday life, in the arts and urban design, and in ordinary activities ranging from cooking to housekeeping.

The Consumption of Wealth: Models

My intention here is not to offer a history of "everyday life" in the eighteenth century. The history of "everyday life" is of course a popular genre in France, but it is open to criticism on the grounds that it applies the same analytic categories to different periods, whereas the real problem is to understand how change comes about in activities that are by nature repetitive. This is a difficult problem to solve, because it forces us to historicize the work process and make invisible habits visible. The goal is to understand the activities that constitute material culture of a particular period along with the latent symbolic meanings of those activities and their underlying social beliefs. As we have seen, the eighteenth century is in some ways a good period for studying changes in material culture because of the expansion of consumption and the debates it provoked, as in the controversy over luxury. Now, however, we need to delve a little more deeply in order to see how, in a world of constraint and necessity, the first signs of change began to emerge. How were the first steps taken toward a new world of possibility? Why was the impossibility of change finally rejected?

Changes in Diet

Changes in material culture are difficult to measure owing to the lack of appropriate sources such as account books and journals. Even when such sources are available (and they are more plentiful for urban than for rural areas and for the wealthy, especially the very wealthy, than for the poor and wretched), they are hard to interpret. Economists since Vauban have looked at the household budgets of typical families, but these raise as many questions as they answer. One can study the ways in which such budgets have been used to construct an average household, but such aggregates, while necessary for understanding change, are not sufficient.

Two facts stand out. First, change in the eighteenth century was more qualitative than quantitative, and prosperity came first to the urban or semiurban fringe of society. Second, "the shift of labor from agriculture to manufacturing implies that at some point in time the prospects of the urban worker were perceived as being in all likelihood better than those of the agricultural laborer."[4] Until the nineteenth century, the bulk of the budget of the vast majority of families went for food: 99 percent of the farm laborer's income was spent on subsistence, and in many cases his survival depended on whether he could supplement his earnings with a small plot of land, a few animals, and additional income from his wife and children. This variability makes it difficult to measure the ratio of income to expenditure and of necessity to luxury for rural and urban families. Michel Morineau calculated that an agricultural laborer at the beginning of the century earned 112 livres for 250 days of work annually, of which 53 percent was spent on grain; with two incomes in the family, the proportion of income spent on grain dropped to 35 percent. Disposable income ranged from about 40 livres in the first case to 90 in the second.

Clearly it is not easy to move from abstract aggregates such as these, which show how vulnerable people were to fiscal pressures, to a more concrete picture of what people ate. Subtle economists have ventured various calculations of what went into the market baskets of families in different social situations. Although the validity of these calculations is difficult to assess, it is worth mentioning the results. Take the family of a Rouen weaver in the first quarter of the eighteenth century: their daily ration consisted of bread (1,222 grams for the husband, 983 for the wife, and 659 for their child), herring (a symbolic as well as nutritious food for people living in coastal towns), and cheese, for a total of 3,000 calories for the workingman and perhaps 2,000 for his wife. At this level of consumption, it is likely that the daily diet was not restricted to just these items 365 days a year. Other fish, starches, vegetables, and on occasion meat probably appeared on the family dinner table from time to time. Variety was possible without any major change in total caloric consumption or dietary balance. All economists agree that certain groups ate better than others: the wealthy of course, city dwellers, soldiers and sailors, and students in *collèges* and *pensions*. To cite just one example, based on the available data, the girls in the convent school founded by Mme de Maintenon and her spiritual successors at Saint-Cyr consumed from 4,000 to 5,000 calories a day, enough to sustain a forced laborer. Such disparities naturally reflected social differences.

According to the same economists, the dietary possibilities changed little in the eighteenth century, although tastes did evolve, first at the top of the social ladder and then lower down. The use of spices and pepper diminished as the consumption of fresh meat increased; heavily salted meat fell out of favor, and sauces became more diverse.[5] In budgets from the reign of Louis XVI, whether recorded at the time or reconstructed by historians, we find little change in consumption; disposable income did not increase much because wages rose more slowly than prices, which rose unevenly: wheat went up more than wine, oil doubled in price, and salt tripled.[6] The standard of living of the "Abbeville weaver," the "farmer from Aunis," and the "Provençal peasant" declined, according to observations instituted to halt that decline (observations that were unreliable, although less so than most historical reconstructions). True, people were no longer dying of hunger, and the population was on the rise.[7] Meanwhile, social and economic theorists had begun to think about consumption as an object of scientific study. Significantly, diversification was noted in household budgets: money was being spent on new necessities such as clothing and furniture, while the preponderance of grain in food expenditures decreased. Contemporary statistics were biased by two concerns of the observers: to solve the problem of distributing assistance to the poor and to reduce the number of non-working days. In a report on the *grand concours* of 1775, whose subject was how "to reduce begging," the academicians of Châlons-sur-Marne calculated that the poor would benefit from a longer working day. The members of the Société d'Agriculture of Aunis and the academicians of La Rochelle agreed. If people wished to live at all, and perhaps even to live better, either they had to work more or wages had to be increased (though the latter possibility opened up a different can of worms).

Despite all the methodological difficulties involved, we can hazard two hypotheses. First, there continued to be a close relation between wages and the price of wheat, and this resulted in widespread support for market controls. This was a source of stability. Nevertheless, given the many aspects of consumption that we cannot observe, together with what we know about the possibilities of change in certain rural and industrial sectors, we can only assume that significant changes in diet were possible. Where more women and children joined the work force, and among the better-off segments of the population, food consumption habits may have evolved.

Two Examples: Rural Auvergne and Paris

Auvergne may be taken as typical of many other rural areas. It was a diverse province in which dietary customs varied widely from region to region.[8] There were grain-producing areas (Limagne), wine-producing areas (the hills of Allier), grassland, and mountainous regions, each with customs of its own. In the Clermontois rye bread dominated, sometimes with a not very appetizing mixture of spring wheat and vetch, along with barley and beans, walnut or hempseed oil, and low-quality imported wine. There was not much meat on dinner tables because cattle were rare; but in Limagne and the hill country, receipts for payments in kind show that many farms kept barnyard animals, so diets included eggs, capon, chicken, and to a lesser extent rabbit. Only the wealthier families kept hogs, and milk cows were virtually unknown. In the hills, moreover, goats were often raised for milk, cheese, and meat, and orchards supplied fruits that physicians blamed for epidemics of dysentery. On the whole, the typical diet offered little variety, consisting mainly of crude bread, watery wine, cheese, vegetables, and perhaps a little meat.

In the mountains there was more diversity. Milk was plentiful enough to be used for making porridge and cheese. Considerable numbers of hogs were raised in the forests on acorns or chestnuts; families customarily kept a single sheep, goat, or cow for milk. A variety of grains was available, along with relatively plentiful herbs and vegetables, and of course potatoes, which fed "the animals and the poor." Fishing and poaching also sustained a diet richer in calories and protein than the low-country diet. The mountain man—the "Gaspard" of legend—was more robust than the plainsman, who suffered from various deficiencies and diseases. The difference was obvious from early childhood.

There was little exchange between plains and mountains, except for cheese, which was sold in the plains, and wine, which found a market in grain country, mountain pasture areas, and cities. In all regions estate inventories reveal a culinary hierarchy determined by wealth. People everywhere cooked in pots that hung from hooks in the fireplace. Some kitchens also had cauldrons and frying pans. In the homes of notables, prosperous peasants, merchants, physicians, and priests, we find dripping pans, spits, various kinds of flatware, fish pans, and other utensils. This range of kitchen equipment may well have corresponded to a range of diets as well as to different capacities for modernization.

A look at working-class Paris (which accounted for three-quarters of the city's population) turns up similar results.[9] Around the hearth we find a variety of objects that tell us a great deal about how meals were prepared and what they consisted of: "vivre à pot et à feu," as the old saying goes. Kitchen utensils found in all households accounted for a significant portion of a family's patrimony: 20 percent in 1715 and 7 percent in 1780 (but, for the same dates, only 5 and 2 percent among domestic servants, who were on the average better off than most other workers). Two things account for this decrease: people were switching to less costly materials and types of cookware, but also an old way of life was dying out and being replaced by a new one. Iron and copper cookware was costly enough to be estimated item by item rather than weighed together like tinware. We find metal objects in all households: an average of ten under Louis XIV compared with six under Louis XVI. In 1715 utensils were generally made of iron, copper, or tin: iron for tripods, fireplace hooks, grills, and frying pans; copper for casseroles and cauldrons; tin for dishes. In 1780 wrought and cast iron objects were still in use, but copper was on the decline and tin even more so; items once made of these materials were replaced by stoneware and ceramics. Cooking methods changed, too, as stoves replaced hearths, and utensils proliferated, suggesting both new foods and more specialized types of preparation. In wealthier bourgeois homes we find casseroles, egg cups, bowls, coffee makers, sugar bowls, and occasionally teapots. At the same time we find fewer implements for grilling meat and less fine silver. Grilled meat had once been a relatively rare delicacy, but now meat was consumed more frequently, generally boiled and usually in different cuts than were used for grilling; 80 percent of estate inventories reflect this change. But inventories of kitchen equipment alone cannot answer the question whether Parisians ate better under Louis XVI than under Louis XIV. For that we need to consider some additional statistics.

In this regard we can look to Lavoisier. Following the lead of many economists beginning with William Petty and Marshal Vauban, many thinkers and administrators took an interest in the problem of supplying large cities with food. Domestic peace depended on it, since food shortage was the leading indicator of social unrest.[10] In order to determine the quality and quantity of food flowing into the capital, economists looked at the records of the *octroi*. From his vantage point at the Ferme Générale, Lavoisier was well informed, and he was able to calculate "a ceiling of per capita resources from which it was possible to deduce the same for provincial metropolises and secondary cities." On the basis of Lavoisier's figures for the year 1780, Robert Philippe figured the daily caloric intake of Paris's estimated 600,000 people at about 2,000 calories, 208 of which came from 52 grams of protein (the minimum daily requirement today is set at 30 grams). Parisians ate a lot of meat; carbohydrates accounted for 50 percent of their normal diet and fats for a third. So far as we can tell, this was a comfortable ration.[11] Parisians were healthy: not a single epidemic struck the city in the eighteenth century, reflecting their resistance to disease. This level of comfort and security of course depended on bread, which accounted for 50 percent of total calories though only a sixth of the typical food budget. The remainder went for meat, large quantities of fish, and an already wide range of items such as eggs, butter, cheese, oil, sugar, coffee, cocoa, wine, spirits, cider, and beer. Thirteen percent of total calories came from meat, fish, and eggs, 10 percent from cheese, 11 percent from alcohol, and 3 percent from sugar. Based on the records of the *octroi*, scholars have found the eighteenth-century Parisian diet to be balanced, distinctive, and modern.

This positive assessment may not be as sound as it appears, however. For one thing, it is based on an estimate of the population of the city. If the population was in fact 500,000 rather than 600,000, the daily ration increases to 2,400 calories; if it was 700,000, the daily ration decreases to 1,700. There is obviously a risk of overestimating average consumption: for example, if the population was 700,000, the average meat consumption drops from 73 to 60 kilograms according to Philippe's calculations, which are based on Lavoisier's data.[12] The variable size of the capital's population leaves some doubt about the overall standard of living. For another thing, the composition of a person's diet of course varied not only with wealth, wages, and employment but also with status and rank. The diet of the poor still consisted mainly of bread. As one moved up the scale of wealth, average caloric consumption increased only slightly, but the money spent on food went to purchase a much wider variety of items. The diet of the poor differed from that of the rich in qualitative as well as quantitative terms. The poor man's diet was "much more vulnerable to price increases than the diet of the well-to-do, who could substitute less expensive items for more expensive ones."[13]

Furthermore, one cannot neglect the hypothesis that consumption of certain major dietary components such as meat remained stable: 170–180 grams per day in 1720 as compared with 165–168 grams per day in 1780, according to actual entry figures. The unique features of the Paris distribution system also have to be taken into account. The royal government generally kept the machinery of supply, especially for bread and meat, well oiled. Although the lower-class diet may have included meat, as Lenoir, the *lieutenant de police*, maintained, it was surely in the form of inferior cuts along with offal; the better cuts were reserved for prosperous artisans, bourgeois, and "people who keep a good table."[14] If some observers, including Louis-Sébastien Mercier, thought that the lower classes ate badly, it was because overall expectations had risen. In the end, the good diet of the rich had a "trickle-down effect" on the mediocre diet of the poor in two ways: through the activity of hucksters *(regrattiers, regrattières)* and the rise of restaurants.

Hucksters bought up excess supplies from noble and bourgeois households, convents, and monasteries and sold them to the poor. Mercier describes one dish spurned by a bishop and left to molder on a huckster's stand until an indigent shopper finally bought it: "One quarter of Versailles feeds itself on dishes served at royal tables." Fruits, vegetables, eggs, and salt were sold in this way on the streets and in markets. Street markets were notable for confusion, filth, and fraud, yet they served a vast population, mainly but not exclusively lower class. They were an element of disorder in the dream of the orderly city, and as such incurred criticism similar to that leveled against cabarets, which the authorities viewed as dens of iniquity while the people saw them as places to gather daily for lunch, dinner, or a snack at any hour of the day or night.

Cabarets were an essential part of lower-class eating patterns: artisans, shopkeepers, journeymen, helpers, stevedores, and laborers frequently ate their meals out. We have Rétif's description of Mother Thorel's greasy spoon on the rue des Mauvais-Garçons. In little over an hour Mother Thorel served nearly 120 people, who gulped down their food at a table seating 30 or 40 diners, hurried along by the proprietress and her daughters: guests had only fifteen minutes to eat. By their dress and habits Rétif was able to distinguish tailor's helpers, factory workers, carpenters, locksmiths, and saddlers. He sampled the food, since "looking is not enough, you have to eat." In any case, he was used to such fare because, while living in the Cour d'Albret, he had taken meals at the corner cabaret. His description of Mother Thorel's establishment contrasts with the usual diatribes: the reality may have been less sordid than the more strident critics would have us believe. In *Les Contemporaines*, in fact, Rétif says that "the great city of Paris is so admirably set up that you can live there on any income." We can only assume that large numbers of people were accustomed to eating out. Thus, even in the same city, modes of consumption could vary widely to suit the needs of different segments of the population. A flexible system of distribution made it possible to resolve the apparent contradiction between widespread poverty and the extensive frequenting of restaurants offering a wide range of fare.

Gastronomy and Good Taste

The eighteenth century benefited from the culinary revolution of the seventeenth century and extended it with a further revolution of its own. Both revolutions had an important impact not only on the elites of France and indeed all of Europe but also on a much larger number of ordinary Frenchmen, who witnessed a substantial enrichment and diversification of their gastronomic possibilities. "In contrast to the crudeness and skimpiness of ordinary meals, the abundance of holiday fare marked occasions such as agrarian festivals, religious holidays, birthdays, weddings, and so on."[15] All sorts of unusual foods could turn up on the festive dinner table. Things usually eaten only by the urban upper classes were often devoured at country feasts, where guests gorged themselves on meat. Rousseau denounced the expansion of taste in terms worthy of an apostle of equality: "Because we demand gravy in our kitchens, the sick must go without bouillon. Because we demand spirits on our tables, the peasant must drink water."[16]

Cookbooks provide a good way to measure the scope of the change in taste. A number of important works, including *Le Cuisinier français*, *Le Pâtissier français*, *Le Confiturier français*, *Le Cuisinier friand*, *L'Ecole des ragoûts*, and *Le Cuisinier royal ou français*, first appeared in the seventeenth century and were still being reprinted and read in the eighteenth century. Two hundred thirty works in gastronomy were published between 1650 and 1789, seventy-five (or 32.6 percent) before 1700 and 156 over the next nine decades. Cookbooks were an important publishing phenomenon, with nearly 300,000 volumes in circulation. They were also a Parisian phenomenon, since nearly 60 percent of the titles were published in the capital in the seventeenth century and 87 percent in the eighteenth century. Significantly, some of these works entered the Bibliothèque Bleue of Troyes in the form of inexpensive editions published by Oudot and Garnier: *Le Cuisinier français* appeared in this format as early as 1680. The seventeenth-century works proved durable: at the height of the Enlightenment they were still promoting a change in taste that had occurred before 1650 and that began to meet with competition from yet another change after 1750. Cookbooks enjoyed the same surge in popularity as scientific and technical publications, and it comes as no surprise to find recipes and menus in works on agronomy such as the *Ménages des champs* and *Délices des campagnes*. Cookbooks succeeded because they captured the desire for a better life, as can be seen by a glance at Menon's *Cuisinière bourgeoise*, which first appeared in 1746 and was frequently reprinted thereafter. Baron Grimm recommended it in a letter he wrote in 1757: "Science and philosophy have taken hold of the cooking pot; the kitchen has entered the realm of ideology."[17]

Given this recognition, we need to take a more careful look at both the purposes for which cookbooks were written and the people who read them. The culinary literature was above all a literature for cooks, intended to be read by other cooks and people who wished to emulate them. François Pierre de La Varenne was cooking for the marquis d'Uxelles when he wrote *Le Cuisinier français*. Menon, the author of the eighteenth century's most aristocratic treatise on cooking, *Les Soupers de la cour*, as well as its most plainly bourgeois work, *La Cuisinière bourgeoise*, wrote especially for young cooks in his *Traité historique et pratique de la cuisine ou le Cuisinier instruit* (1758). The chef was an artist who graced the noblest households with his reputation: "He found himself promoted to the empyrean of science and progress, far above lesser chefs who thought it dishonorable to give the slightest hint that they had borrowed the idea for a dish from some printed book."

Cookbooks helped to codify and publicize rules of service and to define relations between servants and their masters beyond the confines of the aristocratic household. The success of *La Cuisinière bourgeoise* is a direct indicator of this broadening of the culinary horizon. Sophisticated cookbooks spread the table manners and tastes of court society to aristocratic *hôtels* and bourgeois homes. People acquired a new style of dining: they learned how to decorate their tables, orchestrate their meals, and greet and converse with guests. Cookbooks joined books on etiquette and manners and manuals of letter writing as agents in the transformation of custom. Propriety, decency, and taste became aspects of a new etiquette, a way of indicating respect for hierarchy while at the same time allowing for more egalitarian interactions among people united by a sense of belonging to a distinctive elite.[18]

There was no conflict between aristocratic and bourgeois manners in the eighteenth century. In fact, aristocratic tastes spread from the court to the city and from Paris to the provinces. This spread may in fact have accounted for the decrease in the number of cookbooks published and the switch from Parisian publishers to provincial and foreign booksellers. Cookbooks were written by but not necessarily for specialists: amateurs also studied them. A more bourgeois cooking style grew out of the encounter between elite customs and the needs of people made wealthy by the growing economy. "Social mobility had a decisive impact on the evolution of culinary practices."[19] It is not surprising that Menon was the first to address himself explicitly to a bourgeois audience. Notices for the work appealed to people of relatively modest wealth and status, whose expectations had plainly increased. The author of the anonymous preface to the counterfeit Brussels edition of 1774 explicitly indicated the intended audience: "He writes not for the nobility but for the bourgeoisie. But it can be said that he ennobles common dishes by enlivening them with seasoning." So much for the broader audience. Then came more specific targets, including cooks, male and female, servants, and their masters:

> In addition to lessons in cooking, he also provides lessons in service, from which he has just as carefully eliminated everything that might be beyond the reach of the bourgeois household or beyond the abilities of its cooks. In giving rules for heightening the taste of food with typical devices of the art, he has not forgotten to supply further rules for identifying foods that are naturally good, and these, in my view, are among the more substantial parts of his doctrine.[20]

The cookbooks had nothing to offer the urban or rural lower classes, however. What ordinary people ate was beneath mention. Nevertheless, refinements in cooking did reach the lower strata of society through editions of cookbooks sold by hawkers and through the almanacs. Although it is probably true that more people read sophisticated recipes than used them for cooking, their interest "revealed the fascination of such middling groups as rural notables, clergymen, and the minor nobility with the real or imagined culture of the ruling classes." Girard's hypothesis is confirmed by the originality of *La Cuisinière bourgeoise*, which offered a popular version of the customs of the Parisian aristocracy to a broad audience to whose social betterment it thereby contributed. The work addressed itself especially to nonspecialists, including women, "for the purpose of transforming, from time to time at any rate, a routine, everyday activity into a creative act." Between *Les Soupers de la cour* and *La Cuisinière bourgeoise* there was permeability, continuity, and adaptation.[21]

New Cooking, Culinary Mythology

In this way the transition was made from aristocratic cooking to a gastronomy within everyone's reach. The cheap editions of *Le Cuisinier français* held up the magnificent tables of the Grand Siècle for the eighteenth century to admire.[22] French cuisine had gradually freed itself from the habits of the Middle Ages and the Renaissance and moved toward a style of cooking less dominated by spices. Native herbs such as parsley, garlic, savory, thyme, and bay leaf, used with discretion, replaced imported spices. Sugar, vinegar, and verjuice were sometimes added. Sweet-and-sour dishes became less prevalent, and bouillon and butter were used to reduce acidity. Vegetables were common, not only in soups but as an accompaniment to main dishes. Roast meats were joined by fried dishes, casseroles, fricassees, and stews. Such were the meals that the gourmets of the classical period enjoyed, and that one can duplicate today with the help of recipes compiled by historians of cooking and taste.[23] And do not forget to consume them with wine, which people drank diluted with considerable quantities of water, sometimes iced. Wine was still considered an "excellent food," an essential part of the variety and abundance of the "grand style."

The eighteenth century announced its subversive opposition as early as 1739, when Marin published his *Dons de Comus ou les Délices de la table:*

> Modern cooking is based on the older style, but with less fuss, less formality, and just as much variety it is simpler, healthier, and perhaps even more sophisticated. The old cooking was highly complicated and involved an extraordinary attention to detail. Modern cooking is a kind of chemistry. The chef's science nowadays consists in knowing how to decompose meats, make them digestible, and reveal their quintessential qualities, drawing out light and nourishing juices and mixing them together in such a way that no single one dominates and all can be tasted. The cook must unite these juices as a painter unites colors; he must make them so homogeneous that their various flavors yield only a

subtle and piquant taste, indeed, I dare say, a harmonious chord combining all tastes simultaneously.

Note the praise of subtlety, which is associated with both chemistry and painting: the new cuisine saw itself as one triumphant art among many. It distinguished itself first by offering a variety of composite dishes served as hors d'oeuvres and entremets: meat, fowl, game, fish, vegetables, fried dishes, fricassees, stews, rissoles, and pâtés with reduced, light sauces, often slightly acidic. For these side dishes chefs created various *fonds,* or sauce bases: coulis, jus, and bouillons consisting of reduced cooking juices that could be elaborated to make different types of sauce. The new French cuisine was refined and elegant. It was simpler than the old cooking, as one can judge by comparing recipes for the same dish, say, a chicken fricassee, in La Varenne and Menon: preparation gained in both finesse and precision. Bourgeois cooking became lighter, less complicated, and less costly.

It therefore behooves us, when examining estate inventories, to pay attention to the presence of the utensils that made this revolution possible. Brick herb planters, first used in Italy, became a fixture of aristocratic kitchens in the seventeenth century and of bourgeois kitchens in the eighteenth. These provided the herbs for bouillons and simmered sauce bases and made complex new dishes possible. Portable cast-iron herb planters became common in well-to-do Paris homes in the 1750s. Brick planters, built into the wall behind the hearth and near a window, were not included in inventories of movable property since they were part of the house itself. Hence our indicator of change disappears. Nevertheless, we may assume that taste and cooking techniques evolved together and that cookbooks popularized the change by linking the quest for simpler, more flavorful, less expensive dishes of the sort Menon advocated to a veritable culinary mythology.

That mythology called for returning to the childhood of mankind, to "innocent dishes," "good fruits, good vegetables, good cream, and good people," as Rousseau put it in *Emile.*[24] Culinary culture, as A. Girard and Jean-Claude Bonnet have shown, marked a break with nature: it participated in the oppressive order of society and civilization. "Culinary Rousseauism" made its appearance even before Rousseau, for example, in Jaucourt's article "Cuisine" in the *Encyclopédie:*

There is fairly general agreement about a hundred different ways of disfiguring the foods that nature provides, which thereby lose their quality and become, if I may put it this way, pleasant poisons that destroy temperaments and shorten lives. Thus the simple cooking of the earliest stages of the world's existence has lately become a subject for study, a most difficult science on which new treatises are constantly being published with titles such as "French chef," "royal chef," "modern chef," and "gifts of Comus."

History, Jaucourt argued, showed the results of the ancient philosophical struggle between "gastrophiles" and ascetic nature lovers: luxury versus pleasure, East versus West, subversive foreigners (in this case the sixteenth-century Italians) versus domestic moderation, virtue versus illusion. For the *Encyclopédie,* however, comparison by itself was not persuasive. Jaucourt went on to contrast the bizarre profusion and "ancient prejudices" of the past to the culinary triumphs of the Enlightenment, to the new cuisine then advancing in step with the other arts. In the end, our culinary philosopher succeeded in reconciling nature with culture, dietetics with gastronomy (the term itself was not coined until the beginning of the nineteenth century by Grimod de La Reynière, who thereby recorded the final defeat of culinary Platonism and Rousseauism).

Before Jaucourt, *Le Cuisinier français* had tried to reconcile health with diet. The book sought to preserve "health in a good state and excellent disposition" by teaching ways to prepare substantial, well-made, tasty dishes at a reasonable price. People who ate according to its recipes could reputedly do without either physician or apothecary. Among cookbook writers it was a traditional article of faith that good digestion begins in the pantry. The Enlightenment added science to the culinary art, which thus became yet another ornament of the triumphant human spirit. Menon made the point in his *Science du maître d'hôtel confiseur et cuisinier* (1749–1750):

Cooking makes the crude parts of food more subtle and eliminates the earthy juices from the mixtures it uses. It perfects them, purifies them, and in a sense spiritualizes them. Prepared dishes should thus contribute a greater abundance of thinner, more purified spirits to the blood . . . Would it be too much to argue that the preparations of the modern kitchen belong among the physical causes which, from the bosom of barbarity, have called forth among us the reign of politeness, the talents of the spirit, the arts and sciences?

Overshadowed somewhat by the debates about luxury and about the social virtues of science and the arts, another debate erupted between proponents of the new cuisine (including Meusnier de Querlon, Menon, and the *Encyclopédie*) and adversaries (such as Desalleur, the author of *Lettre d'un pâtissier anglais au nouveau cuisinier français*, 1747). Civilization, it was argued, has its culinary side: cooking involves not only the material and corporeal but also the intelligence. Once again the generalization of "luxury" was a source of conflict.

From Luxury to Comfort: New Habits and New Things

In the reflection on cooking symbolized by *La Cuisinière bourgeoise*, two things stand out: that the idea of progress coincided with a new mastery over the body, and that the transformation of taste depended on a domination of space. The emphasis on a healthy diet points up a need for equilibrium and simplicity. In this respect the applied science of cooking was simply an application of the theoretical science of alimentary biology. The first step was to analyze nutrition in terms of the digestive process, whose muscular, physical, and chemical mechanisms became objects of study. Here, Réaumur and Spallanzani made important contributions.

The second stage involved thinking about diet in general. In the second half of the seventeenth century, old ideas about the ritual organization of the dinner table gave way to systematic study of eating habits in the context of a search for a general theory of hygiene.[25] Tronchin and Tissot advocated a "diet of abstinence" after centuries of reliance on "repletion" and bleeding. They argued for a return to natural foodstuffs and a regulated, balanced diet. Eating habits should be adjusted to reflect an individual's age, sex, location, profession, and social status. Physicians compared diets across Europe, as in Tissot's *Avis au peuple sur sa santé* (1761) and *Sur la santé des gens de lettres* (1768). The new theory reflected the need for a simple, natural yardstick of healthy eating; people were told to adjust their diet to their circumstances. Ultimately the new thinking led to recommended daily allowances and to a shift from empirical guidelines to a mathematical chemistry of nutrition.[26] The philosophy of hygiene was also a philosophy of custom, that is, of the balance to be struck between natural and nonnatural things. Eventually this thinking evolved into applied physiology.[27]

In eating as in other matters, the Enlightenment believed that man should dominate nature. When we look at what the *Encyclopédie* had to say about clothing, for example, we discover an order of exchange, a relation between the familiar and the exotic in the textile tradition. Similarly, when we look at what the same work had to say about food, we discover a series of spatial relationships: the texts concentrate on technology and production and ignore the social dimension of eating and the normative aspects of etiquette. The *Encyclopédie* focused not on the artifices of high cuisine, culinary art, and sybaritic luxury but on the innocent art of producing nourishing meals and healthy pleasures.[28] Kitchen objects, garden produce, and the by-products of the barnyard and stable were linked to a whole range of activities. Production, exchange, and industriousness and agronomy were praised. Wealth was simple, but production had many facets.

The *Encyclopédie* thus ratified what *La Cuisinière bourgeoise* was saying at the same time from an essentially Parisian vantage point. The most varied foods came to Paris from such nearby places as Passy, Argenteuil, Belleville, and Montreuil. The orchards, gardens, stables, farmyards, and pigsties in these villages supplied the city with meat, fruits, vegetables, and herbs. Truck farmers delivered peaches, apricots, and cherries to market stalls and street vendors. Beef was imported from western and central France, from Cotentin and Auvergne. Mutton came from Champagne and Beauvais in the spring and from the Ardennes in the winter. Veal was shipped from Caen and Rouen. Shad was fished from the Seine and the tidal basins of Dieppe and Fécamp. The quality of food products came to be associated with their place of origin.

In both the *Encyclopédie* and *La Cuisinière bourgeoise* we are aware of the potential richness and extreme diversity of the food supply: nature, these texts implied, is at our doorstep, its subtly varied flavors and textures available for our delectation.[29] Enlightenment France drew on both familiar, nearby sources of food and more exotic suppliers, importing spices from the Orient and the New World; coffee and chocolate from the Antilles; cheese from Holland and Roquefort; dried vegetables, lemons, and oranges from the Mediterranean. A readiness to experiment and a determination to explore all available sources of food overcame doubts about luxury and put sophisticated, costly, and exotic ingredients on the same plane as simpler, more economical, locally produced ingredients. Artists such as Chardin celebrated ordinary, familiar foods, as in the *Cut Melon*, now in the Louvre, which features the bright orange of the sliced melon, the pinks and yellows of the peaches, the greens and violets of the plums, and the gray-greens and yellows of the pears along with such familiar objects as a bottle and an exotic porcelain dish with a floral pattern. The balanced colors—what Diderot called the "very substance of objects pulverized on the palette"—displayed the fragile sensibility of a moment in which matter and intelligence seemed to be in full harmony.

New Tastes and New Customs

Changing tastes gave rise to new customs. From the most common foods to the most select items such as sugar, coffee, chocolate, and tea, new ingredients found a variety of uses. For the Encyclopedists and other observers, the impetus behind changes in taste was the same as that responsible for the new "still-life" aesthetic in art. Novel recipes confirmed the emergence of a new culinary and descriptive style.

Everyone used sugar, which Italian chefs and bakers had made fashionable. Grown on tropical islands and refined in major port cities, the sweet crystal was a source of colossal profits well into the nineteenth century. It also sustained the slave trade, but on this score the *Encyclopédie* contrived to keep a clear conscience: it looked at the production of sugar, and at all other foodstuffs for that matter, solely in terms of techniques and benefits.[30] Sugar, a colonial product, began to supplant native honeys as early as the seventeenth century, and as its price fell and imported quantities increased, candy and pastry makers came up with imaginative new ways to use it.[31] Marmalades, jellies, and pastes were both marketed independently and incorporated into pastries.

The vogue for jams and sweets called for cooking implements of copper (slotted spoons, ladles, baking sheets, preserve pans), glass (jars), and even porcelain (jam pots). Artisans turned out new utensils first for the luxury market, then for a broader public, and ultimately for everyone, transforming the look of the typical household (as still-life paintings reveal and estate inventories confirm). Pure copper cookware became an object of controversy: it had the visual and psychological advantage of preserving the color of fruit but could be dangerous because of the potential for forming verdigris. Physicians and dealers recommended tinned copper, which caused fruit to turn black but eliminated the risk of poisoning from various compounds of copper. The use of sugar had further consequences that continue to this day. Some of the sweetener went to make sorbet and ice cream, lemonade (available in Paris exclusively from a guild of three thousand *maîtres limonadiers*), and medicinal syrups. On the eve of 1789, the French colonies were probably producing more sugar than their British counterparts: on the order of ninety thousand tons, not counting contraband. Additional sugar was also imported from Spanish, Portuguese, and English sources, for a total of just under four kilograms per capita (the precise figure is open to question, but it gives an idea of the degree of dependency on sugar). Sugar symbolized the social position of the rich and was also used in a surprising variety of ways by the less well-off.[32]

J.-C. Bonnet is right to ascribe the Encyclopedists' emphasis on sugar and sweets to a "collective affirmation of joyous orality," a quality we also find in the lists of sweets in novels by Voltaire and Marivaux. Sweets—sorbets, ice cream, jams, sweet pastries, biscuits, cookies, macaroons, candies, and bonbons—had a sociable connotation, a sense of respectable, lighthearted sensuality that contrasted sharply with the baroque profusion of the great gastronomic feast and the cumbrous gluttony of the bourgeois dinner table. These were the totem foods of the *Encyclopédie* generation, symbols of peaceful civilization.

Coffee had similar qualities: because it was exotic, it symbolized modernity and commerce, and because it was drunk with sugar, its use involved the popularization of a habit previously associated with wealth. In both England and France, people added sugar to bitter, stimulating beverages, partly to disguise their unusual taste and partly because it was traditional to sweeten drinks. The French first began drinking coffee toward the end of the seventeenth century. Coffee was drunk much more in public, as in Italy and the Near East, than in private, where its use was at first contested on medical grounds by many physicians. In Paris, coffee drinking quickly became a habit. People were drawn to the warmth of cafés, and their predilection was encouraged both by the guild of *limonadiers* (who sold coffee as well as lemonade) and the enthusiasm for drinking coffee with sweetened milk. The brown beverage was seen as both a powerful mental stimulant and a substitute for food. The *Encyclopédie* praised its medicinal effects for the obese and for migraine sufferers but also mentioned the need for certain precautions: before drinking coffee, people were well advised to consume a glass of water in order to ensure that the beverage would have a laxative and diuretic effect; sugar was necessary to disguise the unpleasant bitterness of straight coffee; and milk or cream was to be added to improve the nutritive value of the beverage and "inhibit the saline principles." In the thirty-sixth of Montesquieu's *Lettres persanes* (1721), Uzbek describes the extensive consumption of coffee: "Coffee is much used in Paris. It is distributed in a large number of public houses. In some of these, the news is read; in others people play chess. There is one where the coffee is prepared in such a way that it imparts wit to those who drink it: at any rate, no one leaves the place without thinking that he is four times wittier than when he went in."

Such was the combined effect of fashion and intellect. The century would play all possible variations on this theme. The café and cabaret were polar opposites: the *limonadier,* or café keeper, was not a *marchand de vin,* or publican; the clients were more elegant, their manners were more refined and more disciplined, and there was less noise and more concentration.[33] Literary descriptions of cafés tell the same story. They were warm but not boisterous places with tiled floors, paneled walls, chandeliers, small, clean tables and comfortable chairs rather than long tables and benches, newspapers, and central stoves. From the Palais-Royal to the boulevards, from rue Férou to the Montagne-Sainte-Geneviève, there was a café for every taste and budget: the guild register listed some 2,800, or one café for every 250 people (assuming a population of 700,000). Customers liked the clean, civilized interiors, where they were likely to run into a better class of people than in the unsavory cabarets and tobacco shops. Cafés, in other words, were a sign of modernity. In the regular course of things, people thus gathered in one of two places around one of two drinks: either in the cafés around coffee or in the cabarets around wine. The cabarets were chaotic and turbulent, the cafés disciplined. One place was for brawling, promiscuity, and loose morals, the other for silence, decorum, and show. From the fruits of the earth to the beverages of the table to the people who consumed them, the differences were palpable and symbolic of the social tensions of the time. One sees this in Abbé Delille's celebrated poem:

Il est une liqueur au poète plus chère
qui manquait à Virgile et qu'adorait Voltaire,
C'est toi divin café, dont l'aimable liqueur
sans altérer la tête épanouit le coeur.
Ainsi quand mon palais est émoussé par l'âge,
Avec plaisir encor je goûte ton breuvage.
Que j'aime à préparer ton nectar précieux!
Nul n'usurpe chez moi ce soin délicieux.
Sur le réchaud brûlant moi seul tournant ta graine,
A l'or de ta couleur fais succéder l'ébène;
Moi seul, contre la noix qu'arment ses dents de fer,
je fais en te broyant crier ton fruit amer.
Charmé de ton parfum, c'est moi seul qui dans l'onde
infuse à ton foyer ta poussière féconde;
Qui tour à tour calmant, excitant tes bouillons,
suis d'un oeil attentif tes légers tourbillons.
Enfin de ta liqueur lentement reposée
Dans le vase fumant la lie est déposée;
Ma coupe, ton nectar, le miel américain
Que du suc des roseaux exprima l'Africain,
Tout est prêt. Du Japon l'émail reçoit tes ondes
Et seul tu réunis le tribut des deux mondes.
Viens donc divin Nectar, viens donc, inspire moi.[34]

There is a liquor dear to poets,
which Virgil lacked and Voltaire adored:
thou, divine coffee, lovely liquid,
which sets the heart beating without making the head spin.
When my palate is deadened by age,
I still can savor thee.
How I love to prepare thy precious nectar!
No one deprives me of this delightful chore.
On the hot stove I alone roast thy beans,
turning thy golden color to ebony.
I alone, grinding thy bitter fruit between iron teeth,
cause it to cry out.
I alone, charmed by thy fragrance,
infuse the waters with thy fertile dust.
I alone watch thee now swirl,
now settle in the turbulent warmth.

Ultimately the dregs settle
to the bottom of the smoking pot.
My cup, thy nectar, the American honey
that the African has pressed from the sap of the cane—
all is ready. The Japanese enamel receives thee:
thou alone enjoy the tribute of two worlds.
Come, then, divine Nectar, come inspire me.

Here, in the poetic canon of the time, which essentially required adapting new themes to conventional forms, is a fine lesson in material culture. We recognize the gestures and objects and the method of infusion (which resulted in stronger coffee than boiling or percolation) in what is ultimately a meditation on the relation between the physical and the moral— a physiology of habit.

Tea and chocolate deserve a similar analysis, and not just for the sake of completeness. Both had customary associations similar to those of sugar and coffee, and like those substances were exotic, caught on gradually, and aroused controversy over their effects on health. Chocolate, which came to France from Spain and above all Italy, established its presence during the Regency: Jean-Etienne Liotard's 1743 painting of Maria Theresa's maid serving the empress her daily ration of chocolate (*La Belle Chocolatière*, today in Dresden) symbolized the importance of the new confection. Chocolates were sold in Paris grocery shops and cafés as well as chocolate shops. In 1770 Paris got its first chocolate factory, which was joined in 1776 by a second, that of Legrand d'Aussy. Apothecaries also sold chocolates. Millions of pounds of chocolate from the Antilles were consumed in France. Of this total, only 250,000 pounds went to Paris, according to Lavoisier's calculations, or less than 200 grams per person, compared with 2.5 million pounds of coffee and 6.5 million pounds of sugar. Chocolate accounted for a small fraction of the average person's total caloric intake, but its social and symbolic role was immense. Although hot chocolate was a beverage of the rich, it could also be sampled in small quantities in the cafés. Usually consumed in private, chocolate was closely associated with the erotic. In novels and memoirs, including Casanova's, it was represented as an aphrodisiac more effective than either champagne or oysters. In painting hot chocolate was associated with scenes of passion.[35] For the international social elite, the taste for chocolate was linked to the enthusiasm for sweets and for alternating hot and cold drinks. Whether taken together or in succession, such treats helped "to while away the hours of the day and mark the passage of the seasons of the social round."[36]

Tea, which did not enjoy as much of a vogue as coffee or chocolate, was for France (though to a lesser extent than for England) essentially a by-product of trade with China. Some of the tea that France imported was reshipped to London and Dublin. In France, tea was for a long time regarded as a medicinal plant, sold under the auspices of the Faculté de Médecine. It was very expensive: seventy livres for a pound of Chinese tea in 1700, and two hundred livres for a pound of Japanese tea. As the price came down, the market increased. The 1715 edition of *Le Nouveau Cuisinier royal et bourgeois* remarked that "tea is not as common as coffee because of its much higher price," but it gave instructions for its preparation and indicated that tea "is usually drunk in the morning to get the mind going and after meals to aid in digestion." Tea was never as popular in France as in England, where it became the center of a domestic ritual and a staple of the British diet, but it did encourage new forms of sociability and conversation and inspired its own panoply of accoutrements, probably modeled on those of the English.

From Consumption to Objects to Interior Decoration

Coffee, tea, and chocolate were consumed in particular ways—ways that were at first incidental to the use of these substances but later became essential. Estate inventories from Paris show that the required accessories were common in well-to-do and middling households, especially after the Regency, and that the lower classes began to acquire such items before 1780.[37] We can track the growth in consumption by looking at debts owed to chocolatiers and grocers. Common accessories included coffee tins, pewter bowls, roasting pans, hot plates, and cookers, along with coffeepots, cups, and spoons. Silver and porcelain coffeepots were expensive (ranging in price from fifty to two hundred livres). Copper and pewter ones cost only a few sols. The nobility and clergy kept supplies of mocha in their cupboards and armoires. In 1760, 37 percent of estate inventories from the parish of Saint-Germain-l'Auxerrois included at least one coffeepot, compared with only 15 percent from the faubourg Saint-Antoine. Equipment for making tea was rarer: we find it in 2 percent of the inventories from Saint-Germain-l'Auxerrois but as many as 10 percent of those from the wealthier parish of Saint-Eustache. The documents mention tea tins, kettles, and saucers, and pots of porcelain or metal, including copper, pewter, and silver (which could cost as much as a hundred to two hundred livres), porcelain and china teacups, and in wealthier homes complete tea services on the English model. Spending large sums of money on a tea service was a way of exhibiting one's wealth and showing that one kept up with the latest fashions, and the task of serving tea could be assigned to younger members of the household to show them off. The tea ceremony was not so much a private as a social ritual.

We can estimate the extent of use of various substances by the presence of the necessary accessories. Everyone drank coffee both inside and outside the home. The elite drank tea. And only the wealthy and sick drank chocolate, except to a limited extent in cafés and chocolate shops. Rural estate inventories from the Ile-de-France and Vexin reveal the limits of the new beverages' popularity: we find the necessary accessories, generally of cheaper quality than in the cities, in only a few homes, mainly of the wealthier peasants.

Porcelain versus Silver

The link between the consumption of new substances and the possession of novel objects shows how fashions, even frivolous fashions, contributed to economic growth: economic change and cultural change were intimately intertwined. Like clothing, which we looked at earlier, porcelain is a case in point.[38] Louis Dermigny has provided us with a magisterial study of the business done by the Compagnie des Indes in Lorient, where buyers from across Europe came to purchase tea.[39] In it we can follow year by year the distribution of exotic items from China and the East Indies: three-quarters of what was sold went to wholesale markets in Nantes, Lorient, Montpellier, Lyons, Paris, and Geneva. Pepper, tea, coffee, and porcelain were sold mainly to buyers along the Atlantic coast. Silk, wallpaper, rattan, and lacquerware were sold to inland buyers, mostly in northwestern France. Very little went to the south and nothing to the northeast. From this we gain a general idea of the pattern of redistribution, although the sales figures may be somewhat misleading in that shipments could be sold to an intermediate buyer and yet remain in the warehouse in Lorient for delivery to yet another buyer. Despite this, knowledge of trading customs and family and commercial connections gives some assurance that the sales figures accurately reflect the distribution of shipments.

The market for porcelain was linked to the markets for other imported goods, and its growth was determined by the evolution of taste. Although the number of pieces imported remained constant from the Regency to the reign of Louis XVI, the number of different types of items (cups, saucers, bowls, jam jars, teapots) decreased. This suggests that porcelain had become a familiar household item. The reduction in the range of items imported was probably due to the growth of the mass market, with its greater uniformity of taste. After 1730, it became fashionable to buy complete sets: a table service, tea service, or coffee service. The Compagnie des Indes bought shrewdly and was able to sell its imports at high prices: from three hundred to five hundred livres for a two hundred–piece service. Meanwhile, the Chinese adapted their production to Western tastes. Buyers in France, Holland, and England sent metal and earthenware models of desired items to producers in China. Chinese patterns were replaced by European ones, as oriental artists copied designs from Meissen, Rouen, and Moustiers as well as French engravings. At the same time, however, the taste for things oriental remained strong until the reign of Louis XVI, and the new factories at Sèvres and Chantilly continued to turn out fake "china," just as the old ones had done. The import business was sustained by the price differential: a typical Sèvres service sold for four hundred livres at Lazare Duvaux, a supplier of china to the best Paris houses; for the same price the Compagnie des Indes could sell a dozen services. The low cost of Chinese labor made the difference.

Of course, low prices would not have been important had there been no psychological need to own fine china. That need was created in France by porcelain factories established under royal protection after Macquer's voyage and the discovery of kaolin in Saint-Yrieix in 1768; the royal *manufacture* at Sèvres produced a steady output of soft and hard mixes *(pâtes tendres, pâtes dures)*. Porcelain began to replace silver. To be sure, silver dinnerware remained a mark of social status, wealth, and respectability, but it signified "constrained wealth, still daunted by memories of the frequent monetary shocks and shortages of earlier times." Silver was a comforting luxury, a reserve that a family could count on in hard times, a sort of talisman. Porcelain revealed a new style: "It was wealth unconstrained by prudence or timidity, luxury freed from the tyranny of the useful and without ulterior purposes." Society felt sufficiently in control to abandon itself to frivolous pleasures and recreations. That is why porcelain caught on first with established and enlightened families, whereas the nouveaux riches and petits bourgeois continued to insist on silver as proof of their newfound status. Older families, who already owned silver, looked to porcelain for a different purpose: as proof of their intellectual curiosity, aesthetic predilections, and sophisticated taste. "Whereas silver signified earnest patience and attested, spoon after spoon, salt cellar after salt cellar, to slow and steady bourgeois progress, a porcelain service signaled a more rapid rise or a desire for new sensations, and its fragile perfection captured the hint of the eternal in the fugitive that was characteristic of a certain eighteenth-century spirit."[40] Exotic as well as fragile, porcelain reassured Enlightenment society of its possession of the world. It therefore appealed to all segments of society and to people in all regions.

Aesthetics and Comfort:
The Rococo and Neoclassical in the Minor Arts

I have been discussing the intimate connection between the evolution of taste in general—in food, clothing, and furniture—and the proliferation of objects. This is the province of the "aesthetics of the minor arts,"[41] which deals with changing customs and their relation to economic, social, cultural, and intellectual trends. Here, matters of taste—colors, shapes, ornament—run up against social constraints.

The stylistic changes of the period are well known: the dominant rococo—desacralized, sensual, steeped in pagan mythology and erotic and amorous imagery—gave way to a new emphasis on reason and history, a new rigor that swept the fine arts.[42] At various points in the 1750s and 1760s, architecture, painting, and sculpture as well as the minor arts all adopted the new vocabulary and new themes.

The exuberance of detail that contrasted so effectively with the linear narratives of Voltaire's stories, and the sober palace facades that contrasted so dramatically with their airy interiors and sumptuously abundant furnishings, gave way to a new type of equilibrium to which the label "neoclassical" fails to do justice, for the reaction against the old style was animated by a felt need for order and variety—for a more disciplined order and more controlled variety that would respect both the traditional forms and the functional imperatives of majesty. One sees this in the theoretical reflections of an "urbanist" such as Abbé Laugier, the artisan of the anti-rococo reaction, or of Nicolas Cochin, an engraver and draftsman who helped design entertainments for Louis XV and was contemptuous of frivolous, overly elaborate ornament. In Cochin's *Supplication aux orfèvres*, for example, we read:

> Would goldsmiths, when they execute a life-size artichoke or celery stalk on the cover of a cooking pot, kindly refrain from placing it next to a hare the size of a finger? . . . [Would they kindly refrain] from altering the uses of things and remember that a chandelier must hang straight and perpendicular . . . if it is to hold candles and that a candleholder must be concave if it is to collect melting wax and not convex so that the wax drips onto the chandelier? Would domestic sculptors kindly agree, when executing trophies, not to represent a scythe as smaller than a sand clock or a man's head as smaller than a rose? . . . Let us hope at least that when things should be square, [artisans] will not twist them into tortuous shapes, and that when an arch is supposed to be semicircular, they will refrain from corrupting it with those S-shapes that they seem to have picked up from the master writers.

This condemnation of curves and excess by one of the leading illustrators of the time and one of the initiators of the new history painting does not challenge the idea of seeking pleasure through variety and contrast: Cochin is simply asking for a different standard.[43] The artisans and decorators who changed the look of everyday life applied that "different standard" in their work. Two examples will help to make this clear: the art of chair making and the pedagogy of comfort.

Furniture and Decoration

The eighteenth century was at once the golden age and the twilight of furniture making. Furniture makers demonstrated their zeal for perfection at a time of important changes in both supply and demand. The growth of consumption in general had increased the demand for various kinds of furniture, while the first signs of industrialization were beginning to affect production (of textiles and wallpaper as well as furniture). Skilled craftsmen responded to their customers' new concern to move beyond necessities. High-end demand for prestige items drove the transformation of the craft, and this had a secondary impact on less costly items as well, although I do not mean by this to suggest that everyone had equal access to the new styles. Beyond the craftsmen themselves, the general public shared the new sensibility even if they could not afford the more costly items. That the number of pieces of furniture in homes increased is beyond doubt: by a factor of four or five in lower-class homes and by a factor of a hundred in aristocratic households. The eighteenth century developed a taste for the new. The fact that lower-class and upper-class interiors evolved in parallel clearly shows that what took place was a shift in sensibility toward a more individualized appropriation of space.[44]

There is reason to believe that the demand for new furniture was associated with the desire for visible signs of distinction. The city was a kind of spectacle, and people learned to read the signs of status by attending the theater and watching cultural trendsetters. In addition, many people attended the annual Salons, or exhibitions of painting, in the capital. The audience for such cultural phenomena was fragmented and incoherent, a minority susceptible to direction; it did not establish criteria of taste, which emerged from the dialogue among art lovers, artists, and academic institutions, but it did gradually learn the principles. The people who crowded into art exhibits did develop a critical aesthetic. Criticism offered the enlightened minority the abstract tools with which to separate themselves from the concrete but divided public. Artists learned how to engage in dialogue with the growing audience for art exhibits. A rough estimate of the number of people attending the Salons can be obtained from the sales figures for the successful Salon brochures: from 7,696 in 1755, brochure sales increased to 21,940 in 1787 (and assuming that one in three visitors purchased a brochure, as seems likely, this means that 10 percent of the population of Paris visited the Salon that year). The audience for art included men and women of all classes, according to Pidansat de Mairobert in *L'Espion anglais* (1783).[45] It seems likely that the new taste was propagated by printed works, public exhibitions, and word of mouth. We find other examples of this in the theater and fairs.[46]

Craftsmen completed the process. Scattered in villages and towns throughout France, they weighed local traditions against the new ideas wafting in from Paris. In the capital itself, craftsmen were an innovative group. Renowned artists sprang from their midst, as did half the painters in France. The rival carpenters' and cabinetmakers' guilds merged in 1754 and adopted a single set of rules.[47] The combined guild coexisted with independent craftsmen who enjoyed royal protection (whether at the Gobelins or in the faubourg Saint-Antoine) and exemption from the last remaining seigneurial jurisdictions. Most of the carpenters were French, however, while the cabinetmakers constituted a foreign minority. Among them were the Oebens and Rieseners, names that still stand for the highest standards of Parisian furniture making. These skilled craftsmen made do with few tools and minimal resources, yet they were perfectionists capable of working with a broad range of woods and veneers and of adapting both traditional pieces and new designs to changing needs and styles.[48]

The eighteenth century was the golden age of seating, which came in every imaginable style: stools, folding chairs, banquettes, chairs, armchairs, cabriolets (small armchairs), and sofas, to name a few, and each type came in many models and varieties. The straight chair, or *chaise,* from which everything else derived, first appeared at the end of the fifteenth century. Two centuries later, seating design was still dominated by architectural principles and the need for mobility: folding chairs and armchairs and seats in the shape of an X began to compete effectively with the chair with three or four legs and a straight back. If it is true that seating reflects the fundamental character of an epoch, then the older seating, which made no effort to adapt the seat to the body, might be said to reflect hierarchical formality. In the eighteenth century, however, it became possible to sit in more relaxed postures or even partially stretched out, especially in private settings. Modern chairs came in many styles. Uncomfortable benches fell out of favor, and newer chairs came with matching cushions. The intention—to create a comfortable space in which to sit—continued to dominate interior design until recently.

Two revolutions that began in the seventeenth century were completed in the eighteenth. To begin with, furniture making became an art with rules of its own, independent of architecture, which had refused to accommodate itself to the body: "Supple and delicate arabesque motifs ceased to be mere ornament and began to shape the contours of objects themselves," and furniture making became "drawing projected into space." Out of this conjunction of the formal with the material came the light, dynamic style of the Enlightenment. The neoclassical return to antiquity did not mean that furniture making once again became subordinate to architecture: the neoclassical style of ornament and designs using columns and lintels were thoroughly denatured, and the final result was furniture that seemed to defy the laws of gravity.[49]

Furthermore, speculation about "comfort" and a new relationship between furniture and the body also affected seating design (note that the word *confort* did not enter the French language until 1815, but *confortable*, borrowed from English, was probably first used in 1786). Chairs, though in widespread use, did not vary much in style until the Regency and the reign of Louis XV, when rococo was all the rage. Curved, padded backs signaled a new search for comfort, freedom, and a more relaxed seating posture. Sitting comfortably did not mean sitting still: small movements were essential, and in portraits one sees this reflected in more relaxed placement of the legs, which were no longer always held straight. People began to sit less stiffly and self-consciously. Armrests were shortened and curved outward out of respect for women's clothing.[50] Louis XIV–style frames were imaginatively adapted to fit the human body. *L'Art du meuble* by the cabinetmaker Roubo codified the new principles of design. In the *bergère*, or wing chair, seat and armrests now became an arabesque enveloping the body. A settee with a mid-height back, sometimes wide enough to accommodate two people, became the *marquise*, or love seat. Architectural rigor was conjoined with suppleness; cushions further softened the appearance of seating. New designs proliferated: the *duchesse, gondole, canapé, sopha,* and *ottomane,* to name a few. These were suitable for relaxed, private conversation and socializing. A society given to wit and pleasure and in search of happiness in this world as opposed to the next invented a style that turned wood and textiles into light, supple, visually pleasing creations. The relative sobriety of the age of Louis XVI did not reverse these gains. It was not until the nineteenth century (and the mechanization of ornament) that furniture began to be conceived as isolated pieces with no definite relationship to their surroundings, and by then the idea of comfort was out of date.

Interior decoration was dominated by rococo. Neoclassicism lightened the style but did not replace it: it sought models in nature, archaeology, and erudite fantasy,[51] but it encountered resistance from people unwilling to give up their comfortable armchairs, including Louis XV at Versailles, who commissioned the work of many craftsmen. In any case, the charge that the new furniture was uncomfortable was open to discussion, as Roederer noted in his *Lettre sur les meubles à la mode* in 1802.[52] In general, the wealthy became accustomed to an ease of social intercourse that, in Paris at least, influenced the interiors of those lower down the social scale.[53]

New conveniences made life easier and more comfortable.[54] Interiors were redesigned to allow for greater functional diversity and privacy. Furniture designers adopted new styles permitting greater freedom of movement and more rational use, qualities evident in furniture designed for storage as well as for relaxation. And architects began to worry about odors, ventilation, heat, and light.[55] By the second half of the eighteenth century, the apartments of the wealthy had begun to reflect these new concerns. Various devices made it possible to regulate the flow of air into and out of rooms and to improve heating, ventilation, and lighting. People began thinking about water and bodily hygiene. Bathing was no longer exclusively a prerogative of the rich, although it was still a pleasure for sophisticated sensualists. Luxurious *salles d'eau* began to appear in the *hôtels* of the aristocracy, such as the Hôtel Verges in 1782, which had a tiled bathroom with hot and cold running water and a collection of paintings for decoration. The Hôtel de Vauvinaux on rue d'Anjou was similarly equipped.[56] All sorts of new comforts were appearing.[57] We can measure the impact of these changes by looking at the vocabulary of real estate advertisements: N. Coquery has analyzed those published in the *Petites Affiches* from 1755 to 1800.[58]

Published advertisements already contained all the information the market required: location, nature of property, description, and sometimes price. These notices reflected the varying pressures of supply and demand, changes in attitudes toward housing, and new perceptions of the city formulated by architects such as Patte, Soufflot, and Dewailly. The number of ads increased as the paper began to appear more frequently and the city itself grew: from 1,470 in 1755 (an average of 14 per issue), the number rose to 7,521 in 1782 and 10,459 in 1800. The press reflected a veritable real estate fever, which took the form of a sharp increase in rentals (65 percent of all ads in 1800); in 1755, 22 percent of ads concerned apartments as opposed to entire houses or *hôtels,* and the comparable figure for 1782 was 41 percent. All segments of the population were involved: professionals, shopkeepers, artisans, and rentiers, who accounted for 50 to 60 percent of all transactions. All sections of Paris figured in the ads, but the maps show that people were abandoning the boulevards as far back as 1782; the ads made a point of locations in the wealthier parishes and newer neighborhoods, reminding us that the city was growing.

We also discover that the insistence on comfort went hand in hand with increased specialization of living space. In 1755 twenty terms sufficed to identify different kinds of rooms. By 1782 it took twenty-seven, and by 1800 it was up to fifty. Descriptive precision went along with functional variety. The most notable shift, both quantitatively and qualitatively, involved hygiene: new terms included *garde-robe, cabinet de garde-robe, lieux d'aisance, lieux à l'anglaise, cabinet d'aisance, garde-robe à l'anglaise, cabinet de bain,* and *salle de bain.* Two other indicators also showed movement: terms pertaining to decor and ornamentation and terms pertaining to display and view. In 1755 these were mentioned 59 percent of the time, compared with 60 percent in 1782 and 82 percent in 1800. Thus it would appear that private homes were affected by changes comparable to those which revolutionized the look of the city as a whole, but even earlier.

By 1780 people in cities such as Paris and Caen were convinced that social happiness depended in part on urban organization. Theorists looked for solutions by analyzing ancient cities and studying symbols and allegories. Ancients and moderns agreed that the best plan was for the appearance of every part of the city to reflect the need that it served: "Architecture," wrote d'Alembert, "is merely the embellishment with which we hide our deepest needs."[59] Everyone agreed that one consequence of the emergence of new needs was that cities should stress well-being over splendor. These very concrete developments justify the title of this chapter, "Materializing the Intelligence, Abstracting Things," which is intended to suggest the organic unity of material life and culture and the convergence of all the arts. "The nature of the beloved earthly things amongst which we live is such that one cannot reject one without rejecting all the others."[60]

20

❦❦❦

Paris, Capital of the Enlightenment

THERE ARE TWO reasons for ending this book with a chapter on Paris. First, urban culture played an important role in the overall transformation that occurred in France in the eighteenth century. And second, the interpretation of urban culture has been a subject of controversy. Social and cultural historians need to explain how cities construct cultural identities. Clearly, culture has become one of the standard urban functions. There are many reasons for this, beginning with the traditional idea of the city as the matrix of civilization, "touched by the breath of spirit." This was true even in the eighteenth century, when a new feeling for nature and new images of the economy and society changed the way that people looked at cities and their populations. In *La Métropolitée*, published in Amsterdam in 1682, Alexandre Le Maître explained what distinguished a capital from other cities and what constituted the organic relationship between the capital and other parts of a state:

> Capital cities derive their life and glory from all parts of the state and repay all provinces in like kind. What the head is to the body, the prince to his subjects, heaven to earth, a metropolitan city is to towns and townships, villages and hamlets. The head works to preserve all the other members, and all the parts of the body cooperate and act in concert to sustain the head. The prince sacrifices his rest and energy to protect the honor, life, and belongings of his subjects, who are obliged, if need be, to immolate their possessions and their blood for the life

and glory of their prince, and who are like small veins pouring their money into his treasury, which the prince then pours back into all the parts of his state . . . The capital receives but also gives back. It acts, and it also suffers. Without it the state would be without glory, without majesty, without pomp, and without magnificence, forlorn, disorderly, and filled with injustice and plunder.

The capital, where the prince resides, cannot be seen, interpreted, or explained except by analogy with fundamental political relationships. What makes the capital the capital is the concentration of power: "the usual residence of the prince, the seat of Parlement and of the Académie, and center of commerce." Of course, Enlightenment Paris possessed only three of these four characteristics, but major government departments remained in the city even after Louis XV and the court returned to Versailles. Note the mention of the Académie, the symbol of intellectual activity, which Le Maître discusses in greater detail in his fourteenth and fifteenth chapters, on the utility of science and mathematics, and in his twenty-seventh and subsequent chapters on the various aspects of urban intellectual life: religious eloquence, law, medicine, science, philosophy, libraries, and gardens. In this highly "culturalist" vision of urban power, we recognize the essential role that major capitals are supposed to play in history. The very prestige and influence of great cities stems in the first place from material realities, their sheer volume, vitality, and mass: the quantitative becomes the qualitative. Enlightenment Paris amplified the effects of urbanity in general; its growing population, thriving social institutions, and extensive new construction yielded a vast outpouring of new data.

During the eighteenth century, the status of the capital attracted renewed interest as relations between Paris and the provinces took a peculiar turn. People became aware of disparities between cities of different sizes, and provincials began to think of their future as independent of the capital's.[1] Criticism of the capital became a literary leitmotif. In *La Méprise* (1734) Marivaux had written that "Paris is the world; the rest of the earth is nothing but its suburbs," but after 1760, many voices rose in opposition to this myth of the ideal city. That couple of which the seventeenth century had been much enamored, the court and the city, suddenly faced stiff competition. In 1759 Fougeret de Montbron published *La Capitale des Gaules ou la Nouvelle Babylone*, sixty-seven pages of vitriol poured out on Paris. The book broached all the criticisms that we find later in the work of Rousseau, Grimm, Fabre d'Eglantine, and even Mme Necker, who wrote *Les Inconvénients de la vie de Paris* in 1778. A delightful place for the rich, Paris was hell for the poor—and also for horses. Fougeret attacked the city for its luxury, social shortcomings, lack of charity, toadying courtiers, and contribution to the depopulation and wretchedness of the countryside. He was the first to paint a portrait of daily life in the city as simultaneously luxurious and sordid, "picturesque" (the word was new at the time) and animated.[2]

Historians of culture have looked at changes in Paris in two ways. Some insist on the importance of social differentiation, noting the coexistence of high and low culture and of bourgeois and aristocratic culture. Others look for signs of convergence and homogeneity, for a transformation common to all the Parisians who were soon to effect and experience a decisive political change. To reconcile the two points of view, it is best to consider the unequal distribution of cultural opportunities with an eye to constructing oppositions but without invoking the revolution to come; here as elsewhere, presentiments cannot stand in for certitudes that did not yet exist. Three facts make this a particularly interesting area of investigation: the magnitude of the phenomenon (Paris was a beacon not only to France but to all of Europe), the complexity of the urban organism, and the ways in which the spirit of the age affected behavior and things.

Volume, Space, and Time in Paris

The "capital of capitals" stood out first of all for its sheer physical size and vitality. The exact population of the city has been a subject of lengthy controversy, since no census was ever taken, and there are too few documents to which one can apply demographic methods. For the sake of argument, let us accept the estimate of the more conservative statisticians, who put the population of the city in 1780 at 700,000, though the methods used to arrive at this figure are open to doubt.[3] One problem is the difficulty of measuring the vast influx of new residents and the significant size of the "floating population." In the seventeenth century, parish priests began to keep annual records of baptisms, marriages, and births, and these records have been the object of intense speculation by demographers ever since the eighteenth century (Deparcieux, Expilly,

Buffon, La Michodière, Lavoisier, and des Pommelles, to name a few). The records appear to show that in less than a hundred years the population of the capital increased by 100,000 to 150,000 owing to the influx of newcomers who chose to remain. No estimate has yet been given of the number of visitors and temporary immigrants who returned home after a brief stay, taking with them at the very least the *air de Paris*, if not a more durable change.

Newcomers and visitors helped to convey the fascination of the city to the folks back home. The society was complex and not easy to describe: there were domestics (the abbé d'Expilly put their number at close to 35,000 at midcentury), soldiers, laborers, seasonal workers, the permanently and temporarily unemployed, tourists *avant la lettre*, lawyers, students, and men of letters: Paris was a vast caravansary. Demographic change implied cultural exchange, as people from many different places came to Paris and mingled with one another. The influence worked two ways, moreover: many visitors took new customs home with them, and the effects of travel were magnified by the widely read literature of guidebooks, city almanacs, travelogues, and even novels about travel. Because Paris was centrally located and drew immigrants and supplies from a vast area, it embodied all the problems associated with the new social mobility.

There can be no doubt that the spread of innovation associated with this mobility was linked to the complexity of Parisian society, a complexity that was already attracting the attention of analysts. The twelve volumes and more than four thousand pages of Louis-Sébastien Mercier's *Tableau de Paris* still have much to teach us on this score. We learn, for example, of the apparent chaos of the city and of many symbols of disorder, which caused people to study behavior and consumption patterns in search of a political solution. We witness the birth of a method of social observation that was partly ethical, partly political, torn between absolute values and practical choices. Mercier's close scrutiny of the urban organism revealed glaring contrasts, incompatible customs, differences of theoretical and practical knowledge, and conflicts with numerous ramifications in space and time. We also find that new social and economic values were being transmitted in two directions, from the top to the bottom and from the center to the periphery of society. This brings up a theoretical problem involving the apparent divorce between Paris's role as a center of consumption and demand and its role as an economic metropolis: because the cultural and social center did not coincide with the center of the economy, Paris may not have been a capital of the "world economy."

There can be no doubt that Parisians controlled a significant portion of France's wealth, and they paid more taxes than other Frenchmen, an average of 140 livres according to Necker and 120 according to Lavoisier.[4] The variety of the city's functions can be seen in Lavoisier's 1791 calculations of France's "territorial wealth": out of a total net income of 300 million livres per year (not counting payments for services within the capital or income on private loans), 33 percent came from manufacturing, marketing, and sales of real estate, 20 percent from rent, and the rest from wages, interest, and disbursements from the royal treasury. Every year Paris consumed some 260 million livres worth of merchandise and dominated the financial market with bonds, loans to the Church and monarchy, and other loans from sources that ranged from small lenders to farmers-general and major Protestant bankers.[5] The 1780s were a time of febrile speculation, intensified trading, and countless technological and industrial initiatives: "The increase in the monetary mass, accompanied by intense speculation on negotiable securities, proved profitable, if not to all the contractors and entrepreneurs in Paris, then at least to those who had nothing to fear from the English competition unleashed by the commercial treaty of 1788." The city's industrial base was still fragile despite the boost to manufacturing from increased consumption of quality textiles, books, fashion articles, furniture, hardware, metals, porcelain, and glassware. Nevertheless, the capital's role in production and marketing needs to be reevaluated.[6]

Economies of scale were compounded by temporal disparities: the social and cultural reality of the capital was a complex web of interacting temporalities woven by social intercourse in all its forms. The city itself was a composite of different time frames, a human construct in which duration was frozen in stone, and space was experienced in different ways by the horseman and the pedestrian, the coachman and the dandy at the reins of his tilbury, the stagecoach passenger and the harried worker, the policeman on his rounds and the nocturnal observer (such as Rétif de La Bretonne in *Les Nuits*), the tavernkeeper and the quarrelsome journeyman (such as Jacques-Louis Ménétra).

It was in the eighteenth century that man's relation to the space in which he lived was codified and instrumentalized with maps and plans, guidebooks and directories, house numbers and street names (which made it easier to find specific locations despite the growing urban sprawl). Jèze, the publisher of an *Etat ou Tableau de la ville de Paris*, organized information about the city under three heads: "necessity," "utility," and "pleasure." Necessities were those things essential to subsistence, security, and reproduction. Spiritual aids were just as necessary to the soul as physical aids were to the body. Useful things included education (the elements of which were enumerated), the arts, and commerce. Pleasures included shows, walks, concerts, monuments, gardens, and cafés. Crowning the entire edifice was the political and civil "administration," both secular and religious. The Jèze reader thus understood space to be a juxtaposition of various means of fulfilling the many purposes, recreational as well as productive, of both individuals and groups.

Thus the city was experienced as a series of overlapping temporalities, which revealed themselves either simultaneously or in succession. There was church time, in which the organization of the world reflected the eternity of salvation: it was still a daily presence, marked by everyday religious acts as well as by the highly symbolic round of religious holidays. There was also the time of the marketplace, where memory coexisted with action and self-expression with self-control: in recreational activities, celebrations, and riots, people constructed a relation to the present that drew on imagination and myth. And there was economic time—working hours, shipping delays, and so on—the time of traders whose interests reached to the ends of the known world, and the time of artisans whose corporate idiom reflected a certain conception of work and an economic philosophy torn between supervised monopoly and the free market. And finally there was the fluid time of cultural commerce and intellectual exchange, where thought and sociability came together: it gave the century its meaning and justification and gave Paris a leading role as the capital of change.

Once again, the only way we can grasp the practices of the past is through a series of reinterpretations, inventions, and improvisations, a process that resembles everyday life more than it does clear, rational argument. Although it is true that things may have happened at the same time, it is also clear that change did not proceed at the same pace for everyone, from the most rudimentary intellects to the most enlightened minds. In everyday life people met with resistance, just as they did in science. Sometimes the going was slow, while at other times the pace of change picked up. Paris was both the capital of fashion and the place where philosophy became fashionable.

Cultural change can be analyzed in terms of relationships, a preference for change over stability, and the interaction between material and intellectual culture. The reason I choose to look at relationships instead of giving a social analysis of cultural forms is that the latter task has already been performed quite well: the work of Jean Chagniot, Arlette Farge, Jeffrey Kaplow, Stephen Kaplan, and M. Sonnenscher has given us an excellent social topography of Parisian culture. The difficulty right now is to think of Parisian society not as clearly structured (whether by orders, classes, or groups) but as a fluid milieu organized by shifting relationships: contrasts and similarities, antagonisms and convergences. That a particular individual belongs to a particular group is never clear; we need to look at social networks and trajectories if we are to get a handle on how the city itself organized social interaction. The coexistence of diverse temporalities associated with different individuals, groups, and classes suggests a society divided in various ways yet at the same time tending to create homogeneity. The civilizing of manners and the emergence of public opinion are the two most obvious manifestations of this. Both required changes in the cultural attitudes of men and women. The process was one of integration into a new culture, which in turn triggered a response.[7] I do not mean to suggest that this can be understood in terms of popular versus elite or active versus passive or open-minded versus closed-minded. We must rather look at how individuals were transformed by successive experiences. This requires understanding how and where they moved and how long-term processes interacted with specific events.

In Paris, opinions and habits changed, but not at the same pace for all. So did ideas and behavior, political practice and the material environment. The new freedom in family relations and other private interactions seems to me just as important as the conquest of intellectual independence, because, as I have tried to show several times, there was constant interchange between the two spheres. The connection is clear when one looks at reactions to fashion and the debate over luxury: the "culture of appearances" and social uses of clothing can serve as indices, clearly legible yet fundamentally ambiguous, to social values in general and to the conception of the body social as either an organic hierarchy or a civil society. Popular political practices can be used in a similar way: demonstrations and uprisings raise questions about the "moral economy" and culture of the marketplace, the conception of order, and attitudes toward society. Habits of dress reveal the ethics of a society. They can tell us about politics and the demand for liberty and equality.[8] Social turmoil, whether spontaneous or premeditated, gives physical reality to social representations and to notions of order and disorder: the mob reminds the authorities of the rules and sometimes succeeds in enforcing them.[9] I hope that the reader will indulge the vagueness of the foregoing remarks, which are meant simply to recall themes I touched on earlier and will now return to, by way of conclusion, in the Parisian context. In what follows, as in what came before, the central topics are the cultural effects of increased social mobility and accelerated social change and the interaction between culture and politics.

Roots and Identity

Paris, like every other city, reveals the layering of time. Duration is embodied in institutions, or what Pierre Nora aptly calls "lieux de mémoire," sites of memory. Every one of these institutions has a history, a symbolic weight, a source of energy, a spatial extension, a set of practices, and perhaps a network of clients. They may be housed in or represented by monuments—monuments that sometimes take on an independent existence. In the eighteenth century, for example, a bureaucratic and administrative space came into existence in former aristocratic palaces and *hôtels* in Paris. The change in the use of these buildings did not spell an end to their former prestige. In the Louvre, a onetime royal residence, the king housed his academies, including the Académie Française, the Académie des Sciences, the Société Royale de Médecine, and the finest artists and artisans in the kingdom. Much of Parisian culture depended on people's ability to relate to practices associated with these institutions. Social diversification structured these relations, but at the same time institutional activities reshaped the culture.

Religion and Tradition

In Paris, the capital, there was little or no conflict between the temporal and religious authorities: the two coexisted and acted in concert to civilize the people and suppress excesses such as convulsionary Jansenism. The presence of the sacred in the monumental and the vast and enormously valuable real estate holdings of the Church offer striking evidence of the spiritualization of space, yet within that space secular and de-Christianized practices were commonplace. Cathedrals, churches and chapels, abbeys, convents, monasteries, hospitals, and schools were all part of this religious space, as were crosses and statues, holiday celebrations and processions, pilgrimages and miracles, and, last but not least, cemeteries, which became an object of bitter controversy when an administration bent on improving public health attacked these places of worship and commemoration and tried to banish the dead from the sight of the living. Parishes, schools, and hospitals played a particularly important role in shaping representations of the world and influencing social reproduction.

In Paris, the parish provided the framework for the complex religious activities of Christians, or rather Catholics, since Parisian Protestants could practice their faith only in private, primarily in the residences of foreign ambassadors. The vitality of a parish was reflected in charities and bequests, but it did not necessarily obey the rules of space. Parish boundaries followed old political boundaries. People who lived far from the main church often preferred to worship at a chapel or convent. An excessive number of small parishes impeded unity. "Too many churches in the center, too few on the periphery: this was a problem in all old cities."[10] This situation created inequalities within the diocese. What sort of relationship could the curé of Saint-Sulpice, who was more powerful than a provincial prelate, have with the 100,000 or 120,000 members of his congregation? "All Parisian curés are minor bishops," Mercier noted.

There were probably about 1,200 secular clergy, 1,000 regular clergy, and 2,500 nuns in Paris. The typical parishioner knew the unbeneficed priests, vicars, and religious better than the curés and chapter canons. The bishop, for his part, reigned over this entire realm, including fifty-four parishes, four hospitals recording baptisms, and 136 religious houses open to the faithful. Once the conflicts of the early eighteenth century had settled down, the clergy, scattered about the city in much the same way as before, formed a loosely knit group to which Paris offered plenty of career opportunities in the form of numerous benefices and countless official tasks. It was against this backdrop that individuals defined their relation to religion, as Ménétra informs us:

Before tying the knot and putting myself into the harness of marriage, I had a lot of trouble over the wretched *billet de confession*. [There could be no sacrament without a *billet,* which could be obtained only from one's parish, but Ménétra, whose reputation in the parish was poor, could not get one.] Finally, a person I happened to know got me one from a Recollect father in exchange for a few bottles of wine and three books, and I was over the hurdle.

Here we see how a man accustomed to expressing himself freely could allow his anticlericalism to show, but it is also clear that some obligations were inescapable: Father Basuel, the priest who refused to issue the required *billet de confession,* had known Ménétra all his life, and it comes as no surprise that he refused to grant the journeyman either absolution or certification thereof. In Paris there were ways around such obstacles: a certificate could be obtained from a mendicant friar, and the wedding could be held in the church of Ménétra's intended rather than in his home parish.

Christian life depended heavily on the *oeuvre,* or charity fund, main- tained by the parish council, whose members included the parish elite: aristocrats, bourgeois, merchants, and/or artisans, depending on the na- ture of the parish. To belong to the council was a mark of religious commitment, but a costly one, since membership required a substantial donation. After Ménétra had settled in as a master glazier in the parish of Saint-Sauveur, he was approached:

There was a fellow by the name of Bertrand, a master button maker, who was constantly after me to join the confraternity of Saint-Prix, which had set itself up in the parish of Saint-Sauveur. The faith of our fathers was awfully contradictory to have combined in one church a fellow who escaped and a fellow who got caught [Ménétra is punning on *sauveur* and *prix,* "runaway" and "captured"]. You realize how simple they must have been to have combined two so-called saints with such contradictory names. And they wanted to put my name in as a churchwarden of the Holy Sacrament . . . Never having been a pillar of the church, and having very little faith in all clergymen and their beliefs, I had no interest in joining.

Disaffected in practice and critical of church dogma, the glazier in- dulges in anticlerical puns, but his words also show the importance of the parish elite, the way in which new members were recruited, and the influence of true "pillars of the church" and the clergy-controlled confraternities to which they belonged. Just as some parishes were more important than others, not all parishioners were equal: parish council members wielded more influence than the merely devout, who in turn outranked those whose attendance at church was merely dutiful and, a fortiori, those who were estranged from the faith. Certain parishes had traditions of their own, whether "Jansenist" (Saint-Germain-l'Auxerrois, Saint-Médard) or "constitutional" (Saint-Sulpice, Saint-Eustache). Some were more orthodox than others. Some were more tolerant of "popular libertinage" (concubinage, common-law marriage) or "aristocratic" ways (meaning, in some cases, outright debauchery). Respect for form depended on such forces. Wills show that people were less and less attached to traditional religious forms, although in some communities burial customs remained unchanged and belief in miracles persisted. In Paris the educational system and Church charities influenced the evolution of customary practices.

By dint of enormous efforts on the part of the Church, most boys and some girls were able to attend school, as their parents wished. There was a wide range of educational institutions: choir schools, parish schools that charged tuition and were supervised by the head cantor (and in which 402 schoolmasters and mistresses were employed in 1790), charity schools founded by parish priests, secular boarding schools, *collèges* staffed by the teaching congregations, seminaries, and girls' schools run by nuns. Nearly all boys between the ages of seven and fourteen attended one of the smaller schools, though only 10 to 15 percent continued beyond that; a substantial number of girls also received an education. Two problems were never resolved: the relation between schools that charged tuition and those that did not (lack of room in free schools meant that some children who wished to attend could not); and the relative scarcity of educational opportunities for young women, despite definite advances in the education of girls in Paris.[11] Education was a success among the well-to-do elite and socially integrated workers: it trained young Christians of both sexes, prepared youths for the workplace, and on the whole kept people in their place while enhancing their ability to think. Hence the social structure was reproduced, with upward mobility for a minority, but at the same time there was change owing to the acquisition of basic knowledge by growing numbers of people. Paris schools trained docile and industrious students, but they also turned out individuals who eluded norms, contributed to growth, and displayed open if not downright critical minds, like Ménétra.

Still, a significant portion of the population was not fully integrated into society. Paris was the "capital of the poor," a situation that pointed up the failures as well as the successes of migration. There was no shortage of traditional Christian charities to aid the poor: many were able to overcome their hardships in the parish without becoming a burden on the various branches of the Hôpital Général, which saw the number of people it served increase from nine thousand in 1700 to fifteen thousand in 1789.[12] Charitable institutions adhered to the tradition of confining the poor but responded to the growing insistence on more individualized treatment. Even as almsgiving decreased, the poor tax declined, and challenges were raised to the practices of the older hospitals; new private initiatives were launched, new charitable organizations developed, and charity was increasingly secularized. Society accepted the lumping together of paupers and criminals, but at the same time it experimented with new forms of philanthropy that attest to the permanence of the charitable impulse. Public opinion called on the state to aid the poor and recognize their right to work. Meanwhile, the indigent remained a frightening menace. In dealing with the poor, Paris remained wedded to Christian tradition even as it questioned the adequacy of older forms of charity.

Urban Space and Living Space

Because the Ancien Régime created new institutions without abolishing old ones, their number in Paris proliferated. As capital of the tertiary sector, the city offered a job market unlike any other. Relations of dependency and domination were plainly visible. And astute observers like Mercier could divine the social hierarchy from subtle differences in the things people consumed. Forces of emulation and necessity operated on three levels: everyday life, political regulation, and social hierarchy.

Home, street, and neighborhood were the principal arenas of everyday life, or what Arlette Farge calls "fragile life." It would be misleading to say that the lives of the working poor were ruled by necessity while people of property were always civilized in their behavior. The distinctive character of popular life was shaped by family and work.[13] People in poor neighborhoods mingled constantly and watched one another closely, with an eye to protecting the "family honor." Mercier saw the poor man's home as freedom's refuge because the poor were not slaves to calculation, and in many poor families the wife had arrived only recently from the countryside and was still close to nature. True emotional warmth and sexual intimacy could exist within the economic and social unit known as the family. But it was not all sweetness and light. There was also conflict, as we know from countless cases that came to the attention of the authorities for the usual reasons such as violence and drunkenness as well as new reasons that tell us about changes in the division of household chores. In the workplace life was still marked by mobility, frequent job changes, shifting social relationships, and clashes between the authority of employers and the freedom of their employees. As Farge shows in her description of this "fragile life," everyday customs reflect "all the ways in which society dramatizes alliances and ruptures," solidarity and conflict. Feelings were of course not limited to the wealthy and cultivated, and their specific coloration in various milieus revealed the overlapping of different cultural spheres.

The different cultural spheres were in turn subject to political regulation. The city's police played an important role in this regard. Paris's twenty *quartiers* were policed by forty *commissaires*, backed up by *inspecteurs* who reported directly to the *lieutenant de police*. Parisians turned first to the *commissaires*, who recorded complaints, information, and requests for assistance. They had their fingers on the pulse of the neighborhoods, whose moods they gauged and whose ordinary outbreaks of violence they dealt with. The *inspecteurs* took a broader view of the city as a whole. Berryer grouped them into *sections* with specialized functions, and their main responsibilities were to deal with organized crime and vice *(libertinages)*. As representatives of the magistrates, the police were responsible for more than just surveillance. They regulated daily life in "a myriad of small ways."[14] They enforced economic regulations and ideological and social controls and assisted in matters of administration and security. Eyes and ears were essential for preventing disorder and crime before it happened. The police dreamed of a systematic method of surveillance, and one constable, Guillauté, proposed keeping a file on every house in the city with information useful to the authorities. After 1750 there can be no doubt that the city was safe thanks to improved lighting, increased patrols (which often included French and Swiss guardsmen), and an extensive network of paid informers and spies, who kept the authorities informed about the vices of the aristocracy as well as the mischief of the working class. The goal of the police was to make sure that everyone behaved in a way appropriate to his or her age and status.[15] A model for all of Europe, the Paris police did not so much combat crime as govern it. The criminal element adapted to the system with a variety of ruses, while the people remained on their guard. Attitudes toward the police varied: people wanted protection from violence, but they rejected any perceived abuse of authority, sometimes violently, as in the riots triggered by the alleged "abduction of children" by the police in 1749–50, and the disturbances that erupted at the city's customs barriers in 1787–88. In the latter half of the eighteenth century, the overweening police force seems to have lost some of the confidence that the police had enjoyed earlier.

The city's institutions enjoyed a remarkable longevity. For men who dreamed of office as their life's ambition, these institutions were still a source of pride, but in reality they were a mere facade. Without free elections, the *prévôt des marchands* (roughly equivalent to mayor), aldermen, and councilors of Paris cannot be regarded as true representatives of the people.[16] A relic of the past, the bourgeois militia found itself unable even to recruit officers among the neighborhood elite. The city corporation could absorb only a few members of the bourgeoisie who aspired to municipal office: ten offices were reserved for officers of the courts, *maîtres des requêtes,* and royal secretaries; only thirty-two were open to the bourgeois elite, the merchants of the Six Corps, lawyers, notaries, and wealthy rentiers. These honors were avidly sought, but they were hardly an expression of political freedom. Elections were tightly controlled, and electors were not only handpicked but also subject to influence by the court; the *prévôt des marchands* was appointed, moreover. Nevertheless, the post of alderman and certain other municipal offices were attractive because they conferred nobility, yielded considerable income (both overt and covert), and afforded a measure of symbolic and administrative influence. The municipal authorities still organized holiday celebrations and performed other important functions: *ratione loci,* or surveillance of the quays, docks, and boulevards; and *ratione materiae,* or oversight of the food supply, taxes, loans, river traffic, and public works projects, which proliferated as the city grew.

Three things undermined the old municipal institutions, however.

First, the municipal corporation was in no way representative and was for the most part impotent in the face of royal authority. Second, its competence was questioned: it was difficult to tell who was responsible for what, regardless of whether offices were shared among many people or concentrated in the hands of a single individual. And third, the power of the municipality was merely symbolic compared with that of the police, backed by the royal army. After 1780 the monarchy tightened its control over the Paris region without opposition from the traditional elite or the courts, for the maneuver was seen as repairing defects in the old system rather than as extending royal power into new areas. The royal government intervened in Paris in such a way as to keep up the appearance of municipal independence, but its reinforced sovereignty did not succeed in controlling public opinion in the 1780s.[17]

Within Parisian society, hierarchical prerogatives remained fundamental. The observer can choose among several ways of interpreting the city's social hierarchy. Regardless of whether we look at the scale of rents or at the range of wealth as calculated from marriage contracts, estate inventories, and the poor tax, we discover that wealth and status were related and that the city of the rich partly overlapped the city of the poor. When Marcel Reinhart looked at rents for 1788–89, he found that 58 percent fell between forty and two hundred livres for a one-room apartment. Although most people lived in one or two rooms, a good third of the population inhabited comfortable apartments or *hôtels*. The integrated bourgeoisie—the "host of busy, virtuous men who are not corrupted by either opulence or misery," those who would later be called *citoyens actifs*—inhabited apartments that rented for less than two hundred livres. Rich and poor had yet to be separated by the expansion of the city, for the industrious center still combined all the elements of the old tradition. Luxury and indigence rubbed shoulders daily.

This diversity provided an ideal setting for the new science of social observation as practiced by Louis-Sébastien Mercier. Three forms of sensibility were here combined: an aesthetic eye, which saw the urban landscape as organized in terms of masses, volumes, colors, and forms; a medical eye, which applied the diagnostic techniques of medical science to the urban organism; and a social eye, which seized on the occasions offered by urban life to make social judgments. Among those occasions were the religious procession, a spectacle of display, an opportunity to admire the opulence of the Church, but at the same time a "sacrilege for the poor"; and the exchange of glances in the street, whether between people of importance taking one another's measure or people of no account shunning one another's gaze. Submission or insolence, disorder or order, ability or inability: these were the things that city people were always on the lookout for, as Jacques-Louis Ménétra informs us.[18] They were always searching for value contrasts that shaped behavior: contrasts of exchange value, use value, symbolic value, or sign value.[19] For the author of the *Tableau de Paris*, urban society was governed by rules, which he hoped to discover. His "sociology *avant la lettre*" relied on comparing the kinds of commodities that different people consumed and on demonstrating the interdependence of various social roles. The society he describes is a society not of orders but of classes, which can be multiplied by invoking finer and finer criteria.[20] Traditional Parisian society was reshaped by the forces of emulation, distinction, and choice.

The Sensibility of the Marketplace

The value system of the age achieved its most lasting expression in the culture of the marketplace. This had three defining characteristics: it was open to all; it allowed for public forms of expression, such as processions and institutional assemblies, which revealed the structure of society; and it was a culture of spectacle, which combined the values of the market with those of liberality, the values of labor with those of leisure, and the values of the imagination with those of the concrete. From the street to the fairground and the sideshow to the festival, space and behavior were restructured. The streets of Paris captured the attention of its citizens in any number of ways. A simple walk was a show unto itself. Shopwindows, quacks hawking their remedies, posters advertising some event— Paris appealed to both the eye and the ear.

Song was an essential ingredient of Parisian culture. People learned music in many ways: in church choirs, at the Opéra's singing school, in private lessons given by dancing teachers and musicians, at the confraternity of Saint-Julien-des-Ménétriers (which vanished in 1776), and from concerts and opera. Music and singing lessons were part of the "proper upbringing" of children in well-to-do homes. Through the church and workplace music also became part of the repertoire of ordinary people. Published anthologies of song, such as Maurepas's, show the political importance of what people sang. Common people sometimes composed their own songs, as the example of Ménétra once again shows, but mostly they took their music from others, often anonymous songwriters, whose compositions were known to people of all classes.[21] The better the music fit the words, the more easily the song circulated. Songs with repeated refrains were the easiest to remember. In every religious and political debate from the Regency to the crisis of the 1780s, songs played a part. Tunes were constantly recycled, not just for reasons of musical economy but also because the recycling helped to give point to the song's informational content. New words could always be adapted to existing melodies, and a familiar tune was easy to learn and therefore circulated more readily. There were two types of song, two circuits of production, and two circles of diffusion. One, such as newspapers and gazettes, reached a large audience, while the other was confined mainly to the court and ruling circles. Sometimes a successful or significant song crossed over from one circuit to the other, and these crossovers tell us something about the way in which public opinion was formed.

We can observe similar types of convergence in the fairground theater.[22] This type of theater was closely linked to the market, the consumer economy, and the flow of goods. Its stock-in-trade was urban satire, and its success depended on the mingling of different audiences. The theaters of the Saint-Germain, Saint-Ovide, and Saint-Laurent fairgrounds drew spectators of both sexes and of all ages and ranks. They aroused the curiosity of all. The fairground was a place whose status was ambiguous, like that of the boulevards and the Palais-Royal, where spectacles were also staged after 1770: it was a center of commerce but also a place for people to enjoy themselves freely. There was an essential connection between spending money on useful goods and "squandering" it on a show.[23] The mix of genres, the use of burlesque and parody, the contrast with the traditional hierarchies of the legitimate theater, the emphasis on the body and physical strength, and the taste for the strange and exotic proved to be a formula for durable success. The traditional idea of the world as stage and of the theater as a metaphor for the world, upon which philosophers and moralists commented endlessly, was corroborated by the rituals of urban life. Meanwhile, the theater advertised new consumer goods and instructed people in the rules of the marketplace and of propriety.

In Paris, older forms of entertainment survived, new audiences came together (not only in the theater but also in taverns and cafés), and the producers of new spectacles availed themselves of both the spoken word and visual decor, elements made familiar by centuries of religious and urban ritual. Processions and rituals had always defined a public sphere of representation, but already that sphere was being reshaped by new cultural and economic values and by the imposition of novel hierarchies. Between the street and the theater there was a structural continuity in both decor and roles, but this would give way to a new definition of the social personality based on a different equilibrium between public and private.[24]

Politics and Culture: Confusion and Interference

The population of Paris acquired a common culture through joint action. Residents shared a long memory embodied in monuments, traditions, customs, images, and social occasions. Civilization and Christianization had fostered self-control and curtailed violence.

Power dramatized itself in the spectacle of executions, which intimidated potential lawbreakers but also accustomed and desensitized people to the sight of suffering and death. In *Les Nuits de Paris*, Rétif de La Bretonne tells the story of his going to the place de Grève to witness the execution of three men condemned to be broken on the wheel. The fact that this spectacle of torture was staged at night is already a sign of a change in sensibility, that of the author and the cultivated classes. Rétif cannot stand the sight of such barbarity and turns away, but he sees in the faces of his fellow spectators that they are insensible to what is happening, laughing and talking as the men are subjected to horrible suffering. In particular, a young girl becomes the object of his wrath because she makes fun of the screams and gesticulations of the condemned men. Beneath the civilized surface lurk the old terrors: the logic of vengeance has simply been ritualized and turned into a collective act.

Court society did its part to standardize ways of thinking and acting. In the vision of society promoted by the state and enforced by its police, the prince was at the center of everything. Dependency defined the hierarchy of rank; differentiated customs represented it. But the city was also structured by old forms: the *corps* controlled by the king had powerful memories; the aristocracy, which was by no means ruined by economic development as Norbert Elias believed, had its powers of resistance; the old corporations remained active and preserved their economic power without constituting a totally unified milieu of shared interests and practices. The city was also being reshaped by new forces: the values of work, the merits of enterprise and entrepreneurs, the appeal of freedom and economic success, the retreat into privacy, the spread of utilitarian and secular values. Three factors contributed to the cultural confusion and interference that Mercier investigated: the overall increase in cultural capital, the acceleration of circulation, and the tension between public and private affairs. Out of these developments grew a new relationship between culture and politics.

The Cultural Capital of Parisians

As a result of education and the transforming influence of various elites, the people of Paris had the means to examine their own situation and promote their own fortune. Cultural institutions became substantially more productive between the time of Louis XIV and that of Louis XVI, and Parisians became substantially more literate. A majority knew how to read and write, as marriage contracts, wills, and estate inventories prove. By the end of the seventeenth century, people in the upper and middle strata of society could sign these documents. Overall, under Louis XIV, 85 percent of men signed their wills and 60 percent of women; under Louis XVI the comparable figures were 90 and 80 percent, respectively. Estate inventories of the lower classes corroborate this progress, but these figures should not be allowed to conceal the existence of a nonintegrated population, the majority of which was illiterate. The overall literacy of the capital depended on three things, which deserve a closer look in the form of a thorough study of marriage contracts: where people were born (the implication being that improved literacy depended on improved schooling throughout the region from which Paris drew immigrants); the length of time and manner in which their families had lived in the city; and their occupational skills and family ability to avoid social failure. Marginality and poverty, recent arrival from the provinces, marital difficulties, and even large numbers of children: these were the factors that created ghettos of illiteracy. But by and large people read, and needed to read. Listen to Rétif as Monsieur Nicolas is received by his neighbor:

"Well, sir, you must be very learned. Do you know a book entitled *Les Sept Trompettes?*"

"Yes, sir."

"It is an excellent book."

"People no longer admire it as much as they used to."

"That is because the world is so corrupt. But surely people like Father Caussin's *La Cour sainte.* Now that's a book!"

"Not much more than *Les Sept Trompettes:* people see that book as nothing more than an uncritical collection of fables."

"You're joking, sir! It is the most beautiful book I ever read."

"That may be, sir."

"Do me a favor and tell me what people admire nowadays."

"People speak highly, sir, of Buffon's *Histoire naturelle,* of Voltaire's tragedies, of Rousseau's *Emile* and *Héloïse,* and of Racine's tragedies; and of a few of Corneille's, some of Prévost's novels, and Madame Riccoboni's, and Lesage's, and of Marmontel's *Contes moraux.*"

"I don't know any of those books! The world has changed greatly without my being aware of it."

In this dialogue between a devout old man of forty-five and a young typesetter we see not only the appearance of a generation gap but also the multiplication of the city's attractions.

Paris encouraged people to read not only to acquire information but also to improve themselves. The ability to read, write, do sums, and reflect on events—normal accomplishments of the literate and well-to-do—became less uncommon for everyone owing to certain obligations linked to the economy, public life, and the family. For one thing, there was the obligation to work: good jobs and prospects for advancement were already associated with culture. Labor regulations made it essential for workers to be able to deal with the related paperwork: certificates, proofs, certifications of good behavior and morals, applications for leave, and before long the first *livret,* or workman's record book. In a variety of occupations workers had to deal with accounts, estimates, and correspondence if they wished to be paid their due. Advertisements for jobs called for educated servants and workers. Public life imposed similar requirements: one had to be able to read posted notices in order to learn about new laws, the prices of goods, and schedules of shows. The police posted regulations, and Parlement posted important political and legal decisions.

Some of these ubiquitous posters were read more carefully than others.[25] Reading newspapers, on a daily basis after the launch of the *Journal de Paris* in 1776, provided all sorts of information. Papers could be read in cafés and reading rooms, or out loud in more or less public settings. Finally, private life offered opportunities for writing letters: people wrote to their families back home, lovers wrote to each other, and young tradesmen courted women with amorous notes.

As the written word circulated, it conveyed information that transformed society. No aspect of Parisian life went untouched. Here, the work of the official academic institutions had an impact, even though it directly affected only scholars and men of letters—citizens of the Republic of Letters. Because of the way the academies worked, however, and their penchant for calling in experts to propose remedies for urban ills, their influence extended far beyond this immediate audience. Hence, as both Rétif and Mercier observed, the people approved of their government, but only partially; after all, the king favored innovation, science, and utility: "A fine thing, balloons!" (Rétif).

Sharing Cultural Resources

Access to cultural resources was determined by ability and status, economics and connections. Culture was a delicate thing, more readily available to those with family and professional ties to Paris. Three avenues of access were open to everyone: printed matter, theaters, and music.

Paris was the capital of print—of its production certainly and probably also of its consumption. Over the course of the century more than 100,000 titles were published by Parisian printers (including both new editions and reprints). Through use of the *privilège*, or official authorization to publish, the authorities had encouraged concentration of the publishing industry in the capital and granted printers the copyrights to official and well-known texts. This small and wealthy group of royal favorites was reluctant to risk printing any of the more audacious Enlightenment texts without solid official backing, and even then only with caution. But the established printers were prodded, particularly after 1750, by successful newcomers such as Duchesne, Robin, Merlin, and of course Panckoucke, who built a publishing empire on the popularization of the Enlightenment. Demand from the Parisian market soon attracted provincial printers as well, some of whom produced less costly counterfeits of well-known works while others published banned religious and philosophical works. J.-D. Mellot's study of the publishing industry in Rouen shows how the process worked.[26] With the complicity of local authorities and support from one another, Norman booksellers circumvented the censors and supplied books to readers in the capital, while at the same time perhaps encouraging a redistributive exchange that altered the reading habits of provincials and Parisians alike. The lesson was not lost on publishers outside France in places such as Liège, Bouillon, and above all Neuchâtel, who found the lure of the Paris market irresistible, particularly after 1760.

Reading in Paris was not an exclusively private activity, and Parisians did not read only the books they themselves owned. There were many ways to gain access to reading material. Perhaps a quarter of the population owned books, to judge by estate inventories. People read in many places: at school, in churches, at home, in the workshop, and in the street. There were libraries for the scholarly and curious, the Bibliothèque du Roi being the foremost among them, but the majority found other opportunities to read, as Mercier recounts:

> People are definitely reading ten times as much in Paris as they did a hundred years ago, if you consider the host of small bookshops, scattered here and there in little street-corner booths or sometimes right out in the open, that sell old books or some of the new brochures that are constantly appearing. You see groups of readers clustered around the counter as if held there by a magnet. They get in the way of the merchant, who has removed all the chairs so that the customers have to remain standing. But still they stay for hours on end, perusing books, leafing through brochures, and offering opinions on their quality and fate.[27]

This feverish desire to read troubled the author of *L'An 2040*, who expressed the belief that the ability to read, which fostered an ability to argue, ought to be drastically curtailed. Many businesses developed to meet the needs of the exploding market: lending libraries charged fees and cut books into parts in order to rent them to more readers simultaneously; reading rooms offered a variety of fare and sold annual subscriptions for the right to consult newspapers on the premises. "The hands of the multitude are sullying the great works": clearly the general cultural level had risen.

The theaters of Paris contributed to this by establishing a hierarchy of spectacles and audiences.[28] Rétif remarked on this while denouncing the jostling and indecency of fairground theaters, in which he observed an audience composed "of workers, male and female, thieves and prostitutes, urchins and idlers, slackers and foreigners." He also turned up his nose at the "vulgar sensuality of the showgirls," so different from the tasteful decorum of the legitimate theater.[29] The crowds were not barred from the great theaters: seat prices ranged from a few livres for a box to sixteen sols for the pit. Here the bourgeoisie mingled with smartly dressed journeymen and workers. On Sundays and holidays, free performances at the Théâtre Français drew the "rabble" with their different ways. The audience's enthusiasm for the theater worked against restrictions imposed by the government and by theatrical monopolies. After 1759 began the expansion of the boulevards, symbolized by the "comic opera" and the subsequent proliferation of *petits spectacles*. The monarchy gave in to public pressure, but in part because it saw the theater and newer forms of entertainment as a necessary instrument for diverting the urban masses and inculcating discipline by example.[30]

In 1715 Paris theaters drew some 35,000 spectators annually. By the eve of the Revolution the capacity of the city's theaters was much larger, and attendance figures were probably considerably higher. The social composition of the audience had changed. Although the privileged of all sorts still attended, while the absolutely impoverished (some 10 percent of the population, according to Olwen Hufton) did not, the well-to-do, talented, and members of the professions mingled with merchants and master craftsmen.[31] The world of culture—students, men of letters, journalists, actors—met people of other backgrounds. The theater was a cultural melting pot within which the social hierarchy was spatially represented, from balcony to pit and boxes to benches. The "freedom of the pit" and the unruliness of its occupants were major ingredients in the formation of public opinion. A colorful, dynamic, but closely watched society of theatergoers developed its own customs but never forgot reality entirely: the lighting and presence of spies in the hall did not yet allow this, but the politicization of the repertoire was real. This was not because of anything the playwrights did, and the actors added very little; it was because of what the pit could make of any allusion to topical matters. In 1784 *Le Mariage de Figaro* did not yet possess the revolutionary charge that it would later take on; its critique of customs and institutions was irreverent but not entirely new. What made the play a success was the fact that it was banned, together with the situation in which the ban occurred: Louis XVI's comment that "this is despicable, it will never be performed" was made in a period of political crisis and protest.

The theater, like the church, was a place where different elements of society came together. In the church, unanimity was imposed by the service. In the theater, everyone was free to express his opinion, his agreement or disagreement. "What makes the theater subversive is its audience."[32] To that one must add that the theater also benefited from a profound social and cultural transformation. The combination of the new repertoire with the new architecture of the Odéon and its neighborhood tended to elicit more predictable reactions from the audience. The importance of debates about plays is easy to imagine. Closed staging, with its solemn symbolism and ritualized representation of power and grandeur, gave rise to an aesthetic that new theatrical audiences could understand.

One can ask similar questions about music, which also attracted a new audience. The taste for music was fostered by religious training, aristocratic celebrations, and the sociability of the tavern and workplace. Counting rhymes, ballads, Christmas carols, and drinking songs were part of the spectacle of the street. Mercier described their impact:

> Some [street singers] wail holy canticles, while others, oftentimes separated from their rivals by no more than forty paces, belt out bawdy ditties . . . A joyous song draws the audience away from the scapular salesman. He remains alone on his stool, his stick pointing in vain at the horns of the devil, the enemy of the human race. Everyone forgets the salvation he is promising to hasten after the song of perdition. The entertainer of the damned sings of good wine, good food, and love and celebrates the beauties of Margot, and alas, the two-sol piece that hovered between the canticle and the vaudeville will end up in the pocket of the more worldly songster.

This is valuable testimony about the linked pedagogy of song and image and the transformation of sensibility, which was beginning to break out of its traditional mold. Church music, which enjoyed its own success and attracted its own share of talent, was no longer the only form of music capable of attracting an audience. In order to retain its listeners, it was even obliged to go in for showmanship and improvisation and novelties capable of "sending a shiver down the spine," as the archbishop of Paris complained of Daquin. Besides opera, which was an integral part of the royal system of beaux-arts as well as a subject of controversy (French versus Italian, Gluck versus Piccini), there were new forms more intimately integrated into the fabric of urban society. The comic opera enjoyed great success with its pastiches, romances, and melodramas, and concerts for music lovers were staged at first by private individuals and later by organizations: the Concert des Amateurs (1769), Concert des Associés (1770), Concert des Amis (1772), and Concert Spirituel. In this area the Masonic lodges had some influence: some meetings were accompanied by musical rituals or even true concerts, as in the Loge et Société Olympique. As a result, music was no longer limited to the court and church and was less dedicated to the celebration of the absolute. Composers and musicians became increasingly independent of traditional institutions but more dependent on their considerably enlarged audience: Jacques-Louis Ménétra took his children to the Concert Spirituel.[33]

The transformation of reading, the vogue for the theater, and the extension of the fashion for music all tended in the same direction. Both public performance and clandestine circulation of Enlightenment innovations put Parisians in an excellent position to witness the advent of the new culture. The Enlightenment was embraced by the most official of cultural institutions, the academies. For complex reasons, the government protected these, just as economic factors and the need to keep people employed played a role in the toleration of the *Encyclopédie,* and just as the *privilège* and government censorship helped to sustain a publishing industry that printed works critical of the government. Clandestine channels of circulation had been in place since the late seventeenth century, and counterfeit editions and secret publications contributed to the success of both official literature and scandalous pulp. Disapproval itself could advertise a work and contribute to its success, as Diderot noted in his letters on freedom of the press. The censorship of the period 1770–1789 was misguided and increasingly pointless.

In short, owing to many influences—rumors, books, newspapers, pamphlets, plays—a growing number of Parisians entered a new world, even if they were not fully conscious of doing so. The change was facilitated, moreover, by the fact that everyday manners and behaviors were also changing. Capital of luxury and fashion, city of consumption, Paris generated economic pressures that impelled people to embrace novelty: the accelerating pace of material change overwhelmed the values of stability and tradition all the more easily because people increasingly depended on the new economy for their survival. What the "culture of appearances" revealed—namely, the countless side effects of both the market (such as the restructuring of the trades) and nonmarket (gifts, loans, exchanges, thefts)—can also be seen in new dietary needs, fashions in furniture, and methods of hygiene. The "display-window effect" transmitted the fashions of the rich to everyone else, and the pleasures of opulence defined a model to be emulated, affecting the general sensibility and intelligence. The press and "fashion magazines" publicized information on the latest fashions and their commercial ramifications along with philosophical and political commentaries on changing customs, economic development, and even women's protests.

More work remains to be done on these phenomena, but for now I want to emphasize the virtues of imitation and the birth of a new economy, indeed a morality, of consumption. The coexistence of diverse populations, inequalities of rank, and contrasts of wealth fostered new behaviors and attitudes. Style propagated signs of change: lackeys wore handsome uniforms, shoes with buckles, and wristwatches; clerks generally wanted new clothes; printers primped themselves and strapped on swords before going out to dance at a *guinguette*, or suburban café; shopgirls could afford the latest trinkets; and provincials came to the city to enjoy the bright lights and dazzling array of commodities. Parisian society no longer saw itself clearly, because the hierarchy of appearances was difficult to interpret at first glance; and as it became more complicated, people had to learn new ways of deciphering the ambiguities of rank and fortune. Make no mistake: I am not saying that equality arrived, nor do I mean to confuse a change in lifestyle with a social and political revolution. Still, to paraphrase Paul Valéry, it was important to show how a large city which "feeds like a flame on an expanse of land and a people" consumes and transmutes its riches into spirit and creates words and actions by tapping the "deep reservoirs" of consciousness in the men and women who come to it in search of greater freedom and in order "to dissolve themselves and undergo metamorphosis." The debate over luxury, which I discussed earlier, was fundamental, for what was at issue was not just the legibility but the very nature of the social.

Behind the social mask, public space, private space, and representation came together: "In public one confronted the problem of the social order by creating signs. In private one confronted, without entirely resolving, the problem of education and protection by adhering to transcendent principles."[34] The forces that operated in the two spheres were not the same: private behavior was governed by modesty and repudiation of artifice, public behavior by will, artifice, and convention. Rules of behavior established an equilibrium between public and private: certain types of behavior one hid from other people. Control of the instincts distinguished the two spheres, but within a coherent "social molecule." With the affirmation of natural rights and demands for liberty and equality at the end of the eighteenth century came a new principle of differentiation in social life. The personality sought new ways to express itself, beyond the old forms of representation. This enhanced power of self-expression, fostered in part by the democratization of writing, undermined ancient values and helped dissolve the bonds between the individual on the one hand and church and state on the other.

In this context a controversy erupted over the theater and man-as-actor.[35] There were three ways of looking at the relation between the public man and the actor who feigned emotions he did not feel. First, it was a commonplace to compare the world to a theater or stage, hence to identify the individual with the actor. In *Les Lettres persanes,* for example, Montesquieu suggested that there was no distinction between the actors on stage and the spectators in the audience at the Comédie Française. Human life, freed of worries about the afterlife, was morally liberated. Second, by contrast, Diderot related the actor to the public man. In his *Paradoxe sur le comédien,* he says that the actor must dominate his emotions and feelings: his sensibility while acting is different from the feelings he arouses in the spectator. What counts in social interaction is independence. The individual can change his style of speech as he changes his clothing; he can avail himself of conventions of language and repetition. Here we are one step closer to secularization: "If the meaning of the actor's acting did not depend on the text, it would also have a meaning independent of the actor and his feelings." Finally, Rousseau completed this idea by connecting it with urban life. He condemned Paris and urban civilization generally, the mixture of street and stage. He thereby formulated the first theory of the modern city as an instrument of expression. In his response to the article on Geneva in the *Encyclopédie,* he showed how the theatrical values implicit in the idea of the *theatrum mundi* destroyed civilization and morality by justifying inauthenticity and corruption, just as luxury and the "culture of appearances" also did.

The theater thus robs the individual of his identity. Material conditions—the central market, the social division of labor—influenced Parisian morals indirectly by corrupting individual wills. In this respect Paris differed from smaller cities. Social interpretation was more complex in the capital, so that it was harder to understand individuals there solely on the basis of the material conditions of their existence. Because of the concentration of capital, the gap between the poor, exhausted from trying to imitate the rich, and the rich, indifferent to the poor, was greater than it was elsewhere. Listen to Rousseau: "In a large city, full of scheming, idle people, without religion or principles and with imaginations depraved by idleness, leisure, owing to love of pleasure and immensity of need, engenders nothing but monsters and inspires nothing but crimes. In a large city morality and honor count for nothing because each person can easily conceal his behavior from the public eye and accredit his own account."[36] Note the use of the word "accredit," which suggests the extent to which, in the moralist's eye, appearances and language were as universal as that substitute for money, credit. The diatribe is noteworthy not so much for what it says as for the fact that at a crucial juncture, the "birth of the modern city," Rousseau insisted that the city-as-theater was contrary to nature because the urban denizen took the actor as his model. Hence he called upon the future citizen to adopt a mode of life that would combine the values of private authenticity with those of the general will, that would wed need to self-control in such a way as to restore authenticity in a new organic whole. Rousseau failed to see that "in this same metropolis, the forces that were already undermining the principles of appearance typical of the Ancien Régime were moving toward quite opposite goals, toward the celebration of liberty and the absence of constraint."[37]

Paris, Capital of Change

Two things emerge from the debate about the theater, actors, and acting. First, Ancien Régime values were still in force, still legitimate. Indeed, they were backed by the law and the apparatus of church and state. They had conscious supporters and even more unconscious ones. Second, a questioning of those values was already under way, because more people were enjoying greater access to information, because new social hierarchies were emerging, and because it was becoming more difficult to perceive hierarchies and differences between individuals.

Therein perhaps lay the cultural crisis. The rupture with the past had in some respects already taken place: censorship was accomplishing nothing, and a realm of freedom was being established through increasingly intense, rapid, and eloquent consumption of commodities. Sensibilities had changed, as we know from changes in wills, no matter how one interprets them. New solidarities were emerging. A public sphere of critical reason was operating in the capital's intellectual salons and academic institutions. In the former, free expression reigned, and people were learning how to debate under conditions of apparent equality. Opinions could also be expressed freely in the institutions of the arts and art criticism, in learned societies and Masonic lodges. In all these places what was most important was the change in customary habits, the mingling of different arts, the coupling of intellectual curiosity with polite manners, and the acceptance of forms of social control not dependent on traditional religious and political justifications.

There were more than a hundred Masonic lodges in Paris between 1773 and 1793. Ninety-two of these were subsidiary to the Grand Orient. We do not know how many subsidiaries the Grande Loge had: probably more than a hundred.[38] There were at least 8,292 members of the Grand Orient, and, based on estimates of the membership of the Grande Loge, the total number of Masons was probably twice that, or 2 percent of the population of the city and probably 4 to 5 percent of the male population. Freemasonry was therefore quite influential, especially since it involved all segments of society: the clergy (who accounted for 4 percent of recruits to "blue" Masonry), the nobility (22 percent), and the Third Estate (64 percent). In any given lodge, aristocrats mingled with people of modest means, soldiers, and *parlementaires,* members of the comfortable bourgeoisie, artisans and shopkeepers (12 percent), but above all men of talent and ability, court personnel, traders (44 percent), artists, and a substantial number of wage earners, including clerks and people employed in commerce and manufacturing, managers employed by noble families, and nonnoble officers in the military (5 percent). What was novel about the Paris lodges was that they broadly welcomed people of all sorts involved in social change, including entrepreneurs and service-sector employees. Although the distribution of these people among the various lodges remains to be studied, it is clear that the Masonic idea was broadly shared and that rationalist and spiritualist tendencies were able to find common ground. By 1785, according to Lenoir, the *lieutenant de police*, the lodges were seen as "innocent recreations." Still, the new values were honored here, and the initiation of Voltaire, who was formally installed as the king of the Republic of Letters by the Nine Sisters Lodge on April 7, 1778, points up the contrast between the indifference of the police and the turmoil just below the surface. For the Parisian elite, public space was already a reality.

Did that same public space exist for the lower classes? In other words, can we define the cultural frontiers of the political? By lower classes *(classes populaires)* I mean more than just wage earners. The category merges into the middle classes, where work, family, friends, and recreation were also central elements of life. Both groups were presumably excluded from politics by their obedience to the secular and religious authorities. But both were also affected by the decline of ignorance.[39] In the barracks and the garrets, people were beginning to read. Nevertheless, Rétif, Mercier, and a few other observers of changing mores always add that "the people" lacked the aptitude for politics owing to their volatility and lack of self-control, indeed their very "naturalness." We have the testimony of the police and eyewitnesses on that score. We hear first of all of a change of mood, an increased frequency of complaints and bad temper and an awareness of being excluded even as material needs grew more numerous and sophisticated. And we also find religious attitudes that shocked the clergy, which never totally overcame the idolatry and "fanaticism" of the Parisians (there is enough evidence here to fill several books). If there was a crisis of faith in the eighteenth century, there was also a religious side to politics, which survived attempts to suppress it, and a shift toward more private forms of religion free from prejudice and superstition. The religion of the people of Paris suffered from two bad examples: the libertinage of the high nobility and a portion of the clergy, and the inability of the clergy to respond to the questions of their most intellectually rigorous parishioners. "I sometimes put questions to the priests, who always responded in words of one syllable, either to shut me up or cut me off by saying these things are mysteries," Ménétra noted in his journal.[40] Although reason did not triumph universally, it made progress everywhere.

Attitudes toward authority also changed, as can be seen from the increase in the number of strikes, plots, and work-related conflicts. Agitation in the workplace was nothing new, but it increased after 1760 as workers mobilized to defend their wages and obtain the right to change jobs and to work shorter hours.[41] Explosions such as the disturbances over the *octroi*, the Réveillon riots, and coordinated strikes reflect both the greater organizational capacity of workers and their readiness to man the barricades and even take the offensive in hard times. Professional pride and the spirit of independence ran counter to the official policy of economic controls and supervised professionalization, with discipline enforced by the guild hierarchy and the police, at a time when crumbling guild structures, urban growth, and economic crisis (1787–1789) were further compounding the difficulties and making the future even more uncertain. Ultimately, the endemic fever was exacerbated by doubts about the king. A clerk in the department responsible for regulating the book trade wrote to M. de Villedeuil, then the department head: "One observes that the songs sold in the street for the amusement of the populace instruct them in the system of liberty. Rabble of the most vile sort, mistaking themselves for the Third Estate, no longer respect the high nobility. No measure can be more useful than to subject these Ponts-Neufs to severe censorship in order to stifle this spirit of independence." The lucid policeman thus corroborates our contention that political songs had long been in circulation even as he attempts to inform his superiors of their harmful effects.

What forms did libertarian agitation take? Rétif notes more and more incidents in the streets, which he then records in *Les Nuits:* when a woman is whipped by clerks from the Palais, a mob chases "hostile citizens" on the quai des Orfèvres; on December 26, 1787, a plot against English prisoners is exposed, and eight people are arrested; when Necker is recalled, disturbances erupt across the city; the Palais-Royal has to be closed because tensions are running so high. Rétif interprets these phenomena in two ways. On the one hand, the people are immature. Their agitation is mere childishness, and it is their misreading of Rousseau that is to blame: "*Emile* has given us a generation that speaks loudly and reduces its elders to silence." On the other hand, any popular unrest is an evil that can lead to disaster.[42] More evidence needs to be examined with an eye to understanding how the recycling of phrases, texts, and objects that originally were either not political or not intended for the lower classes gave rise to new forms of political expression. Examples from Ménétra's journal have already been discussed, but other evidence exists. The cobbler Joseph Charon mentions some of these in his *Lettres ou Mémoires historiques,* about disturbances that broke out in Paris in August and September 1788. The excluded were mired in poverty and even some of the more settled were affected, but the crucial point is that political ideas and discontent descended "from men of the world of the highest rank to the very lowest ranks through various channels." Charon notes that "people acquired and dispensed enlightenment that one would have searched for in vain a dozen years earlier . . . and they have acquired notions about public constitutions in the past two or three years." The year 1766 marked the failure of Turgot and 1786 the failure of reform.

I shall end with two questions: How far did public opinion go? And how much change was there? Already, as Charon's text proves, ordinary events were triggering profound shifts in opinion. Political crisis and economic crisis developed together, not separately. The moment was defined by three concurrent processes: the collapse of surveillance, the explosion of free expression, and the propagation of criticism through the institutions of cultural sociability. Criticism erupted everywhere: in the press, in songs, in rumors. There was debate over the very nature of the tension. Public opinion was fragile, torn between reason and credulity, confusion and order, permanence and evanescence, the controlled and the uncontrolled. All this was at the heart of the first, irrational political outbursts and the early activities of the patriotic and popular societies at the end of 1788. The genuine liberties "granted pell-mell under the pressure of events could only favor radicalization of political agendas."[43] Debate could then begin in the press and memoranda. On December 27 the Council gave in to the agitation and agreed to a doubling of the Third Estate in future Estates General. But the people, who interpreted in economic and social terms a debate that passed them by, were still excluded from the Third Estate. The contradiction between the general cultural evolution and the negative response of the majority grew worse. Resolution of this contradiction was essential if cultural sociability was to be transformed into political sociability, where form mattered more than ideology and education more than indoctrination. This would become the problem of Jacobinism. The future of the whole society depended on the depth of cultural change. As Montesquieu said, it is "the general spirit of a nation" that governs historical change. Social habits *(les moeurs)* were opposed to violence, but habit always needed the added force of law to keep violence in check. It was social habits—compounded of intelligence and sensibility, of the materiality of things and the intellectuality of behavior—that determined whether there would be social progress or social corruption. Paris was not France, but it contributed its share.

NOTES

INTRODUCTION

1. Yves Coirault, *L'Optique de Saint-Simon* (Paris, 1965).

2. J. de Witte, ed., *Journal de l'abbé de Véry* (Paris, 1933).

3. Alphonse Dupront, *Les Lettres, les sciences, la religion et les arts dans la société française de la deuxième moitié du XVIIIe siècle* (Paris: CDU, 1963).

4. William Doyle, *The Origins of the French Revolution*, 2nd ed. (Oxford: Oxford University Press, 1988).

5. Denis Richet, *La France moderne: l'esprit des institutions* (Paris, 1973).

6. Louis Dumont, *Essais sur l'individualisme* (Paris, 1983); in English, *Essays on Individualism* (Chicago: University of Chicago Press, 1986).

7. Roger Chartier, *Les Origines culturelles de la Révolution française* (Paris, 1991); Daniel Mornet, *Les Origines intellectuelles de la Révolution française* (Paris, 1933).

1. KNOWING FRANCE

1. Georges Durand, *Etats et institutions, XVIe–XVIIIe siècle* (Paris, 1969), p. 8.

2. René Pomeau, *Politique de Voltaire* (Paris, 1963).

3. Fernand Braudel, *L'Identité de la France*, 3 vols., vol. 1, *Espace et histoire* (Paris, 1986); in English, *The Identity of France*, trans. Sian Reynolds (New York: Harper & Row, 1988–1990).

4. Daniel Nordman and Jacques Revel, "La Formation de l'espace français," in André Burguière and Jacques Revel, eds., *Histoire de France*, vol. 1, *L'Espace français* (Paris, 1989), pp. 33–174.

5. Montesquieu, *Pensées*, 542.

6. Robert Shackleton, *Montesquieu: A Critical Biography* (London: Oxford University Press, 1961).

7. Nordman and Revel, "La Formation."

8. C. Brun, "La Figure de la France" (master's thesis, University of Paris I, 1992), typescript.

9. Jean Boutier, Alain Dewerpe, and Daniel Nordman, *Un Tour de France royal: le voyage de Charles IX (1564–1566)* (Paris, 1984).

10. Nordman and Revel, "La Formation," p. 76.

11. Michel Antoine, *Louis XV* (Paris, 1989).

12. Antoine Picon, *L'Invention de l'ingénieur moderne: l'Ecole des ponts et chaussées, 1747–1841* (Paris, 1992).

13. Nordman and Revel, "La Formation," p. 77.

14. Numa Broc, *La Géographie des philosophes géographes et voyageurs français au XVIIIe siècle* (Paris, 1975).

15. Pierre Goubert and Daniel Roche, *Les Français et l'Ancien Régime*, 2 vols., vol. 2, *Sociétés et cultures* (Paris, 1984).

16. Broc, *La Géographie*.

17. Marie-Noelle Bourguet, *Déchiffrer la France: la statistique départementale à l'époque napoléonienne* (Paris, 1988).

18. J. Molinier; see also G. Arbellot and Bernard Lepetit, eds., *Atlas de la Révolution française*, vol. 1, *Routes et communications* (Paris, 1987).

19. Jean-Claude Perrot, ed., *La Richesse territoriale de la France de Lavoisier* (Paris, 1991).

20. J. Boissière, "Population et économies du bois dans la France moderne" (doctoral thesis, University of Paris I, 1993), 4 vols., 1:50–92, 262–292; R. Dainville, ed., *Le Langage du géographe* (Paris, 1978); *La Cartographie, reflet de l'histoire* (Paris, 1986).

21. Marc Bloch, "Les Plans parcellaires," *Annales, HES* (1929).

22. Jean Nicolas, *La Savoie au XVIIIe siècle*, 2 vols. (Paris, 1979).

23. Anne Blanchard, *Les Ingénieurs du "Roy" de Louis XIV à Louis XVI: étude du corps des fortifications* (Montpellier, 1979).

24. Jean-Claude Perrot, *Genèse d'une ville moderne: Caen au XVIIIe siècle*, 2 vols. (Paris and The Hague: Mouton, 1975).

25. Daniel Roche, *Le Peuple de Paris: essai sur la culture populaire au XVIIIe siècle* (Paris, 1981).

26. Nordman and Revel, "La Formation," p. 112.

27. Monique Pelletier, *La Carte de Cassini* (Paris, 1990).

28. Fénelon, *Examen de conscience sur les devoirs de la royauté: oeuvres complètes* (Paris, 1971).

29. Louis Trénard, *Introduction à l'édition des mémoires des intendants pour l'éducation du duc de Bourgogne* (Paris, 1975).

30. Bourguet, *Déchiffrer la France*.

31. Ibid., p. 30.

32. Darluc, *Histoire de la Provence* (Marseilles, 1787).

33. Jean-Claude Perrot, *Genèse d'une ville moderne* (Paris, 1975), 1:140.

34. François Dagognet, *Le Catalogue de la vie* (Paris, 1970).

35. Ibid.

36. Antoine Laurent de Jussieu, *Exposition d'un nouvel ordre des plantes: mémoire de l'Académie royale des sciences* (Paris, 1774).

37. Dagognet, *Le Catalogue de la vie*.

2. MASTERY OF SPACE

1. Pierre Dockès, *L'Espace dans la pensée économique du XVIe au XVIIIe siècle* (Paris, 1969).

2. *Encyclopédie,* vol. 3 (1753), p. 690.

3. Karl Marx, *Capital,* chap. 24.

4. Henri Cavaillès, *La Route française, son histoire, sa fonction* (Paris, 1946), pp. 54–56.

5. Antoine Picon, *Architectes et ingénieurs au siècle des Lumières* (Marseilles, 1988), p. 97.

6. Bernard Lepetit, *Chemins de terre et voies d'eau, réseaux de transports, organisation de l'espace* (Paris, 1984).

7. Arthur Young, *Travels in France* (London: G. Bell, 1889).

8. Picon, *L'Invention.*

9. J.-M. Goger, "La Politique routière en France de 1716 à 1815" (thesis, Ecoles des Hautes Etudes en Sciences Sociales, 1988), typescript, 5 vols. (esp. vols. 1 and 2). See also idem., *Le Temps de la route exclusive en France: histoire, économie, société* (1992), pp. 553–570.

10. Guy Arbellot, "La Grande Mutation des routes de France au milieu du XVIIIe siècle," *Annales E.S.C.* (1971), 765–791.

11. Picon, *L'Invention,* p. 50.

12. Goger, "La Politique routière."

13. Fernand Braudel, *Civilisation matérielle et capitalisme* (Paris, 1967), p. 32.

14. Abel Poitrineau, "L'Economie du transport fluvial: une esquisse," *Revue historique,* no. 577 (1991), 105–120.

15. "Hommes," *Encyclopédie* (1757).

16. Daniel Roche, "Le Temps de l'eau rare, du Moyen Age à l'époque moderne," *Annales E.S.C.* (1984), 383–399.

17. Ibid.

18. Jean-Claude Perrot, *Une Histoire intellectuelle de l'économie politique (XVIIe–XVIIIe siècle)* (Paris, 1992).

19. Picon, *L'Invention,* p. 220.

20. Anne-Marie Cocula, *Les Gens de la rivière de Dordogne, de 1750 à 1850,* 2 vols. (Lille, 1979).

21. Picon, *L'Invention.*

22. La Font de Saint-Yenne, *Commentaires sur le salon* (Paris, 1746).

23. Nordman and Revel, "La Formation," pp. 33–174.

24. Peter Sahlins, *Boundaries: The Making of France and Spain in the Pyrenees* (Berkeley, 1989).

25. Nicole Lemaître, *Un Horizon bloqué: Ussel et la montagne limousine aux XVIIe et XVIIIe siècles* (Ussel, 1968).

26. Anne Zink, "Les Forains sous l'Ancien Régime: l'indifférence à la différence, les forains dans la France du Sud-Ouest," *Annales E.S.C.* (1988), 149–172.

27. Gérard Bouchard, *Le Village immobile: Sennely en Sologne au XVIIIe siècle* (Paris, 1972), p. 351.

28. Georges Durand, *Vin, vigne et vignerons en Lyonnais et Beaujolais, XVIe-XVIIIe siècle* (Lyons, 1979), p. 237.

29. Arlette Farge, *Le Vol d'aliment à Paris au XVIIIe siècle* (Paris, 1974), p. 161.

30. Annik Pardailhé-Galabrun, *La Naissance de l'intime: 3,000 foyers parisiens, XVIIe–XVIIIe siècle* (Paris, 1988); in English, *The Birth of Intimacy*, trans. Jocelyn Phelps (Philadelphia, 1991).

31. J. Vassort, "Une Société provinciale face à son devenir: le Vendômois au XVIIIe et XIXe siècle," 2 vols. (thesis, University of Paris I, 1992), typescript.

32. Dominique Margairaz, *Foires et marchés dans la France pré-industrielle* (Paris, 1988).

33. J. Thomas, "L'Age d'or des foires et des marchés: commerce, politique et sociabilité dans le Midi toulousain (vers 1750–vers 1914)," 3 vols. (thesis, Toulouse-le-Mirail, 1989), typescript.

34. Abel Chatelain, *Les Migrants temporaires en France de 1800 à 1914*, 2 vols. (Lille, 1976).

35. Anne-Marie Moulin, *Les Maçons de la Haute-Marche au XVIIIe siècle*, publication of the Institut d'Etudes du Massif Central (Clermont-Ferrand, 1986).

36. Laurence Fontaine, *L'Histoire du colportage en Europe du XVIe au XIXe siècle* (Paris, 1993); *Le Voyage et la mémoire: colporteurs de l'Oisans au XIXe siècle* (Lyons, 1984).

37. Jean-Pierre Poussou, *Bordeaux et le Sud-Ouest au XVIIIe siècle: croissance économique et attraction urbaine* (Paris, 1983).

38. Perrot, *Genèse.*

39. Vassort, "Une Société provinciale."

40. Jean-Pierre Gutton, *La Société et les Pauvres: l'exemple de la généralité de Lyon* (Paris, 1971), pp. 447, 448.

41. François Dagognet, *Le Nombre et le lieu* (Paris, 1984), pp. 22, 23.

42. Perrot, *Genèse*, 2:533–600.

43. Picon, *L'Invention*, p. 297.

44. François Dagognet, *Pour une théorie générale des formes* (Paris, 1975), p. 61.

3. TIME AND HISTORY

1. François Furet, "L'Ensemble Histoire," in François Furet, ed., *Livre et société dans la France du XVIIIe siècle* (Paris and The Hague, 1970), 2:95–100.

2. Reinhart Koselleck, *Futures Past*, trans. Keith Tribe (Cambridge, Mass.: MIT Press, 1985).

3. Furet, "L'Ensemble Histoire."

4. Pascal, "De l'esprit géométrique," in *Pensées*.

5. Fernand Braudel, *Ecrits sur l'histoire* (Paris, 1977).

6. Marcel Lachiver, *Les Années de misère: la famine au temps du grand roi* (Paris, 1991).

7. Vassort, "Une Société provinciale," p. 272.

8. Nicole Pellegrin, *Les Bachelleries dans le Centre-Ouest: organisations et fêtes de jeunesse* (Poitiers, 1982), p. 277.

9. Ibid.

10. E. Gutton, *L'Etat et la mendicité dans la première moitié du XVIIIe siècle: Auvergne, Beaujolais, Forez, Lyonnais* (Lyons, 1973).

11. Krzystof Pomian, *L'Ordre du temps* (Paris, 1984), pp. 231–267.

12. Jacques Le Goff, *Pour un autre Moyen Age* (Paris, 1977), trans. Arthur Goldhammer as *Time, Work, and Culture in the Middle Ages* (Chicago, 1978).

13. Perrot, *Une Histoire intellectuelle*.

14. Pomian, *L'Ordre du temps*, p. 163.

15. Judith E. Schlanger, *Les Métaphores de l'organisme* (Paris, 1971), pp. 53, 54.

16. David Landes, *Revolution in Time: Clocks and the Making of the Modern World* (Cambridge, Mass., 1983).

17. Daniel Roche, *La Culture des apparences: une histoire du vêtement, XVIIe-XVIIIe siècle* (Paris, 1989), p. 84.

18. Vassort, "Une Société provinciale," p. 330.

19. Ibid., p. 335.

20. Gaston Saffroy, *Bibliographie des almanachs et annuaires administratif, ecclésiastiques et militaires français de l'Ancien Régime* (Paris, 1959).

21. V. Sarrazin, "L'Histoire dans les almanachs" (master's thesis, University of Paris I, 1988), typescript.

22. Pierre Rétat, *Regards sur la presse et histoire au XVIIIe siècle, l'année 1734* (Lyons, 1978), p. 26.

23. Pomeau, *Politique de Voltaire*, p. 54.

24. Jean Ehrard and G.-P. Palmade, *L'Histoire* (Paris, 1964), p. 33.

25. François Furet and Mona Ozouf, "Mably et Boulainvilliers: deux légitimations historiques de la société française au XVIIIe siècle," *Annales E.S.C.* (1979), 438–450.

26. Georges Benrekassa, *Montesquieu, la liberté et l'histoire* (Paris, 1987), p. 79.

27. Nicolas Lenglet-Dufresnoy, *Méthode pour étudier l'histoire* (Paris, 1735), pp. 470–475.

28. Rétat, *Regards sur la presse*, p. 9.

29. Pierre Chaunu, *La Civilisation de l'Europe des Lumières*, 2 vols. (Grenoble, 1971), pp. 281–282.

30. Dominique Julia and L. Donnat, "Le Recrutement d'une congrégation monastique, les bénédictins de Saint-Maur, esquisse d'histoire quantitative: Saint-

Thierry, une abbaye du VIe au XXe siècle," Actes du colloque international d'histoire monastique, Reims-Saint-Thierry, October 11–14, 1976 (Saint-Thierry, 1979), pp. 505–594.

31. Blandine Barret-Kriegel, *Les Historiens de la monarchie*, 4 vols. (Paris, 1988); vol. 3, *Les Académies de l'Histoire;* vol. 4, *La République incertaine.*

32. Ibid.; Dieter Gembicki, *Histoire et politique à la fin de l'Ancien Régime: Jacob-Nicolas Moreau, 1717–1803* (Paris, 1967).

33. Ira Owen Wade, *The Intellectual Development of Voltaire* (Princeton: Princeton University Press, 1969).

34. Pomeau, *Politique de Voltaire.*

35. Keith Michael Baker, *Condorcet, from Natural Philosophy to Social Mathematics* (Chicago, 1975).

4. PEASANT FRANCE AND MERCHANT FRANCE

1. Pierre Chaunu, *La Civilisation de l'Europe des Lumières* (Paris and Grenoble, 1974).

2. E. W. Fox, *L'Autre France: l'histoire en perspective géographique* (Paris, 1973), p. 27.

3. Marx, *Capital,* bk. 1.

4. Jean-Pierre Hirsch, *Les Deux Rêves du commerce: entreprise et institution dans la région lilloise, 1780–1800* (Paris, 1991), p. 9.

5. Perrot, *Genèse,* 2:951.

6. Henri Mendras, *La Seconde Révolution française* (Paris, 1989).

7. Henri Mendras, *La Fin des paysans* (Paris, 1984), pp. 14, 15.

8. Florian, "Essai sur la pastorale," preface to *Estelle* (Paris, 1788), pp. 6, 7. Thanks to Yves Castan for pointing out this wonderful text.

9. J. Mulliez, "Le Blé, mal nécessaire," *Revue d'histoire moderne et contemporaine* (1979), 3–47.

10. Karl Marx, *The Eighteenth Brumaire of Louis Bonaparte,* trans. Daniel De Leon (New York, 1951).

11. Mendras, *La Fin des paysans,* pp. 18, 19.

12. Ibid.

13. Emmanuel Leroy-Ladurie, *Histoire de la France rurale,* vol. 2, *L'Age classique des paysans* (Paris, 1975), p. 406.

14. Perrot, *Une Histoire intellectuelle,* p. 232.

15. Ibid., p. 214.

16. Mendras, *La Fin des paysans,* p. 214.

17. Hervé Le Bras and Emmanuel Todd, *L'Invention de la France: atlas anthropologique et politique* (Paris, 1981).

18. Perrot, *Une Histoire intellectuelle.*

19. Ibid., p. 215.

20. Robert Muchembled, *Culture populaire et culture des élites* (Paris, 1978); *L'Invention de l'homme moderne* (Paris, 1988).

21. Yves Castan, "Criminalités paysannes et urbaines en Languedoc au XVIIIe siècle" (doctoral thesis, Toulouse, 1961), typescript.

22. Michel Bernard, *Introduction à une sociologie des doctrines économiques des physiocrates à Stuart Mill* (Paris, 1963).

23. Herbert Lüthy, *La Banque protestante en France, de la révocation de l'édit de Nantes à la Révolution* (Paris, 1959–1960), 2 vols., vol. 2, *De la Banque aux Finances*, pp. 15–45.

24. Ibid., p. 768.

25. L. Salleron, *Oeuvres complètes de Quesnay*, 2 vols. (Paris, 1958).

26. Mulliez, "Le Blé, mal nécessaire."

27. Geneviève Bollème, *Les Almanachs populaires aux XVIIe et XVIIIe siècles: essai d'histoire sociale* (Paris and The Hague, 1969).

28. Geneviève Bollème, "Littérature populaire et littérature de colportage en France au XVIIIe siècle," in Furet, ed., *Livre et société*, pp. 61–92.

29. Ibid., pp. 80, 81.

30. Bollème, *Les Almanachs populaires*, pp. 84, 85.

31. Jacques Pineaux, *Proverbes et dictons français* (Paris, 1956), p. 108.

32. Bouchard, *Le Village immobile*.

33. Anne Fillon, "Louis Simon, étaminier (1741–1820), dans son village du Haut-Maine au Siècle des lumières," 2 vols. (thesis, Le Mans, 1983), typescript.

34. A. Sauvy, "Le Livre aux champs," in Roger Chartier and Henri-Jean Martin, eds., *Histoire de l'édition française*, vol. 2, *Le Livre triomphant* (Paris, 1984), p. 561.

35. Daniel Roche, *Journal de ma vie: l'autobiographie d'un compagnon vitrier, Jacques Louis Ménétra* (Paris, 1982).

36. Dagognet, *Pour une théorie*.

37. See Chapter 16.

38. Mendras, *La Fin des paysans*.

39. Duhamel du Monceau, *Traité de l'exploitation du bois* (Paris, 1761), pp. iv, v.

40. V.-D. Musset-Pathay, *Bibliographie agronomique* (Paris, 1810).

41. Marquis de Mirabeau, *L'Ami des hommes, ou Traité de la population* (1758), pp. 33–39.

5. THE KINGDOM OF EXCHANGE

1. Voltaire, *Lettres philosophiques*, ed. René Pomeau (Paris: Garnier-Flammarion, 1964), pp. 66, 67.

2. Fox, *L'Autre France*.

3. Pierre Léon, *Economies et sociétés préindustrielles*, vol. 2, *1650–1780: les origines d'une accélération de l'histoire* (Paris, 1970).

4. Joel Cornette, *Un Révolutionnaire ordinaire: Benoît Lacombe, négociant, 1759–1819* (Paris, 1986).

5. Hirsch, *Les Deux Rêves du commerce*.

6. Cornette, *Un Révolutionnaire ordinaire*, p. 88.

7. Ibid., pp. 141–147.

8. Hirsch, *Les Deux Rêves du commerce*.

9. P. Minard, "Les Inspecteurs des manufactures et les politiques industrielles de la monarchie française" (master's thesis, University of Paris I, 1986).

10. Lüthy, *La Banque protestante en France*.

11. C. Theré, "Etude sociale des auteurs économistes, 1561–1789," 4 vols. (thesis, University of Paris I, 1990).

12. Perrot, *Une Histoire intellectuelle*, pp. 59, 60.

13. Jean-Claude Perrot, "Le Livre d'économie politique," in Chartier and Martin, *Histoire de l'édition française*, 2:306–309.

14. Eli F. Heckscher, *Mercantilism*, trans. Mendel Shapiro, 2nd ed., 2 vols. (London, 1955).

15. Georges Weulersse, *Le Mouvement physiocratique en France de 1756 à 1770: La Physiocratie à la fin du règne de Louis XV, 1770–1774* (Paris, 1959); *La Physiocratie sous les ministères de Turgot et de Necker, 1774–1781* (Paris, 1950); *La Physiocratie à l'aube de la Révolution, 1781–1792* (Paris, 1985).

16. Michel Foucault, *L'Archéologie du savoir* (Paris, 1969); in English, *The Archaeology of Knowledge*, trans. A. M. Sheridan (New York, 1972).

17. Simone Meysonnier, *La Balance et l'Horloge: la genèse de la pensée libérale en France au XVIIIe siecle* (Paris, 1989).

18. Ibid., pp. 181–209.

19. Weulersse, *Le Mouvement physiocratique*, 1:53.

20. Luc Boltanski and Laurent Thévenot, *De la justification: les économies de la grandeur* (Paris, 1991), pp. 240–252.

21. Lüthy, *La Banque protestante en France*, 2:408–410.

22. Daniel Roche, *Les Républicains des Lettres: gens de culture et Lumières au XVIIIe siècle* (Paris, 1988).

23. Lüthy, *La Banque protestante en France*, 2:387.

24. Serge Chassagne, *Le Coton et ses patrons: France, 1760–1840* (Paris, 1991); Denis Woronoff, *L'Industrie sidérurgique en France pendant la Révolution et l'Empire* (Paris, 1984).

25. Hirsch, *Les Deux Rêves du commerce*.

26. P. Jeannin, "Distinction des compétences et niveau des qualifications," in Franco Angiolini and Daniel Roche, eds., *Culture et formations négociantes dans l'Europe moderne* (Paris, 1995).

27. Dominique Julia, "Les Ressources culturelles, les réseaux scolaires," in Burguière and Revel, *Histoire de France*, 1:379–405.

28. Maurice Garden, *Lyon et les Lyonnais au XVIIIe siècle* (Lyons, 1970), pp. 465–467.

6. THE CITY, CRUCIBLE OF CHANGE

1. Braudel, *Espace et Histoire.*

2. *Encyclopédie*, vol. 17 (1765), p. 279.

3. Bernard Lepetit, *Les Villes dans la France moderne (1750–1830)* (Paris, 1988), p. 22.

4. Jean-Claude Perrot, "Les Economistes, les philosophes et la population," in Jacques Dupâquier, ed., *Histoire de la population française*, vol. 2 (Paris, 1988), pp. 499–552.

5. M. Moheau, *Recherches et considérations sur la population de la France* (Paris, 1778), p. 58.

6. Ibid., p. 99.

7. Lepetit, *Les Villes,* pp. 91, 92.

8. Ibid., pp. 50, 51.

9. I borrow the expression "galloping statistics" from Mona Ozouf.

10. Jean-Pierre Bardet, *Rouen au XVIIe et XVIIIe siècle: les mutations d'un espace social* (Paris, 1983).

11. Poussou, *Bordeaux et le Sud-Ouest.*

12. Garden, *Lyon et les Lyonnais.*

13. Moulin, *Les Maçons.*

14. Antoinette Fauve-Chamoux, "Comportement parental en milieu urbain (XVe-XIXe siècle), *Annales E.S.C.* (1985), 1023–41.

15. Jean-Claude Perrot, "Rapports sociaux et villes au XVIIIe siècle," *Annales E.S.C.* (1968), 241–268.

16. Louis-Sébastien Mercier, *Tableau de Paris* (Paris and Amsterdam, 1782–1788), 1:1.

17. Lepetit, *Les Villes,* pp. 80, 81.

18. Max Weber, *Economy and Society,* trans. Ephraim Fischoff et al., vol. 1, *The City* (Berkeley, 1978).

19. Jean Meyer, *Etudes sur les villes en Europe occidentale,* 2 vols., vol. 2, *Milieu du XVIIe siècle à la veille de la Révolution française* (Paris, 1987).

20. Lemaître, *Un Horizon bloqué.*

21. John McManners, *French Ecclesiastical Society under the Ancient Regime: A Study of Angers in the Eighteenth Century* (Manchester, 1960), p. 7.

22. Braudel, *L'Identité,* 1:214.

23. François-Yves Besnard, *Souvenirs d'un nonagénaire* (Paris, 1880).

24. Perrot, *Genèse,* 2:236.

25. Braudel, *L'Identité,* 1:222.

26. Perrot, *Genèse*, 1:529.

27. Garden, *Lyon et les Lyonnais*.

28. Georges Gusdorf, *Les Sciences humaines et la pensée occidentale*, vol. 7, *Naissance de la conscience romantique au siècle des Lumières* (Paris, 1976), pp. 269–371.

29. Ibid., pp. 369–371.

30. Perrot, *Genèse*, 1:15–27.

31. V. Milliot, "Les Représentations de la ville dans la littérature de colportage" (master's thesis, University of Paris I, 1983); idem., "Les Cris de Paris: le peuple apprivoisé" (thesis, University of Paris I, 1991).

32. Lepetit, *Les Villes*, pp. 83–85.

33. Adam Smith, *The Wealth of Nations* (New York, 1994).

34. "Hommes," *Encyclopédie*, p. 525.

35. Lepetit, *Les Villes*, pp. 85–101.

36. Philippe Guignet, *Le Pouvoir dans la ville au XVIIIe siècle: pratiques politiques, notabilité et éthique sociale de part et d'autre de la frontière franco-belge* (Paris, 1990).

37. Perrot, *Genèse*.

7. THE REGULATED KINGDOM

1. Montesquieu, *Pensées*, 2099.

2. Durand, *Etats et institutions;* Richet, *La France moderne*.

3. Durand, *Etats et institutions*.

4. Daniel Roche, *Le Siècle des Lumières en province: académies et academiciens provinciaux (1680–1789)* (Paris, 1978).

5. Richet, *La France moderne*.

6. Alexis de Tocqueville, *L'Ancien Régime et la Révolution;* in English, *The Old Regime and the French Revolution*, trans. Stuart Gilbert (Garden City, N.Y., 1955).

7. Pierre Goubert, *L'Ancien Régime* (Paris, 1969–1973); vol. 1, *La Société;* vol. 2, *Les Pouvoirs* (1973).

8. A. Guéry and R. Descimon, "Un Etat des temps modernes," in Burguière and Revel, *Histoire de France*, vol. 2, *L'Etat et les pouvoirs* (Paris, 1989), p. 243.

9. Françoise Mosser, *Les Intendants de finance* (Paris, 1978).

10. Tocqueville, *L'Ancien Régime*.

11. Pierre Legendre, *L'Administration du XVIIIe siècle à nos jours* (Paris, 1969).

12. Michel Antoine, *Le Conseil du roi sous le règne de Louis XV* (Paris, 1970); *Le Conseil royal des finances au XVIIIe siècle* (Paris, 1973); *Le Gouvernement et l'administration sous Louis XV* (Paris, 1978).

13. Antoine, *Le Conseil du roi*, pp. 177–210.

14. Ibid., p. 631; Legendre, *L'Administration*, p. 154.

15. Roland Mousnier, *La Vénalité des offices sous Henri IV et Louis XIII* (Paris, 1971).

16. Guéry and Descimon, "Un Etat," p. 202.

17. Jean-Pierre Samoyault, *Les Bureaux du secrétariat d'Etat des Affaires étrangères sous Louis XV* (Paris, 1971).

18. Yves Durand, *Les Fermiers généraux au XVIIIe siècle* (Paris, 1971), p. 121.

19. Mousnier, *La Vénalité des offices.*

20. Durand, *Etats et institutions*, p. 111.

21. Vivian R. Gruder, *The Royal Provincial Intendants: A Governing Elite in Eighteenth-Century France* (Ithaca, N.Y., 1968).

22. P.-Y. Legras, "L'Intendance de Lyon au milieu du XVIIIe siècle, 1739–1750" (master's thesis, University of Paris I, 1983).

23. Michel C. Kiener and Jean-Claude Peyronnet, *Quand Turgot régnait en Limousin: un tremplin pour le pouvoir* (Paris, 1979).

24. Denis Diderot, *Mémoires pour Catherine II* (Paris, 1966), pp. 159, 160.

25. Alain Viala, *Naissance de l'écrivain* (Paris, 1985).

26. Roche, *Le Siècle des Lumières en province.*

27. Alphonse Dupront, *Art et Société en Europe au XVIIIe siècle* (Paris: CDU, 1964), 2:96.

28. André Monglond, *Pèlerinages romantiques* (Paris, 1968); Pierre Trahard, *Les Maîtres de la sensibilité française au XVIIIe siècle, 1715–1789*, 4 vols. (Paris, 1931–1933).

8. THE KING AND HIS SUBJECTS

1. Mary Douglas, *How Institutions Think* (Syracuse, N.Y.: Syracuse University Press, 1986).

2. Ibid.

3. Louis Althusser, *Montesquieu: la politique de l'histoire* (Paris, 1964); Georges Benrekassa, *Montesquieu: la liberté et l'histoire* (Paris, 1987), pp. 87, 88.

4. Shackleton, *Montesquieu.*

5. Jean Ehrard, *Politique de Montesquieu* (Paris, 1965), p. 11.

6. Montesquieu, *De l'esprit des lois* (Paris, 1962).

7. Pomeau, *Politique de Voltaire*, p. 85.

8. Montesquieu, *Considérations* (1734), bk. 9.

9. Benrekassa, *Montesquieu*, p. 127.

10. Hans Lüthy, *Le Passé présent: combat d'idée de Calvin à Rousseau* (Monaco, 1965), pp. 186–187.

11. Louis Marin, *Le Portrait du roi* (Paris, 1981).

12. Antoine, *Le Conseil du roi.*

13. Ibid.

14. Ibid., p. 611.

15. Evelyne Lever, *Louis XVI* (Paris, 1985), pp. 25–30.

16. Louis-Sébastien Mercier, *Des notions claires sur les gouvernements* (Paris, 1787), 2:369, 370.

17. Norbert Elias, *La Dynamique de l'Occident,* trans. (Paris, 1975); orig. German, *Wandlungen der Gesellschaft* (Bern, 1969).

18. Roger Chartier, "Formation sociale et économie psychique: la société de Cour dans les procès de civilisation," preface to Norbert Elias, *La Société de cour* (Paris, 1985), pp. i–lxxvii.

19. Jacques Benigne Bossuet, *Politique tirée des propres paroles de l'Ecriture sainte* (Paris, 1709).

20. March Bloch, *Les Rois thaumaturges* (Paris, 1923).

21. Ibid., citing Frazer.

22. Michele Fogel, *Les Cérémonies de l'information dans la France du XVIe au milieu du XVIIIe siècle* (Paris, 1989).

23. Ibid., p. 410.

24. M. T. Dremière, "Portrait et représentation de 1650 à 1800," 2 vols. (thesis, University of Paris III, 1986), typescript, p. 366.

25. Michel Martin, *Les Monuments équestres de Louis XIV* (Paris, 1986); Daniel Rabreau, "La Statue équestre de Louis XV d'Edme Bouchardon," *L'Information d'histoire de l'art,* no. 2 (1974), 69–97.

26. Keith Michael Baker, ed., *The Political Culture of the Old Regime* (Oxford, 1985).

27. Richet, *La France moderne,* p. 156.

28. Ibid., p. 156; Baker, *Political Culture;* Gail Bossenga, "La Révolution française et les corporations: trois exemples lillois," *Annales E.S.C.,* no. 2 (1988), 405–426.

29. Pierre Rosanvallon, "L'Utilitarisme français et les ambiguïtés de la culture politique pré-révolutionnaire," in Baker, *Political Culture,* pp. 435–440.

30. Arlette Farge, *Dire et mal dire: l'opinion publique au XVIIIe siècle* (Paris, 1992).

31. Michel Vovelle, "La Représentation populaire de la monarchie," in Baker, *Political Culture,* pp. 77–88.

32. Robert Darnton, *The Forbidden Best-Sellers of Pre-Revolutionary France* (New York, 1995).

33. Chartier, *Les Origines culturelles.*

9. The King and the People

1. Stephen Kaplan, *Le Pain, le peuple et le roi: la bataille du libéralisme sous Louis XV* (Paris, 1986), pp. 21–24.

2. Louis Dumont, *Homo hierarchicus: un essai sur le système des castes* (Paris, 1966), pp. 318, 319; *Essai sur l'individualisme,* p. 71.

3. F. Hincker, *Les Français devant l'impôt sous l'Ancien Régime* (Paris, 1971).

4. David D. Bien, "Offices, Corps, and a System of State Credit: The Use of Privilege under the Ancient Regime," in Baker, *Political Culture.*

5. A. Guéry, "Les Finances de la monarchie française sous l'Ancien Régime,"

Annales E.S.C. (1978), 216–239; M. Morineau, "Budgets de l'état et gestion des finances royales en France au XVIIIe siècle," *Revue historique* (1980), 289–336.

6. Jean Meyer, *Le Poids de l'état* (Paris, 1983), p. 144.

7. M. Burguière, "Louis XVI's Receivers General and Their Successors," *French History*, no. 1 (1987), 238–256.

8. Jean-Claude Perrot, "Cours inédit" (University of Paris I, 1990–91).

9. A. Guéry, "Le Roi dépensier: le don, la contrainte et l'origine du système financier de la monarchie française d'Ancien Régime," *Annales E.S.C.*, no. 6 (1984), 1241–69.

10. Voltaire, *Le Siècle de Louis XIV* (Paris, 1957), p. 708.

11. Durand, *Les Fermiers généraux en France.*

12. Mercier, *Tableau de Paris*, 11:204, 205.

13. Daniel Dessert, *Argent, pouvoir et société au Grand Siècle* (Paris, 1984).

14. Ibid.

15. Perrot, "Cours inédit."

16. Joel Cornette, *Le Roi de guerre: essai sur la souveraineté dans la France du Grand Siècle* (Paris, 1993).

17. A. Dubois, *Journal du curé de Rumegies, 1686–1739* (Paris, 1965).

18. Emmanuel Leroy-Ladurie, *L'Ancien Régime: histoire de France* (Paris, 1990), 3:336–337.

19. Lucien Bély, *Espions et ambassadeurs au temps de Louis XIV* (Paris, 1900), pp. 695–751.

20. Jean Chagniot, *Paris au XVIIIe siècle*, Nouvelle Histoire de Paris series (Paris, 1988), pp. 5–7; *Paris et l'armée au XVIIIe siècle: étude politique et sociale* (Paris, 1985).

21. Leroy-Ladurie, *L'Ancien Régime*, pp. 339–341.

22. Emile G. Léonard, *L'Armée et ses problèmes au XVIIIe siècle* (Paris, 1958).

23. Chevalier d'Arc, *De la noblesse militaire* (Paris, 1976), pp. 97, 98.

24. Blanchard, *Les Ingénieurs du "Roy."*

25. Michel Foucault, *Surveiller et punir: naissance de la prison* (Paris, 1975); in English, *Discipline and Punish: The Birth of the Prison*, trans. Alan Sheridan (New York, 1995).

26. Guéry and Descimon, "Un Etat des temps modernes," p. 455.

27. Philippe Sueur, *Histoire du droit public, XVe–XVIIIe siècle*, 2 vols., vol. 1, *La Constitution monarchique;* vol. 2, *Affirmation et crise de l'etat sous l'Ancien Régime* (Paris, 1989).

28. Emmanuel Guillaume, *Justice seigneuriale et vie quotidienne dans la vallée du Mont-Dore au XVIIIe siècle* (Clermont-Ferrand, 1992).

29. Montesquieu, *L'Esprit des lois*, 6:5.

30. Robert Mandro, *Magistrats et sorciers* (Paris, 1968).

31. Nicole Castan, *Justice et répression en Languedoc à l'époque des Lumières* (Paris, 1980), p. 299.

32. Foucault, *Surveiller*, pp. 78, 79.

33. Hans-Jürgen Lusebrink, *Histoires curieuses et véritables de Cartouche et de Mandrin,* "Bibliothèque bleue" (Paris, 1984).

34. Bernard Schnapper, *Voies nouvelles en histoire du droit: la justice, la famille, la répression pénale, XVIe–XXe siècle* (Paris, 1991), pp. 186–205.

35. Ibid., pp. 202, 203.

36. Foucault, *Surveiller.*

37. Olwen Hufton, *The Poor of Eighteenth-Century France, 1750–1789* (Oxford, 1974).

10. The End of Rebellion

1. Jean Nicolas, ed., *Mouvements populaires et conscience sociale, XVIe–XIXe siècle* (Paris, 1985).

2. Hincker, *Les Français devant l'impôt,* p. 68.

3. R. Huard, "Existe-t-il une 'politique populaire'?" in Nicolas, *Mouvements populaires,* p. 61.

4. Pierre Ronzeaud, *Peuple et représentation sous le règne de Louis XIV* (Aix-en-Provence, 1988).

5. Philippe Sassier, *Du bon usage des pauvres: histoire d'un thème politique, XVIe–XXe siècle* (Paris, 1990), pp. 62–105.

6. J. Fabre, "L'Article 'Peuple' dans l'*Encylopédie* et le couple Coyer-Jaucourt," in H. Coulet, ed., *Images du peuple au XVIIIe siècle* (Aix-en-Provence, 1973), pp. 11–24.

7. Ronzeaud, *Peuple,* pp. 277ff.

8. C. de Rochefort, *Dictionnaire général* (Amsterdam, 1685).

9. Daniel Roche, *Le Peuple de Paris: essai sur la culture populaire* (Paris, 1981), pp. 278–284.

10. Coulet, *Images du peuple.*

11. Sassier, *Du bon usage,* p. 127.

12. Jean Meslier, *Oeuvres complètes,* 3 vols. (Paris, 1970), 2:152, 153.

13. See Turgot, "Travail," in *Encyclopédie.*

14. Daniel Roche, "Peuple des mots, peuple des images: les représentations du peuple de l'Ancien Régime à la Révolution: peuple, plèbe, populace," *Revue française d'histoire du livre* (1990), 15–32.

15. Milliot, "Les Cris de Paris."

16. Emile Lousse, *La Société d'Ancien Régime: l'organisation et représentation corporatives* (Louvain, 1943).

17. Jean-Pierre Gutton, *La Sociabilité villageoise dans l'ancienne France* (Paris, 1979); Charles Petit-Dutaillis, *Les Communes françaises* (Paris, 1947).

18. Yves Castan, *Honnêté et relations sociales en Languedoc, 1715–1780* (Paris, 1974).

19. Pierre de Saint-Jacob, *Les Paysans de la Bourgogne du Nord* (Paris, 1963).

20. L. Fontaine, "Droits et stratégies: la reproduction des systèmes familiaux dans le Haut-Dauphiné (XVIIe–XVIIIe siècle)," *Annales E.S.C.*, no. 6 (1992), 1259–77.

21. Yves-Marie Bercé, *Fête et révolte: des mentalités populaires du XVIe au XVIIIe siècle* (Paris, 1976).

22. O. Journeaux, "Villageois et autorités," *Droit et cultures*, no. 19 (1990), 101–118.

23. H. Root, "The Rural Community and the French Revolution," in Baker, *Political Culture*, pp. 141–156.

24. Huard, "Existe-t-il une 'politique populaire'?"

25. Harvey Chisick, *The Limits of Reform in the Enlightenment: Attitudes toward the Education of the Lower Classes in Eighteenth-Century France* (Princeton, 1981).

26. Roger Chartier, *Lectures et lecteurs dans la France d'Ancien Régime* (Paris, 1987), pp. 271–346.

27. Bercé, *Fête et révolte*.

28. Daniel Roche, ed., *Journal de ma vie* (Jacques-Louis Ménétra's journal) (Paris, 1982); in English, *Journal of My Life*, trans. Arthur Goldhammer (New York, 1986).

29. Philippe Minard, *La Fin de l'inspection des manufactures: premières hypothèses sur le dérèglement d'une institution de commerce: états, finances et économie pendant la Révolution française* (Paris, 1989), pp. 295–303.

30. Roger Chartier, "Culture populaire et culture politique dans l'Ancien Régime," in Baker, *Political Culture*, pp. 243–260.

31. Stephen Kaplan, "Réflexions sur la police du monde du travail, 1700–1815," *Revue historique*, no. 261 (1979), 297–331.

32. G. Sabatier, "De la révolte du Roure (1670) aux masques armés (1789), la mutation du phénomène contestataire en Vivarais," in Nicolas, *Mouvements populaires*, pp. 121–148.

33. Hincker, *Les Français devant l'impôt*.

34. M. Huvert, "Gabelous et faux sauniers en France à la fin de l'Ancien Régime: essai statistique et sociologique sur le faux saunage dans le ressort de la commission de Saumur, 1764–1789," 2 vols. (thesis, University of Rennes II, 1975), typescript, p. 509; Philippe Savoie, "Contrebande et contrebandiers dans l'Ouest et le Centre de la France au XVIIIe siècle: les archives de la Commission de Saumur, 1742–1789" (master's thesis, University of Paris VIII, 1975), typescript.

35. N. Schapira, "Contrebande et contrebandiers dans le Nord et l'Est de la France, 1740–1789: les archives de la Commission de Reims" (master's thesis, University of Paris I, 1991), typescript.

36. Savoie, "Contrebande," and Schapira, "Contrebande."

37. Hans-Jürgen Lusebrink, "Images et représentations sociales de la criminalité au XVIIIe siècle: Mandrin," *Revue d'histoire moderne et contemporaine* (1979), 345–364.

38. François-Xavier Emmanuelli, *Pouvoir royal et vie régionale en Provence au déclin de la monarchie: psychologie, pratique administrative, défrancisation de l'intendance d'Aix, 1745–1790*, 3 vols. (Lille, 1974).

11. God, the King, and the Churches

1. Michel de Certeau, *La Formalité des pratiques: du système religieux à l'éthique des Lumières,* La Società religiosa nell'età moderna (Naples, 1973), pp. 447–509; *L'Ecriture de l'histoire* (Paris, 1975); *La Fable mystique* (Paris, 1982).

2. M. Valensise, "Le Sacre du roi: stratégie symbolique et doctrine politique de la monarchie française," *Annales E.S.C.,* no. 3 (1986), 547–577.

3. Assembly of the Clergy, 1765, in *Actes sur la religion,* p. 205.

4. Certeau, *La Formalité,* p. 38.

5. Claude Michaud, *L'Eglise et l'argent sous l'Ancien Régime: les receveurs du clergé de France aux XVIe et XVIIe siècles* (Paris, 1991).

6. Michel Peronnet, *Les Evêques de l'Ancienne France,* 2 vols. (Lille, 1977), 2:721–847.

7. Dominique Julia, "Les Deux Puissances: chronique d'une séparation de corps," in Baker, *Political Culture,* pp. 293–310.

8. Jean Queniart, *Les Hommes, l'Eglise et Dieu dans la France du XVIIIe siècle* (Paris, 1978).

9. Perronnet, *Les Evêques.*

10. Augustin Sicard, *L'Ancien Clergé de France,* 3 vols. (Paris, 1905).

11. Julia, "Les Deux Puissances," p. 307.

12. Alphonse Dupront, "Vie et création religieuse dans la France moderne (XIVe–XVIIIe siècle)," in M. François, ed., *La France et les Français* (Paris, 1972).

13. Dominique Julia, "Le Catholicisme, religion du royaume, 1715–1789," "Lumières et religions," "La Déchristianisation, pesée d'un phénomène, des indicateurs de longue durée," and "Jansénisme et déchristianisation," in Jacques Le Goff and René Rémond, eds., *Histoire de la France religieuse, XVIIIe–XIXe siècle* (Paris, 1991), 3:11–49, 145–155, 183–207, and 249–262.

14. M. Cottret, "L'Idée de la primitive Eglise au XVIIIe siècle," 2 vols. (thesis, University of Paris X, 1979), typescript.

15. Julia, "Le Catholicisme."

16. Catherine-Laurence Maire, *Les Convulsionnaires de Saint-Médard: miracles, convulsions et prophéties à Paris au XVIIIe siècle* (Paris, 1985).

17. C. Mabillat, "Les Convulsionnaires" (thesis, University of Paris I, 1982), typescript.

18. René Tavenaux, *Le Jansénisme en Lorraine, 1640–1789* (Paris, 1960).

19. Edmond Preclin, *Les Jansénistes du XVIIIe siècle et la Constitution civile du clergé* (Paris, 1929).

20. Certeau, *La Formalité des pratiques,* pp. 65, 66.

21. Hans Georg Gadamer, *Vérité et méthode;* in English, *Truth and Method,* trans. William Glen-Doepel (London, 1975).

22. Jean-Marie Goulemot, "Démons, merveilles et philosophie à l'âge classique," *Annales E.S.C.*, no. 6, 1223–50.

23. Paul Vernières, *Spinoza et la pensée française avant la Révolution* (Paris, 1959).

24. Philippe Lefebvre, *Les Pouvoirs de la parole: l'Eglise et Rousseau, 1762–1848* (Paris, 1992), p. 10.

25. Dominique Julia, "Le Prêtre au XVIIIe siècle," *Recherche de sciences religieuses,* no. 58 (1970), 522.

26. Ibid., p. 528.

27. Ibid., pp. 521–534; Julia, "Le Catholicisme," pp. 387–389.

28. Jean Delumeau, *Le Péché et la peur: la culpabilisation en Occident, XIIIe–XVIIIe siècle* (Paris, 1983); in English, *Sin and Fear: The Emergence of a Western Guilt Culture, 13th–18th Centuries,* trans. Eric Nicholson (New York, 1990).

29. Queniart, *Les Hommes,* pp. 154–178.

30. *La Théorie de l'intérêt de l'argent* (Paris, 1780).

31. Lefebvre, *Les Pouvoirs de la parole,* p. 11.

32. A. Monod, *L'Apologétique en France au XVIIIe siècle* (Paris, 1916).

33. O. Robert, "Le Franc de Pompignan et l'apologétique au siècle des Lumières," 2 vols. (thesis, University of Paris I, 1983), typescript.

34. Rivarol, *De l'homme intellectuel et moral* (Paris, 1791).

12. ELITES AND NOBILITIES

1. Roland Mousnier, *Fureurs paysannes: les paysans dans les révoltes, du XVIIe siècle* (Paris, 1967).

2. Dumont, *Homo hierarchicus.*

3. Ibid., p. 34.

4. Denis Richet, *De la Réforme à la Révolution: études sur la France moderne* (Paris, 1991), p. 391.

5. Roland Mousnier, *Les Hiérarchies sociales de 1450 à nos jours* (Paris, 1973), p. 39; in English, *Social Hierarchies: 1450 to the Present,* trans. Peter Evans (London, 1973).

6. "Ordre," *Encyclopédie,* 11:595–616.

7. Jules Flammermont, *Les Remontrances du Parlement de Paris au XVIIIe siècle,* 3 vols. (Paris, 1888–1898), 3:287–291.

8. Anne Zink, *Azereix: la vie d'une communauté rurale à la fin du XVIIIe siècle* (Paris, 1969).

9. Robert Darnton, *The Great Cat Massacre and Other Episodes in French Cultural History* (New York: Basic Books, 1984), pp. 107–145.

10. Perrot, *Genèse,* 1:243–249.

11. François Bluche and Jean-François Solnon, *La Véritable Hiérarchie sociale de l'ancienne France: le tarif de la première capitation (1695)* (Geneva, 1983).

12. A. Guéry, "Etat, classification sociale et compromis sous Louis XIV: la capitation de 1695," *Annales E.S.C.* (1986), 1041–60.

13. Jean-Claude Perrot, "Cours sur les finances et les institutions financières au XVIIIe siècle," unpublished ms. (1992); Perrot, *Une Histoire intellectuelle*, pp. 31–50.

14. Mercier, *Tableau de Paris*, vol. 11.

15. Guy Chaussinand-Nogaret, *La Noblesse au XVIIIe siècle, de la féodalité aux Lumières* (Paris, 1976), p. 68.

16. Jean Meyer, *La Noblesse bretonne au XVIIIe siècle*, 2 vols. (Paris, 1966).

17. Robert Forster, *The House of Saulx Tavanes: Versailles and Burgundy, 1700–1830* (Baltimore, 1971).

18. Meyer, *La Noblesse bretonne*.

19. Monique Cubells, *La Provence des Lumières: les parlementaires d'Aix au XVIIIe siècle* (Paris, 1984).

20. François Bluche, *Les Magistrats du Parlement de Paris au XVIIIe siècle, 1715–1771* (Paris, 1960).

21. William Doyle, *The Parliament of Bordeaux and the End of the Old Regime, 1771–1790* (London, 1974).

22. Maurice Gresset, *Gens de justice à Besançon: de la conquête par Louis XIV à la Révolution française, 1674–1709*, 2 vols. (Paris, 1978).

23. Jean Egret, *Le Parlement de Dauphiné et les affaires publiques dans la deuxième moitié du XVIIIe siècle* (Grenoble, 1970).

24. Montesquieu, *L'Esprit des lois*, bk. 3, 5.

25. Chaussinand-Nogaret, *La Noblesse*, pp. 200–223.

26. Richet, *La France moderne*.

27. Ibid.

28. Gaston Roupnel, *La Ville et la campagne au XVIIe siècle: etude sur les populations du pays dijonnais* (Paris, 1955).

29. Jean Meyer, "Noblesse française au XVIIIe siècle," *Acta poloniae historica* 26 (1977), 15–21.

30. André Lespagnol, *Messieurs de Saint-Malo: une élite négociante au temps de Louis XIV* (Saint-Malo, 1990).

31. Buffon, *Actes du Colloque international* (Paris, Montbard, and Dijon, 1992), pp. 13–81.

32. J. Hecht, *Pierre de Boisguilbert ou la naissance de l'économie politique*, 2 vols. (Paris, 1964), pp. 267–289.

33. G. Richard, *Noblesse d'affaires au XVIIIe siècle* (Paris, 1974).

13. Public Space

1. François Furet, *Penser la Révolution française* (Paris, 1978); Chartier, *Les Origines culturelles*.

2. Tocqueville, *L'Ancien Régime*, trans. Gilbert, pp. 145–146.

3. Furet, *Penser la Révolution française*.

4. Ibid., p. 147.

5. Keith Baker, *Au tribunal de l'opinion: essais sur l'imaginaire politique au XVIIIe siècle* (Paris, 1992).

6. Ibid.

7. Roche, *Le Siècle des Lumières en province*.

8. Jürgen Habermas, *L'Espace public: archéologie de la publicité comme dimension constitutive de la société bourgeoise* (Paris, 1978); in English, *The Structural Transformation of the Public Sphere*, trans. Thomas Berger with the assistance of Frederick Lawrence (Cambridge, Mass., 1989).

9. Baker, *Political Culture*.

10. Dominique Julia and Daniel Milo, "Les Ressources culturelles," in Burguière and Revel, *Histoire de la France*, pp. 379–510.

11. Roger Chartier, Dominique Julia, and Marie-Madeleine Compère, *L'Education en France du XVIe au XVIIIe siècle* (Paris, 1976).

12. Ibid.

13. Dominique Julia, "Une Réforme impossible," *Actes de la recherche en sciences sociales* (1983), 53–76.

14. Maurice Agulhon, *Pénitents et Francs-Maçons de l'ancienne Provence* (Paris, 1968).

15. E. François and R. Reichardt, "Les Formes de sociabilité en France du milieu du XVIIIe siècle au milieu du XIXe siècle," *Revue d'histoire moderne et contemporaine* (1987), 453–472.

16. Furet, *Penser la Révolution française*.

17. J. Boutier and P. Boutry, "La Diffusion des sociétés politiques en France, 1789, An III, une enquête nationale," *Annales historiques de la Révolution française* (1986), pp. 365–398.

18. Ran Halévi, *Les Loges maçonniques dans la France d'Ancien Régime* (Paris, 1984); G. Gayot, *La Franc-Maçonnerie française, textes et pratiques, XVIIIe-XIXe siècle* (Paris, 1980).

19. Roche, *Le Siècle des Lumières en province*.

20. Reinhart Koselleck, *Le Règne de la critique*, trans. (Paris, 1979).

21. Ibid., p. 79.

22. Roche, *Les Républicains des Lettres*, p. 166.

23. Mona Ozouf, "L'Opinion publique," in Baker, *Political Culture*, pp. 419–434.

24. Elias, *La Société de cour*.

25. Philippe Stewart, *Le Masque et la parole: le langage de l'amour au XVIIIe siècle* (Paris, 1973).

26. Immanuel Kant, *Anthropology from a Pragmatic Point of View*, trans. Victor Dowdell (Carbondale: University of Illinois Press, 1996), p. 190; translation modified.

14. CRISES IN STATE AND SOCIETY

1. Baker, *Au tribunal de l'opinion*.

2. Jean-Jacques Rousseau, *Considérations sur le gouvernement de Pologne*, in *Oeuvres complètes*, vol. 3 (Paris).

3. *Encyclopédie* 5:337–349.

4. Schlanger, *Les Métaphores de l'organisme*.

5. Jean-Marie Goulemot, *Discours, histoire et révolution: représentations de l'histoire et discours sur les révolutions de l'âge classique aux Lumières* (Paris, 1975).

6. Leroy-Ladurie, *L'Ancien Régime*.

7. Jean Meyer, *Le Régent* (Paris, 1985).

8. Baker, *Au tribunal de l'opinion*.

9. Leroy-Ladurie, *L'Ancien Régime*.

10. Edgar Faure, *La Banqueroute de Law, 17 juillet 1720* (Paris, 1977).

11. F. Hincker, *Expériences bancaires sous l'Ancien Régime* (Paris, 1973).

12. Jacques Necker, *De l'administration des finances de la France* (1784), 3 vols. (Paris, 1984), 3:340–343.

13. Baker, *Au tribunal de l'opinion*.

14. Dale Van Kley, *The Jansenists and the Expulsion of the Jesuits from France, 1757–1765* (New Haven: Yale University Press, 1975); idem, "The Jansenist Constitutional Legacy in the French Pre-Revolution," in Baker, *Political Culture*, pp. 169–203.

15. Montesquieu, *L'Esprit des lois*, bk. 5, 10.

16. Jean Egret, *Louis XV et l'opposition parlementaire* (Paris, 1970).

17. Roger Bickart, *Les Parlements et la notion de souveraineté nationale au XVIIIe siècle* (Paris, 1932), pp. 249, 250.

18. François Furet, *La Révolution, 1770–1880: histoire de France* (Paris, 1988).

19. Ibid.

20. Lüthy, *La Banque protestante*, 2:370, 371.

21. Ibid., p. 35.

22. Furet, *La Révolution*, pp. 59, 60.

15. LIFE TRIUMPHANT

1. Vivian R. Gruder, "Les Pamphlets 'populaires' à la veille de la Révolution," *Revue d'histoire moderne et contemporaine* (1992), 161–197.

2. Dupront, *Les Lettres*.

3. Jean Starobinski, *L'Invention de la liberté, 1700–1789* (Paris and Geneva, 1964); in English, *The Invention of Liberty, 1700–1789*, trans. Bernard C. Swift (Cleveland, 1964).

4. Jean-Claude Perrot, *De la richesse territoriale du royaume de France: Lavoisier texte et documents* (Paris, 1988), pp. 500–508.

5. François Lebrun, *Les Hommes et la mort en Anjou, XVIIe–XVIIIe siècle* (Paris, 1971).

6. Y. Blayo, "Mouvement naturel de la population française de 1740 à 1829," *Population: démographie historique* (1975), 15–64.

7. J.-Y. Grenier, Jacques Dupâquier, and André Burguière, "Croissance et déstabilisation," in Dupâquier, *Histoire de la population française*, 2:437–499.

8. Michel Morineau, *Les Faux-Semblants du démarrage économique: agriculture et démographie dans la France du XVIIIe siècle* (Paris, 1971).

9. J.-M. Moriceau, "Les Fermiers de l'Ile-de-France, XVIe–XVIIIe siècle," 2 vols. (thesis, University of Paris I, 1993), typescript.

10. Mulliez, "Le Blé, mal nécessaire."

11. Pierre Darmon, *La Longue Traque de la variole: les pionniers de la médecine préventive* (Paris, 1986).

12. Jacques Gélis, *L'Arbre et le fruit: la naissance dans l'Occident moderne* (Paris, 1984); *La Sage-Femme ou le médecin: une nouvelle conception de la vie* (Paris, 1980).

13. Jean Meyer, "L'Enquête de l'Académie de médecine sur les épidémies," in Jean-Paul Desaive et al., *Médecins, climat et épidémies à la fin du XVIIe siècle* (Paris, 1972), pp. 9–20; Pierre Goubert, *La Médicalisation de la société française, 1770–1790* (Waterloo, Ontario, 1982).

14. André J. Bourde, *Agronomie et agronomes en France au XVIIIe siècle*, 3 vols. (Paris, 1967).

15. François Dagognet, *Des révolutions vertes: histoire et principe de l'agronomie* (Paris, 1973).

16. Michel Morineau, "Ruralia," *Revue historique*, no. 2 (1992), 359–384.

17. Perrot, *Une Histoire intellectuelle.*

18. Moriceau, "Les Fermiers."

19. Bourde, *Agronomie.*

20. Claire Salomon-Bayet, "L'Institution de la science," *Annales E.S.C.*, no. 5 (1975), 1028–44; *L'Institution de la science et l'expérience du vivant: méthode et expérience à l'Académie royale des sciences, 1666–1793* (Paris, 1976).

21. Georges Canguilhem, *Etude d'histoire et de philosophie des sciences* (Paris, 1968), pp. 9–23.

22. Steven Shapin and Simon Schaffer, *Leviathan and the Air-Pump: Hobbes, Boyle, and the Experimental Sciences* (Princeton, 1985); Salomon-Bayet, "L'Institution de la science" and *L'Institution de la science.*

23. M.-N. Bourguet, "Voyages, statistiques, histoire naturelle: l'inventaire du monde au XVIIIe siècle," 2 vols. (habilitation thesis, University of Paris I, 1993), typescript.

24. B. Jammes, "Le Livre des Sciences," in Martin and Chartier, *Histoire de l'édition française*, 2:206–217.

25. Dupront, *Les Lettres.*

26. Roger Hahn, *The Anatomy of a Scientific Institution: The Paris Academy of Sciences, 1666–1863* (Berkeley, 1971); Charles Gillispie, *Science and Polity in France at the End of the Old Regime* (Princeton, 1980).

27. Salomon-Bayet, "L'Institution."

28. Georges Gusdorf, *Les Sciences humaines et la pensée occidentale*, vol. 5, *Dieu, la nature, l'homme au siècle des Lumières* (Paris, 1972).

29. Turgot, *Tableau philosophique des progrès successifs de l'esprit humain* (Paris, 1750).

30. Jean Ehrard, *L'Idée de nature en France, dans la première moitié du XVIIIe siècle*, 2 vols. (Paris, 1963).

16. THE LIBERTIES OF INDIVIDUALS

1. Dumont, *Essai sur l'individualisme.*

2. Ibid., pp. 85–102.

3. Louis Dumont, *Homo aequalis* (Paris, 1977), pp. 24, 25.

4. Claude Lévi-Strauss, preface to André Burguière et al., *Histoire de la famille*, 2 vols. (Paris, 1986), 1:9–14.

5. Ibid.

6. Jack Goody, *The Development of the Family and Marriage in Europe* (Cambridge, 1983).

7. Jean Delumeau and Daniel Roche, *Histoire des pères* (Paris, 1990), p. 129.

8. J.-C. Bonnet, "Le Réseau culinaire dans l'*Encyclopédie*," *Annales E.S.C.*, no. 5 (1976), 891–915.

9. François Chatelet, introduction to Hélène Vérin, *Entrepreneurs, entreprise: histoire d'une idée* (Paris, 1982), pp. 7–8.

10. Ibid.; Joseph Schumpeter, *A History of Economic Analysis* (London, 1954); Perrot, *Une Histoire intellectuelle.*

11. Vérin, *Entrepreneur*, p. 115.

12. Richard Cantillon, *Essai sur la nature du commerce en général* (London, 1755), pp. 28–32.

13. Ibid., pp. 28, 29.

14. Vérin, *Entrepreneur*, p. 171.

15. Ibid., pp. 90–99.

16. Georg Simmel, *Philosophie de l'argent*, trans. (Paris, 1987), p. 19; in English, *The Philosophy of Money*, trans. Tom Bottomore and David Frisby (London, 1990).

17. Ibid., p. 550.

18. Pierre Vilar, *Or et monnaie dans l'histoire* (Paris, 1974).

19. G. Thuillier, "Pour une histoire monétaire de la France au XIXe siècle: les monnaies de cuivre et de billon," *Annales E.S.C.*, no. 1 (1959), 65–91.

20. R. Bigot, "Aux origines du mont-de-piété parisien: bienfaisance et crédit, 1777–1789," *Annales E.S.C.* (1932), 113–127.

21. Pierre Goubert, *Beauvais et le Beauvaisis, de 1600 à 1730: contribution à l'histoire sociale au XVIIe siècle,* 2 vols. (Paris, 1958).

22. Pierre Léon, *Structures économiques et problèmes sociaux du monde rural dans la France du Sud-Est* (Paris, 1966).

23. Mona Ozouf, "Egalité" and "Liberté," in François Furet and Mona Ozouf, eds., *Dictionnaire critique de la Révolution française* (Paris, 1988), p. 697; in English, *A Critical Dictionary of the French Revolution,* trans. Arthur Goldhammer (Cambridge, Mass.: Harvard University Press, 1989).

24. Roche, *Le Siècle des Lumières,* pp. 166–181.

25. Dumont, *Essai sur l'individualisme,* pp. 95–102.

26. Ozouf, "Egalité," "Liberté," pp. 713–767.

27. Philippe Lejeune, *L'Autobiographie en France* (Paris, 1971); *Le Pacte autobiographique* (Paris, 1975).

28. Starobinski, *L'Invention de la liberté,* p. 137.

29. Dremière, "Portrait et représentation."

30. Starobinski, *L'Invention de la liberté,* p. 136.

31. Laurent Versini, *Laclos et la tradition: essai sur les sources et les techniques des "Liaisons dangereuses"* (Paris, 1965).

32. J. Hebrard, "La Lettre représentée: les pratiques épistolaires populaires dans les récits de vie ouvriers et paysans," in Roger Chartier, ed., *La Correspondance* (Paris, 1991), pp. 279–372.

33. Beatrice Fraenkel, *La Signature: genèse d'un signe* (Paris, 1992), p. 189.

34. Ibid., pp. 272–278.

35. Marcel Mauss, *Sociologie et anthropologie* (1950), 4th ed. (Paris, 1968), p. 361.

17. CONSUMPTION AND APPEARANCE

1. J.-P. Lethuillier, "Prénoms et Révolution: enquête sur le corpus falaisien," *Annales de Normandie,* no. 4 (1990), 413–436.

2. Starobinski, *L'Invention de la liberté.*

3. J.-Y. Grenier, "Modèles de la demande sous l'Ancien Régime," *Annales E.S.C.* (1987), 487–528.

4. Georg Simmel, *La Tragédie de la culture,* trans. (Paris, 1988).

5. Pierre Léon, "La Réponse de l'industrie," in *Histoire économique et sociale de la France,* vol. 2, *1660–1789* (Paris, 1970), pp. 217–266.

6. Chassagne, *Le Coton et ses patrons,* pp. 22–23.

7. Roche, *Le Peuple de Paris;* Pardaillé-Galabrun, *Naissance de l'intime.*

8. Roche, *Le Peuple de Paris,* pp. 242–274; Farge, *Dire et mal dire.*

9. Roche, *La Culture des apparences.*

10. J.-V. Alter, *L'Esprit anti-bourgeois sous l'Ancien Régime* (Geneva, 1970).

11. G. Galliani, "Rousseau, le luxe et l'idéologie nobiliaire," in *Studies on Voltaire*

(Oxford, 1989); Albert Cherel, *Fénelon au XVIIIe siècle en France: son prestige, son influence* (Paris, 1917).

12. Fénelon, *Télémaque*, bk. 22.

13. André Morize, *L'Apologie du luxe au XVIIIe siècle et "Le mondain" de Voltaire* (Paris, 1909), pp. 46–48.

14. Cantillon, *De la nature*, pp. 73–83.

15. Ibid., pp. 115–116.

16. Paulette Carrive, *Bernard Mandeville: passions, vices, vertus* (Paris, 1980).

17. Ibid., p. 105.

18. Albert Hirschman, *Bonheur privé, action publique* (Paris, 1983).

19. Ibid., p. 81.

20. Perrot, *Une Histoire intellectuelle*, pp. 333–358.

21. Galliani, "Rousseau, le luxe et l'idéologie nobiliaire."

22. Roche, *Le Siècle des Lumières en province;* Jean-Claude Perrot, "L'Economie politique et ses livres," in Martin and Chartier, *Histoire de l'édition française*, 2:240–260.

23. Michel Launay, *Jean-Jacques Rousseau, écrivain politique* (Cannes, 1971); *Jean-Jacques Rousseau et son temps* (Paris, 1969).

24. Jean Starobinski, *Jean-Jacques Rousseau, la transparence et l'obstacle* (Paris, 1957), p. 354; in English, *Jean-Jacques Rousseau, Transparency and Obstruction*, trans. Arthur Goldhammer (Chicago, 1988).

25. Edward Twitchell Hall, *Beyond Culture* (Garden City, N.Y., 1976); *The Hidden Dimension* (Garden City, N.Y., 1966).

26. Hirschman, *Bonheur privé*, pp. 99–102.

27. Roche, *Le Siècle des Lumières en province;* Jacques Proust, *Diderot et l'Encyclopédie* (Paris, 1967).

28. Gilbert Simondon, *Du mode d'existence des objets techniques* (Paris, 1969).

29. Ibid., p. 93.

30. Ibid., pp. 101–103.

18. Desacralization, Secularization, Illuminism

1. Paul Hazard, *La Crise de la conscience européenne, 1680–1715* (Paris, 1935); *La Pensée européenne au XVIIIe siècle, de Montesquieu à Lessing*, 3 vols. (Paris, 1946).

2. Gusdorf, *Les Sciences humaines*, vol. 5, *Dieu, la nature, l'homme au siècle des Lumières.*

3. Pierre Chaunu, *L'Europe des Lumières* (Grenoble, 1971), p. 299.

4. Ernst Cassirer, *La Philosophie des Lumières*, trans. (Paris, 1966); in English, *The Philosophy of Enlightenment*, trans. Fritz C. A. Koelln and James P. Pettegrove (Princeton, 1979).

5. Bernard Groethuysen, *Origines de l'esprit bourgeois en France*, trans. (Paris, 1927); in English, *The Bourgeois*, trans. Mary Ilford (New York, 1968).

6. Chaunu, *L'Europe des Lumières*, p. 299.

7. Michel Foucault, *Les Mots et les choses: une archéologie des sciences humaines* (Paris, 1966); in English, *The Order of Things: An Archaeology of the Human Sciences* (New York, 1970).

8. Gusdorf, *Les Sciences humaines*, 5:26–38.

9. Peter Gay, *The Enlightenment: An Interpretation* (New York, 1967), pp. 253, 254.

10. McManners, *French Ecclesiastical Society*, p. 19.

11. Alphonse Dupront, *Du sacré* (Paris, 1987), pp. 422, 423.

12. Julia, "Jansénisme," pp. 251–253.

13. Philippe Ariès, *L'Homme devant la mort* (Paris, 1977); Michel Vovelle, *Piété baroque et déchristianisation en Provence au XVIIIe siècle* (Paris, 1973); *La Mort en Occident de 1300 à nos jours* (Paris, 1983).

14. Pierre Chaunu, *Mourir à Paris, XVIe, XVIIe, XVIIIe siècles* (Paris, 1979).

15. Louis Chatellier, *L'Europe des dévots* (Paris, 1987).

16. Chartier, *Les Origines*.

17. Certeau, *La Formalité*, pp. 43, 44.

18. Alphonse Dupront, *Art et société en Europe au XVIIIe siècle* (Paris, 1965), p. 225.

19. Gusdorf, *Les Sciences humaines*, 5:40–45.

20. René Pomeau, *La Religion de Voltaire* (Paris, 1956).

21. Ibid.

22. Paul Vernière, *Spinoza et la pensée française avant la Révolution* (Paris, 1954).

23. Dupront, *Les Lettres*.

24. Pierre-Maurice Masson, *La Religion de Jean-Jacques Rousseau*, 3 vols. (Paris, 1916), 1:21.

25. Charles Guyot, "La Pensée religieuse de Rousseau," in Samuel Baud-Bovy et al., *Jean-Jacques Rousssseau* (Neuchâtel, 1962), pp. 127–152.

26. Pierre Trahard, *Les Maîtres de la sensibilité française au XVIIIe siècle*, 4 vols. (Paris, 1932), 3:110.

27. Sylvain Menant, "De l'*Encyclopédie* aux *Méditations*," in Michel Delon, Robert Mauzi, and Sylvain Menant, *Littérature française* (Grenoble, 1984), 6:267–320.

28. Claire Salomon-Bayet, *Jean-Jacques Rousseau, ou l'impossible unité* (Paris, 1972), pp. 65, 66; Guyot, *La Pensée*, p. 149.

29. Henri Gouhier, *Les Méditations métaphysiques de Jean-Jacques Rousseau* (Paris, 1970), pp. 244–259.

30. Mauzi, *L'Idée*.

31. Turgot, *Deuxième Lettre à un grand vicaire sur la tolérance* (Paris, 1754).

32. Michel Delon, *L'Idée d'énergie au tournant des Lumières, 1770–1820* (Paris, 1988), p. 19.

33. Jean-Jacques Rousseau, *Essai sur l'origine des langues* (Paris, 1990).

34. Louis-Sébastien Mercier, *De la littérature et des littérateurs* (Paris, 1778), p. 21.

35. Denis Diderot, *Fragments échappés du portefeuille d'un philosophe;* quoted in Delon, *L'Idée.*

36. Delon, *L'Idée,* p. 32.

37. Ibid., p. 427.

38. Ibid., pp. 516–521.

39. Jean Deprun, *La philosophie de l'inquiétude en France au XVIIIe siècle* (Paris, 1979).

40. Trahard, *Les Maîtres,* pp. 275–290.

41. Jules Michelet, *Histoire de France* (Paris, 1833–1846), 15:340.

42. Deprun, *L'Inquiétude,* p. 122.

43. Dupront, *Art et société,* p. 24.

44. E. J. Mannuci, *Gli altri Lumi: esoterismo e politica nel settecento francese* (Palermo, 1988).

45. Foucault, *Les Mots et les choses,* pp. 32–55.

46. Robert Darnton, *Mesmerism and the End of the Enlightenment in France* (Cambridge, Mass.: Harvard University Press, 1968); Vincenzo Ferrone, *I Profeti dell'illuminismo: le metamorfosi della ragione nelle tardo settecento italiano* (Bari, 1989).

47. Darnton, *Mesmerism,* p. 120.

19. Materializing the Intelligence, Abstracting Things

1. Goulemot, *Discours,* pp. 438, 439.

2. René Pomeau, *Candide* (Oxford, 1980), pp. 64–69.

3. Starobinski, *L'Invention de la liberté,* p. 15.

4. Michel Morineau, "Budgets populaires en France au XVIIIe siècle," *Revue d'histoire économique et sociale,* nos. 2–4 (1972), 468–489.

5. Jean-Louis Flandrin, *Chronique de platine: pour une gastronomie historique* (Paris, 1992), pp. 213–249.

6. Morineau, "Budgets," pp. 450–470.

7. Perrot, *Une Histoire intellectuelle.*

8. A. Poitrineau, "L'Alimentation populaire en Auvergne au XVIIIe siècle," in Jean-Jacques Hemardinquer, *Pour une histoire de l'alimentation* (Paris, 1970), pp. 146–153.

9. Roche, *Le Peuple de Paris;* Jeffry Kaplow, *Les Noms des rois: les pauvres de Paris à la veille de la Révolution* (Paris, 1974); in English, *The Names of Kings: The Parisian Laboring Poor in the Eighteenth Century* (New York, 1972).

10. Perrot, *De la richesse,* pp. 190–197.

11. R. Philippe, "L'Alimentation de Paris au XVIIIe siècle," *Annales E.S.C.* (1974), 60–67.

12. M. Lachiver, "L'Approvisionnement de Paris en viande au XVIIIe siècle," in *La*

France d'Ancien Régime: études réunies en l'honneur de Pierre Goubert, 2 vols. (Toulouse, 1984), 1:345–354.

13. Philippe, "L'Alimentation."

14. Kaplow, *Les Noms des rois*, p. 135.

15. Jean-Robert Pitte, *Gastronomie française: histoire et géographie d'une passion* (Paris, 1991), p. 50.

16. Michel Onfray, *Le Ventre des philosophes* (Paris, 1989).

17. A. Girard, "La Cuisinière bourgeoise: livres culinaires, cuisine et société au XVIIe et XVIIIe siècle," *Revue d'histoire moderne et contemporaine* (1977), 437–523.

18. Claudine Marenco, *Manières de table, modèles de moeurs: XVIIe–XXe siècle* (Paris, 1992).

19. Girard, "La Cuisinière."

20. Menon, *La Cuisinière bourgeoise suivie de l'office, à l'usage de tous ceux qui se mêlent de dépenses de la maison* (Brussels, 1774; rpt. Poitiers, 1881), pp. 480–498.

21. A. Peters, afterword to Menon, *La Cuisinière bourgeoise*.

22. Jean-Louis Flandrin, Philip Hyman, and Mary Hyman, *Le Cuisinier français* (Paris, 1983).

23. Flandrin, *Chronique de platine*.

24. Jean-Jacques Rousseau, *Emile*, in *Oeuvres complètes*, vol. 4 (Paris), p. 465.

25. J. Lambert, "Le Chirurgien de papier," 3 vols. (thesis, University of Paris I, 1991), typescript.

26. Jean-Pierre Aron, "Biologie et alimentation à l'aube du XIXe siècle," in Hemardinquer, *Pour une histoire de l'alimentation*, pp. 23–28.

27. Lambert, "Le Chirurgien," 1:187.

28. J.-C. Bonnet, "Le Réseau culinaire dans l'*Encyclopédie*," *Annales E.S.C.*, no. 5 (1976), 891–915.

29. Peters, afterword to Menon, *La Cuisinière bourgeoise*, pp. 487–492.

30. Bonnet, "Le Réseau culinaire," p. 905.

31. Jean Meyer, *Histoire du sucre* (Paris, 1989).

32. Sidney W. Mintz, *Sweetness and Power: The Place of Sugar in Modern History* (New York, 1985).

33. Roche, *La Culture*, pp. 255–265.

34. Abbé Delille, *Les Trois Règnes de la Nature* (Paris, 1808).

35. N. Harwich, *Histoire du chocolat* (Paris, 1992).

36. Piero Camporesi, *Le Goût du chocolat: l'art de vivre au siècle des Lumières*, trans. (Paris, 1991); in English, *Exotic Brew: The Art of Living in the Age of Enlightenment* (Cambridge, Mass., 1994).

37. Pardaillé-Galabrun, *Naissance de l'intime*, pp. 300–303; Roche, *Le Peuple de Paris*, pp. 143–145.

38. Roche, *La Culture des apparences*.

39. Louis Dermigny, *Le Commerce à Canton au XVIIIe siècle, 1719–1833,* 3 vols. (Paris, 1964).

40. Ibid., 2:577.

41. Bernard Deloche, *L'Art du meuble: introduction à l'esthétique des genres mineurs* (Lyons, 1980).

42. Chaunu, *L'Europe des Lumières.*

43. Starobinski, *L'Invention,* pp. 39–40.

44. Chaunu, *L'Europe des Lumières,* p. 482.

45. U. van de Sandt, "Les Salons au XVIIIe siècle," *Revue de l'Art* (1986).

46. Goubert and Roche, *Sociétés et cultures.* Robert M. Isherwood, *Farce and Fantasy: Popular Entertainment in Eighteenth-Century Paris* (Oxford, 1986).

47. Pierre Verlet, *L'Art du meuble à Paris au XVIIIe siècle* (Lyons, 1983), pp. 14, 153, 154.

48. Pierre Verlet, "Le Commerce des objets d'art et les marchands merciers à Paris au XVIIIe siècle," *Annales E.S.C.,* no. 12 (1958), 10–28.

49. Bernard Deloche, *Le Mobilier bourgeois à Lyon, XVIe–XVIIIe siècle* (Lyons, 1983), pp. 14, 153, 154.

50. Siegfried Giedion, *La Mécanisation au pouvoir,* trans. (Paris, 1980), pp. 269–278; in English, *Mechanization Takes Command* (New York, 1969).

51. Svend Eriksen, *Early Neo-Classicism in France: The Creation of the Louis Seize Style in Architectural Decoration, Furniture and Ormolu, Gold and Silver and Sevres Porcelain,* trans. Peter Thornton (London, 1974).

52. Mario Praz, *Goût néoclassique,* trans. (Paris, 1989), pp. 261, 262; in English, *On Neoclassicism,* trans. Angus Davidson (Evanston, Ill., 1969).

53. Pardaillé-Galabrun, *Naissance de l'intime,* p. 397.

54. Jean-Pierre Goubert, ed., *Du luxe au confort* (Paris, 1988).

55. Georges Vigarello, "Confort et hygiène en France au XIXe siècle," in Goubert, *Du luxe au confort,* p. 52.

56. Pardaillé-Galabrun, *Naissance de l'intime,* p. 358.

57. Roche, "Le Temps de l'eau rare," pp. 383–399.

58. N. Coquery, "Les Annonces des *Petites Affiches* à la fin du XVIIIe siècle" (master's thesis, University of Paris I, 1982).

59. Perrot, *Genèse,* 2:700, 701.

60. Praz, *Goût néoclassique,* p. 257.

20. PARIS, CAPITAL OF THE ENLIGHTENMENT

1. Perrot, *Genèse,* 2:1028.

2. Raymond Trousson, *Introduction à Fougeret de Montbron: le cosmopolite ou le citoyen du Monde* (Bordeaux, 1970).

3. Chagniot, *Paris au XVIIIe siècle*, p. 221.

4. Morineau, "Budget de l'Etat," pp. 289–336.

5. Perrot, *De la richesse*.

6. Chagniot, *Paris*, pp. 71–92, 299–316.

7. Dupront, *Les Lettres*.

8. Nicole Pellegrin, *Les Vêtements de la liberté* (Paris, 1989).

9. Arlette Farge and Jacques Revel, *Logiques de la foule: l'affaire des enlèvements d'enfants, Paris 1750* (Paris, 1988).

10. Gabriel Le Bras, preface to Adrian Friedmann, *Paris, ses rues, ses paroisses du Moyen Age à la Révolution* (Paris, 1959), pp. 1–2.

11. Martine Sonnet, *L'Education des filles au siècle des Lumières* (Paris, 1987).

12. Roche, *Le Siècle des Lumières en province*.

13. Arlette Farge, *Vivre dans la rue à Paris au XVIIIe siècle* (Paris, 1979); *La Vie fragile: violence, pouvoirs et solidarités à Paris au XVIIIe siècle* (Paris, 1986).

14. F.-J. Guillauté, *Mémoire sur la réformation de la police en France soumis au roi en 1749*, ed. J. Seznec (Paris, 1974).

15. Chagniot, *Paris*, p. 142.

16. Ibid., p. 93.

17. J.-L. Gay, "L'Administration de la capitale entre 1770 et 1780" and "La Tutelle de la royauté et ses limites," *Paris et Ile-de-France*, no. 8 (1956), 299–370; no. 9 (1957–58), 283–363; no. 10 (1959), 181–247; no. 11 (1960), 363–405; no. 12 (1961), 135–218.

18. Roche, *Journal de ma vie*.

19. Perrot, "L'Economie politique."

20. Mercier, *Tableau*, 11:39.

21. C. Grasland, "Recherches sur la chanson politique à l'époque de la Régence" (master's thesis, University of Paris I, 1986), typescript.

22. Isherwood, *Farce and Fantasy*.

23. M. Vénard, *La Foire entre en scène* (Lyons, 1978).

24. Richard Sennet, *Les Tyrannies de l'intimité*, trans. (Paris, 1979).

25. Paolo Piasenza, *Polizia e città: strategie d'ordine, conflitti e rivolte a Parigi tra sei e settecento* (Bologna, 1990).

26. J.-D. Mellot, "Livres et société à Rouen, XVIe–XVIIIe siècle," 4 vols. (thesis, University of Paris I, 1992), typescript.

27. Mercier, *Tableau*, 12:151, 152.

28. Henri Lagrave, *Le Théâtre et le public à Paris de 1715 à 1750* (Paris, 1972).

29. Rétif de La Bretonne, *Les Nuits de Paris* (Paris, n.d.), pp. 1296, 1297.

30. Martine de Rougemont, *La Vie théâtrale en France au XVIIIe siècle* (Paris, 1988), p. 232.

31. Hufton, *The Poor of Eighteenth-Century France*.

32. Rougemont, *La Vie*, p. 232.

33. Bruno Brevan, *Les Changements de la vie musicale parisienne de 1774 à 1799* (Paris, 1980); Georges Snyders, *Le Goût musical en France au XVIIe et au XVIIIe siècles* (Paris, 1968).

34. Sennett, *Les Tyrannies,* p. 89.

35. Ibid., pp. 91–106.

36. Jean-Jacques Rousseau, *Lettre à d'Alembert* (1758).

37. Sennett, *Les Tyrannies,* p. 103.

38. Alain Le Bihan, *Loges et chapitres de la Grande Loge et du Grand Orient de France* (Paris, 1986); *Les Francs-Maçons parisiens du Grand Orient de France (fin du XVIIIe siècle)* (Paris, 1973).

39. Roche, *Le Peuple.*

40. Roche, *Journal,* pp. 409–412.

41. Steven Laurance Kaplan, *La Bagarre: Galiani's "Lost" Parody* (The Hague, 1983), pp. 30–68.

42. Rétif de La Bretonne, *Les Nuits,* pp. 3181, 3197, 3252, 3255.

43. Chagniot, *Paris,* p. 525.

INDEX

Abeille, 504–505

Absolutism, 2, 5, 8, 12, 153, 210, 212, 242, 264, 266, 270, 369, 390, 468; opposition to, 212–213, 288, 408, 475, 482; governmental, 222, 228, 563; enlightened, 262, 277–280, 289, 393–395; crisis and future of, 451, 452, 470; authoritarian, 457, 464; science and, 513

Absolutist society, 323

Academic model, 440

Academic movement, 242

Academies, 21, 102, 155, 189, 235, 244–245, 253, 281, 282, 305–306, 317, 322, 323, 409–410, 648; location, 106–107, 438–439; salons and, 151, 545; academic life and sociability, 169–172; political, 281–283; effect on justice system, 311, 315; Jews and, 366; membership standards, 439; reform, 440–441; scientific, 498, 508, 512–514; supplanted by agricultural societies, 504–505; criticism of, 516; purpose of, 517; luxury debate, 567; economic discourse, 572; culture and, 665. See also Institutions: academic; Learned societies

Acting and actors, 668

Adanson, Michel, 40

Administrative debate and crisis, 320, 464–466

Advertisements, 639–640

Aesthetics and style, 634–635, 636. See also Art; Fashion; Interior decoration

Agriculture, 114, 123, 126–127, 137–139, 289, 386, 417, 460, 498–499, 549, 565; revolution, 112, 121, 494–495; crops, 115, 124–125; livestock, 125, 235, 502; economy / capitalism, 142, 235–236, 412–413; production, 206, 553; tax, 295; societies, 504–505

Agronomy, 125–126, 131, 137–138, 153, 235, 413, 432, 487, 498, 499–507, 625; progress and innovation, 135–136; reform through, 499–507; books on, 503–504; influence of, 505–506

Aguesseau, Henri François, Chancellor d' / d'Aguesseau circle, 105, 106, 215, 218, 255, 261, 408, 464

Agulhon, Maurice, 434–435

Aiguillon, duc d', 4, 469

Alembert, Jean Le Rond d', 36, 339, 444, 476, 604; academies and education, 433, 440, 511; as architect, 514, 640; on egalitarianism, 540; on consumption, 574, 576

Almanacs. See Book(s): almanacs and yearbooks

Althusser, Louis, 252

Angivilliers, comtesse de, 152

Animal husbandry. See Agriculture: livestock

Anjou, duc d', 453

Antin, Louis Antoine de Pardaillan de Gondrin, duc d', 456

Antireformist sentiment, 466–468

Antoine, Michel, 218, 219, 258–259, 260, 264

Anxiety theory, 595, 602–604

Apologetics, 382, 384–389

Apprenticeship, 424, 425, 428, 431

Arc, chevalier d', 304, 417

Architecture, 514, 604, 634, 637–638, 639, 640

Argenson, René-Louis, marquis d', 37, 154, 219, 220, 223, 261, 307–308, 328, 351, 375, 408, 417, 458, 464, 465, 571

Aristocracy, 156, 253. See also Nobility

Aristotle, 75, 86, 326

Army, royal, 655

Art, 443, 545, 549; painting, 54–55, 77, 84–85, 112, 156, 184, 201, 529, 586, 626, 630, 634, 635–637; monuments, statues and sculpture, 272–273, 275–277, 634, 648; painting (royal portraits), 273–275; painting (narrative), 330–332; education, 433; painting (portraits), 542, 545–546, 638; religious, 586; exhibitions, 636

Artists, 439, 636–637, 648

Arts, 624, 669; minor, 634–635